WITHDRAWN
FOR SALE

EUROPEAN
URBANIZATION
1500–1800

EUROPEAN URBANIZATION 1500–1800

Jan de Vries

METHUEN AND CO. LTD
London

First published in 1984 by
Methuen & Co. Ltd
11 New Fetter Lane, London EC4P 4EE

© 1984 Jan de Vries

Typeset in Great Britain by
Scarborough Typesetting Services
and printed in the United States of America

All rights reserved. No part
of this book may be reprinted
or reproduced or utilized in any form
or by any electronic, mechanical or other means, now
known or hereafter invented, including photocopying
and recording, or in any information storage
or retrieval system, without permission
in writing from the publishers.

British Library Cataloguing in Publication Data

De Vries, Jan
European urbanization, 1500–1800
1. Urbanization – Europe – History
I. Title
307.7′6′094   HT131
ISBN 0-416-36290-7

FOR
NICHOLAS
AND
SASKIA

CONTENTS

List of figures x
List of tables xii
Foreword xvi

I THE PROBLEM OF THE CITY
   IN EARLY MODERN EUROPE

1 The problem of the city in early modern Europe 3
   The post-medieval pre-industrial city:
   a term too awkward to endure 3
   Urbanization 10

II THE URBAN POPULATION OF EUROPE

2 Assembling the data base 17
   The challenge 17
   Limits and boundaries 19
   Thresholds 21
   Sources 22
   Estimates, interpolations and assignments 24

3 The contours of European urbanization I 28
   The data base 28
   Extensions backward and forward 40

4 The contours of European urbanization II 49
   The 'tip of the iceberg' problem 49
   Direct evidence 54

CONTENTS

*The indirect estimation of cities with
under 10,000 inhabitants* 66
European urbanization 1300–1980 69

III THE PROPERTIES OF THE URBAN SYSTEM

5 Cities, systems and regions 81
6 The development of an urban hierarchy 85
     Techniques and interpretations 85
     Europe's rank-size distributions 95
     Rank-size distributions of individual countries 107
7 Stability and discontinuity in European urban growth 121
     The issues 121
     Transition matrices 123
     The growing cities 136
     Stability and change in the very long run 142
8 The spatial pattern of European urbanization 151
     The measurement of urbanization 151
     Potential 154
     European potential surfaces 158
     The long-term development of Europe's urban core 167

IV DYNAMICS OF URBAN GROWTH

9 Demography of the early modern city 175
     The status of historical urban demography 175
     The law of urban natural decrease and its critics 179
     Assessment 182
     The reproductive value of urban migrants 197
10 Migration and urban growth 199
     The linchpin of the urban economy 199
     Estimating net urban migration 200
     The context of pre-industrial urban migration 213
     Push, pull, and potential migration 214
     Pre-industrial migration options 217
     A three-sector pre-industrial migration model 221
     Urbanization, proletarianization and protoindustrialization 231
     The economic consequences of the protoindustrial urban system 240
     Dualism, parasitism and regionalism 246

viii

CONTENTS

V CONCLUSIONS

11 Conclusions 253
   The making of the urban system 253
   What sort of urban system did Europe get? 260
   What sort of urban system will Europe get? 264

APPENDICES

1 The data base 269
2 Sources 288
3 Distribution of cities by size category, aggregate urban population and transition matrices, by territory 305
4 Urban population of eastern-most Europe *c.*1800 338

Notes and references 341
Bibliography 367
Index 394

FIGURES

1.1	The growth of world urban population	6
2.1	The sixteen territories of Europe	20
4.1	Example of a rank-size distribution: Europe in 1750	51
4.2	Rank-size distribution for Europe in 1700	53
4.3	Rank-size distributions for the Netherlands, 1849 and 1970	55
4.4	Rank-size distribution of cities in several territories of non-Mediterranean Europe *c.*1800	56
4.5	Northern European rank-size distributions for 1500, 1600, 1750 and 1800	68
4.6	Urban percentage in Europe, northern Europe and Mediterranean Europe to 1800	74
4.7	Population of Europe by size of settlement, 1300–1980	77
6.1	Urban population by city-size categories, 1500–1890	86
6.2	Rank-size distributions: Europe, 1300–1979	94
6.3	Rank-size distributions: northern Europe, 1500–1600	97
6.4	Rank-size distributions: Mediterranean Europe, 1500–1600	97
6.5	Rank-size distributions: northern Europe, 1600–1750	99
6.6	Rank-size distributions: Mediterranean Europe, 1600–50	99
6.7	Rank-size distributions: Mediterranean Europe, 1600–1750	100
6.8	Rank-size distributions: northern Europe, 1750–1800	100
6.9	Rank-size distribution of US city populations, 1790–1950	103
6.10	Scatter diagram of cities by size in 1600 and 1750	104
6.11	Scatter diagram of cities by size in 1750 and 1800	105
6.12	Population growth ratios by city rank, 1500–1979	106

FIGURES

6.13	Rank-size distributions: Spain, 1500–1979	109
6.14(a)	Rank-size distributions: Italy, 1500–1979	110
(b)	Rank-size distributions: northern Italy and southern Italy, 1500–1800	111
6.15	Rank-size distributions: France, 1500–1979	113
6.16	Rank-size distributions: Germany, 1500–1978	115
6.17	Rank-size distributions: the Netherlands, 1500–1978	117
6.18	Rank-size distributions: England and Wales, 1500–1979	119
8.1	Urban potential in Europe, 1500	160
8.2	Urban potential in Europe, 1600	162
8.3	Urban potential in Europe, 1650	163
8.4	Urban potential in Europe, 1750	164
8.5	Urban potential in Europe, 1800	164
8.6	High urban potential zones in 1500 and 1750	165
8.7	High urban potential zones in 1600 and 1800	165
8.8	Zones of expanding and contracting potential: 1500, 1600 and 1750	166
8.9	The urbanization of north-western Europe in the very long term, 1000–1900	169
8.10	Night-time satellite photograph of Europe	170
8.11	Two versions of the European metropolitan core	171
10.1	The relationship of the rural natural rate of increase to the percentage of the rural surplus population destined for urban migration, per fifty-year period	216
10.2	Growth trajectories of urbanization when the urban rate of natural increase is below and above 0	233
10.3	Shares of European population in four categories, 1500–1900	239
11.1	Three phases of early modern urbanization	256
11.2	Rank-size distributions for Europe, 1800; China, 1843 (Skinner); Russia, c. 1800 (Rozman); and Japan, c. 1800 (Rozman)	262
11.3	Two modes of European urbanization, 1000–the future	265

TABLES

2.1 Number of unknowns by territory and by year, 1500–1800 26
2.2 Assignment of unknowns to size category, 1500–1800 27
3.1 Number of cities with at least 10,000 inhabitants, by territory, 1500–1800 29
3.2 Total population of all cities with at least 10,000 inhabitants, by territory, 1500–1800 30
3.3 Percentage of total European urban population, by region, 1500–1800 32
3.4 Number of cities by size category, 1500–1800 33
3.5 Urban population by size category, 1500–1800 34
3.6 Total population of Europe, by territory and region, 1500–1800 36
3.7 Urban percentage of total population, by territory and region, 1500–1800 39
3.8 Number of cities, aggregate urban population and urban percentage, by territory, 1800–1980 45
3.9(a) Number of cities by size categories: all of Europe 48
(b) Total urban population by size categories: all of Europe 48
4.1 Estimated total population of all 379 cities of the data base, 1500–1800 50
4.2 Cities by size category in several territories of non-Mediterranean Europe c. 1800 56
4.3 Distribution of urban population by size category around 1800: cities of 5000 and over 57
4.4 Distribution of urban population by size category around 1800: cities of all sizes 59
4.5 Cities of East Anglia by size category, 1520–1801 60

TABLES

4.6	Cities of Electoral Saxony by size category, 1300–1843	61
4.7	Cities of Denmark by size category, 1672–1845	63
4.8	Cities of the Netherlands by size category, 1500–1859	64
4.9	Cities of England and Wales by size category, 1520–1851	64
4.10	Cities of France by size category, 1750–1851	65
4.11	Estimated number and total population of cities with 5000–9999 inhabitants, 1500–1800	67
4.12	Number of cities by size category, 1300–1890	70
4.13	Urban population by size category, 1300–1979	72
4.14	Comparison of the growth of cities above and below 40,000 inhabitants, 1500–1800	76
7.1	Transition matrices: number of cities in population size categories at fifty-year intervals, 1500–1800	125
7.2	Transition matrices for north and west Europe: number of cities in population size categories at fifty-year intervals, 1500–1800	127
7.3	Transition matrices for central Europe: number of cities in population size categories at fifty-year intervals, 1500–1800	128
7.4	Transition matrices for Mediterranean Europe: number of cities in population size categories at fifty-year intervals, 1500–1800	129
7.5	Summary of the transition matrices	130
7.6	Transition matrices: number of cities in population size categories, 1500–1600	132
7.7	Transition matrices: number of cities in population size categories, 1600–1750	133
7.8	Transition matrices: number of cities in population size categories, 1750–1800	134
7.9	Summary of the transition matrices in three periods	135
7.10(a)	Accounting for urban population growth in Europe	137
(b)	Accounting for urban population growth in northern Europe	138
(c)	Accounting for urban population growth in Mediterranean Europe	139
7.11	Fastest growing cities, in three periods, 1500–1800	140
7.12	Transition matrices: number of cities in population size categories, 1500–1800	143
7.13	The relative importance of 'new' and 'old' cities, by size category, 1500–1800	145
7.14	Transition matrix: Europe, 1800–1979	147

TABLES

7.15	The relative importance of 'new' and 'old' cities, by size category, 1800–1979	148
8.1	Urbanization index results	154
8.2	Coefficients used to modify the distance between city pairs in the calculation of potential	158
8.3	Cities with the highest potential values (expressed in percentage of peak value for each period), 1500–1800	159
9.1(a)	Cross-tabulation of Amsterdam brides and grooms by place of birth, 1801, 1806	187
(b)	Partner-choice among Amsterdam-born brides and grooms, 1601–1800	188
9.2	Partner-choice characteristics in four cities	191
9.3	Age at first marriage in Amsterdam for native-born and migrant brides and grooms, 1796	191
9.4	Amsterdam demographic characteristics compared to those of the 'Kingdom of Holland'	194
9.5	London demographic characteristics compared to those of England, 1550–1824	195
10.1	A model of net rural–urban migration: northern Europe, 1500–1890	203
10.2	Migration and natural increase in Caen, 1753–95	205
10.3	A model of net rural–urban migration: Mediterranean Europe, 1500–1800	208
10.4	Annual losses abroad in the service of the Dutch East India Company	211
10.5	Three-sector model fifty-year simulation results, assuming no intersectoral migration	225
10.6	Three-sector model fifty-year simulation results, assuming farm to urban migration just sufficient to maintain initial urban population	226
10.7	Three-sector model fifty-year simulation results, assuming migration to urban sector only just sufficient to maintain initial urban percentage	227
10.8	Three-sector model fifty-year simulation results, assuming that all surplus farm and rural–industrial population migrates to the urban sector	228
10.9	Three-sector model fifty-year simulation results, assuming all farm surplus population migrates to rural–industrial sector	229
10.10	Three-sector model fifty-year simulation results: the effect of changing the urban rate of natural increase from −0.005 to 0 and +0.005, assuming that all farm and rural surplus	

TABLES

	migrates to the urban sector 232
10.11	Natural increase and net inmigration in the growth of the population of Amsterdam, 1700–1900 235
10.12	Natural increase and net inmigration in the growth of the population of Berlin, 1711–1900 236
10.13	Natural increase and net inmigration in the growth of the population of Stockholm, 1721–1910 237

FOREWORD

When I embarked on this study I had no intention of writing a book, and as it expanded to become one I often felt that it could better be written by a committee. Now that it is finished I am hard pressed to explain how I came to write it.

This book began as an effort to satisfy my curiosity about the number and size of Europe's larger cities. As an agrarian historian with an interest in cities as markets for agricultural products, I was struck by the imbalance between how little is known and how much is asserted about the role of cities in the pre-industrial economy. I then began, over ten years ago, to gather and save references to city population totals. Since then, matters have got completely out of hand, and I now present a study that immodestly aspires to function as a framework for urban history. All this I blame on my environment.

An invitation to present a paper at the International Conference on Urbanization and Functional Differentiation, organized by a group of Dutch historians and geographers in 1979, introduced me to urban historians and acted as a catalyst to make me think more deeply about some of the issues latent in the materials I had assembled over the years. Thereafter, my efforts to analyse and interpret the data on urban population were repeatedly stimulated, corrected and advanced by contact – both formal and informal – with colleagues at the University of California at Berkeley, other campuses of the University of California, and Stanford University.

This study would surely have assumed a different, more limited form were it not for the establishment at Berkeley of the Graduate Group in Demography, the support given by the Institute of International Studies to the Berkeley–Stanford Demography Seminars, and the long-standing Berkeley–Stanford Economic History Seminars (supported by nothing more than the purses of the participants). These initiatives have brought together historians, economists, sociologists, anthropologists and demographers to create the intellectual environment that made this study possible. Thus, before turning to acknowledge individuals I wish to express my appreciation to the 'faceless bureaucrats' who have helped make my university a good place to do research.

I profited, often in ways unsuspected by my benefactors, from the comments of many individuals, among them the late Allan Sharlin, Tom Smith, Carlo Cipolla, Claude Fisher, Ronald Lee, Ken Wachter and Gene Hammel at Berkeley; G. William Skinner and Paul David at Stanford; and, elsewhere, David Ringrose, Jeffrey Williamson, Charles Tilly and Franklin Mendels.

I collected my thoughts and wrote this book while a Fellow at the Netherlands Institute for Advanced Study. For this second opportunity to enjoy the excellent facilities of NIAS I am very grateful. A year in the Netherlands also enabled me to gain access to research materials and renew academic contacts whose impress on this study will be apparent. Long discussions with Ad van der Woude and the many suggestions of Paul Klep helped me improve this book, but, even more, they have supplied me with ideas for further work on the subject of European urbanization.

This project has seen a succession of students come and go, each of them supported by the modest but welcome Committee on Research grants awarded by the University of California. Polly Pfar, Bonnie Bishop and Louise Schneider hunted for obscure journals and helped bring to heel the unruly scholarly apparatus. John Brega prepared the computer programs and performed a wide variety of computational work with efficiency and good humour. I am grateful to them all.

Finally, a note of warning. Every month brings new information to light requiring revision in the quantitative description of European urbanization presented here. Most of these changes are minor refinements, but some are – and will be – more consequential. I like to imagine a conference convening, say, in a decade's time, at which urban historians of the various European countries present the latest findings on historical urban population and demography. They will, I am certain, find much to correct in this volume. If I have done my work well they will improve upon, but not cast aside, the broad lines of the interpretation I offer here. But even if it should come to pass that my analysis is found to be steeped in grievous error, I will continue to take comfort in having presented a quantitative basis for the study of European urban history, one that can be examined, tested, altered and built upon by later investigators.

Berkeley, California
January 1984

I
THE PROBLEM OF THE CITY IN EARLY MODERN EUROPE

1
THE PROBLEM OF THE CITY IN EARLY MODERN EUROPE

THE POST-MEDIEVAL PRE-INDUSTRIAL CITY: A TERM TOO AWKWARD TO ENDURE

This book is a history of European urbanization in the sixteenth, seventeenth and eighteenth centuries. It is not an urban history, if that means a history of individual cities and what occurs in them. The number of such studies now available is no longer small, but they are subject to limitations that hinder making generalizations and comparisons that transcend the experience of a unique place. This problem has long been recognized. H. J. Dyos urged in 1966 that

> The study of urban history must mean not merely that study of individual communities, fixed more or less in time and space – what might be called the urban aspect of local history; but the investigation of altogether broader historical processes and trends that completely transcend the life cycle and range of experience of particular communities.[1]

The identification and analysis of these 'broader historical processes' has not yet been carried very far. As a consequence the framework for the study of urban history remains poorly developed. I shall argue here that the basic framework for urban history should be a history of urbanization.

One can gain an intuitive understanding of the basic problem that needs to be resolved in order to supply a history of urbanization in these centuries by pondering the contradictory terminology currently in use. Historians conventionally call the three centuries after 1500 'modern', or more specifically 'early modern'. Hence the title of this chapter. The label is a general one; it is not at all specific to the urban history of these centuries. Is it appropriate?

THE PROBLEM OF THE CITY IN EARLY MODERN EUROPE

Most social scientific studies of urban development refer to the city before nineteenth-century industrialization as 'pre-modern'. But here again, this is simply a reflection of a scholarly convention to refer to *all* aspects of life before the industrial revolution as pre-modern. In a pre-modern society the cities must also have been pre-modern. Is this usage justifiable?

The character of the pre- or early modern city is not clarified by available works of urban history. In writings about European cities the urbanism of these centuries often seems lost between two well-mapped urban landscapes – those of the medieval city and the industrial city.

The medieval city has been the object of an original and influential literature that goes back to Henri Pirenne and Max Weber.[2] It identifies the medieval city as a new and unique phenomenon and in so doing ascribes to the middle ages an important function in bringing about the modern world. This historical tradition stresses the city's autonomy, a characteristic allowing it to function first as an incubator of capitalism in an otherwise hostile (feudal) environment and later as a vehicle for capitalist progress. Pirenne put it this way:

> The essential character of the European bourgeoisie was, indeed, the fact that it formed a privileged class in the midst of the rest of the population. From this point of view the medieval town offers a striking contrast both to the ancient town and to the town of today. . . . Once outside the gates and the moat [of the medieval town] we are in another world, or more exactly, in the domain of another law.[3]

More recently the economic historian M. M. Postan emphasized the same elements of medieval urbanism:

> [*The medieval towns*] were non-feudal islands in the feudal seas; places in which merchants could not only live in each other's vicinity and defend themselves collectively but also places which enjoyed or were capable of developing systems of local government and principles of law and status exempting them from the sway of the feudal regime.[4]

The influence of this tradition can also be found in the work of Fernand Braudel, who begins his discussion of the city in *Capitalism and Material Life* by asking 'Why were [western cities] like steam engines while the others were like clocks . . .?', and later asserts that 'Capitalism and towns were basically the same things in the West'.[5]

After the demise of feudalism the specific character of the medieval town changes (i.e. it ceases to be 'closed', an island in a feudal sea) but not its long-run mission. Thus the later history of the medieval city anticipates its role in industrial capitalism. The long-distance interregional trade of the middle ages becomes the intercontinental trade of the sixteenth and later centuries;

4

the limited communications role of the 'closed' city develops into a more complex and influential social and cultural function as the city becomes legally, physically and economically more 'open'. In this way the medieval city – a unique creation – lays the foundations for the later emergence of industrial capitalism.

The industrial city has inspired an extensive literature written primarily by social scientists fascinated by its power, novelty and apparent irresistibility.[6] The dynamic character of the industrial city is seen as quantitatively so different from that which preceded it that it amounted to a qualitative difference. It justifies restricting the term 'urbanization' to 'the spatial dimension of the industrial and technological revolutions of the past two centuries'.[7] Moreover, this urbanization is incorporated with industrialization, secularization and centralization into the all-encompassing concept of modernization, with the result that the city of earlier times becomes at once pre-industrial and pre-modern.

Good social science has managed to go beyond adherence to the concept of a static traditionalism embracing an undifferentiated pre-modern past, but the terminology persists, and continues to emphasize the size of the chasm separating the society – and the city – of ancient, medieval and traditional peasant Europe from that of the industrial epoch. A typical example of this viewpoint is found in David Clark's *Urban Geography*:

> In adopting a long-term perspective, it is apparent that the process of urban growth has undergone two major changes of pace. The first, known as the agricultural [i.e. Neolithic] revolution, occurred in the Near and Middle East around the fifth millennium BC and is associated with the emergence of identifiable towns and cities. The second, known as the industrial revolution, occurred first in Britain in the late eighteenth century, and led to the growth of the large metropolis. These revolutions separate what Sjoberg has termed the pre-agricultural, the traditional and the urban-industrial societies. They distinguish different technological environments each of which is associated with a specific settlement response.[8]

Clark illustrates this thumbnail sketch of world urbanization with a figure (figure 1.1) that serves to call attention even more insistently towards two elements of the traditionalism-modernization school: the static, undifferentiated character of traditional urban life (following G. Sjoberg's *The Pre-Industrial City*) and the dynamic world-changing character of the industrial city.[9]

These two traditions in urban history, each based on an assertion of the novelty and power of a particular type of city, are not compatible with each other. Moreover, their incompatibility resides to a large extent in what is

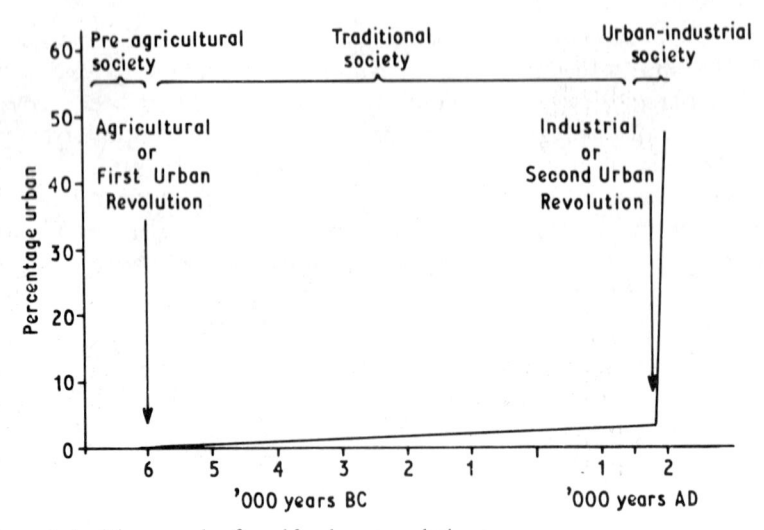

Figure 1.1 The growth of world urban population

Source David Clark, *Urban Geography* (London, 1982), 49 (reproduced by courtesy of Croom Helm Ltd).

implied about the character of the 'post-medieval, pre-industrial city', a city with which neither tradition is directly concerned. One's view of this city depends on one's assessment of the rival claims of the medieval and industrial cities.

Efforts to resolve the contradictions just identified can be grouped under two headings, both of which identify the city of early modern Europe as a species of failure. The first alternative is to see the early modern city as a deposed vehicle of progress. Fernand Braudel, whose utterances on this subject are not free from ambiguity, advances this position in *The Mediterranean and the Mediterranean World in the Age of Philip II*. There, after celebrating the dynamism of the medieval city of the West, he observes of the sixteenth century:

> The cities were no longer undisputed rulers of the world. Their reign, which had lasted throughout the early rise of Europe and the Mediterranean, from the eleventh to the fourteenth century, was beginning to be challenged at the threshold of modern times by the territorial states . . . which modern times suddenly projected to the centre of the stage.
> . . . all towns without exception saw their liberties being whittled away by the extension of the territorial states, which were expanding even more rapidly than the towns, surrounding them, subjugating them or even chasing them from acquired positions.[10]

The medieval city had played an important role in causing feudal society to come unglued. But the nation state subordinated it and harnessed it. The cities then saw their distinctive municipal culture dismissed as a medieval relic by right-thinking servitors of the modern state. At the same time the concentrations of money and resources achieved by that state allowed many cities to become parasitic, living as rentiers off these concentrations.[11] In short, the vital, creative medieval city was real, but it ultimately succumbed, so that 'the capital cities would be present at the forthcoming industrial revolution as spectators'.[12]

The second variant of this urban failure position holds that the ease with which the productive medieval city was transformed into the rentier, consumer city of the early modern period is a demonstration that the medieval city had not, in fact, possessed the potential ascribed to it by Pirenne, Postan and their followers. As John Merrington has argued, the medieval city was no 'non-feudal island' or vehicle of capitalist progress; it was a part of the feudal order.[13] The opposition of town and country had strict limitations that precluded a breakthrough to industrial capitalism. Indeed, the town's merchant capitalism was dependent on the continued existence of pre-capitalist economic forms in the larger society. In the terminology of Merrington, the medieval city was not 'external' to feudal society, it was 'internal'. He then goes on to claim that:

> Nothing reveals better the limits of this municipal economy than its decline and involution in the context of the growing world market and the establishment of territorial state sovereignty from the sixteenth century. . . . This was accomplished by an internal involution toward rentier forms of wealth, the flight of urban capitalism into land, state bonds, and tax farming which transformed the urban elite into a landed elite or rentier aristocracy, merged in turn with the absentee nobility itself. Urban capital becomes usury capital. Usury feeds off the old mode [of production] without altering it. It depends, like merchant capital, on a pre-capitalist market.[14]

The two variants of the 'failure case' differ in their assessments of the medieval city of the West, but they are in agreement that the rise of the national state 'reduced the urban merchant economies of the feudal mode to a shrinking sphere of operations'[15] at the same time that it offered opportunities for parasitism: 'feeding off the old mode without altering it'. They are further agreed that the industrial city represents an historical discontinuity. A new mode of production nurtured in the countryside matured, with the invention of industrial machinery, into an urban factory economy. This opens the way to an accelerated permanent urbanization based on the 'concentration of the motive power of society in big cities' (Marx) and the subordination of agriculture as merely one branch of industry. The dominance of the town is no longer externally imposed: it is now reproduced as part of the accumulation process.[16]

A new technology removed for the first time the fetters to autonomous urban growth, and raised up a new urban hierarchy. Thus urbanization in the industrial era was no linear extension of the earlier urban world which, indeed, had demonstrated its impotence in the sixteenth, seventeenth and eighteenth centuries.

These thumbnail sketches of interpretative frameworks for urban history present the European city of the early modern era as either a preparation for and lineal ancestor of urban-industrial society, or as an obstacle to the achievement of such a society, an obsolete relic from the past. The first view, in its simple form, lacks the power to convince. It is an affirmation of the importance of the medieval city to the modern world, or it reflects a belief in gradualism and continuity in history. But either way it must ignore a great deal. It has the further disadvantage of not being capable of saying anything specific about the character of post-medieval, pre-industrial urbanism. This latter shortcoming also affects the crude 'traditional city' concept. The versions presented by Braudel and by Merrington, however, have the virtue of emphasizing the different character of the city in the early modern period. The question here is whether their characterizations are valid. In my view the 'failed city' approach, whether based on the internal impotence or the external subordination of the city, suffers from two weaknesses. It is too dependent on our image of the early modern city derived from urban history, that is from the study of individual, usually major cities. It is based on a too-limited and selective number of observations. Secondly, this position relies on the concept of an industrial revolution – or new mode of production – as a quite sudden historical discontinuity, a concept that a large amount of recent scholarship now casts into serious doubt.[17]

The post-medieval, pre-industrial city was clearly no longer a 'non-feudal island in a feudal sea'. Nor was it the centre of technological change, social modernization and proletarianization that the nineteenth-century city is taken to be. Yet we now know that the large-scale redeployment of capital and labour, indeed the emergence of a proletariat and of widespread industrial production, did not begin with the first urban factories. These things arose much earlier, selectively transforming regions throughout Europe. The physical setting of much of this 'protoindustrialization' was of course rural. But large-scale rural-industrial production for distant markets depended on communications and co-ordination, that is, on cities. It is more useful to stress the *regional* context of these new developments rather than simply their *rural* setting. It follows that an assessment of the place of urban settlements in the economy and society of early modern Europe requires an examination of urban–rural interactions in a regional framework.

The differences that emerge when the early modern city is compared to those attributes of the medieval city that have attracted the attention of historians usually leads one to regard the early modern city as less potent and less original. But cities possess more dimensions than those usually emphasized in studies of individual towns. They need to be seen in a fuller context. Philip Abrams expressed this point directly with his observation that 'cities are implicated in a nodal manner in the larger system of society, economy, and government'.[18] This formulation recommends a critical re-examination of the notion of the medieval city as an 'island in a feudal sea'. It also calls attention to the links among the nodes and the interaction of this complex – i.e. of cities as a collective entity – with the society, economy and government. In other words, while the city may have become less than it had been, the system of cities became more.

The recent works of the sociologist Gilbert Rozman, the anthropologist G. William Skinner and the geographers Brian Robson and Allan Pred all emphasize the importance of networks, or systems of cities.[19] They argue, each in his own way, that the economic, social and administrative functions of cities are carried out in hierarchic, or at least interconnected frameworks. More importantly, the characters of those structures condition the sort of role that cities, *taken collectively*, can play.

Of these scholars, Rozman makes the largest claims for the study of systems of cities. He develops a seven-stage model of 'pre-modern urban development' that leads a society from its pre-urban condition to the threshold of modernity.[20] In the first three of his stages (following the initial non-urban stage) administrative cities come into being, forming a hierarchic pattern of governance 'from the top down'. There follow, as part of a total process that can take a millennium or be telescoped into a much briefer period, three stages in which commercial towns and market-places are created 'from the bottom up' and are organized to secure an economic articulation of the society. The last of these stages features the emergence of regional centres that make possible an integration at the national level of numerous small marketing systems. These stages are derived from Rozman's studies of China, Japan and Russia. He also provides a brief application of the model to England and France, and claims that the final stage of pre-modern urban development was achieved in the sixteenth century in China, the sixteenth or seventeenth century in England and France, the seventeenth century in Japan and the eighteenth century in Russia.

What interests us here is Rozman's assertion that a mature urban system is a 'pre-modern' achievement rather than a product of the industrial epoch. In his view, a certain very long-term process of urban network creation is a necessary preparation for entry to the modern industrial world. It is necessary because certain societal functions require an urban network for their efficient performance.

What are these functions? Rozman is vague on this point; he is much more specific about the relative merits of alternative designs of a complete urban network. We can, however, turn to G. William Skinner, a critic of Rozman's oddly abstract yet descriptive model, for a reasonable answer to the question. The emergence of an urban system is a crucial step in regional development, that is, 'the process whereby regional resources of all kinds, social and cultural as well as economic and political, were multiplied, deployed with greater effectiveness and exploited with increased efficiency'.[21] This work, based on non-western urbanization, carries the ironic implication that the era of the 'subordinate city', or 'parasitic city', simultaneously marked the emergence of the 'generative urban system', that is, the efficient articulation of regional economies by networks of cities which make possible just the sort of mobilization of labour, capital and information referred to by Skinner.

Philip Abrams provides another way of expressing what I believe amounts to much the same thing when he calls for a consideration of cities as part of the 'complex of domination': 'Towns become interesting as moments in a process of usurpation and defence, consolidation, appropriation and resistance; as battles rather than as monuments.'[22]

With whatever rhetoric it now appears that we should seek to understand the European city from the sixteenth to the early nineteenth centuries in the context of the history of urbanization rather than the context of urban history. This formulation is based on the insight that the distinctive, individual contributions of cities are not simply microcosms of the collective, general functions of cities.[23] Both the discussion of the inadequacies of existing interpretative frameworks for the early modern city and the arguments based on the study of non-western urban development lead me to this view. The design of this book rests on the proposition that the problem of the city in early modern Europe can be resolved only in the context of the history of urbanization.

URBANIZATION

If this is to be a history of urbanization we must have a clear idea of what urbanization is. A conventional starting-point is the definition of Hope Eldridge Tisdale, offered in 1942.

> Urbanization is a process of population concentration. It proceeds in two ways: the multiplication of points of concentration and the increase in size of individual concentrations.[24]

It is the regrouping of a population over time from a dispersed to a concentrated settlement pattern that Tisdale had in mind in her 'ruthless analytical pruning' of the concept of urbanization.

While this is clear enough, it does leave some unanswered questions. First of all, the 'points of concentration'. A regrouping of population that reduces the population density of certain rural zones while it increases the density of others is obviously not what Tisdale wished to call urbanization. The points of concentration must be cities, and this forces us to be as clear as possible about what cities are. The number of ways cities can vary among themselves is sufficiently great that a specific, unambiguous definition is not achievable. What is possible is the identification of certain commonly accepted quantifiable dimensions that distinguish cities from other forms of settlement: population size, density of settlement, share of non-agricultural occupations and diversity of non-agricultural occupations.[25] All four of these criteria are continuums, so that one must draw a line at some point dividing cities from non-cities. This cannot help but be arbitrary. But a settlement must score sufficiently high in *all four* of these criteria to be a city, a requirement that does not make the task easier, but does reflect the existence of a broadly shared intuitive understanding of what constitutes an urban place. For instance, a large mining settlement may fulfil the first three criteria, but not the fourth, and so is not in itself a city. For the same reason a large dormitory suburb is not a city, although it is likely to be part of *another* city.

So long as urbanization proceeds via increases in the size of existing cities, lack of agreement about which places are cities is unlikely to affect the outcome greatly. This is not true when urbanization takes the form of increasing the *number* of cities. Then our understanding of the tempo and timing of urbanization will be sensitively affected by the criteria applied. In the following chapter more will be said about the identification of cities *in practice*, for now we can say that urbanization is a process of population concentration in more and/or bigger cities.

A second problem with Tisdale's definition is that it leaves open the possibility that the growth of cities in number or absolute size will be exceeded by the growth of a dispersed, rural population. Can one speak of urbanization if cities are growing, but the percentage of the population located in these points of concentration is falling? Philip Hauser, who noted this problem in 1965, thought not and added to Tisdale's two points the proviso 'as a result, the proportion of the population living in urban places increases'.[26]

After all this work we still have little more than a statistical definition of urbanization: a shift of population from rural to urban locations such as to increase the relative size of the latter. This might better be called *urban growth* or *demographic urbanization*, for urbanization in general usage implies something more than this.

THE PROBLEM OF THE CITY IN EARLY MODERN EUROPE

Today one speaks of 'the urbanization of society'. The implication is that urbanization is a process that involves people in 'urban' behaviour, modes of thought and types of activities whether they live in cities or not.[27] This usage refers to the conduct of individuals, and can be called *behavioural urbanization*. It is of interest to this historical study because of the perception that, in the last century at least, the urban way of life has reached out far beyond the physical city to urbanize society, while in earlier times the 'towns were deeply penetrated by the countryside'.[28] This can justify the use of the apparently nonsensical phrase, the urbanization of the cities, when referring to behavioural urbanization. It is an obvious illustration of why a durable definition of a city is such a troublesome illusive task.

Finally, one can refer to *structural urbanization*, that process of change in the organization of society that fosters nodal concentration of population. Structural urbanization places its emphasis on the concentration of *activities* at central points in contrast to demographic urbanization's emphasis on the concentration of *population*. These are obviously related but one can distinguish, at least in theory, between a larger number of people performing a number of urban functions and a growth in the number of urban functions attracting people to cities and transforming rural settlements into urban ones. The latter reflects changes in society associated with the development of large-scale, co-ordinated activities.[29] Charles Tilly advances a definition of urbanization that emphasizes this structural dimension.[30] The operation of a centralized state, the conduct of a religion with a professional priesthood, the control of water for irrigation, the production of goods in a factory system, and the channellings of exchange through a pervasive market, are all examples of activities that foster urbanization. They do so because they require the appearance of co-ordinators (social positions devoted to co-ordinating large-scale activities, such as bishops, merchants, bankers, provincial governors), communications lines (to permit co-ordinators to carry out this work) and cross-cutting relationships (social relationships that cross the boundaries of kinship, locality and traditional alliances).

Tilly's approach cannot be disentangled from behavioural urbanization (cross-cutting relationships and the impersonal, instrumental behaviour they foster is a prime example of what distinguishes urban from rural ways of life) and demographic urbanization (people concentrate at points of co-ordination and control). But he relates these clearly to the spread and growth of particular activities most of which require not simply *a* point of concentration but *networks* of such points, together with communications systems to connect them.

The three-headed definition of urbanization recommends itself by its combination of comprehensiveness and specificity. But possession of a definition does not necessarily mean that the thing defined exists. We have

THE PROBLEM OF THE CITY IN EARLY MODERN EUROPE

already noted that some scholars hold that urbanization is closely linked to the 'industrial and technological revolutions of the past two centuries'.[31] The implication of this formulation is that cities before the industrial revolution neither experienced changes nor inflicted them on society on a large enough scale, or on a sustained enough basis to warrant the use of the term urbanization. This position can be sustained only when the definition of urbanization is narrow and presentist. With the definition presented here it is possible to proceed under the assumption that urbanization is a more general historical process, but one whose specific characteristics vary over time. Thus each epoch of urbanization can be thought of as having distinct demographic, behavioural and structural dimensions. The problem of the early modern city can then be approached by placing it in the context of the specific features of early modern urbanization, rather than by applying the standards of contemporary urbanization. Similarly, the limits and future of modern urbanization might become clearer when it is placed in a context of several epochs of urbanization.

It is the task of this book to describe and analyse the distinctive features of urbanization in the early modern period. Part II sets out to provide a comprehensive account of Europe's demographic urbanization. There a data base is presented that lays the foundation for the rest of the study. It will be shown that an urban system gradually came into being, and the analysis of the properties of that system, performed in Part III, will establish the uniqueness and importance of structural urbanization in these centuries. Part IV pursues dynamic and interactive aspects of demographic and structural urbanization, and touches on the limited, highly uneven incidence of behavioural urbanization. Behavioural urbanization, partly because of the sources and methodology used in this study and partly because of its apparently limited role, is not a major object of study in this book. Ultimately, the objective of this book is to provide a history of urbanization that can serve as a framework for urban history in the early modern period and as a background for the better understanding of the urbanization process in the modern world.

II
THE URBAN POPULATION OF EUROPE

2
ASSEMBLING THE DATA BASE

THE CHALLENGE

The first requirement of any study of urbanization is comprehensive data on the number and size of cities. What is now known about the pre-nineteenth-century urban population of Europe? The short answer to this question must be: surprisingly little. The meagreness of the existing literature is surprising because historians and social scientists have never been hesitant to make sweeping statements about the historical evolution of urban populations. But the information, if any, on which these statements rest tends to be merely illustrative. There exists no satisfactory general statistical description of European urbanization before 1800. The first step of this study, therefore, must be to provide such a description.

This negative appraisal may seem odd to some readers who are aware of the impressive advances made since the late 1950s in the study of historical demography. First, the technique of family reconstitution laid a firm foundation for a deeper, technically sophisticated understanding of family and community demographic behaviour. More recently, the inverse projection technique has been applied with success to reconstruct the population history of a large territory.[1] But neither of these foundation stones of modern historical demography have been of much assistance to the issue at hand. Family reconstitution concerns itself with the vital rates of a population, not the size thereof; inverse projection does estimate total population size but it shares with family reconstitution technical limitations that lay imposing obstacles in the path leading to its application to urban populations. These problems receive more extended discussion in chapter 9; for now it is sufficient to note that the new technical sophistication of demographic history has not enlarged substantially the available stock of knowledge about historical urban populations. Indeed, the new techniques, by attracting the attention of scholars to the rural settings where they are most readily applicable, may be said to have retarded research in urban population.

Standing as testimony to the plausibility of the last assertion is the fact that the last major study of European historical urban demography is Roger Mols's *Introduction à la démographie historique des villes d'Europe du 14ᵉ au 18ᵉ siècle*.[2] This three-volume opus was published in 1954–6, just before the successful application of the family reconstitution methodology by Louis Henry ushered in a new age of research. Mols's compendious study is, by modern standards, eclectic and sometimes impressionistic. Moreover, since his chief interest was urban *demography* rather than urban *population* history, the material he presents on the latter tends to be illustrative rather than comprehensive.

Since the publication of Mols's informative book two studies of urban population have appeared. *Three Thousand Years of Urban Growth*, by Tertius Chandler and Gerald Fox, is a massive collection of information about the size of cities.[3] Its unsystematic character and, even worse, the authors' reliance on suspect sources and their completely uncritical use of such sources renders the volume all but unusable. More systematic is the work of Paul Bairoch. He has published urban population estimates for Europe in several of his works (most fully in *Tailles de villes*), but their value to others remains limited because of the highly aggregative form of the published information (the smallest geographical unit is Europe as a whole) and the absence of any mention of sources or discussion of methodology in the works thus far published.[4]

Studies of urban population in individual countries and regions are more abundant than those for Europe as a whole. But even at this level the information at our disposal is limited and uneven. Only Italy can boast of a comprehensive, scholarly overview of historical census data extending back before the eighteenth century, in the form of Karl Beloch's three-volume *Bevölkerungsgeschichte Italiens*.[5] Beyond that one must descend to the level of the province, where Paul Klep's *Bevolking en arbeid in transformatie*, concerning Brabant, and Karlheinz Blaschke's *Bevölkerungsgeschichte von Sachsen bis zur industriellen Revolution* stand out among the very few studies that trace urban populations over long periods of time.[6]

In this book I attempt to remedy the unsatisfactory state of historical urban population studies by providing a statistical description of European urban growth before the nineteenth century that is as comprehensive, systematic and as accurate as possible.[7] The heart of this study is a data base consisting of population estimates for all European cities which numbered at least 10,000 inhabitants at some time between 1500 and 1800. The populations of all cities satisfying this minimum size rule, 379 in all, are presented at fifty-year intervals from 1500 to 1800.

ASSEMBLING THE DATA BASE

This short paragraph introducing the data base that will function as the keystone to this book must unavoidably provoke in the reader a number of questions about the procedures used and the assumptions made to enable an existing literature characterized by incompleteness and error to be replaced by a book worthy of serious attention. In the four sections that follow I provide a step-by-step description of my method and attempt to anticipate the questions of the sceptical reader.

LIMITS AND BOUNDARIES

In setting the outer limits of 'Europe' in this study of European urbanization, practicality has played a much more important role than principle. The 379 cities identified as having contained at least 10,000 inhabitants at some point in the period 1500–1800 are located in that portion of Europe that might best be described as Latin Christendom. Russia and Orthodox Europe are excluded. I defend this decision by arguing that through most, if not all, of the period 1500–1800 the cities of the Russian and Ottoman empires possessed characteristics so distinctive that it would be misleading to include them in a single study with western and central Europe.[8]

Complicating matters is the fact that the line separating European urbanism from that of Muscovy and the Ottomans was not stationary over the three centuries covered by this study. This and other practical considerations combined to form the outer limits displayed in figure 2.1.

Hungary, which should of course be included in Latin Christendom, is excluded because of the difficulty of gaining information for the sixteenth and seventeenth centuries, when most of Hungary was under Ottoman control. Poland is included, but not Lithuania, with which it was politically joined for much of the time. Lithuania's exclusion and that of the Baltic states is required by a combination of insufficient information and boundary changes.

The line separating Europe from non-Europe for the purposes of this study is one that I have extended as far east as possible while at the same time keeping at a manageable level the problem of assembling comparable data over the time period 1500–1800.[9]

The internal boundaries used in this study, much as the outer limits, have been drawn for their analytical value tempered – indeed severely constrained – by necessity. The smallest units of analysis are sixteen territories. They sometimes correspond to modern national states, sometimes combine several states and sometimes split them into parts.

At this point I am eager to insert the exculpatory proviso printed on international route maps found aboard aircraft to the effect that the boundaries shown have absolutely no political significance. For purposes of compatibility

Figure 2.1 The sixteen territories of Europe

and ease of analysis it is important that boundaries be used that remain fixed for the entire three-century period. Ideally, the boundaries should have been so drafted as to delimit functional regions. Quite apart from the special difficulties that stand in the way of doing this for Europe (see pp. 83–4), the nature of most historical data on territorial population required that most of the sixteen territories assume the contours of political units. But not just any political units. It is noteworthy that historical population data tend to be more abundant for 'the state' in certain of its successive configurations than in others. The most important example of this is of course Germany. Historical population estimates are numerous for the territory of the Wilhelmine Reich but much more spotty for other – more modest – definitions of 'Germany'.

In order to enable the calculation of rates of urbanization and related statistics I drafted the boundaries of the sixteen territories in a manner calculated to allow effective use of the available historical population estimates. In the case of Poland I could find no consistently workable solution to this problem. Correspondingly, the reader must be aware that the identification of Polish cities is arbitrarily limited (many are listed here as German) while the boundaries encompass a territory for which historical population estimates are seriously limited.[10]

For purposes of analysis the data for the sixteen territories is often grouped into four regions: Mediterranean Europe (Iberia and Italy), central Europe (France, Germany and Switzerland), north and west Europe (Scandinavia, the British Isles and the Low Countries) and eastern Europe (Poland, Czechoslovakia and Austria). The last three of these regions, embracing all of Europe north of the Pyrenees and Alps, are sometimes grouped together to form northern Europe.

The separation of Europe into a northern and Mediterranean component is a convention employed with sufficient frequency that it is unlikely to generate controversy. In contrast, the virtues of the divisions that I make *within* northern Europe are probably not so readily apparent. The groupings 'north and west' and 'central' are not intended to imply that the urban worlds of France and Germany or Sweden and Belgium are essentially the same. The reasons for this division are found primarily in the observed differences in the rates of total population growth and the overall urban growth of the two groupings. Eastern Europe is distinctive from the two other northern regions both in its very limited urbanization and in the limitations of its historical evidence. As a consequence certain of the generalizations made in this study will be based on analyses of a smaller 'Europe' that excludes the eastern region.

THRESHOLDS

A study of urban population needs not only boundaries delimiting territories but also boundaries distinguishing urban settlements from all other places of habitation: that is to say, it needs a definition of cities. Legal definitions are convenient since the burden of identifying cities is then placed on someone else. Cities then are those places that contemporaries say are cities by the conferral of city charters or some other administrative distinction. This is how people usually defined cities in early modern Europe; indeed, today the large majority of the 133 territories from which data are assembled by the United Nations continue to adhere to purely administrative criteria.[11] This is an undesirable basis for the study of urbanization, particularly in earlier centuries, because such distinctions of urban and rural almost always exaggerate the functionally urban population. Occasionally very large places fail to receive urban charters for some anomalous reason (The Hague, Dutch seat of government, officially became a city only in the nineteenth century), but more commonly one finds scores of small settlements whose urban privileges reflect hopes that never materialized.

A functional definition is to be preferred, and I provided one in the introductory chapter. Cities, I argued there, are places that have populations, population densities, percentages of the workforce in non-agricultural occupations and a measure of diversity in the occupational structure, all of which are *sufficiently large*. The question of where to draw the line along these four quantitative criteria to separate urban from non-urban places is not a trivial one. But for present purposes we do not need to answer it because at best the first two and usually only the first of the listed criteria are commonly available in the period before 1800.

As a practical matter our definition of a city will be based on size and density. The data base assembled for this study includes only densely housed places of 10,000 or more inhabitants. This size threshold is not intended to serve as a definition of cities. Rather, I chose it as a practical threshold that permits a substantial number of cities to be studied systematically. A higher threshold – say 100,000 – would include so few cities that the result might be highly unrepresentative. A lower threshold – say 3000 – would embrace very nearly all of the functionally urban population, but historical evidence of the populations of the many hundreds of such cities is unavailable. Moreover, at this level it becomes important to know about the occupational attributes, in order to avoid erroneously including non-urban places. Consequently I selected 10,000 inhabitants as a minimum level that combined feasibility with representativeness. By representativeness I mean representative of the entire set of functional cities. The size and number of that larger universe will be estimated indirectly, using a methodology to be explained in chapter 4. In summary, a serviceable definition of urban population in early modern Europe is the inhabitants of densely housed settlements of at least 2000 or 3000 population. The 10,000-inhabitant threshold used here is a practical device intended to permit the reconstruction of a subset of the total urban population that is sufficiently representative to allow indirect estimation of the 'unobserved' subset.

SOURCES

Boundaries, limits and thresholds are of little account without reliable sources on which to base the compilation of urban population estimates. It was fully twenty years ago that Eric Lampard, a leader in the then infant field of urban history, proclaimed that 'an autonomous social history ought to begin with the study of population, its changing composition and distribution in time and place'.[12] If in the intervening decades little has been done in the historical study of cities to heed his counsel the explanation may well have been given by Lampard himself two years before issuing the call cited above.

ASSEMBLING THE DATA BASE

The demographer, of course, is no magician; he cannot produce reliable results from unreliable sources. All census enumerations, for example, are subject to a variable degree of error: undercounts here, overcounts there, and occasional confusions of categories by the counters and counted everywhere. These shortcomings in the data are compounded for the historical demographer. Census categories are changed, items covered at one date are dropped at another and sometimes reappear later under a different title. Once the historian gets back before the first official census in any country, he must rely, for the most part, on fugitive sources, particular counts that have no claim to comprehension, such as directories, parish registers of births and deaths, 'books of souls', various lists of tax-payers, the wildest estimates of contemporaries, and so forth. If he lacks numerological powers, the historical demographer, nevertheless, has had to develop all the arts of the conjurer in manipulating even the official census data to make his results consistent and comparable over time. This fact alone accounts for the paucity of historical studies of urbanization.[13]

How, then, do I propose to produce reliable results from the sources at hand? In assembling the data base my approach has been one of traditional historical source criticism supplemented by certain rules of thumb to aid in making decisions in cases where my expertise is insufficient to assess contradictory evidence. In the course of handling a literature as extensive as that of the urban history of all of Europe, such cases were not rare. At this point I must emphasize that no *a priori* judgements or assumed relationships influenced the assembly of the data base. The decision to include each city, and the estimations of its population, were in all cases based on historical evidence.

The search procedure for all cities of at least 10,000 inhabitants consisted of two parts. The first part began with the national censuses held by most countries around 1800. These comprehensive sources served as a benchmark: the cities meeting the minimum size criterion in 1800, numbering 364, became the object of a search for evidence concerning their earlier population history. The second part of the process consisted of identifying cities that had once numbered at least 10,000 inhabitants but no longer did so in 1800. No systematic approach could assist in the identification of these cities. In canvassing the historical literature I have succeeded in identifying 15 such cities, but it is easily possible that I have missed some. The reader should be aware that the greater difficulty inherent in finding all category II cities (cities that no longer had 10,000 inhabitants in 1800) may have biased the data base in favour of slightly overestimating the growth of the number of cities whose populations exceed the threshold level.

Altogether the data base consists of 379 cities. I relied on the historical literature to determine the probable populations of all these cities except those in the Netherlands, the one area where my own archival research, or that of others, in some cases supplements published material.

The preferred sources consisted of those demographic studies or town histories that based population estimates on specific archival documents, such as censuses, tax records, lists of communicants or parish records of baptisms and burials. Where such studies needed to make assumptions – about household size, age of communicants, crude birth-rate – they did so in a way that permitted replication and, if needed, alteration.

Less desirable, but also accepted for this study, were secondary works, usually town histories, where the historian makes population estimates based on his general knowledge about the city in question. These estimates cannot be verified or corrected; their acceptability hinges on the authority of the scholar.

A third type of source, one I have sought to exclude from this study, is both uncheckable and of questionable authority. Many population estimates of unknown provenance have assumed lives of their own through frequent repetition. General histories, encyclopedias and other compendia frequently provide this sort of 'data'. Regrettably, it must be admitted that certain widely accepted population figures for the early sixteenth century which are repeated here are probably of this type.

When more than one source offers population estimates for a town in a given time period I use the preferred source, and if the authority of the sources are equivalent, I use the more recent source. For example, the 1600 population of the Spanish city of Ecija can be estimated on the basis of a hearth-count taken throughout Castile in 1591. Tomas Gonzalez used this source in his *Censo de poblacion* published in 1829. Since then the historian Henry Kamen has estimated the city's population using the 1591 hearth-count and other information in *Spain in the Later Seventeenth Century, 1665–1700* (London, 1980). I regard Kamen as the preferred source. Kamen also presents estimates of the population of Barcelona, but because he does not offer an explanation of why his estimates are to be preferred to those of J. N. Biraben, who provides a detailed examination of the evidence concerning the population history of Barcelona in *Les Hommes et la peste* (Paris, 1975), I continue to rely on the latter, older source. The sources on which I have based each city's population estimates are listed in appendix 2.

ESTIMATES, INTERPOLATIONS AND ASSIGNMENTS

For each of the 379 cities with at least 10,000 inhabitants at some time during the period 1500–1800, I sought evidence of their populations. In order to achieve the uniformity needed for an analysis of changes in urban structure

ASSEMBLING THE DATA BASE

and growth the population estimates were grouped at fifty-year intervals. The figures presented for each date refer to evidence drawn from within ten years of the date in question. For example, the figures for 1650 are based on evidence found for the period 1640–60.

Of course, not all evidence is conveniently grouped in these twenty-year periods. When the only available evidence refers to years outside the twenty-year periods (say, for 1625 and 1680) an *interpolated* estimate is made, using straight-line method, for the intervening fifty-year interval date, 1650. Thus, if a city is found to have 25,000 inhabitants in 1625 and 32,000 in 1680, the interpolated estimate for 1650 is (in thousands): $25 + (7/55 \times 25) = 28$.

A data base of population estimates for 379 cities at seven fifty-year intervals requires 2653 observations. The sources at our disposal allow for direct estimates or interpolated estimates in 2274 cases; 379 spaces in the data base, 14.3 per cent of the total, cannot be estimated using the standards outlined above. Unfortunately these lacunae are not distributed evenly across space and time. Table 2.1, which displays the distribution of unknown cases by territory and year, indicates that they are concentrated in the earlier years, as one would expect, and in France, Spain and Portugal.

A data base consisting of direct and interpolated estimates will probably long remain incomplete in the limited but awkward way summarized in table 2.1. In order to permit a full analysis of urban growth over the three centuries the unknown cases need to be dealt with. For this purpose the city population data have been grouped in size categories so defined that each category encompasses a doubling of population. Thus the first category is 10,000–19,900 with successive categories at 20,000–39,900, 40,000–79,900, 80,000–159,900, 160,000–319,900 and 320,000 and over.

Each of the 2274 known cases finds its place in one of these categories (or in the category for all cities under 10,000) and I have assigned each of the 379 unknown cases to its most likely category. For example, a city whose population in 1500 was 11,000 and in 1650 was 18,000, but whose population in the intervening years is unknown, would be assigned to category I (10,000–19,900) as long as the city's history offers no reason to believe otherwise. Not all cases are as straightforward as this one, but the broadness of the size categories minimizes the number of problematical decisions that need to be made.

The distribution of assignments of unknown cases by size category is displayed in table 2.2. There it is evident that the great majority of the 379 unknown cases involve the smaller cities: 138 of them were assigned to category 0 (under 10,000) and 178 to category I (10,000–19,900). These two categories together account for 84 per cent of all unknowns. Only five cases were assigned a rank of III (40,000–79,900), four of them involving the elusive Andalusian city of Granada.

Table 2.1 Number of unknowns by territory and by year, 1500–1800

Territory	Total number of cities	1500	1550	1600	1650	1700	1750	1800	Total number of unknowns	% of all spaces
1 Scandinavia	6	1	1	2	1	1	0	0	6	14.3
2 England and Wales	44	0	0	0	1	0	2	0	3	1.0
3 Scotland	8	1	1	0	2	1	0	0	5	8.9
4 Ireland	8	0	0	0	0	0	2	0	2	3.6
5 Netherlands	21	0	0	0	0	0	0	0	0	0
6 Belgium	20	1	1	5	2	2	1	0	12	8.6
7 Germany	56	2	7	6	6	6	10	0	37	9.4
8 France	78	26	31	31	33	0	3	0	124	22.7
9 Switzerland	4	0	0	0	0	0	0	0	0	0
10 Northern Italy	34	10	3	1	10	11	2	0	37	15.5
11 Central Italy	11	3	1	1	0	0	0	0	5	6.5
12 Southern Italy	30	10	5	3	4	6	6	1	35	16.7
13 Spain	43	28	11	0	12	12	24	0	87	28.9
14 Portugal	5	3	2	3	0	3	1	2	14	40.0
15 Austria-Bohemia	8	2	3	1	2	2	0	0	10	10.1
16 Poland	3	0	0	0	0	1	1	0	2	9.5
Region										
1–6 North and west	107	3	3	7	6	4	5	0	28	3.7
7–9 Central	138	28	38	37	39	6	13	0	161	16.7
10–14 Mediterranean	123	54	22	8	26	32	33	3	178	20.8
15–16 Eastern	11	2	3	1	2	3	1	0	12	14.3
Europe	379	87	66	53	73	45	52	3	379	14.3

ASSEMBLING THE DATA BASE

Table 2.2 Assignment of unknowns to size category, 1500–1800

Size category	Year						
	1500	1550	1600	1650	1700	1750	1800
0 Under 10,000	29	21	11	32	23	22	0
I 10,000–19,900	47	35	28	27	18	20	3
II 20,000–39,900	11	9	14	13	3	8	0
III 40,000–79,900	0	1	0	1	1	2	0
IV 80,000–159,900	0	0	0	0	0	0	0
V 160,000–319,900	0	0	0	0	0	0	0
VI 320,000 and over	0	0	0	0	0	0	0
1 Total number of cities assigned to categories I–VI	58	45	42	41	22	30	3
2 Estimated population ('000s)	908	753	748	763	374	590	40
3 Assigned cities as % of all cities	38	27	19	21	10	12	1
4 Estimated assigned population as % of total urban population	26	17	13	12	5	7	0.3

In order to produce estimates of total urban population the populations of the unknown cases are assumed to equal the average population of the known cities in the size category to which the unknown cases have been assigned. Thus, the cities assigned to category I are assumed to have 13,000 inhabitants for the purpose of calculating aggregate urban population.

These assignment procedures are not without their risks. But the fact that the great majority of unknown cases involves the smaller cities limits the sort of biases that are likely. Errors in assignment may affect the *number* of cities in category I, but they are unlikely greatly to alter estimates of the total urban population. Consider the data for 1650: for this year 21 per cent of all cities with 10,000 or more inhabitants were assigned, but the small average size of these cities had the consequence that only 12 per cent of the total urban population was accounted for by cities for which no specific information is available.

3

THE CONTOURS OF EUROPEAN URBANIZATION I

THE DATA BASE

The product of the procedures described in the last chapter is the data base displayed in appendix 1: a large table listing 379 cities with estimates of their populations at fifty-year intervals. A second table shows the size catagories in which each city falls or to which it is assigned. This data base forms the foundation for the description and analysis that follows.

Of the perhaps 3000–4000 settlements in Europe that were vested with city rights of one form or another, or were otherwise acknowledged to be urban places around 1500, only 154 were inhabited by 10,000 or more people, and only 4 contained as many as 100,000. These cities, far from being well distributed over the face of Europe, were geographically very concentrated. Italy alone accounted for 44 of the 154, while France and Belgium accounted for another 44. Indeed, the larger cities of Europe were primarily to be found in that part of Europe that had known an extended period of Roman occupation and city-building. If we abandon for a moment the boundaries that form the basis for territorial analysis in this study (as in figure 2.1) and divide Europe, as the Romans did, at the Rhine and Danube rivers, the Romanized zone below those rivers accounted in 1500 for over 71 per cent of all cities above the 10,000 level, and all four cities at or above the 100,000 level.[1]

Throughout the sixteenth century, populations grew in a context of vigorous economic expansion. In some regions of Europe this continued until nearly the middle of the seventeenth century. During this 'long sixteenth century' the number of cities with at least 10,000 inhabitants rose by over 40 per cent to 220 in 1600 and perhaps more in the decades immediately following. This urban growth was well distributed over nearly every part of Europe;

Table 3.1   Number of cities with at least 10,000 inhabitants, by territory, 1500–1800

Territory	1500	1550	1600	1650	1700	1750	1800
1 Scandinavia	1	1	2	2	2	3	6
2 England and Wales	5	4	6	8	11	21	44
3 Scotland	1	1	1	1	2	5	8
4 Ireland	0	0	0	1	3	3	8
5 Netherlands	11	12	19	19	20	18	19
6 Belgium	12	12	12	14	15	15	20
7 Germany	23	27	30	23	30	35	53
8 France	32	34	43	44	55	55	78
9 Switzerland	1	1	2	2	3	4	4
10 Northern Italy	21	22	30	19	22	29	33
11 Central Italy	9	9	9	11	10	11	11
12 Southern Italy	14	15	20	20	19	25	30
13 Spain	20	27	37	24	22	24	34
14 Portugal	1	4	5	5	5	5	5
15 Austria-Bohemia	3	3	3	3	4	6	8
16 Poland	0	1	1	1	1	2	3
Region							
1–6 North and west	30	30	40	45	53	65	105
7–9 Central	56	62	75	69	88	95	135
10–14 Mediterranean	65	77	101	79	78	94	113
15–16 Eastern	3	4	4	4	5	7	11
Europe	154	173	220	197	224	261	364

as a consequence it left unaltered the historic predominance of the old urbanized core of 'Roman' Europe. In 1600, just as a century earlier, 71 per cent of all cities above the 10,000 population threshold were located south of the Rhine–Danube line.

Between the beginning and middle decades of the seventeenth century Europe experienced, on a selective basis, sharp demographic reversals: first in the Mediterranean lands (1596–1602, 1630, 1647–52), later in central Europe (during the Thirty Years' War), still later in Denmark and Poland (1656–60).[2] Elsewhere, population growth slowed or ceased. In this environment the number of cities standing above the 10,000 population threshold ceased to grow and in the hardest-hit areas decreased.

In the aftermath of these dramatic reversals, a new process of urban expansion slowly got under way. Viewed from a Europe-wide perspective this renewed process of urban expansion differed profoundly from the sixteenth century expansion. By 1750 the number of cities of 10,000 or more inhabitants exceeded the 1600 peak by only 41 (or 18 per cent), but now the territories beyond the Rhine and Danube held over 35 per cent of these cities and the older urbanized lands no longer possessed a disproportionate number of the very large cities. This altered balance was a combined result of selective urban contraction and growth.

The last half century covered by the data base is one of renewed vigorous population growth in nearly all of Europe. The growth of the number of cities qualifying for inclusion in the data base, which had been gradual in the century after 1650, now intensified and became more general. By 1800 there were 364 European cities with 10,000 or more inhabitants, a 40 per cent increase over 1750. This rapid expansion of the number of such cities did not, of course, end in 1800: by 1850 there were 878, in 1890 there were 1709.

The number of European cities with at least 10,000 inhabitants more than doubled in the three centuries after 1500. However, this long-term expansion

Table 3.2 Total population of all cities with at least 10,000 inhabitants, by territory, 1500–1800 ('000s)

Territory	1500	1550	1600	1650	1700	1750	1800
1 Scandinavia	13	13	26	63	115	167	228
2 England and Wales	80	112	255	495	718	1,021	1,870
3 Scotland	13	13	30	35	53	119	276
4 Ireland	0	0	0	17	96	161	369
5 Netherlands	150	191	364	603	639	580	604
6 Belgium	295	375	301	415	486	432	548
7 Germany	385	534	662	528	714	956	1,353
8 France	688	814	1,114	1,438	1,747	1,970	2,382
9 Switzerland	10	12	25	22	39	60	63
10 Northern Italy	638	711	897	614	778	924	1,032
11 Central Italy	287	286	362	384	399	448	489
12 Southern Italy	377	501	714	579	584	787	1,074
13 Spain	414	639	923	672	673	767	1,165
14 Portugal	30	138	155	199	230	209	252
15 Austria-Bohemia	60	67	90	100	180	294	410
16 Poland	0	10	15	20	15	36	103
Region							
1–6 North and west	552	704	976	1,628	2,107	2,481	3,895
7–9 Central	1,083	1,360	1,801	1,988	2,500	2,987	3,798
10–14 Mediterranean	1,746	2,275	3,051	2,448	2,663	3,135	4,012
15–16 Eastern	60	77	105	120	195	330	513
Europe	3,441	4,416	5,933	6,184	7,465	8,933	12,218

was neither linear nor general. The data base makes possible not only the charting of the number of cities but also the calculation of Europe's total population resident in cities of 10,000 and more inhabitants. The figures presented in table 3.2 consist of summations of the 'known' populations and population estimations for the 'unknown' cities following the procedures described above in the final section of chapter 2.

Table 3.2 shows that Europe's 154 cities above the threshold size in 1500 contained just under 3.5 million inhabitants. In the following century Europe's urban population rose to nearly 6 million, growing much more rapidly than the number of eligible cities (70 per cent and 40 per cent respectively). Moreover in the seventeenth century, when the number of cities above the threshold level experienced a substantial decline, the size of the urban population did not: it continued to grow. There was no fifty-year interval when the urban population failed to grow. By 1800 12.2 million persons resided in the 364 cities of 10,000 or more inhabitants, a 3.5-fold increase over 1500.

The distribution of these urban people over the various states and regions of Europe was no more even than the distribution of the cities themselves. In 1500 and throughout the sixteenth century fully half of all the people resident in cities of at least 10,000 inhabitants lived in Italy and Iberia. About one-third lived in France, Germany and Switzerland (the 'central' region), and one-sixth in Scandinavia, the British Isles and the Low Countries. This rough balance was undisturbed by the rapid economic expansion of the sixteenth century. In the eighteenth century a rough balance again characterized the distribution of urban population among the major regions: north and west, central, and Mediterranean Europe each claimed about one-third of the total. The discontinuity implied by these two distributions occurred suddenly and dramatically in the first half of the seventeenth century. Then the changes in the number of cities with at least 10,000 inhabitants described above, and regional differences in urban growth-rates quickly caused the north and west region, led by England and the Dutch Republic, to increase its share of the total urban population to over one-quarter, while the Mediterranean lands fell from over half to under 40 per cent. Throughout this era, the central zone held firm with a one-third share of the total urban population.

The data base uncovers an urban Europe (of relatively large cities) which in 1500 consisted of 154 cities and 3.5 million persons, half of whom lived in Italy and Iberia and only one-fifth of whom lived beyond the Rhine and Danube. By 1800 this urban Europe comprised 364 cities with 12.2 million inhabitants. The Mediterranean region had lost its urban predominance in a dramatic structural transformation during the first half of the seventeenth century, and now held little more than one-third of the urban population.

Table 3.3 Percentage of total European urban population, by region, 1500–1800

Region	1500	1550	1600	1650	1700	1750	1800
North and west	16.0	15.9	16.5	26.4	28.3	27.8	31.9
Central	31.5	30.8	30.3	32.1	33.3	33.4	31.0
Mediterranean	50.7	51.5	51.4	39.6	35.8	35.1	32.9
Eastern	1.7	1.7	1.8	1.9	2.6	3.7	4.2
British Isles	2.7	2.8	4.8	8.8	11.7	14.6	20.6
Low Countries	12.9	12.8	11.2	16.5	15.1	11.4	9.4
Rest of northern Europe	33.7	32.9	32.6	35.1	37.4	38.9	37.1
Mediterranean	50.7	51.5	51.4	39.6	35.8	35.1	32.9

The character of urban growth after 1600 also undermined the dominance of the larger zone of long-term Roman urbanization. In 1800 the urban population located north of the Rhine and Danube was rapidly approaching 50 per cent of the European total.

Demographic urbanization, according to Tisdale's definition (p. 10), is the result of an increase in the number and/or an increase in the size of cities. We have already noted the increase in the number of cities whose population exceeded the minimum size threshold; the even greater increase of the total urban population implies that the average size of Europe's cities also grew. Or, to be more precise, the urban growth process that caused so many cities to cross the 10,000 population threshold (increasing the number of cities in the data base) also increased the number of cities in the higher size categories (increasing the average size of cities in the data base). The size-distribution of European cities will be analysed in detail in chapter 6; my purpose here is simply to describe the evolving pattern of city sizes that stands behind the overall increase of urban population.

The size categories used throughout this study (introduced on p. 25) each cover a range of population such that the upper limit of each category is double its lower limit. Thus, the range of category I is 10,000–19,900, II is 20,000–39,900, III is 40,000–79,900, IV is 80,000–159,900, V is 160,000–319,900, and VI is 320,000 and above. Table 3.4 presents the frequency distributions of the number of cities by size category, while table 3.5 presents the total urban population of the cities within each size category for the four regions and for Europe as a whole. These data for the sixteen territories are presented in appendix 3.

In Europe as a whole the rate at which the number of cities in each size category increased varied directly with the level of the size category. Thus, while the number of cities of 10,000–19,900 doubled over the three centuries, the number of cities of 20,000–79,900 (categories II and III) grew by

Table 3.4 Number of cities by size category, 1500–1800

Size category	1500	1550	1600	1650	1700	1750	1800
Region 1	*North and west Europe*						
I	20	18	25	20	26	37	60
II	7	8	11	17	14	14	24
III	3	2	3	6	10	10	16
IV	0	2	0	0	1	2	2
V	0	0	1	1	1	1	2
VI	0	0	0	1	1	1	1
Total	30	30	30	45	53	65	105
Region 2	*Central Europe*						
I	38	41	41	39	47	45	78
II	15	14	22	20	29	34	40
III	2	6	11	9	10	12	11
IV	1	1	0	0	1	2	5
V	0	0	1	0	0	0	0
VI	0	0	0	1	1	1	1
Total	56	62	75	69	88	94	135
Region 3	*Mediterranean Europe*						
I	40	40	56	50	41	52	63
II	13	22	25	14	20	25	27
III	9	12	13	7	8	9	10
IV	3	2	6	7	7	7	9
V	0	1	1	1	2	1	3
VI	0	0	0	0	0	0	1
Total	65	77	101	79	78	94	113
Region 4	*Eastern Europe*						
I	1	2	2	1	3	4	5
II	2	2	1	2	1	2	3
III	0	0	1	1	0	1	2
IV	0	0	0	0	1	0	0
V	0	0	0	0	0	1	1
VI	0	0	0	0	0	0	0
Total	3	4	4	4	5	8	11
All of Europe							
I	99	101	124	110	117	138	206
II	37	46	59	53	64	75	94
III	14	20	28	23	28	32	39
IV	4	5	6	7	10	11	16
V	0	1	3	2	3	3	6
VI	0	0	0	2	2	2	3
Total	154	173	220	197	224	261	364

Note
For distributions of cities by size category per territory, see appendix 3.

Table 3.5 Urban population by size category, 1500–1800 ('000s)

Size category	1500	1550	1600	1650	1700	1750	1800
Region 1	*North and west Europe*						
I	252	227	326	276	330	498	802
II	180	218	288	445	383	385	654
III	120	90	162	332	539	530	1,006
IV	0	170	0	0	80	183	183
V	0	0	200	175	200	210	385
VI	0	0	0	400	575	675	865
Total	552	704	976	1,628	2,107	2,481	3,895
Region 2	*Central Europe*						
I	502	550	536	516	614	629	1,053
II	391	385	557	519	749	908	1,036
III	90	295	488	523	530	670	578
IV	100	130	0	0	97	204	519
V	0	0	220	0	0	0	0
VI	0	0	0	430	510	576	581
Total	1,083	1,360	1,801	1,988	2,500	2,987	3,798
Region 3	*Mediterranean Europe*						
I	539	549	734	698	570	721	897
II	363	588	671	361	518	689	722
III	494	671	706	390	408	529	499
IV	350	256	659	823	786	891	957
V	0	212	281	176	381	305	510
VI	0	0	0	0	0	0	427
Total	1,746	2,275	3,051	2,448	2,663	3,135	4,012
Region 4	*Eastern Europe*						
I	13	23	28	13	42	53	64
II	47	54	27	47	39	43	78
III	0	0	50	60	0	59	140
IV	0	0	0	0	114	0	0
V	0	0	0	0	0	175	231
VI	0	0	0	0	0	0	0
Total	60	77	105	120	195	330	513
All of Europe							
I	1,306	1,348	1,624	1,503	1,556	1,901	2,816
II	981	1,244	1,543	1,372	1,689	2,025	2,521
III	704	1,056	1,406	1,305	1,477	1,788	2,223
IV	450	556	659	823	1,077	1,278	1,659
V	0	212	701	351	581	690	1,126
VI	0	0	0	830	1,085	1,251	1,873
Total	3,441	4,416	5,933	6,184	7,465	8,933	12,218

Note
For urban population by size category per territory, see appendix 3.

260 per cent, while the number of cities with at least 80,000 inhabitants (categories IV, V and VI) grew more than sixfold. In 1500 Europe numbered but four cities with at least 100,000 inhabitants – Paris, Milan, Venice and Naples – and three of these are thought to have stood near that minimum figure. By 1600 the number of 100,000-plus cities had doubled to eight, and by 1800 it had more than doubled again to seventeen. By then three great cities, London, Paris and Naples, surpassed the 320,000 threshold of the largest size category, a category without members until the mid-seventeenth century.

A corollary to this pattern of city size evolution is the progressive concentration of the total urban population in the larger cities. Between 1500 and 1800 the number of inhabitants of cities in category I (10,000–19,900) doubled; the total population of cities in category II and III 20,000–79,900) almost tripled, and the total population of cities in categories IV and above (at least 80,000) rose tenfold.

This European-wide pattern is a composite of numerous localized patterns of city growth that display considerable variability. In such territories as Belgium, Italy, Spain, Austria and Bohemia the number of cities in categories I and II (10,000–39,900) grows slowly at best until 1750; in England, Scotland, the Netherlands and Switzerland, the number of such cities increases, in one period or another, by leaps and bounds. But every territory except two (Belgium and Switzerland) develops over time one or more representatives in the upper size categories (80,000 and above). Such cities were originally highly concentrated in Italy. As late as 1600, five of the nine were located there. Cities of 80,000 or more inhabitants never became truly numerous (in 1800 there were twenty-five), but they did come to be remarkably well distributed across Europe, with at least one in fourteen of the sixteen territories by the end of the eighteenth century.

So far I have presented the urban population as an autonomous entity, thereby perhaps giving the false impression that cities grew and increased in number in isolation from the larger non-urban society. This has been done to highlight certain features of the long-term process of urban growth. If Tisdale's definition of urbanization were sufficient an exclusive focus on the number and size of cities would, indeed, be warranted. But, as noted above, most students of urbanization regard demographic urbanization as a growth of cities *that results in an increase in the proportion of the total population residing in urban places.* Thus, the next step in this description of Europe's urban growth must be to express it in relation to the total population.

Do we know enough about the total population of the European states and regions to make these calculations? It must be emphasized that improving our knowledge of total population sizes has not been the chief interest of modern historical demography. The available material is by no means

Table 3.6 Total population of Europe, by territory and region, 1500–1980 (in millions)

	1500	1550	1600	1650	1700	1750	1800	1850	1890	1939	1980
Territory											
1 Scandinavia	1.5	1.7	2.0	2.6	2.9	3.6	5.0	7.9	11.4	16.9	22.3
2 England and Wales	2.6	3.2	4.4	5.6	5.4	6.1	9.2	17.9	29.0	41.8	49.2
3 Scotland	0.8	0.9	1.0	1.0	1.0	1.3	1.6	2.9	4.0	4.8	5.2
4 Ireland	1.0	1.1	1.4	1.8	2.8	3.2	5.3	6.6	4.8	4.3	4.9
5 Netherlands	0.95	1.25	1.5	1.9	1.9	1.9	2.1	3.0	4.5	8.9	14.0
6 Belgium	1.4	1.65	1.6	2.0	2.0	2.2	2.9	4.4	6.1	8.8	9.8
7 Germany	12.0	14.0	16.0	12.0	15.0	17.0	24.5	34.4	49.4	69.5	78.1*
8 France	16.4	19.0	19.0	20.0	19.0	21.7	27.0	35.8	38.4	41.2	53.5
9 Switzerland	0.65	0.8	1.0	1.0	1.2	1.3	1.7	2.4	3.0	4.3	6.3
10 Northern Italy		4.7	5.4	4.3	5.7	6.5	7.2				
11 Central Italy	10.5	2.5	2.9	2.7	2.8	3.1	3.6	24.0	30.5	42.9	56.9
12 Southern Italy		4.2	4.8	4.3	4.8	5.7	7.0				
13 Spain	6.8	7.4	8.1	7.1	7.5	8.9	10.5	15.0	17.6	25.9	37.2
14 Portugal	1.0	1.2	1.1	1.2	2.0	2.3	2.9	3.8	5.1	7.7	9.9
15 Austria-Bohemia	3.5	3.6	4.3	4.1	4.6	5.7	7.9	12.9	17.6	22.3	22.7
16 Poland	2.5	3.0	3.4	3.0	2.8	3.7	4.3	6.0	9.0	15.0	35.2**
Region											
1–6 North and west	8.3	9.8	11.9	14.9	16.0	18.3	26.1	42.7	59.8	85.5	105.4
7–9 Central	29.0	33.8	36.0	33.0	35.2	40.0	53.2	72.6	90.8	115.0	137.9
10–14 Mediterranean	18.3	20.0	22.3	19.6	22.8	26.5	31.2	42.8	53.2	76.5	104.0
15–16 Eastern	6.0	6.6	7.7	7.1	7.4	9.4	12.2	18.9	26.6	37.3	57.9
Europe	61.6	70.2	78.0	74.6	81.4	94.2	122.7	177.0	230.4	314.3	405.2

* East and West Germany only; not directly comparable with earlier figures.
** Post-1945 Poland; not directly comparable with earlier figures. Territories 7 and 16, taken together, continue to cover approximately the same area.

Sources

Scandinavia. Finland: H. Gille, 'The demographic history of the northern European countries in the eighteenth century', *Population Studies* 3 (1949–50). 19; Sweden: ibid.; Norway: Michael Drake, *Population and Society in Norway, 1735–1865* (Cambridge, 1969), 9; Ståle Dyrvik, 'Historical demography in Norway, 1660–1801: a short survey', *Scandinavian Economic History Review* 20 (1972), 27–44; Denmark: Aksel Lassen, 'The population of Denmark in 1660', *Scandinavian Economic History Review* 13 (1965), 1–30; Aksel Lassen, 'The population of Denmark, 1660–1960', *Scandinavian Economic History Review* 14 (1966), 134–67.

England and Wales. E. A. Wrigley and R. S. Schofield, *The Population History of England, 1541–1871: a Reconstruction* (London, 1981), 566, 531–5.

Scotland. J. G. Kyd, *Scottish Population Statistics*, Scottish Historical Society, third series, vol. XLIV (1952), 1–81.

Ireland. Cormac O'Grada, 'The population of Ireland, 1700–1900: a survey', *Annales de démographie historique* (1979), 287; L. M. Cullen, 'Population trends in seventeenth century Ireland', *Economic and Social Review* 6 (1975) 149–65.

Netherlands. J. A. Faber *et al.*, 'Population changes and economic development in the northern Netherlands: a historical survey', *A.A.G. Bijdragen* 12 (1965), 47–110.

Belgium. Roger Mols, 'Die Bevölkerungsgeschichte Belgiens im lichte der heutigen forschung', *Vierteljahrschrift für Sozial- und Wirtschaftsgeschichte* 46 (1959), 491–511; W. P. Blockmans *et al.*, 'Tussen crisis en welvaart: sociale veranderingen 1300–1500', *Algemene geschiedenis der Nederlanden*, vol. 4 (Haarlem, 1980), 44–5.

Germany. F. W. Henning, *Das vorindustrielle Deutschland, 800 bis 1800. Wirtschafts- und Sozialgeschichte*, vol. 1 (Paderborn, 1977), 182; Charles Wilson and Geoffrey Parker (eds) *An Introduction to the Sources of European Economic History, 1500–1800* (Ithaca, NY, and London, 1977), 191.

France. E. Le Roy Ladurie, 'De la crise ultimate à la vraie croissance, 1660–1789', in E. Le Roy Ladurie and M. Morineau (eds), *Histoire de la France rurale*, vol. 2 (Paris, 1975), 576; J. C. Toutain, *La Population de la France de 1700 à 1959* (Paris, 1963), 54–5, 16, 19; see also Jacques Dupâquier, *La Population rurale du bassin parisien à l'époque de Louis XIV* (Paris, 1979), 163–6.

Switzerland. Wilhelm Bickel, *Bevölkerungsgeschichte und Bevölkerungspolitik des Schweiz, seit dem Ausgang des Mittelalters* (Zurich, 1947); H. C. Peyer, 'Die Wirtschaftliche Bedeutung der fremden Dienste für die Schweiz', in J. Schneider (ed.). *Wirtschaftskräfte und Wirtschaftswege*, vol. II (Cologne, 1978), 708.

Italy. Karl Julius Beloch, *Bevölkerungsgeschichte Italiens* (Berlin, 1937–61), vol. 3, 354–5.

Spain. B. Vincent, 'Recents travaux de démographie historique en Espagne (XVIe–XVIIIe siècles)', *Annales de démographie historique* (1977), 473; for estimate for 1650 see Henry Kamen, *Spain in the Later Seventeenth Century, 1665–1700* (London, 1980), 39, 46.

Portugal. José-Gentil Da Silva, 'Au Portugal: structure démographique et developpement économique', *Studi in onore di Amintore Fanfani*, vol. II (Milan, 1962), 490–510; Nuno Alves Morgado, 'Portugal', in W. E. Lee (ed.), *European Demography and Economic Growth* (New York, 1979), 333.

Austria. *Statistisches Handbuch für der Republik Österreich*, vol. 39 (Vienna, 1978), 9.

Czechoslovakia. Alois Mika, 'On the economic status of Czech towns in the period of late feudalism', *Hospodářské Dějiny* 2 (1978); Ludmila Kárníková, *Vývoj obyvatelstva v českých zemích 1754–1914* (Prague, 1965), 327.

Poland. Irena Gieysztorowa, 'Research into the demographic history of Poland: a provisional summing-up', *Acta Poloniae Historica* 18 (1968), 5–17; A. Eisenbach and B. Grochulska, 'Population en Pologne (fin XVIIIe début XIXe siècle)', *Annales de démographie historique* (1965), 111; J. Topolski and A. Wyczanski, 'Les fluctuations de la production agricole en Pologne aux XVIe–XVIIe siècles', *Actes du colloque préparatoire* (1977).

Data for 1850–1979 from Adna F. Weber, *The Growth of Cities in the Nineteenth Century: a Study in Statistics* (New York, 1899); B. R. Mitchell, *European Historical Statistics, 1750–1970* (London, 1975); *Geographical Digest* 19 (1981), 25–39; supplemented by *Statistisk årsbok, 1979, Sveriges officielle statistik* (Stockholm, 1979); *Folke- og Boligtelling 1970* (Oslo, 1974); *Statistical Abstract of Ireland, 1970–71* (Dublin, 1974); *Statistisch zakboek 1980* (The Hague, 1981); *Statistisches Jahrbuch 1980 der Deutschen Demokratischen Republik* (Berlin, 1980); *Statistisches Jahrbuch 1979 für die Bundesrepublik Deutschland* (Stuttgart and Mainz, 1979); *Recensement général de la population de la France* (Paris, 1975); *Statistisches Jahrbuch der Schweiz, 1979* (Basle, 1979); *Eidgenössesches Volkszählung, 1900* (Berne, 1904); *Censo de la población de España, 1897* (Madrid, 1899); *Anuario Estatístico, 1973* (Lisbon, 1973); *Statistisches Handbuch für der Republik Österreich*, vol. 39 (Vienna, 1978); *Mittheilungen aus dem Gebiete des Statistik* (Vienna, 1852); *Statistická rocenka. Československé socialistické republiky, 1979* (Prague, 1979), and *Annuaire statistique de la Republique Polonaise, 1923* (Warsaw, 1924).

unimpeachable, and even when acceptable, its usefulness for our own purposes is often undermined by recurring boundary changes.

Table 3.6 displays the best estimates I have found for the total populations of the territories whose urban populations are the object of this study. The population estimates are presented at the same fifty-year intervals as the urban populations. Quite a number of estimates of the total population of Europe are in circulation. In comparing the figures presented here with the estimates of others, it is necessary to remember that the outer limits of Europe are here more restrictive than in most other cases. It also bears emphasizing that the totals presented here derive exclusively from the estimates for the various territories. No independent assumptions have been made about the probable course of Europe's total population.

The data in tables 3.2 and 3.6 make possible the calculation of the percentage of total population resident in cities of at least 10,000 inhabitants for each fifty-year interval from 1500 to 1800 for each of the sixteen territories and four regions, and for Europe as a whole. In reading these tables one must take into account the weaknesses in the data, particularly the estimates of total population. It is possible to guard against seeking to achieve a spurious precision by focusing attention wherever possible on the urban growth patterns of the larger territorial aggregates: the estimate for Spain in 1650, for example, is probably less reliable than the estimate for the Mediterranean region in 1650. Similarly, one can be more confident of the *direction of change* in urbanization over time shown by table 3.7 than of the calculation of the *absolute level* of urbanization for any one period.

In 1500 the percentage of the total population residing in cities of at least 10,000 inhabitants varied enormously by district. In the vast expanses of Britain's 'Celtic fringe', Scandinavia and eastern Europe, cities of such a size were all but unknown. No more than 1 per cent of the population lived in them. At the other extreme stood the Low Countries and Italy, where these cities claimed 13–23 per cent of total population. The great bulk of Europe – Iberia, France, Germany and England – held an intermediate position, with 3–5 per cent of the population located in the cities. In Europe as a whole fewer than 6 per cent of the total population lived in 154 cities with at least 10,000 inhabitants.

The three centuries that follow, viewed globally, could be described as an epoch of steady, gradual urbanization. In every single fifty-year interval the urban percentage rose, reaching 10 per cent by 1800. Moreover, in comparing 1500 with 1800, all four regions shared to some extent in these gains, as did fifteen of the sixteen territories, Belgium forming the sole exception.

This image of a gradual, broadly based process of urbanization, seemingly confirmed by table 3.7, is a statistical artefact. Further inspection of these

Table 3.7 Urban percentage of total population, by territory and region, 1500–1800

	1500	1550	1600	1650	1700	1750	1800
Territory							
1 Scandinavia	0.9	0.8	1.4	2.4	4.0	4.6	4.6
2 England and Wales	3.1	3.5	5.8	8.8	13.3	16.7	20.3
3 Scotland	1.6	1.4	3.0	3.5	5.3	9.2	17.3
4 Ireland	0	0	0	0.9	3.4	5.0	7.0
5 Netherlands	15.8	15.3	24.3	31.7	33.6	30.5	28.8
6 Belgium	21.1	22.7	18.8	20.8	23.9	19.6	18.9
7 Germany	3.2	3.8	4.1	4.4	4.8	5.6	5.5
8 France	4.2	4.3	5.9	7.2	9.2	9.1	8.8
9 Switzerland	1.5	1.5	2.5	2.2	3.3	4.6	3.7
10 Northern Italy			15.1	16.6	14.3	13.6	14.2	14.3
11 Central Italy	12.4	11.4	12.5	14.2	14.3	14.5	13.6
12 Southern Italy			11.9	14.9	13.5	12.2	13.8	15.3
13 Spain	6.1	8.6	11.4	9.5	9.0	8.6	11.1
14 Portugal	3.0	11.5	14.1	16.6	11.5	9.1	8.7
15 Austria-Bohemia	1.7	1.9	2.1	2.4	3.9	5.2	5.2
16 Poland	0	0.3	0.4	0.7	0.5	1.0	2.5
Region							
1–6 North and west	6.6	7.2	8.2	10.9	13.1	13.6	14.9
7–9 Central	3.7	4.0	5.0	6.0	7.1	7.5	7.1
10–14 Mediterranean	9.5	11.4	13.7	12.5	11.7	11.8	12.9
15–16 Eastern	1.1	1.2	1.4	1.7	2.6	3.5	4.2
Europe	5.6	6.3	7.6	8.3	9.2	9.5	10.0
British Isles	2.0	2.4	4.2	6.5	9.4	12.3	15.6
Low Countries	18.5	19.5	21.5	26.1	28.6	24.7	23.0
Rest of northern Europe	3.3	3.5	4.3	5.0	6.1	6.5	6.4

figures will raise doubts about both the gradualness of the process and about its broad diffusion.

The tempo of demographic urbanization was not steady; nor did it gradually gain in momentum over the span of 300 years – a scenario that would by some accounts stand as a fitting prelude to the ignition of modern industrialization.

Rather, urban growth began slowly in the first half of the sixteenth century (an age of urban decay in many places, the rapid growth of rural population notwithstanding), quickened its pace dramatically in the century from 1550 to 1650, and then decelerated, reaching a low point in the first half of the eighteenth century. This description fits the non-Mediterranean regions of Europe. In Iberia and Italy urban growth was rapid throughout the sixteenth century only to collapse, as is well known, in the seventeenth. In this region the eighteenth century is one of a slow and only partial recovery of the earlier level of urbanization.

The curious feature of this chronology is not the divergence between the Mediterranean countries and the rest of Europe: it is the fact that major increases in the percentage of the population resident in cities in non-Mediterranean Europe was at least as much a phenomenon of demographic stagnation and decline as it was of demographic expansion. The second half of the sixteenth century was the only period in which rapid population growth and rapid urbanization occurred together. The latter half of the eighteenth century was not such an era; in almost all areas it was at best a period of very sluggish urban growth. On the other hand, the major gains of northern European urbanization were made during the seventeenth century, particularly during the first half, when total population grew little if at all.

This portrait of urban and rural populations following divergent paths, and of major gains in urbanization being made in an era of 'crisis' rather than in one of general economic expansion, is not the expected one, and is certainly difficult to reconcile with the concept of a benign, gradual process of long-term urbanization. In later chapters the implication of these insights into the character of European urbanization will be pursued more fully.

When one examines the course of urban growth country-by-country, only one area stands out as truly experiencing a long-term, gradually accelerating process of urbanization: the British Isles (including Ireland). Every other territory achieved most of its gains in a relatively brief period (Spain, 1500–1600; the Netherlands, 1550–1650; France and Scandinavia, 1600–1700; Austria 1650–1750), whereafter further urbanization – if there was any – occurred on a more modest scale.

This motley pattern of regional urban growth yielded in 1800 a Europe in which the lightly urbanized fringe lands of the sixteenth century had become endowed with sufficient large cities to raise their urban percentage to the 4–6 per cent range, and in which the historic zones of high urbanization, the Low Countries and Italy, were joined by Great Britain. In comparison with 1500 it is now harder to identify a large region of 'typical' urbanization, but France and Germany might still be held up as the largest territories whose urban characteristics seem intermediate to the extremes of European experience.

EXTENSIONS BACKWARD AND FORWARD

Backward

Before analysing in greater detail some of the features of European urban growth uncovered by the data base, it will be useful to place urbanization from 1500 to 1800 in a larger context by assembling such data as are available about the course of urban growth before 1500 and after 1800.

Medieval urbanism has attracted an enormous amount of scholarly attention, but so far the fruits of this interest have assumed a quantitative cast only very occasionally. Apart from some of the larger cities – such as Florence, Venice and Ghent – little is known about the details of urban population. Perhaps little is knowable. Still, the available information about the process of town foundings (as marked by the granting of municipal charters) and expansion (as marked by the rebuilding of town walls) does allow for a few basic observations.[3]

The revival of European urban life that began in the tenth century did not constitute a reinvention of urban settlement. Even so strong a proponent of the novelty of the medieval city as Henry Pirenne assures us that the Carolingian period knew sites of concentrated habitation, or nodes of military and administrative activity. He insists that these nodes, often fortresses or remnants of Roman urbanism,

> did not show the slightest urban character. [Its] population comprised, aside from the knights and clerics who made up its essential part, only men employed in their service and whose number was certainly of very little importance. It was a fortress population; it was not a city population.[4]

He goes on to observe that 'everything indicates that the population of the burgs (fortresses) never consisted of more than a few hundred men and that the towns probably did not pass the figure of two or three thousand souls'.[5]

We need not enter into the debate about how these early medieval nodes acquired their unique urban characteristics, nor need we accept as accurate Pirenne's guesses of the size of these places. It is clear none the less that around the year 1000 concentrated non-rural populations were very small. With the probable exception of Italy, no territories in Latin Christendom then possessed cities of 10,000 or more inhabitants. It is much more hazardous to guess at what the total population of these small burgs and ecclesiastical seats might have been. But for our purposes it will be sufficient to take the total urban population (i.e. in towns of whatever size) to be well under 5 per cent and the percentage in cities of at least 10,000 to be close to zero.

From the tenth century through the thirteenth century the records of the chartering of cities and of the expansion of their walls testify to a vigorous urban growth. This process of city foundings came to an end by the early fourteenth century, except in the northern and easternmost reaches of Europe where it continued into the seventeenth century. Consequently it would be of great interest to know about the number of cities and their populations at this time – at the end of the great era of urban expansion and just before the demographic catastrophe to come in 1347.

Europe's population on the eve of the Black Death is a subject that has attracted the curiosity of many scholars. As a consequence, quite a number of estimates are available of the size of the larger cities. In addition, two historians in independent studies have sought to identify systematically all cities of at least 10,000 inhabitants around the year 1300.

The Belgian medievalist Léopold Genicot offers a survey of the literature concerning the cities of Latin Christendom.[6] He categorizes cities according to his confidence in the veracity of the sources, identifying 64 cities of at least 10,000 inhabitants with certainty, an additional 19 'probablement', and 16 more where the assertions found in the literature cannot be verified. Thus, the number of European cities of at least 10,000 inhabitants in 1300 stood somewhere between 99 and 64. Genicot went on to identify 4 to 6 of these cities as containing at least 50,000 inhabitants and another 21 to 34 in the 20,000–50,000 class. His survey implies that Europe's cities of 10,000 and above together contained no more than about 2 million inhabitants.

Josiah Cox Russell, in *Medieval Regions and Their Cities*, approached the task rather differently from Genicot.[7] He asserted the applicability of a specific *ad hoc* relationship between the size of the largest city of a region and the number and size of smaller cities in that region. Much depends on the validity of his formula and on his specification of Europe's regions, for wherever direct evidence failed him he relied on these concepts to estimate the number of cities of at least 10,000 inhabitants that *must have* existed.

His results are intriguing. Europe in the early fourteenth century, with a total population somewhat in excess of the 1500 figure, numbered 125 cities above the 10,000 population threshold containing a total population of about 3 million. Four cities numbered at least 100,000 inhabitants, the same 4 that could make that claim in 1500. Italy and Iberia together accounted for 55 per cent of the total urban population (about the same as in 1500 and 1600), while France and Germany (central Europe) accounted for 33 per cent of the total urban population (again, the same share that I have found for the entire early modern period). In summary, Russell's approach describes an urban pattern for *c.* 1300 that is very similar to my differently assembled data for 1500. In only one important respect did the pre-plague urban structure differ significantly from that of 1500: the number of cities identified by Russell as having at least 10,000 inhabitants was 30 fewer than in 1500. Consequently the total urban population stood at about 85 per cent of the 1500 figure while the total population of 1300 is widely believed to have been larger than two centuries later.

Genicot's survey almost certainly undercounts the number of eligible cities, since he lists only those that he can positively identify on the basis of direct evidence. Russell, in an effort to achieve a more comprehensive overview, applies a 'theory', one that cannot inspire complete confidence in the outcome. But even his results, which run the risk of exaggerating the number and size of cities in 1300, present a portrait of pre-plague urbanism in which the urban population is substantially smaller – and a smaller portion of the total – than in 1500. The implications of this finding are interesting. Despite the dramatic disruptions to the European population brought about by the Black Death and the consequent transformation of rural settlement patterns that took place in several regions (the *Wüstungen*), the urban population grew while its overall distribution seems to have remained remarkably stable, or to have reconstituted itself by 1500 to much as it had been two centuries earlier. Indeed, when Genicot's list of cities of 1300 is compared with the data base in 1500, only 8 cities listed by Genicot as certain of having 10,000 inhabitants are not on the 1500 list.

Just as in the seventeenth century, when the percentage of the total population living in cities of at least 10,000 inhabitants rose as a consequence of city growth in the face of a declining rural population, the late fourteenth and fifteenth centuries were witness to an increased overall level of urbanization (from something under 5 per cent in 1300 to 5.6 per cent in 1500) in an environment of declining rural population.

Forward

The challenge of extending the study of European urban growth backward from 1500 resides in the scarcity of data. In extending the study forward from 1800 into the nineteenth and twentieth centuries data availability is no longer a severe problem; now the challenge is to achieve uniformity and comparability in the data as cities proliferate and spill over their boundaries to transform vast territories into urbanized regions.

The explosive and ultimately all-embracing character of modern urbanization is well known and has been described and analysed in many publications.[8] The number of cities above the 10,000 population threshold rose from 364 in 1800 to 878 in 1850 and reached 1709 in 1890. By then the overall growth of population was such that the 10,000 threshold had ceased to have anything like the same sort of meaning as an indicator of urbanity that it had possessed in earlier times. Moreover, after 1890 the growth of large cities increasingly took the form of suburbanization and the creation of metropolitan districts. New procedures are needed to measure the size of such cities and these make comparisons with the past difficult.

The following statistics of European urbanization since 1800 will make clear the nature of the problem. The number of cities of 100,000 or more inhabitants grew from 17 in 1800 to 43 in 1850 and to 101 in 1890. By 1979 the same territory numbered 390 such cities. The percentage of the total population resident in these cities rose from 3.2 per cent in 1800 to 13.3 per cent in 1890 and, using a narrow definition of city population, to 33.8 per cent in 1979. If we direct our attention to the larger number of cities with at least 50,000 inhabitants in 1979 the urban percentage rises to 41.8 per cent. But when the metropolitan rings of these 840 cities of at least 50,000 inhabitants are added, the urban percentage doubles. Four-fifths of all western and central Europeans now reside in the direct sphere of influence, i.e. in the labour market of a large city.[9] If one were to employ similar criteria to 1800, the 840 largest cities (which of course include many cities far under the 10,000 population level) and their rural environs might embrace about one-fifth of the total population.

The inherent difficulty of comparing late-twentieth-century urban population data with those of the late eighteenth century makes it advisable to limit such comparisons to the simplest issues. This problem is less severe with nineteenth-century evidence. Until the late nineteenth century all but the very largest cities continued to maintain coherent physical forms. This facilitates comparisons with the results of the data base for 1500–1800, although it must be emphasized that a city of 10,000 inhabitants in 1890 was by no means the *functional* equivalent of a city that size in 1800.[10]

The data presented in tables 3.8 and 3.9 are drawn from published works and census materials and have been arranged to faciliate comparison with the results of the data base analysis. The pattern of urban growth displayed in these tables calls into question the conventional use of 1800 as a dividing line between what is sometimes called pre-modern and modern urbanization. In designing this study I uncritically accepted the validity of this convention, but it now appears that the middle of the nineteenth century – one might say the beginning of the railway age – is a worthier candidate for the title of threshold to the era of universal urbanization.

Until the mid-nineteenth century massive urbanization is almost wholly confined to Great Britain. In fact a large number of societies, such as the Scandinavian countries, the Low Countries, Italy and Austria, made only modest gains, or indeed none at all until after 1850. Moreover, until 1850 the most rapid growth of urban population occurred in the smaller cities, those in the 10,000–19,900 category. This suggests that a large proportion of urban growth up to 1850 was a reflection of the general rise of population then being experienced. Cities grew rapidly because the population of all settlements was rising rapidly, and this alone caused many small cities to pass the 10,000 inhabitant threshold. After 1850 this 'illusory' urbanization played a much smaller role; then the pace of urban growth in nearly every European country was such as to alter fundamentally the place of cities in their societies. An obvious indication of the cities' new position is the fact that urban growth began to be sufficient to put a permanent halt to the absolute growth of rural population. This occurred in England in the 1860s; by the eve of the Second World War it was general to all of Europe.

Table 5.8 Number of cities, aggregate urban population and urban percentage, by territory, 1800–1980

	1800 (10,000 and over)			1850 (10,000 and over)		
	Number	Population	Urban %	Number	Population	Urban %
Territory						
1 Scandinavia	6	228	4.6	12	00,456	5.8
2 England and Wales	44	1,870	20.3	148	7,310	40.8
3 Scotland	8	276	17.3	18	928	32.0
4 Ireland	8	369	7.0	14	672	10.2
5 Netherlands	19	604	28.8	28	885	29.5
6 Belgium	20	548	18.9	26	900	20.5
7 Germany	53	1,353	5.5	133	3,719	10.8
8 France	78	2,383	8.8	165	5,174	14.5
9 Switzerland	4	63	3.7	8	185	7.7
10–12 Italy	74	2,595	14.6	183	4,875	20.3
13 Spain	34	1,165	11.1	99	2,590	17.3
14 Portugal	5	252	8.7	10	501	13.2
15 Austria-Bohemia	8	410	5.2	17	862	6.7
16 Poland	3	103	2.4	17	560	9.3
Region						
1–6 North and west	105	3,895	14.9	246	11,151	26.1
7–9 Central	135	3,798	7.1	306	9,078	12.5
10–14 Mediterranean	113	4,012	12.9	292	7,996	18.6
15–16 Eastern	11	513	4.2	34	1,422	7.5
Europe	364	12,218	10.0	878	29,617	16.7
British Isles	60	2,515	15.6	180	8,910	32.5
Low Countries	39	1,152	23.0	54	1,785	24.1
Rest of northern Europe	152	4,539	6.4	352	10,956	11.0

(continued)

Table 3.8—continued

	1890 (10,000 and over)			1890 (20,000 and over)		
	Number	Population	Urban %	Number	Population	Urban %
Territory						
1 Scandinavia	37	1,510	13.2	16	1,233	10.8
2 England and Wales	356	17,964	61.9	185	15,564	53.7
3 Scotland	37	2,072	50.3	17	1,708	42.7
4 Ireland	18	845	17.6	8	720	15.0
5 Netherlands	34	1,504	33.4	19	1,317	29.2
6 Belgium	61	2,106	34.5	21	1,580	25.9
7 Germany	382	13,947	28.2	142	10,827	21.9
8 France	232	9,940	25.9	105	8,096	21.1
9 Switzerland	15	480	16.0	8	384	12.8
10–12 Italy	215	6,457	21.2	66	4,163	13.6
13 Spain	174	4,710	26.8	51	3,049	17.3
14 Portugal	15	649	12.7	3	471	9.2
15 Austria-Bohemia	101	3,489	18.1	32	2,570	14.6
16 Poland	32	1,310	14.6	12	1,050	11.7
Region						
1–6 North and west	543	25,941	43.4	266	22,122	37.0
7–9 Central	629	24,367	26.8	255	19,307	21.3
10–14 Mediterranean	404	11,816	22.2	120	7,683	14.5
15–16 Eastern	133	4,799	18.0	44	3,620	13.6
Europe	1,709	66,923	29.0	685	52,732	22.9
British Isles	411	20,821	55.0	210	17,992	47.6
Low Countries	95	3,610	34.1	40	2,897	27.4
Rest of northern Europe	799	30,676	23.8	315	24,160	18.8

1980 (100,000 and over)

	Number	Population	Urban %	Urban % by national definition
Territory				
1 Scandinavia	23	7,329	32.9	66
2 England and Wales	55	24,958	50.7 }	77
3 Scotland	4	1,627	31.2	
4 Ireland	3	1,057	21.6	49
5 Netherlands	21	6,541	46.7	77
6 Belgium	7	2,798	28.6	72
7 Germany	82	25,417	32.5	78
8 France	55	23,332	43.6	76
9 Switzerland	7	2,173	34.4	57
10–12 Italy	47	16,127	28.3	48
13 Spain	40	13,431	36.1	59
14 Portugal	2	1,062	10.7	29
15 Austria-Bohemia	11	4,833	21.3	53
16 Poland	30	9,500	27.0	55
Region				
1–6 North and west	113	44,310	42.0	73
7–9 Central	144	50,922	36.9	76
10–14 Mediterranean	89	30,620	29.4	50
15–16 Eastern	44	14,333	24.7	54
Europe	390	140,185	34.6	65
British Isles	62	27,642	46.6	75
Low Countries	28	9,339	39.2	75
Rest of northern Europe	167	72,584	45.3	75

THE URBAN POPULATION OF EUROPE

Table 3.9(a) Number of cities by size categories: all of Europe

Size category	1800	1850	1890
10,000–19,900	206	551	1,024
20,000–99,900	141	284	584
100,000 and over	17	43	101
Total	364	878	1,709

Table 3.9(b) Total urban population by size categories: all of Europe ('000s)

Size category	1800	1850	1890
10,000–19,900	2,816	7,388	14,190
20,000–99,900	5,425	10,971	21,871
100,000 and over	3,977	11,259	30,861
Total	12,218	29,617	66,922

Source See table 3.8.

4
THE CONTOURS OF EUROPEAN URBANIZATION II

THE 'TIP OF THE ICEBERG' PROBLEM

The statistical description of European urbanization provided thus far depends on the information contained in the data base of the 379 largest cities in the period 1500–1800. This I then placed in a broader framework by gathering information on the larger cities before 1500 and after 1800. These large cities accounted for the lion's share of certain important urban functions (such as banking, long-distance trade, higher governmental activities, manifestations of high culture) and they concentrated within their walls and precincts a large part of the total urban population.

For many purposes of urban analysis this data base is sufficient. But not for all. Throughout the centuries covered by this study settlements with populations far under the 10,000 threshold were unquestionably 'urban', indeed were primarily responsible for such urban functions as agricultural marketing and distribution, education and religious services, inland transportation and many types of industrial production. That is to say, such cities functioned as integral parts of the larger urban system. Moreover, by their large number these smaller cities must have accounted for a substantial portion of the total urban population. It is unlikely that any generalization about the tempo of urban growth and the character of urbanization in these centuries can safely be made without some attempt to 'deepen' this study to uncover the contours of the large and still unknown urban world of cities with less than 10,000 inhabitants.

The importance of this subject to the calculation of rates of demographic urbanization is immediately apparent from table 4.1. As the number of cities above the 10,000 inhabitant threshold rises from 154 in 1500 to 364 in 1800

Table 4.1 Estimated total population of all 379 cities of the data base, 1500–1800

	1500	1550	1600	1650	1700	1750	1800
Number of cities with at least 10,000 inhabitants	154	173	220	197	224	261	364
Aggregate population	3,441	4,416	5,933	6,184	7,465	8,933	12,218
Number of cities with under 10,000 inhabitants	225	206	159	182	155	118	15
Assumed average population ('000s)	5	5	6	7	7	7.5	8
Aggregate population	1,125	1,030	954	1,274	1,085	885	120
Aggregate population of the 379 cities	4,566	5,446	6,887	7,458	8,550	9,818	12,338
% of total population	7.4	7.8	8.8	10.0	10.5	10.4	10.1

the number of remaining cities falls from 225 to 15. Several of these cities were new urban creations; they either did not exist or were mere villages until some point between 1500 and 1800. But most of them were simply cities of under 10,000 inhabitants, often only slightly under that level. They formed a small and dwindling subset of a much larger set of such cities.

If Europe's urban population were defined as the population of all 379 cities in the data base, regardless of their size in any particular year, the course of population growth displayed in table 4.1 would be altered as follows: the population of cities with at least 10,000 inhabitants grew by 350 per cent over the three centuries, but the 379 cities grew by only 270 per cent. Likewise, the urban percentage when defined as the population residing in cities with at least 10,000 inhabitants rises from 5.6 in 1500 to 10.0 in 1800. The same rate defined as the percentage of total population residing in the 379 cities shows much less movement, from 7.4 in 1500 to 10.1 in 1800. Finally, while the original approach yields a pattern of ever-rising demographic urbanization, the new one shows the growth to have been concentrated in the century after 1550 with utter stagnation in the eighteenth century.

It is of obvious importance to this study to know more about the number and populations of the cities of under 10,000 inhabitants. Yet, as I argued in chapter 2, a direct approach to this task would surely fail. The investment of time and effort searching for sources would yield so little, and leave a data base so full of holes that no dependable conclusions could be drawn from it. I propose here the use of an indirect approach to estimate the size of the smaller cities. This strategy does not permit anything to be said about *particular* cities, but it promises reasonably accurate estimations of the total number and the aggregate population of such cities *as a group*.

The problem before us is to infer something about a large, mainly unobserved mass from our knowledge of a small, observed part of it. This is rather like estimating the size of the submerged part of an iceberg from one's observation of its exposed tip. The key to any such exercise is to know something about the structure and other regular properties of the phenomenon under investigation.

My strategy relies on an often-observed and much-discussed regularity in the distribution of cities when ranked in order of their size. A full discussion of theories about 'rank-size distributions' and an analysis of the historical development of these distributions in urban Europe is presented in chapter 6. Here my use of the rank-size distribution concept is limited to the specific task at hand. In nearly all large territories the large cities are few in number and small cities are numerous. Indeed, the smaller the size class the more numerous are the cities in that class. This logical tendency in the distributions of cities by size often yields a statistical pattern that conforms roughly to that shown in figure 4.1, where cities are plotted in order of their size on a graph, both axes of which are logarithmically scaled.[1]

Some scholars have argued that the cities of a large, well-integrated society

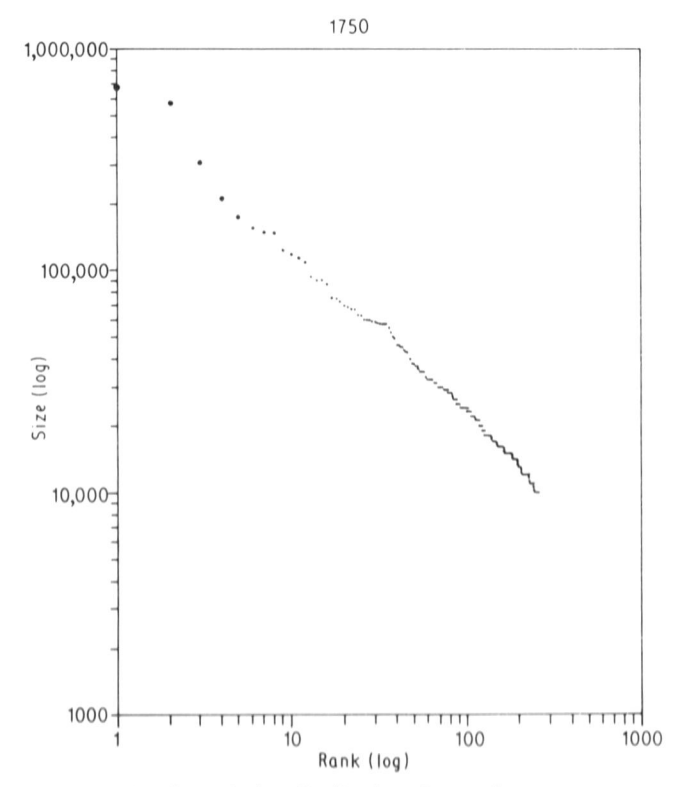

Figure 4.1 Example of a rank-size distribution: Europe in 1750

will not simply conform to this pattern in general, but will tend to conform to a specific version of it, where the second largest city is half the size of the largest, the third-ranked city is one-third the size of the largest and so on, so that the size of a city of any particular rank will tend to be the reciprocal of its rank times the population of the largest city.[2] This 'rank-size rule', if it really were a rule, would solve our problem. Knowing the size of the largest city of Europe or of the larger European countries would be sufficient to estimate the number and size of smaller cities down to any desired minimum size.

Needless to say, matters are not so simple. The data base for cities in the period 1500–1800 is large enough to demonstrate (as will be done in chapter 6) that the urban hierarchies of Europe are inconsistent with the expectations of the rank-size rule. But the general proposition that there existed structured distributions of cities ranked by size is not inconsistent with what can be observed of the cities in the data base. The question then is how can that structure best be described?

Rather than relying on a 'rule' I propose that the slope of the rank-size distribution be empirically determined for large numbers of cities in each time period that concerns us. (Size is of importance here because the smaller the territory examined the less likely is the distribution to be regular.) When this slope is estimated, using least-square regression, for the cities above the 10,000 population threshold, the number of smaller cities can be 'predicted' by extending the slope below the threshold into the unobserved region.

In using this technique for the purpose of estimating the number of small cities it is advisable to exclude the very largest cities from the calculation of the regression line, since a few large cities of anomalous size can greatly influence the slope of the overall distribution in ways that only reduce its dependability in estimating the number of smaller cities.[3] When these procedures are followed a relationship of rank to size can be empirically established that is likely to have a direct application to that range of the rank-size distribution which includes the unknown cities below the threshold level of the data base.

Figure 4.2 can serve to illustrate the method just described. The dots show all of the cities of 10,000 or more inhabitants in 1700 ranked by size on a double logarithmic graph. A least-squares regression line was fitted to all of these observations *except* the twenty largest cities. The high coefficient of determination (R^2) assures us that the coefficients of the regression equation do a good job of 'explaining' the relationship of rank and size among the cities of rank 21 through 223. In the regression equation $y = a + bx$, where y is city population and x is city rank, the coefficient that interests us is b, the slope of the regression line, which relates rank to size. It can be used to predict the size of cities of ranks below 223, or to predict the rank of cities at specified levels of population below 10,000.

This same procedure was used for Europe as a whole at each fifty-year

THE CONTOURS OF EUROPEAN URBANIZATION II

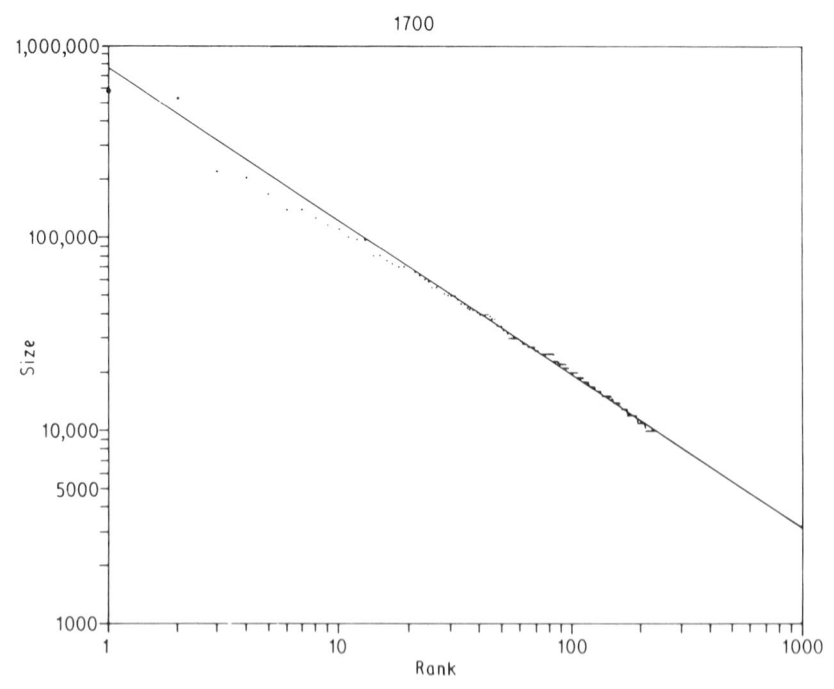

Figure 4.2 Rank-size distribution for Europe in 1700

interval from 1500 to 1800 and for northern Europe and Mediterranean Europe separately, in which cases the excluded cities were the largest 9-11 rather than the largest 20.[4]

The theoretical justification for this method and its technical execution should now be clear. A practical question remains. How far can and should the regression line be extended from the known into the unknown range? Two factors must be considered in answering this question. The first requires us to consider again that 'tar baby' of urban studies, the definition of a city. When is a place so small that it is unlikely to carry out many urban functions? In my discussion of this issue in chapter 2 I argued that four distinct quantitative indicators should form the basis for separating urban from rural places. So long as the threshold level used for *one* of those criteria, population, is as high as 10,000 the others hardly need to be examined. At that size level in early modern Europe it is very unlikely that the place in question would not also qualify on the bases of the three other criteria. As one descends to lower population levels the possibility increases that a place does not qualify in terms of its occupational structure or settlement density. Many urban places then had populations of less than 2000, but many villages did too. So long as the only criterion systematically available to us is population size it is advisable to be prudent. By not extending the investigation below the 5000 population level few rural places will be erroneously included, although many small urban places will be arbitrarily excluded. In northern Europe one might hazard to extend the investigation further, say to the 2000 population level. But this would be too hazardous in Mediterranean Europe, where many 'Agrocities' of southern Italy and Andalucia would erroneously be included. Thus our examination of European urbanization will generally extend no further than cities of 5000.

The second issue concerns the range in which the regression equation of the rank-size distribution is likely to provide valid estimates. One might secure general agreement that the rank-size relationship based on cities of 60,000 to 10,000 inhabitants is a good predictor of the number of cities of 8000 inhabitants, but will the same relationship hold at 5000? 3000? 2000? And if not, how should we expect the slope of the regression equation to change in this range of the distribution?

DIRECT EVIDENCE

To answer these questions, and to be assured that the proposed technique of indirect estimation merits acceptance, empirical evidence is called for. The following pages are therefore devoted to assembling and analysing the available aggregative evidence on the smaller cities of Europe.

Rank-size distributions for large urban systems of the later nineteenth and twentieth centuries can be of assistance so long as we bear in mind the altered scale of urban settlement that they reflect. That is, small cities in a Europe of 400 million inhabitants are bound to be much larger than in a Europe of 100 million. The Dutch distributions for 1849 and 1970 (figure 4.3) nicely illustrate this point. In 1849 a regular rank-size relationship is evident down to a size of about 3000. Below that point the distribution curves downward more steeply, indicating that the number of cities under 3000 is less than would be predicted by the rank-size relationship observed at higher levels. This is sometimes called the 'lower limb' of the rank-size distribution. In 1970 the entire distribution assumes a more curved form and the point below which city size drops off rapidly with increasing rank is much higher than in 1849, at about 25,000.

In general, modern rank-size distributions are not regular throughout but bend downward - form a lower limb - at some point. Theorists of rank-size distributions sometimes take this to be an indication of the 'demarcation between urban and rural settlement'. That is, the distribution itself is thought to provide an 'internal' definition of the urban threshold.[5] Of course, it is always possible that this lower limb phenomenon does not signal

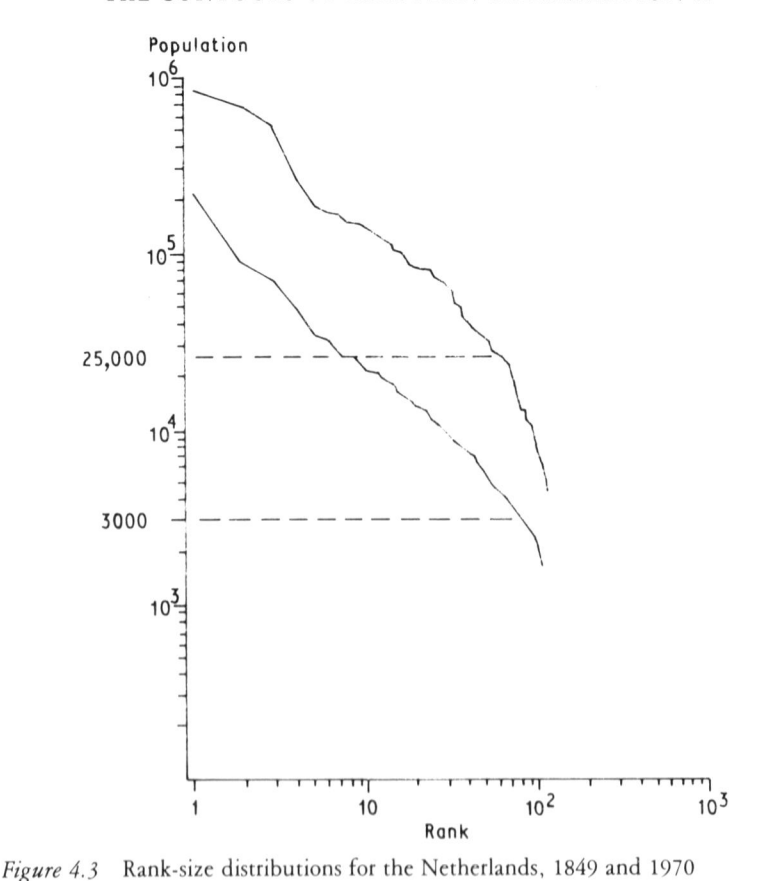

Figure 4.3 Rank-size distributions for the Netherlands, 1849 and 1970

Source C. Deurloo and G. A. Hoekveld, 'The population growth of the urban municipalities in the Netherlands between 1849 and 1970, with particular reference to the period 1899–1930', in H. Schmal (ed.), *Patterns of European Urbanisation since 1500* (London, 1981), 257, fig. 9.1.

a change in the character of settlements, but simply reflects the existence of very small cities in certain regions of low population density or deviant economic structure. For present purposes it is enough to note that this lower limb phenomenon often exists, and that the threshold level at which it begins is not constant.

Was this also the case before the mid-nineteenth century, and if so, where did the threshold level stand? We can hope to answer these questions using census materials from around 1800 that are available for many parts of Europe. The largest aggregation of tolerably reliable data that I have been

THE URBAN POPULATION OF EUROPE

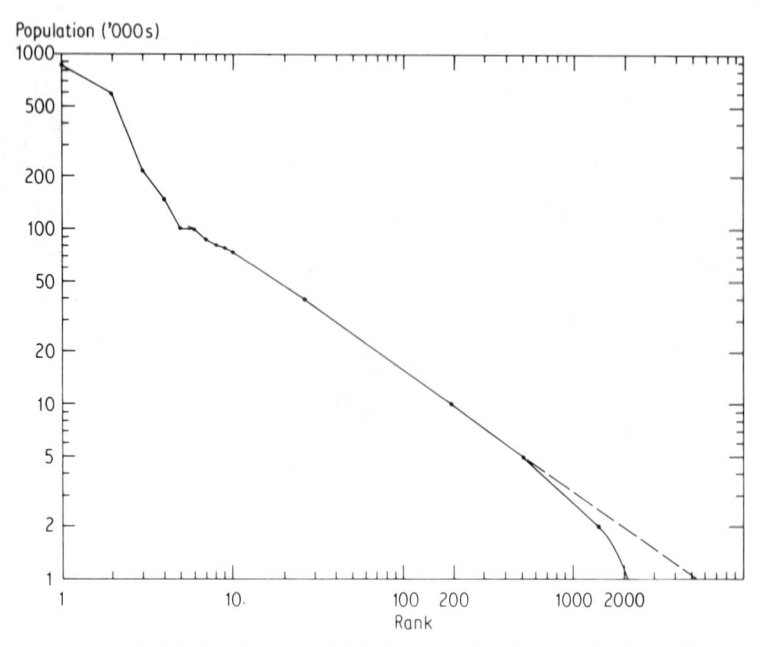

Figure 4.4 Rank-size distribution of cities in several territories of non-Mediterranean Europe *c.* 1800

Table 4.2 Cities by size category in several territories of non-Mediterranean Europe *c.* 1800

Size category	Number of cities	Aggregate population in millions
10,000 and over	186	6.04
5000–9999	310	2.10
2000–4999	894	2.70
Under 2000	*c.* 1300	1.50
Total	*c.* 2700	12.34

The total population of these territories was 58.1 million. Hence, the urban % was:

cities 10,000 and over	10.4%
cities 2000 and over	18.7%
all cities	21.2%.

The territories included are: Scandinavia, England and Wales, the Netherlands, Prussia, Saxony, the 'left Bank' of the Rhine, France and Bohemia.

able to muster covers the Scandinavian countries, England and Wales, the Netherlands, Prussia, Saxony, the 'left bank' of the Rhine, France and Bohemia. These territories embrace most of non-Mediterranean Europe. Table 4.2 summarizes the number and size of the cities found in these territories around 1800 and figure 4.4 displays their rank-size distribution.

Table 4.3 Distribution of urban population by size category around 1800: cities of 5000 and over

	Germany, 1792		France, 1806	
	No.	% of total	No.	% of total
1 Cities 10,000 and over	60	6.5	83	9.1
2 Cities 5000–9999	116	2.9	144	3.4
3 Population of cities of 5000–9999 as a % of cities of 10,000 and over		45		37

	Switzerland, 1800		Netherlands, 1795		England and Wales, 1801	
	No.	% of total	No.	% of total	No.	% of total
1	4	3.7	19	28.8	44	20.3
2	6	2.3	18	6.2	60	4.7
3		62		22		23

	Scandinavia, 1800		Belgium, 1792	
	No.	% of total	No.	% of total
1	6	4.6	20	18.9
2	8	1.3	26	8.2
3		28		43

Sources Wilhelm Franke, 'Die Volkszahl deutscher Städte, ende des 18. und anfang des 19. Jahrhunderts', *Zeitschrift des preussischen statistischen Landesamts* 62 (1922), 102–21; René Le Mée, 'Population agglomérée et population éparse au début du XIX siècle', *Annales de démographie historique* (1971), 455–510; Wilhelm Bickel, *Bevölkerungsgeschichte und Bevölkerungspolitik des Schweiz, seit dem Ausgang des Mittelalters* (Zurich, 1947); A. M. van der Woude, 'Demografische ontwikkeling van de noordelijke Nederlanden 1500–1800', in *Algemene geschiedenis der Nederlanden*, vol. V (Haarlem, 1980), 139; Brian T. Robson, *Urban Growth: an Approach* (London, 1973); Grethe Authén Blom (ed.), *Urbaniseringsprosessen i Norden*, vol. 2 (Oslo, 1977).

In this sample the rank-size distribution of northern European cities of at least 10,000 inhabitants predicts well the number of smaller cities down to the 5000-inhabitant level. Below that size the observed numbers become systematically less than predicted. The rank-size equation overestimates the number of cities of 2000 or more inhabitants by 37 per cent. Below the 2000 level the distribution falls off ever more sharply.

A portion of this observed divergence probably reflects differences among countries in the identification of urban places. Perhaps this can be taken to indicate that contemporary Europeans were agreed that places of 5000 inhabitants were indisputably urban, but that places of 2000–4000 were not invariably thought to function as cities. In any event, at this time the position of small cities in the larger urban hierarchy could vary enormously from region to region. Table 4.3 presents summary data on all cities of 10,000 and over and of 5000–10,000 in several countries around 1800. It is immediately apparent from line 3 that the small cities were of little consequence in some countries while they were sufficiently numerous to account for a larger share of the urban population in others.

When we press further into the hazy world of small cities, market towns and large villages, less dependable data stand at our disposal. Table 4.4 displays what is available and shows us dramatic differences in the position of small cities in the total urban hierarchy of the various states and territories. In the Netherlands and England cities in the 2000–5000 class were not much more numerous than the larger cities and the aggregate population of cities in the 2000–9900 class was little more than half of the population found in the cities of 10,000 and above. In France cities of 3000–9900 inhabitants were four times as numerous as the larger cities. When the places (many of dubious urban character) of 2000–3000 are added we find that as many Frenchmen lived in cities of under 10,000 inhabitants as lived in the larger cities. In Germany these smaller cities actually housed considerably more people than the larger ones, while in the Scandinavian lands cities of *under* 2000 must have weighed quite heavily on the urban scale. The entry for Austria and Czechoslovakia dates from 1851, but is included to indicate that even at this late date the urban population of the more agrarian regions of central Europe was still largely to be found in the hundreds of very small cities that dotted the landscape.

How did the position of small cities change over the three centuries preceding 1800? Did they always stand in a relationship to the larger places similar to that just described for 1800? The historical material available to respond to these questions is not abundant, but it is worth assembling and studying with some care. The plausibility of the indirect estimation results will depend on what is found in the scarce direct evidence.

John Patten's detailed study of urban places in East Anglia (the English counties of Norfok and Suffolk) is a good place to begin.[6] He identifies forty-nine urban settlements in 1520. None of these had as many as 10,000 inhabitants. Norwich, the largest city, numbered no more than about 8000; five towns fell in the 2000–5000 range and all the others were smaller. By 1603

Table 4.4 Distribution of urban population by size category around 1800: cities of all sizes

	Prussia, 1801		Austria-Czechoslovakia, 1851	
	No.	% of total	No.	% of total
1 Cities 10,000 and over	18	7.8	16	8.2
2 Cities 5000–9999	37	4.2		
3 Cities 3000–4999	75	4.9	240	9.0
4 Cities 2000–2999	122	4.7		
5 Cities under 2000	722	?		
6 Cities of 2000–9999 as a % of cities of 10,000 and over		177		110

	France, 1806		England and Wales, 1801		Scandinavia, 1800	
	No.	% of total	No.	% of total	No.	% of total
1	83	8.8	44	20.3	6	4.6
2	144	3.5	60	4.7	8	1.3
3	185	2.5	150*	6.7*	29	2.3
4	315	2.6				
5					165	c. 2.5
6		98		54*		78

	Netherlands, 1795		Germany, left bank of Rhine, 1806	
	No.	% of total	No.	% of total
1	19	28.8	4	6.6
2	18	6.2	11	4.5
3	34	4.4	25	5.0
4				
5	28	1.3		
6		37		144

* Cities of 2500–4900.

Sources See note 14; also *Mittheilungen aus dem Gebieleder statistik* (Vienna, 1852); Léopold Krug, *Abriss der neuesten Statistik des preussischen Staats* (Halle, 1804).

Norwich had nearly doubled in size and nine other cities had surpassed the 2000 level. By 1670 Norwich was joined by Great Yarmouth in the category of cities with at least 10,000 inhabitants, and by 1801 Ipswich and King's Lynn had also passed that threshold. If we fix our gaze on the very largest towns, and observe that the share of the population resident in cities of at least 10,000 grows from 0 in 1520 to over 15 per cent in 1800, we are sure to acquire a distorted picture of urban growth in East Anglia. When all towns of 2000 and over become the measure, the urban percentage does not quite double, and if all the little market towns are added East Anglian urban growth over three centuries shows nothing more than an irregular rise from about 25 to 30 per cent.

It must be borne in mind that the total population of the region grew from 200,000 to 500,000. Consequently, the average size of East Anglian towns rose a great deal, but there was no growth in the number of towns over these three centuries. Urban growth primarily took the form of a redistribution of population among the towns and only secondarily an increase in the percentage of the population resident in the towns.

A similar pattern of urban change is observable in the much larger territory of Electoral Saxony. Karlheinz Blaschke's study permits us to reconstruct the number of cities and the distribution of urban population at three dates: 1500, 1750 and 1843.[7] Here, as in East Anglia, the number of urban settlements remained essentially unaltered (151 in 1550, 148 in 1843). Similarly, the percentage of the total population in cities of 10,000 and more rose from 0 in 1550 to over 10 in 1750 as Leipzig and Dresden grew in size. Here

Table 4.5 Cities of East Anglia by size category, 1520–1801

Size category	Number of cities			
	1520	1603	1670	1801
10,000 and over	0	1	2	4
5000–9999	1	4	5	5
2000–4999	5	5	8	11
Under 2000	43	40	34	29

Threshold size	Urban population as a % of total population			
10,000 and over	0	6	10	15
5000 and over	4	14	17	16
2000 and over	12	16	20	21
All urban places	c. 25	26	32	c. 30

Source John Patten, *English Towns, 1500–1700* (Folkestone, 1978), 251; Census of 1801.

Table 4.6 Cities of Electoral Saxony by size category, 1300–1843 (population in '000s)

Size category	1300 Number	1300 Population	1550 Number	1550 Population	1750 Number	1750 Population	1834–1843* Number	1834–1843* Population
10,000 and over	0		0		4	108.5	5	154.1
5000–9999	2	10.0	8	55.0	6	42.7	16	104.1
2000–4999	7	16.5	10	29.4	39	107.0	56	176.3
Under 2000	94	50.9	133	87.0	101	113.8	71	93.6
Total for all cities	103	77.4	151	171.4	150	372.0	148	528.1
Total population		395.2		556.7		1020.0		1595.7

								193.6
								628.1
								1857.0

Urban population as a % of total population

Threshold size								
10,000 and over		0		0		10.6		9.7	8.3
5000 and over		2.5		9.9		14.8		16.2	13.9
2000 and over		6.7		15.2		25.3		27.2	23.4
All cities		19.5		30.8		36.5		33.1	33.8

* Blaschke cites the total urban population in 1843 as 628,100. His table 10, providing data for each city, yields a total that is 100,000 smaller. This discrepancy apparently results from his use of 1834 data for individual cities and 1843 data for the overall totals. But it is not obvious how this discrepancy is to be reconciled. Consequently, I have presented two columns. The second is Blaschke's for 1843; the first is my suggested revision, based on Blaschke's data in table 10 and the 1834 census as reported in Adna F. Weber, *The Growth of Cities in the Nineteenth Century: a Study in Statistics* (New York, 1899), 9.

Source Karlheinz Blaschke, *Bevölkerungsgeschichte von Sachsen bis zur industriellen Revolution* (Weimar, 1967), 70, 78, 91, 98, 138–41.

too, the percentage of the total population living in all 150 towns grew much less dramatically; indeed, it actually declined in the century after 1750.

Denmark's historical records do not allow us to look further back than the mid-seventeenth century.[8] Then only Copenhagen's population exceeded 10,000 while the remaining urban places (69 in 1672) without exception numbered fewer than 2000 inhabitants. In Denmark the number of urban foundations continued to increase modestly through the seventeenth century (some ten new towns were founded), but urban growth up to 1769 was accounted for in its entirety by the capital city. Thereafter, and particularly in the first half of the nineteenth century, the pattern was reversed. Copenhagen's relative position actually declined slightly, while from among the fixed complement of smaller places a handful grew to the 2000–9900 range. While Denmark's urban population remained a constant percentage of the total (19.8 per cent in 1769, 20.8 per cent in 1845), the cities of 2000–9900 more than doubled their share of the total population from 3.3 to 7.1 per cent. After the mid-nineteenth century Copenhagen renewed its rapid metropolitan growth, but it was then accompanied by the rise of several regional centres.

The Dutch Republic experienced a phenomenal rate of urban growth in the century after 1550.[9] This is observable in the more than doubling of the percentage of the population in cities of at least 10,000 inhabitants at the same time that the total population also doubled. But the stock of urban centres from which the growing cities were drawn remained essentially stable, so that the complement of smaller places was necessarily drawn down. The population of cities with 2500–10,000 inhabitants, which equalled 90 per cent of the population of larger cities in the early sixteenth century, equalled no more than one-third of the population of larger cities by 1800. As in the earlier examples, overall urban growth was much more muted than was the growth of the larger cities.

The overall trends of urban growth in England and Wales can be sketched on the basis of surveys and estimates made by Patten, Law, Corfield, and Clark and Slack.[10] The number of cities of 2500 or more inhabitants rose enormously, from 35 in 1600 to 130 in 1750 to 521 in 1851. But these were drawn in large part from a universe of market towns and boroughs that their historians Allan Everett and C. W. Chalkin estimate at approximately 700 in the sixteenth century and rather fewer, 600, around 1700.[11] The populations of these little centres can hardly be estimated, and in any event their urban character must in many instances be doubted. It is noteworthy, however, that the urban growth of this most rapidly urbanizing society of Europe made use of a generous endowment of long-existing nodes. Here, too, our understanding of the level and pace of urbanization is sensitively affected by how far down we reach into that fund.

Table 4.7 Cities of Denmark by size category, 1672–1845 (population in '000s)

Size category	1672 Number	1672 Population	1769 Number	1769 Population	1801 Number	1801 Population	1845 Number	1845 Population
10,000 and over	1	41.5	1	80.0	1	101.0	1	127
5000–9999	0		2	10.4	} 9	35.3	5	35
2000–4999	0		7	16			9	62
All cities under 10,000	69	71.2	70	78.7	70	91.8	67	155
Total for all cities	70	113.7	71	158.7	71	192.8	68	282
Total population	(1642)	600		800		929		1357

Threshold size	Urban population as a % of total population
10,000 and over	c. 7.0	10.0	10.9	9.4
2000 and over	c. 7.0	13.3	14.7	16.5
All cities	c. 19.0	19.8	20.8	20.8

Source See note 8.

Table 4.8 Cities of the Netherlands by size category, 1500–1859

Size category	c. 1500 Number	c. 1500 % of total	c. 1675 Number	c. 1675 % of total	c. 1750 Number	c. 1750 % of total	1795 Number	1795 % of total	1859 Number	1859 % of total
10,000 and over	11	15.8	19	33.6	18	30.5	19	28.8	29	28.8
2500–9999	27	14.2	46	11.8	43	10.7	43	9.1	68	10.2
Under 2500	c. 52	5.6	c. 30	1.8	?	?	37	2.8	20	1.3
Total	c. 90	35.6	c. 95	47.2	—	—	99	40.7	117	40.3

Source See note 9, and M. C. Deurloo et al., *Zicht op de Nederlandse stad* (Bussum, 1981), 47, 97–8.

Table 4.9 Cities of England and Wales by size category, 1520–1851 (population in '000s)

	1520 Number	1520 Population	1520 % of total	1600 Number	1600 Population	1600 % of total	1700 Number	1700 Population	1700 % of total	1750 Number	1750 Population	1750 % of total	1801 Number	1801 Population	1801 % of total	1851 Number	1851 Population	1851 % of total
London	1	55	1.9	1	200	4.5	1	575	10.6	1	675	11.1	1	865	9.4	1	2,685	15.0
Other cities																		
10,000 and over	4	40	1.4	5	55	1.3	10	143	2.6	20	346	5.7	43	1,005	10.9	151	4,625	25.8
5000–9999	5	30	1.1	14	85	1.9	22	145	2.7	30	210	3.4	60	420	4.6	135	945	5.3
2500–4999	?			15	45	1.0	37	120	2.2	79	245	4.0	150	480	5.2	234	750	4.2
Urban population																		
5000 and over	10	125	4.4	20	340	7.7	33	863	16.0	51	1,231	20.2	104	2,290	24.9	287	8,522	46.1
2500 and over	—			35	385	8.8	70	983	18.2	130	1,476	24.2	254	2,770	30.1	521	9,005	50.3
Total population		2,850			4,400			5,400			6,100			9,200			17,900	

Source See note 10.

Table 4.10 Cities of France by size category, 1750–1851 (population in millions)

Size category	c. 1750 No.	c. 1750 Population	c. 1750 % of total	1806 No.	1806 Population	1806 % of total	1836 No.	1836 Population	1836 % of total	1851 No.	1851 Population	1851 % of total
20,000 and over	31	1.63	7.8	33	1.80	6.4	43	2.66	8.1	63	3.80	10.9
10,000–19,999	23	0.32	1.5	50	0.65	2.3	73	1.02	3.1	102	1.40	4.0
5000–9999	106	0.75	3.6	144	0.98	3.5	273	1.86	5.7	291	2.00	5.7
All cities 5000 and over	170	2.70	12.9	227	3.43	12.2	389	5.54	16.9	456	7.20	20.6
3000–4999	124	0.40	1.9	185	0.70	2.5	(143)			(146)		
All cities 3000 and over	294	3.10	14.8	412	4.13	14.7	532			602		

Sources 1750: data base; Gilbert Rozman, *Urban Networks in Russia, 1750–1800, and Premodern Periodization* (Princeton, NJ, 1976), 230; Jacques Dupâquier, *La population rurale du bassin parisien a l'époque de Louis XIV* (Paris, 1979), *passim*. Dupâquier's calculations show that in the entire 'bassin parisien' 20.4 per cent of the population lived in all towns of 2000 or more inhabitants. In 1806, 21.0 per cent lived in such towns. 1806: René Le Mée, 'Population agglomérée et population éparse au début du XIX siècle', *Annales de démographie historique* (1971), 455–510. 1836, 1851: Adna F. Weber, *The Growth of Cities in the Nineteenth Century: a Study in Statistics* (New York, 1899), 76.

THE URBAN POPULATION OF EUROPE

For France it is possible to explore the pattern of small city growth only after the mid-eighteenth century. It is in the decades after 1750 that the urban growth of England and Saxony was chiefly accounted for by small cities; the same seems to hold true for France. Between the 1750s and 1836 the population of cities of at least 10,000 doubled in number and rose from 9.3 to 11.2 per cent of the total population (but not until first falling to under 9 per cent during the Napoleonic era). Smaller cities, on the other hand, grew in number and aggregate population at a much faster rate. Cities of 5000–9900 rose from just over 100 in the 1750s to 273 in 1836. In the same period these places grew from 3.6 to 5.7 per cent of the total population, and from an urban population only one-third as large as that of the larger cities to one half as large. Thereafter, the larger cities began once again to grow more rapidly than the smaller ones, as the data for 1851 make clear.

The information available on the number and size of small cities in the period 1500–1800 is neither comprehensive nor unimpeachable. But it permits us to suggest answers to the questions posed earlier regarding the range over which the rank-size distribution for cities of at least 10,000 can be applied, and the nature of the relationship between large and small city growth. Regarding the first question, we have seen that regression-based estimations of the number of cities with 5000–10,000 inhabitants are likely to be accurate, while below the 5000 level the regression slope is likely substantially to overestimate the number of cities. In northern Europe around 1800 the true number of cities of at least 2000 inhabitants was 73 per cent of the predicted number. Since the error was entirely located in the 2000–5000 range, it amounted to a 58 per cent overstatement of the number of cities in that size category. Regarding the second question, we have seen that the relative position of cities with fewer than 10,000 inhabitants was not stable, nor was the direction of change always the same. Until the mid- to late-eighteenth century the relative position of small cities diminished, often substantially. Thereafter it improved in many countries until some point in the first half of the nineteenth century.

THE INDIRECT ESTIMATION OF CITIES WITH UNDER 10,000 INHABITANTS

It is now time to return to the indirect estimation procedure developed earlier in this chapter. Does it yield estimates of the number of cities with less than 10,000 inhabitants that can be regarded as credible on the basis of the fragmentary direct evidence reviewed above? Table 4.11 displays the results of that estimation procedure for northern regions, Mediterranean lands and for Europe as a whole.

Table 4.11 Estimated number and total population of cities with 5000–9999 inhabitants, 1500–1800 (population in '000s)

Year	Northern Europe Number	Northern Europe Estimated population	Mediterranean Europe Number	Mediterranean Europe Estimated population	Europe* Number	Europe* Estimated population	Total Number of cities 5000 and over
1500	255	1734	108	734	363	2468	517
1550	213**	1700	111	755	(361)	2455	534
1600	250	1700	116	789	366	2489	586
1650	237	1612	104	707	341	2319	538
1700	219	1489	112	762	331	2251	555
1750	275	1870	132	898	407	2768	668
1800	410	2788	134	911	544	3699	908

* The estimates for Europe as a whole are the summations of the estimates for northern and Mediterranean Europe. Direct estimates based on the regression equations for the overall European rank-size distribution vary from this only in details.
** The 1550 regression line crosses those for 1500 and 1600, thereby yielding an improbably small estimated number of cities. In further calculations the number of cities of 5000–9999 inhabitants in northern Europe is set at 250.

THE URBAN POPULATION OF EUROPE

It would be foolish to regard these estimates as accurate in their details. Their usefulness resides in the overall pattern that emerges, and in the consistency of that pattern with the diverse evidence available about Europe's pre-industrial urban hierarchy. The estimates show that cities in the size category 5000–9900 were much more numerous than all cities of 10,000 and above in every time period and in both northern and Mediterranean Europe. Such cities increased in number modestly during the sixteenth century, but fell off thereafter so that a sustained growth in their numbers took place only after 1700.

By these estimates, Europe numbered just over 500 cities of at least 5000 inhabitants in 1500 and not many more than that in 1700. Only in the eighteenth century, particularly after 1750, does that number rise rapidly to reach about 900 by 1800. This pattern reflects the fact that the rank-size distributions for 1500 to 1750, when extended 'downward' from the 10,000 population threshold, tend to converge at a common point of origin (see

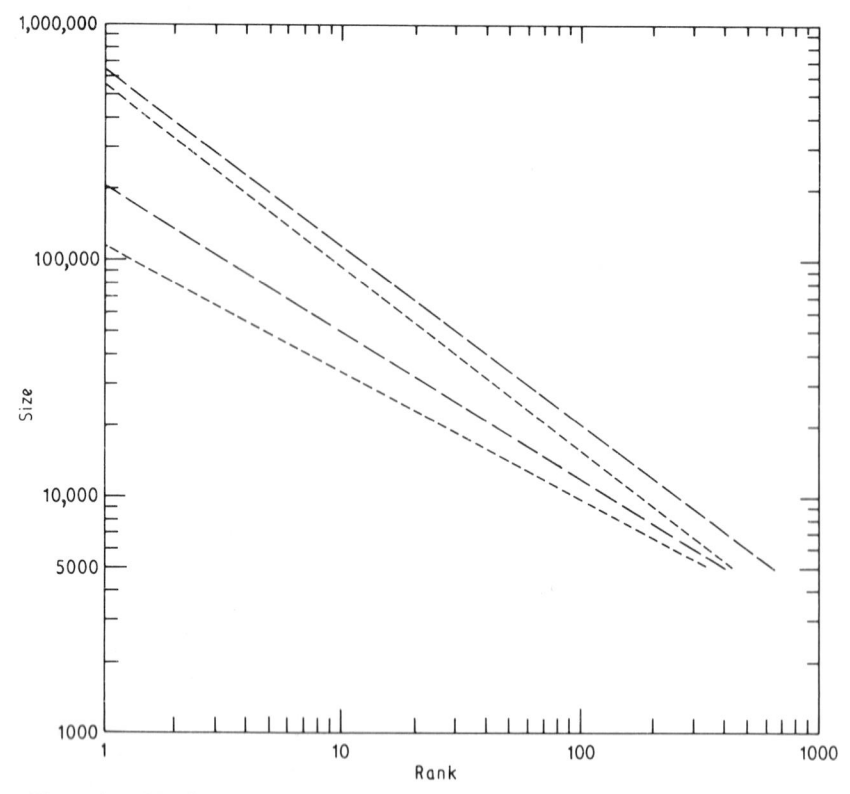

Figure 4.5 Northern European rank-size distributions for 1500, 1600, 1750 and 1800

figure 4.5). This is another way of saying that the total number of cities in those years was roughly constant, and this in turn is completely consistent with our knowledge of the timing of city founding in Europe.

The high middle ages endowed most of Europe with a stock of urban settlements and market towns that was little altered until the rise of the factory system. It is true that the monarchical states of the sixteenth and seventeenth centuries founded some new cities, but while a few became places of importance, the number was insufficient to have an impact on the European totals. It is also true that in such areas as Highland Britain, Ireland, Scandinavia and eastern Europe the process of founding towns was not yet completed by 1500. Here the stock of cities continued to grow into the seventeenth century. Sweden's urban foundations increased in number from 53 in 1580 to 85 in 1680; Norway added 27 urban places in the three centuries after 1500; Finland, which had only 7 medieval urban foundations, added 23. But the great majority of these settlements were and always remained tiny. The 1800 census shows that of Sweden's 32 'new cities' founded in the century after 1580, the population of 15 was still below 1000, 10 contained 1000–2000, and the two largest did not exceed 3200 inhabitants.[12]

One can imagine urban Europe in the early modern era as consisting of 3000–4000 marketing and administrative nodes, most of which had been established in the middle ages. These urban settlements came close to exhausting the stock of geographical locations that had much potential to serve urban functions under the technological and commercial conditions of the age. Beginning in the late eighteenth century new demographic and economic conditions allowed a new wave of mostly *de facto* city formation to occur. Until then the history of European urbanization was played out in that stock of 3000–4000 mostly rudimentary urban places.

EUROPEAN URBANIZATION 1300–1980

If the above estimates, justifications and generalizations can be accepted, we are now in a position to extend the analysis of European urbanization from the cities of at least 10,000 inhabitants in the period 1500–1800 'downward' to the many hundreds of smaller cities, as well as 'outward' in time to the middle ages and to the twentieth century. I believe that the strategy followed above generates more reliable estimates of urban population than any others now available, but one must not regard these numbers as precise. Later research may well show the number of cities or the aggregate urban population to be in error; I am confident, however, that such revisions will not alter the insights acquired here into the structure of the urban population and the trends of its development over time. Table 4.12 presents an overview of the number of cities in Europe and their distribution over selected size

Table 4.12 Number of cities by size category, 1300–1979

Size category	c. 1300	1500	1550	1600	1650	1700	1750	1800	1850	1890	1979
Europe											
1 million and over	—	—	—	—	—	—	—	—	2	4	24
100,000–999,000	4	4	3	8	10	11	12	17	41	97	366
40,000–99,000	15	14	23	29	24	32	36	47	⎱ 284	584	—
20,000–39,000	33	37	46	59	53	64	75	94	⎰		—
10,000–19,000	73	99	101	124	110	117	138	206	551	1024	—
5000–9000	—	363	(361)	366	341	331	407	544	—	—	—
Total	—	517	534	586	538	555	668	908	—	—	—
Northern Europe											
1 million and over	—	—	—	—	—	—	—	—	2	4	18
100,000–999,000	1	1	1	2	3	4	5	9	28	81	283
40,000–99,000	4	5	10	15	16	22	26	32	⎱ 213	480	—
20,000–39,000	16	24	24	34	38	44	50	67	⎰		—
10,000–19,000	47	59	61	68	61	76	86	143	343	740	—
5000–9000	—	255	(250)	250	237	219	275	410	—	—	—
Total	—	344	346	369	355	365	442	661	—	—	—
Mediterranean Europe											
1 million and over	—	—	—	—	—	—	—	—	—	—	6
100,000–999,000	3	3	2	6	7	7	7	8	13	16	83
40,000–99,000	11	9	13	14	8	10	10	15	⎱ 71	104	—
20,000–39,000	17	13	22	25	15	20	25	27	⎰		—
10,000–19,000	26	40	40	56	49	41	52	63	208	284	—
5000–9000	—	108	111	116	104	112	132	134	—	—	—
Total	—	173	188	217	183	190	226	247	—	—	—

categories from 1300 to 1979. Table 4.13 presents estimates of the total urban population for the same period. The inclusion of cities of under 10,000 inhabitants has the effect of substantially revising the contours of urban growth revealed by the original data base. Immediately apparent is the already noted stability in the number of cities until the eighteenth century and the very large size of the total population located in the smaller cities. For every 100 residents of European cities of at least 10,000 population in 1500, there were 70 inhabitants of cities of 5000–9900. In northern Europe cities of 5000–9900 housed fully as many urbanites as all the larger cities.

From 1500 to 1700 the rapid growth of very large cities greatly reduced the numerical weight of the unchanging complement of smaller cities. By the latter date Europe could count only 30 residents of cities in the 5000–9900 category for every 100 in cities of 10,000 and above.

The following century brings a respite from the seemingly irresistible trend toward concentration in ever larger cities. Particularly in the century 1750–1850 the relative importance of small cities improves as the number of such cities grows for the first time since the middle ages. This is partly the result of the creation of new factory towns, but quantitatively more important is the impact of demographic and economic trends on the many hundreds of long-existing rudimentary urban settlements, elevating them to a level that allows us to include them in this study.

By examining only the largest cities it is easy to gain the impression that urban growth in the century after 1750 was both rapid and characterized by the emergence of true metropolises. After all, London grew some fivefold over this period. In the broader context of tables 4.12 and 4.13 the emphasis must be placed elsewhere. The number of small cities more than tripled, after being almost fixed in number for centuries. This allowed the aggregate urban population of such cities to rise, and even their share of total urban population to increase, a phenomenon that is unique in the entire period 1500–1980 (see figure 6.1).[13]

So far I have emphasized the changing relationship of large to small cities. How does the new information about the smaller cities alter our understanding of the relationship of the urban to the rural population? Obviously the addition of such a large urban population to the numbers presented in table 3.5 increases substantially the urban percentage of the total population. In 1500 the population resident in cities of at least 10,000 inhabitants stood at 5.6 per cent of the total European population, but when the threshold is lowered to 5000 the percentage rises to 9.6; in northern Europe the change is from 4.0 to 8.0 per cent.

In 1800 the inclusion of the smaller cities has less impact on these statistics than in 1500, but they are still important. Cities of 10,000 and above contained 10.0 per cent of the European population; cities of 5000 and above

Table 4.13 Urban population by size category, 1300–1979 ('000s)

Size category	c. 1300	1500	1550	1600	1650	1700	1750	1800	1850	1890	1979
Europe											
100,000 and over	(400)	450	500	1,270	1,914	2,390	2,860	3,977	11,259	30,861	140,185
40,000–90,000	(750)	704	1,324	1,496	1,395	1,830	2,147	2,904	} 10,971	21,871	
20,000–39,000	(890)	981	1,244	1,543	1,372	1,689	2,025	2,521			
10,000–19,000	(950)	1,306	1,348	1,624	1,503	1,556	1,901	2,816	7,388	14,190	
5000–9000	—	2,468	2,455	2,489	2,319	2,251	2,768	3,699			
Total		5,909	6,871	8,422	8,503	9,716	11,701	15,917			
Northern Europe											
100,000 and over	(100)	100	130	420	1,005	1,399	1,751	2,513	8,875	26,840	109,565
40,000–99,000	(200)	210	556	700	915	1,246	1,531	1,975	} 8,325	18,209	
20,000–39,000	(430)	618	656	872	1,011	1,171	1,336	1,799			
10,000–19,000	(610)	767	799	944	805	986	1,180	1,919	4,452	10,057	
5000–9000		1,734	1,700	1,700	1,612	1,489	1,870	2,788			
Total		3,429	3,841	4,582	5,348	6,291	7,668	10,994			
Mediterranean Europe											
100,000 and over	(300)	350	370	850	909	991	1,109	1,464	2,384	4,021	30,620
40,000–9,000	(550)	494	768	796	480	584	616	929	} 2,646	3,662	
20,000–39,000	(460)	363	588	671	361	518	689	722			
10,000–19,000	(340)	539	549	734	698	570	721	897	2,936	4,133	
5000–9000		734	755	789	707	762	898	911			
Total		2,480	3,030	3,840	3,155	3,425	4,033	4,923			

contained 13.0 per cent. In northern Europe cities of 5000 and above accounted for 12.1 per cent, in the Mediterranean lands it was 15.8 per cent.

The urban population of Europe before the onset of modern industrialization was larger than is often assumed. In an article seeking to place contemporary urban society in a historical context Eric Lampard expressed the view that

> Before the nineteenth century it is doubtful whether cities, say, of 5,000 and more inhabitants at any time accounted for more than three percent of world population, or more than 15–20 percent of population on a local or regional basis.[14]

We have already had occasion to note that the Dutch Republic, Belgium, and northern and central Italy all had reached or exceeded the 15 per cent level – even before taking cities of 5000–9900 into account – long before 1800 (see table 3.7). Now we can observe that all of Europe came very close to the 15 per cent level by 1800. The Mediterranean region had exceeded it already in the sixteenth century, while in northern Europe the urban percentage was approaching 15 per cent, even when such lightly urbanized areas as Scandinavia and the eastern countries are included.

Another indication of the underestimation of Europe's urban population is Lampard's statement that no more than 3 per cent of the world's population lived in cities of 5000 or more inhabitants. This is based on an often-cited assertion that the world's cities of at least 5000 population numbered 27 million inhabitants, or 3 per cent of an assumed world population in 1800 of 900 million.[15] Our figures show that Europe alone could claim an urban population of nearly 16 million. It does not seem plausible that the rest of the world could have contained an urban population of no more than 11 million. Indeed, the information now available (summarized in note 15) suggests strongly that world urbanization circa 1800 stood at over twice the generally accepted level. This finding implies that nineteenth-century world urbanization was much slower than earlier thought: the percentage urban doubled over the century instead of quadrupled. Moreover (assuming the accuracy of twentieth-century world urbanization calculations), nearly all of the increase up to 1900 must have been accounted for by Europe and regions of European settlement.

The addition of the smaller cities to the information provided by the data base shows not only that pre-industrial Europe was more urban than had been thought, but also that its overall rate of urbanization was more muted. Figure 4.6 makes this very clear. When we restrict our view to cities of at least 40,000 inhabitants, Europe's urban population rises from less than 2 per cent to 5.6 per cent of the total over the three-century period 1500–1800. When cities of at least 10,000 are used as the standard, the figures rise from 5.6 to

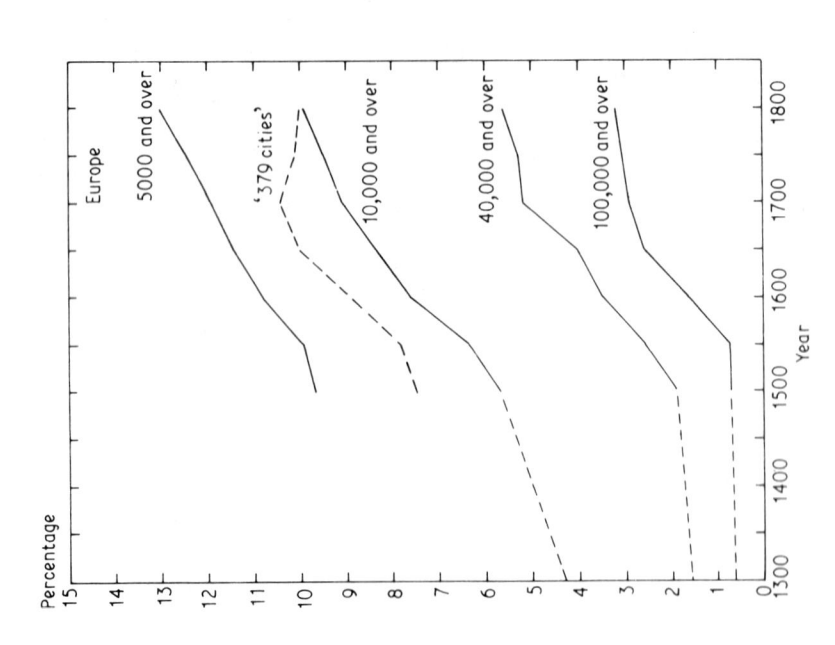

Figure 4.6 Urban percentage in Europe, northern Europe and Mediterranean Europe to 1800

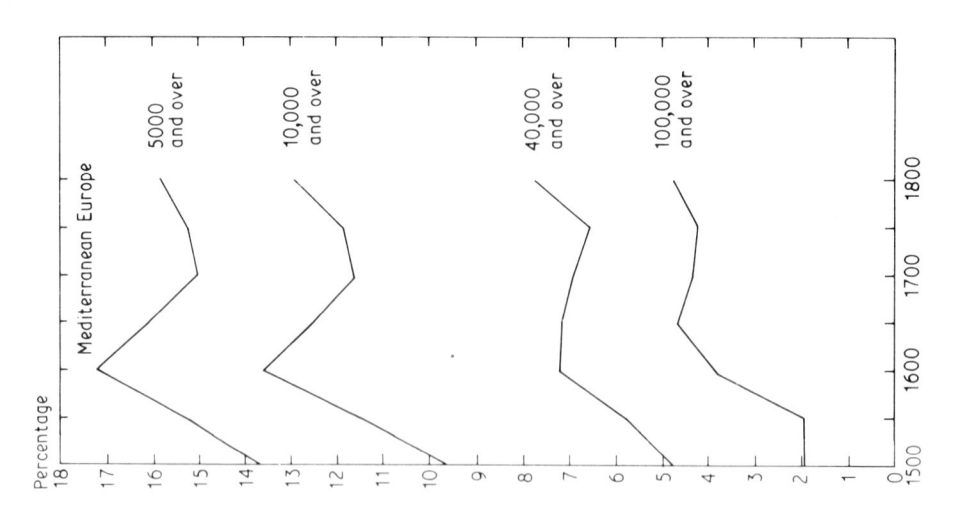

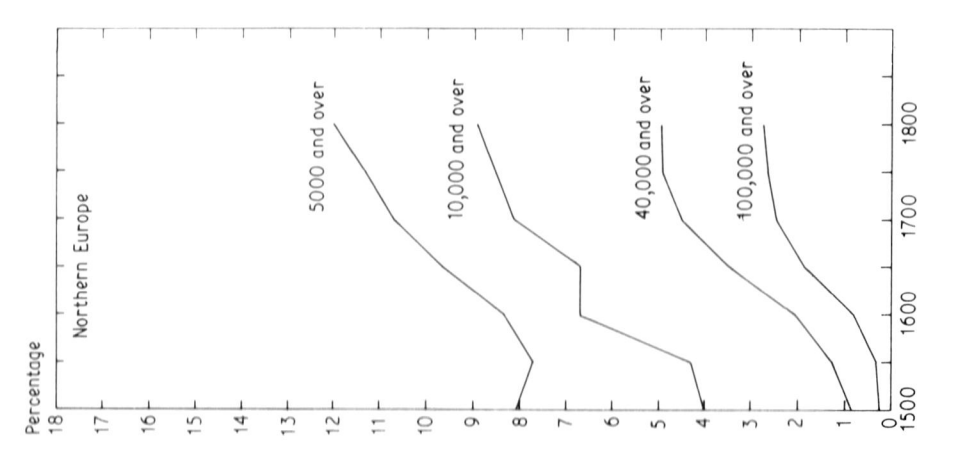

Table 4.14 Comparison of the growth of cities above and below 40,000 inhabitants, 1500–1800

	1500	1550	1600	1650	1700	1750	1800
Estimated number of cities, 5000–39,000	499	508	549	504	512	620	844
Estimated number of cities 40,000 and over	18	26	37	34	43	48	64
Percentage of European population in cities							
over 5000	9.6	9.8	10.8	11.4	11.9	12.4	13.0
over 40,000	1.9	2.6	3.5	4.4	5.2	5.3	5.6
5000–39,000	7.7	7.2	7.3	7.0	6.7	7.1	7.4

10.0 per cent; when the standard becomes cities of 5000 and above, the pace of urbanization slows to a crawl, taking 300 years to rise from 9.6 to 13.0 per cent. These figures are for Europe as a whole. Obviously, there were important regional differences in the course of urbanization. In the Mediterranean region cities of 5000 and over barely budged from the 15–16 per cent range during the entire three-century period; in northern Europe this was different.

This pattern of urbanization rates can serve to emphasize the highly selective character of urban growth in these centuries. Table 4.14 divides the entire urban population into two groups: cities of 5000–39,000 inhabitants and cities of 40,000 and above. The 500-odd cities of the smaller size category actually lost ground relative to the total population in the course of the sixteenth and seventeenth centuries. This de-urbanization was repaired in the eighteenth century by the addition to the ranks of over 200 'new' cities, but the final percentage was no higher than that of three centuries before. The entire relative increase of Europe's urban population can be attributed to the cities of 40,000 and above (including, of course, initially small cities that cross the 40,000 threshold in the course of time). There were only 64 such cities in 1800, but they obviously played a special role in the urbanization of Europe.

European urban growth, which had been very modest, from all we can tell, in the fourteenth and fifteenth centuries, became all-embracing in the century after 1850. The intervening period was not simply an extension of one or the other of these neighbouring epochs. It displayed a distinctive growth process characterized by differentiation. This differentiation had three dimensions: territorial, functional and temporal. The tempo of urban growth varied by region; the potential for growth varied by the function and

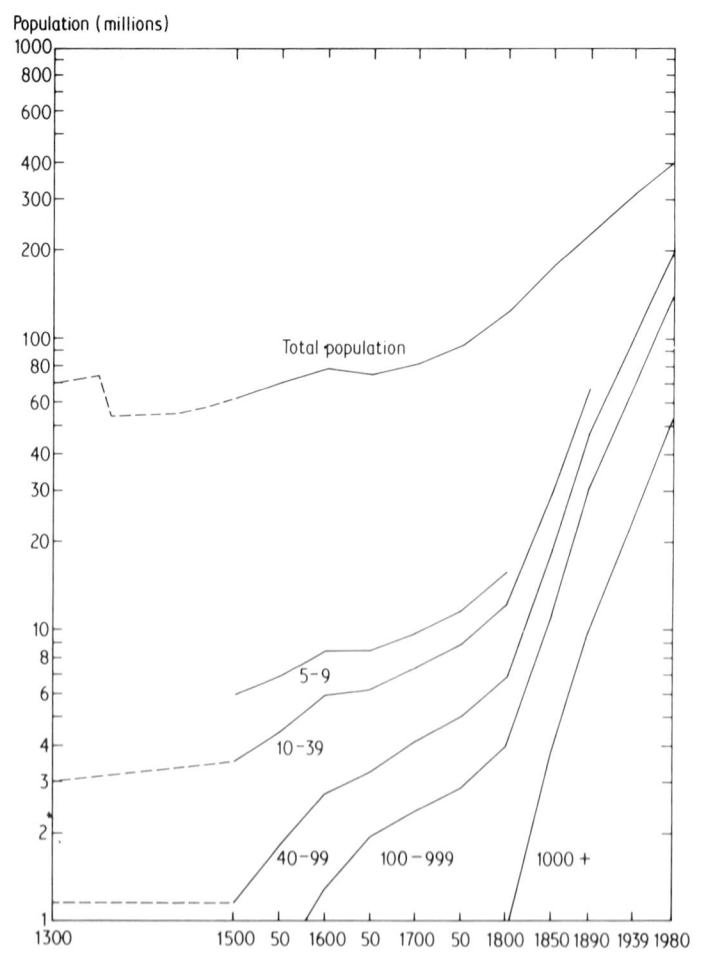

Figure 4.7 Population of Europe by size of settlement, 1300–1980 (settlement size in '000s)

size of the city; and in successive periods the process literally 'shifts gears', first fostering concentration, then fostering diffusion.

The implication of these statements is that the fate of individual early modern cities cannot be fully understood when studied in isolation since they were part of a structured system or, better put, were in the process of forming such a system. Part III examines the properties of the European urban system.

III
THE PROPERTIES OF THE URBAN SYSTEM

5
CITIES, SYSTEMS AND REGIONS

In part II data were assembled to present a series of statistical portraits of urban Europe from the middle ages to the present, with the chief focus of attention being the period 1500–1800. I traced the contours of European urbanization in terms of the number of cities, their populations, the size of the total urban population and the relationship of urban to non-urban populations.

Contemplation of the assembled data base generates many questions about the character of past urban growth. For instance, we have observed already that major gains in the most conventional yardstick of urbanization, the percentage of the total population resident in cities, occurred in areas in which the overall population experienced stagnation or decline. Large-city growth also occurred when the larger society experienced little or no net urbanization, suggesting that rapidly growing cities did so as much at the expense of smaller cities as of the rural population. These observations give rise to questions about the growth process by which Europe became urbanized. In addition, we observed that the rise in the number of cities above 10,000 inhabitants was accompanied by a geographical redistribution of Europe's total urban population. This causes one to wonder about the relative stability of the network of cities.

In this part I present an analysis of the just-described pattern of European urban growth in the period 1500–1800, with excursions backward to 1300 and forward to the present. Three successive chapters treat, in turn, the evolution of the size distribution of European cities, its causes and consequences; the patterns of stability and discontinuity, emphasizing the extent to which cities persist in their positions within urban hierarchies and the role of 'new entrants' in successive time intervals; and, finally, the spatial patterns of urban growth and changes in the geographical concentration of urban life over time.

THE PROPERTIES OF THE URBAN SYSTEM

Before proceeding it is necessary to consider briefly the definitions of three terms that will figure prominently in what follows: city, system and region.

The first term, *city*, we have pondered already. In chapter 2 a practical definition was adopted, one based exclusively on population with the proviso that geographically extensive rural parishes with large populations be excluded. I thereby hope to leave to others the frustrating task of putting their fingers on the essence of 'cityness'.

Unfortunately, no such simple evasive manoeuvre can get us past the two remaining terms. The concept of *system*, as in a system of cities or an urban system, is now much used by geographers and other social scientists.[1] Pred provides a satisfying definition of a system of cities:

> a . . . set of urban units [historically, cities; today presumably metropolitan areas] that are interdependent, or bound together by economic interactions, in such a way that any significant change in the economic activities, occupational structure, total income, or population of one member unit will directly or indirectly bring about some modification in the economic activities, occupational structure, total income, or population of one or more of the other members of the set.[2]

The elements of the system are cities, and these are dependent on each other, as Pred describes it, in an organized complexity. Their interdependence implies that the cities are differentiated – that they vary sufficiently in their specializations and functions not to be faithful replicas of each other. Besides interdependence and differentiation, the concept requires closure; the system must have boundaries and this leads directly to the third concept, the *region*.[3]

First, I must make clear the limited way in which I intend to use the concept of system. If one wished simply to discuss a group of cities, one could do without the word 'system'. System implies that the whole (the urban system) is more than – or at least *other* than – the sum of its parts (the aggregate of cities). This means that urbanization is not simply a phenomenon generated by the sum of the cities, but also by the way in which those cities are 'arranged'. This I shall seek to demonstrate in the following chapters.

Many geographers go much further than this to apply general systems theory to the study of cities. Here the object is to adduce the state of the system, usually in terms of entropy maximization. The point of such exercises is to identify likely steady-states. Such applications of 'social physics' to the study of urban systems will not be pursued here. The historical and comparative study of urbanization shows clearly enough that an urban system must be thought of as adaptive rather than mechanistic, which is to say that a learning process in society subtly and often unpredictably alters the nature of responses to given stimuli.[4]

CITIES, SYSTEMS AND REGIONS

A social system is also distinguished from a physical system in never being truly closed. It always stands open to impulses from the external environment. Still, the identification of urban systems would be wholly arbitrary if no criterion could be applied to establish a sufficient degree of closure. What are the appropriate boundaries of an urban system? Pred's definition refers to 'a national or regional set of urban units'.[5] In his work, as in that of most geographers, national boundaries are most frequently used to limit the urban system.

National systems are usually the largest urban systems studied, reflecting the modern tendency to regard state boundaries as the single most potent factor in channelling human interaction. Nested within national systems, particularly in large countries, are regional subsystems. Here the concept of the 'natural region' comes into play to identify groupings of cities so arranged that they interact with each other much more than with cities in other natural regions. Finally, these subregions can be thought to contain local systems that are identified by daily commutation patterns which establish the boundaries of functioning labour markets.[6]

The challenge to the historian of European urbanization is to translate this contemporary hierarchy of nested urban subsystems into an historically appropriate form. The third and smallest subsystem can logically be redefined as the periodic marketing circuit, or as an agricultural supply hinterland. At any rate an extensive literature exists on the relationship of towns to their rural hinterlands, marketing networks and the like.

In further aggregation, what criteria would provide sufficient closure to satisfy the requirements of the urban system concept? Regions can be defined either by ecological factors (watersheds, mountains or other physical features) or by economic and social organization (flows of information and commodities, or travel patterns of people). The former criterion has the virtue of yielding regions of unchanging boundaries, and requires only information that is easily obtainable regardless of the historical period being studied. In other respects the economic region would probably be preferable. But in the study of European regions of the sixteenth to the eighteenth centuries one soon confronts a unique difficulty, for the political fragmentation of many areas meant that any delimitation of Europe's natural regions would be crisscrossed with administrative boundaries that to some extent impeded commercial and social interaction. One would need to add to that numerous linguistic or religious boundaries of particular importance in the constraining of migration patterns. How is one to demarcate natural regions in such an environment?

In this study I take the position that Europe can be divided up into hundreds of micro-regions – often the size of a province, with a regional centre and a number of subordinate market towns – but it cannot be divided into generally accepted and durable macro-regions. The sixteen 'territories' and four 'regions' used here to organize and present the data on urban population have not been identified by any formal criterion of regional science; they are a compromise between the practical limitations of the data and the more obvious divisions created by state boundaries.

Europe has never formed a single polity; nevertheless it has had a real identity and a real unity. That unity was religious and cultural, but also economic. The very fragmentation of political authority allowed economic linkages to play a vital role in organizing society.[7] The (regrettable) dominance of the nation state in nineteenth- and twentieth-century Europe should not blind us to the fact that state boundaries and linguistic frontiers counted for something less in earlier centuries. They were sufficiently real to muddle any regional analysis, but not sufficient to prevent us from regarding Europe as a whole to be capable of fashioning a single urban system.

This urban system always possessed important subsystems to be sure, but its outer boundaries were much more important than any interior boundaries. The outer boundaries were to the east those with the Ottoman empire and Russia. In other directions we assume the Mediterranean Sea and the Atlantic Ocean to form the boundaries, but one must not forget the existence of colonial cities as part of Europe's urban system.[8]

The single most important interior boundary was probably that separating the Mediterranean region from northern Europe. The four 'regions' into which I have divided Europe allow for a crude separation of these two great zones. However, the three regions into which I have divided northern Europe (north and west; central; eastern) should not be interpreted as functional regions. They have been identified on the basis of their differing histories of urban growth (and for practical considerations) rather than their regional affinities.

To summarize: the units of analysis are Europe's cities, particularly the 379 that at some time between 1500 and 1800 possessed a minimum of 10,000 inhabitants. The analysis is based on the assumptions that Europe formed a potential urban system, that its two most important regions were the Mediterranean lands and northern Europe, and that, as a practical matter, smaller subregions must be defined largely on the basis of administrative boundaries.

6

THE DEVELOPMENT OF AN URBAN HIERARCHY

TECHNIQUES AND INTERPRETATIONS

The changing character of European urbanization described in part II occurred partly through an increase in the number of cities and partly through changes in the size of individual cities. Because the number of cities participating in this system is large, a study of the dynamics of urban growth cannot readily proceed by the examination singly of each city's growth characteristics. The way in which each city grew or declined ultimately determined the overall size distribution of the system of cities. But in this and succeeding chapters these growth experiences will be analysed with methods emphasizing their behaviour as elements in a system of cities.

The distribution of urban population by city-size categories as displayed in figure 6.1 is an unambiguous testimony that the relative importance of large and small cities was far from stable. It also suggests that these changes were far more dramatic in the 150 years before 1700 than in the 150 years thereafter. But figure 6.1 is silent about the sort of city creation or city growth which brought about the new distributions of urban population.

A more informative display of the distribution of city sizes is achieved by arranging all the cities of a system by descending order of their populations. Because there are many small and few large cities, with a tendency for the number of cities in each size class to decrease as city size increases, the pattern formed by cities so arranged corresponds to the general form of a Pareto distribution:[1]

$$N(\bar{P}) = AP^{-q}$$

where $N(\bar{P})$ is the cumulative percentage of cities above a lower threshold

THE PROPERTIES OF THE URBAN SYSTEM

level of city population $\bar{P}$, and A and q are constants. Expressed in logarithmic form this is:

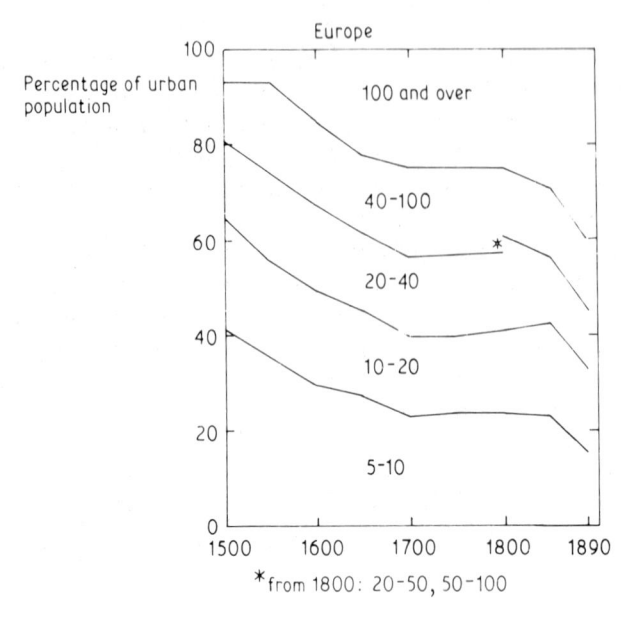

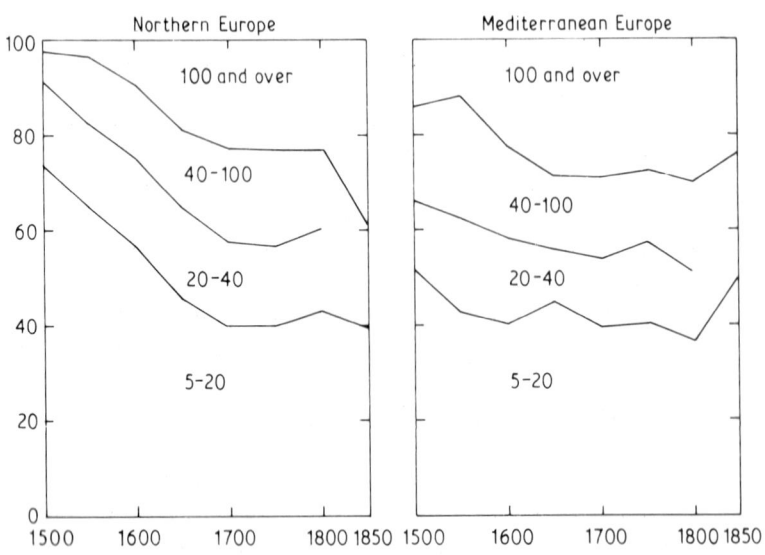

$$\log N(\bar{P}) = \log A - q \log P$$

Figure 6.1 Urban population by city-size categories, 1500–1890

A related distribution (differing from the Pareto distribution in that it does not require a threshold level), the lognormal distribution, is commonly used in studies of the size distribution of cities. It can be expressed as a rank-size distribution:

$$P = K(R)^{-q}$$

where R is city rank, q and K are constants, and P is city size. This is identical to the Pareto distribution except that the rank of cities is being used instead of a cumulative percentage of the cities. For computational purpose, this may be expressed in logarithmic form as:

$$\log P = \log K - q (\log R)$$

The values of K and q can be estimated as a simple linear regression by ordinary least squares. If the array of cities arranged in order of their size yield a good fit, the city-size distribution can be represented by a straight line on logarithmic paper with a slope of $-q$, and is called a lognormal distribution. A remarkable variety of other aspects of human life (such as wealth-holding by individuals and the number of publications of university professors) conforms to distributions of this type.

A special case of the lognormal distribution has attracted much attention. In 1949 the geographer Zipf observed that the city-size distribution for the United States was such that the population of the city of rank R equalled the population of the largest city divided by its rank. This has the property that

$$K = R \cdot P = P_1$$

where P_1 is the population of the first-ranked city. It is equivalent to a lognormal distribution of slope -1. In this rank-size rule, as Zipf and later geographers have dubbed it, the population of the second largest city of an urban system is expected to be half that of the largest, the third ranked city, a third that of the largest, and so on.[2]

Not all distributions of city sizes are linear, certainly not over the entire range of city sizes. At the smallest city sizes we have already had occasion to note that the curve often bends downward, forming a 'lower limb' of the distribution. This has sometimes been interpreted as 'the demarcation between urban and rural' settlements, and accepted as an internally defined minimum population threshold for inclusion in the urban system.[3]

More interest and importance is attached to departures from the lognormal at the upper end of the distribution, i.e. among the largest cities. Geographers have come to regard the lognormal distribution of city size to be a norm toward which urban systems should move and at which they should remain. Zipf sought to provide his empirical demonstration of the rank-size rule with a theoretical explanation. More recently Brian J. L. Berry has supplied mathematical demonstrations that the lognormal distribution and specifically its special case, the rank-size rule, is consistent with central place theory (which is concerned with how settlements should be spatially arranged) and that it 'is the most probable distribution and represents the steady state equilibrium' of an urban system whose individual elements (cities) vary in size in a stochastic process.[4] 'When many forces act [on cities] in many ways with none predominant a lognormal distribution is found', says Berry.[5]

He is relying here on the concept of entropy maximization to justify the expectation of a lognormal rank-size distribution. Related to this is the notion that city size is the product of a stochastic process. This underlies Gibrat's 'law of proportionate effect', which holds that city growth is proportional, on average, to city size. More precisely, all cities of a given size are thought to have an equal probability to grow at the same rate.[6]

All of these arguments lead their exponents to expect lognormal patterns to evolve, and once achieved to persist. Yet empirical studies show that many national city-size distributions are not lognormal and these countries span the full range of levels of economic development and levels of urbanization.[7] Theorists fall back then on the assertion that lognormal distributions seem most common in national systems that are very large, that have a long history of urbanization, and that are economically and politically complex, that is to say, where the forces acting on city size can be expected to be numerous and varied.[8]

The upshot of all this (often strained) theorizing is to identify departures from lognormal distributions as symptomatic of disorder. In theory these deviations can take many forms, but by far the most common and most discussed non-lognormal distribution in modern urban systems is primacy, where the largest or several largest cities are 'too large'.

The existence of overgreat cities in the modern world cannot simply be ascribed to underdevelopment, low urbanization or some other indicator of backwardness, since countries at all levels of income and urbanization exhibit primacy. But this has not inhibited geographers and sociologists from identifying primacy as a symptom, or even as the generator of some sort of problem: political instability,[9] colonial domination,[10] impoverishing economic imbalance,[11] and, of course, combinations of these.

The study of city-size distributions has focused mainly on contemporary evidence. The assertions made about the dynamic properties of the size distribution of cities (which in my view is the most interesting aspect of this field of study) are either based on historical studies spanning at most several decades,[12] or, more commonly, on cross-sectional comparisons.[13] Most social scientists regard modern urbanization as a relatively recent phenomenon. Moreover, the geographic literature of rank-size distribution speaks to the phenomenon of pre-industrial urban systems only indirectly, via the shopworn assumption that presently less-developed economies share features of developed economies in their pre-industrial past. There is, then, reason to wonder whether the generalizations and theories just reviewed can fruitfully be brought to bear on urbanization before the Industrial Revolution.

The phenomenon of primacy in pre-industrial Europe is an obvious example of the problem we face. Nationalism, (neo)colonial relations and the process of economic development figure prominently in existing theories of primacy. How can that phenomenon be interpreted in a society where none of these forces is present in anything like its modern form? It will also be useful to know whether urban-systems growth in earlier centuries obeyed the law of proportionate effect. That is, can changes in city size be understood as the outgrowth of numerous random factors, or were systematic factors at work? And if the latter is true, what could those factors have been?

Recent work by anthropologists on city-size distributions offers ideas that may be more directly appropriate to the historical study of urbanization. Anthropologists, notably G. William Skinner, have come to see settlement patterns as influential in shaping social interaction and cultural institutions, and this perception has led them from the study of small-scale periodic market networks to the design of systems of cities.

The most comprehensive work on city-size distributions and their interpretation is that of Carol Smith.[14] She enriches the lognormal-versus-primacy concepts of the geographers with an approach based on the distinction between pre-modern and modern urban systems. Primacy, she argues, might be present in either type of society, but its meaning would differ according to the sort of remaining city-size distribution to which it was grafted. She distinguishes three types of city-size distribution: lognormalcy, 'convexity' and 'concavity'. Overly large primate cities might preside over each of these three types.

The lognormal distribution is by now familiar. It should be noted here that Smith uses this term to refer to the special case of the rank-size rule, a lognormal distribution with a slope of -1. Her concave distribution is one where the largest cities are smaller than would be consistent with the rank-size rule. Primacy in this case means that the first-ranked city is overly large relative to the other large cities but is still not as large as would be true in a fully developed rank-size rule. The less common convex distribution arises when the larger cities are consistently 'too large' and fashion a curve that exceeds a slope of -1.

Smith argues that 'stable lognormal systems are restricted to the developed economic systems of the modern world, whereas concave distributions are characteristic of the pre-modern world as well as the underdeveloped economic systems of the modern world'.[15] Primacy can arise in both 'worlds' but she believes that modern primacy is likely to be stable and not necessarily undesirable because it is based on the concentration of 'infrastructure' – government institutions, economic enterprises and urban functions generally. Pre-modern primacy, on the other hand, is more likely to consist of a concentration of population in one place without a corresponding concentration of infrastructure. One might speak of an unwarranted primacy. Unlike modern primacy it is likely to be a transitional condition; Smith reasons that pre-modern primacy will give way to lognormalcy as the society develops, or the primate city will acquire the infrastructure to warrant its bloated population.

Berry had sought to explain lognormal distributions as the result of numerous random forces acting on the cities of an urban system. Presumably the larger and more complex a society, the more likely are these conditions to obtain. If one argues that these conditions were less likely to obtain in the past, particularly in pre-industrial times, then one would not expect lognormality. The city-size distribution would vary from it in innumerable unspecifiable ways. Smith adds content to this chaos of unspecified 'forces' by basing her distinction of modern and pre-modern urban systems squarely on the underlying forms of economic organization. In modern economies freely mobile labour can migrate to seek its best economic opportunities. The resulting dispersion of migrants among recipient locations, she supposes, will correspond generally to Berry's numerous, random forces. In pre-capitalist and, hence, pre-modern economies labour mobility was institutionally restricted, either because it was tied to the land (serfdom, slavery) or because urban institutions (guilds, apprenticeship, town citizenship) inhibited entry. Urban migration under such conditions, Smith reasons, will be small, thereby yielding a concave distribution of city sizes, and it may also be selective, yielding a primate city where the governing élites for some reason do not erect barriers to entry. The resulting non-lognormal distributions she calls *immature* since they betoken a lack of urban-system integration.

Here we have a more specific formulation than is provided by geographers of how urban systems can be expected to have developed over time. But it too is not without problems, both theoretical and practical. The practical problems involve the objective identification of city-size distributions as primate, lognormal or concave. Once we review these problems the theoretical problems should become more readily apparent.

The techniques used to describe city-size distributions vary with the interests of investigators. If one is primarily interested in testing for the existence of primacy, attention tends to focus on the largest cities of the distribution. The primacy index of urban sociologists simply expresses the population of the largest city as a percentage of the largest four.[16] Several investigators have improved upon this very crude measure by applying the rank-size rule (a lognormal distribution of slope −1) fitted to the largest city.[17] The sizes of lower-ranked cities are then compared to the expectations of the rank-size rule. If they fall under the line, primacy and probably a non-lognormal distribution is indicated. Robson aptly comments on this approach that it 'makes the unreasonable assumption that all places other than the largest may be out of kilter'.[18]

When the focus of interest is less on the existence of primacy and more on the relative position of larger numbers of cities in a distribution, the techniques used also change. Skinner, following the lead of C. H. Harris's study of Russian urban growth, proceeds by fitting the rank-size rule to the *smallest* city. He determines a lower population threshold for urban settlements and this effectively calibrates the expected distribution. Carol Smith also uses this technique, identifying convexity, primacy, and so on, in relation to a lower threshold rank-size rule. As Smith herself emphasizes, this approach is very sensitive to the lower threshold selected. Since there is little to guide the investigator in the choice of the lower threshold, scholars using the same technique can differ in their characterization of all but the most well-behaved city-size distributions.

This method (with its assumption that all but the *smallest* city may be out of kilter) and that based on the largest city both share additional weaknesses that are particularly important to Smith's interpretation of pre-modern primacy. The weakness flows from incorporation of the rank-size rule. When using the Harris–Skinner–Smith technique, the selection of the 'smallest city' determines everything else about the expected urban system. One knows the number of cities, of course, since it is the rank of the smallest city, and the rank-size rule then determines the expected size of all larger cities and the expected total urban population of the society. Given the total population of the society the method also 'expects' a particular level of urbanization, but it generates these expectations in total independence of such data as total population, land area and economic system.

Suppose that a pre-modern, agrarian society with 2 million inhabitants in a territory of 100,000 km^2 had 100 cities. The smallest of these cities performed administrative, marketing and service functions for extensive rural hinterlands, for which they needed a minimum of 2000 inhabitants. To adhere to the rank-size rule the largest city would have 200,000 inhabitants and the entire urban sector just over 1 million, that is, over 50 per cent of the population would need to live in cities. If 25 per cent is the effective upper limit of urbanization for this society, given its technology and occupational structure, and if 100 urban settlements are needed to serve the agrarian economy, then its largest cities must be smaller than predicted by the rank-size rule (a lognormal distribution of slope −0.73 with the largest city at 50,000 inhabitants would be compatible).

In this example as originally presented, the city-size distribution would appear to Smith as immature, its concave shape betraying an imperfect mobility of labour to flow to the larger towns. Yet the true explanation for the 'concavity' would be the overall constraint on unlimited urbanization.

So long as the number of cities remained roughly fixed, general population growth and/or structural changes allowing the urban percentage to rise would probably shift the distribution in the direction of the rank-size rule. Of course, the factors identified by Smith that can cause rural–urban migration to be selective of certain towns could still operate to generate primacy, but Smith's characterization of pre-modern city-size distributions as generally concave and, hence, immature is flawed. The weaknesses of her analysis flow from adherence to the rank-size rule as a standard and from the treatment of the urban system in isolation from the technological and spatial setting in which it finds itself.

The best way to describe rank-size distributions is by statistically estimating the regression line of rank on size. The slope of a lognormal rank-size distribution should be empirically derived rather than assumed to have a slope of −1. It can be objected, as Smith does,[19] that the anomalous size of one or a few of the largest cities will strongly influence the slope of the regression line, rendering the results difficult to use in the determination of just which cities are too large or too small. In the application of this technique that follows I have regressed size on rank over the entire array of cities *excluding* the very largest cities (the twenty largest for Europe as a whole, the ten largest for northern Europe). This was done to assure that the regression would be a dependable predictor of the number of cities below the threshold level of 10,000 population (see chapter 4), and to permit comparison of the development over time of the great body of middle-sized cities and the handful of very large cities that empirical investigation had shown to follow a unique course.

One final question of interpretation remains to be considered. The concave distribution, particularly one in which several of the largest cities are of the same approximate size, may signal one of Smith's immature pre-modern urban systems or it may signal the improper specification of an urban system. Clearly, there is a hazy line separating a poorly integrated urban system (Smith's immaturity) and the conflation of separate urban systems (the improper specification of the system).[20] But what does one make of a city-size distribution that is lognormal, but of a slope less than −1? Does it also betoken 'immaturity', i.e. a poor integration of the constituent cities? It is true that when clearly separate urban systems are merged the resulting city-size distribution will always have a lower slope than each system has separately. But it is fallacious to deduce from this fact the inverse proposition that all *true* urban systems must conform to the rank-size rule.

The rank-size distribution is a blunt instrument with which to evaluate the process of growth and change in urban systems. The danger is great that these beguiling arrays will not simply be misinterpreted but also overinterpreted.

The hazards of misinterpretation stem from the difficulty of establishing the boundaries of the urban system, from using an inappropriate technique to analyse the distribution (to determine which cities are too large and too small), and from the temptation to examine the urban system disembodied from the specific society in which it functions, in particular from such data as the society's size, economic structure, number of cities and level of urbanization.

Overinterpretation is likely because rank-size distributions can vary from each other in many details without this being of far-reaching importance to the way the system functions. Robson goes so far as to reject these distributions entirely as a useful tool of analysis:

> Indeed, in the whole of the work on city sizes, there is much confusion, great difficulty in distinguishing the different distributions, many problems in drawing inferences about processes which might give rise to them and even doubt about the goals of the exercise itself because of the notorious difficulty of arguing about the processes underlying static cross-sectional forms when so often, according to the principle of equifinality, many different processes give rise to identical endproduct forms . . . the study of size distributions appears to be an elaborate maze which ends only in a cul-de-sac.[21]

This critical review of the concepts and techniques available for the analysis of the structure of urban systems will end on a note of cautious optimism. Rank-size distributions can help us gain insight into the process of urban growth, but only if certain pitfalls are avoided. Neither Zipf's rank-size rule nor Smith's method of distinguishing modern and immature urban systems have independent value. The adequacy of an urban system cannot be judged on the basis of an abstract standard or ideal.

Rank-size distributions are a product of empirical investigation and it seems wise to continue to insist that their use be empirically based. For this reason the technique used to characterize a rank-size distribution is of the first importance. Regression over the bulk of the cities of the urban system I hold to be the preferred method because it makes a minimum of assumptions about the appropriate shape of the distribution and permits differences among them to be viewed unobstructed by a filter of abstract standards.

The second precaution that can limit erroneous inference-making is to emphasize the diachronic study of rank-size distribution for a given system over the cross-sectional comparison of different urban systems. The latter has its place, no doubt, in illustrating gross differences in the design of urban networks, but for most purposes the study of a given system over time has the advantage of limiting the number of unobserved variables that influence the

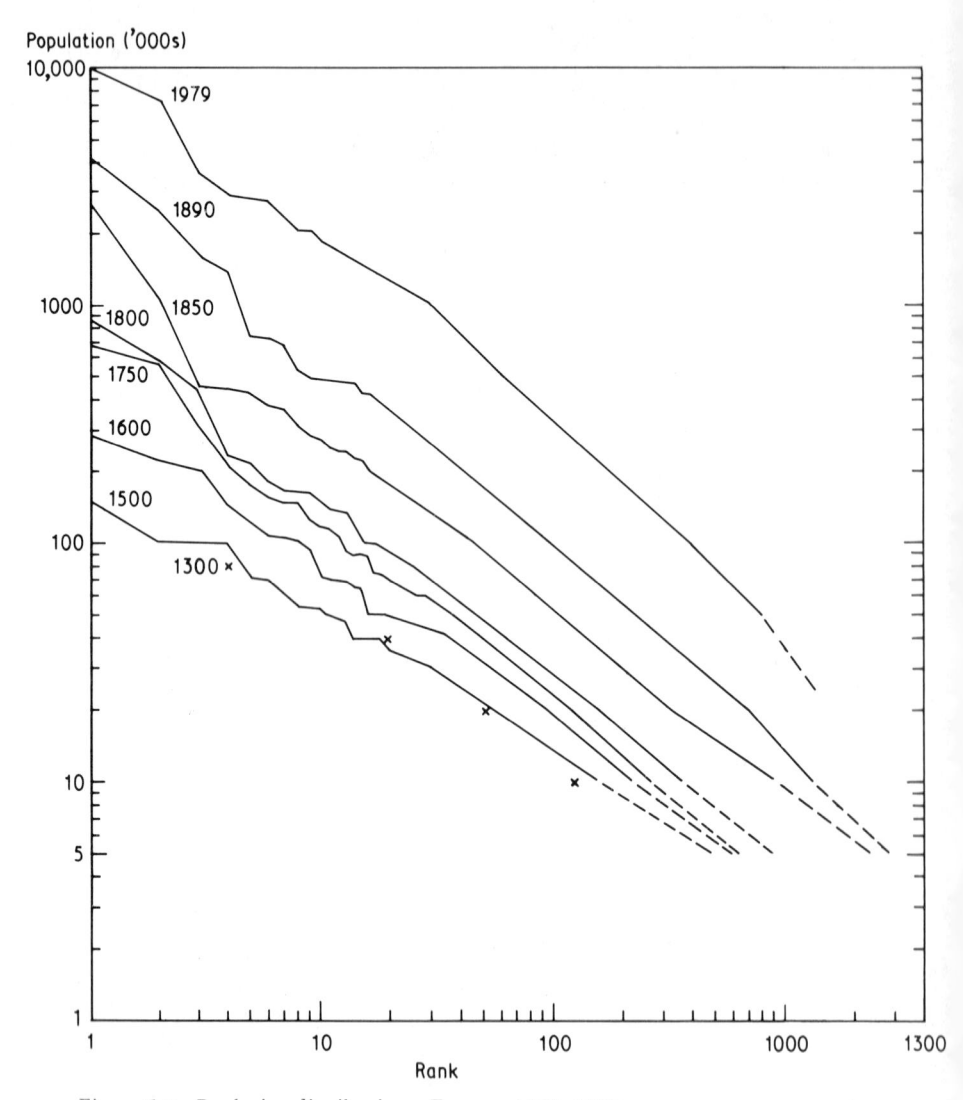

Figure 6.2 Rank-size distributions: Europe, 1300–1979

structure of the urban system, and, hence, of reducing the probability of drawing unwarranted inferences.

In the section that follows I will employ rank-size distributions (with the caution and scepticism that the above discussion calls for) to order the mass of data on city growth and examine hypotheses about the process of European urbanization.

EUROPE'S RANK-SIZE DISTRIBUTIONS

In this section rank-size distributions will be presented and analysed first for Europe as a whole and for the largest subdivisions (northern and Mediterranean Europe). Thereafter attention will focus on a selection of national urban systems. In chapter 11 the European experience will be compared to several other major urban systems of the world.

Figure 6.2 displays selected rank-size distributions for Europe as a whole from the early fourteenth century to the present day. What is it safe to conclude from this figure about the long-term process of urban growth?

In 1500 the cities of Europe from approximately rank 20 downward formed a loglinear distribution, albeit with a very shallow slope coefficient (-0.63). The inclusion of the larger cities would have reduced the slope coefficient yet further, for these cities all fell below the regression line fashioned by the smaller cities, while the four largest cities endowed the distribution with very nearly a flat top. To lend some perspective to the 1500 data, I have plotted in outline form J. C. Russell's estimates of the number of Europe's early-fourteenth-century cities by size categories. Russell's estimates, based on independent data and using techniques that differ from mine, generate a city-size distribution that is strikingly similar to mine for 1500. Only his estimate of the number of cities with 10,000–20,000 inhabitants – probably the least secure of his estimates – differs significantly from the 1500 pattern.

The 1300 and 1500 distributions both reflect a low level of integration among the various regions of Europe. In Smith's parlance these are textbook examples of an 'immature' pre-modern system. To the extent that medieval European urbanism raised up a number of small, relatively autarchic urban systems, their aggregation into a single rank-size distribution would of course yield a flat-topped curve with a shallow slope. More noteworthy is the persistence of this characteristic to all of Europe in 1500. Indeed, the apparent long-term stability of the medieval urban hierarchy through all the vicissitudes of Black Death and 'feudal crisis' sets one to wondering about the relationships of the towns to the rest of late-medieval European society.[22]

THE PROPERTIES OF THE URBAN SYSTEM

In 1500 the low level of subsystem integration is present in its most exaggerated form in northern Europe, particularly in those territories beyond the ancient boundaries of substantial Roman urbanization (the Rhine and Danube). Nearly a dozen cities of 20,000–45,000 inhabitants shared the top-ranked positions in this vast expanse: some, like Copenhagen and London, standing at the head of the rather sketchy urban hierarchies of Scandinavia and Britain; others, like Cologne, Nuremberg and Utrecht, enjoying the benefits of administrative, ecclesiastical and economic power and privilege over more limited regions; and still others, the Hanseatic cities, participating in a trading alliance that specifically sought to avoid the subordination of all members to one great merchant centre. In general it would be unreasonable to assert the existence of one, or of only a small number, of urban systems in early-sixteenth-century Europe.

The following century of economic and demographic expansion brought with it substantial urban growth. The 1600 rank-size distributions for Europe and its major regions all shift vigorously upward and to the right, signifying both increases in the population of cities (the upward shift) and the entry of new cities – that is, the passage of existing cities over the 10,000 population threshold (which results in a rightward shift of the distribution). Cities of every size and in every region participated in this process of urban growth. There was a tendency for the larger cities to grow rather more rapidly than smaller cities. What is more noteworthy, however, is the emergence of several cities from the pack of leading medieval cities to assume positions at the top ranks of the rank-size distributions.

These phenomena are reflected in the greater slopes of the 1600 distributions as compared to 1500 (for Europe -0.72 in 1600, -0.63 in 1500) and in the disappearance of the flat top, as Naples, Paris, London and Amsterdam (in the process of rising as Antwerp declines) grew to achieve population levels unknown to medieval urbanism.

In comparing the 1500 and 1600 distributions, one is tempted to hypothesize that in the intervening century the level of economic integration was rising, and that an urban hierarchy was developing that would begin linking together the numerous regional urban systems. This process is certainly more apparent in northern Europe than in the Mediterranean area (see figures 6.3 and 6.4). In the latter case, the large size attained by Naples in 1600 should not be interpreted to mean that she had assumed functions at the peak of a Mediterranean or even of an Italian system of cities. One is left then with five or six cities of roughly the same size (Venice, Genoa, Milan, Seville, Lisbon and soon Madrid), each presiding over a regional or colonial system.

Rather different was the pattern of urban growth emerging in northwestern Europe. There, an irregular, flat-topped rank-size distribution was replaced within a century by a more nearly loglinear distribution, with

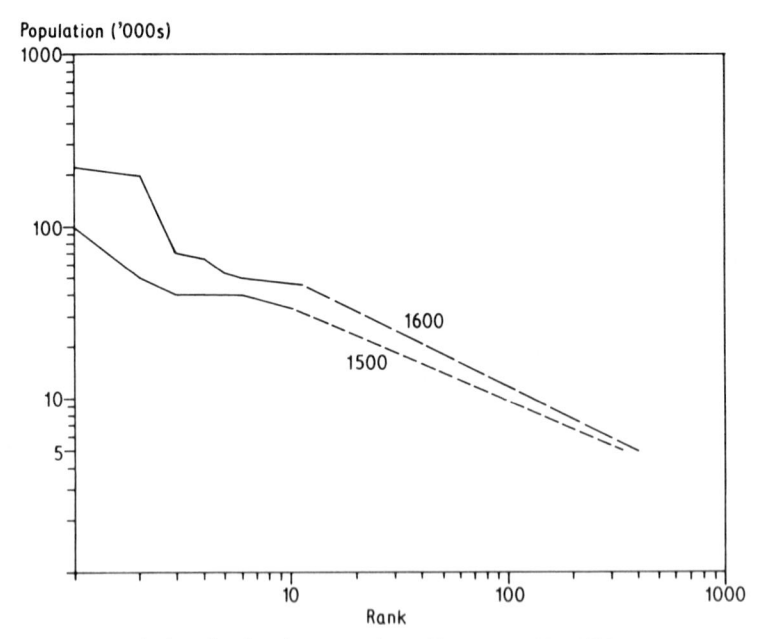

Figure 6.3 Rank-size distributions: northern Europe, 1500–1600

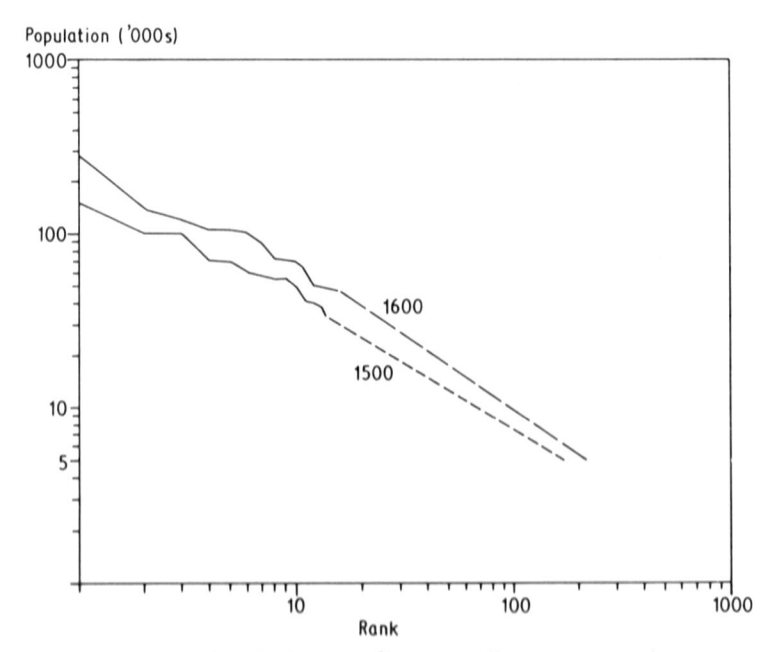

Figure 6.4 Rank-size distributions: Mediterranean Europe, 1500–1600

London, the largest city, actually displaying a primacy not only in the context of the British Isles but in the urban hierarchy for all of north-western Europe. It would be misleading to infer from this that London somehow directly dominated all of this large territory, but one can conclude that in the course of the sixteenth century north-western Europe's larger cities were becoming more integrally tied to one another, in the sense that forces at work in one city now affected more powerfully and with less delay the activities and relative standing of the other cities than had been the case a century earlier.

The patterns observed in the sixteenth century persisted into the early decades of the seventeenth century, but in the following period, and particularly in the decades surrounding 1650, these patterns of urban growth dissolved, to be replaced by a dramatic reordering of Europe's urban hierarchy. An urban growth process in which cities in every size class and in all regions participated gave way to a rigorously selective urban growth. The rank-size distribution for northern Europe became much more steeply sloped (1600, −0.62; 1650, −0.71; 1700, −0.77) as the larger cities grew while the smaller cities stagnated (see figure 6.5).

At the same time Mediterranean Europe suffered a sharp drop in the size of its cities, leading to a contraction of the number of cities above the 10,000 population threshold and to a somewhat less steeply sloped rank-size distribution (1600, −0.85; 1650, −0.81; 1700, back to −0.84; see figure 6.6). Even in the face of this widely shared urban collapse, certain large cities managed to continue their growth, or to recover quickly and resume their former position. By 1750 the rank-size distribution is strikingly similar to that of 1600 (see figure 6.7), except that the nine or ten largest cities have all improved their position relative to the rest of the distribution.

Europe's urbanization clearly assumed a new character during the seventeenth century. The rank-size distributions call attention both to the divergent paths followed by northern and Mediterranean urbanization and to the sharply increased concentration of urban population in the largest cities of the urban system everywhere. By the early eighteenth century a hierarchy of cities is in place, featuring dominant cities that not only stand at the head of extended urban subsystems but perform functions that serve to integrate Europe into a single, albeit loosely coupled, urban system.

The extent of Europe-wide urban hierarchy-formation achieved by the early eighteenth century was not surpassed in later decades. The slopes of the 1700 and 1750 rank-size distributions (−0.8) represent a high point that was not reached again − let alone exceeded − until 1890. When we allow the rank-size distributions to be our guide, the century after 1750 − the century of the Industrial Revolution − distinguishes itself with a pattern of urban growth altogether distinct from that which had preceded it from 1500 to 1750 and from that which was to follow in the century after 1850.

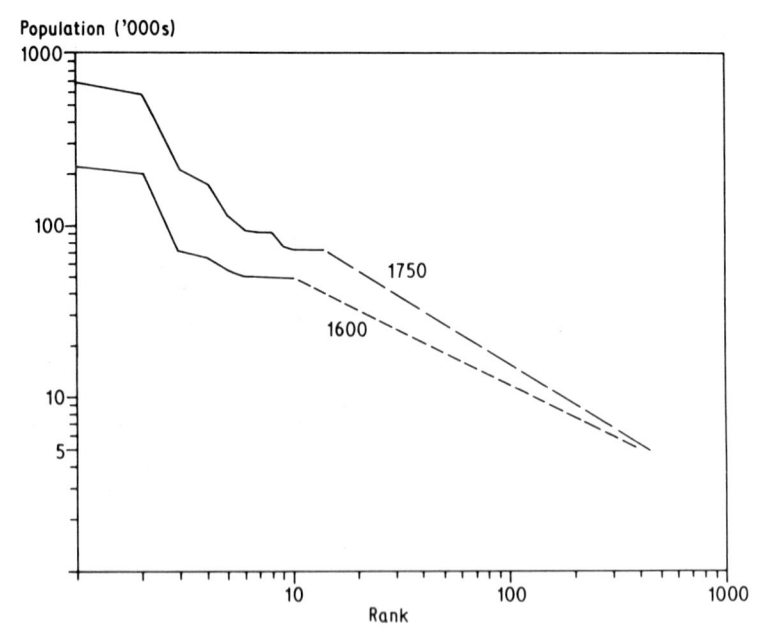

Figure 6.5 Rank-size distributions: northern Europe, 1600–1750

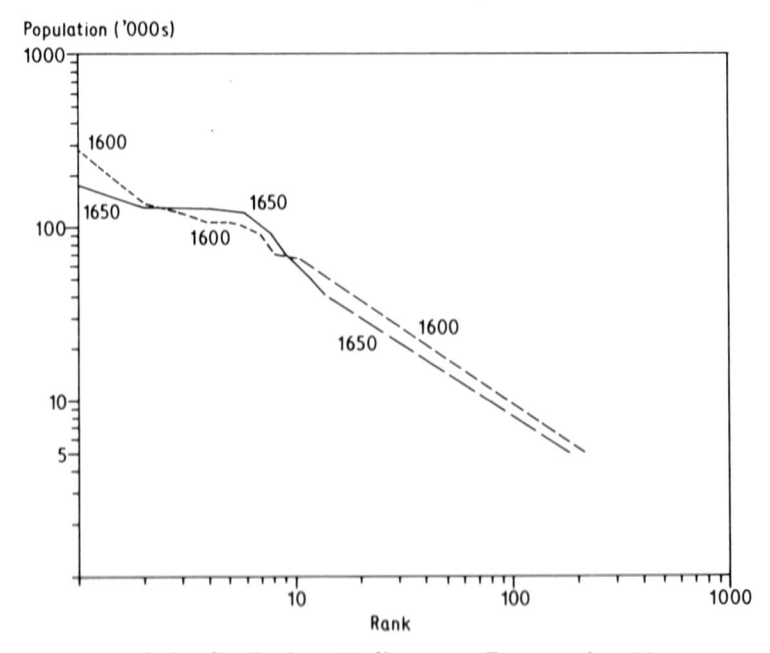

Figure 6.6 Rank-size distributions: Mediterranean Europe, 1600–50

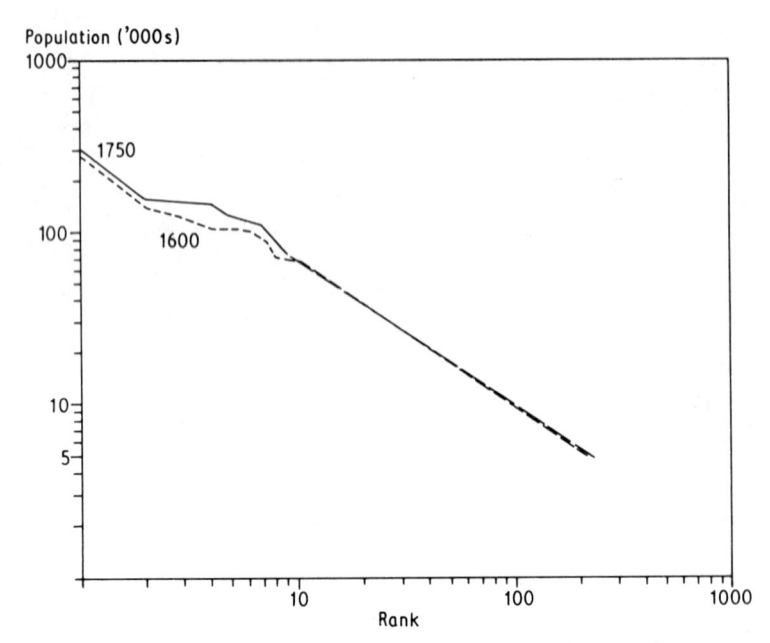

Figure 6.7 Rank-size distributions: Mediterranean Europe, 1600–1750

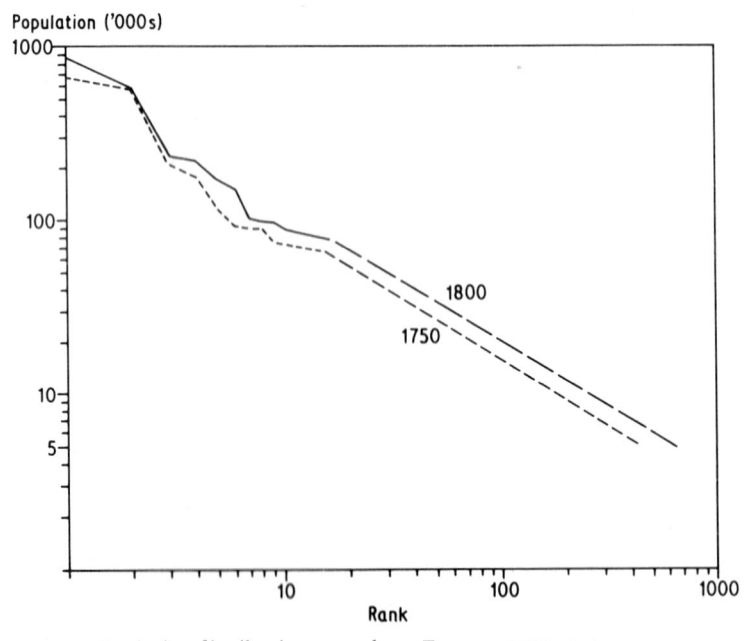

Figure 6.8 Rank-size distributions: northern Europe, 1750–1800

THE DEVELOPMENT OF AN URBAN HIERARCHY

From 1500 to 1750 urban growth in Europe as a whole can be summarized as a process of selective city-growth which step-by-step converts a strikingly 'concave' rank-size distribution (one of low slope and of flat top) to one approaching lognormality and with a much steeper slope. The rank-size distribution literally rotated clockwise from a pivot at the lower right, signifying the roughly stable number of cities in Europe's urban universe throughout this period. This is a rather abstract way of saying that urban growth was concentrated in the larger cities, and in those whose growth persisted long enough for them to become large, and that urbanization was not characterized by the 'birth' of numerous new cities.

The century after 1750 differs in that it is now the smaller cities which grow disproportionately while, as a related phenomenon, the emergence of new urban settlements enlarges the stock of European cities. Until 1800 this new pattern of urban growth is essentially a characteristic of northern Europe (see figure 6.8). In the first half of the nineteenth century the Mediterranean cities join in. Not only did numerous small cities and new urban places grow vigorously in this era, but most of the dozen or so largest European cities were conspicuous for the sluggishness of their expansion. Again, this was primarily a feature of the late eighteenth century in northern Europe and of the early nineteenth century in the south. Europe's overall rank-size distribution in 1850 remains lognormal, but at a somewhat lower slope than before, while the largest city, London, for the first time attains an unambiguous primacy over the entire distribution. These characteristics are all true for the north and west of Europe in an exaggerated form; in the Mediterranean region the 1850 distribution, while also of a lower slope than a century earlier, continues to be distinctly 'concave' in its higher ranks.

The end of the 'interlude' of urbanization from below varies in its timing from region to region. In England urban growth led by the larger cities reasserts itself by the 1820s, in France in the 1840s, and in the Mediterranean countries, for which the data are less precise, probably after 1850. The contours of nineteenth- and twentieth-century urbanization are well known from a long list of publications, not least of which is Adna F. Weber's pioneering work, *The Growth of Cities in the Nineteenth Century: a Study in Statistics* (New York, 1899). One of Weber's conclusions was that 'the process of concentration of population is centralizing in its tendencies; that is, the large cities are growing more rapidly than the small cities and absorbing the great bulk of the urban increase'.[23] This process is commonly attributed to the effects of industrialization, so that the 'age of the great city' is thought to find its origins in the Industrial Revolution. The pattern of rank-size distributions here under discussion urges a rather different interpretation. The dominant position of large cities, signalled by their absorption of 'the great bulk of the urban increase', was an achievement of the seventeenth century. The era of the Industrial Revolution actually reversed that process, or held it in check, until roughly with the coming of the railways large-city growth reasserted itself. Even then, the process of nineteenth-century urban concentration should not be exaggerated. The 1890 rank-size distribution (based on Weber's data, corrected in a few instances) is perhaps the most nearly loglinear throughout its length of any observable in figure 6.2. The growth of large cities below first-ranked London eroded that city's position of primacy. But that growth, very much concentrated in Germany and France, roughly restored the sort of rank-size distribution (as defined by slope and approximation to loglinearity) prevailing in the mid-eighteenth century.

Twentieth-century urban systems are enormously difficult to compare to those of earlier times. Since the elements of the system are generally no longer cities but metropolitan areas, the rank-size distributions and other statistical descriptions of urban structure can vary considerably according to how wide a net is cast in the calculation of metropolitan population. The rank-size distribution shown for 1979 is based on the population data reported in national censuses. Wherever the documents offered a choice, I used the population for metropolitan areas, but no steps were taken to bring the various national reporting conventions into conformity with a single standard. The overall distributions surprise us in their general similarity to those of earlier centuries. The slope remains distinctly below -1 (-0.81) and is concave at the top — for the first time since the seventeenth century.

In the review of geographers' efforts to infuse rank-size distributions with meaning, the expectation figured prominently that in large urban systems the growth of cities of a given size class will, on average, be proportional to their initial size. This 'law of proportionate effect' underlies Berry's expectation that urban systems whose cities grow 'as a result of the operation of a large number of independent growth influences' ultimately will achieve lognormal distributions (no matter what the initial configuration) and that the steady state of such an urban system will also be a lognormal distribution of city sizes.[24] A classic case of the evolution of such an urban system is the rank-size distribution for United States cities in the period 1790–1950, displayed in figure 6.9. Decade by decade the rank-size distributions remain parallel to each other. Their preservation of the same overall slope signifies that the average growth rate for cities in each size class is proportional to initial size. To achieve this constancy there must also exist a long-run balance between the growth of the component cities (the cause of the vertical shifts) and the rate at which new cities are introduced to enlarge the urban system as a whole (the cause of the horizontal shifts).

By now it must be abundantly clear that the European pattern does not conform to any of these expectations. To begin with, there was no regular introduction of new cities. From the high middle ages to the mid-eighteenth

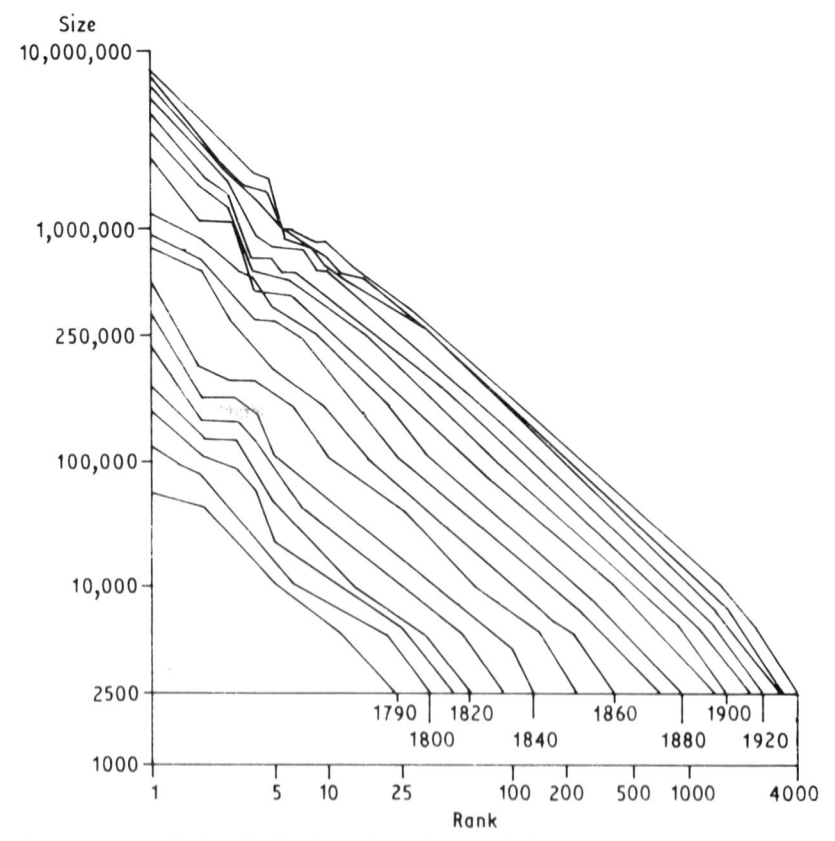

Figure 6.9 Rank-size distribution of US city populations, 1790–1950

century the number of cities in this long-settled part of the world changed but little. The era of early industrialization augmented that stock of cities, but by the mid-nineteenth century the pace of new addition slowed once again. In conformity with this, the distributions of figure 6.2 tend to group around two pivots, one for the 1500–1750 distributions, and a second, further to the right, for the post-1850 distributions. Each pivot locates a relatively stable stock of cities.

The next feature deserving emphasis is that there is no period in which urban growth can be characterized as proportional to initial city size. The constant changes of the slope of rank-size distributions indicate this in a general way. These distributions are the products of growth-rates that varied distinctly by size of city. To illustrate the significance of what is visually difficult to distinguish and what must appear as trivial differences in slope, two techniques are of use.

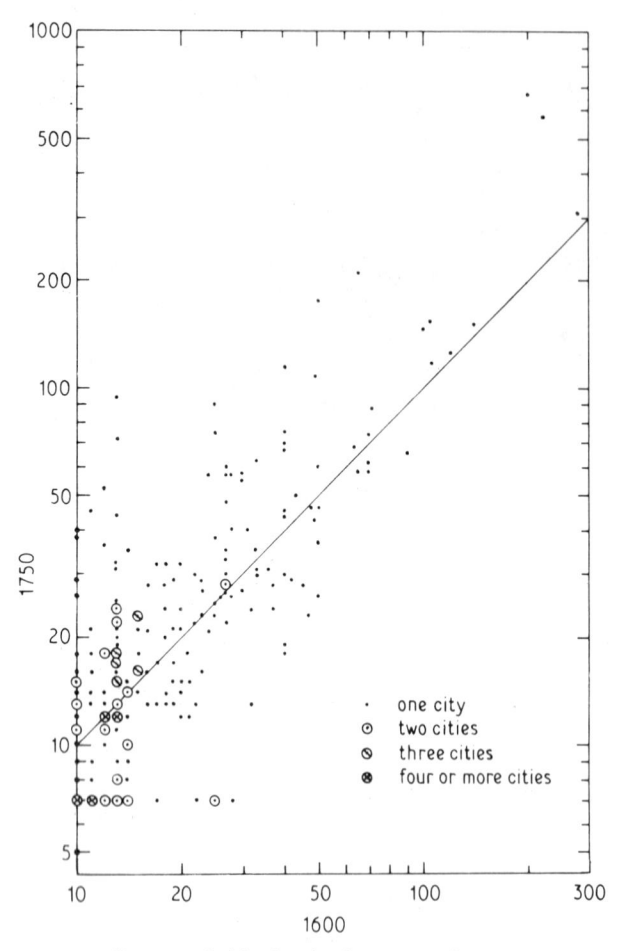

Figure 6.10 Scatter diagram of cities by size in 1600 and 1750

Figures 6.10 and 6.11 plot the scatter diagram of European cities by size for the intervals 1600–1750 and 1750–1800 respectively. Each city is represented by a point determined by its size in the initial year (measured on the abscissa) and at the end of the period (measured on the axis). By using a double logarithmic scale the convenient result is achieved that if, on average, cities of all sizes grew by an amount proportional to their initial size, the observations would cluster around a regression line sloping upward to the right at a 45-degree angle. In the special case of no overall growth, the 45-degree line passes through the origin; in a growing system of cities the intercept of the regression line would pass through the axis to the left of the origin. Such a regression line would demonstrate that the law of proportionate effect holds. A regression line that is not parallel to the 45-degree line suggests the existence of a systematic relationship between growth and size: an angle of over 45 degrees signifies that growth-rates rise with initial size, while an angle smaller than 45 degrees signifies that growth-rates vary inversely with initial size. Clearly, the 1600–1750 scatter diagram for northern Europe shows that the growth-rates of the larger cities substantially exceeded those of smaller cities while the 1750–1800 scatter diagram shows just the opposite.

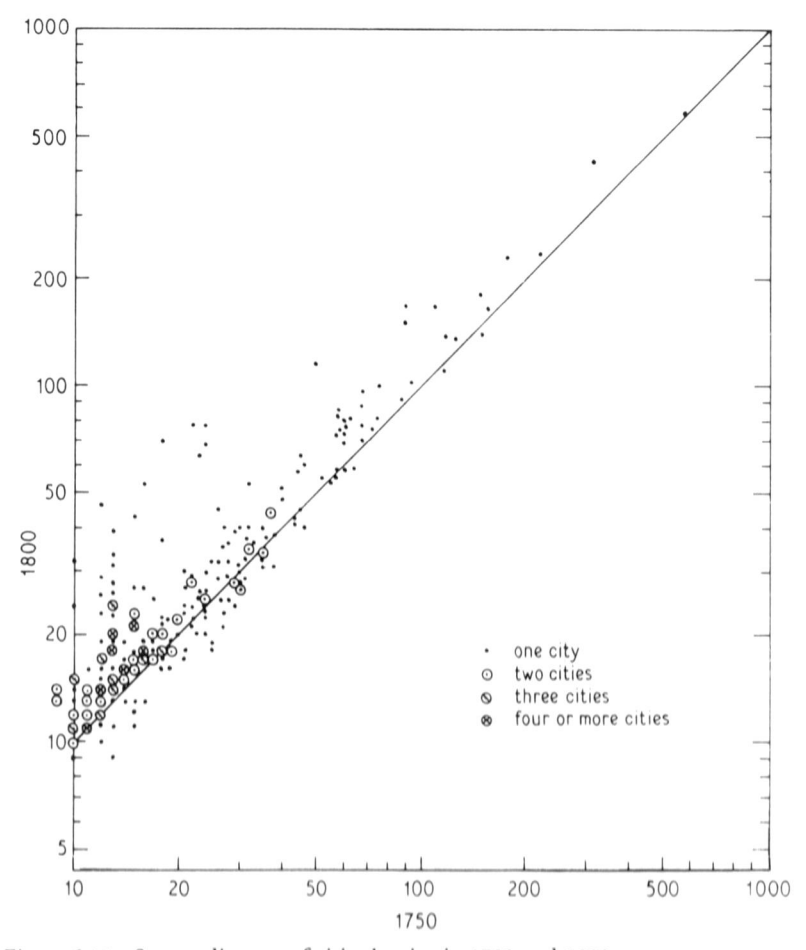

Figure 6.11 Scatter diagram of cities by size in 1750 and 1800

THE PROPERTIES OF THE URBAN SYSTEM

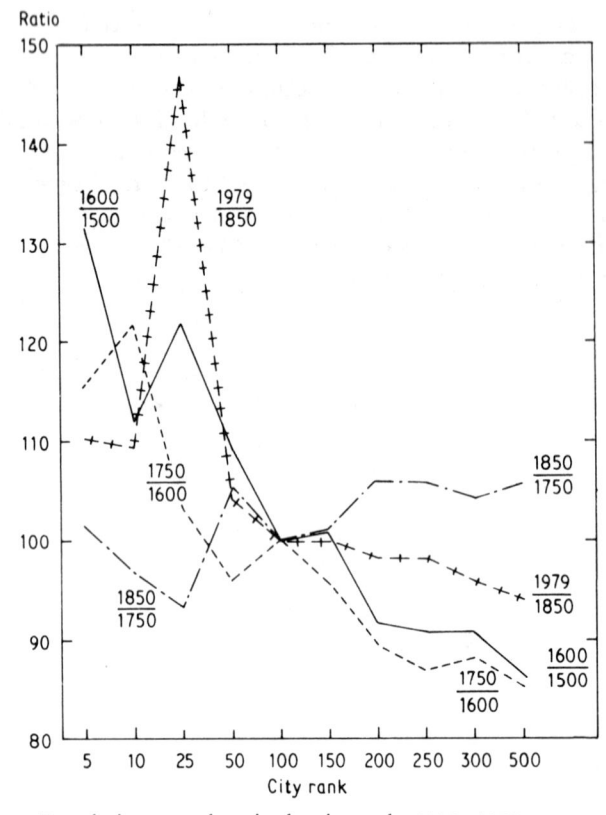

Figure 6.12 Population growth ratios by city rank, 1500–1979

A second technique to identify the pattern of growth by city size is presented in figure 6.12. For selected time intervals I calculated the percentage by which cities at several ranks grew. Thus, if the tenth largest city in Europe possessed 60,000 inhabitants in 1600 while the city of that rank in 1500 had 30,000, the value of rank 10 for the period 1500–1600 is 60/30 = 2.0. The higher the ratio, the more rapid is the growth of cities at that rank. For present purposes it is not the level of the ratios that concerns us but the pattern of the ratios by rank for each interval. To facilitate comparisons among the intervals the ratios are expressed as a percentage of the ratio at rank 100. If urban growth is concentrated in larger cities, the figure will show a diminution of the ratios as one moves from higher to lower ranks, i.e. from larger to smaller cities. This is, indeed, the case for the intervals 1500–1600 and 1600–1750. For the interval 1750–1850 the curve, while irregular, moves in the opposite direction. That is, the smaller cities grew more rapidly than the larger cities.[25]

THE DEVELOPMENT OF AN URBAN HIERARCHY

After 1850 the relationship of growth to city size reassumes, in a more muted way, the general pattern common to the centuries before 1750. The peculiar bulge at rank 25 is related to the twentieth-century tendency for large cities just below the status of the largest metropoli to enjoy particularly favourable growth possibilities.

The rank-size distributions do not by themselves 'explain' anything. Their value resides in their power to describe specific aspects of the process of urban growth and to test hypotheses about that process. The pattern of growth revealed by the changing slopes of the regression lines demonstrate that the forces affecting that growth were anything but random and independent. Those forces were systematic in the sense that urban growth was usually highly selective of certain types of cities in certain regions, and in the sense that the growth impulses changed systematically several times. Around 1600 a large-city-biased but very widespread urban growth suddenly gave way to an era in which many cities declined while growth came to be concentrated rigorously in a small number of northern cities. In the mid- to late eighteenth century this pattern of growth yielded in favour of a small-city-biased growth. By the mid-nineteenth century at the latest, a more general growth process, moderately biased in favour of large cities, emerged.

This analysis of European rank-size distributions establishes certain of the broad contours of urban growth. It must be recalled, however, that it says nothing specifically about the behaviour of the elements of the urban system – the individual cities. The cities of any particular rank-size distribution in time t can, in theory, redistribute themselves to conform with a new distribution in time $t + 50$ in many different ways. In chapter 7 I will try to reveal the specific patterns of city behaviour that generated the urban growth process outlined by these distributions. Before proceeding with this task, the analysis of the rank-size distributions will be completed by examining the national and regional entities into which Europe is divided.

RANK-SIZE DISTRIBUTIONS OF INDIVIDUAL COUNTRIES

I have argued that the cities of Europe were fashioned into a single urban system in the course of the sixteenth and seventeenth centuries. But it would be foolish to suppose that the interactions among distant cities could then have been intense. The claims for the existence of systemic relations are most impressive when Europe is viewed from a global perspective; the urbanism of Russia and the Ottoman empire, let alone of more distant cultures, seems to be clearly distinguishable from that of Europe. From a perspective within Europe, the system must appear as loosely coupled, composed of many subsystems whose internal patterns of urban hierarchy and growth differed one from another in important ways. But by how much did they stand apart from one another? Are the Europe-wide distributions illusory artefacts consisting of national or regional urban systems displaying characteristics that are disguised by overaggregation? Or can the study of the urban subsystems complement the analysis presented above for Europe as a whole?

To confront these issues, we now proceed to the analysis of several national urban systems. This smaller scale will permit us to push beyond the contemplation of the urban growth process to a consideration of what the changing shapes of the distributions can suggest about how a regional or national economy was organized and exploited by its system of cities. Here the interpretative concepts of primacy, lognormality and concavity (discussed in the first section of this chapter) will come into play as we enquire whether the nations and regions of Europe experienced any characteristic progression of rank-size distributions as their economies became more market-oriented, capitalistic, industrial or modern.

Spain

During its sixteenth-century rise as a European and colonial power, Habsburg Spain's substantial urban growth did not alter the concave shape of its rank-size distribution, the form that Carol Smith regards as symptomatic of an immature urban system. In the seventeenth-century demographic, economic and political collapse of Spain, the rank-size distribution of its suffering cities shifted to approximate lognormality at a slope near −1 that is, it corresponded to the rank-size rule. This surprising result proved to be quite durable. In the nineteenth and twentieth centuries Spain's urban system has approximated the rank-size rule with the notable exceptions of Madrid and particularly Barcelona, which have stood above the rest of the distribution as primate cities.

Obviously Spain in 1650 did not really suddenly find itself endowed with a modern urban system. The new distribution was the composite product of two distinct events: first, the decay of many regional centres with the result that vast areas of Castile came to be drained of commercial facilities and services, and second, the rapid growth of Madrid as the parasitic administrative centre of a vast empire.[26] It would be foolish to infer from the shape of these rank-size distributions alone that Spain's urban system after 1600 had become better integrated or in some other sense more modern. Likewise, neither of the just-mentioned trends at work in the seventeenth century can wholly be accounted for by factors internal to Spain; the urban collapse was part and parcel of a larger phenomenon of Mediterranean eclipse[27] while the rise of Madrid was obviously related to the European and colonial empire of the Habsburgs.

THE DEVELOPMENT OF AN URBAN HIERARCHY

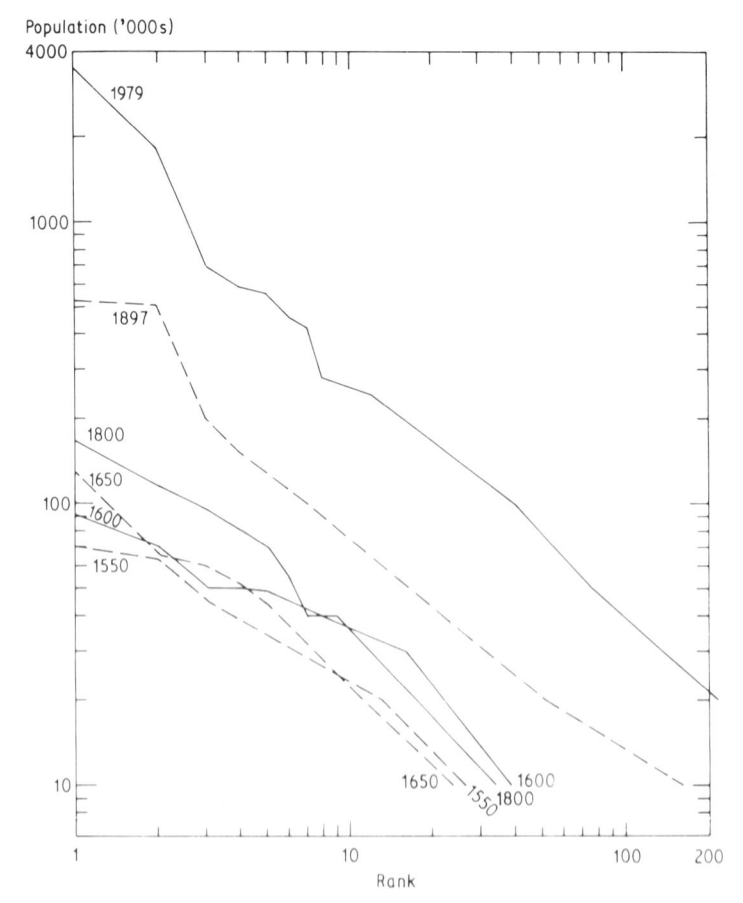

Figure 6.13 Rank-size distributions: Spain, 1500–1979

Italy

Since Italy formed easily the most urbanized large area of Europe in 1500, the character and evolution of its urban hierarchy is of special interest. Italy was then the home of three of Europe's four cities of 100,000 or more inhabitants and of ten of Europe's eighteen cities of at least 40,000. Given Italy's division into numerous political jurisdictions one might question the legitimacy of treating this 'geographical expression' as a single urban system. For this reason, after considering Italy as a whole, the consequences of further disaggregation will be explored by a brief survey of two important subregions:

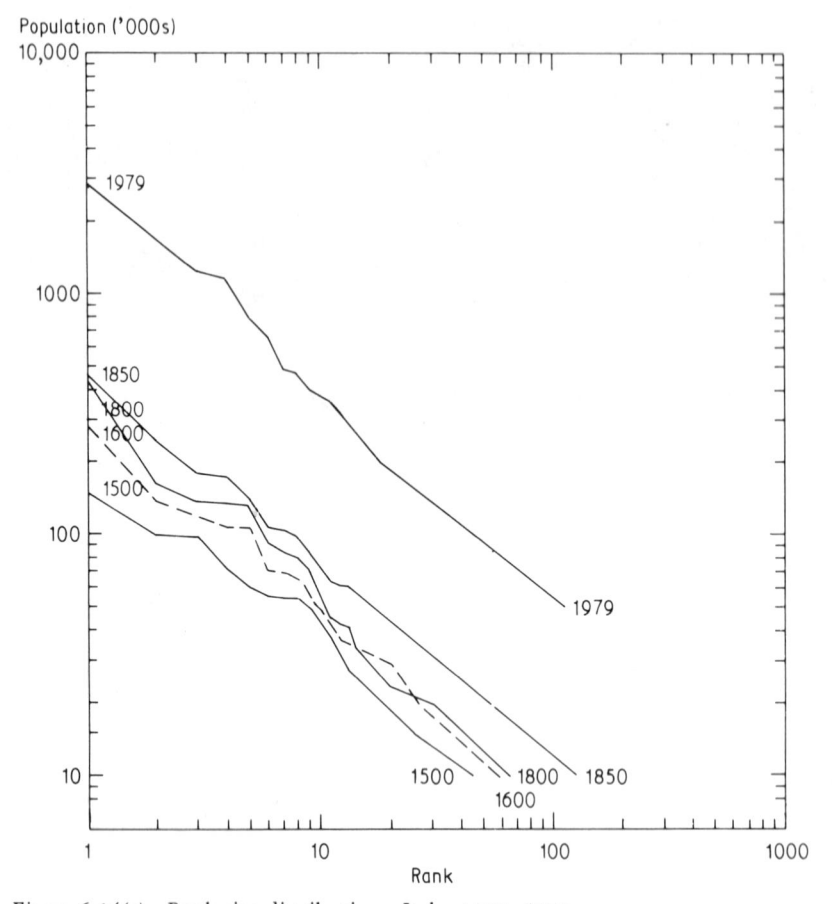

Figure 6.14(a) Rank-size distributions: Italy, 1500–1979

northern Italy (territory 10) and southern Italy, essentially the old Kingdom of Naples (territory 12).

In 1500 the cities of Italy formed a concave rank-size distribution of the type suggesting the presence of several relatively autonomous subsystems headed by the many large cities of similar size: Naples, Venice, Milan, Palermo, Genoa, Rome and Florence. The upper reaches of Italy's rank-size distribution showed the signs of Smith's 'immature' pre-modern system, despite the relatively advanced character of Italy's economy and despite the fact that Venice and Genoa each headed urban systems largely located outside Italy, as did, in a rather different way, Rome. Such 'imperialism' would seem to invite the creation of primacy,[28] but Italy's urban hierarchy remained decidedly decentralized.

THE DEVELOPMENT OF AN URBAN HIERARCHY

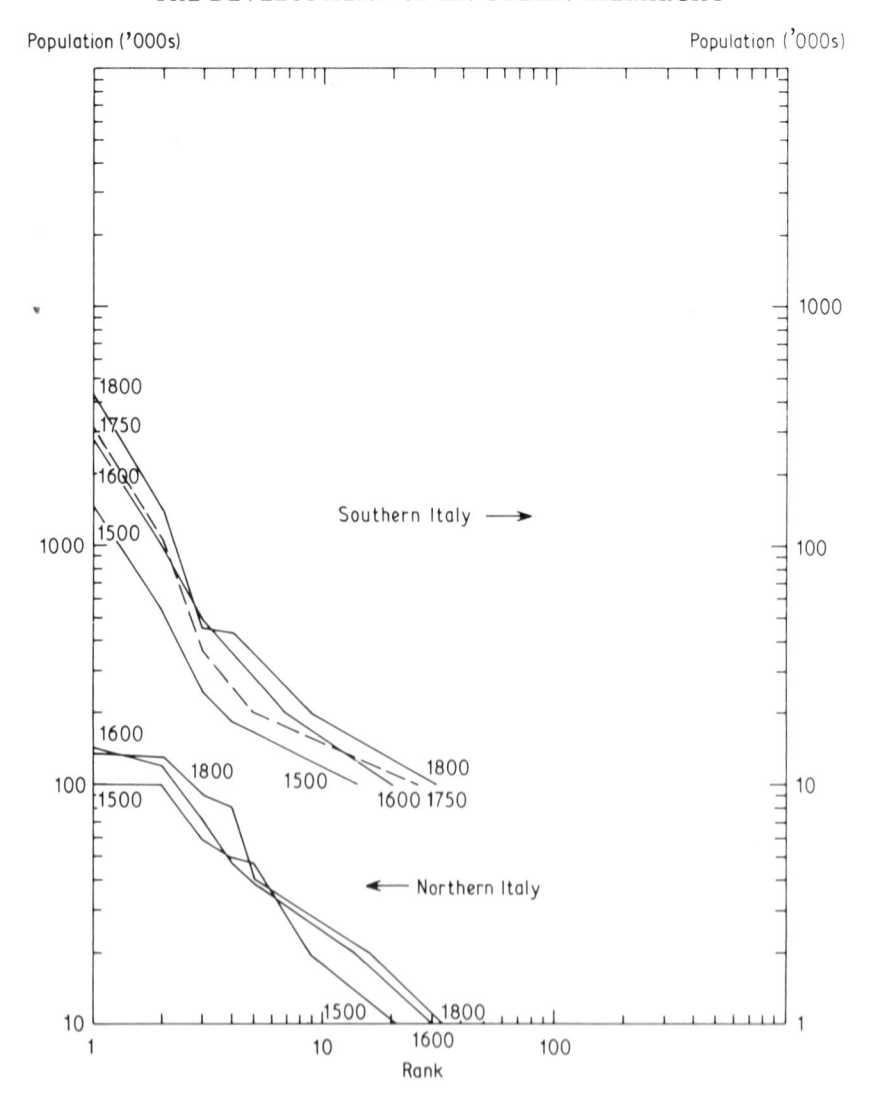

Figure 6.14(b) Rank-size distributions: northern Italy and southern Italy, 1500–1800

By 1600 the system had expanded and the larger cities in particular grew with vigour, but without substantially altering the concave character of the rank-size distribution. The demographic reversals of the seventeenth century and the limited recovery that followed caused the rank-size distributions up to 1800 to hover in a very narrow range. With the notable but hard to explain exception of the largest city, Naples, which grew substantially, Italy's cities seem to fluctuate in size in random ways. This changed the details but not the general contours of the rank-size distributions, which remained concave with the body of the distribution (below rank 5) close to the rank-size rule.

The rapid growth of smaller cities in the first half of the nineteenth century transformed the rank-size distribution for the first time to one loglinear throughout its entire length, but at a substantially lower slope than before (-0.81). Modern urban growth since the political unification of the Italian peninsula (1860) has resulted, perhaps ironically, in a slight reversion to the older, pre-nineteenth-century pattern. In 1979, just as in 1500, the body of the distribution is loglinear near slope -1 while the largest cities – the largest three in this case – are 'too small'.

When the urban hierarchies of northern and southern Italy are examined separately two distinctive, sharply contrasting patterns emerge. In the city-rich, heavily urbanized north, the shared leaderships of 1500 became even more pronounced in later periods as Genoa and Turin gradually joined Venice and Milan to assume the top positions in rank-size distributions whose slopes became, if anything, less steep over time. In the Kingdom of Naples the primacy of the capital city dominated an otherwise very concave distribution which, interestingly enough, assumed almost exactly the same general form in 1800 as it had in 1500.

In the context of Carol Smith's mode of analysis, southern Italian urbanization was peculiar not so much because of Naples' enormous size but because of the underdevelopment, after Palermo, of cities of intermediate rank. In other words, rather than wonder how Naples became so large, historians should wonder why cities of intermediate rank were not larger. Of course this can be argued only by asserting that the rank-size rule should be the standard by which to judge the urban hierarchy. Then Naples in 1500 and again from 1650 to 1750 is roughly at the 'appropriate' size for the largest city of a well-behaved urban hierarchy.

No matter what technique is used to interpret Italian urban systems, we are left with a puzzling result; southern Italy supported one enormous city, whose size is hard to justify; northern Italy possessed several cities whose extensive international functions in the sixteenth century might easily have resulted in primacy, but the rank-size distribution remained distinctly concave. The combination of those distributions into one 'Italian' urban system appears to be highly misleading. If the subsystems of the Italian peninsula are to be related to each other, it should be in a Mediterranean rather than an Italian context.

France

France is the one large European nation where one might expect to find a

THE DEVELOPMENT OF AN URBAN HIERARCHY

hierarchy of cities that corresponds to the expectations of central place theory, and presumably the rank-size rule. Administrative centralization as pursued by the absolutist monarchs of the seventeenth and eighteenth centuries plus the agricultural marketing requirements of a large territorial state both lend plausibility to this expectation. In 1500 the rank-size distribution shows Paris, the largest city, to be slightly primate, a primacy that would become

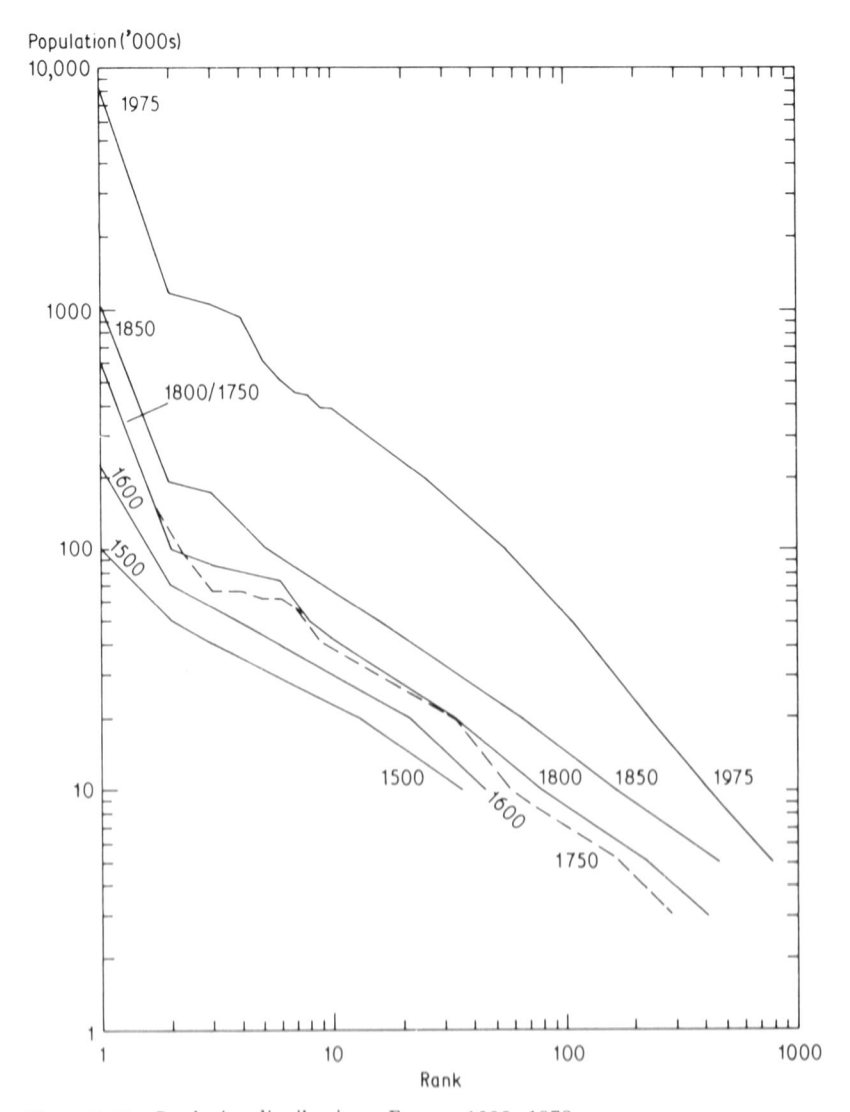

Figure 6.15 Rank-size distributions: France, 1500–1979

steadily more pronounced right up to 1750. But it shows the rest of the distribution to have a very shallow slope (-0.56), and this rises only very slightly up to 1850 (-0.66).

This long-persisting pattern of city sizes illustrates well the problems involved in accepting Carol Smith's concept of pre-modern primacy. She would describe the French urban system as concave and immature, and interpret the fact that nearly all the cities fall short of the population expectations of the rank-size rule as a consequence of labour market imperfections that limit the flow of rural labour into the cities, particularly the provincial centres. However, a hierarchy of cities conforming to the rank-size rule in 1500 would have required the largest city to number 360,000 inhabitants (instead of 100,000) and the total population in cities of at least 10,000 inhabitants to be three times larger than in fact it was. Yet no large territory could have supported 30 per cent of its population in cities under the economic conditions of that time.

Smith's technique is to calibrate the rank-size rule to the *smallest* city. Alternatively, one might draft the rank-size rule line from the largest city, Paris. In 1500 the second-ranked city, Lyons, conforms perfectly, being one-half the size of Paris, and Rouen, the third largest city, is not far from its 'expected' size either. But this procedure yields the absurd conclusion that France 'ought' to have numbered only ten cities of 10,000 or more inhabitants in 1500 (it possessed over thirty). Clearly France needed many cities to organize effectively its vast territory, but could not, in those centuries, support one-third of its population in urban occupations and locations. The 'solution' to these constraints was the type of rank-size distribution already evident in 1500 that continued to characterize France until the mid-nineteenth century.

Only after 1850 is this durable pattern altered. Then, while Paris preserves its primate status, cities of intermediate size grow to account for a much larger portion of the total urban population. But even at the present day, the distribution below rank 1 forms a curve that falls short of the rank-size rule.

Of the national rank-size distributions examined thus far, the French is the only one that appears comprehensible in the context of developments internal to France. Despite this its contours suggest to the analyst of twentieth-century urban systems a lack of national cohesion. Ironically, the Spanish and Italian urban hierarchies often seem to conform better to the modern ideal. But a cursory familiarity with the histories of those countries is sufficient to expose this as an illusion. Rather, they are the product of various political and economic factors that serve to demonstrate that the urban subsystems were often smaller than the nation and exposed to important influences from abroad. In other words, they were part of a European urban system.

THE DEVELOPMENT OF AN URBAN HIERARCHY

Germany

In the sixteenth and seventeenth centuries politically fragmented Germany possessed a large number of regional centres, but no city to integrate these centres either politically or economically. The severely concave rank-size distribution of 1600 illustrates this situation with unimpeachable clarity.

Between the seventeenth and early nineteenth centuries – long before German unification – varied developments, such as the rise of the Prussian state, the commercial initiatives of the city-state of Hamburg and a broadly diffused agricultural development and demographic growth, had the composite effect of transforming the rank-size distribution of 1600 into one approximately lognormal with a slope in 1800 of −0.67. The point to

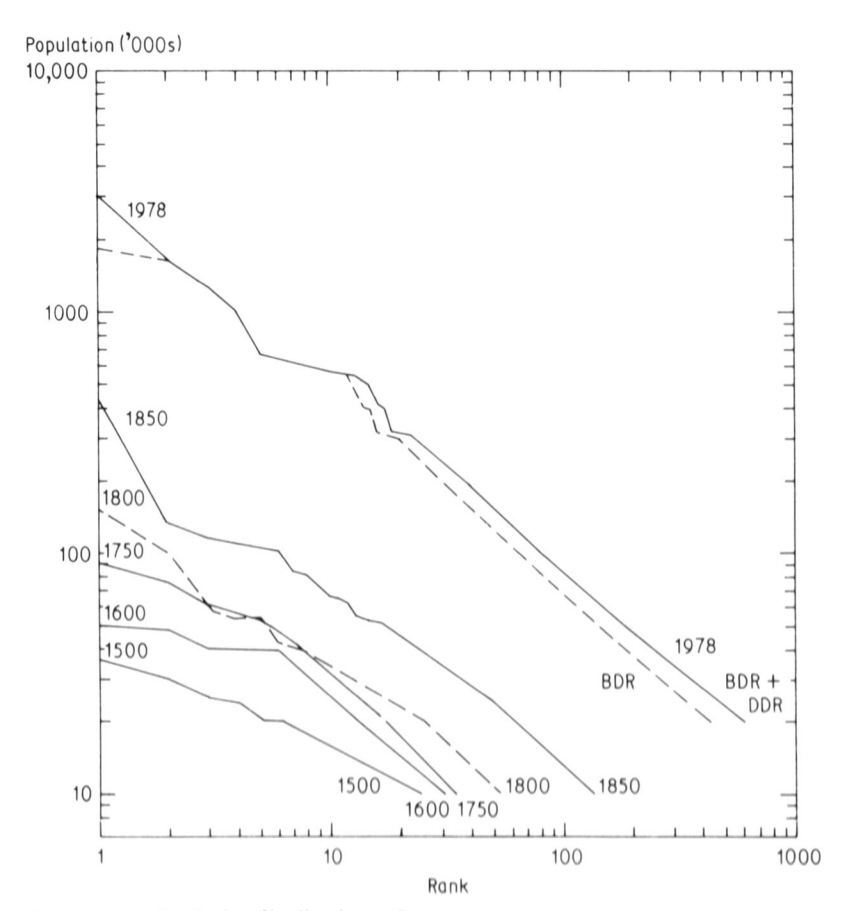

Figure 6.16 Rank-size distributions: Germany, 1500–1978

emphasize here is that competition among several cities striving to assume new functions for large parts of central Europe had the effect of endowing 'the Germanies' with a well-ordered urban hierarchy in the absence of a unified state.

The characterization of Germany's modern rank-size distribution depends to a large extent on how one treats the two Germanies, divided Berlin, and the industrial cities of the *Ruhrgebiet*. If the numerous, contiguous Ruhr cities are treated as one metropolitan area, Germany possesses a giant primate city, arguably the largest on the European continent.[29] If this is not done, Germany has a large number of middle-sized cities. If the two Berlins are recognized to be two separate places, as indeed they now are, the primate city of the German empire dissolves. If the Federal Republic is regarded as the successor to the more extensive 'Germany' of earlier times, historical comparisons of the urban hierarchies become misleading, if not meaningless. To illustrate how the results can vary, figure 6.16 displays two 1978 rank-size distributions. The dashed lines represents the Federal Republic plus West Berlin, and treats the Ruhr cities as separate urban elements. The solid line presents East and West Germany combined, and merges the two Berlins into one city. The distribution for West Germany alone shows the industrial heart of Europe to possess, of all things, an immature pre-modern urban system. The distribution for the two Germanies combined is very similar to the 1800 distribution: both are generally loglinear and both have quite shallow slopes (-0.78 in 1978).

The similarity of the pre-industrial, pre-unification (1800) urban hierarchy to the industrial, post-unification (1978) urban hierarchy is particularly noteworthy because G. K. Zipf, whose work sought to establish the rank-size rule as a standard by which to measure the social and economic developments of a nation, used the evolving urban hierarchy of the German empire from 1870 to 1939 as a particularly clear example of increasing economic specialization and integration.[30] In that period Germany's rank-size distribution became more linear and more steeply sloped. But this was in large part the result of German annexations; once the political structure changed, so did the rank-size distribution. Yet who would argue that the complexity of economic life or the efficiency of transport and communications among cities has been reduced since 1939?

The Netherlands

In 1500 the urban settlements of what would later form the Dutch Republic fashioned an immature urban hierarchy. Those cities were in fact part of a larger urban system centred in the southern Netherlands. The only city that

THE DEVELOPMENT OF AN URBAN HIERARCHY

could lay claim to functions spanning a large part of the northern Netherlands was the ancient ecclesiastical centre of Utrecht, probably the largest city of the region.

The well-known economic, political and cultural flowering of this area in the late sixteenth and seventeenth centuries was accompanied by the fashioning of a well-integrated urban system which by 1650 displayed a tolerable

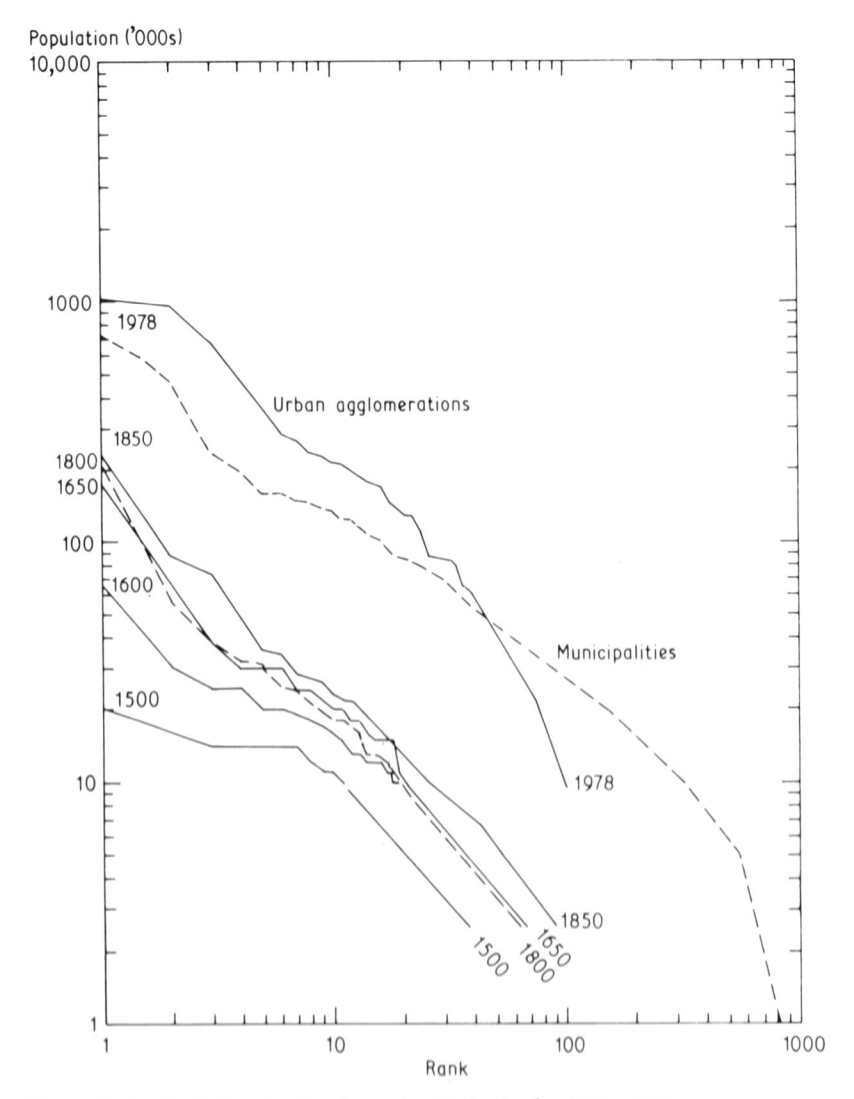

Figure 6.17 Rank-size distributions: the Netherlands, 1500–1978

conformity to a loglinear distribution at a slope approaching −1. Such an urban system could be formed in the Republic, while for France and other territories I have argued that it was not feasible, because of two specific factors. First, the Netherlands is geographically diminutive, which means that the number of market towns and regional centres needed to serve the territory is small. Second, the major Dutch cities assumed functions that served much of Europe and made them capable in turn of drawing resources, particularly breadgrains, from distant places. This effectively exempted the Netherlands from the ceiling of urbanization that the technological limitations of the age imposed on Europe as a whole. To put it another way, the major Dutch cities of the mid-seventeenth century stood at the head of an urban system that actually extended far beyond the Republic's borders. Once again, we see that a well-behaved national rank-size distribution is actually the artificial product of forces acting on a much larger scale.

As the international position of the Dutch economy faltered in the eighteenth century, the character of her urban hierarchy changed to one in which the largest cities became too small to preserve a loglinear distribution. The exception to this process was the largest city, Amsterdam, whose relative success in preserving an international role converted it into a primate city in the context of the Dutch urban system.

So far the rise and decline of the Dutch economy seems to be mirrored faithfully by the integration and later disarticulation of its urban system. But what is one to make of the contemporary situation? The rank-size distribution of urban agglomerations is far from the ideal of lognormality. Using the methodology of Harris, Skinner and Smith one would conclude that the modern urban system is more concave than it has been since the sixteenth century. To muddy the waters further I have included the rank-size distribution of all Dutch municipalities (i.e. all urban and rural jurisdictions). This illustrates just how sensitive these distributions are to one's specification of the urban unit. The safest conclusion to draw from this evidence is that the Dutch urban system is so integrated into that of the surrounding countries that it cannot be analysed meaningfully in isolation. In this respect, little has changed since the sixteenth century.

England and Wales

The rank-size distributions for England form what is perhaps the only case that generally conforms to the developmental expectations that geographers from Zipf to Barry have nurtured about how urban hierarchies should evolve. Between 1500 and 1850 a sketchy, highly irregular urban hierarchy became a concave distribution with very pronounced primacy by the eighteenth

THE DEVELOPMENT OF AN URBAN HIERARCHY

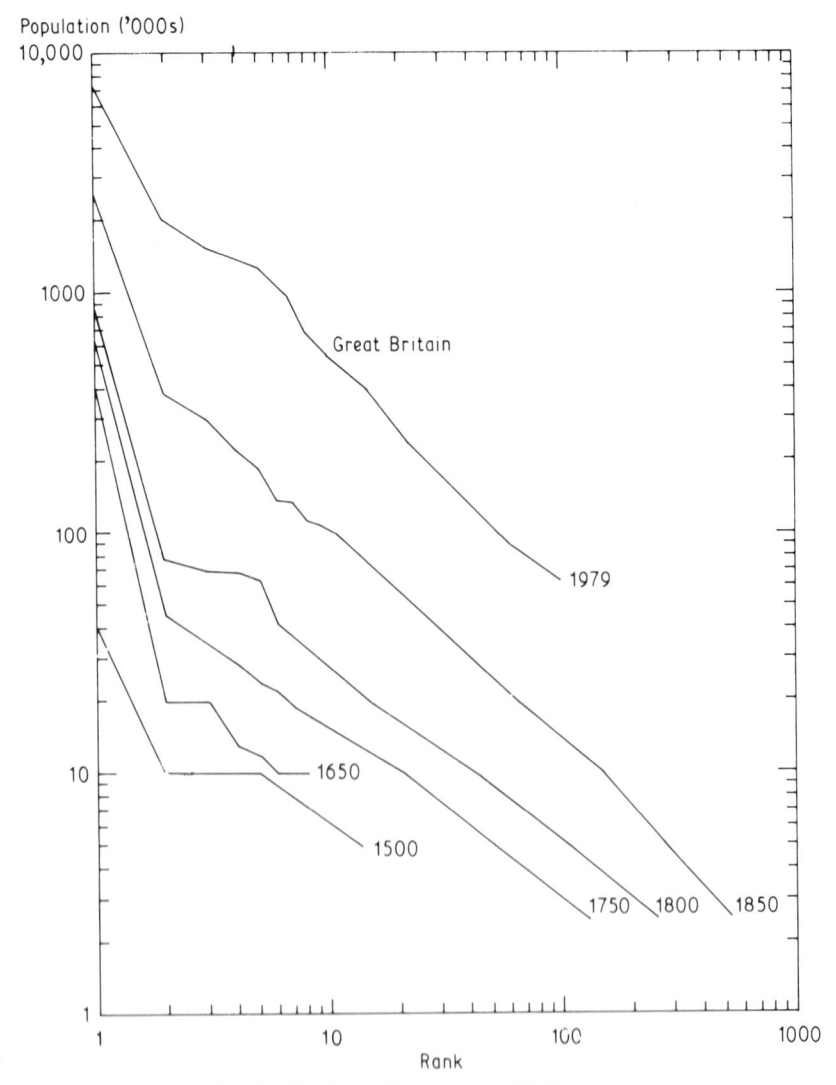

Figure 6.18 Rank-size distributions: England and Wales, 1500–1979

century, and emerged from the Industrial Revolution with an urban system that had gone far in the direction of approximating the rank-size rule. Indeed, the present-day rank-size distribution for Great Britain (including Scotland) conforms to the rule more closely than that of any other European nation.

THE PROPERTIES OF THE URBAN SYSTEM

Summary

What can we conclude from these efforts to 'read' the national rank-size distributions? The most obvious result of this survey is the absence of any common pattern of national urban evolution. Both a developmental model and a pre-modern – modern dichotomy seem to mislead at least as often as not. The bewildering variety exhibited by these diachronic examples may be explained in part by weaknesses in our definitions of the elements of the system and our limited ability to specify the proper boundaries of a system. More fundamental is the fact that every urban hierarchy is adapted to a specific society, topography and technology. These interact with each other in ways that are too complex to be comprehended by existing theories of rank-size distribution. As a consequence, the existence of primacy, concavity or the rank-size rule cannot be ascribed to any particular condition. Each case seems to have its own specific explanation.

A second conclusion that seems warranted is of particular importance to the larger strategy of this study. The historical evolution of the national rank-size distributions can hardly ever be understood without recourse to factors that impinge from beyond the borders of the nation itself. Time and again we have observed that the evolving urban hierarchy of a nation reflects a composite of regional, i.e. subnational, and international forces. The comprehensive Europe-wide focus of this study is hereby warranted, in the sense that it is more likely to provide insight into the urbanization process than to obscure real factors by overaggregation.

7

STABILITY AND DISCONTINUITY IN EUROPEAN URBAN GROWTH

THE ISSUES

The ruins of a once important city – whether it is the abandoned site of a city of antiquity or a mining town – are highly evocative to modern people. We are inclined to engage in playful speculations about future archaeologists uncovering the physical remains of New York or some other modern city. This fascinates us because it seems so utterly unlikely. How can a place so busy and populous, a place to which society has committed so much of its capital and talent, and hence its future, ever be stripped of its functions and abandoned? Such an event is correctly understood to betoken an enormous discontinuity in the history of a civilization. Of course cities can experience a loss of relative position that changes their character utterly without suffering actual abandonment. Cities might be viewed as vessels which in the course of time come to be filled with completely different substances. This too represents a kind of discontinuity, but one less obvious and more subject to interpretation than actual abandonment.

The issue of instability and discontinuity is embedded in the study of urban growth. Changes in the level of urbanization and shifts in the rank-size distribution of an urban system are products of numerous changes in the populations of individual cities, yet neither of those descriptions of urban growth actually reveals anything about the processes by which the individual cities achieve those new situations. The analysis of rank-size distribution in chapter 6 demonstrated the unreasonableness of the 'law of proportionate effect' and its implications that city growth should be interpreted as a stochastic process. However, the analysis of that chapter could say nothing about whether the systematic factors driving urban growth were disruptive or stabilizing in their effects. For example, when we observed that the slope of the rank-size distribution for 1750 was much steeper than that for 1600 it was not clear whether this was because growth rates were positively correlated to the initial size of cities or because some cities, of whatever initial rank, grew very rapidly to become the largest cities in Europe. These reflections give rise to a series of questions that will guide the following study of patterns of change in the size of Europe's cities. To what extent has urban growth since the middle ages been subject to instability and discontinuity in the fortunes of individual cities? Has the urban system become more stable over time; is the modern urban hierarchy more stable than that of pre-modern urbanism? Was there a specific discontinuity-inducing event, such as the Industrial Revolution, that forms a watershed between two urban systems? Finally, and related to the last question, when did the current complement of leading cities first assume their positions at the head of Europe's urban system?

Herodotus was convinced that discontinuity was endemic to the urban world of antiquity:

> The cities that were formerly great have most of them become insignificant; and such as are at present powerful, were weak in olden time. I shall therefore discourse equally of both, convinced that human happiness never continues long in one stay.[1]

Among modern students of urban history perceptions on this issue vary. John Patten, in his study of English towns in the sixteenth and seventeenth centuries, wrote that 'Towns existed in a world that made them inherently frail, both demographically and economically'.[2] This inherent frailty he elevated to one of the three themes of his book. The urban organism had no adequate defences against the epidemics, disasters and displacements of trade flows that always had the potential of pulling the rug out from under the legs on which a city's position in the urban hierarchy rested. What is less clear in Patten's account is whether this frailty reflected anything more than random shocks that could affect cities individually, but did not necessarily disrupt the overall character of the urban system.

A very different sort of discontinuity in urban history is put forward by Fernand Braudel, most succinctly in his *Afterthoughts on Capitalism and Material Civilization*. He speaks of Europe and later the whole western world as a system organized around a focal point – a city functioning as a sort of economic capital (distinct from the administrative capitals of Europe's numerous *political* units). The history of this capitalist system, he believes, consists of long periods in which a city dominates and co-ordinates the system, followed by crises, periods of 'de-centring and re-centring', in which another city emerges to succeed the dethroned economic capital of western capitalism. He asserts that in the past 500 years the mantle of greatness passed, at intervals, from Venice to Antwerp, to Genoa, to Amsterdam, to London, and most recently to New York.[3] Braudel says little about how the de-centring re-centring process might affect the subsidiary cities of the urban system. But it seems clear that his structural approach envisions eras of stability punctuated by relatively brief periods in which many cities are frail and vulnerable to the loss of their relative position while others see opportunities to ascend to positions of greater importance.

The geographer Allan Pred, in his work on the emerging system of cities in the United States, stresses stability and continuity.[4] In each regional system, the leading cities of today asserted their dominance already at the embryonic stage of urban systems building. Permanence and continuity in the context of furious, seemingly chaotic growth are what impress Pred about urbanization in the first decades of the new nation.

These authors are not necessarily contradicting each other. It is, in fact, possible to accept the views of all of them, for each is focusing on a different dimension of urban stability and each is observing it on different time scales (and, in the case of Pred, on a different continent). For example, the urban frailty that impresses Patten may be most characteristic of the smaller cities of a region, while the leading centres, as Pred observes in the early decades of the American republic, have a tenacious hold on their position. Likewise, it may be that the regional rank-size distributions are stable, but that cities that always remain at the head of their regional economy can experience dramatic changes in their position in national and international urban systems. In this sense the insights of Pred and Braudel can be thought of as complementary.

If these interpretations have validity then we should expect the study of discontinuity in urban systems to be highly sensitive to the scale of the analysis. Stability at the regional or national level may be consistent with instability at the international level while the behaviour of larger cities may be entirely at variance with that observed among smaller cities. In the analysis that follows attention will be focused on the European urban system as a whole. Hence we will be incapable of observing *all* relevant sorts of perturbations in the urban system. But the data base should suffice to indicate whether urban instability was chronic or episodic and whether certain types of cities were more vulnerable than others.

TRANSITION MATRICES

Transition matrices offer the most efficient way to observe the patterns of population change of nearly 400 cities over three centuries. Each matrix describes how a specified number of cities, classified by size category, are redistributed among the size categories over a given period of years.

The matrices below each span an interval of fifty years. In the column at the far right one reads the distribution of cities by size category in the initial year, in the bottom row the distribution of cities by category in the final year of the interval. The matrix itself displays how the transition was made from the initial to the final distribution. The rows show how the cities that began the period in any given size category were distributed among the size categories fifty years later; the columns indicate where the cities in any given size category at the end of the interval had started from fifty years earlier. For example, in the first transition matrix covering the entire data base of European cities, row 1 shows what became of the 99 cities of 10,000–20,000 inhabitants in 1500. Four of these cities descended to category 0 (cities of under 10,000 inhabitants), 80 remained in the same category, 14 grew sufficiently to attain category II (cities of 20,000–40,000) and one city jumped two categories to reach the 40,000–80,000 level. Column 1 of the same matrix shows that of the 101 cities of 10,000–20,000 inhabitants in 1550, 80 had been in the same size category in 1500 while 21 had emerged from the netherworld of cities under 10,000 inhabitants.

Row and column 0 enumerate only those cities of under 10,000 inhabitants which at some time between 1500 and 1800 entered the charmed circle of larger cities. Thus of the 225 cities of under 10,000 in 1500, 21 grow to enter category I while 2 grow sufficiently to enter category II, leaving 202 behind. Meanwhile column 0 informs us that 4 cities that had been in category I fall below the 10,000 population threshold to leave 206 cities in the category in 1550. Interval by interval, the number of these category 0 cities 'waiting in the wings' diminishes, but it does fall to zero. By 1800, 15 cities that once contained at least 10,000 inhabitants had fallen from grace to become the sole remaining occupants of category 0.

Because of the large size of each category, the population of cities that rise or fall to a neighbouring category must on average experience a substantial change. The categories have been so defined that a city moving from the midpoint of any category to the midpoint of the next will always have doubled its population. Correspondingly, at the end of any fifty-year interval most cities remain in the category in which they had begun, and shifts of more than one category are infrequent. If all cities remained in their original size category during an interval only the diagonal cells of the matrix beginning at the upper left and extending to the extreme lower right would be filled. Cities advancing one category from their initial positions are registered in the diagonal series of cells to the right of that just mentioned, while cities advancing two categories are registered in the diagonal series of cells one step further to the right. Declining cities are registered in analogous cells to the left of the central diagonal. Beside each of the six transformations for Europe as a whole (table 7.1) the cities that rise or fall by at least two categories in any fifty-year period are identified by name.

Table 7.1 Transition matrices: number of cities in population size categories at fifty-year intervals, 1500–1800

Cities rising or falling by at least two size categories

			1550						
		0	1	2	3	4	5	6	T
	0	202	21	2	0	0	0	0	225
	1	4	80	14	1	0	0	0	99
1500	2	0	0	28	8	1	0	0	37
	3	0	0	2	10	2	0	0	14
	4	0	0	0	1	2	1	0	4
	5	0	0	0	0	0	0	0	0
	6	0	0	0	0	0	0	0	0
	T	206	101	46	20	5	1	0	379

148 MAGDEBURG	7	1	3
332 BURGOS	13	0	2
342 MADRID	13	0	2
367 LISBOA	14	2	4

			1600						
		0	1	2	3	4	5	6	T
	0	157	48	1	0	0	0	0	206
	1	2	71	28	0	0	0	0	101
1550	2	0	5	28	13	0	0	0	46
	3	0	0	2	14	4	0	0	20
	4	0	0	0	1	2	2	0	5
	5	0	0	0	0	0	1	0	1
	6	0	0	0	0	0	0	0	0
	T	159	124	59	28	6	3	0	379

| 82 MIDDELBURG | 5 | 0 | 2 |

			1650						
		0	1	2	3	4	5	6	T
	0	147	12	0	0	0	0	0	159
	1	33	76	14	1	0	0	0	124
1600	2	1	21	33	4	0	0	0	59
	3	1	1	6	17	2	1	0	28
	4	0	0	0	1	5	0	0	6
	5	0	0	0	0	0	1	2	3
	6	0	0	0	0	0	0	0	0
	T	182	110	53	23	7	2	2	379

6 STOCKHOLM	1	1	3
68 AMSTERDAM	5	3	5
148 MAGDEBURG	7	3	0
362 VALLADOLID	13	3	1
336 CUENCA	13	2	0

(continued)

Table 7.1—continued

Cities rising or falling by at least two size categories

	1700							
	0	1	2	3	4	5	6	T
1650 0	147	32	3	0	0	0	0	182
1	8	81	18	3	0	0	0	110
2	0	4	42	7	0	0	0	53
3	0	0	1	18	4	0	0	23
4	0	0	0	0	6	1	0	7
5	0	0	0	0	0	2	0	2
6	0	0	0	0	0	0	2	2
T	155	117	64	28	10	3	2	379

60 CORK	4	0	2
61 DUBLIN	4	1	3
115 BERLIN	7	1	3
123 DRESDEN	7	1	3
240 VERSAILLES	8	0	2
333 CADIZ	13	0	2

	1750							
	0	1	2	3	4	5	6	T
1700 0	111	40	4	0	0	0	0	155
1	7	93	17	0	0	0	0	117
2	0	5	51	8	0	0	0	64
3	0	0	3	22	3	0	0	28
4	0	0	0	2	7	1	0	10
5	0	0	0	0	1	2	0	3
6	0	0	0	0	0	0	2	2
T	118	138	75	32	11	3	2	379

8 BIRMINGHAM	2	0	2
27 LIVERPOOL	2	0	2
185 BREST	8	0	2
370 GRAZ	15	0	2

	1800							
	0	1	2	3	4	5	6	T
1750 0	13	101	4	0	0	0	0	118
1	2	101	31	4	0	0	0	138
2	0	4	59	12	0	0	0	75
3	0	0	0	23	9	0	0	32
4	0	0	0	0	7	4	0	11
5	0	0	0	0	0	2	1	3
6	0	0	0	0	0	0	2	2
T	15	206	94	39	16	6	3	379

7 BATH	2	0	2
22 HULL	2	0	2
25 LEEDS	2	1	3
29 MANCHESTER	2	1	3
35 PLYMOUTH	2	1	3
40 SHEFFIELD	2	1	3
59 BELFAST	4	0	2
66 WATERFORD	4	0	2

STABILITY AND DISCONTINUITY IN EUROPEAN URBAN GROWTH

The results of the six transition matrices for Europe as a whole are summarized in table 7.5. Here one can see clearly that five of the six intervals spanning the period 1500–1800 share several similarities. About three-quarters of the cities of at least 10,000 inhabitants remained in their initial category; 15–25 per cent moved upward at least one category and 5–7 per cent declined to a lower category. When the rapid underlying growth of the overall population in the periods 1550–1600 and 1750–1800 are taken into account, the minor differences among the intervals seem easily explainable.

Table 7.2 Transition matrices for north and west Europe: number of cities in population size categories at fifty-year intervals, 1500–1800

1550

	0	1	2	3	4	5	6	T
0	76	1	0	0	0	0	0	77
1	1	17	2	0	0	0	0	20
2	0	0	6	1	0	0	0	7
3	0	0	0	1	2	0	0	3
4	0	0	0	0	0	0	0	0
5	0	0	0	0	0	0	0	0
6	0	0	0	0	0	0	0	0
T	77	18	8	2	2	0	0	107

(rows labeled 1500)

1700

	0	1	2	3	4	5	6	T
0	54	7	1	0	0	0	0	62
1	0	17	2	1	0	0	0	20
2	0	2	11	4	0	0	0	17
3	0	0	0	5	1	0	0	6
4	0	0	0	0	0	0	0	0
5	0	0	0	0	0	1	0	1
6	0	0	0	0	0	0	1	1
T	54	26	14	10	1	1	1	107

(rows labeled 1650)

1600

	0	1	2	3	4	5	6	T
0	66	10	1	0	0	0	0	77
1	1	13	4	0	0	0	0	18
2	0	2	5	1	0	0	0	8
3	0	0	1	1	0	0	0	2
4	0	0	0	1	0	1	0	2
5	0	0	0	0	0	0	0	0
6	0	0	0	0	0	0	0	0
T	67	25	11	3	0	1	0	107

(rows labeled 1550)

1750

	0	1	2	3	4	5	6	T
0	39	13	2	0	0	0	0	54
1	3	21	2	0	0	0	0	26
2	0	3	9	2	0	0	0	14
3	0	0	1	7	2	0	0	10
4	0	0	0	1	0	0	0	1
5	0	0	0	0	0	1	0	1
6	0	0	0	0	0	0	1	1
T	42	37	14	10	2	1	1	107

(rows labeled 1700)

1650

	0	1	2	3	4	5	6	T
0	62	5	0	0	0	0	0	67
1	0	15	9	1	0	0	0	25
2	0	0	8	3	0	0	0	11
3	0	0	0	2	0	1	0	3
4	0	0	0	0	0	0	0	0
5	0	0	0	0	0	1	0	1
6	0	0	0	0	0	0	0	0
T	62	20	17	6	0	1	1	107

(rows labeled 1600)

1800

	0	1	2	3	4	5	6	T
0	2	36	4	0	0	0	0	42
1	0	24	9	4	0	0	0	37
2	0	0	11	3	0	0	0	14
3	0	0	0	9	1	0	0	10
4	0	0	0	0	1	1	0	2
5	0	0	0	0	0	1	0	1
6	0	0	0	0	0	0	1	1
T	2	60	24	16	2	2	1	107

(rows labeled 1750)

THE PROPERTIES OF THE URBAN SYSTEM

One matrix, that for the interval 1600–50, exhibits characteristics markedly different from all of the others. In this interval only 60 per cent of the cities remained in their initial size category, while nearly 30 per cent fell in rank and the remaining 10 per cent rose. This interval is also distinguished by a very small number of 'new' cities – cities that for the first time pass the 10,000 population threshold. Related to this was the uniquely large number of cities whose population declined below the 10,000 population threshold.

Table 7.3 Transition matrices for central Europe: number of cities in population size categories at fifty-year intervals, 1500–1800

1500 → 1550

	0	1	2	3	4	5	6	T
0	73	9	0	0	0	0	0	82
1	3	32	2	1	0	0	0	38
2	0	0	12	3	0	0	0	15
3	0	0	0	2	0	0	0	2
4	0	0	0	0	1	0	0	1
5	0	0	0	0	0	0	0	0
6	0	0	0	0	0	0	0	0
T	76	41	14	6	1	0	0	138

1650 → 1700

	0	1	2	3	4	5	6	T
0	50	18	1	0	0	0	0	69
1	0	29	8	2	0	0	0	39
2	0	0	19	1	0	0	0	20
3	0	0	1	7	1	0	0	9
4	0	0	0	0	0	0	0	0
5	0	0	0	0	0	0	0	0
6	0	0	0	0	0	0	1	1
T	50	47	29	10	1	0	1	138

1550 → 1600

	0	1	2	3	4	5	6	T
0	62	14	0	0	0	0	0	76
1	1	26	13	0	0	0	0	41
2	0	0	9	5	0	0	0	14
3	0	0	0	6	0	0	0	6
4	0	0	0	0	0	1	0	1
5	0	0	0	0	0	0	0	0
6	0	0	0	0	0	0	0	0
T	63	40	22	11	0	1	0	138

1700 → 1750

	0	1	2	3	4	5	6	T
0	41	8	1	0	0	0	0	50
1	3	35	9	0	0	0	0	47
2	0	2	23	4	0	0	0	29
3	0	0	1	8	1	0	0	10
4	0	0	0	0	1	0	0	1
5	0	0	0	0	0	0	0	0
6	0	0	0	0	0	0	1	1
T	44	45	34	12	2	0	1	138

1600 → 1650

	0	1	2	3	4	5	6	T
0	62	1	0	0	0	0	0	63
1	6	33	2	0	0	0	0	41
2	0	5	16	1	0	0	0	22
3	1	0	2	8	0	0	0	11
4	0	0	0	0	0	0	0	0
5	0	0	0	0	0	0	1	1
6	0	0	0	0	0	0	0	0
T	69	39	20	9	0	0	1	138

1750 → 1800

	0	1	2	3	4	5	6	T
0	2	42	0	0	0	0	0	44
1	1	33	11	0	0	0	0	45
2	0	3	29	2	0	0	0	34
3	0	0	0	9	3	0	0	12
4	0	0	0	0	2	0	0	2
5	0	0	0	0	0	0	0	0
6	0	0	0	0	0	0	1	1
T	3	78	40	11	5	0	1	139

STABILITY AND DISCONTINUITY IN EUROPEAN URBAN GROWTH

The transition matrices for several of the larger countries also show interesting features, but for our purposes it will suffice to examine three of the large regions into which I have divided Europe: the north and west, the central zone and the Mediterranean lands (see table 7.5).

Each of these regions shows considerable regularity in the interval-by-interval patterns of change and stability, with the exception once again of the interval 1600–50. In this period the percentage of cities remaining stationary

Table 7.4 Transition matrices for Mediterranean Europe: number of cities in population size categories at fifty-year intervals, 1500–1800

1550

	0	1	2	3	4	5	6	T
0	46	10	2	0	0	0	0	58
1	0	30	10	0	0	0	0	40
2	0	0	8	4	1	0	0	13
3	0	0	2	7	0	0	0	9
4	0	0	0	1	1	1	0	3
5	0	0	0	0	0	0	0	0
6	0	0	0	0	0	0	0	0
T	46	40	22	12	2	1	0	123

(rows labeled 1500)

1600

	0	1	2	3	4	5	6	T
0	22	24	0	0	0	0	0	46
1	0	29	11	0	0	0	0	40
2	0	3	13	6	0	0	0	22
3	0	0	1	7	4	0	0	12
4	0	0	0	0	2	0	0	2
5	0	0	0	0	0	1	0	1
6	0	0	0	0	0	0	0	0
T	22	56	25	13	6	1	0	123

(rows labeled 1550)

1650

	0	1	2	3	4	5	6	T
0	16	6	0	0	0	0	0	22
1	27	27	2	0	0	0	0	56
2	1	16	8	0	0	0	0	25
3	0	1	4	6	2	0	0	13
4	0	0	0	1	5	0	0	6
5	0	0	0	0	0	1	0	1
6	0	0	0	0	0	0	0	0
T	44	50	14	7	7	1	0	123

(rows labeled 1600)

1700

	0	1	2	3	4	5	6	T
0	37	6	1	0	0	0	0	44
1	8	34	8	0	0	0	0	50
2	0	1	11	2	0	0	0	14
3	0	0	0	6	1	0	0	7
4	0	0	0	0	6	1	0	7
5	0	0	0	0	0	1	0	1
6	0	0	0	0	0	0	0	0
T	45	41	20	8	7	2	0	123

(rows labeled 1650)

1750

	0	1	2	3	4	5	6	T
0	28	17	0	0	0	0	0	45
1	1	35	5	0	0	0	0	41
2	0	0	19	1	0	0	0	20
3	0	0	1	7	0	0	0	8
4	0	0	0	1	6	0	0	7
5	0	0	0	0	1	1	0	2
6	0	0	0	0	0	0	0	0
T	29	52	25	9	7	1	0	123

(rows labeled 1700)

1800

	0	1	2	3	4	5	6	T
0	9	20	0	0	0	0	0	29
1	1	42	9	0	0	0	0	52
2	0	1	18	6	0	0	0	25
3	0	0	0	4	5	0	0	9
4	0	0	0	0	4	3	0	7
5	0	0	0	0	0	0	1	1
6	0	0	0	0	0	0	0	0
T	10	63	27	10	9	3	1	123

(rows labeled 1750)

Table 7.5 Summary of the transition matrices

Europe

	Period					
Movement	*1*	*2*	*3*	*4*	*5*	*6*
Up 3						
Up 2	4	1	2	6	4	8
Up 1	46	95	34	62	69	158
Stay in category	120	116	132	151	177	194
Down 1	7	10	61	13	18	6
Down 2			2			
Down 3			1			
Enter from category 0	23	49	12	35	44	105
Exit to category 0	4	2	35	8	7	2
Stay in category 0	202	157	147	147	111	13
1 New entrants as % of cities over 10,000 at beginning of period	14.9	28.3	5.4	17.8	19.6	40.2
2 Cities rising by at least 1 as % of cities at beginning of period	17.5	27.2	10.9	16.8	13.0	23.4
3 Cities staying in category as % of cities at beginning of period	77.9	67.1	60.0	76.7	79.0	74.3
4 Cities falling by at least 1 as % of cities at beginning of period	4.5	5.8	29.1	6.6	8.0	2.3

North and west

	Period					
Movement	*1*	*2*	*3*	*4*	*5*	*6*
Up 3						
Up 2		1	2	2	2	8
Up 1	6	16	18	14	19	50
Stay in category	24	19	25	35	39	47
Down 1	1	5		2	8	
Down 2						
Down 3						
Enter from category 0	1	11	5	8	15	40
Exit to category 0	1	1	0	0	3	0
Stay in category 0	76	66	62	54	39	2

(continued)

Table 7.5—continued

North and west

Movement	Period					
	1	2	3	4	5	6
1	3.3	36.7	12.5	17.8	28.3	61.5
2	16.7	20.0	37.5	17.8	11.3	27.7
3	80.0	63.3	62.5	77.8	73.6	72.3
4	3.3	16.7	0	4.4	15.1	0

Central

Movement	Period					
	1	2	3	4	5	6
Up 3						
Up 2	1			3	1	
Up 1	14	33	5	28	22	58
Stay in category	47	42	57	56	68	74
Down 1	3	1	13	1	6	4
Down 2						
Down 3			1			
Enter from category 0	9	14	1	19	9	42
Exit from category 0	3	1	7	0	3	1
Stay in category 0	73	62	62	50	41	2
1	16.1	22.6	1.3	27.9	10.2	44.7
2	10.7	30.7	5.3	17.7	15.9	17.0
3	83.9	66.1	75.7	80.9	77.3	78.7
4	5.3	1.6	18.9	1.4	6.8	4.3

Mediterranean

Movement	Period					
	1	2	3	4	5	6
Up 3						
Up 2	3			1		
Up 1	25	45	10	18	23	44
Stay in category	46	52	47	58	68	68
Down 1	3	4	48	9	4	2
Down 2			2			
Down 3						
Enter from category 0	12	24	6	7	17	20
Exit to category 0	0	0	28	8	1	1
Stay in category 0	46	22	16	37	28	9
1	18.5	31.2	5.9	8.9	21.8	21.3
2	24.6	27.3	4.0	15.2	7.7	25.5
3	70.8	67.5	46.5	73.4	87.2	72.3
4	4.6	5.2	49.5	11.4	5.1	2.1

THE PROPERTIES OF THE URBAN SYSTEM

Table 7.6 Transition matrices: number of cities in population size categories, 1500–1600

Europe

				1600				
		0	1	2	3	4	5	6	T
1500	0	156	62	6	1	0	0	0	225
	1	3	61	32	3	0	0	0	99
	2	0	1	19	15	2	0	0	37
	3	0	0	2	9	2	1	0	14
	4	0	0	0	0	2	2	0	4
	5	0	0	0	0	0	0	0	0
	6	0	0	0	0	0	0	0	0
	T	159	124	59	28	6	3	0	379

Mediterranean

				1600				
		0	1	2	3	4	5	6	T
1500	0	22	33	2	1	0	0	0	58
	1	0	23	17	0	0	0	0	40
	2	0	0	5	6	2	0	0	13
	3	0	0	1	6	2	0	0	9
	4	0	0	0	0	2	1	0	3
	5	0	0	0	0	0	0	0	0
	6	0	0	0	0	0	0	0	0
	T	22	56	25	13	6	1	0	123

Northern Europe

				1600				
		0	1	2	3	4	5	6	T
1500	0	134	29	4	0	0	0	0	167
	1	3	38	15	3	0	0	0	59
	2	0	1	14	9	0	0	0	24
	3	0	0	1	3	0	1	0	5
	4	0	0	0	0	0	1	0	1
	5	0	0	0	0	0	0	0	0
	6	0	0	0	0	0	0	0	0
	T	137	68	34	15	0	2	0	256

in their initial category falls to a low point in both north and west Europe and the Mediterranean lands, but in the latter nearly half of the cities of at least 10,000 inhabitants fall to a lower category, and 28 per cent fall below the 10,000 inhabitants threshold. In north and west Europe *no* cities decline to lower categories while 37.5 per cent rise to a higher category. In this era of dramatic change the lands of the central zone show greater stability. The impact of the Thirty Years' War is reflected in the fall to a lower category of 18 per cent of the cities of 10,000 and above in 1600, but then, as in nearly every other of the intervals, the central zone was characterized by a larger percentage of cities remaining in their initial categories and a relatively small number of newcomers to the ranks of cities with at least 10,000 inhabitants.

A clearer image of the pattern of city growth can be gained by grouping the fifty-year interval matrices along the lines suggested by the evolution of rank-size distributions and the course of urbanization rates described in earlier chapters. Tables 7.6, 7.7 and 7.8 present transition matrices for Europe as a whole, northern Europe, and the Mediterranean lands in each of the three periods: 1500–1600, 1600–1750 and 1750–1800. Table 7.9 displays a summary of the patterns disclosed by these transition matrices.

In the sixteenth century, when the total population of Europe grew by about 30 per cent or 0.26 per cent per annum, city growth was vigorous and regionally well distributed. The underlying rural population growth of the era seems to have supported urban populations, as indicated by the scarcity of cities that fall into lower categories and by the large number of new cities emerging into the data base from below the 10,000 population level.

The third period, spanning the second half of the eighteenth century, was also one of rapid general population growth; total population grew twice as rapidly as in the sixteenth century, rising by 30 per cent in fifty years. In this era urbanization proceeded in a different way than it had in the sixteenth century. The cities of 10,000 and over grew in a restrained manner: only 4 out of 259 (Leeds, Manchester, Plymouth and Sheffield) moved more than one category, and the basic pattern was much the same in both northern and

Table 7.7 Transition matrices: number of cities in population size categories, 1600–1750

Europe

		0	1	2	3	4	5	6	T
1600	0	91	54	11	2	1	0	0	159
	1	25	72	22	4	1	0	0	124
	2	2	10	36	10	1	0	0	59
	3	0	2	6	15	3	2	0	28
	4	0	0	0	1	5	0	0	6
	5	0	0	0	0	0	1	2	3
	6	0	0	0	0	0	0	0	0
	T	118	138	75	32	11	3	2	379

Mediterranean

		0	1	2	3	4	5	6	T
1600	0	9	10	2	1	0	0	0	22
	1	18	33	5	0	0	0	0	56
	2	2	8	14	1	0	0	0	25
	3	0	1	4	6	2	0	0	13
	4	0	0	0	1	5	0	0	6
	5	0	0	0	0	0	1	0	1
	6	0	0	0	0	0	0	0	0
	T	29	52	25	9	7	1	0	123

Northern Europe

		0	1	2	3	4	5	6	T
1600	0	82	44	9	1	1	0	0	137
	1	7	39	17	4	1	0	0	68
	2	0	2	22	9	1	0	0	34
	3	0	1	2	9	1	2	0	15
	4	0	0	0	0	0	0	0	0
	5	0	0	0	0	0	2	0	2
	6	0	0	0	0	0	0	0	0
	T	89	86	50	23	4	2	2	256

THE PROPERTIES OF THE URBAN SYSTEM

Mediterranean Europe. The rapid urban growth of the period found its location elsewhere, in the large number of new cities. Of the 106 such cities, 4 out of every 5 were in northern Europe, and of these 36 per cent were in the British Isles.

The long period standing between the two just discussed differed from them in that overall population growth was very slow (less than half the annual rate of the sixteenth century and less than one-quarter that of the late eighteenth century) and highly uneven in its incidence among regions. In this environment one might expect, other things remaining equal, that relatively few cities would rise to higher categories, that such change as did occur would be concentrated in one-cell movements, and that few small cities would rise to cross the 10,000 population threshold.

At first glance the summary data for Europe as a whole seems to be consistent with these expectations. But this picture of sluggish urban growth dissolves as soon as the northern and Mediterranean regions are viewed separately. Evidence of the Mediterranean zone's urban collapse of 1600–50

Table 7.8 Transition matrices: number of cities in population size categories, 1750–1800

Europe

1750 \ 1800	0	1	2	3	4	5	6	T
0	13	101	4	0	0	0	0	118
1	2	101	31	4	0	0	0	138
2	0	4	59	12	0	0	0	75
3	0	0	0	23	9	0	0	32
4	0	0	0	0	7	4	0	11
5	0	0	0	0	0	2	1	3
6	0	0	0	0	0	0	2	2
T	15	206	94	39	16	6	3	379

Mediterranean

1750 \ 1800	0	1	2	3	4	5	6	T
0	9	20	0	0	0	0	0	29
1	1	42	9	0	0	0	0	52
2	0	1	18	6	0	0	0	25
3	0	0	0	4	5	0	0	9
4	0	0	0	0	4	3	0	7
5	0	0	0	0	0	0	1	1
6	0	0	0	0	0	0	0	0
T	10	63	27	10	9	3	1	123

Northern Europe

1750 \ 1800	0	1	2	3	4	5	6	T
0	4	81	4	0	0	0	0	89
1	1	59	22	4	0	0	0	86
2	0	3	41	6	0	0	0	50
3	0	0	0	19	4	0	0	23
4	0	0	0	0	3	1	0	4
5	0	0	0	0	0	2	0	2
6	0	0	0	0	0	0	2	2
T	5	143	67	29	7	3	2	256

Table 7.9 Summary of the transition matrices in three periods

Europe

Movement	1500–1600		1600–1750		1750–1800	
Up 3 or more		1	1	3		
Up 2	6	6	7	11	4	4
Up 1	51	62	37	54	57	101
Stay in category	91		129		194	
Down 1	6		42		6	
Down 2			4			
Over 10 at beginning date	154		220		261	
Rise above 10		69		68		105
Fall to below 10	3		27		2	
Stay below 10	156		91		13	
1 New entrants as % of cities at beginning of period	44.8		30.9		40.2	
2 Cities rising by at least 1 as % of cities at beginning of period	37.0		20.5		23.4	
3 Cities staying in category as % of cities at beginning of period	59.1		58.6		74.3	
4 Cities falling by at least 1 as % of cities at beginning of period	3.9		20.9		2.3	

Northern Europe

Movement	1500–1600		1600–1750		1750–1800	
Up 3 or more			1	2		
Up 2	4	4	7	9	4	4
Up 1	25	29	29	44	33	81
Stay in category	55		70		124	
Down 1	5		11		4	
Down 2			1			
Over 10 at beginning date	89		119		167	
Rise above 10		33		55		85
Fall to below 10	3		7		1	
Stay below 10	134		82		4	
1		37.1		46.2		50.9
2	32.6		31.1		22.2	
3	61.8		58.8		74.3	
4	5.6		10.1		2.4	

(continued)

Table 7.9—continued

Mediterranean

Movement	1500–1600		1600–1750		1750–1800	
Up 3 or more		1		1		
Up 2	2	2		2		
Up 1	26	33	8	10	24	20
Stay in category	36		59		68	
Down 1	1		31		2	
Down 2			3			
Over 10 at beginning date	65		101		94	
Rise above 10		36		13		20
Fall to below 10	0		20		1	
Stay below 10	22		9		9	
1		55.4		12.9		21.3
2	43.1		7.9		25.5	
3	55.4		58.4		72.3	
4	1.5		33.7		2.1	

Note
For each period the left-hand column summarizes the experience of cities with at least 10,000 inhabitants at the beginning of the period; the right hand column summarizes the experience of new entrants.

remains plainly evident a century later. Few cities rose to higher categories and newly emergent cities were also scarce. Meanwhile in northern Europe the percentage of cities that rose to higher categories reached its peak while newly emerging cities were much more numerous than in the sixteenth century.

A second way in which the matrices for 1600–1750 differed from the others is in the much greater dispersion of individual city performances around the average urban growth-rate. A simple way to measure this dispersion is to count the number of occupied cells more than one step away from the central diagonal in each of the three transition matrices for Europe as a whole. For the sixteenth century there are 5, for 1750–1800 only 2 and for 1600–1750, 8. The number of cities falling into these cells was 13 in the sixteenth century, 8 in the late eighteenth century, and 26 in the period 1600–1750.

THE GROWING CITIES

The patterns of stability and change uncovered by the transition matrices make clear that in each period the cities that pushed Europe's urbanization forward were distinct in number, rate of growth, and location within the matrix. It is now time to ask which cities, and what types of cities these were.

STABILITY AND DISCONTINUITY IN EUROPEAN URBAN GROWTH

Because of the way urban growth is being measured in this study, 'new' cities always play a role in increasing the urban population, both by their own growth and by the transfer of the population they had before crossing the 10,000 inhabitant threshold. Table 7.9 shows that the new entrants (net of those cities that drop below the threshold size) are particularly important in the sixteenth century and again after 1750. However, the regional patterns look rather different. In northern Europe new cities rise in importance in each successive period, while in the Mediterranean area the many entrants of the sixteenth century are followed by net removals in the seventeenth, and only slow recovery thereafter.

The largest cities at the beginning of each period are also likely candidates to play a major role in increasing the total urban population. Given their large initial weights, even small percentage gains can account for a great deal of urban growth. The ten largest cities – of Europe and of northern and Mediterranean Europe separately – were modest contributors to total urban growth in the sixteenth century and played, if anything, an even smaller role

Table 7.10(a) Accounting for urban population growth in Europe ('000s)

	1500–1600	1600–1750	1750–1800
Change in total population	16,400	16,200	28,500
% change	26.6	20.8	30.3
% change per annum	0.24	0.13	0.53
Change in urban population	2,490	3,000	3,290
% change	72.4	50.6	36.8
Change in urban/change in total population	15.2	18.5	11.5
Urban population change			
Added by new entrants	977	1,145	1,430
Deducted by dropouts	91	637	78
Net addition of new entrants	886	508	1,352
Added by 10 largest cities at beginning of period	428	973	440
Added by 10 largest cities at end of period	716	1,261	615
Added by 22 fastest-largest growers	1,031	2,018	1,147
% of total urban growth accounted for by:			
net new entrants	35.6	16.9	41.1
largest 10 (beginning)	17.2	32.4	13.4
largest 10 (end)	28.8	42.0	18.7
fastest 22 in growth	41.4	67.3	34.9

after 1750. Once again the 1600–1750 periods stands out: in the Mediterranean the ten largest cities of 1600 account for all *net* urban growth in the following 150 years; north of the Alps and Pyrenees they account for only one-third of all net growth, but this too is more than in any other period.

We must pause here for a moment to consider another definition of the 'ten largest cities' – those which are largest at the *end* of a period. If there are no additions or subtractions from this group during a period, this is of course the same as the ten largest at the beginning. In this case the data shown in tables 7.10(a)–(c) for the two definitions of ten largest cities would be the same. The amount of divergence in the results of these two categories provides a crude measure of the amount of discontinuity in the rankings of the very largest European cities. Here once again the greatest discontinuity is displayed in the middle period. In this era more fast-growing cities entered the top of the urban hierarchy, displacing older larger cities, than in the other periods.

This brings us to the category of 'fastest growers'. At first glance it stands to reason that the fastest growing cities will always account for the lion's share of

Table 7.10(b) Accounting for urban population growth in northern Europe ('000s)

	1500–1600	1600–1750	1750–1800
Change in total population	12,400	12,000	23,800
% change	28.9	21.5	35.2
% change per annum	0.25	0.13	0.60
Change in urban population	1,190	2,920	2,410
% change	70.2	101.3	41.6
Change in urban/change in total population	9.6	24.3	10.1
Urban population change			
Added by new entrants	455	904	1,170
Deducted by dropouts	78	182	52
Net addition of new entrants	377	722	1,118
Added by 10 largest cities at beginning of period	324	943	388
Added by 10 largest cities at end of period	455	1,445	436
Added by 10 fastest-largest growers	503	1,537	658
% of total urban growth accounted for by:			
net new entrants	31.7	24.7	46.4
largest 10 (beginning)	27.7	32.3	16.1
largest 10 (end)	38.2	49.5	18.1
fastest 10 in growth	42.3	52.6	27.3

urban growth, but this is not necessarily so. If small cities grow most rapidly, the growth of dozens of them may not exceed the small percentage gains, but enormous absolute increase, of a handful of the largest cities. The nature of the data base limits our ability to identify all rapidly growing cities. Since the initial size of cities that emerge from below the 10,000 population threshold is not always known, it is impossible to be precise about their actual growth-rates. In the analysis that follows we will seek to identify all cities that at least double in population in each time period. To avoid making arbitrary assumptions and uncheckable errors, the identification of fast-growing cities will be limited to those of at least 20,000 inhabitants at the end of each time period. Table 7.11 lists the cities that at least double in size during each period and adds a second list of those cities whose rates of growth were lower, but which added at least 30,000 inhabitants. One can think of table 7.11 as identifying those cities that contribute most to total urban growth in each period.

The exceptional character of the 1600–1750 period is once again evident. In this era of slow and regionally uneven overall population growth more

Table 7.10(c) Accounting for urban population growth in Mediterranean Europe ('000s)

	1500–1600	1600–1750	1750–1800
Change in total population	4,000	4,200	4,700
% change	21.9	18.8	17.7
% change per annum	0.20	0.12	0.33
Change in urban population	1,300	80	880
% change	74.5	2.6	28.0
Change in urban/change in total population	32.5	1.9	18.7
Urban population change			
Added by new entrants	522	241	260
Deducted by dropouts	13	455	26
Net addition of new entrants	509	−214	234
Added by 10 largest cities at beginning of period	301	127	253
Added by 10 largest cities at end of period	435	236	339
Added by 10 fastest-largest growers	528	357	381
% of total urban growth accounted for by:			
net new entrants	39.2	−267.5	26.6
largest 10 (beginning)	23.2	158.8	28.8
largest 10 (end)	33.5	295.0	38.5
fastest 10 in growth	40.6	446.3	43.3

Table 7.11 Fastest growing cities, in three periods, 1500–1800

1 Cities that at least doubled in population during each interval

1500–1600	1600–1750	1750–1800
Amsterdam	Amsterdam	Glasgow
Berlin	Berlin	Liverpool
London	London	Barcelona
Madrid	Madrid	Bath
Paris	Paris	Belfast
Turin	Turin	Birmingham
Augsburg	Brest	Dundee
Bordeaux	Bristol	Graz
Catania	Cadiz	Hull
Danzig	Clermond-Ferrand	Leeds
Haarlem	Copenhagen	Limerick
Hamburg	Cork	Magdeburg
Lecce	Dresden	Manchester
Lisbon	Dublin	Nottingham
Magdeburg	Glasgow	Plymouth
Messina	The Hague	Portsmouth
Middelburg	Leipzig	Sheffield
Seville	Königsberg	Sunderland
	Liège	Warsaw
	Liverpool	
	Livorno	
	Lyons	
	Malaga	
	Nancy	
	Nantes	
	Newcastle	
	Nîmes	
	Norwich	
	Prague	
	Rotterdam	
	Stockholm	
	Toulon	
	Versailles	
	Vienna	

2 Cities that did not double, but added at least 30,000 inhabitants to their populations

1500–1600	1600–1750	1750–1800
Naples	Hamburg	Berlin
Palermo	Lille	Dublin
Rome	Lisbon	Lisbon
Rouen	Rome	London
		Madrid
		Naples
		Seville
		Vienna

(continued)

STABILITY AND DISCONTINUITY IN EUROPEAN URBAN GROWTH

Table 7.11—(continued)

	1500–1600		1600–1750		1750–1800	
	No.	Population ('000s)	No.	Population ('000s)	No.	Population ('000s)
Urban population growth accounted for by:						
cities that at least doubled	18	770	34	2253	19	1230
cities that added at least 30,000	4	261	4	164	8	626
Total	22	1031	38	2417	27	1856
% of total urban growth		41.4		80.6		56.4

cities at least doubled their population than in any other, and this occurred at the same time that more cities suffered losses of population than in any other period. Overall, the 38 cities listed in the table accounted for 80 per cent of Europe's net urban growth in the period 1600–1750. In no other period was urban growth so thoroughly concentrated in a handful of the many hundreds of cities comprising the urban system.

What sorts of cities were these rapid growers? Since most cities, and particularly large cities, carry out a wide range of social and economic functions, any general scheme of categorization is bound to assign many cities rather arbitrarily. For this reason I have resisted making more than the most basic of designations: the rapidly growing cities are here identified simply as capitals, ports, capitals *and* ports, and others. Cities in this last category generally combine industrial with commercial and administrative functions.

In every period capitals and ports contribute substantially to Europe's urban growth, but in the period 1600–1750 they are pre-eminent. Thirty of the 38 rapidly growing cities were either capitals or ports or both. Of the 8 other cities only Lyons combined rapid growth with large size. The others were all at the margin of inclusion in the category of rapid growers. Their aggregate growth amounted to only 7 per cent of the growth of the 38 cities.

Of the ports, Atlantic ports active in inter-continental trade are most conspicious in 1600–1750. Seven such ports made the list in 1500–1600, 13 in 1600–1750, and 7 in 1750–1800. Of the Mediterranean ports, the only ones to grow in the seventeenth century were those dominated by northern European merchants instead of natives: Cadiz, Livorno and Malaga.

The list of rapidly growing capitals in 1600–1750 includes nearly all the great capital cities of twentieth-century western and central Europe. Only Brussels, Oslo and Berne – the latter two for obvious reasons – are not found on the list, and it includes only two capital cities that do not now function as national capitals (Turin and Dresden).[5]

In comparing the lists of rapidly growing cities in the three periods a striking difference emerges between the capitals and all other cities. Among the capitals there is a great continuity, or persistence, in growth performance. Altogether, 16 capital cities appear in at least one of the three lists. Four of these cities rank, either because of their rapid growth or their large absolute growth, in all three lists. Six capitals appear in two lists. Among the 25 ports which find themselves on the list in at least one period only 5 are listed twice, and none more than twice. Finally, the lists of 'other' cities are completely different in each period: none of the 25 cities appears in more than one list. Clearly, being the governmental centre for a large territory conferred on a city a long-term, stable growth that no other functions were capable of. The irresistible expansion of government is not a phenomenon of recent origin. At the other extreme, commercial and industrial functions carried out in inland cities were the most vulnerable to altered circumstances. Rapid growth on such bases was never more than 'temporary' by the temporal standards being used here.

STABILITY AND CHANGE IN THE VERY LONG RUN

An overview of the urban growth process can be gained by constructing a single transition matrix for the three centuries before 1800. It will permit an examination of the issue of continuity versus discontinuity in the very long run by showing the place in 1800 of the cities with at least 10,000 inhabitants in 1500. How diverse were the fates of those cities? To what extent were they overshadowed in 1800 by new cities? To lend some perspective to the answers we get to these questions the chapter will end with a similar analysis of European urban growth in the 180 years *after* 1800.

The transition matrix shows that Europe's 154 cities of at least 10,000 inhabitants in 1500 were joined in the following three centuries by 216 new cities. In 1800 the 'old' cities formed but 41 per cent of those at or above the population threshold, and in northern Europe they were overshadowed even more, comprising only 36 per cent of the 250 cities possessing at least 10,000 inhabitants in 1800.

One's impression of the performance of the large cities of 1500 is a bit more positive when one inspects the transition matrix to determine the changes of size category experienced by the 154 cities. Only 6 of them fell below 10,000 inhabitants and only 3 others declined to a lower size category, while altogether half rose at least one size category.[6]

Since the total population of Europe approximately doubled over the three centuries, one might assume that a city maintaining its relative standing in

STABILITY AND DISCONTINUITY IN EUROPEAN URBAN GROWTH

the urban hierarchy would at least double in size, i.e. rise some time between 1500 and 1800 to the next higher size category in the transition matrix. A more stringent test of the persistence of the old cities is thus made by asking how many of the 158 cities of at least 20,000 inhabitants in 1800 had numbered among the 154 cities of 10,000 or more inhabitants in 1500? Table

Table 7.12 Transition matrices: number of cities in population size categories, 1500–1800

Europe

1500 \ 1800	0	1	2	3	4	5	6	T
0	9	159	38	16	1	2	0	225
1	6	46	37	5	4	1	0	99
2	0	1	17	14	3	2	0	37
3	0	0	2	4	6	1	1	14
4	0	0	0	0	2	0	2	4
5	0	0	0	0	0	0	0	0
6	0	0	0	0	0	0	0	0
T	15	206	94	39	16	6	3	379

The 154 cities of 10,000 and over in 1500: 6, 47, 56, 23, 15, 4, 3
%: 23, 60, 59, 94, 67, 100

Mediterranean

1500 \ 1800	0	1	2	3	4	5	6	T
0	5	42	7	2	1	1	0	58
1	5	19	13	3	0	0	0	40
2	0	1	6	3	2	1	0	13
3	0	0	2	2	4	1	0	9
4	0	0	0	0	2	0	1	3
5	0	0	0	0	0	0	0	0
6	0	0	0	0	0	0	0	0
T	10	62	28	10	9	3	1	123

The 65 cities of 10,000 and over in 1500: 5, 20, 21, 8, 8, 2, 1
%: 32, 75, 80, 89, 67, 100

Northern Europe

1500 \ 1800	0	1	2	3	4	5	6	T
0	4	117	31	14	0	1	0	167
1	1	27	24	2	4	1	0	59
2	0	0	11	11	1	1	0	24
3	0	0	0	2	2	0	1	5
4	0	0	0	0	0	0	1	1
5	0	0	0	0	0	0	0	0
6	0	0	0	0	0	0	0	0
T	5	144	66	29	7	3	2	256

The 89 cities of 10,000 and over in 1500: 1, 27, 35, 15, 7, 2, 2
%: 19, 53, 52, 100, 67, 100

143

7.12 displays the 1800 size categories of the large cities of 1500 at the bottom of each transition matrix. While the 154 cities of 1500 comprised only 41 per cent of the cities of 10,000 or more in 1800, they accounted for two-thirds of the cities of 20,000 and over. In the Mediterranean countries the old cities dominate every size category from 20,000 (i.e. category II and up); only 11 of the 51 such cities did not number among the large cities of 1500. In northern Europe the hold of the old cities was weaker, but everywhere the old cities dominated the larger size categories. To put it another way, the numerous small cities of 1500 with few exceptions did not penetrate the upper reaches of the urban hierarchy. Table 7.13 shows this clearly. The older cities, while numerically inferior to the 216 cities that surpassed the 10,000 population threshold during the period 1500–1800, accounted for 64 per cent of the population resident in the cities of at least 10,000 and accounted for 22 of the 25 cities of 80,000 and more inhabitants.

The transition matrix allows for a ready identification of the cities that combined rapid growth with persistence, and those whose decline was substantial and irrevocable. If we continue to regard a one-cell upward movement as a norm for the three-century period, then the cities of noteworthy change can be defined as those that rose by at least three categories or fell by one or more categories. Twenty-five cities satisfy the growth criterion, i.e. expanded their populations by at least eightfold, and 9 satisfy the decline criterion, i.e. suffered on average a halving of their initial population. The rapid risers include 12 capitals (including Turin, Madrid and Dublin, the only cities to rise from under 10,000 inhabitants to 80,000 or more), 10 ports (of which only Amsterdam rose by more than three categories) and 3 other cities – Nîmes, Manchester and Birmingham. All 9 declining cities were inland towns and none was a capital.

The foregoing analysis of continuity and instability in the urban system cannot readily be summarized in a few words. Continuity is obviously a matter of degree, and one's perceptions depend in part on which aspect of this complex phenomenon is selected for emphasis. Thus, *ex ante* the large cities of 1500 experienced much variability, so that their position in 1800 is difficult to predict, but *ex post* it was very likely that a large city of 1800 had numbered among the larger cities of 1500. Before offering a final assessment on the stability or fragility of early modern European cities it will be helpful to develop a comparative perspective by applying the techniques just used to the era since 1800. By constructing a transition matrix for the period 1800–1979 we can observe the patterns of city growth that are characteristic of the industrial age. Specifically, we will observe the extent to which the large cities of 1800 remain the large cities of today, and compare the results to the period 1500–1800.

Before embarking on this investigation some thought must be given to the

Table 7.13 The relative importance of 'new' and 'old' cities, by size category, 1500–1800

Size category in 1800 ('000s)	Number of cities					Aggregate population of cities ('000s)			
	Cities of 10,000 and over in 1500	Cities under 10,000 in 1500	Total number in 1800	Column 2 as % of column 4		Population of 'old' cities in 1800	Population of 'new' cities in 1800	Total population	Column 6 as % of column 8
1	2	3	4	5		6	7	8	9
10–19	46	160	206	22.3		738	2,078	2,816	26.2
20–39	57	37	94	60.6		1,586	935	2,521	62.9
40–79	23	16	39	59.0		1,240	983	2,223	55.8
80–159	15	1	16	93.4		1,577	82	1,659	95.1
160–319	4	2	6	66.7		791	335	1,126	70.2
320 and over	3	0	3	100.0		1,873	0	1,873	100.0
Total	148	216	364	40.7		7,805	4,413	12,218	63.9
5–9.9	6	c. 529	c. 535			c. 45	3,654	3,699	1.2
Total urban population 5000 and over						7,850	8,067	15,917	49.3

problem of determining which modern cities are the functional equivalents of the 364 cities of at least 10,000 inhabitants in 1800. The rapid population growth and intense urbanization of the nineteenth and twentieth centuries make absurd the continued use of a 10,000 population threshold. Another approach is to establish the size threshold at such a level that the number of 1979 cities is roughly equal to the number of cities with at least 10,000 inhabitants in 1800. This approach is probably overly exclusive, for it implies that there are no more locations carrying out certain urban functions in a modern industrial society than there were in the predominantly agrarian society of 1800.

Any population threshold for 1979 will have arbitrary qualities. We will begin here by examining the 390 modern cities of 100,000 and above, and ask how many of them numbered among the 364 cities of at least 10,000 inhabitants in 1800. Later, a brief glimpse of the smaller cities will provide a broader context for the analysis.

The relevant data are displayed in tables 7.14 and 7.15. The transition matrix, whose size categories necessarily differ from those used for the earlier centuries,[7] impresses us with the wide dispersion of growth-rates observable for cities of almost every initial size category. Thus, among the cities with 20,000–39,000 inhabitants in 1800 were those that grew to over 1 million, others that were unable even to double their population, and a remarkably even distribution of the remaining cities among all the intervening size categories. As a result of this great variance, the 364 cities with a minimum population in 1800 of 10,000 contributed 214 cities to the 390 with 100,000 and more inhabitants in 1979, while fully 137 failed to achieve that threshold level. (The remaining 13 cities cannot be analysed separately because of their inclusion in the metropolitan population of others.) This implies that the 214 large cities of 1800 were joined by 176 new cities that had possessed under 10,000 inhabitants in 1800.

The 1800–1979 matrix bears many statistical similarities to that of 1500–1800. In both cases the old cities experience great variance in their growth performance and they are joined by a larger number of newcomers. Likewise, in both cases the new cities do not generally penetrate far up the urban hierarchy and come to account for only a modest portion of the total urban population. Table 7.15 shows this clearly. The 214 old cities make up only 55 per cent of all cities of 100,000 and over in 1979, but they account for 77 per cent of the 140 million inhabitants of such cities. The newcomers are dominant only in the cities of 100,000–200,000 inhabitants; they account for less than one-third of the cities of 200,000–500,000, while among the 59 cities of 500,000 and over, only 4 were cities of under 10,000 in 1800. Once again, *ex ante* the fate of a large city of 1800 is difficult to predict; *ex post* the large city of today is very likely to have been a leading city in 1800.

Table 7.14 Transition matrix: Europe, 1800–1979 (population in '000s)

	Size category in 1979									
	Under 50	50–99	100–199	200–299	300–499	500–999	1000–1999	2000–3999	4000 and over	Total with 100 and over in 1979	Total, all cities
Size category in 1800											
Under 10	*	c. 375	131	28	13	4	0	0	0	176	551*
10–19	58	57	46	16	9	5	0	0	0	76	191
20–39	6	16	28	24	12	9	1	0	0	74	96
40–59	0	0	3	8	4	7	2	0	0	24	24
60–99	0	0	2	0	6	7	7	1	0	23	23
100–199	0	0	0	0	1	2	5	3	0	11	11
200–399	0	0	0	0	0	1	2	0	0	3	3
400 and over	0	0	0	0	0	0	1	0	2	3	3
Total with 10 and over in 1800	64	73	79	48	32	31	18	4	2	351/390	
Total, all cities	64*	448	210	76	45	35	18	4	2		902

* Cities with populations under 10,000 in 1800 *and* under 50,000 in 1979 have not been studied. The totals of this row and column are incomplete.

Table 7.15 The relative importance of 'new' and 'old' cities, by size category, 1800–1979

Size category in 1979 ('000s)	Number of cities				Aggregate population of cities ('000s)			
	Cities of 10,000 and over in 1800	Cities under 10,000 in 1800	Total number in 1979	Column 2 as % of column 4	Population of cities in column 2	Population of cities in column 3	Total population of all cities	Column 6 as % of column 8
1	2	3	4	5	6	7	8	9
100–199	79	131	210	37.6	10,550	18,401	28,951	36.4
200–299	48	28	76	63.2	11,721	6,577	18,298	64.1
300–499	32	13	45	71.1	12,638	4,763	17,401	72.6
500–999	31	4	35	88.6	20,900	2,669	23,569	88.7
1000 and over	24	0	24	100.0	51,966	0	51,966	100.0
Total	214	176	390	54.9	107,775	32,410	140,185	76.9
50–99	73	c. 375	448	16.5	5,550	24,375	29,925	18.5
Under 50	64	*	N.A.	N.A.	2,086	N.A.	N.A.	N.A.
Merged cities	13	—	—					
Total, cities of 50,000 and over	287	551	838	34.3	113,325	56,785	170,110	66.6

* Cities with populations under 10,000 in 1800 *and* under 50,000 in 1979 have not been studied.

STABILITY AND DISCONTINUITY IN EUROPEAN URBAN GROWTH

Urban growth since 1800 has differed from that which preceded in one important respect: in the kinds of cities that have enjoyed rapid growth and suffered from prolonged stagnation. The 176 new cities that grew to exceed the 100,000 level were overwhelmingly industrial and were highly concentrated in specific regions, such as the West German *Ruhrgebiet*, northern England, northern Spain and industrial areas of Sweden and Poland. The four cities that rose from under 10,000 to over 500,000 inhabitants are all of this type: Lodz, Dortmund, Duisburg and Essen. Among the old cities that grew rapidly, only Oslo (capital of newly independent Norway), Munich and Zurich were not primarily centres of industrial activity.

If we now consider the 137 cities of at least 10,000 inhabitants in 1800 that have failed to reach 100,000 inhabitants, we find a large number of commercial and administrative centres in regions that remain agrarian (or deindustrialize). Half of all these cities (72) were places of 10,000–20,000 inhabitants in 1800 that had ranked among the large centres of Europe for at least a century. These languishing centres, many destined to become thriving tourist attractions after the Second World War, are particularly numerous in France, Italy, Spain and Belgium. Many port cities have also experienced below-average growth as trade has tended to become concentrated in a small number of very large harbour complexes. The relative stagnation of each of these ports has its own particular explanation, but such places as Cork, Cadiz, Middelburg, Rochefort, La Rochelle and Livorno are all of this general type.

Even though such a large number of old cities failed to reach the 100,000 population level, they formed but a small percentage of the smaller cities. The lower portion of table 7.15 shows that some 375 new cities of 50,000–100,000 inhabitants dominate this category.[8] Yet when our analysis is expanded to include these smaller cities, the basic patterns described above do not change. The large cities of 1800 then account for only one-third of Europe's 838 cities of 50,000 and over, but two-thirds of the 170 million urban-dwellers. Compare this to the large cities of 1500, which accounted for two-fifths of the 364 cities of 10,000 and over in 1800, and almost two-thirds of the 12 million urban-dwellers.

What conclusions can be drawn from this analysis of stability and discontinuity in the European urban system? Perhaps the most unexpected finding is that post-1800 urban growth, although on a wholly different scale from pre-1800 urban growth, displays many elements of continuity with the past. Regionally dominant cities, particularly those possessing formal political functions, have tended to hold their positions through thick and thin. At the Europe-wide level and viewed in the long run, the rankings of cities by size show substantial changes, but this has rarely been brought about by small cities rising to assume the functions of established larger cities. Rather, the rearrangements in the upper reaches of the urban hierarchy were typically the result of differential growth in the regional economies which caused the dominant city of a fast-growing region to surpass the dominant city of a slow-growing region. The dominant cities of each region remained the same, but their standing relative to each other changed. This process usually spanned many decades, even centuries. The most obvious exceptions to this general pattern are the rise of Madrid to the head of Castile's urban hierarchy, supplanting Toledo, and arguably the rise of Amsterdam in the Low Countries.[9] Far below this rarified stratum, among the cities just above the threshold levels used in this study, much more movement and discontinuity is evident. Competition among ports, the fortunes of industries, the effects of the Reformation and of government centralization, and accidents of history and of nature have caused such cities to rise and fall relative to each other. At this level we see the effects of the 'new' cities, those locations from the stock of several thousand existing in 1500 which became the bearers of novelty and the reflectors of structural change. These new cities were particularly numerous in the nineteenth century – witness the 551 cities of less than 10,000 inhabitants in 1800 that today have at least 50,000. But relative to the number of large cities, the earlier centuries had also experienced a steady stream of growing cities passing over the 10,000 population threshold.

Between these two levels we find the cities of intermediate rank, just below the apexes of their urban subsystems. They have developed beyond the provision of basic urban services by specialization in transport functions, industrial production or ecclesiastical administration, but are not possessed of central governmental functions. Such cities (examples are Augsburg, Brescia, Bremen, Bristol, Ghent, Magdeburg, Malaga, Reims) deserve more detailed study *in the context of their urban hierarchies* so that the periods of urban turbulence that alter their positions for better or worse can be better understood.

What this statistical examination shows is that the era of the Industrial Revolution was not a unique urban watershed, introducing shocks to so many cities as to create a new urban system. In most regions the disruptions of that era were well within the pre-nineteenth-century experience of the European urban system. A complex, international urban system predated the era of industrialization; this study has shown that its construction was a gradual process, but the best candidate for the period of its consolidation is the seventeenth century. It is, therefore, a mistake to regard the rapid growth of industrial towns in the nineteenth century as creating the modern urbanized society of the advanced nations. On the contrary, the construction of an urban system was (as I shall argue in chapter 10) a precondition for modern industrial growth. The rise of specifically industrial cities was dramatic and novel, but highly localized (on coal-fields and in textile districts) and episodic (the period of rapid growth was brief). Few became central places in the urban system; most remained subordinate to long-existing regional centres.

8
THE SPATIAL PATTERN OF EUROPEAN URBANIZATION

THE MEASUREMENT OF URBANIZATION

The urbanization of Europe in the three centuries after 1500 occurred at varying rates of growth, was selective with regard to the types of cities that ascended to higher levels of size and importance, and featured the construction of a new hierarchical pattern, or rank-size distribution of cities. Urban growth also exhibited pronounced spatial features: its incidence was geographically highly uneven. I have sought to expose these developments by comparing urban growth sometimes in two large regions (Mediterranean and northern Europe), and sometimes in four regions (Mediterranean, central, north and west, and eastern Europe). It is important to go further than that, for European urbanization in these centuries, instead of being an all-conquering force, was as regionally selective as we have already seen it to be selective in other respects.

The most direct way to uncover the spatial patterns of European urbanization involves comparing the percentage of total population resident in cities, region-by-region. The necessary information is presented in table 3.7, where the urban population in each of the sixteen territories is expressed as a percentage of the estimated total population of its territory. The table shows great regional differences in urbanization and striking differences in the tempo of change: the urbanization rate rose rapidly in certain territories, such as England, Scotland and the Netherlands, while it hardly moved in others, such as Belgium and Italy.

Much more could be said along these lines if we calculated urbanization rates for smaller geographical entities than 'Scandinavia', 'Germany' or 'Spain'. The frequent absence of total population data for smaller territories makes a more fine-grained analysis impractical for this study. But, even if it were possible, it would not be particularly enlightening. Indeed, these simple percentages can mislead as often as they inform. The following example demonstrates the need for caution in making comparative statements about levels of urbanization. The population of London grew from 40,000 to 575,000 in 1500–1700. In that period it singlehandedly accounted for nearly all of the rise of England and Wales's level of urbanization from 3.1 to 13.3 per cent. Now, if England and Wales were divided into, say, four regions, the urban percentage in south-eastern England would show an increase from something like 8 or 9 per cent in 1500 to about 40 per cent in 1700. Meanwhile, the figures for the three remaining regions would start at from 0 to 2 per cent and increase very little, if at all, over the two centuries that follow.

Which of these two approaches is the more accurate? In 1500 London's growth probably had little direct demographic and economic impact on the northern and western extremities of England and Wales. One could defend the proposition that the regional urbanization figures are the more telling. By 1700 London's growth had a national – indeed, an international – impact that would make reliance on the regional urbanization figures more misleading than informative. Of course London's growth was extraordinary, but we have observed that the growth of large national capitals and international trading cities was a major feature of urban growth throughout Europe. Finding the appropriate regional context in which to measure levels of urbanization when cities such as Paris, Amsterdam and Lisbon are involved is obviously neither simple nor a matter of little consequence. Once one rejects the handy assertion that the nation state is the natural unit of analysis, and the anachronism that *what would later become* the nation state is the natural unit of analysis, one must confront the issue of what constitutes an urban system or subsystem. In our earlier discussion of this issue it became clear that in Europe the concept of the natural region cannot often help us, and for that reason the boundaries of urban subsystems are subject to considerable change.

The simple comparison of urban percentages is inadequate in a second respect as well: it tells us very little about the phenomenon of urbanization as a social and economic process. When using the term urbanization in more than a simple statistical sense (see pp. 11–12), we are interested in knowing, among other things, the density with which an area is covered with cities, the intensity of communication among those cities and the range of urban functions performed in the cities. Population data alone cannot answer these questions in all their aspects, but simple calculations of the percentage of a territory's population residing in cities can be faulted for making insufficient use of the data base at our disposal: such percentages hide too much from us.

For example, they tell us that in both south-eastern England and the Dutch Republic about 40 per cent of the population resided in cities in 1700. They say nothing about the fact that the Republic was then covered with 19 cities of over 10,000 inhabitants (and scores of smaller ones) while the English region's urban population was concentrated entirely in one city, with all the others being very much smaller.

These limitations have provoked scholars to devise alternative measurement formulae: Arriaga proposed an urbanization index that, in his view, provides superior insights in comparing urban populations across time and among nations.[1] It gives extra weight to larger cities (more truly urban, in Arriaga's view) by multiplying the simple urban percentage *(U)* by a coefficient that is the sum of the squares of the population of each city *(X_i)* divided by the simple sum of those city populations. His urbanization index is, thus:

$$IU = \frac{\sum_{i=1}^{n} x_i^2}{\sum_{i=1}^{n} x_i} \times U$$

Paul Klep, in his study of long-term developments in the population and economy of Brabant, employs this index in his analysis of urbanization in that important Belgian province.[2] Using a conventional measure of urbanization he found that the population of the 9 municipalities of at least 5000 inhabitants in 1526 stood at 39 per cent of the total population, while the 28 such municipalities of 1856 also registered 39 per cent. But, he reasoned, the largest cities at the latter date were many times larger than their counterparts in the sixteenth century. Brabant had really become more urban, but the conventional measure did not reflect this. The urbanization index presents a very different picture: it rises from 8.25 in 1526 to 52.98 in 1856.

Is this really an improvement? Obviously it depends a great deal on one's definition of urbanization. The Arriaga index does not simply weigh more heavily larger cities – for this one is better advised to use higher population thresholds, or a moving threshold – it gives almost *all* weight to the very largest city or cities. Thus, in the comparison of south-eastern England and the Netherlands discussed above, this index would rank the former, with one huge city, as far more urbanized than the Netherlands, where no one was far from a city of substantial size performing sophisticated economic and social functions. Table 8.1 displays some calculations that illustrate further the biases of this index. Germany, whose modest urban population of 1600 does not rise much by 1800, shows a doubling of its urbanization index, which is

Table 8.1 Urbanization index results

$$\text{Index of Urbanization } (IU) = \frac{\sum_{i=1}^{n} x_i^2}{\sum_{i=1}^{n} x_i} \times U$$

x_i = *population of city i*

U = *urbanization rate* ($\sum_{i=1}^{n} x_i$ / total population)

		IU	U (%)
Germany	1600	1.13	4.2
	1800	2.60	5.5
England	1600	8.76	5.5
	1800	90.15	21.1
Spain	1600	4.00	10.8
	1650	5.50	10.2
Brabant*	1600	17.37	41.0
	1800	12.87	30.0

* From Paul M. M. Klep, *Bevolking en arbeid in transformatie* (Nijmegen, 1981), 84–6; including all cities of at least 5000 inhabitants.

solely accounted for by the growth of Berlin and Hamburg. England in 1600 was comparable to Germany in the relative size of its urban population, but because of its concentration in London, England's urbanization index stands well above the German figures. The high English figure increases tenfold by 1800 and one is tempted to interpret this as a reflection of the burgeoning industrial towns that were, indeed, urbanizing important English regions. But the index would have grown almost just as much if none of those towns had existed: 96 per cent of the coefficient value is attributable to London alone. Finally, consider Spain. From 1600 to 1650 the number of cities with at least 10,000 inhabitants fell by 13 and their aggregate population by 25 per cent. But the growth of one city, Madrid, counteracts all of that to raise the index from 4.0 to 5.5.

Very large cities are certainly not without importance, but such cities standing alone – a Vienna or Lisbon – influence society very differently from those interacting intensely in a dense network of subordinate cities. Arriaga's index does not capture this any better than do the conventional measurements.

POTENTIAL

In the remainder of this chapter I will describe and apply a technique that is capable of sidestepping the knotty problems of regionalization while it provides a comprehensive view of spatial differences in the incidence of important dimensions of urbanization.

Potential is a geographer's concept that expresses the 'potential' of a location for interacting with all other locations. It may be thought of as a measure of the accessibility of a location to people, or markets, in all other locations. In the use to be made of the concept here, the locations consist entirely of cities. Thus, potential measures the accessibility of a city to the inhabitants of all other cities.[3]

The potential of city i for interaction with all cities, n in number, within a bounded region is computed as the summation of the separate potentials of i with each of the n cities, including itself. The potential (V) varies directly with the population of city j (M_j) and varies inversely with the distance separating city i from city j (d_{ij}). The measure of a city's size may of course be refined, by adjusting the number of inhabitants by their average purchasing power or some other indicator of economic strength. Likewise, the distance factor should ideally be adjusted to reflect the real cost faced by persons in i and j in communicating with each other, if this should vary among the locations of a region. In symbols:

$$V_i = M_1/d_{i1} + M_2/d_{i2} + \ldots M_j/d_{ij} \ldots M_n/d_{in} + M_i/d_{ii}.$$

That is: $V_i = \sum_{j=1}^{n} M_j/d_{ij} + M_i/d_{ii}.$

The last element of the equations refers to the potential of city i itself. Clearly, d_{ii} cannot be 0, since this would force V_i to infinity. Geographers employ several conventions to deal with this problem, the most common being to set d_{ii} equal to half the distance between i and its nearest neighbour. My approach to this problem will be discussed below.

Once the potential (V_i) for every location is calculated in turn, the resulting set of values can serve as a measure of the relative position of each place with respect to all other places. In this study potential is calculated for all European cities of at least 10,000 inhabitants at each of the seven by now very familiar dates from 1500 to 1800. The maps of urban potential that can be drafted on the basis of this information will serve to indicate the position of Europe's cities *relative to each other*, with respect to their nearness to urban population in the aggregate and to the urban functions and markets that are associated with such people.

Since potential is a general concept with various applications to, among other things, marketing, migration and communications, one is easily left to wonder how the potential values should be interpreted. In the historical application at hand I propose the following. One can imagine an urban field of influence extending around a city. The larger the city, the more extensive the field. When many cities exist in a given area their fields might overlap, generating economic possibilities for both the intervening countryside and the cities of the region that are absent where the cities stand in relative isolation. Those new possibilities arise when cities can interact intensely with each other as elements of an urban system. By plotting on a map the potential values for all cities, a potential surface is created from which we can identify the areas in which urbanization takes the form of urban-system creation and where cities, despite their growth, remain relatively isolated from each other. By comparing the potential surfaces at successive dates we can identify where the more intense, systematic urbanization spreads to, where it retreats from, and how the locations of greatest urban potential change. In brief, the potential surface illustrates how location and communication are important along with population in determining a city's capacity for interaction with other places.

Before proceeding attention must be given to two problems attached to the use of this technique. In calculating potential it is misleading to suppose that only *other* cities contribute to the potential of a city. The city's own population is also relevant; indeed, the more difficult communications are, the larger the city itself looms in its total potential. If each city's own population were ignored, the absurd result would be that the potential of a small place near a large city would exceed that of the large city itself. We have already noted what happens when a city's own population is divided by a distance of 0. What, then, is to be done?

In the calculations that follow d_{ii} is the same for every city: 20 km. I settled on this value as a result of experimentation. With d_{ii} equal to 20, results were generated that stood midway between all potential (V_i) being concentrated in city i itself and city i having no discernible effect on its own potential. It should also be noted that in the application at hand 20 km will also function as a *minimum* value for d_{ij}. Those city pairs closer than 20 km to each other (for example, Greenwich and London, The Hague and Delft) are constrained to take this minimum value.

The second problem concerns the distance factor itself. In its simplest form the potential equation assumes that the terrain over which cities interact with each other is akin to a featureless plain where all movement is equally difficult in direct proportion to distance. The computer model employed to calculate the distance between each city pair (d_{ij}) is consistent with this: for each city we noted the co-ordinates of latitude and longitude and on this basis calculated the direct 'great circle' distances.

This assumption is particularly inappropriate to the period under study, when the costs of overland transportation greatly exceeded those of inland navigation, which in turn exceeded the cost of sea-borne transportation. In order to lend greater realism to the study I have adjusted the distances between each city pair to reflect the relative cost of actually moving goods, people and information between them. Adjusting each of the $\frac{1}{2}(379^2 - 379) = 71{,}631$ d_{ij}'s individually was not possible. In place of this I employed the following procedure to achieve a rough approximation of the 'true' distance between each city pair.

Each city has been coded according to its location:

Code	Type of location
1	Atlantic or Baltic seaport
2	Mediterranean seaport
3	inland city on navigable waterway
4	land-locked city

Each city pair generates a combination of these code numbers, such as 3 – 3 for two cities on navigable waterways, or 1 – 2 for a Baltic port and a Mediterranean port. The next step is to establish coefficients to be used for the adjustment of the direct distance between any two cities. I reasoned that the high cost of overland transportation between two land-locked cities had the effect of increasing the 'real' distance separating them while, at the other extreme, the relative ease of sea-borne communications had the effect of shortening the effective distance between two Atlantic ports or two Mediterranean ports. As a standard I took communication between cities on navigable waterways. The coefficient for this most frequently occurring combination I set at 1.0. That is, the direct distances were left unadjusted. The distances between two land-locked cities needed a coefficient greater than one to reflect the relative difficulty of communication, while the distances between seaports required a coefficient below one to reflect the relative ease of communication. Other combinations would require coefficients with values between these two extremes. These intermediate combinations are self-evident, except perhaps for Atlantic–Baltic ports and Mediterranean ports. These have been separately coded, and communications between these two types of ports treated less favourably than communication among ports within the same zone, in order to deal with the fact that distances have been computed 'as the crow flies' while oceanic communications between northern and Mediterranean ports involve a highly circuitous route that counteracts the lower per-kilometre cost of sea-borne transportation.

While the ordering of city pairs by their relative cost of per-kilometre transportation is straightforward enough, the actual assignment of coefficients with specific values is not. The transformation of an ordinal to a cardinal ranking (table 8.2) can claim no more authority than that of a 'guesstimate'. This attempt to approximate the real effort needed to communicate between

Table 8.2 Coefficients used to modify the distance between city pairs in the calculation of potential

	City pair codes	Distance coefficients
Worst case	4–4	1.6
	1–4 2–4 3–4	1.3
Neutral	3–3 1–2	1.0
	1–3 2–3	0.8
Best cases	1–1 2–2	0.5

every city pair is just that – an approximation. But it does succeed in adding a measure of realism to the computation of urban potential.[4]

EUROPEAN POTENTIAL SURFACES

I have calculated the urban potential of every city of at least 10,000 inhabitants, using the potential equation modified as just described, at fifty-year intervals from 1500 to 1800. In each period the absolute potential values have been recast as percentages of the highest potential value. The examination of the results will proceed by first identifying for each period the cities with highest potential and then by plotting the potential values for all eligible cities and analysing the resulting spatial patterns of high and low potential.

The cities with the highest potential values in each of the seven periods are identified in table 8.3. In 1500 Venice possessed the highest potential of all European cities, with Milan a close second. Fifty years later Venice continued to stand at the apex of the urban potential rankings, but a northern centre, Antwerp, was a very close second. By 1600 the honours of highest potential had shifted to the north. The city identified as possessing the greatest potential, Rotterdam, was then a small place of no great importance. Its high score was the result of its being located in the middle of an extensive urban zone which numbered several cities with potential values close to 100, most notably Amsterdam. This Low Countries zone of high potential did not stand alone. Paris then acted as a second northern centre of high potential while the northern Italian cities, led by Venice and Milan, as well as Naples in southern Italy, all possessed comparable high potential values.

This broadly shared leadership did not last long. By 1650 the southern cities had dropped out of contention while the cities of Holland held the top positions, with Paris close behind. London now joined these others as a contender for the status of city with the highest potential value. In 1700 these three places, Paris, central Holland and London continued to monopolize the ranks of cities with potential within 10 per cent of the highest value, but now London stood at the apex. In the course of the eighteenth century London consolidated its position as the city with the highest potential. No other city came within 10 per cent of London's potential value in 1750; by 1800 the nearest competitor, Paris, mustered a potential value less than three-quarters that of London.

The meaning of this evolution in the location of highest potential values displayed in table 8.3 may become more clear when it is compared to the succession of cities acting as the centre of gravity of the European 'world economy' postulated by Fernand Braudel in *Afterthoughts on Capitalism and Material Civilization*.[5] Braudel's approach to the issue of stability and discontinuity in the European economy was introduced in chapter 7. The concept of centring and decentring that he puts forward involves the reign of a city at the apex of European capitalism, followed by relatively brief episodes of decentring in which leadership is contested, the old champion falls, and a new centre – always a city – is established.

Braudel argues that Venice, having assumed the functions of centre in the fourteenth century, held onto its position until the early sixteenth century. The leadership position then passed to Antwerp, only to revert after a relatively brief reign of fifty years to the Mediterranean area again. This time, after the mid-sixteenth century, the leader was Genoa, the beneficiary of Habsburg commercial policy. Genoa's leadership was also of short duration. A decentring of the world economy in the period 1590–1610 was resolved

Table 8.3 Cities with the highest potential values (expressed in percentage of peak value for each period), 1500–1800

City	1500	1550	1600	1650	1700	1750	1800
London	54.0	59.2	86.4	92.7	100.0	100.0	100.0
Amsterdam	72.9	75.3	98.1	99.3	90.0	77.7	68.3
Rotterdam	0	0	100.0	100.0	92.0	79.7	70.9
Antwerp	95.7	98.4	93.3	86.7	81.3	70.3	67.0
Paris	76.2	74.0	92.9	95.1	93.6	89.9	73.6
Venice	100.0	100.0	94.4	54.6	53.2	52.9	44.2
Milan	98.1	76.6	90.1	51.4	50.9	49.7	43.4
Naples	82.4	84.5	96.0	49.8	47.1	51.8	50.3

only as Amsterdam consolidated its position as the centre of European capitalist economic activity. This consolidation in Amsterdam possessed a durability that the previous centres had lacked. Only after a protracted period of rivalry between Amsterdam and London did the locus of leadership change once again. According to Braudel London's position became clearly preeminent toward the end of the eighteenth century. London's leadership spanned the nineteenth century and continued into the twentieth, until the mantle crossed the Atlantic Ocean to New York in the crisis of 1929.

It is noteworthy that among all the cities identified by Braudel only London was the largest city of Europe at the time of its pre-eminence. Clearly he had more in mind than size alone in his assessments of the economic importance of these cities. The potential model used here relies entirely on population data, since no other quantitative indicators of a city's importance are generally available. Despite this, the potential values follow Braudel closely in the identification of the cities at the apex of Europe's capitalist system.

In 1500 and again from 1650 to 1800 the potential values conform nicely with Braudel's qualitative assessments, while Antwerp's brief reign is

Figure 8.1 Urban potential in Europe, 1500

adequately reflected in that city's high score in 1550. Around 1600 Braudel argues that strong destabilizing forces created an environment in which several centres vigorously contested for the leadership of the European economic system. None could uphold for very long a durable recentring. The widely shared top potential values of 1600, with seven cities within hailing distance of the highest score, are surely consistent with Braudel's vision.

To my mind this convergence of a qualitative assessment with the results of a rather formalistic quantitative technique lend credence to the interpretation that I have sought to place on this application of the potential concept.

Thus far the discussion has focused exclusively on the cities of highest potential. It is now time to examine the results of the potential analysis for the entire set of European cities. Figures 8.1–8.5 display the potential surfaces for five of the seven dates from 1500 to 1800. The potential surfaces are formed by isolines, each isoline encircling a zone in which the potential values of all cities equal or exceed the stated percentage of the location of highest potential. Consider the potential map for 1500 (figure 8.1). It shows that cities with potential values of at least 80 per cent of the peak are located throughout northern Italy, at Naples and in a triangle of the Low Countries whose corners are formed by Dordrecht, Tournai and Leuven. Isolines of lower value form irregular, progressively larger zones around these cores. At the potential isoline of 40 the north-western and Mediterranean zones are precariously joined by an urban corridor extending from the Atlantic coast of France to Languedoc, and at potential isoline 30 the southern Italian urban zone centred on Naples is also absorbed. At that potential level only the urban centres of Andalucia stand in apparent isolation. Potential isoline 30 forms an irregular zone that excludes most of Scandinavia, Celtic Britain, Ireland, Castile, Portugal and eastern Europe. This suggests that cities in these vast territories interacted only weakly with each other and with the more centrally located cities.

At this point attention must be drawn to the fact that the potential values have been, and must be, calculated in a bounded territory. The influence of cities beyond the boundaries that might affect the potential of certain European cities is necessarily excluded from the results reported here. How would more expansive boundaries affect the potential surfaces displayed in the figures? Certainly the cities of the Balkan peninsula and the eastern Mediterranean (among them Constantinople) would augment the potential of the Italian cities. The only other possibilities are the overseas colonial cities. Whether the intensity of their links with the Atlantic ports compensated sufficiently for their great distance to alter materially the potential surfaces shown in the figures remains an open question.

In other respects the boundaries used in this study are probably not guilty of greatly distorting the results reported here. The Russian cities are so few

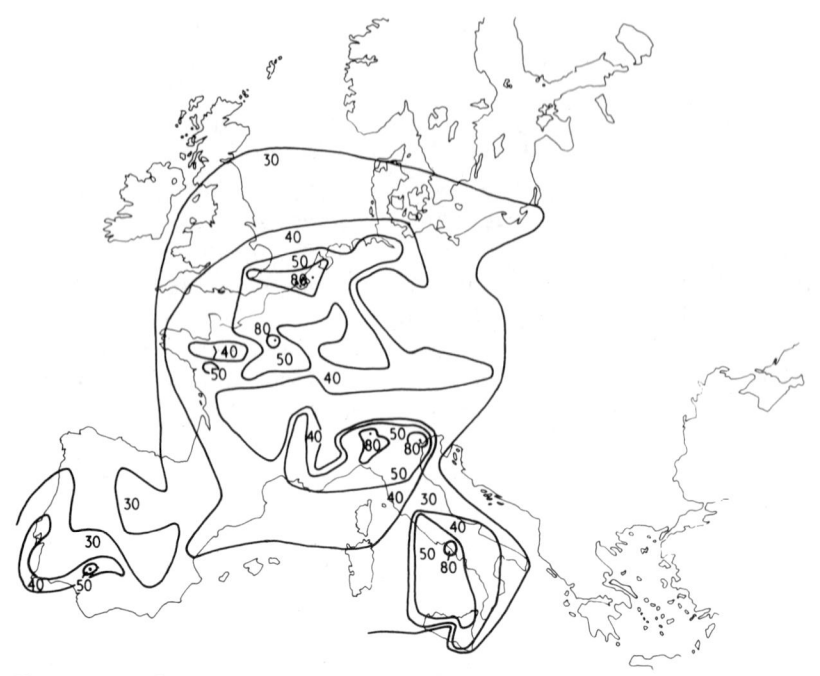

Figure 8.2 Urban potential in Europe, 1600

and far removed that they could do little to increase the low potential values of the eastern European cities.[6]

The potential surface in 1600 (figure 8.2) features a potential isoline 30 that distinguishes peripheral from central zones much as in 1500, except that rather more of eastern Europe falls within the isoline and, more dramatic, the isoline reaches out in the Iberian peninsula to include the cities of Andalucia and Portugal. The potential surface of 1600 is most interesting: it shows that sixteenth-century Iberian urbanization had been sufficient to fashion a new subsidiary peak embracing Lisbon and the cities of the Guadelquivar. The city of highest potential in this region, Seville, did not yet approach the values found in more centrally located areas, but there was now a fourth locus of urbanization to set beside those in the Low Countries, northern Italy and southern Italy, all of which possessed comparable peak potential values.

A comparison of the potential maps for 1600 and 1650 (figure 8.3) conveys the dramatic effects of the seventeenth-century urban crisis. The recent urban growth of Iberia is undone as the subsidiary peak of 1600 all but disappears. The long finger of high urban potential extending through the south German cities is withdrawn, and, most importantly, the relative potential values of the Italian cities sink away, so that the highest Italian values are little more than half of the highest northern values.

A century later, in 1750 (figure 8.4), the potential surface shows that the northern Italian and Neopolitan urban systems remain much as the seventeenth-century collapse had left them. The cities of the Iberian peninsula register potential values above 20 only along the coasts and in Catalonia. Apart from Madrid the Castilian interior is a vast territory of very low potential that finds its counterparts only at the extreme margins of eastern and northern Europe. Standing in sharp contrast to all this is the northwestern urban zone which is expanding north and west to embrace most of the British Isles and east, more or less along the Elbe, to incorporate the cities of Prussia and Saxony. By 1800 (figure 8.5) the Atlantic reorientation of the potential surfaces is complete, reflecting the rise of Britain's industrial cities.

Figures 8.6, 8.7 and 8.8 are intended to identify more clearly several principal long-term spatial developments. The first two identify the 'core' zones of urbanization in selected periods. The criterion used for 1500 and 1600 is a minimum potential value of 50; in 1750 and 1800 the minimum potential value of 30 appears to be roughly analogous.[7] In 1500 three zones

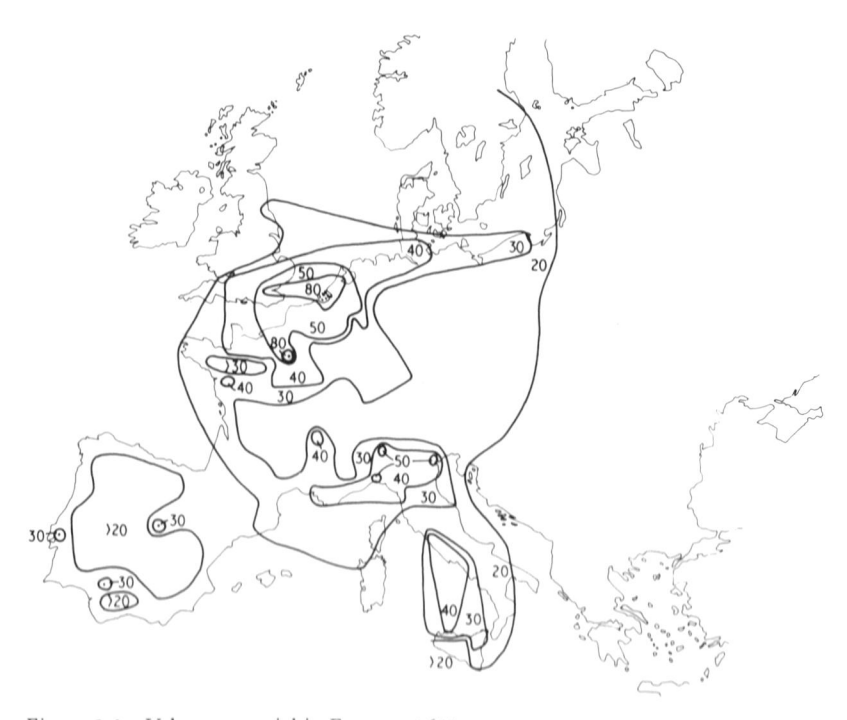

Figure 8.3 Urban potential in Europe, 1650

Figure 8.4 Urban potential in Europe, 1750

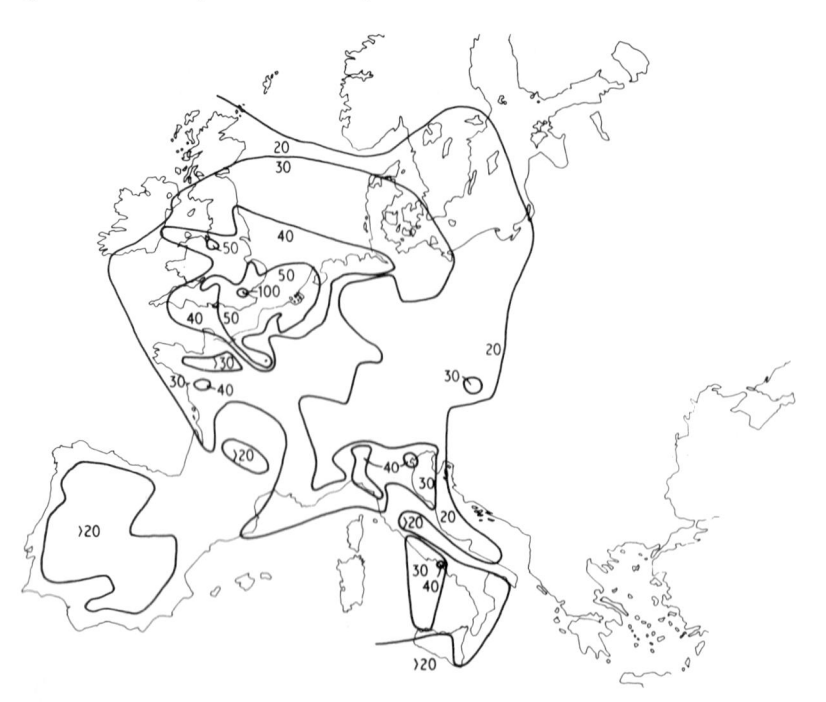

Figure 8.5 Urban potential in Europe, 1800

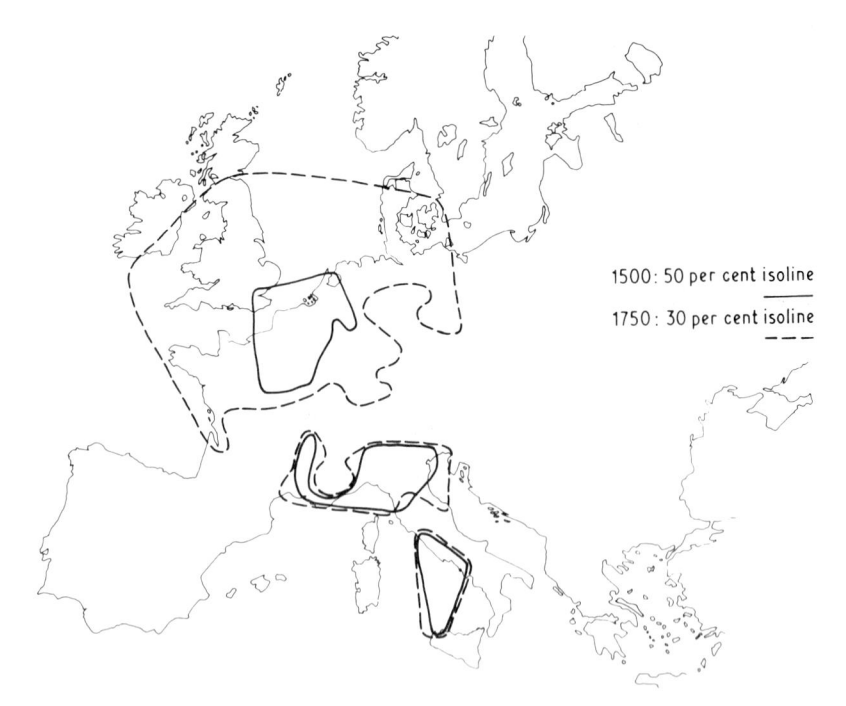

Figure 8.6 High urban potential zones in 1500 and 1750

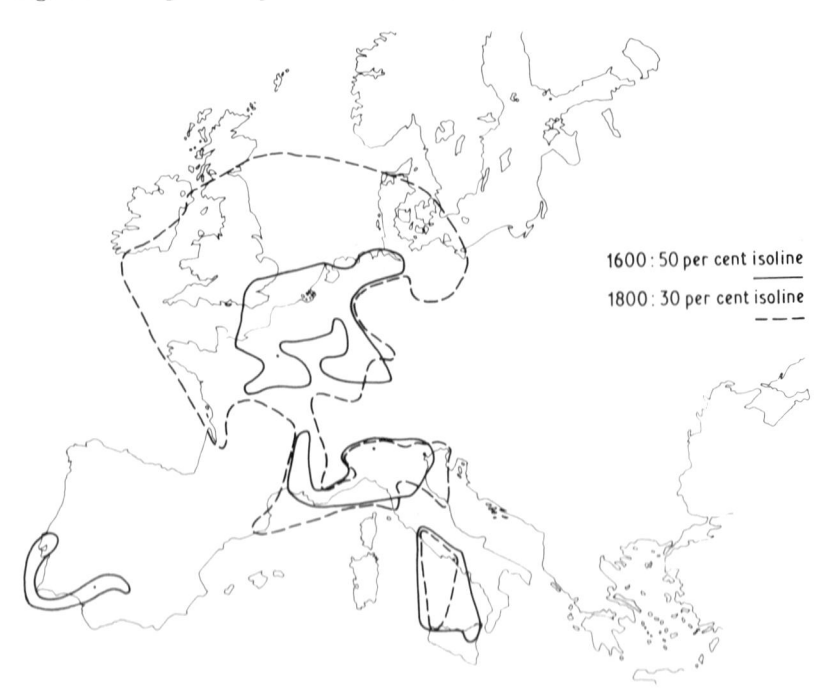

Figure 8.7 High urban potential zones in 1600 and 1800

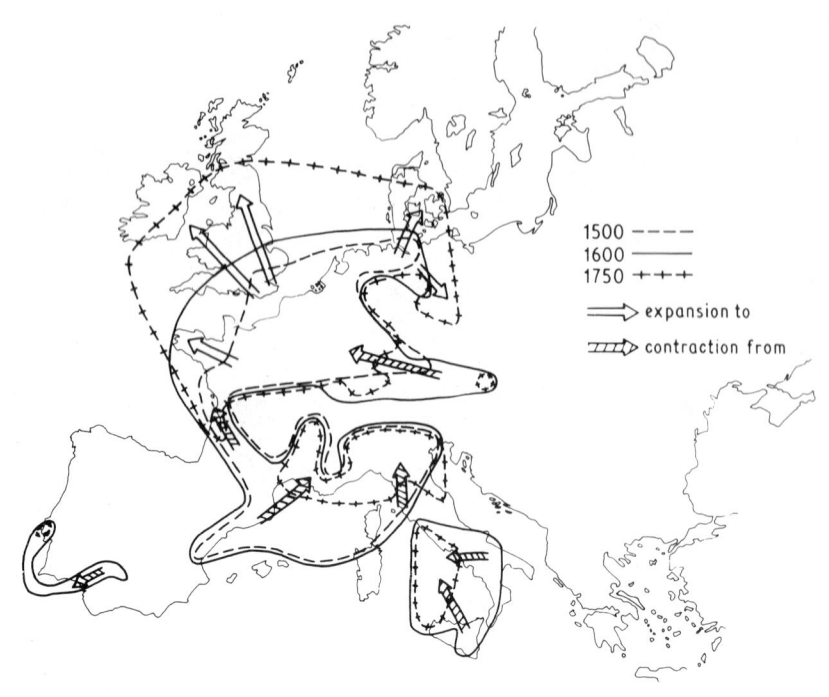

Figure 8.8 Zones of expanding and contracting potential: 1500, 1600 and 1750

existed, each with chief cities of very high potential. In 1600 a fourth zone had been added in Iberia, although it was not yet the full equivalent of the others. By 1750 the Iberian urban core had disappeared while those in Italy were, if anything, smaller than before. In contrast the northern core had expanded enormously in every direction except the south. The Loire river continued to define the southern boundary. In 1800 the core zones were not much altered, but a new corridor connecting the northern to the now subsidiary Mediterranean core had opened up, making use of the Rhône–Saône river system and its canals.

Figure 8.8 calls our attention to the main areas from which high potential value contracted and to which it expanded. Date one claim that it identifies areas of relative urbanization and de-urbanization? Using those terms in their conventional senses such a statement would be misleading. But if urbanization is a phenomenon produced by cities in the aggregate and by their systematic interactions, then we might be justified in arguing that the areas that came to be embraced by relatively higher potential values were exposed to an urban life that offered new possibilities for the introduction of more complex economic and social relations.

THE SPATIAL PATTERN OF EUROPEAN URBANIZATION

The last statement must be regarded as tentative, even speculative. But the analysis of Europe's potential surfaces over a period of three centuries also furnishes us with a number of simple, apparently robust generalizations.

(1) The cities of Europe formed a polynuclear urban system in the sixteenth century, but thereafter came to be fashioned into a single-centred system focused on north-western Europe. The decisive period for this transformation was the first half of the seventeenth century.

(2) The zones of high urban potential came to be orientated more and more to the Atlantic and North Sea coasts of Europe; the inland cities of central Europe tended to lose relative standing.

(3) Although political boundaries were not taken into account in this application of the potential model, the results suggest that they would have had to be very potent barriers to communication indeed to alter the persistent isoline patterns that linked the northern French cities to the urban centres of the Low Countries, the cities of Catalonia to France and Italy, and the cities of southern France to northern Italy (until 1800). Related to this centripetal force working with particular vigour on the cities of France is the long-term inability of Paris to become the centre of an urban zone. Its large size notwithstanding, Paris always stood alone as a subsidiary peak in the north-western European zone of intense urban interaction. There is little evidence that a national urban system existed in *ancien régime* France.

THE LONG-TERM DEVELOPMENT OF EUROPE'S URBAN CORE

It remains to consider in more detail the historical development of Europe's urban core. We have seen in chapters 3 and 4 that our image of the process of urbanization is sensitively affected by both the lower threshold employed for the measurement of urban population and the geographical units in which urban growth is charted. When we look at only the largest cities in Europe as a whole, urban growth appears to be rapid and continuous. When we examine each of the sixteen 'territories' separately, we find that all except Belgium made some gain in its level of urbanization, but that nearly everywhere those gains were distinctly concentrated in relatively brief periods: Spain, 1500-1600; the Netherlands, 1550-1650; France and Scandinavia, 1600-1700; Austria, 1650-1750. Only one area stands out as an exception to this pattern of irregularity and discontinuity, experiencing a long-term, gradually accelerating process of urbanization: the British Isles. And only in England did this process exhibit sufficient intensity to elevate its urban percentage to the level of northern Italy and the Low Countries.

It is difficult to resist linking this unique British urbanization process to her equally unique Industrial Revolution, and interpreting it as the opening salvo of the universal urbanization that has spread over the western world since the mid-nineteenth century. Britain's uninterrupted urban growth during the sixteenth, seventeenth and eighteenth centuries must then appear as the bridge between an old and new, a pre-modern and modern world. Yet the preceding analysis of urbanization, based on the potential concept rather than on comparisons of 'national' histories, gives us reason to suspect that this interpretation of Britain's unique urban history is excessively anglocentric and presentist.

Urban growth before the mid-nineteenth century, when viewed with the wide-angled lens of this study, can be divided into two distinct processes. The first, 'basic urbanization', is a general process of city development and urban hierarchy-formation. It is associated with at most a very slow increase in the urban population to a limit of about 7–10 per cent of the total. In the potential maps this process is observed in the enlargement of the area embraced by the middle-value isolines. Thus in large regions of France and Germany, which in 1500 already possessed a full complement of regional urban centres, the growth of the urban percentage was modest, despite the rapid growth of individual cities. In the vast expanses of northern and eastern Europe urban growth was much more rapid. But it began from very low initial levels, so that the net achievement by 1800 was simply to share in the 'basic urbanization' long characteristic of central Europe.

The second urbanization process consisted in the intense growth of a regional cluster of cities creating an 'urban civilization'. This resulted in urbanization levels two to four times the norm of 'basic urbanization' and appears in the potential maps as regional peaks in the pattern of isolines.

We have already identified and discussed these exceptional concentrations of urban life. The Mediterranean lands had developed no less than three such zones by the end of the sixteenth century, but the ensuing crisis brought their further development to a halt. In time they became subordinate to Europe's single urban core. In this sense we can speak of the modern urban system as having its origins in the seventeenth century.

That single urban core has developed over many centuries, and began in the southern Low Countries (Flanders, Brabant and adjacent regions now in northern France). In the early sixteenth century, when this study begins, the urban civilization of Flanders–Brabant was reaching its apogee. It found its origins in the tenth century, and grew rapidly to the fourteenth, whereafter it experienced changes in structure and emphasis associated with the rise of Antwerp. In the centuries covered by this study these cities experience crisis and decline. But it is only superficially similar to the contemporaneous crisis of the Mediterranean cities, for in this case it is directly related to the competition of cities in the adjacent northern Netherlands. Those cities had developed as small textile, fishing and shipping centres in the fourteenth and fifteenth centuries and they grew in association with the dominant cities to the south, but they possessed original characteristics that allowed them to grow rapidly and displace the southern cities in the sixteenth and early seventeenth centuries. In this study we observe only the final, triumphant phase of this process, as the northern Netherlands urban civilization achieves urbanization rates that exceed those of the south. After 1650 this region, too, approaches a ceiling, and this ceiling, too, is related to competition from another incipient urban civilization across the North Sea. England's urban settlements counted for little in 1500. In the sixteenth and seventeenth centuries London's growth and thereafter the rise of the industrial towns and Atlantic ports carried the process of urban growth forward. By 1800 England's

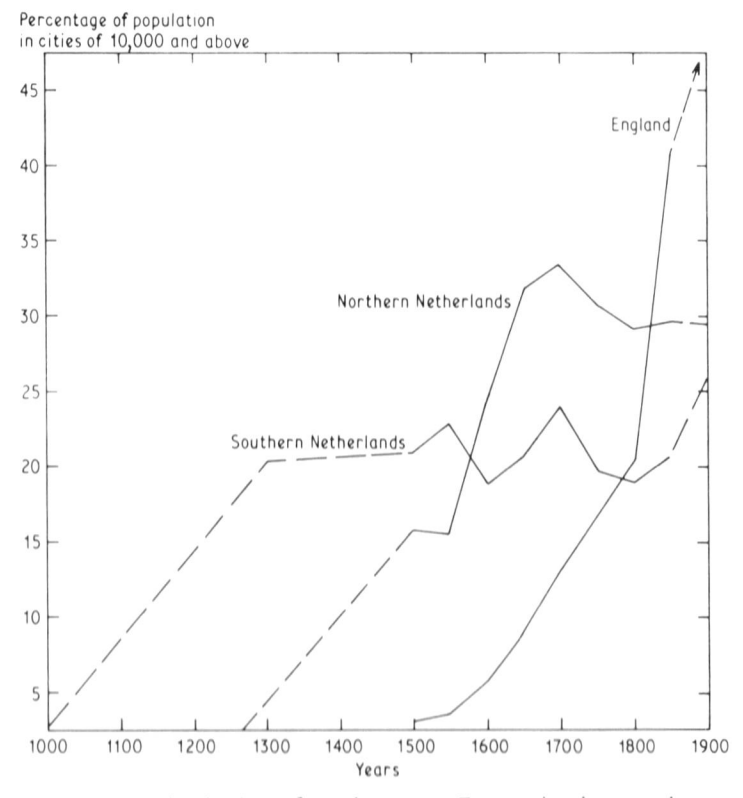

Figure 8.9 The urbanization of north-western Europe in the very long term, 1000–1900

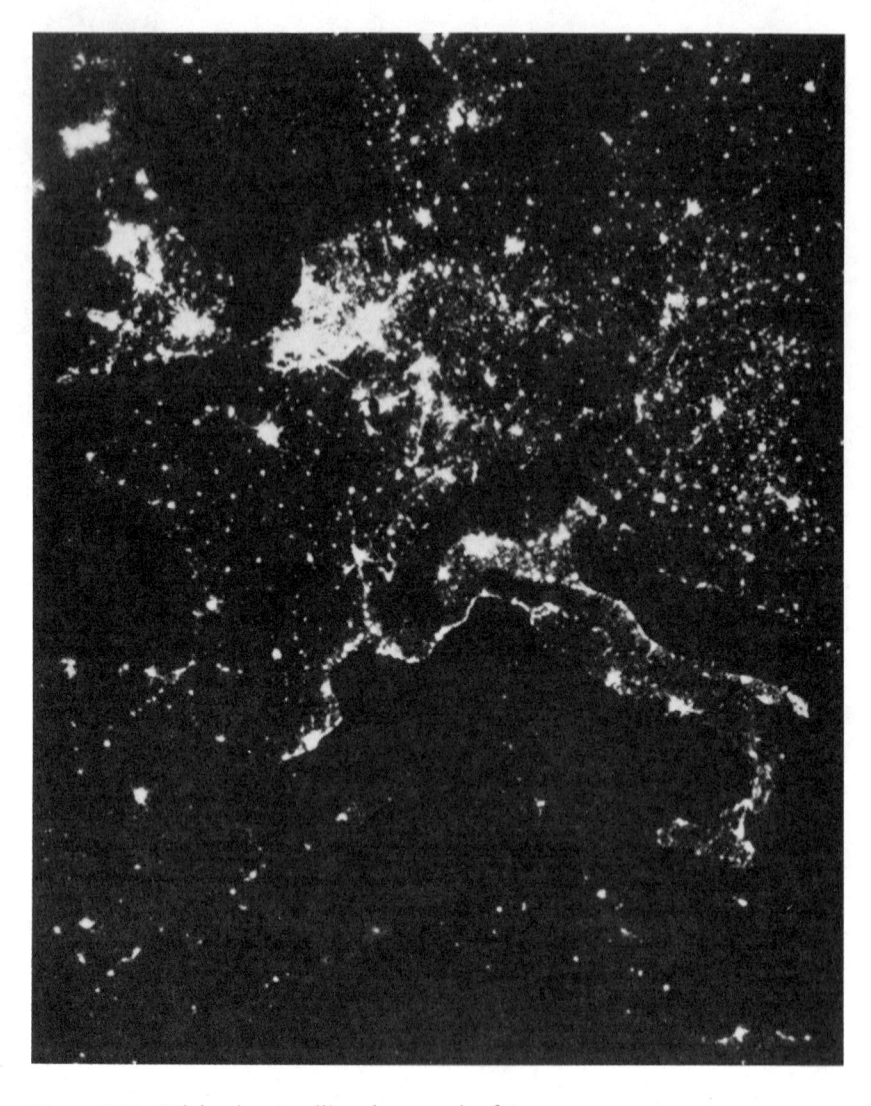

Figure 8.10 Night-time satellite photograph of Europe
Source US Air Force Defense Meteorological Satellite Program, 1977.

THE SPATIAL PATTERN OF EUROPEAN URBANIZATION

levels of urbanization approach those of the Dutch; by 1850 they had become the highest of any European country (see figure 8.9).

England's urban civilization is the only one created within the chronological limits of this study. For this reason England stands out in the statistical material presented in chapters 3 and 4 as unique in its steady process of urban growth. But when viewed in an even longer time perspective, the British 'breakthrough' appears as part of a sequential pattern with origins that reach far into the past. The urban civilization that emerged in Flanders supported itself as head of a northern European commercial system; that of the Dutch Republic built upon this, presiding over a more far-reaching European and colonial system that succeeded in subordinating all rivals; that of Britain took

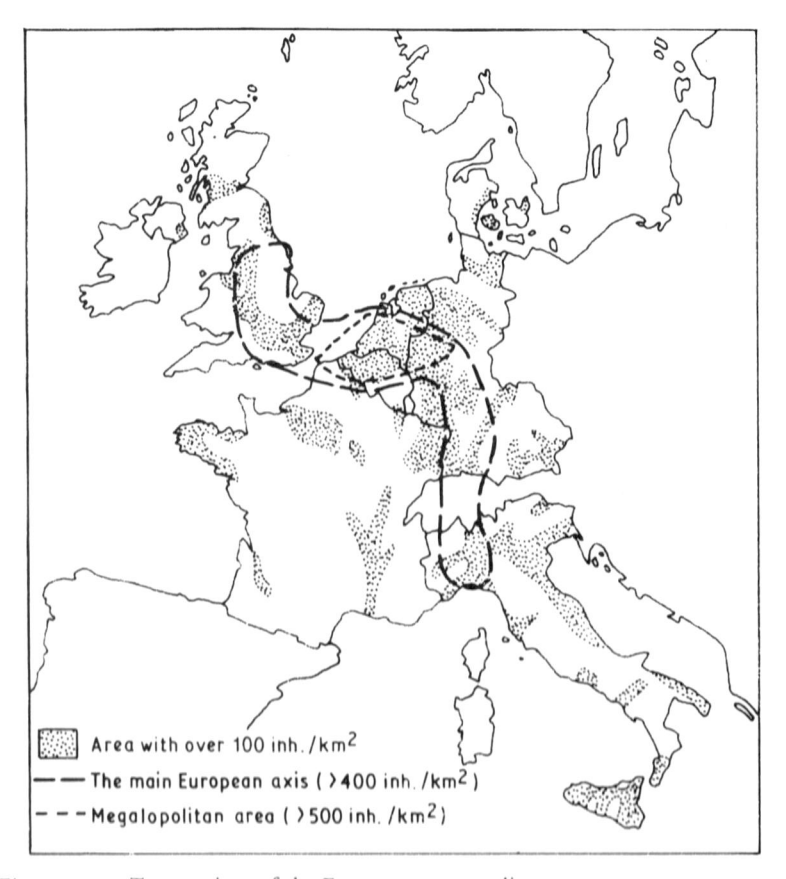

Figure 8.11 Two versions of the European metropolitan core

Source M. C. Deurloo *et al.*, *Zicht op de Nederlandse stad* (Bussem, 1981), 126 (reproduced by courtesy of Unieboek bv).

this over and added the critical dimension of a dynamic Atlantic economy. By 1800 Europe's urban core displayed a more pronounced maritime orientation than ever before, the culmination of a centuries-long process.

The potential map of 1800 can be called a culmination because after 1850 a new phase of urban core development got under way – the rapid growth of German, particularly *Ruhrgebiet*, cities – that reversed the seaward orientation of the previous centuries, shifting the weight of intense urbanization toward the continent for the first time since the sixteenth century.

This process continued well into the twentieth century giving rise to the modern pattern of urban concentration displayed in figure 8.10, a night-time satellite photo of Europe in which industrial and urban areas are indicated by night lighting. The continental reorientation relative to 1800–50 is readily apparent from figure 8.11, in which the 'main European axis' is shown extending from the urban core of 1800 through West Germany, to northern Italy.

The phenomenal growth of this new coal- iron- and railway-based civilization was partially camouflaged by the generalized European-wide urbanization set in motion by Britain's industrial revolution. In this sense the British achievement marked the beginning of a new era. But it was the industrial urbanization of Germany that reversed the long-term Atlantic drift of the urbanization process. In this sense the British achievement marked the culmination of the process that had begun in the sixteenth century.

British urban growth is, thus, by no means without interest and importance. But it is probably more correct to emphasize the continuity between the successive Flemish, Dutch, British and German phases in the development of Europe's urban core than to emphasize the differences. The great discontinuity must be sought in the seventeenth century, when Europe's polynuclear urban system was made to give way to the leadership of one of its centres, that of north-western Europe.

IV
DYNAMICS OF URBAN GROWTH

9
DEMOGRAPHY OF THE EARLY MODERN CITY

THE STATUS OF HISTORICAL URBAN DEMOGRAPHY

Up to now this description and analysis of European urban growth has taken the city as its basic unit of observation. We have enquired into the characteristics of cities – their size, setting and principal functions among others – in order to understand better the patterns of urbanization. This chapter enquires into the sources of urban population change, a subject that requires us to shift our attention from the city to the individual and the family.

The demographic characteristics of urban populations in the early modern period are not well known. In fact, the impressive advances made in historical demography during the last twenty years have only made more acute our sense of ignorance about fertility, mortality and nuptiality among city-dwellers. It is worth pausing for a moment to consider how this has come about.

Family reconstitution, a powerful technique permitting accurate calculation of age-specific vital rates, has greatly deepened our understanding of demographic behaviour among villagers, but the technique is subject to limitations that have kept it from being widely applied to the study of urban populations. The reconstitution of families is time-consuming, a fact that encourages the study of small groups – village populations numbering in the hundreds rather than cities with populations in the thousands. Small communities are also preferred to limit the danger of mistaken identity that is present when documents for separate events are linked together to reconstitute the demographic life of a family. In addition, the technique requires that a substantial percentage of the families in the settlement to be studied do not migrate. Widespread mobility makes impossible the full reconstitution of sufficient families from the data found in parish registers. Since urban people are commonly more mobile than country folk, few urban parish registers – even when they are complete – can satisfy the requirements for the use of the technique. As if this were not enough, there is the further problem of defective data. Urban parish registers vary in quality, of course, but they are generally less adequate than rural registers, particularly for the study of mortality. The author of one of the few detailed studies of urban mortality, Alfred Perrenoud, summarizes the obstacles as follows: defective registration (the product of administrative breakdown in the face of a task that exceeds the capability of the registration system) and inaccurate data that flow from specific urban social phenomena such as the placement of infants with rural wet-nurses (*mise et nourice*), the abandonment of infants and the role of institutional mortality (in hospitals, homes for the aged, orphanages, prisons and garrisons).[1]

Such work as has been done either focuses on a high social class, where genealogies aid in reconstituting patrician families,[2] or consists of partial reconstitutions. These are reconstitutions that do not span more than a single generation – from the marriage of a couple (rather than from their birth) to what is thought to be the birth of the couple's last child. They can provide accurate estimates for only a limited range of vital rates.[3]

A second type of study that has extended our knowledge of past demographic behaviour can be placed under the heading of 'population reconstruction'. Annual or even monthly totals of baptisms, burials and marriages form the basis for this type of study, which is aggregative rather than being based on the study of individual families. The challenge is to relate these known flows of events to the underlying, but unknown, population at risk. Ideally, periodic censuses specifying the age structure, sex composition and marital status of the population provide the needed information. In the absence of censuses, family reconstitution creates a population at risk, the members of the reconstituted families. When reconstitution is not possible, or is impractical, what alternatives remain available? Until recently attempts to link the flows of events to the stock of people have relied on improvised *ad hoc* methods.

This 'naïve' population reconstruction is not without its achievements. A good example is A. M. van der Woude and G. J. Mentink's *De demografische ontwikkeling te Rotterdam*, where the authors succeed in establishing the probable levels and directions of change of the city's population, crude birth- and death-rates, and child mortality.[4] It is indicative of the high effort-to-results ratio typical of such work that the careful and exhaustive demographic analyses of several French urban history monographs (on Nantes, Amiens and Lyons) are generally unable to do more than this.[5] Indeed, most such studies, the painstaking work of collecting and correcting the data notwithstanding, say nothing at all about urban demography. Instead, they *assume* the existence of certain rates in order to infer the size of the total population.[6]

The recent development by Ronald Lee of the technique of 'inverse projection' and the 'aggregative back projection' of E. A. Wrigley and R. S. Schofield permit for the first time a more rigorous estimation of demographic variables from aggregate data *and* at least one comprehensive census of the population.[7] The application of this technique by Wrigley and Schofield in *The Population History of England, 1541–1871: a Reconstruction* represents the most ambitious work of aggregative historical demography yet produced, but this study specifically excludes London. It was the authors' view that the use of London's parish records posed too many problems for the successful application of the technique they pioneered. Apart from their doubts about the quality of London's parish registers, Wrigley and Schofield feared that their technique could not be applied with success to urban data because of the problem of migration. To use aggregative back projection assumptions must be made about the age structure of migration. In a large national population the scope of migration was likely to be sufficiently small that erroneous assumptions would not much damage the final results. In cities, where migration assumed an altogether larger importance, the possibility for error seemed unacceptably large.

In fact, later testing of aggregative back projection on parish register data for the city of Stockholm (where the results can be checked against known population totals) yielded satisfactory results for certain purposes.[8] One can nurture the hope that just as partial family reconstitutions have proved feasible in Geneva and London, so aggregative back projection might be applicable to the parish records of some large cities. But the fact remains that until now most demographic historians have shied away from the study of urban populations. If the technical problems that adhere to the application of the two techniques just discussed are not sufficient to deter the scholar, the sheer size of the undertaking usually is.

The relative impotence of urban historical demography is ironic when one considers that seventeenth- and eighteenth-century demographers, or social arithmeticians, expressed great interest in (or more correctly concern about) the demographic conditions of the cities. Records of baptisms, burials and the causes of death were kept for many places, and these were occasionally supplemented by special-purpose censuses.

The fruit of this early statistical work, supplemented by modern tallies from parish records and fiscal documents, constitutes by far the most common type of contribution to the study of urban demography. The greatest single compendium of such material is Roger Mols's three-volume *Introduction à la démographie historique des villes d'Europe du 14e au 18e siècle*.[9] The data assembled by Mols, which can now be supplemented by many more recent articles, include breakdowns of urban population by age categories and civil status, and they sometimes permit the calculation of the average size of households. However, the coverage of European cities is so patchy and the available observations show such variance that most generalizations about urban population structure must be hedged with qualifiers.

There are two exceptions to this. In two important cases the materials assembled by Mols seem to reveal basic, widely shared urban demographic characteristics. First, the urban sex ratios (the number of males per 100 females) are generally well below 100, and where it is possible to trace the sex ratio of a city over time they exhibit some tendency to decline. As one moves from west to east this rule gradually ceases to hold. In the eighteenth century Berlin had more males than females, the result of the large military presence in the Prussian capital. In Warsaw even the civilian population's sex ratio stood above 100 until the early nineteenth century, while Russian cities were overwhelmingly dominated by males.[10] Rome, as one might expect, was also a notable exception to the rule.[11]

Urban sex ratios below 100, a characteristic that continues to the present day, distinguish European urban life from that of many other world civilizations. Chinese and Indian cities have long attracted many more men than women; the same is true of the recent urban growth of Africa.[12] This characteristic female surplus in European cities has implications for migration patterns, nuptiality (i.e. substantial female celibacy in cities) and, arguably, total fertility.

The second common characteristic of European cities in early modern times was a chronic excess of deaths relative to the number of births. Mols's study provides many pages of baptism to burial ratios for dozens of seventeenth- and eighteenth-century cities. Such data almost always show a burial surplus until some point between 1775 and 1850.[13] Except in the rare cases when these data can be linked to independent information on the size of the urban population, they can say nothing about the *level* of mortality or fertility. Even when the size of the population is known they yield only crude birth- and death-rates, which is a critical limitation given the large amount of variation observable in the age composition and civil status of urban populations. Moreover, the accuracy of these counts of baptisms and burials is open to question. They are commonly uncorrected for omissions, such as births not baptised because of early death or religious scruples, or still births included among the burials. In short, data of this sort are abundant but they usually give no clues as to the underlying factors causing the excess of burials over baptisms. Still, the gap is there, and is often of such a magnitude that adjustments to deal with possible flaws cannot explain it away.

The gap has not gone unnoticed; indeed, the implied inability of cities to sustain themselves by natural generation constitutes what is easily the single most widely noted demographic feature of early modern cities.

THE LAW OF URBAN NATURAL DECREASE AND ITS CRITICS

The book commonly accepted as the first important English treatise on demography, John Graunt's *Natural and Political Observations and Conclusions made upon the Bills of Mortality* (1662) was an analysis of London's demography and particularly of its chronic shortfalls of births and periodic outbursts of appalling mortality. Graunt concluded that London's mortality regularly exceeded that of the countryside, but he also thought that London's fertility levels stood below those found among the more robust and virile rural-dwellers.[14]

A century later Johan Peter Süssmilch, a Lutheran chaplain to the Prussian army, pursued Graunt's interests further by bringing together historical and contemporary data on cities all over Europe.[15] He, too, established that a large excess of deaths constituted the normal state of affairs in Europe's cities. Most important for present purposes, Süssmilch attributed this condition squarely to the unhealthiness of cities, which caused urban death-rates to exceed those found in rural locations. The divine order, he argued, enforced laws of population, one of which was a tendency for mortality to rise with the density of population. Among the evidence which he used to bolster his case was a calculation made by Gregory King, pertaining to England at the end of the seventeenth century, which reckoned that London's crude death-rate was 42 per 1000 inhabitants, while the lesser cities and market towns suffered the lower rate of 33 per 1000, and the villages only 31 per 1000.[16] Süssmilch argued that it was far better that a nation's urban population be spread among many small cities (for which he praised Saxony) than to be concentrated in a Vienna, Berlin or Paris. Indeed, he contended that the demographic impact of such large cities was equivalent to annual outbreaks of bubonic plague.

The succeeding generations have adopted Süssmilch's assessment with remarkably little change. The nineteenth-century British demographer William Farr held, just as Süssmilch, that mortality was density-dependent, although for Farr this was a statistical rather than a divine law.[17] In recent times a prominent exponent among the many scholars who hold these same views is the demographer Kingsley Davis. In 'Cities and mortality' he states that

> until very recently city populations did not reproduce themselves. They depended on migrants from rural villages not only to give them their

growth but even to maintain their population. City mortality was generally so high that the fertility, whatever it was, was insufficient to come even close to providing replacement.[18]

This three-century tradition has culminated in several recent efforts to base explanations of long-term socio-economic change in pre-industrial societies on the consequences of chronic excess urban mortality. E. A. Wrigley, in an influential article, sought to demonstrate that London, because of its combination of rapid growth and excess mortality in the century after 1650, drew to itself such an enormous flow of migrants that stimulating influences of various sorts penetrated into even very distant corners of England.[19] In a study of the Dutch rural economy I applied a version of Wrigley's model to argue that the combined demographic deficits of the numerous Dutch cities laid such a claim on the natural increase of the countryside that population growth eventually became nearly impossible, and challenges to the entrenched economic interests of the stagnant cities became less likely.[20]

This venerable orthodoxy of urban natural decrease, given perhaps an excess of attention as the 'only child' of historical urban demography, is vulnerable to criticism. As we have seen the evidence in its support is abundant in quantity but unimpressive in quality. When in 1955 Roger Mols assembled and discussed a great mass of crude birth- and death-rates, baptism–burial ratios and the like, it could fairly be said that more was known about historical urban demography than about rural demography. But since then the family reconstitution technique being developed as Mols's book was published and the recently developed breakthrough in aggregative population reconstruction have enormously enlarged our knowledge of historical rural demography while, as we have noted, their application to urban settings has been beset by nettlesome obstacles.

Modern historical demography is capable of measuring detailed vital rates – age specific and, sometimes, social-class specific. Moreover the numerous village studies completed in the past twenty-five years of continuing research have uncovered an unanticipated variability – it is hard to resist adding a dismaying variability – in demographic behaviour among villages and over time.[21] From this perspective most of the literature on historical urban demography is technically unimpressive and its chief finding of urban natural decrease is based on wholly inadequate foundations: without knowledge of nuptiality behaviour and age-specific fertility and mortality rates the observation that deaths exceeded births in a city cannot be convincingly interpreted.

Allan Sharlin issued the first challenge to the orthodox position in a short, bold article in which he asserted that early modern European 'cities would not have declined in population without immigration'.[22] He did not deny the reality of the numerous baptism and burial tallies that registered excess deaths, and hence he did not deny that rural–urban migration took the dimensions claimed in studies such as Wrigley's on London. Instead, Sharlin argued that city populations could generally be divided into two groups: permanent residents and temporary migrants.

> For the former, births exceeded deaths, at least at a modest level, while the reverse was true of the latter. The permanent residents, consisting of natives and some migrants, lived out their lives in the city – married, had children and died – and enjoyed some measure of natural increase. The temporary migrants who came to the cities, on the other hand, were preponderantly artisan journeymen and servants, and people of that status could seldom marry by the standards of early modern society. Given the high mortality conditions of the times, they contributed their due share of deaths to the vital registers of the cities, but as illegitimate fertility was substantially lower than legitimate, deaths outnumbered births by a very large amount.[23]

In other words, the so-frequently observed excess of deaths relative to the number of births occurred *because* of migration rather than the other way around. This was so, argues Sharlin, because of specific social institutions and customs governing the lives of servants, apprentices and journeymen and controlling access to the rights of urban citizenship in European cities before the nineteenth century.

Sharlin's message is clear: if the detailed vital rates now known for scores of villages were available for a number of large cities they would not show 'a radical discrepancy in mortality conditions, but differences in the proportions married', with the consequence that the total number of births would be lower than in a rural population where most women of child-bearing years married.

Another way of understanding Sharlin's model of urban migration is to consider an American retirement community such as St Petersburg, Florida. The excess of deaths over births recorded there is not a reflection of the city's unhealthiness, for the demographic characteristics of the permanent residents is normal. It is the migrants to the city – in this case the old-age pensioners – who create the statistical illusion of a city unable to reproduce itself. This is so because (1) their own births are, of course, registered elsewhere, (2) they give birth to no children in St Petersburg (in this case because their children were born elsewhere), but (3) they do die in St Petersburg. Sharlin's 'temporary migrants' have a demographic effect similar to Florida's pensioners: they typically migrate to the cities in their teens and 20s, but social controls prevent them from marrying there, and although many expect their urban stay to be temporary, substantial numbers of them die there.

Sharlin finds support for this model of urban migration in data for Frankfurt-on-Main which show that from 1650 to 1800 burgers usually registered an excess of births while non-burgers (by his own admission 'an inexact surrogate for temporary migrants')[24] registered shortfalls of births so large that the city as a whole consistently experienced natural decrease.

The second voice to be raised in criticism of the conventional urban natural decrease position is that of the Dutch economic and demographic historian A. M. van der Woude. While Sharlin seeks an improved explanation for an admitted excess of deaths in the early modern city, van der Woude is not convinced that this excess of deaths is such a constant and universal characteristic as is often maintained.[25] That is, he attacks the 'law' of urban natural decrease, whether divine or otherwise.

His argument is based on the observation that in most European cities the surplus of deaths gives way to a modest surplus of births during the first half of the nineteenth century. Van der Woude argues that since the circumstances of urban life (with respect to housing, sanitary provisions, medical knowledge and provision, scope of population concentration and demographic structure) had not improved substantially from those prevailing in the previous century, a substantial rise in urban fertility must explain the change. This, at any rate, is what occurred in the cities of the Netherlands and 'that which occurred in the first half of the nineteenth century was in principle also possible before the mid-seventeenth century'.[26] Van der Woude agrees that excess mortality was the rule in the Netherlands (and in Europe) from the mid-seventeenth century to the end of the eighteenth century, but he rejects the proposition that this reflected a law of urban natural decrease.

Like Sharlin, van der Woude directs our attention to the birth-rate, but while Sharlin argues that social institutions caused urban birth-rates to be systematically lower than rural ones, van der Woude reasons that birth-rates could vary, and that if they changed enough around 1800 to end a period of urban natural decrease, they could just as well have changed earlier to bring that period on. In short, van der Woude seeks to integrate historical urban demography with the long-term 'secular trends' of economic and demographic behaviour that are now widely used as a framework for the analysis of rural history.[27] On the strength of this rural model he hypothesizes that sixteenth-century urban fertility stood at a sufficiently high level to allow cities to contribute in some measure to their own growth.[28]

ASSESSMENT

Both Sharlin and van der Woude affirm that urban demography must be studied in its historical context: for Sharlin that context is the sociology of the early modern city, for van der Woude it is the secular trend of economic life that affects city and countryside alike. Their scepticism of a dogma whose inadequate demonstration scholars have sought to repair chiefly by frequent repetition is certainly warranted. But while scepticism is effective in exposing the scope of our ignorance, it does not constitute a basis for a new understanding of pre-industrial demography. The real service of the two critics is their insistence that the demography of the pre-industrial city be studied as an historical process rather than reduced to a mechanistic 'law' based on assumed 'natural' conditions. This requires that the historical process be specified and its operation demonstrated. Their efforts along these lines will now be considered in more detail.

Sharlin advances a model based on the internal social structure of the city which generates nuptiality behaviour (with its implications for total fertility) specific to the two groups into which urban populations can be divided: the permanent residents and the temporary migrants. His supporting evidence for this model is drawn from one city, Frankfurt. Obviously there is a need for more evidence to permit the testing of Sharlin's urban migration model.

In his recent study of Madrid's role in the economic development of Spain, David Ringrose offers an interesting portrait of the Castilian capital's demographic structure that appears to offer support for Sharlin's views.[29] Ringrose also divides the population of his city into two distinct groups. Independently of Sharlin he comes to the conclusion that in Madrid there coexisted a stable inner core of nobles, merchants, government officials and artisans and a fluctuating envelope of immigrants and transients employed in domestic service and unskilled labour. The core consists of permanent resident families enjoying the stable economic benefits that flowed from long-distance trade and the imperial government. The envelope consists of a more marginal population dependent on Castile's unstable regional economy that supplied Madrid with foodstuffs and raw materials. These people suffered from both poverty and insecurity, which combined to make their life chances decidedly unfavourable. Although the envelope could expand and contract according to the fortunes of Madrid's economy, Ringrose believes this dual structure characterized the city from at least the seventeenth until the mid-nineteenth century.

Ringrose is unable to establish the mortality and fertility rates of the two groups. He can show, for 1787, that in parishes with high concentrations of immigrants the proportion of females who were married was marginally lower than in parishes dominated by permanent residents. This suggests that total fertility among immigrants was a bit lower than among native-born *Madrilenos*, and Ringrose believes that the migrants experienced higher mortality rates. The relative importance of these determinants of the rate of natural increase remains an open question, but it is clear that the core population was in a better position to reproduce itself than was the envelope.

So far Madrid seems to conform in a general way to Sharlin's expectations. But on further inspection Ringrose's evidence and analysis offer less support than first appears to be the case. The Madrid case study can, in fact, help illustrate two major problems with Sharlin's proposed model.

The 'law' of urban natural decrease had treated the urban population as a single unit. Sharlin and Ringrose both recognize structural divisions: each identifies a relatively prosperous, economically secure group that can reproduce itself. But are they not simply observing the nearly universal tendency for higher socio-economic groups to secure for themselves higher life expectancies than their economically less fortunate brethren? Both Roger Finlay's partial family reconstitutions for London in the period 1580–1650 and Alfred Perrenoud's more comprehensive efforts for Geneva in the seventeenth and eighteenth centuries report enormous differences in the infant and child mortality of rich and poor.[30] In Geneva during the period 1650–84, life expectancy at birth, a comprehensive measure of mortality, stood at 26.5 years for the families of Geneva-born women and only 22.7 for the families of immigrant women. Almost all of that difference could be attributed to the relatively greater weight of the working class in the immigrant population. Life expectancy at birth among the working class – irrespective of their place of origin – stood at 20.5 years, while for the 'middle class' it was 26.0 years, and among the upper class 36.8 years.

This pattern of life expectancy had a direct effect on the ability of these segments of the population to reproduce themselves. The net reproduction rate for Geneva-born women in 1650–84 stood just below unity, while among immigrant women it was a desperately low 0.6. But, once again, it was the class composition of these two groups, and not 'immigrant status', that accounted for the bulk of the difference. The upper class could easily reproduce itself (NRR = 1.2), the middle-class net reproduction rate hovered around unity, and the working-class rate stood at 0.6. The low net reproduction rate of the immigrant group was chiefly a consequence of the fact that over 70 per cent of that population was working class while hardly any were upper class; among Geneva-born women less than 40 per cent were working class while about 20 per cent were upper class, by Perrenoud's definitions.

The ability of the urban well-to-do to reproduce themselves is, by itself, not incompatible with chronic urban natural decrease. On the contrary, it is just the sort of more nuanced account that one should expect from the application of a more exacting methodology to the study of urban populations. Urban communities, far more than rural communities, are composed of differentiated socio-economic groups which can be expected to exhibit distinct demographic patterns. The demographic characteristics of an urban population should always be regarded as the composition of the behaviour of the several socio-economic groups that make up that population.[31]

The differences observed between permanent and temporary, or core and envelope populations are of little analytical value if they simply reflect differences commonly found between rich and poor. To save the urban migration model it must be shown that these social categories have a real existence and that certain structural features of urban society cause them to persist. Of course, this is exactly what Sharlin's analysis proposes: there exists a group, temporary migrants, which faces social institutions and conventions inhibiting its merger via marriage into the permanent population. As a consequence it experiences low nuptiality and all that flows therefrom.

The distinctiveness of the two coexisting city populations specified by Sharlin is obviously a matter of degree, as he states.[32] But the more that immigrants are able to marry, the less the urban fertility rates will be lower than those of the countryside and the less useful is Sharlin's model. The question before us is, then, whether such structural groups (as distinct from ubiquitous socio-economic differences) are a common feature of the early modern city.

Ringrose, an historian, develops the concept of core and envelope populations to explain conditions specific to Madrid, not to identify a structure common to pre-industrial urban life in general. Indeed, he argues that other cities lacked such pronounced dichotomies in their social structures. Barcelona, for example, possessed a more diversified economy than did imperial Madrid and as a consequence it provided more opportunities for immigrants to achieve economic stability and to form families.[33]

Beside cities such as Frankfurt, where, Sharlin argues, immigrants filled jobs as servants and apprentices that were incompatible with married status, and Madrid, where the economic instability of the 'envelope economy' undermined family life, were there cities where immigrants were likely to settle, marry and become integrated into the urban community – indeed where the continuation of the community depended on it?

In those cities whose marriage registers record the birthplaces of brides and grooms, historians regularly find that non-natives account for about half of all those marrying. In Lyons, 48 per cent of the grooms and 40 per cent of the brides marrying in 1728–30 had been born elsewhere. In Grenoble in 1780 the comparable figures were 63 per cent for grooms and 54 per cent for brides. In the German industrial town of Barmen in 1815 the non-native-born accounted for 64 per cent of the grooms and 54 per cent of the brides. In Amsterdam, where 650,000 men and women married between 1601 and 1800, less than half, 48 per cent, had been born there. In the first half of the seventeenth century, when Amsterdam grew vigorously, two-thirds of the brides and grooms were not natives of the city. But in the eighteenth century, when the city's population fluctuated around a stable average level, immigrants continued to account for nearly half of all marriage partners.[34] This information is evocative of a city in which immigrants do not remain excluded from the demographic life of the city. But by itself it is not sufficient to establish firmly what it evokes. Since the data refer only to those who marry, we know nothing about the number of immigrants who did not. This is a serious limitation, but if it can be shown that the migrants were not constrained to marry only other migrants, but had substantial access to natives as marriage partners, the hypothesis that pre-industrial urban society was typically more 'open' than Sharlin supposed will gain in plausibility.

We will consider first intermarriage of natives and migrants in Amsterdam. A sample of marriage bans assembled by Herman Diederiks for the years 1801 and 1806 (when the decaying urban economy of the city was of diminishing attractiveness to immigrants) allows us to examine the functioning of the Amsterdam marriage market by constructing a cross-tabulation of brides and grooms by their place of birth.[35] The sample consists of 655 marriages in which both partners were marrying for the first time. Their birthplaces are presented in table 9.1 in a cross-tabulation. In each cell two numbers are presented: the observed number of marriages between partners from the specified locations (o = observed) and the number that *would have* occurred if place of birth had been a factor of no relevance in the choice of a marriage partner (e = expected). Thus, the cell for Amsterdam grooms marrying brides from the western provinces of the Netherlands informs us that twenty-six such couples are found in the sample while, given the number of Amsterdam men and provincial women looking for spouses,[36] a 'blindfolded pairing' of couples would have yielded thirty with those places of origin.

The data so arranged allow us to note several interesting features of the Amsterdam marriage market that speak to the issue of how insulated natives and migrants were from each other. Amsterdam-born men of marriageable age were scarce (the city's overall sex ratio was 80). They enjoyed considerable choice of brides and manifested a distinct preference for Amsterdam-born women: 80 per cent married such women. At the other end of the marriage market hierarchy were German-born women. They were scarce in relation to the number of German-born men. This plus their probable isolation as servants, Lutherans and German-speakers caused them to be married to German men at three times the 'expected' rate. Only 21 per cent of them married Amsterdam-born men.

Between these two exclusivist groups we find a very different pattern. Intermarriage among people of different places of origin was widespread, in the sense of not being wildly at variance with the pattern that random pairing would have generated. The key to this open marriage market was the Amsterdam-born woman. We have already noted that her male counterpart was relatively scarce.[37] Out of necessity many women had to find marriage

Table 9.1(a) Cross-tabulation of Amsterdam brides and grooms by place of birth, 1801, 1806

	Grooms born in									Total brides
	Amsterdam		Western Netherlands*		Germany		Other			
	o	e	o	e	o	e	o	e		
Brides born in Amsterdam	314	275	36	43	55	84	60	63		465
Western Netherlands	26	30	11	6	9	9	5	7		51
Germany	11	31	5	6	30	10	7	7		53
Other	36	51	9	7	25	16	16	12		86
Total grooms	387		61		119		88			655

Note
The data in the table refer *only* to marriages in which *both* the bride and groom are marrying for the first time. When marriages to widows and widowers are included, the number of first-marrying brides in the sample rises to 779 (16 per cent of brides married widowers) and the number of first-marrying grooms rises to 734 (11 per cent of grooms married widows).
* Western Netherlands includes Holland and Utrecht.

o = observed cases
e = expected cases if place of birth had no influence on the choice of partner

Source Data from Herman A. Diederiks, *Een stad in verval. Amsterdam omstreeks 1800* (Amsterdam, 1982), 77–83.

Table 9.1(b) Partner-choice among Amsterdam-born brides and grooms, 1601–1800

Brides Between 1601 and 1800, 184,947 Amsterdam-born women married for the first time in Amsterdam. Migrants from the places listed supplied *husbands* as follows:

Place of birth	Number marrying in Amsterdam	Marrying Amsterdam-born women — Number	Marrying Amsterdam-born women — %	Expected* % marrying Amsterdam-born women	Difference between observed and expected %
Holland cities	16,282	9,535	58.6	50.7	+7.9
Groningen–Friesland cities	5,303	2,508	47.3	50.7	−3.4
Overijssel–Gelderland cities	11,908	4,918	41.3	50.7	−9.4
Hamburg–Bremen–Lübeck	6,555	2,665	40.7	50.7	−10.0
Niedersachsen	21,755	8,049	37.0	50.7	−13.7

Grooms Between 1601 and 1800, 127,609 Amsterdam-born men married for the first time in Amsterdam. Migrants from the places listed supplied *wives* as follows:

Place of birth	Number marrying in Amsterdam	Marrying Amsterdam-born men — Number	Marrying Amsterdam-born men — %	Expected* % marrying Amsterdam-born men	Difference between observed and expected %
Holland cities	15,007	5,323	35.5	49.3	−13.8
Groningen–Friesland cities	5,050	1,422	28.2	49.3	−21.1
Overijssel–Gelderland cities	16,093	3,770	23.4	49.3	−25.9
Hamburg–Bremen–Lübeck	4,141	638	15.4	49.3	−33.9
Niedersachsen	15,148	2,424	16.0	49.3	−33.3

* Expected means the number that would arise, on average, if place of birth were of no relevance to partner choice.

Source Data drawn from Simon Hart, *Geschrift en getal* (Dordrecht, 1976), 180–1.

partners among immigrant men (and widowers). Thus we find Amsterdam brides marrying provincial grooms in numbers consistent with expectations, marrying German grooms somewhat less readily, and taking satisfaction with immigrant widowers in large numbers. Marriages between first marrying brides/grooms and widowers/widows are not included in table 9.1, but the Diederiks sample includes them: besides the 655 women marrying new grooms, 124 married widowers. In contrast, the 655 men marrying new brides were supplemented by only 79 who married widows. Three-quarters of this difference was accounted for by the excess of Amsterdam-born women marrying widowers – many from Germany – over Amsterdam-born men marrying widows.

Altogether, 37 per cent of Amsterdam-born brides in the 1801–6 sample entered into their first marriages with migrants to the city. Among *all* first marriages contracted in 1796 the comparable percentage was 38. In that year 38 per cent of all marriages united two Amsterdam-born persons, in 29 per cent both partners came from elsewhere, and in 33 per cent an Amsterdammer married a migrant. In 70 per cent of those cases, the Amsterdammer was a woman.[38]

Diederiks's sample of partner choice in Amsterdam is comprehensive but focuses only on two years; a second study by Simon Hart is selective in that it focuses on the marriage partners of migrants from a limited number of places, but it does so for all such migrants to Amsterdam throughout the seventeenth and eighteenth centuries. Table 9.1b shows a pattern of integration of migrants with native-born Amsterdammers that generally confirms the 1801–6 findings: female migrants to Amsterdam found little favour among Amsterdam-born men, who expressed a pronounced distaste for foreign women. With male migrants the situation was different. The more distant from Amsterdam their place of birth, the less likely they were to find an Amsterdam-born wife, but even foreign men married Amsterdam women at rates approaching those that one would expect to find if the spouse's place of birth was a matter of no importance.

These data allow us to say nothing directly about the number of migrants who were prevented from marrying at all, but the evidence reviewed here is not consistent with the view that integration into the established community via marriage was an unattainable achievement for migrants. German migrants faced tangible barriers, but certainly the men among them (and two German men married for every German woman) enjoyed substantial access to Dutch and Amsterdam-born partners. Indeed, the city's demographic survival required male migrants.

Migrants figured rather less prominently in the marriage market of seventeenth- and eighteenth-century Geneva: they comprised 40 per cent of all grooms and 36 per cent of brides in a sample of 12 per cent of all marriages concluded between 1625 and 1810 drawn by Perrenoud. In Geneva the number of native-born men and women was roughly in balance, so that over 70 per cent of Geneva-born brides and grooms married Geneva-born spouses. Consequently, while only 38 per cent of Amsterdam marriages united two natives to the city in 1796, 46 per cent of the marriages concluded in Geneva did so. But in both cities about one-third of the marriages united a migrant and a native. Perrenoud was also able to calculate the celibacy rates for Genevan and immigrant women: between 1625 and 1810 they were almost always *lower* among immigrants (who stayed on to die in Geneva after the age of 50) than among Geneva-born women.

In the rapidly growing German industrial city of Barmen native-born brides and grooms were greatly outnumbered by those born elsewhere. But the native-born did not bias their partner-choice towards each other. The pattern of partner choice replicated almost exactly the results to be expected from a 'blindfolded pairing' of the prospective brides and grooms.

Partner choice can also be investigated in the German city of Würzburg, but here our source is a census of all residents – regardless of where they married – rather than only the marriages contracted within the city. The entrance of those immigrant couples who had married elsewhere plus the departures from the city of couples who had married there is readily apparent in the pattern that emerges from the analysis of the Würzburg census of 1701. Only 16 per cent of married couples present that year consisted of native-born spouses, while 35 per cent consisted of partners both of whom had been born elsewhere. What is more remarkable – signifying substantial integration of migrants and natives in the city – is the 44 per cent of all couples where one of the partners is a native and the other is a migrant. Just as in Amsterdam, two of every three such unions brought together a native-born bride and a migrant groom. The small inland city of Würzburg shared with the large port of Amsterdam a distinct shortage of native-born grooms.

A second dimension of marriage market behaviour that addresses the issue of dualism in the urban population is the age at which brides and grooms marry. In an analysis of all Amsterdam brides and grooms marrying for the first time in 1796, Diederiks uncovered a pattern (displayed in table 9.3) that was the same for both men and women: life-long Amsterdammers found each other soonest, while natives marrying outsiders married a bit later. Immigrants married substantially later, but here, once again, the immigrant marrying a city-born partner married younger than one marrying another immigrant. The same general pattern obtained among merchant seamen marrying in Amsterdam in 1676–7. Simon Hart's study of this important segment of the city's population found the average age at first marriage among Amsterdam-born seamen to be 27.7 years, that of seamen from elsewhere in the republic 28.2, and seamen from abroad 29.0 years. In

Table 9.2 Partner-choice characteristics in four cities

	Geneva 1625–1811	Amsterdam 1796	Barmen 1815	Würzburg* 1701
Both born in city (%)	47	38	16	16
Native bride–migrant groom	16 ⎱ 30	23 ⎱ 33	30 ⎱ 50	30 ⎱ 44
Native groom–migrant bride	14 ⎰	10 ⎰	20 ⎰	14 ⎰
Both migrants	22	29	34	39
% of native grooms marrying native brides	77	79	45	54
% of native brides marrying native grooms	74	62	35	35
% of migrant grooms marrying native brides	42	44	47	43
% of migrant brides marrying native grooms	39	25	37	27
Number of marriages	3385	1428	192	1885

* All examples except Würzburg refer to marriages contracted within the city in a given year or period. The Würzburg evidence refers to the birthplaces of all married couples *present* in the city in 1701.

Sources Geneva: Alfred Perrenoud, 'Croissance ou déclin? Les mécanismes du non-renouvellement des populations urbaines', *Histoire économie et société* 4 (1982), 585; *Amsterdam:* Herman A. Diederiks, *Een stad in verval. Amsterdam omstreeks 1800* (Amsterdam, 1982), 92; *Barmen:* Wolfgang Köllmann, *Bevölkerung in der industriellen Revolution* (Göttingen, 1974), 192–3; *Würzburg:* Stadtarchiv, Volkzählung von 1701.

Table 9.3 Age at first marriage in Amsterdam for native-born and migrant brides and grooms, 1796

	Brides		Grooms	
	Age	Number	Age	Number
Average for all	26.1	1428	28.3	1428
Amsterdam-born				
spouse Amsterdam-born	24.5	538	26.0	538
spouse migrant	25.6	329	27.6	143
Migrant				
spouse Amsterdam-born	26.6	143	29.7	329
spouse migrant	28.4	418	30.5	418

Source Herman A. Diederiks, *Een stad in verval. Amsterdam omstreeks 1800* (Amsterdam, 1982), 92.

Geneva the average age at first marriage in every period between 1625 and 1772 was some 4.5 years older for immigrant women than for native-born women.[39]

This progression of marriage ages may reflect the age at which migrants entered the city, about which nothing is known,[40] and the extra search-time needed by newcomers to find a partner may also have played a role. But it may also reflect the existence of differences in the size of obstacles that stand in the way of establishing the economic basis for marriage. If the economic opportunities available to native Amsterdammers were superior to those available to migrants, the natives could marry earlier. A migrant seeking to speed the process of acquiring a stable economic position would then do well to marry a native; those migrants unable to do so would have to wait longer. Indeed, Diederiks presents evidence that Germans, who were less likely than Dutch migrants to marry native Amsterdammers, married later than any other group.[41]

This nuptiality behaviour is potentially of great importance. If the relationship of migration distance to marriage age is more generally observable, it raises yet another question about the representativeness of family reconstitution studies that exclude migrants, and it raises the possibility that variation in the frequency and range of migration in a society can systematically affect nuptiality – and hence total fertility.

It is here that we return to the possible importance of the Amsterdam evidence to Sharlin's hypothesis. The shorter span of fertile years that immigrant couples in Amsterdam lived in the married state would have had the result, *ceteris paribus*, that fewer children would have been born to them than to Amsterdam-born couples.[42] Sharlin had argued that the social system characteristic of the pre-industrial European city prevented marriage. Via nuptiality, total urban fertility was unusually low. The information surveyed here cannot test this hypothesis directly, but it strongly suggests that migrants, while not a structurally separate group inhibited from marrying, did marry later than town natives. It lends plausibility to the hypothesis that in places receiving many migrants from far away, average completed family size would be lower than otherwise.

But how much lower? Is, as Sharlin asserts, nuptiality and fertility behaviour the key to understanding pre-industrial urban demography, or is it a minor feature in comparison to urban mortality and the distinctive age structure of urban population?

In the case of Amsterdam the baptism and burial data available for the eighteenth century can assist us, although it must be emphasized that they are not without their weaknesses. They show a persistent baptism–burial gap amounting to a total of 100,000 excess burials in the course of the eighteenth century.[43] Censuses held in 1795 and periodically thereafter permit us to observe that crude death-rates then hovered near 40 per 1000 while crude birth-rates fluctuated in the low-30s per 1000.[44] Assuming a Christian population of about 200,000 throughout that century, the long-term rate of natural decrease must have been about 5 per 1000. But which of the vital rates, fertility or mortality, can be held 'responsible' for this?

In 1811 it is possible to compare crude birth- and death-rates for Amsterdam and the rest of the then Kingdom of Holland. This imperfect evidence, displayed in table 9.4, clearly identifies mortality as the culprit: the more urban the region the higher the mortality. On the other hand, crude birth-rates are, if anything, higher in the urbanized areas than in the more rural provinces. The second panel of table 9.4 allows us to say a bit more about mortality. The Christian population of Amsterdam was 11.6 per cent of the population of the Kingdom of Holland, but accounted for some 15 per cent of the recorded deaths. Moreover, there is little in the patterns of death by age to suggest that the high mortality was a consequence of an enormous influx of migrants who did not marry and thereby reduced urban fertility. The bulge in deaths of persons in their 30s and 40s is easily accounted for by an annual net immigration of the 1464 persons representing the difference between baptisms and burials in the period. When this is done the pattern of deaths is compatible with a desperately low life expectancy at birth of about 26 years whose major determinant is very high infant and child mortality.[45] The calculations being reported here are hypothetical in that they depend on certain assumptions about the number of migrants and their ages. But the assumptions would need to be very far from the mark for the results to be overturned.

Another, more comprehensive, indicator of the extraordinary level of mortality in a large city was assembled for London by Wrigley and Schofield in their *Population History of England*. Table 9.5 expresses the totals of births and deaths recorded in London as percentages of all English births and deaths. These percentages can then be compared to London's population as a percentage of the total population of England. In every twenty-five-year period from 1550 to 1824 the percentage of baptisms celebrated in London follows faithfully the percentage of the English population resident in London. Burials, on the other hand, occurred in London at a rate out of all proportion to the population of the metropolis. Column 6 shows that London burials exceeded baptisms by at least 35–40 per cent in every period.

This evidence is by no means sufficient to reject Sharlin's hypothesis. It is theoretically possible that the age distribution and celibacy rates of London were always such as to generate this 'mirage' of excessive mortality. But the assumptions would have to be extreme ones: in order for London's population to generate so many deaths at normal mortality rates, its age structure would have to be biased to very old ages.

More precise statements can be made on the basis of Perrenoud's study of Genevan urban demography. In 1687–1704 (to take but one of the several periods for which he presents data) the net reproduction rate for the city as a

Table 9.4 Amsterdam demographic characteristics compared to those of the 'Kingdom of Holland'

(a) Regional birth- and death-rates, 1811

	Crude birth-rate	Crude death-rate	Natural rate of increase	% urban
Amsterdam	33.6*	45.4	−11.8	100
North Holland, Utrecht	33.7	35.8	−2.1	} 63
South Holland	34.1	34.2	−0.1	
Friesland	30.1	24.7	+5.4	} 27
Groningen, Drenthe	31.8	26.5	+5.3	
Kingdom of Holland	32.9	30.9	+2.0	

(b) Deaths by age

Age categories	Kingdom of Holland, 1811	Amsterdam Christian population 1777–97	Amsterdam as % of Kingdom
0	12,420	1,880	15.1
1	2,924	610	20.9
2–9	6,452	996	15.4
10–19	2,324	294	12.7
20–29	3,538	473	13.4
30–39	3,817	609	16.0
40–49	4,275	696	16.3
50–59	4,493	687	15.3
60–69	5,320	733	13.8
70–79	5,214	611	11.7
80–89	2,235	270	12.1
90–99	302	40	13.6
100	7	2	
Total	53,321	7,871	14.8
Population ('000s)	1,725	c. 200	11.6

* The Amsterdam crude birth-rate is calculated for 1812.

Sources F. J. B. d'Alphonse, *Aperçu la Hollande* (1811), reprinted in Bureau voor der Statistiek, *Bijdragen tot de Statistiek van Nederland*, no. 1 (The Hague, 1900), 553; for Amsterdam, Herman A. Diederiks, *Een stad in verval* (Amsterdam, 1982), 19, 60; for Amsterdam burials, *Nieuwe Nederlandsche Jaarboeken* (1778–98).

whole was 0.83, insufficient for reproduction. This was the product of a net reproduction rate for Geneva-born women close to unity (0.94) and a very low 0.66 for immigrant women. Was fertility or mortality chiefly responsible for this low net reproduction rate? Immigrant women did not remain unmarried more frequently than native women, but they did marry later (30.2 years versus 26.3 for Genevoise) and had smaller completed families. In the longer period 1625–1727 Geneva-born women in Perrenoud's sample had on average 7.7 children while immigrant women had an average of 6.0. Just as immigrant fertility was lower, so was immigrant mortality higher. Life expectancy at birth was 28.9 years for the children of immigrants and 31.4 years for those of Genevan women. But in every case the dominant factor accounting for these differences in mortality, nuptiality and fertility was the class composition of the immigrant and native populations. Once one controls for the larger weight of the lower class among the immigrants the bulk of the difference is accounted for. And then the severe mortality experienced by the lower class stands out as the single most important factor in depressing the Genevan net reproduction rate below the replacement level.[46]

We turn now to the critique of van der Woude. To the extent that he is advancing hypothetical historical possibilities, they cannot be refuted. However, it is possible to scrutinize his attempt to illustrate the way in which urban natural increase may have occurred in earlier centuries in Amsterdam,

Table 9.5 London demographic characteristics compared to those of England, 1550–1824

Period	Population ('000s) England	Population ('000s) London	London as % of England	London baptisms as % of England	London burials as % of England
1550–74	3011	80	2.7	2.8	5.1
1575–99 } 1600–24 }	4110	200	4.9	4.2 / 6.3	6.8 / 8.7
1625–49 } 1650–74 }	5228	400	7.7	7.7 / 8.5	11.5 / 14.6
1675–99 } 1700–24 }	5058	575	11.4	10.3 / 12.3	15.0 / 16.9
1725–49 } 1750–74 }	5772	675	11.7	11.5 / 10.1	17.2 / 15.7
1775–99 } 1800–24 }	8664	865	10.0	9.8 / 9.7	13.8 / 13.1

Source E. A. Wrigley and R. S. Schofield, *The Population History of England, 1541–1871: a Reconstruction* (London, 1981), table 6.4 and A3.1.

a city whose rate of natural decrease in the period 1650–1800 was substantial. Van der Woude's argument is based on changes in the sex ratio of first marriages in the city. In the first half of the seventeenth century only 95 brides married for the first time for every 100 first-marrying grooms. From 1676 to 1800 there were always 104–108 such brides for every 100 grooms.[47] Obviously the *total* ratio of brides to grooms was always 100. When the number of women marrying for the first time was less than the number of men, as before 1650, it implied that the city attracted many more men seeking brides than the available supply of not-yet-married women could accommodate. Many of those men married widows. When the ratio exceeded 100, from 1676 on, the opposite was true: eligible bachelors were relatively scarce, forcing many women to marry widowers. With this measure of relative scarcity in the urban marriage market, van der Woude goes on to reason that before 1650 most urban women must have married, and married relatively young. As the city ceased to grow, and the changing economic structure began to attract more women migrants than men, the marriage age rose and spinsterhood became more common as women found it increasingly difficult to find husbands. On this basis, van der Woude argues that Amsterdam before 1650 had a surplus of men eager to marry, a large number of children and a relatively young age structure. The crude birth-rate must have been higher before the mid-seventeenth century than was thereafter the case, and it might well have been sufficiently high to generate some measure of natural increase.[48]

The hypothesized high pre-1650 crude birth-rate has two causes: a higher total fertility (the result of more nearly universal marriage of women) and a large number of people of child-bearing age (the result of large-scale migration to the city). Only the first of those factors speaks directly to the traditional expectation that urban populations could not replace themselves. In periods of intense in-migration, the urban marriage market may be such that celibacy is rare and marriage age young. The second factor does not damage the orthodox position. *Age-specific* mortality and fertility rates could have remained constant, always insufficient for a *stable* population to reproduce itself, while changes in age structure brought about by the volume of migration could alter the crude rates as van der Woude hypothesizes. His argument can explain an *episode* of urban natural increase, but the episode would last only so long as massive in-migration lasted, inflating the number of households of child-bearing age. Such an event is not inconsistent with a correctly formulated statement of the urban natural decrease hypothesis.

It is interesting to note that rural–urban migration is central to the analyses of both van der Woude and Sharlin. For the former it permits births to exceed deaths while for the latter it has the opposite effect. The reason for the difference is that van der Woude assumes that most in-migrants marry and raise families while Sharlin assumes that most must remain single. The data available to assess these positions are still very limited. But those presented here cast doubt on the postulated existence of a large, distinct class of temporary migrants who were barred from marrying. More plausible is the suggestion that total urban fertility may have varied over time because of changes in the sex-composition and total volume of rural–urban migration. It is, however, by no means clear that this argument can contribute to a dethronement of mortality as the chief determinant of urban natural decrease.

THE REPRODUCTIVE VALUE OF URBAN MIGRANTS

Once it is accepted that migration to the cities was substantial, and that a substantial portion of such migrants married and raised families (i.e. when the extreme form of Sharlin's position is rejected), then a full account of the urban population's ability to reproduce itself must not stop simply with arguments about celibacy and age at first marriage.

The character of historical urban fertility can best be studied in the context of a model that makes use of the concept of 'reproductive value'. Reproductive value is a measure of the contribution that a female makes to the ultimate population.[49] Its calculation requires the assumption of constant age-specific rates of fertility and mortality ('stable population' assumptions). In the application proposed here, it must also be assumed that these constant rates apply equally to native-born and immigrant residents of a city. Then, the reproductive value of a woman at age x (V_x) is the number of children expected to be born to that woman given a life table (age-specific mortality schedule) and age-specific fertility rates. Reproductive value is akin to the net reproduction rate, but while the latter expresses the expected contribution of a new-born girl to the size of the next generation, V_x does so for women at any age x. The reproductive value of a new-born infant is set at 1 ($V_x = 1; x = 0$). The reproductive value at any other age is thus expressed in relation to that at birth. Such a form measures the 'relative contribution of each age to the ultimate trajectory of the population' so long as it retains its age-specific rates of births and deaths.[50] The reproductive value for most populations starts at unity for age 0 and rises to a peak at the onset of child-bearing. It then falls gradually, reaching zero when the child-bearing years are past.

This knowledge can assist us in assessing the overall impact of migration on the reproduction of an urban population. The reproductive value of migrants will ordinarily exceed that of children just born for the simple reason that 'when a birth is added to the population, the child has a chance of growing up and becoming a parent in about 20 years; when a migrant aged 20 enters he or she can become a parent immediately'.[51] To actually measure that impact one must know the age distribution of migration to the city as well as the age-specific birth- and death-rates required to calculate V_x. Keyfitz and Philipov, using data from the contemporary developing countries of India, Sri Lanka and Mexico, reckoned the reproductive value of the average migrant (V_x weighted by the age distribution of migrants) to exceed that of a just-born child by some 20 per cent. Under the very much higher infant mortality and later onset of child-bearing characteristic of pre-industrial Europe, the difference would surely be even greater.

Other things remaining equal, the rate of natural increase in places experiencing immigration of people of child-bearing years should be substantially higher than in places that are not – let alone places experiencing out-migration. If this is true, the issue before historical urban demography can be formulated as follows: under what conditions would this expectation be confounded?

For instance, Sharlin's belief that many 'temporary migrants' did not marry would have the effect of reducing their reproductive value. However, if the weighted average of migrants' reproductive value stood at 1.2, such celibacy among migrants would have to exceed that of permanent residents by over 20 per cent in order to bring the migrants' contribution to population growth below that of the permanent residents. The argument that urban fertility was depressed by the effects of migration on marriage age (suggested by the Amsterdam data) or by the sex-composition of migration (suggested by van der Woude) must now take into account the compensating effects of migration on age distribution before concluding that total fertility was lower in cities than elsewhere.

The value of this formal approach lies in its potential for quantifying the size of the phenomenon needed to reject the orthodox position that the chief factor preventing urban populations from reproducing themselves was extraordinary mortality. I am sceptical that the effects suggested by the critics reviewed here can prove sufficient to overturn the orthodox position, but until historical urban demography has at its disposal a number of age-specific vital rates separately calculated by social class and place of birth the questions raised by these critics will remain unanswered. All of this notwithstanding, and however these questions ultimately are answered, Sharlin and van der Woude must be credited with exposing the inadequate foundations on which the conventional wisdom rests, and pointing the way to forms of interpretation that are based on history and demography rather than on dogma.

10
MIGRATION AND URBAN GROWTH

THE LINCHPIN OF THE URBAN ECONOMY

Historical urban demography places a great deal of emphasis on migration. Indeed, it sometimes appears that historians pause to examine urban fertility and mortality only long enough to satisfy themselves and their readers that the demographic phenomenon of real importance – the one worthy of serious study – is migration. It is worth pausing for a moment to consider the implications of this for pre-industrial urbanization.

Wrigley and Schofield, in their extraordinary study of English population history, concluded that the key variable in the regulation of total population before the late-nineteenth-century demographic revolution was nuptiality.[1] Among the triptych of vital events – births, deaths and marriages – marriage is the pre-eminently *social phenomenon*. As a consequence, they were able to develop a model of pre-industrial English society in which demographic and economic forces were mediated through the institution of marriage. In their view conscious social acts affecting the decision to marry and the age at marriage regulated the pace of population growth in response to economic conditions.[2] In short, the English exercised a substantial element of control over their numbers.

Migration is also undisputably a social phenomenon. When we identify it as the key regulator of city populations, it follows that any model of the urban sector's role in the pre-industrial economy must place migration in the role of mediator of economic and demographic forces. That is, the growth or decline of cities cannot be ascribed to the effects of mortality, a force that might be relatively autonomous *vis-à-vis* economic variables. Nor is urban growth generated internally out of natural increase. On the contrary, city populations rose or fell *despite* the behaviour of these vital rates, and this was possible because of the enormous impact of migration. It is through migration flows that the cities adjusted their labour forces to the economic possibilities, and that the cities' social and cultural influences could be diffused through overwhelmingly rural societies.

This emphasis on migration is not directly questioned by the critics of the urban natural decrease model. Sharlin and van der Woude challenge conventional views about the functional roles of migration in the internal demography of the cities, but they do not question conventional views about the scope of rural–urban migration flows. Sharlin acknowledges this in so many words;[3] van der Woude argues only that urban natural increase was likely (in the sixteenth century) in those cities that were recipients of massive inmigration.

The importance of migration to the study of urban growth is undisputed – although the specific demographic role of the migrant is now an object of discussion. Cities before the nineteenth century did not exhibit autonomous and self-reinforcing growth processes of the sort that now frighten the observers of the massive and burgeoning cities of Asia, Africa and Latin America.[4] Then, a city's ability to expand its population depended on the extent to which its economic conditions permitted it to hold its existing residents and attract inmigrants from competing cities and the countryside.[5] If this reasoning is correct, migration flows among the cities and between urban and rural sectors were the linchpin of the urban economy and, together with nuptiality behaviour, the key social decisions that governed population size.

ESTIMATING NET URBAN MIGRATION

Study of urban migration is severely hampered by source limitations that make the calculation of total migration flows an unattainable goal. Unlike fertility, mortality and marriages, the incidence of which is governed by well-known regularities and for which comprehensive records are, in principle, available, migration is a more unruly phenomenon which no single historical or contemporary source records in a comprehensive fashion. For example, town archives might possess lists of new (adult male) citizens or new guild apprentices, the marriage records might record the birthplace of brides and grooms, and urban church records might list new and departed members. Each of these sources is highly selective by age, sex and occupation. Each captures only a certain type of migrant. But even if all were available for a single city they would expose only a portion of the total immigration population – and, what is worse, a portion whose relationship to the total is unknown.[6]

Perhaps for this reason demographic historians have relied upon hypothetical calculations of the *net* flows of migration, using for this purpose simple models relating urban natural increase or decrease, total population change, and the age distribution of migrants. One begins with the fundamental identity $r = (b - d) + (i - o)$, where r, the change of population, is equal to births (b) minus deaths (d) plus inmigrants (i) minus outmigrants (o). If r is known and $b - d$ (the natural increase) is known or assumed, then $i - o$ (*net* migration) can be calculated. The first and most well-known of these calculations is E. A. Wrigley's 'Simple model of London's importance in changing English society and economy, 1650–1750'.[7] He begins by noting the growth of the city over the course of the century (275,000 or an average of 2750 per year). Then, on the basis of information provided by the bills of mortality, he sets the rate of natural decrease to be 10 per 1000. The average annual net migration can then easily be reckoned to be about 8000. Wrigley goes on to assume that the average age of these migrants was probably around 20. This means that the migrants can be regarded as the survivors of a birth cohort half again as large (given the mortality conditions of that time). This permits him to calculate that the survivors to adulthood of 29,000 annual births (17,000 in London, 12,000 in the rest of England), or one-sixth of all English births, were destined to die in London.

I made similar calculations of the net migration to the cluster of large cities of central Holland (the modern 'Randstad Holland') in the period 1650–1800, where it appeared that the number of migrants needed just to prevent the region's urban population from falling required that the rural population produce a yearly excess of births over deaths representing a rate of natural increase of 7 per 1000 inhabitants, the survivors of which would have to migrate to the cities.[8] Since such a rate of natural increase was rarely attained, let alone surpassed in pre-industrial times, the urbanized provinces of the Netherlands found themselves in a position that all but excluded rural growth.

The estimation of net migration to London or the cities of Randstad Holland is of obvious interest, given the enormous size of these urban concentrations. But we must not forget that those cities stood at the head of urban networks all of whose cities participated in a complex process of human movement. Ravenstein's second law of migration emphasizes its step-wise character, by which rural-dwellers move to a metropolis only after intermediate periods of residence in smaller cities closer to home.[9] His formulations are based on nineteenth-century experience, but the brief, cabined glimpses of migration flows permitted to us by early modern documents are not inconsistent with them.[10]

If migration fields overlap and link rural areas with small cities and both of these with larger cities in complex channels of movement, it makes sense to estimate net rural to urban migration for nations or large regions as a whole rather than to focus only on the attraction of migrants to individual cities.

Table 10.1 displays my attempt to capture the broad trends of net rural to urban migration in northern Europe from 1500 to 1890. It is based on the urban and total population data assembled in chapter 3. The calculations based on these data all proceed from assumptions that it is hoped capture the basic conditions of early modern demography and society. The resulting estimates of net migration flows and of their relationships to the rural population can pretend to nothing more than the identification of plausible orders of magnitude and directions of change. The suggested trends and turning-points are probably more to be trusted than the absolute levels.

The assumptions on which table 10.1 rests can be summarized as follows:

(1) Cities of at least 10,000 inhabitants are assumed to suffer an average net natural decrease of 5 per 1000 throughout the period 1500–1890. Alternative assumptions applied to particular periods are identified in the table.

(2) Births and deaths in cities of 5000–10,000 inhabitants are assumed to just suffice to generate the observed growth of such cities, i.e. they are neither net sources nor recipients of migrants. In this model the entire net migration to the cities of 10,000 and over comes from the population resident in places of under 5000 inhabitants.

(3) The rate of natural increase of this rural population is that implied by the observed growth of rural population plus the calculated net outmigration in each fifty-year period.

(4) The rural births 'earmarked' for urban migration shown in line 7 are estimates of the number of rural births necessary to allow the net migration estimates of line 6, under the assumption that the average age of migration is 20, and that rural infant and child mortality is such that of 1000 births some 667 can be expected to survive to the age of 20. In the late nineteenth century the mortality assumption differs: in period 8 (1850–90), 800 of every 1000 births survives to age 20.

(5) The estimates of annual rural births in line 10 are based on the simple assumption that the crude birth-rate (CBR) is 35 per 1000, reduced to 28 per 1000 in the period 1850–90.

Consider now the estimates presented in column 3, for the period 1600–50. The net growth of population resident in cities of at least 10,000 inabitants is 854,000 (line 1). The net additions of cities with this minimum size was six, which means that a portion of the increase is a transfer of urban population resident in those seven cities in 1600. Throughout I assume that each such city brought 7000 already existing urban residents with it (line 2).

Table 10.1 A model of net rural–urban migration: northern Europe, 1500–1890 ('000s, except where noted)

Line		1 1500–50	2 1550–1600	3 1600–50	4 1650–1700	5 1700–50	6 1750–1800	7 1800–50	8 1850–90
1	Total growth of urban population	446	741	854	1,066	966	2,408	13,499	33,444
2	Transfer population	77	175	42	196	189	595	2,352	5,033
3	Net growth of urban population	369	566	812	870	807	1,813	11,147	28,411
4	Net growth per year	7.4	11.3	16.2	17.4	16.1	36.3	222.9	710.3
5	Birth deficit per year	9.7	12.6	16.5	21.2	26.3	34.9	74.5	191.9
6	Total net migration	17.1	23.9	32.7	38.6	42.4	71.2	297.4	902.1
7	Rural births 'earmarked' for urban migration	25.7	35.9	49.1	57.9	63.6	106.8	446.1	1,353.3
8	Total population (in millions)	46.8	53.0	55.4	56.8	63.2	79.6	113.6	155.3
9	Rural population (in millions)	43.1	48.7	50.4	51.0	56.2	70.3	104.3	109.0
10	Annual rural births (CBR = 35)	1,509	1,705	1,764	1,785	1,967	2,461	3,650	3,820
11	% of rural births destined for urban migration	1.7	2.1	2.8	3.2	3.2	4.3	12.2	35.5
12	Rural increase + migration (in millions)	7.30	5.96	0.17	4.59	9.86	24.02	41.02	51.21
13	Estimated rural natural rate of increase (%)	0.34	0.24	0.01	0.18	0.34	0.67	0.83	1.00
14	Annual average birth surplus	146.0	119.2	3.4	91.8	197.2	480.4	820.4	1,024.2
15	% of rural surplus destined for migration	17.6	30.2	(49.1/3.4)	63.1	32.3	22.2	54.4	132.1
16	% to migrate under altered assumption				79.0[1]			44.8[2]	85.3[3]

[1] Urban NRI = −1.0. This causes the annual birth deficit to rise to 42,400, raising the rural increase + migration to 5.65 million and the rural NRI to 0.21 per cent.
[2] Urban NRI = 0. Annual birth deficit falls to 0.
[3] Urban NRI = 0; survivors to age 20 assumed to be 800 per 1000 births.

These must be subtracted (line 3). The total urban population growth in the period is thus 812,000, or an average of 16,200 per year (line 4).

The annual urban deficit, 16,500, is produced by multiplying the total urban population midway between 1600 and 1650 by −0.5 per cent, the rate of natural decrease (line 5);[11] 16,500 migrants to replenish the urban population plus 16,200 to achieve the observed urban growth equals an average net migration to the cities of 32,700 (line 6). This flow of migrants, under the assumptions about average age at migration and rural mortality stated above, requires half again as many rural births, or 49,100 (line 7).

The total population of northern Europe midway between 1600 and 1650 can be set at 55.4 million and the rural population (resident in places of under 5000 inhabitants) at 50.4 million (lines 8 and 9). A crude birth-rate of 35 per 1000 population among the rural population yields an average annual flow of 1,764,000 births (line 10). The survivors of 2.8 per cent of each birth cohort would eventually migrate to the cities, never to return (line 11). Of course, many more might migrate temporarily, but this model is not designed to capture such migration flows.

Line 12 displays the net growth of the rural population over the fifty-year period *plus* the total number of out-migrants (line 6 × 50). An approximation of the rate of natural increase of the rural population (line 13) is based on this figure. The period 1600–50 differs from the others in that the rural population actually declines by over 1.4 million. However, once the net migration to the cities of 1.6 million (32,700 × 50) is added, the rural natural increase is found to be (just barely) positive at the rate of 0.01 per cent per annum.

The annual number of rural births in excess of replacement needs (i.e. that could be earmarked for emigration without causing rural depopulation) is displayed in line 14. In 1600–50 that number is miniscule. Finally in line 15, the number of rural births earmarked for migration to the cities (line 7) is expressed as a percentage of the total number of 'surplus' births (line 14). This serves as an indicator of the urban sector's share of the total number of rural births in excess of replacement needs. In 1600–50 this calculation far exceeds 100 per cent; an annual rural natural increase of 3400 was swamped by a yearly outflow representing the survivors of 49,100 births. Migration was then the proximate cause of rural population decline.

The calculations for each of the seven other periods can be read and interpreted in the same way as for 1600–50.

The calculations of table 10.1 demonstrate that in northern Europe as a whole net rural–urban migration involved few country-dwellers, despite steady, gradual growth, until the nineteenth century. This reflects the simple fact that the urban population remained quite small relative to the rural population through the seventeenth and eighteenth centuries. Of all those born in the countryside, 3–4 per cent moved permanently to the cities, i.e. died there. Many others, of course, were temporary migrants, working as servants, labourers or apprentices before returning to a rural location.

These figures are net in two other senses. They are based on the net growth of the cities, and do not take into account the fact that the growing cities increased their numbers by more, thus compensating for the declining cities. Unless the outmigrants from declining cities all moved to the growing cities, we have underestimated total rural–urban migration. In addition, the calculations are based on the net population changes over fifty-year periods. This understates the migration flows in cases where a city's population rises to a peak before the end date and falls back to a lower figure.

Jean-Claude Perrot's masterful study of Caen illustrates this problem nicely.[12] Caen's population rose by 3000 between 1753 and 1795. In this period the parish records record 47,000 baptisms and slightly fewer deaths. Thus Caen was able to reproduce itself and even contribute to its modest growth. Net annual average migration to Caen could not have exceeded a handful of people. But Perrot has more detailed information at his disposal showing that the city grew from 32,000 in 1753 to 41,000 in 1775, whereafter it fell to 38,000 at the outbreak of the French Revolution and further to 35,000 in 1795. Table 10.2 shows that the net migration in the twenty-one years after 1753 was no less than 7332, or 350 per year. Thereafter, the net flow was out of Caen. Perrot was also able to identify the number of residents born elsewhere at the census dates and on this basis he could estimate the apparent 'gross permanent' migration for each interval. Since inmigrants comprised 25 per cent of Caen's population in 1789, after the city had lost 3000 inhabitants in the previous fourteen years, it was clear that all immigration had not ceased. That decline had to be the net result of a large immigration outweighed by a slightly larger outmigration. (Excluded from these

Table 10.2 Migration and natural increase in Caen, 1753–95

	1753–74	1775–89	1790–5
1 Net change in population	+8,858	−3,063	−2,799
2 Natural increase	+1,526	−430	+1,211
3 Net migration (1−2)	+7,332	−2,633	−4,010
4 Immigrants as % of total population at end date	21.7	25.0	5.8
5 Apparent emigration (6−3)	1,532	12,582	6,039
6 'Gross permanent' migration (end pop. × 4)	8,864	9,949	2,029

Source Jean-Claude Perrot, *Genèse d'une ville moderne. Caen au XVIIIe siècle* (Paris, 1975), vol. II, 165.

numbers are those who entered Caen only to leave again before 1789. In this sense we have 'gross permanent' rather than true gross migration.) All in all, Caen, whose net inmigration in 1753–93 amounted to no more than a few hundred people, experienced a 'gross permanent' immigration of 20,842 and an emigration of 20,153.

Clearly, when we say that 3 per cent of rural births were destined for permanent urban migration, this number probably should be doubled or tripled to represent those who spent some substantial amount of time in the city but did not die there. If this is so, 6–10 per cent of rural youngsters eventually got a taste of city life in seventeenth-century northern Europe. Of course, these percentages could vary enormously by region, a matter to be discussed in more detail below.

The above calculations and speculations say something about the limited but certainly non-trivial social and cultural influence that cities in northern Europe could exert on the countryside via migration. If, say, 8 per cent of a rural population cohort moves to a sizeable city for at least a few years, most rural-dwellers will be likely to have some personal contact with a compatriot living in, or having lived in, a city. Most, but certainly not all. And the more regionally uneven the density of migration, the more peasant societies will have differed with regard to their familiarity with urban life.

Another approach to assessing the demographic impact of rural–urban migration focuses on its relationship to the natural increase of, rather than the size of, the rural population. Here I make the simple assumption that the pool of rural-dwellers eligible for migration is normally some proportion – perhaps all – of the surplus, that is, survivors to the age of independence in excess of rural society's replacement needs. The economic as opposed to the cultural role of migration is emphasized when we ask what proportion of this migration-eligible rural population moved permanently to the cities?

In the sixteenth century the cities of northern Europe attracted few migrants relative to the size of the rural 'surplus'. The movement to the cities measured in these terms gathered momentum later in the century and reached a peak in the following century. In the first half of the seventeenth century the model shows rural–urban migration contributing to the absolute decline of the rural population; later in the seventeenth century the cities continued to take the bulk of the rural surplus. The frequent outbreaks of plague in the third quarter of the seventeenth century, then almost always urban phenomena, might possibly justify altering the model's assumption that the rate of natural decrease was 0.5 per cent. If it reached 1.0 per cent in 1650–1700, the flow of migrants to the cities would have absorbed nearly 80 per cent of the rural surplus.

In the eighteenth century the portion of the rural surplus attracted to the cities fell off dramatically, reaching a low point in the second half of the century. Many cities grew rapidly after 1750; indeed, the era is often treated as the beginning of modern urbanization. But the high and rising rate of natural increase of the rural population (line 13) was such that the cities actually attracted the smallest share of the rural surplus since the early sixteenth century. Even in the first half of the nineteenth century, as cities grew at rates unprecedented in European experience, their claim on the rural population was less compelling than it had been in the seventeenth century.

In the nineteenth century most cities had ceased to experience negative rates of natural increase. Many contributed, at least in a modest way, to their own growth so that the assumptions on which line 5 is based are clearly invalid. The obviously impossible estimate of rural–urban migration for the period 1850–90 (line 15) is testimony to the fact that other assumptions are needed. The altered assumptions (that the natural rate of increase = 0 and that the survivors to age 20 per 1000 births = 800) produce lower urban shares of rural surplus (line 16), but even these probably overestimate somewhat net rural–urban migration.

These estimates represent averages for northern Europe as a whole. Since this vast territory certainly did not constitute a single migration field – that is, Irishmen were unlikely to migrate to Vienna and Swedes rarely moved to Bordeaux – the nature of rural–urban migration surely varied greatly from region to region. But, by basing the calculations of table 10.1 on a very large territory including many lightly urbanized regions, the basic finding that seventeenth-century urban growth siphoned off nearly all the rural surplus is all the more remarkable.

When the same sort of analysis is applied to the Mediterranean region very different patterns emerge (see table 10.3). The high overall level of urbanization in Iberia and Italy has the expected consequence of requiring the survivors of some 5 per cent of the rural births to migrate to the cities, a figure which is no higher in 1800 than in 1500. In the sixteenth century this outflow represented two-thirds of the rural surplus, but after the urban crisis of the first half of the seventeenth century the outflow settled down to about one-third of the rural births in excess of replacement requirements.

According to the model the Mediterranean area's rural population fell substantially in the first half of the seventeenth century. This fall would have been worse were it not that the cities suddenly ceased to attract migrants in these decades. This is difficult to accept, since we know from other evidence that the cities of the Mediterranean lands did not lose their 428,000 inhabitants to outmigration but to a frightful plague-inflicted mortality, which reached such levels that a massive migration from country to city could do nothing more than limit the absolute decline of the urban population.

This is not the scenario presented by the model so long as we adhere to the

Table 10.3 A model of net rural–urban migration: Mediterranean Europe, 1500–1800 ('000s, except where noted)

Line		1 1500–50	2 1550–1600	3 1600–50	4 1650–1700	5 1700–50	6 1750–1800
1	Total growth of urban population	529	765	−582	193	483	878
2	Transfer population	84	168	−154	−7	112	133
3	Net growth of urban population	445	597	−428	200	377	745
4	Net growth per year	8.9	11.9	−8.6	4.0	7.4	14.9
5	Birth deficit per year	10.1	13.3	13.7	12.8	14.5	17.9
6	Total net migration	19.0	25.2	5.1	16.8	21.9	32.8
7	Rural births 'earmarked' for urban migration	28.5	37.8	7.7	25.2	32.9	49.2
8	Total population (in millions)	19.2	21.2	21.0	21.2	24.7	28.9
9	Rural population (in millions)	16.4	17.8	17.5	17.9	21.0	24.4
10	Annual rural births (CBR = 35)	574	623	613	627	735	854
11	% of rural births destined for urban migration	5.0	6.1	1.3	4.0	4.5	5.8
12	Rural increase + migration (in millions)	2.15	2.76	−1.85	3.84	4.20	5.44
13	Estimated rural natural rate of increase	0.27	0.31	−0.21	0.42	0.39	0.43
14	Annual average birth surplus	43.0	55.2	−37.0	76.8	84.0	108.8
15	% of rural surplus destined for urban migration	66.3	68.5	(5.1/−37.0)	32.8	39.2	45.2
16	% to migrate under altered assumption			(46.4/4.4)*			

* Urban NRI = −2.0 per cent in 1600–50. This causes the annual birth deficit to rise to 55,000, raising the rural increase + migration to 0.22 million and the rural NRI to +0.02.

original assumptions. From table 10.3 it appears that net migration in the period 1600–50 fell to almost nothing (5100 per year) while the rural rate of natural increase turned fiercely negative. But there is reason to reconsider the assumption that the urban rate of natural increase was −0.5 per cent per annum in these eventful decades. The plagues of 1596–1602 and 1647–52 in Spain, and in 1630 and 1649 in Italy, brought death to hundreds of thousands. Half a million (urban- *and* rural-dwellers) died in each of the Spanish disasters.[13]

In these decades the urban rate of natural increase was far worse than the postulated −0.5 per cent. If we set it at −2.0 per cent, the annual migration to the cities reaches more than twice the level of the sixteenth century and comfortably accounts for the entire *observed* decline of the rural population. In other words, if the urban mortality assumption is revised in this way, the rural population musters a small positive rate of natural increase, but is drawn down by a massive migration to the cities.

It is instructive to compare the experience of northern and Mediterranean Europe in this crucial period. The calculations of the model reveal the rural rate of natural increase in both north and south to have stood close to zero. In both areas rural decline occurred because of migration to the cities, but in much of northern Europe this flow of countryfolk was attracted by new opportunities in vigorously growing cities while in the Mediterranean lands it was attracted by the vacant positions available in plague-devastated cities.

The estimates displayed in tables 10.1 and 10.3 are based on assumptions that might be substantially in error, and which obviously cannot capture important short-run changes in urban demography. It would be foolish to attempt subtle adjustments to such rough-and-ready calculations. Yet there is one important type of rural–urban migration missed entirely by this model that ought to be discussed. The migration estimates are related directly to the level of excess mortality observed in the cities. We have already noted that temporary migrants – those who return to a rural location before their death – cannot be estimated. A second important unobserved migration stream is those who enter a city and die abroad or at sea in the service of the merchant marine, a trading company or the navy. Their deaths are not ordinarily recorded in a town's parish register, yet they are arguably part of the urban economy and society. This phenomenon is restricted to port cities, and its importance surely varied enormously from country to country. No comprehensive data stand at our disposal, but two recent studies provide intriguing glimpses into the phenomenon.

A systematic analysis of the records of all the sailings to and from Asia, carried out by the Dutch East India Company (VOC) from its founding in 1602 until its demise in 1795, provides us with data on the number of men who set sail for Asia and the number returning. In addition, the company's muster rolls provide information about the places of origin of these employees. J. R. Bruijn and others at Leiden University who have prepared and analysed this mass of documentation present us with a striking finding: over the two-century existence of the VOC nearly 1 million men embarked from Dutch ports and of this number nearly 700,000 died before returning, either at sea or, more commonly, while stationed on Java or at some other colonial post.[14] For two centuries an annual average of some 3500 men, mainly young men, died abroad. The number of casualties was actually substantially higher in the eighteenth century than in the seventeenth. These records say nothing of course about mortality among the men serving in the Dutch West India Company, the navy, the private merchant marine, and in whaling and fishing. It must not be expected that these other groups experienced sea-borne or overseas mortality at anything approaching the macabre levels observed among the servants of the VOC. Their periods of duty abroad were much shorter and they did not often face the hazards of tropical diseases. But in the eighteenth century, when the number of VOC servants reached a peak, there were always many more men employed in the other seafaring branches.[15] By their sheer numbers, they must have added several hundreds of overseas deaths per year to the figures presented in table 10.4 of the average annual deaths of VOC personnel.

If all these unfortunate seamen had migrated from rural areas to Amsterdam, Rotterdam and other VOC ports, they would have to be added to the migration streams estimated earlier in table 10.1. In fact many of these seamen were natives of the Dutch cities.[16] This implies that each year the deaths of many hundreds of urban residents occurred overseas and went unrecorded *in patria*. Now, in terms of the urban migration model discussed above, the places of these city-born sailors who died abroad were taken by migrants to the cities who did not sign up with the VOC. Their deaths are 'mistaken' for the deaths of the native-born men who actually disappeared across the seas. Thus the entire number of VOC deaths can be added to the permanent rural–urban migration streams estimated in table 10.1.

In the first half of the eighteenth century the migrants who met their death in the service of the VOC alone are equal in number to one-tenth of all net rural–urban migration in northern Europe. In the province of Holland, van der Woude reckons that, on average, some 20 per cent of every eighteenth-century cohort of 20-year-old males met their death overseas while in the service of the VOC.[17]

Some surviving scraps of data from Amsterdam, by far the largest recruitment centre of the VOC, can help illustrate the process at work. In the 1730s the Amsterdam parish registers record an annual average of 6800 baptisms. This is certainly an underestimate of the true number; in any event Jewish births are not included. About 3500 of these recorded births were boys while

Table 10.4 Annual losses abroad in the service of the Dutch East India Company

Period	Average losses per year	From the Dutch Republic %	Number	Of these, from Holland %	Number	Of these, from 19 cities %	Number
1602–20	1140						
1620s	1840						
1630s	2050						
1640s	2570						
1650s	2780						
1660s	2380						
1670s	3090						
1680s	2400						
1690s	2610						
1700s	2830	76	2150	75	1613	88	1419
1710s	3560	76	2700	77	2100	88	1850
1720s	3630	73	2650	73	1935	90	1741
1730s	4220	61	2575	73	1880	88	1654
1740s	5240	59	3100	74	2294	87	1996
1750s	5190	50	2600	71	1846	88	1624
1760s	5970	56	3350	65	2178	87	1894
1770s	4970	47	2350	66	1551	87	1349
1780s	4630	54	2500	69	1725	88	1518
1790–95	3083	48	1500	64	960	87	835
Average deaths per annum 1700–95	4384		2591		1857		1619
Deaths per 1000 of the population in 1795			1.2		2.4		3.4

Note
The average annual losses equals the number of persons departing from the Republic minus the number departing from Asia or the Cape, reduced by 6 per cent to represent losses on the return voyage. The number of deaths of Dutchmen, Hollanders and urban Hollanders is assumed to be proportional to their numbers among the employees.

Source J. R. Bruijn, 'De personeelsbehoefte van de VOC overzee en aan boord, bezien in Aziatisch en Nederlands perspectief', *Bijdragen en Mededelingen betreffende de geschiedenis der Nederlanden* 91 (1976), 220–3.

3300 were girls. The city's marriage records show that twenty-five years after these births occurred, in the period 1756–65, an annual average of 1100 Amsterdam-born men and 1410 Amsterdam-born women were married.[18]

Nearly 45 per cent of women born in the city survived and stayed on to marry in the city of their birth. Given the city's high infant and child mortality,[19] the likelihood of some out-migration and of some celibacy, one could hardly expect the percentage to have been higher. In contrast, only 30 per cent of Amsterdam-born men married in the city. Infant and child mortality may well have been higher for boys than girls,[20] but that can explain only a small portion of the yawning gap between the number of native men and native women marrying in the city.

The probable cause of this chronic demographic feature of the city[21] is that many men went to sea in their teens and early 20s – before marriage – never to return. The demographic 'hole' created by their departure was filled by the thousands of migrants who accounted for half of all those marrying in eighteenth-century Amsterdam and, as shown in detail in chapter 9, became the husbands of a large portion of Amsterdam-born women.

The other northern European country that may have experienced sea-borne mortality on a large scale is England. Wrigley and Schofield, in their *Population History of England*, provide estimates of net foreign migration for five-year periods from 1541 to 1871.[22] Migration carries a special definition in their study: it is simply all those born in England who apparently did not die there. 'Apparently', because the estimates are a residual of their complex procedure for the reconstruction of English population and are not based on direct evidence. Their measure of 'deaths abroad' is obviously not equivalent to the VOC death series of table 10.4. The English estimates include emigrants and the deaths of fishermen and soldiers serving abroad. Most such persons were not urban residents and were unconnected to the urban economy. Moreover, the estimates are *net* figures, reduced by the entry to England of foreigners – such as Scots, Welshmen and Irishmen.

Wrigley and Schofield's estimates of net migration (i.e. net overseas death) show substantial fluctuations over time, but almost always exceed 5000 a year. Isolating that portion of this minimum figure that represents the deaths abroad of urban seamen would be sheer guesswork, but it is certainly not absurd to suppose that it could have equalled the 4000 per annum level suffered by the servants of the Dutch East India Company alone. England was far more populous than the Dutch Republic, so this flow of sea-borne deaths would have borne less heavily on it than on the Republic. But England's *urban* population was not, until after 1700, larger than the Republic's, so the maritime impact on rural–urban migration might have been roughly similar, particularly in the seventeenth century.

This maritime drain surely affected other parts of Europe, but, except for Portugal and perhaps Spain, it seems unlikely that it could have assumed the scope observed in the Dutch Republic and inferred for England. The effect of all this is to increase substantially the estimated net rural–urban migration in north-western Europe during the seventeenth and eighteenth centuries. On the order of 6000–10,000 permanent migrants – predominantly young men – should be added to the net figure of annual migrants calculated in table 10.1 for the period 1600–1800. Until the mid-eighteenth century this increases the net urban migration for all of northern Europe from 15 to 30 per cent.

MIGRATION AND URBAN GROWTH

THE CONTEXT OF PRE-INDUSTRIAL URBAN MIGRATION

Why did migration to the cities assume the magnitudes and follow the trends just identified? This question cannot be answered directly; it requires that we place rural–urban migration in a larger context of European social and economic change. Then we can hope to identify the factors regulating the migration phenomenon and, ultimately, assess the place of urban growth in the pre-industrial society.

The flows of migration sustaining Europe's cities and allowing them to grow were an integral part of a larger process of geographical mobility, and geographical mobility of all types was intimately related to the achievement, or imposition, of occupational and social mobility. I have already remarked on the fact that the net flows of rural–urban migration estimated above were part of a larger, probably much larger, stream of gross rural–urban migration. This in turn was embedded in a yet more general migration phenomenon continually redistributing population among villages and market towns.

One of modern historical demography's key findings is that the pre-industrial European population was highly mobile.[23] Large numbers of people – in city and countryside alike – moved, sometimes repeatedly, in search of spouses, work, skills, and sometimes religious freedom, physical security or sheer survival.[24] The predominance in most of Europe of nuclear family organization, with its requirement that most children leave the home to establish separate households, endowed even apparently somnolent peasant hamlets with a measure of geographical mobility.[25] These numerous moves did not ordinarily involve long distances but, usually in a step-wise fashion, some people eventually found themselves far from home indeed. As one would expect this is particularly evident in the largest cities. In London over a quarter of all indentured servants entering the city between 1683 and 1759 came from over 200 kilometres away.[26] Over a quarter of all persons marrying in Amsterdam in the seventeenth and eighteenth centuries had been born beyond the borders of the Dutch Republic; 4 per cent came from the Scandinavian countries.[27] Even in the smaller and declining city of Leiden, 25–30 per cent of eighteenth-century immigrants came from abroad, and in the still smaller German town of Ansbach almost 40 per cent of new burgers in the period 1645–1700 had been born over 100 kilometres away.[28]

These numerous criss-crossing currents of geographical mobility were integrally related to the evolution of regional occupational structures and the experience of social mobility. The simplest model relating geographical and social mobility focuses exclusively on rural–urban migration and treats it as both a measure of the growth of non-agricultural occupations and of downward social mobility. This model is often associated with the 'enclosure' phenomenon, which, in turn, many interpret as the institutional means by which peasants were separated from the means of production and made available for migration to the cities. Karl Marx, who placed such great emphasis on enclosures, recognized that the proletariat thus created 'could not possibly be absorbed by the nascent manufactures as fast as it was thrown upon the world'.[29] That is, he emphasized that there was an historical delay between the rise of a proletariat and the rise of the industrial city. Despite this, rural–urban migration has commonly been held to incorporate both occupational change (from agriculture to industry) and downward social mobility (from peasant to proletarian). In this way migration off the land and the growth of the proletariat becomes part of a single process leading to urbanization.

This simple model is inadequate for the analysis of social mobility in pre-industrial Europe, whatever may be its merits for more recent times. It rests on a misunderstanding of the character of both rural society and the pre-industrial city. The achievement of occupational diversity and of pronounced social stratification *within* rural society has been a major theme of recent work in agrarian history.[30] Moreover, the identification of the city as the dynamic agent in economic change – the advanced sector in a two-sector model of economic development – now seems misleading when applied to the pre-industrial era. More will be said about these propositions below; for now it is sufficient to observe that the social mobility associated with migration to the city in pre-industrial Europe nested within a much larger process of social stratification and occupational redistribution.

The challenge before us now is to explain rural–urban migration, and thus the incidence of urban growth, in an historical setting where it is but one, not necessarily dominant factor in the related processes of physical and social mobility that were altering the economic structure and social stratification of early modern Europe.

PUSH, PULL, AND POTENTIAL MIGRATION

The motivation to migrate, whether to cities or elsewhere, is frequently analysed by investigating in turn those factors 'pushing' people out of their places of initial residence and those that 'pull' them into a place observed to be attracting migrants.[31] Push migration requires the existence of an involuntary element in the decision. It implies that survival, or the survival of a cherished value, motivates the migrant. In pull migration superior opportunities in some other place attract the mover, who is now motivated by the possibility of betterment.

In an agrarian society the push to depart is usually associated with population growth. In practice the rate of growth at which such a force begins to be felt varies considerably, depending on, among other factors, inheritance customs, the opportunities available for intensification of land use, and market conditions affecting the local demand for labour. Although an absolute reduction in the demand for labour in agriculture could sometimes occur (and occurs often in modern society), it is safe to assume that in the past push forces generally arose as a rural society's reproduction exceeded the replacement rate, and such forces became stronger the higher was the rate of natural increase.

Nathan Keyfitz and Dimiter Philipov, in a study of the determinants of urban population growth in modern developing societies, concluded that

> the overflow from the countryside is decisive for the growth of cities. In any discussion of the degree to which the cities grow through their own natural increase, it has to be recognized that they grow much more through the natural increase of the countryside.[32]

Keyfitz and Philipov's finding applies with added force when the initial level of urbanization is low. Then push migration from an enormous reservoir of rural population can swamp all other forces acting on the rate of urban population growth. An important implication of this type of rural–urban migration is that the rate of urban population growth bears no particular relationship to the expansion of urban employment opportunities. This forms the backdrop to the well-known pathological features of twentieth-century Asian, African and Latin American urbanization.

Was the pace of rural–urban migration in pre-industrial Europe governed by the rate of rural natural increase? The association of rates of rural and urban growth is by itself no proof of push migration, of course, since both might be part of a more general process of development. Nevertheless, if the association is absent, it is difficult to place great weight on the push factor. No sophisticated test of this association is possible since our observations come only at fifty-year intervals and the estimates of migration are subject to a substantial margin of error. Figure 10.1 displays such information as we have, relating the rural rates of natural increase to the percentage of that increase migrating to cities. The resulting pattern is clear, and clearly inconsistent with the push hypothesis.

In northern Europe the relative strength of rural–urban migration is inversely related to the rate of rural natural increase until 1800. In the Mediterreanean lands the same inverse relationship is present, although all observations except one are clustered around narrow ranges of both rural natural increase and migration rates. In both regions the highest migration rates occur when rural natural increase is zero or negative. Of course, this is simply a statistical consequence of the way in which migration is being measured. When the urban population is small relative to the rural sector it is obviously

DYNAMICS OF URBAN GROWTH

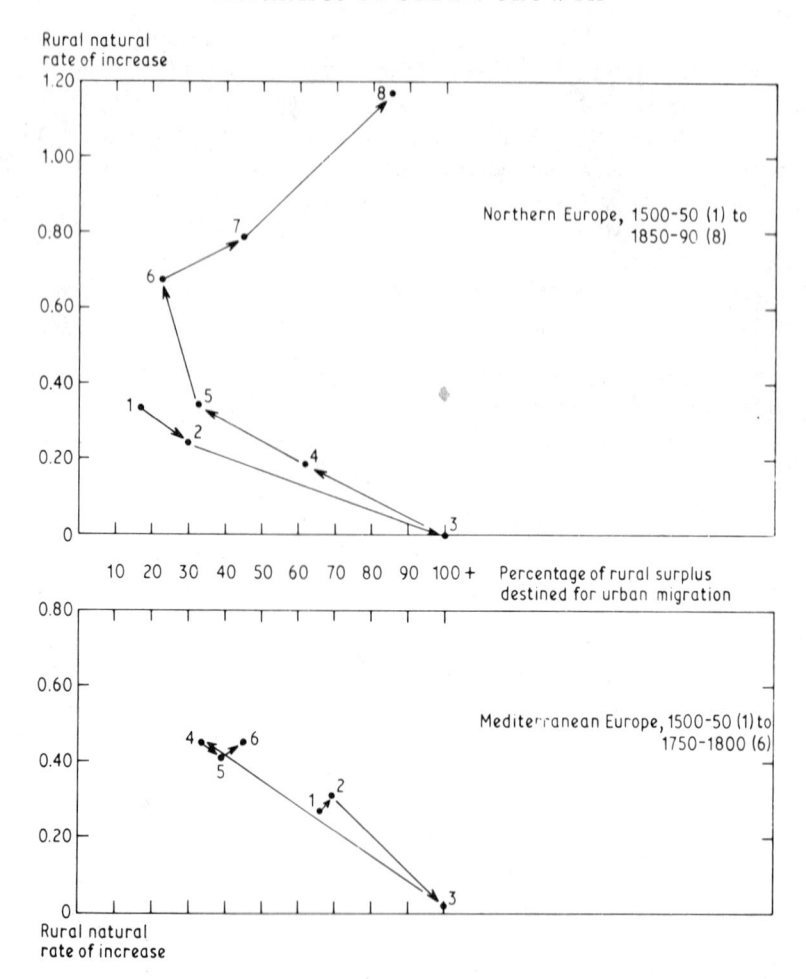

Figure 10.1 The relationship of the rural natural rate of increase to the percentage of the rural surplus population destined for urban migration, per fifty-year period

difficult for a high percentage of a large rural natural increase to migrate to the cities. But, as Keyfitz and Philipov note, it is precisely under such conditions that one would expect the rural increase to dominate the pattern of urban growth. The absence of such a relationship strongly suggests that urban growth as a whole was not dominated by survival chances in the countryside.

As a basis for the analysis of migration in the pre-industrial society, the push explanation seems insufficiently insightful and generally unconvincing. Instead of trying to determine how many people are forced to leave their homes, it should prove more useful to estimate how many are *potential migrants*. Potential migrants (or migration-eligible persons) are those who are likely to consider it and, depending on conditions, i.e. after weighing the 'pull' factors, may migrate or stay in place. In modern society this group 'at risk' of permanent migration is probably close to 100 per cent of the total population, but in a pre-industrial society I shall argue that it is small enough to be of use in analysing the migration phenomenon.

The potential net migration out of an agrarian society before the mechanization of agriculture could not long exceed that portion of population growth in excess of replacement needs (the surplus births referred to in line 12 of tables 10.1 and 10.3). An upper limit to net migration would be the departure of the entire surplus, with the consequence that there would be no agrarian population growth. Stationary agricultural populations are common enough, but in the very long run, apart from those seventeenth-century episodes when rural natural increase approached or fell below zero in some areas, the agricultural population of Europe grew absolutely until the late nineteenth century at the earliest.[33]

A lower limit on net migration is reached when no potential migrants leave the agrarian sector. If our understanding of pre-industrial urban demography is correct, this would result in an absolute de-urbanization. This too has been observed in certain regions (such as eighteenth-century Flanders and Brabant), but in large areas over long time-periods the absolute growth of urban population has been all but universal.

PRE-INDUSTRIAL MIGRATION OPTIONS

If we take the rural natural increase to approximate the pool of potential net migration, the next step is to consider the alternatives faced by the potential migrant. What forces were pulling at him or her, how compelling were they, and how did their relative attractiveness change over time?

A detailed account of all the options that may have been important in pre-industrial Europe is beyond the scope and needs of this study.[34] I will proceed by grouping the many specific options into three basic categories, each of which has distinctive implications for the evolution of occupational structure, social stratification and the scope of rural–urban migration, and, hence, urban growth. On this basis I will present a simple model that relates these categories of options to each other and calls attention to certain demographic and social implications of alternative migration behaviour.

The city

The potential migrant could become an actual migrant by leaving agriculture and his locality behind to seek his fortune in a city. Under the demographic conditions of the pre-industrial era the pull exerted by cities may be divided into two parts: replacement opportunities and growth opportunities.

Most cities offered a fairly steady supply of employment opportunities simply to replenish a labour force systematically being depleted by the high urban mortality levels. In the migration model described in tables 10.1 and 10.3 this component of the urban demand for labour is represented by line 5.

One might suppose that job opportunities in unhealthy cities would not exert a compelling attraction to potential migrants, but the available evidence is unambiguous in demonstrating just the opposite. Most cities that suffered severe crises of mortality, suddenly losing 20–40 per cent of their populations in outbreaks of plague or other epidemic diseases, attracted sufficient replacement migrants to regain their pre-crisis population levels within a matter of years. When in 1625 London lost over 35,000 souls to plague alone, the response of rural Englishmen was such that the loss was made good by 1627, London's very rapid growth could resume.[35] In Venice after the plague of 1570 'replacement by immigration happened so fast that the effect of the momentarily smaller labour pool on the wage rate was completely nullified for journeymen by the end of the decade, and shortly thereafter for *maestri*'.[36] When Venice was again struck by plague in 1630, losing 40,000 inhabitants, its economy was anything but buoyant. Nevertheless, within twelve years of that event a net immigration of 23,000 compensated for further natural decrease and restored half of the loss, while between 1642 and 1655 another 39,000 migrants brought the city's population to 158,000. Richard Rapp, who analysed the census documents on which this reconstruction is based, concluded that 'within twenty years the population had restabilized at 140,000–160,000, which may be said to represent the normal level'.[37]

Smaller regional centres often displayed the same powers of recuperation. In the English city of Colchester 'it is quite clear that whilst epidemics of plague might have provoked flight from centres of infection, they equally drew an influx of strangers, some vagrant, to fill empty houses when the crisis was over, and to restore the seemingly shattered population'. In the last plague visitation of 1665–6 some 4500–5000 people died in Colchester. The estimates of its population show a fall from 10,305 in 1662 to 4114 in 1666. 'Yet after only five years it had climbed again with astonishing rapidity to 9,526, levelling out to reach nearly 10,000 by 1675.'[38]

The opportunities created by urban disasters were exceptional, but less dramatic replacement opportunities must have existed wherever there were cities. Although little is known about this, one is tempted to speculate that where the level of urbanization was high, as in northern Italy and the Low Countries, the size and regularity of this hazardous demand for labour might have evoked a permanent expectation of migration to the city among agrarian households in the region, fashioning, as it were, well-trodden migration paths to connect supply and demand.

While replacement migration may have been ubiquitous the same was surely not often true of the incidence of 'growth migration'. To attract migrants beyond replacement needs pre-industrial cities needed capital investment and analogous commitments of state and church to expand employment opportunities. Allan Pred, in his study of nineteenth-century United States urban growth, reasons that the growth of individual cities 'depended on the extent to which the ever changing supply of employment opportunities in their local economies permitted them both to attract migrants and to hold in-migrants and potential out-migrants away from competing cities'.[39] The differential success of individual cities is based on patterns of investment, disinvestment and reinvestment which find a reflection in shifting migration streams. This approach is obviously of particular relevance to the pre-industrial era, when few if any cities could expand on the basis of their own natural increase and when the differences in growth-rate among cities was particularly great.

Our concern here is not so much with the growth of individual cities as with the growth of the urban sector as a whole. Correspondingly, instead of being attentive, as is Pred, to competition among cities for the pool of migrants *already committed* to urban migration, we are here concerned with competition for potential migrants among alternative types of 'destinations'.

For the urban sector to attract growth migrants its economic and social functions had to increase in importance and/or increase in number. At issue here is not merely the transfer of capital from declining to growing cities, but investment decisions and political commitments that affect the place of cities in the organization of the entire economy.

(2) Agriculture

An alternative to urban migration for the potential migrant was to remain in his rural locality and base his livelihood on agriculture, although not necessarily in precisely the same capacity as his parents. In many discussions of migration the assumption is made that this option is closed, that the migrant is pushed out. The advantage of the potential migrant concept is that it permits us to see remaining in agriculture as a possibility whose attractions the individual weighs against the other accessible options, and whose relative attractiveness may vary over time.

The possibilities in agriculture for someone who will not inherit a family farm and cannot acquire one through marriage are day labourer or servant status, labour for one's siblings as a subordinate member of an extended family, and perhaps becoming a farmer on a small-holding, particularly where partible inheritance is practised. The intensification of production per unit of land and the corresponding increase in the demand for labour that came about through the suppression of fallow, the introduction of new crops and crop rotations, and investment in land improvements, unquestionably 'attracted' many potential migrants to stay where they were, albeit in a different social status. The appeal of staying put varied a good deal over time and place, for the economic incentives to adopt more labour-absorbing agricultural practices were neither constant nor universal, depending as they did on relative prices and access to markets.

Protoindustry

A third option of great importance to this analysis pulled at many potential migrants in early modern Europe. A large and growing portion of industrial production, particularly in the many branches of the textile industry, took place in a decentralized setting of rural cottages. Despite the dispersed, small-scale character of this production it was neither orientated to local markets nor pursued by independent artisans. The hallmark of this rural industrial activity was its co-ordination by urban merchants and its dependence on distant markets. Economic historians have recently come to see the spread of such rural industrial activity as a distinct phase in industrial development, prior to and preparatory to the rise of the factory system.

This protoindustry, a term suggested by Franklin Mendels to emphasize its distinctiveness from other forms of industrial organization, is important to the present study because of the nature of its links to both the agricultural and urban sectors, and its consequent impact on migration, social stratification and occupational structure.[40]

Protoindustry is intimately related to the agricultural sector by physical proximity and the involvement of its labour force in agricultural production, certainly during periods of peak-labour demand. The boundary separating the two sectors should be thought of as a broad transition zone, and the expansion of protoindustry inevitably involved the recruiting of marginal farmers and agricultural labourers, the sort of people likely to qualify as potential migrants. Enrolment into rural industrial work may have involved short-distance migration for some, but it was primarily an act, or more commonly a gradual process, of social rather than physical mobility.

Protoindustry's relationship to the urban economy appears to be one of oppositions. Its expansion reduced the volume of urban industrial employment and it met with the bitter opposition of many cities.[41] But at the same time the capital investment in and the co-ordination of rural production, the performance of the final, most skill- and capital-intensive stages of production, and the commercial activities needed to market the goods, all took place in cities. That is, protoindustry (in contrast to casual rural handicrafts production for local use) required the commercial organization of a regional economy by a city, and its expansion created the basis for a *selective* urban growth.

This third 'destination' pulling at the potential migrant was historically specific. While rural–urban migration is a very nearly universal phenomenon, the pull of protoindustry had a history that assumed importance in the sixteenth century and on which the curtain was drawn rather briskly around the mid-nineteenth century.[42] In this era the pull of protoindustry had far-reaching effects on both rural and urban society such that it forms the strategic element of the model being developed here. The thickening of cottage industry in regions found to be propitious (the factors encouraging it are not yet well understood, but involve population density, inheritance custom and soil fertility) had its counterpart in the strengthening of commercial agriculture in other areas. Likewise, protoindustry's rise was a consequence of city-centred investment that simultaneously undermined urban industrial employment while it selectively strengthened urban commercial and service functions.

Finally, the expansion of protoindustry profoundly affected rural social structure. The rural households dependent on industrial employment, that is, on wage labour, adopted patterns of marriage and fertility behaviour quite different from the norms of peasant society. Several historical studies document a protoindustrial demographic regime in which earlier marriage led to a total fertility level higher than was common in farming communities.[43] As a consequence, protoindustrial communities commonly experienced higher rates of natural increase than did land-based peasant communities.

A THREE-SECTOR PRE-INDUSTRIAL MIGRATION MODEL

The constituent parts of the model of pre-industrial migration can now be tied together. The natural increase of the agrarian population formed a pool of net potential migration, facing options of moving to the city, finding a place in agriculture, or becoming dependent upon rural industrial activity. Of course, these options were not all available in all places, or at all times. Nor, indeed, does my identification of these alternatives as options or attractions pulling on the potential migrant imply that they were *attractive*. On the contrary, the potential migrant may have faced a grim future whatever option he chose: to subsist as a cottar with a small scrap of land, as an unskilled casual labourer in the city, or from irregular work in the putting-out system. Finally, we must not forget that in certain regions people succeeded in putting off making a commitment to one of these options (at least for a time) by combining all three in their family economy. Heurlingen in Lower Saxony and Westphalia can serve as an example of marginal farm families, where the wives and children worked in linen production while the men set off, after sowing their crops, to seek seasonal work in the cities of Holland, returning home in time to harvest their own crops.[44]

Each of the three options had distinct implications for geographical mobility and social mobility. Only the urban migration option was likely to involve movement over substantial distances and, of course, affect directly the rate of urban growth. No simple statement will suffice to describe the impact of these options on social mobility and social stratification. Depending on circumstances, the move to a city might involve downward social mobility (farmer to wage labourer) or not (farmer to guild craftsman or merchant). The decision to remain in agriculture is similarly ambiguous. Only in the case of entry into protoindustry does the direction of change appear to be obvious.[45] Whatever the social class implications of these changes, the impact on occupational structure is clear enough: both geographical migration to the city and social mobility to rural industry involve a shift out of primary production.

Each of the three options also had implications for the future demographic character of the society. If we take as a norm the fertility and mortality behaviour of agricultural communities, then urban populations are distinguished by their high mortality while protoindustrial communities are distinguished by their high fertility, the product of low marriage age, more frequent marriage, higher levels of illegitimacy and perhaps higher marital fertility. It follows that each of these three categories possessed distinct intrinsic rates of natural increase with $r > f > 0 > u$, where r is the rural-industrial, f the farm, and u the urban rate of natural increase.

In this three-sector model of the pre-industrial society the critical variable – shaping the society's aggregate demographic behaviour, social stratification and urbanization – is migration. The act of leaving agriculture for protoindustry, or either of these for the city, affects the relative size of the three sectors in future years and, hence, the overall rate of population growth (the weighted average of the rates of natural increase of the three sectors). This in turn affects the relative importance of artisanal and peasant social classes versus 'proletarianized' rural-industrial communities. Here we have come full circle to our original interest. Migration, the linchpin of the urban economy and regulator of urban growth, is now embedded in a model that permits us to examine the many consequences of the decision to migrate or *not* to migrate.

The following equations describe the three-sector migration model and make possible simple simulation exercises that will prove helpful in explaining the implications of specific migration behaviour.

$$PF_t = [PF_{t-1}(1 - \beta)](1 + f)$$
$$PR_t = [(PR_{t-1} + \beta PF_{t-1})(1 - \alpha)](1 + r)$$
$$PU_t = (PU_{t-1} + \alpha PR_{t-1})(1 + u)$$
$$P_t = PF_{t-1} + PR_{t-1} + PU_{t-1} - \alpha(r - u)PR_{t-1} - \beta(f - r)PF_{t-1} - \alpha(\beta PF_{t-1})(1 + r)$$

Where

P = total population
PF, PR, PU = population of the farm, rural and urban sectors respectively
$f, r, u,$ = rates of natural increase of the farm, rural and urban sectors respectively
α = migration from rural to urban sector
β = migration from farm to rural sector

Migration from the farm to the urban sector is a combination of α and β. No migration flow out of the urban sector is provided for in the model.

The first three equations account for the growth, interval-per-interval, of the three sectors. Each sector's population is augmented or diminished by its own rate of natural increase and the migration flows α and β. The fourth equation accounts for total population change, which is simply a weighted average of the growth-rates of the three sectors, the weights changing according to the intrinsic sectoral growth-rates and the size of the migration flows that redistribute population among the sectors.

With this three-sector accounting model we can isolate the impact of migration behaviour on urbanization, proletarianization and total population growth, and assess its importance relative to other factors. To proceed, simulation values must be selected for the initial size of the three sectors, and each sector's intrinsic rate of natural increase. Then the effects of alternative migration assumptions (values of α and β) can be observed and compared.

I will report overleaf on a selection of the many sector weights and growth-rates that were fed into the model.

Consider first the case in which there is no net intersectoral migration, that is, where sectoral change and total population growth is entirely the result of the initial weights and the sectoral growth rates. After fifty years the total population and the relative size of the three sectors would be as shown in table 10.5.

These simulations can be used as a point of reference, but not as an approximation of historical reality. There apparently always was some migration to the cities, for the drastic declines in the urban population

Initial weights

Sector

Farm	Rural-industrial	Urban
90	0	10
75	10	15
50	25	25
33	33	33

Sectoral rates of natural increase (per annum)

Sector

Farm	Rural-industrial	Urban
0.005	0.008	−0.005
0.005	0.010	−0.010
0.008	0.012	−0.005

recorded in table 10.5 are observed nowhere. Note that differences in the initial weights alone account for variations in the overall rate of population growth of 16–27 per cent, and that the third set of growth-rates generates an overall rate of growth approximately double that of the first two.

Assume now that potential migrants in the farm sector are attracted to the cities only for replacement purposes. Only when the replacement needs of the cities exceed the farm surplus does rural-industrial migration to the cities occur. Table 10.6 displays the results. The postulated migration flow is insufficient to prevent the percentage of the population living in cities from falling, but it does redistribute enough persons to areas of high mortality to dampen population growth, sometimes substantially (by 66 per cent in the worst case), and it siphons off all surplus population in the farm sector in the circled cases.

A larger flow of migrants out of the farm sector is required to maintain the urban population at its initial *percentage* of the total population. The results of this migration assumption are displayed in table 10.7. When compared to the preceding case we find that total population growth is further dampened, and there are now four cases (circled) in which an excess of the entire farm surplus is needed to allow the cities to grow at the rate of total population.

Table 10.5 Three-sector model fifty-year simulation results, assuming no intersectoral migration

Initial weights			Rates of natural increase													
			F 0.005	R 0.008	U −0.005			F 0.005	R 0.010	U −0.010			F 0.008	R 0.012	U −0.005	
			Popu-lation	%				Popu-lation	%				Popu-lation	%		
F	R	U		F	R	U			F	R	U			F	R	U
90	0	10	123.3	93.7	0	6.3		121.5	95.0	0	5.0		141.8	94.5	0	5.5
75	10	15	122.8	78.4	12.1	9.5		121.8	79.0	13.5	7.5		141.5	78.9	12.8	8.3
50	25	25	120.9	53.1	30.8	16.1		120.4	53.3	34.2	12.6		139.4	53.5	32.6	14.0
33	33	33	118.4	36.1	41.9	21.9		117.8	36.3	46.6	17.1		136.1	36.5	44.5	19.1

Table 10.6 Three-sector model fifty-year simulation results, assuming farm to urban migration just sufficient to maintain initial urban population

Initial weights			Rates of natural increase														
			F 0.005	R 0.008	U −0.005				F 0.005	R 0.010	U −0.010				F 0.008	R 0.012	U −0.005			
			Popu-lation	%					Popu-lation	%					Popu-lation	%				
				F	R	U			F	R	U				F	R	U
F	R	U															
90	0	10	122.7	91.8	0	8.1	119.8	91.7	0	8.3	141.0	92.9	0	7.1
75	10	15	121.9	75.5	12.2	12.3	119.2	73.6	13.8	12.6	140.3	76.4	12.9	10.7
50	25	25	119.3	47.8	31.2	21.0	116.1	43.1	35.4	21.5	137.2	48.7	33.1	18.2
33	33	33	116.3	28.7	42.7	26.7	110.7	30.1	39.8	30.1	133.3	29.6	45.4	25.0

Table 10.7 Three-sector model fifty-year simulation results, assuming migration to urban sector only just sufficient to maintain initial urban percentage

Initial weights			Rates of natural increase												
			F 0.005	R 0.008	U −0.005			F 0.005	R 0.010	U −0.010			F 0.008	R 0.012	U −0.005
			Popu-lation	%				Popu-lation	%				Popu-lation	%	
F	R	U		F	R	U			F	R	U			F	R	U
90	0	10	122.1	90.0	0	10.0		119.1	90.0	0	10.0		139.6	90.0	0	10.0
75	10	15	122.1	72.7	12.3	15.0		118.1	71.1	13.9	15.0		138.3	71.9	13.1	15.0
50	25	25	118.2	43.5	31.5	25.0		114.2	43.8	31.2	25.0		134.3	41.2	33.8	25.0
33	33	33	114.6	29.1	37.6	33.3		109.0	30.6	36.1	33.3		129.3	25.8	40.9	33.3

Table 10.8 Three-sector model fifty-year simulation results, assuming that all surplus farm and rural–industrial population migrates to the urban sector

Initial weights			Rates of natural increase												
			F 0.005	R 0.008		U −0.005		F 0.005	R 0.010		U −0.010		F 0.008	R 0.012		U −0.005
F	R	U	Popu-lation	%				Popu-lation	%				Popu-lation	%		
				F	R	U			F	R	U			F	R	U
90	0	10	117.7	76.4	0	23.6		113.8	79.1	0	20.9		128.3	70.1	0	29.9
75	10	15	116.6	64.3	8.6	27.1		113.0	66.4	8.8	24.8		127.5	58.8	7.8	33.3
50	25	25	114.5	43.7	21.8	34.5		110.0	45.5	22.7	31.8		125.4	39.9	19.9	40.2
33	33	33	111.8	29.7	29.7	40.5		106.5	31.2	31.2	37.6		122.0	28.1	28.1	43.8

Table 10.9 Three-sector model fifty-year simulation results, assuming all farm surplus population migrates to rural–industrial sector

Initial weights			Rates of natural increase									
			F 0.005	R 0.008	U −0.005	F 0.005	R 0.010	U −0.010	F 0.008	R 0.012	U −0.005	
F	R	U	Popu-lation	%		Popu-lation	%		Popu-lation	%		
				F	R	U		F	R	U		F	R	U
90	0	10	125.3	71.7	22.1	6.2	125.1	71.9	23.3	4.8	145.1	71.9	22.7	5.4
75	10	15	124.5	60.2	30.5	9.4	124.7	60.1	32.7	7.3	145.6	51.3	40.7	8.0
50	25	25	122.0	40.9	43.1	16.0	122.4	40.8	46.8	12.4	142.0	35.1	51.2	13.7
33	33	33	119.1	28.0	50.3	21.8	119.1	28.0	55.1	16.9	137.9	24.1	57.1	18.8

In both tables 10.6 and 10.7 the only growing sector is the rural-industrial: it grows from 33 to 40 and 25 to 33.8 per cent of the total population in the best cases, and in all cases its growth is entirely accounted for by natural increase. The only migration flows allowed for so far are to the urban sector.

If the opportunities offered by the cities were sufficient to attract all potential migrants in both the farm and rural-industrial sectors, how rapidly would the urban sector grow? Table 10.8 answers this question for the specified assumptions. When the entire non-urban surplus migrate to the cities, the farm and rural-industrial sectors naturally decline in relative size and the urban sector grows. What is more noteworthy for our purposes is the fact that the resulting urban growth is spectacular when the farm sector is large and the urban sector initially small, but becomes diminishingly small as the urban sector grows in relative size. The causes for this are obvious enough, but it is interesting to note that under the second set of sectoral growth-rates the possibilities for further urban growth are nearing exhaustion at 37.6 per cent. The simulation shows that the inflow to the cities of the entire non-urban surplus for fifty years was capable of increasing the urban percentage from 33.3 to only 37.6 per cent, and while in the first decade the urban sector had grown by 5 per cent, by the fifth decade its growth had fallen to 2.8 per cent. Where urban mortality was less severe, as in the first set of sectoral growth-rates, and where non-urban growth was more rapid, as in the third set, the urban ceiling was higher. But, in all three cases, the simulation exercise shows the urban population to be approaching asymptotically a maximum level located between 40 and 50 per cent of the population.

Related to the exhaustion of the potential for further urbanization is the depressive effect exerted by this migration pattern on the rate of total population growth. The effect of migration alone is to reduce the growth of population after fifty years by 40–60 per cent of the 'no-migration' case (table 10.5). This is the demographic price paid to maintain a large pre-industrial urban population.

Consider now the case in which migration no longer flows exclusively from country to city, but where some or all of the surplus farm population 'migrates' (i.e. experiences social mobility or, perhaps, expropriation) to the rural-industrial sector. Table 10.9 displays the extreme case in which the farm population remains at its initial absolute level and the entire surplus flows into the rural-industrial sector. This migration behaviour generates the most rapid total population growth of the cases considered since it enlarges through migration the sector with the highest intrinsic rate of natural increase. The rural-industrial sector is capable of rapid growth: from 0 to 23 per cent of the total population, or from 33 to over 50 per cent in fifty years' time. As the rural-industrial sector is enlarged, a progressively smaller portion of its growth is accounted for by migration (less than half in the fifty years period where r = 0.012 and the rural-industrial sector's initial size = 33), but because of its high intrinsic growth-rate this sector's growth is not capped by a ceiling as was the case when migration flowed exclusively to the cities.

The statistical patterns generated by these simulations can be summarized as follows.

(1) The results are sensitive to the initial values given to the sector sizes and growth-rates. The larger the rural-industrial and urban sectors relative to the farm sector and the more divergent the intrinsic rates of natural increase, the more powerful is the impact of migration on the rates of total population growth and on changes in the relative size of the three sectors.

(2) Despite this, variation in migration behaviour by itself is nearly always capable of altering the values of total population and sectoral share by as much as can variation in initial weights or in the sets of rates of natural increase by themselves.

URBANIZATION, PROLETARIANIZATION AND PROTOINDUSTRIALIZATION

Urbanization

In this model the rate of urbanization is determined principally by (1) the urban rate of natural increase, (2) the size and rate of natural increase of the farm sector, and (3) the migration choices as summarized by the values of α and β. Under pre-industrial conditions the urban rate of natural increase is assumed to be negative, and when this is so the second element becomes particularly important. When the farm sector is large and its rate of growth high, the potential for rapid urban growth is great: recall Keyfitz and Philipov's assertion that 'the overflow from the countryside is decisive for the growth of cities'.[46] Despite this, we have argued that Europe's urban growth was rarely driven by this exogenous force.

It must not be forgotten that the size of the rural sector can affect the growth of cities only via migration, and here the historical setting of pre-industrial Europe becomes decisive. The three 'migration' options described above had the effect of allowing a substantial urbanization to occur only in the special case where the surplus farm population did not take up rural-industrial pursuits. Even then, the flow of migrants may not have sufficed to increase the relative position of the urban sector if that sector was large and subject to a deeply negative rate of natural increase. In short, a great deal had to be overcome to achieve a net increase in the urban share of the total population. It required a specific type of migration behaviour, one that had as side

Table 10.10 Three-sector model fifty-year simulation results: the effect of changing the urban rate of natural increase from −0.005 to 0 and +0.005, assuming that all farm and rural surplus migrates to the urban sector

Initial weights			Rates of natural increase												
			F 0.005	R 0.008	U −0.005			F 0.005	R 0.008	U 0			F 0.005	R 0.008	U +0.005
			Population	%				Population	%				Population	%	
				F	R	U			F	R	U			F	R	U
F	R	U	(from table 10.8)												
90	0	10	117.7	76.4	0	23.6		120.0	75.0	0	25.0		124.2	72.5	0	27.5
75	10	15	116.6	64.3	8.6	27.1		121.7	61.6	8.2	30.2		126.7	59.2	7.9	32.9
50	25	25	114.5	43.7	21.8	34.5		123.8	40.4	20.2	39.4		130.6	38.3	19.4	45.5
33	33	33	111.8	29.7	29.7	40.5		121.6	27.4	27.4	45.2		137.8	24.2	24.2	51.6

Comparing case 3 (urban NRI = +0.005) to case 1 (urban NRI = −0.005)

F	R	U	Total population growth after fifty years is higher in case 3 by	Urban population growth after fifty years is higher in case 3 by
90	0	10	5.5%	23.0%
75	10	15	7.9	32.0
50	25	25	14.1	37.5
33	33	33	23.3	42.7

effects the limiting of total population growth and the limiting of changes in the relative size of the three sectors.

In view of these comments it is instructive to examine the effect on the three-sector model when the urban sector's intrinsic rate of natural increase ceases to be negative, as in fact occurred in the first half of the nineteenth century. Table 10.10 displays the results achieved in the case where all migration is to the urban sector (table 10.8) modified by a change of the urban rate of natural increase from its initial negative figure to zero and +0.5 per cent per annum.

Obviously, the effect of a change in the urban sector's growth-rate is greater the larger its initial size. Thus when the urban rate of natural increase is raised from −0.005 to +0.005 in a society that is initially 10 per cent urban, the difference after fifty years is to increase the per cent urban from 23.6 to 27.5. But when the society is initially 33 per cent urban the effect after fifty years is to raise the attained urbanization level from 40.5 to 51.6 per cent. In short, it has the effect of lifting the ceiling that had prevented the urban sector from growing far beyond 40 per cent of the total population (see figure 10.2). Instead of rising at diminishing rates to an upper limit, the urban share can rise in the pattern of a logistics curve to encompass, theoretically, nearly all of society.

The other important implication of this exercise is that the rapid urban growth of the nineteenth century need not have been accompanied by a major change in migration flows. That is, the quickened pace of urban growth in the nineteenth century did not so much signal an increase in rural–urban migration as it reflected a change in the internal demography of the European city. The calculations of migration flows in table 10.1 illustrate this point. The share of the rural surplus apparently claimed by the growing cities of the first half of the nineteenth century was but little higher than in the previous century. Only after 1850 did the attractive power of cities become sufficient to begin to put an end to rural population growth.

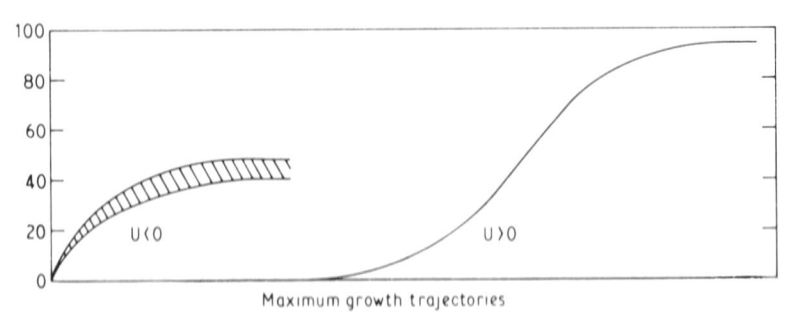

Figure 10.2 Growth trajectories of urbanization when the urban rate of natural increase is below and above 0

If the results of these simulations can be confirmed by empirical investigation, they will require a modification of the conventional view that nineteenth-century urbanization was principally fed by an unprecedented increase in migration, constituting a 'mobility revolution'. Andrei Rogers offers a representative and succinct presentation of this view when he speaks of a 'vital revolution', defined as the societal transition from high to low birth- and death-rates, and a 'mobility revolution', a transition from low to high migration rates. Urbanization, then,

> results from a particular spatial interaction of the vital and mobility revolutions. It is characterized by distinct urban–rural differentials in fertility–mortality levels and patterns of decline, and by a massive largely voluntary net transfer of population from rural to urban areas through internal migration.[47]

The analysis presented here would diminish the importance of change in the migration *rate* (because it was *initially* higher than the mobility revolution concept can admit to) and emphasize instead change in the urban–rural differentials in fertility and mortality.

Tables 10.11, 10.12 and 10.13 display calculations that chart the course of natural increase and net migration as contributors to the population changes experienced by three large cities in the eighteenth and nineteenth centuries. Amsterdam, Stockholm and Berlin differed greatly in their demographic fortunes. The population of Amsterdam was long stagnant. By 1900 it formed a smaller percentage of its national population than it had in 1700. Stockholm grew rapidly, particularly in the late nineteenth century. Berlin ranked among the fastest-growing large cities of Europe in both centuries. Yet, in all three cities, net inmigration when expressed per 1000 of the city's population remained remarkably constant throughout this era of 'mobility transition'. The chief factor affecting the rate and timing of population growth in these three cities was natural increase.

These rough calculations are far from the last word on this subject. On the contrary, they are no more than an initial exploration of available data. However, they suggest that the presumed increase in mobility in the nineteenth century deserves a sceptical re-examination. It may well be that gross mobility rose in this period (by 1880–1900 *gross* inmigration in Berlin and Amsterdam was seven to eight times the *net* inmigration), but it is far from obvious that urban growth now depended *more than before* on inmigration.

Wilbur Zelinsky's claim that 'the course of the mobility transition closely parallels that of the demographic transition . . .' is strongly at variance with the evidence and models presented above.[48] The urban demographic transition, which differed in timing and intensity from the rural demographic transition, dominated the process of urbanization in its early stages. The

Table 10.11 Natural increase and net inmigration in the growth of the population of Amsterdam, 1700–1900

Population totals ('000s)

	Population	Natural increase	Net inmigration	Net population change
1700	c. 220			
1795	221	−100**	+101	+1
1815	180	−33	−8	−41
1860	238	+8	+50	+58
1880	313	+43	+31	+75
1900	511	+92	+64	+156*

Average population change per annum

	Natural increase	Net inmigration	Net change
1700–95	−1,053	+1,063	+10
1796–1815	−1,650	−400	−2,050
1816–60	+170	+1,119	+1,289
1861–80	+2,130	+1,570	+3,750
1881–1900	+4,618	+3,183	+7,801*

Average annual change per 1000 population

	Natural increase	Net inmigration	Total population
1700–95	−4.8	+4.8	+0.005
1796–1815	−8.3	−2.0	−10.3
1816–60	+0.8	+5.4	+6.2
1861–80	+7.7	+5.7	+13.4
1881–1900	+11.2	+7.7	+18.9

* The 198,000 increase in population includes 42,000 gained via annexations. This gain has been subtracted from the net population change and subsequent calculations.
** The excess of burials over baptisms in this period amounts to over 154,000. The Jewish population was included in the burial records, but not in the baptism records. On the basis of the number of Jewish births in the period 1765–95, there may have been 30,000 births in the entire period. To take this and other possible sources of under-registration into account, I have reduced the excess of deaths by 54,000.

Sources Data derived from Bureau van statistiek der gemeente Amsterdam, *Statistiek der bevolking in Amsterdam tot 1921* (Amsterdam, 1923), 136–7, 179; Herman A. Diederiks, *Een stad in verval. Amsterdam omstreeks 1800* (Amsterdam, 1982), 26; T. van Tijn, *Twintig jaren Amsterdam* (Amsterdam, 1965), 110, 278; J. Postmus, *Een onderscheid naar de omvang en aard van de bevolkingsconcentratie in Nederland* (Amsterdam, 1928), 79–82.

mobility revolution was characterized, from the rural perspective, at least as much by a change in destination of migrants as by an increase in the migration rate. From the urban perspective it may have manifested itself in an increased circulation of migrants (i.e. gross migration) but not necessarily in an increased rate of net migration.

Table 10.12 Natural increase and net inmigration in the growth of the population of Berlin, 1711–1900

Population totals ('000s)

	Population	Natural increase	Net inmigration	Net population change
1700	57			
1815	190	−32	+165	+133
1837	283	+25	+68	+93
1856/58	434/459	+58	+118	+176
1880	1,124*	+176	+478	+654*
1900	1,888	+305	+459	+764

Average population change per annum

	Natural increase	Net inmigration	Net change
1711–1815	−301	+1,568	+1,267
1816–37	+1,118	+3,109	+4,227
1838–58	+2,776	+5,605	+8,381
1856–80	+7,340	+19,917	+27,273*
1881–1900	+15,255	+22,970	+38,225

Average annual change per 1000 population

	Natural increase	Net inmigration	Total population
1711–1817	−2.4	+12.7	+10.3
1816–37	+4.7	+13.1	+17.8
1838–58	+7.5	+15.1	+22.6
1856–80	+9.4	+25.6	+35.0*
1881–1900	+9.8	+14.7	+24.5

* The 690,000 increase in population includes 36,000 gained via annexations. This gain has been subtracted from the net population change and subsequent calculations.

Sources Heinrich Schwippe, 'Zum prozess der sozialräumlichen Innerstädtischen Differenzierung im Industrialisierungsprozess des 19. Jahrhunderts', in H. J. Teuteberg (ed.), *Urbanisierung im 19. und 20. Jahrhunderts* (Cologne–Vienna, 1983), 263; Adna F. Weber, *The Growth of Cities in the Nineteenth Century: a Study in Statistics* (New York, 1899), 234.

Table 10.13 Natural increase and net inmigration in the growth of the population of Stockholm, 1721–1910

Population totals ('000s)

	Population	Natural increase	Net inmigration	Net population change
1721	45			
1780	76	−41	+72	+31
1810	65	−30	+19	−11
1860	110	−38	+82	+44
1880	168	+5	+53	+58
1910	344	+68	+108	+176

Average population change per annum

	Natural increase	Net inmigration	Net change
1721–80	−677	+1,192	+515
1781–1810	−980	+637	−343
1811–60	−760	+1,748	+988
1861–80	+262	+2,637	+2,899
1881–1910	+2,351	+3,614	+5,965

Average annual change per 1000 population

	Natural increase	Net inmigration	Total population
1721–80	−11.3	+20.0	+8.7
1781–1810	−14.0	+9.1	−4.9
1811–60	−8.7	+20.1	+11.4
1861–80	+3.8	+19.0	+22.8
1881–1910	+9.2	+14.0	+23.2

Source   Statistik Årsbok för Stockholms Stad, 1964–5 (Stockholm, 1965), 56.

Proletarianization

The chief alternative type of migration behaviour whose properties are being explored here is that which channels most of the surplus farm population into rural industry rather than into the cities (table 10.8 versus table 10.9). The difference between the two migration modes is striking. Whereas farm–urban migration ($\beta + \alpha$) tends to be self-limiting and preserves existing structures, entry into rural industry (β) is potentially explosive, lifting ceilings on both the rate of total population growth and the rate at which sectoral shares (and, hence, economic structure) can shift. This dynamic demographic character can be largely attributed to the fact that the enrolment of dispossessed or otherwise footloose countryfolk into the ranks of a rural proletariat plays a major role in its rapid growth only in the initial stages, when the rural-industrial sector is very small. Once immigration swells the sector's size, natural increase quickly takes over to play the major role in further growth.[49]

The implications of this proletarian demographic regime have not been lost on interpreters of European social history. Articles by Charles Tilly, 'Demographic origins of the European proletariat', and David Levine, 'The English proletariat makes itself', develop arguments that are closely related to the findings emerging from the three-sector model developed above.[50] Together they sustain the position that proletarianization was primarily a rural rather than an urban phenomenon, that the decisive period of proletarianization was before the mid-nineteenth century rather than thereafter, and that the bulk of the proletariat can be 'accounted for' by the natural increase of proletarians rather than downward social mobility or 'expropriation'. From this perspective the nineteenth-century growth of an urban proletariat should be seen as the transfer to the cities of an existing rural proletariat rather than a new creation.

The present model lays particular emphasis on the changing relative strength of the urban and protoindustrial 'destinations' in determining the timing, location and scope of the rise of the proletariat. We exaggerate, of course, in supposing that migration to the cities did not increase the number of dependent wage-earners. But the economic structure of all but the largest cities did inhibit the rapid growth of a true proletariat while their demographic conditions checked such growth for other reasons. It must also be emphasized that the spread of protoindustry did not turn peasants into proletarians in a single moment of decision. It made its mark on social stratification gradually, sometimes over the course of generations. If we keep these qualifications in mind it makes sense to regard urbanization and proletarianization as *alternatives* rather than as associated phenomena.

Protoindustrialization

I have argued that the course of European pre-industrial urbanization depended on the character of migration. With the help of the three-sector model it can now be added that the development of a proletariat also depended on migration behaviour, which can now be analysed on the basis of α and β, migration to the urban and rural-industrial sectors respectively.

From the results of the migration estimation exercises summarized in tables 10.1 and 10.3 (line 15) it appears that α, directing migrants to the cities, came to be very large in the course of the sixteenth century, peaking in the early seventeenth century when the cities attracted to themselves nearly all of the rural surplus. Thereafter the attractive power of the cities, particularly in northern Europe, deteriorated. Regionally, the continued rapid growth of a selection of large cities (London, Madrid) and the maintenance of extremely high levels of urbanization (Dutch Republic, The Veneto) kept α high, but elsewhere α falls, sometimes to the point of bringing about de-urbanization (Brabant and Flanders, southern Germany, much of Spain). In the course of the seventeenth and eighteenth centuries β assumes greater importance than α.

The net effect of the shifting migration patterns, described here in highly generalized terms, was nothing less than to restructure the European economy. Figure 10.3 represents an effort to highlight one aspect of that process of restructuring. It displays the probable changes in the relative size of the three sectors that have been the basis of the preceding analysis. The urban

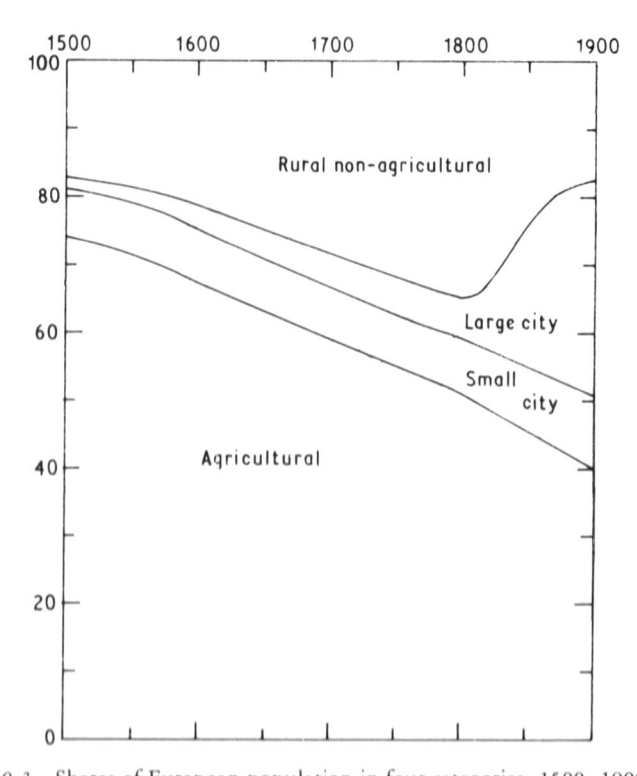

Figure 10.3 Shares of European population in four categories, 1500–1900

population, divided into large (40,000 and over) and small (5000–39,000) components, follows the course uncovered in chapters 4 and 7. Its growth was almost entirely located in the handful of rapidly expanding ports and capitals; the great bulk of Europe's cities in the aggregate barely kept pace with overall population growth.

Figure 10.3 also splits the non-urban population into two segments: the by-now familiar farm and rural-industrial sectors. Of course, much less is known about the relative size of these two groups than about the urban–rural split. In dividing Europe's non-urban population into these two categories I make the assumption that the rural population not primarily engaged in agriculture stood at about 20 per cent in the early sixteenth century and rose to 40 per cent by 1800, only to fall again to 30 per cent by the end of the nineteenth century. This scenario is consistent with a continued increase in the absolute size of the agricultural labour force (about 46 million in 1500, 53 million in 1600, 63 million in 1800, 92 million in 1890). The implied diminution of the farm sector's share of the total population (from 74 per cent in 1500 to 51 per cent in 1800) may not be excessive.

In the interpretation of the figure it is necessary to keep in mind that it represents a composite of regional patterns that varied a great deal. A few areas became intensely urban, some were overwhelmed by a swarming proto-industrial population, others specialized in commercial agriculture, serving the new markets in both the cities and the zones of rural industry. This growth of regional differentiation and specialization is directly related to the changing character of urban life in the seventeenth and eighteenth centuries. Rural locations attracted labour and capital away from the cities, but the investors and the co-ordinators of these new forms of activity were generally urban people. Ironically, for protoindustrialization and de-urbanization to proceed there had to exist serviceable networks of communications and transportation linking towns to their hinterlands and to each other. That is, there had to exist an urban system capable of organizing the landscape into economic regions.

THE ECONOMIC CONSEQUENCES OF THE PROTOINDUSTRIAL URBAN SYSTEM

Once the appropriate urban network was in place, the constraints that had confined much industrial production to urban settings loosened, and the advantage of rural production could be exploited. Those advantages were considerable. In the first place lower production costs could be achieved through nearness to raw materials, exploitation of labour with low opportunity costs, and avoidance of urban taxes and guilds. At the same time, the constraint imposed on non-agricultural expansion by agriculture's inelastic supply responses to increased demand for foodstuffs could be loosened, if not dissolved, by the availability of rural-industrial labour for work in agriculture during the seasons of peak labour demand. Finally, rural industry economized on the need for fixed capital investment, most notably in urban structures.

The placement of the three sectors (with the urban sector split into two parts) in figure 10.3 makes it easier to see how nineteenth-century urbanization and industrialization proceeded. After the early-industrial hiatus stimulating small-city growth (see pp. 101–6), the renewed but now much faster growth of large cities did not so much draw upon the agricultural population as on the *already existing* rural wage-earners. In this perspective the seventeenth- and eighteenth-century era of selective urban growth and widespread regional de-urbanization stands out as a critical link between an agrarian-artisanal world and modern industrial society. The nineteenth century ushered in a dramatic increase in the conventional measure of urbanization, but it did not mark a break in the long-term process of 'de-agriculturalization'. This had been proceeding apace for a long time, facilitated by the construction of an urban system that made it possible to restructure the economy without incurring the costs of massive urbanization. Should nineteenth-century urbanization perhaps be viewed more as a change of strategy than of substance?

This urban restructuring in the context of protoindustrial expansion had unique consequences worthy of further discussion on two key elements of the urban economy: capital investment and food supply.

Discussions of capital stock and investment usually emphasize such productive assets as machinery and inventories. Little attention is paid to the capital requirements of urban growth in the form of residential construction and expansion of the urban infrastructure. No modern visitor to a well-preserved pre-industrial city can fail to be impressed by the enormous commitment of labour and capital embodied in its structures and fabric, but apart from some speculative calculations of the cost of medieval cathedral building, economic historians have devoted little attention to the financing and organization of urban construction.[51] This is to be regretted because one of the foremost characteristics of urbanization is its expense.

The potential importance of the subject becomes obvious when one contemplates the financial requirements of nineteenth-century urbanization. Urban construction, broadly defined, motivated a very large portion of the international lending that then assumed such vast proportions. Indeed, W. Arthur Lewis claims that the capital-importing nations can most consistently be distinguished from the capital-exporting nations on the basis of their rates of urban growth. He observes that the international lenders registered rates of urban growth (which he defines as the annual change of the urban population divided by the total *urban* population) below about 3 per cent per annum, while the intense urban growth of borrowers exceeded that level and, Lewis argues, exceeded the upper limit to self-financed urban construction.[52]

The maximum rate of urban growth consistent with the financial possibilities of the pre-industrial economy is not known. We can only guess that it was probably lower than in the nineteenth century. It is none the less interesting to observe that the annual rates of urban growth in early modern times were almost invariably very much lower than 3 per cent. In northern Europe as a whole they reached 0.6 per cent in the first half of the seventeenth century and no more than that in the late eighteenth century.[53] For smaller regions the rate of growth to be financed could substantially exceed that – in the northern Netherlands it reached 1.2 per cent in 1550–1600 – but throughout the century after 1650 the rates were much lower, suggesting that the investment requirements for urban construction were modest. The non-agricultural population was then growing apace, but without placing substantial demands on the capital supply.

The dependability of the food supply was never far from the minds of early modern Europeans, and securing the food requirements of urban populations was a constant object of government policy.[54] Cities sought to ensure their food supplies through combinations of fiat (forced marketing, taxation) and encouragement (investment in transport facilities, efficient marketing institutions).[55] But did not the technical conditions of agriculture set limits to the feasible growth of non-agricultural populations that no amount of regulations concerning provision could overcome?

Just where those limits lay in the period that concerns us cannot be determined with accuracy, and is probably less important than the size of the annual variations around the mean. It is still of some value to have a rough idea of agriculture's ability to sustain non-food producers. This issue can be explored in a preliminary way with the help of a central economic parameter of a pre-industrial economy, the yield ratio. This relationship of the number of kernels of grain harvested for every seed sown, when placed in the context of a simple model of agrarian production, generates some interesting results concerning the limits of pre-industrial urbanization.

Consider a rural society consisting of five-member households, farming on average 8 hectares of arable land in three-course rotations, sowing 200 litres of seed to the hectare, and requiring 250 litres of bread grain per person per year (about half a kilo of bread per day). Such a household would produce less than its own survival needs if the yield ratio of the harvest were $3:1$, it could feed 1.4 non-farmers per farm household at a yield ratio of $4:1$, and could feed 3.5 extra persons per farm household at a ratio of $5:1$. In other words, the sustainable non-agricultural population could rise from 0 at the

3 : 1 ratio to 22 per cent of the total population at 4 : 1, to 41 per cent at ratio of 5 : 1.[56]

These calculations of the sustainable non-agricultural population exaggerate the real possibilities. Obviously, to support all but the simplest economy many crops needed to be produced besides grain. What is more, the very process of urbanization required a progressive diversion of resources from food production. For example, if the portion of grain output being consumed not on the farm but in the city rises from 15 to 30 per cent, the resources devoted to transporting that grain would have to double. The land devoted to hay and oats production for the horses used in transporting the bread grains could not be used for food production. In addition, many other non-food products were needed to allow an urban population to carry out its non-agricultural activities. All of these factors require that we deflate the results of the yield ratio exercise.

The subject of historical seed-yield ratios cannot here be examined in depth. But it is interesting to observe that in the seventeenth and eighteenth century ratios around 4 : 1 were common in central and eastern Europe while slightly higher ratios seem to have been most common in westernmost Europe. Indeed, in the Low Countries and southern England the ratios considerably exceeded 5 : 1.[57]

So long as the yield ratios hovered between 4 : 1 and 5 : 1, the agricultural limits to urban growth must have been very real indeed. The belief that urbanization faced strict limits is reinforced by the recent studies of preindustrial agricultural output that are based on the records of tithe collections. These investigations commonly find that grain output (the chief product subject to this levy) did not increase in any sustained way over extended periods of time.[58] Le Roy Ladurie bases his concept of an 'histoire immobile' on the proposition that in France

> cereal production in the sixteenth and seventeenth centuries never greatly exceeded a kind of ceiling which remained in place for several centuries. In *L'Histoire économique et sociale de la France*, I put forward certain figures for this 'ceiling': 50 million quintals of grain in the area covered by present-day France at the beginning of the fourteenth century, and 60 million quintals during the long seventeenth century [a period ending in the 1720s] . . .[59]

In this same spirit the Polish historians Topolski and Wyczanski reckon Polish grain production actually to have been slightly lower in 1789 than it had been in the 1570s.[60]

Agricultural production was not everywhere so constrained as these estimates suggest. English grain production certainly grew a great deal.[61] Moreover, the 'immobility' evoked by Le Roy Ladurie is itself rather misleading, since the unbudging levels of grain production often went hand-in-hand with a diversion of productive resources into increasing the output of livestock products, wine, industrial raw materials, maize, rice and potatoes.

The achievement of the agricultural sector before the nineteenth century should not be sought in an enormous increase of grain production in response to a burgeoning urban market. After all, the total population of all of northern Europe's cities of 5000 and more inhabitants only rose from 8 per cent of the total in 1500 to 11 per cent in 1800. Moreover, when such a 'market opportunity' presented itself in the Mediterranean area during the course of the sixteenth-century urban boom, the agricultural supply response was, to say the least, disappointing.[62] This market impact remained confined to specific regions affected by the enormous growth of London, Paris and the cities of Holland.

The key achievement of agriculture before the nineteenth century was located in diversification in the context of regional specialization. The role of the cities in this process had less to do with the growth of their markets, *per se*, than with the intensification of transportation and communications links among themselves and with their hinterlands. I have emphasized that the modest overall growth of urban population during the early modern period did not imply a correspondingly modest growth of non-agricultural population. Indeed, figure 10.3 implies that the number of non-food producers supported by each farmer rose steadily from about 0.35 in 1500 to 0.7 in 1700 to 1.0 in 1800. This apparently spectacular increase in agricultural productivity suggests that urbanization did not really face a ceiling to its expansion, but it must be emphasized that this agricultural achievement occurred in the context of protoindustrialization, where most of the growing non-agricultural population lived in close proximity to agriculture. This labour force was thereby capable of responding to the seasonal peaks in the demand for agricultural labour. It was thereby less vulnerable to subsistence crises at the same time that it could contribute to yield improvements through its strategic participation in agricultural production.

We are observing here a strategy of economic diversification and probably of income growth that limited the society's exposure to the demographic and economic hazards of high urbanization such as struck Mediterranean Europe at the end of the sixteenth century. A pre-condition for this rise of the rural proletariat was an urban system capable of organizing space on a large scale, but its direct consequence was widespread de-urbanization relieved by a selective urban growth in a limited number of larger cities. In both the countryside and among the cities, a process of differentiation and specialization was set in motion.

It is fascinating to observe the parallel between this European phenomenon of the seventeenth and eighteenth centuries and the experience of

MIGRATION AND URBAN GROWTH

Japan in the eighteenth and early nineteenth centuries. Thomas Smith, in a stimulating study of pre-modern growth in Tokugawa, Japan, called attention to Japan's de-urbanization in this era of spreading rural industry and argued that no economic growth could have occurred in a society devoid of foreign trade and experiencing no population growth 'without a considerable degree of de-urbanization'.[63] He went on to argue that

> The expansion of the economy in the absence of foreign trade and population growth induces the decline of towns. For, as per capita income rises, so inevitably does the demand for the products of secondary industry and services, which therefore require more labour. Labour cannot be withdrawn from farming for obvious reasons, including the danger of widespread starvation. It can nonetheless be found in ample supply and good quality and in a stable social environment in the form of peasant family members, who can rarely be kept busy fulltime in farming. As industry and trade spread in the country, therefore, by-employments on the farms begin to reduce the annual flow of migrants to the towns, and the towns, unable to sustain themselves by natural increase, lose population.[64]

This description sounds familiar; it is the very phenomenon being analysed and simulated here for Europe in a period that begins and ends about a century earlier than in Japan.

Smith argued that pre-modern growth in Japan, accompanied by de-urbanization, affected social class relations and culture as well as economic structure in ways that contributed significantly to what he regarded as the major differences between the processes of economic development of Japan and Europe. He contrasted the stagnation and decline of many Japanese cities to the situation in Europe where, following the conclusions of Roger Mols, he observed that 'The major cities of Europe as a whole grew in number and size in every century from 1300 to 1800' (with the possible exception of the period 1350–1450). In the seventeenth and eighteenth centuries he concluded 'the growth of urban population in western Europe is not in doubt'.[65] The data assembled in this study do not contradict this last statement; but we can now be more precise and demonstrate that this growth issued from an exceedingly narrow range of stimuli and affected only a handful of Europe's many hundreds of cities. The smaller cities of Europe as a whole, and vast regions of Europe (particularly inland regions), experienced the same general fate as Smith observed for Japan.

Not only did most cities stagnate or decline in both areas, but they did so for much the same set of reasons: a transfer of industrial production to the countryside, and the rise of numerous villages and local market towns as nuclei of the putting-out system. In this way, just as Smith notes of Japan, an industrial labour force could be recruited without withdrawing it totally from the agricultural sector. At the same time, the heavy burden of capital investment associated with urban growth could also be avoided. In the absence of major technical innovations and rapid population growth, pre-modern industry achieved a growth of output and a reduction of production costs by effecting organizational changes, a primary consequence of which was to cut short the flow of migrants to, and investment in, the cities. But in Europe as well as in Japan this could occur only because of the prior achievement of an urban system featuring a hierarchy of cities and a substantial level of urbanization.

DUALISM, PARASITISM AND REGIONALISM

This pattern of development furnishes us with an important clue about the true economic position of the early modern city. To see it more clearly we must first push aside two rival concepts that have long muddied the waters of urban studies: dualism and parasitism.

Cities did not, by themselves, constitute a superior economy whose relative growth would transform society. On the contrary, beyond a certain – albeit necessary – point, further urbanization imposed demographic costs, famine risks and investment burdens. And what were the benefits that could be placed besides these costs? If we follow Braudel's interpretation, the answer must be that there were few compelling benefits: 'These enormous formations are more linked to the past, to accomplished evolutions, faults and weaknesses of the societies and economies of the *ancien régime* than to preparations for the future.'[66] The new era would be launched by 'innumerable small proletarian towns' as indeed the study of rank-size distributions in chapter 6 confirms.

Obviously, the concept of 'dualism', so often employed in development economics, is inappropriate to the analysis of early modern urbanization. Dualism asserts the existence of an advanced urban sector and a backward rural sector. It interprets the problem of development as a task requiring the shifting of labour and other resources from the one to the other sector, from a lower to a higher use.[67] This transfer does more than simply improve the average level of productivity, it also makes the society more dynamic. '[The towns] exhibit a spirit different from that of the countryside. They are the main force and the chief locus for the introduction of new ideas and new ways of doing things.'[68]

The early modern European city was clearly no conduit of a more advanced economy or technology, as might be true in today's developing countries. Furthermore, there is little reason to believe that rural migrants to the cities of pre-industrial Europe were necessarily put to a higher use than their compatriots remaining in the countryside. Hence, one cannot assume that incremental urbanization in this era *necessarily* denotes incremental economic growth.[69]

I have little reason to belabour this point, because few historians of early modern Europe hold such a view, however appealing it has been to theorists of modern economic development. What does attract many historians is the proposition that European cities in these centuries, particularly the larger cities, were important not as centres of production but as centres of consumption. The enormous appetite of cities for consumer goods, and the tendency for fashion, emulation and luxury to flourish in an urban setting is sometimes regarded as a stimulus to economic development in its own right. A great city's consumption needs reshape marketing patterns in its hinterlands while urban tastes, once diffused to the countryside, generate social change more generally.

But, just as often, the city as a consumer is evaluated more negatively, as a 'parasite'. This 'inverse dualism' is rarely specified in any detail. It often seems to be a moral judgement on urban society rather than a description of the urban economy. To the extent that it is the latter, a parasitic city must be one that lives from its host, that is sustained by the rest of society without offering an equivalent of useful goods and services in return.[70] A direct implication – generating a hypothesis that is, in theory, testable – is that society would have been better off without such cities.

This notion of a parasitic urban economy seems to derive from 'economic base theory', an approach to explaining urban growth favoured by geographers.[71] In this approach the urban economy is divided into two parts, a basic sector and a non-basic sector. The basic sector consists of all activities concerned with the production of goods and services destined for consumption outside the city. The income derived from such 'city-forming' activities pays for imports to the city (such as foodstuffs), but also supports 'city serving', non-basic activities within the city (i.e. bakers, policemen, urban transport). The size of the total urban economy depends on the size of the basic sector and the strength of the multiplier, the number of non-basic workers supported by each basic worker. The smaller the leakage of expenditures out of the city economy, the larger the multiplier. Presumably, the larger and more complex the city, the fewer the leakages, the stronger the multiplier.

Economic base theory is not a very satisfactory approach to urban growth for several reasons. In practice, it is not possible to separate consistently basic activities from non-basic ones. More importantly, the leakages of one city are the support of basic activities somewhere else. It makes an important difference to the growth of an urban *system* whether that place is another city or not. Finally, and this is where the issue of parasitism comes in, exported goods and services that are not produced and distributed in the exchange economy ('public goods', but also, in the modern economy, functions internal to a multi-divisional firm) tend to figure prominently in the economic life of cities. What is their 'value' to the rest of society? Is the city exporting education or indoctrination, salvation or hocus-pocus, management or coercion, justice or tyranny? Even if these questions could be answered objectively, urban base theory would be no more valid than the mercantilist proposition that a (national) economy can only grow by expanding its exports. Exports are not unimportant, but such a crude formulation cannot form the basis for an understanding of economic growth.

A parasitic city, then, must be one with the ability to draw unwarranted income to itself. We can use as an example an imperial city full of noble courtiers and highly placed clerics. Tax receipts, church revenues and the rents of landed estates flow to the city, there maintaining wealthy households and institutions which, in turn, attract to themselves an army of servants, retainers, craftsmen and entertainers. Clearly, this vast edifice of urban consumption and employment rests on a foundation of compulsory transfers of revenue. But would the rest of society be better off in the city's absence?

The answer is less obvious than one might at first suppose.[72] The fact is that the above sketch of a parasitic city fits a large number of different places. It fits Madrid, and Ringrose argues convincingly that the maintenance of that city placed a real burden on Castile.[73] But it also fits London, which F. J. Fisher argues was the 'engine of growth' of the English economy and which E. A. Wrigley describes as 'a potent engine working toward change', part of a positive feedback relationship that gave birth, ultimately, to the Industrial Revolution.[74] What made the one parasitic and the other dynamic? The answer is not to be found in their sources of income, which did not differ so greatly, but in their patterns of expenditure, and particularly in their investment behaviour.

The concentration of many people in one place creates market opportunities and these have not gone unnoticed. But the mere existence of great centres of consumption never sufficed to transform economic life. A large city draws resources from a wide area, but whether that transfer becomes a burdensome levy or an agent of development depends on the existence of investments that lower production costs, improve transportation and encourage specialization. Sometimes such investments have tended to concentrate population in certain cities (such as the seventeenth-century Atlantic ports and nineteenth-century factory towns); sometimes they have created more opportunities in the countryside (via investment in protoindustry, canal and road construction, agricultural intensification).

In both cases, it is not the 'city' that is industrializing or the 'countryside' that is progressing. Rather it is a society, usually best viewed in a regional context, that is developing via the mobilization of its resources by individuals with access to an urban system. Assessments of the early modern city will continue to lose their way among the ambiguous and contradictory features that have been noted in this study so long as the city continues to be examined in isolation. The fate of individual cities was something distinct from that of the urban system, and the city's function in the process of economic growth can only be understood in a broader, regional context.

V
CONCLUSIONS

11
CONCLUSIONS

THE MAKING OF THE URBAN SYSTEM

In the course of writing this book I have wandered rather far from my initial concern, which was to satisfy my curiosity about the number of cities and their sizes before the nineteenth century. Once I was in a position to describe the patterns of urban growth for the period 1500–1800 (part II) it became apparent that the cities of early modern Europe formed a larger entity – an urban system – that called for study in its own right (part III). This urban system was, of course, not an autonomous historical actor, but a product of decision-making: of people and their migration patterns; of the controllers of capital and their investment behaviour; of the state and its political decisions. I investigated only the first of these three determinants of urbanization in detail (part IV). Investment behaviour in particular merits much more attention than could be given to it here. But in each of these areas of decision-making I sought to show that the key to understanding urban change is to focus on the general processes and their differentiated effects on the system of cities rather than on the fate of individual cities. Thus I presented the demographic growth of cities as part of a general model of migration, and I suggested that the investment of capital in a city is not simply a discrete event but is commonly part of a larger process of organizational change or of the diffusion of an innovation.

In chapter 1 I raised the question of the place of the 'post-medieval pre-industrial city' in European history. Was it modern or traditional? Was it a harbinger of industrial capitalism or parasitic on obsolete social forms? The answer I propose is based on the proposition that the individual city cannot be the only unit of analysis in the early modern era, for the city was then in the process of becoming part of a system of cities. When one's attention is focused on a city, the assessment of its character is likely to be based on the city's relationships to the rest of society: to its hinterland, to the state, to the foreign trade sector, and so on. When one focuses attention on cities in the aggregate, the assessment tends to lean more heavily on the internal structure of the urban system, and on how a city functions within that system. This second approach is emphasized here; it allows us to portray the history of urbanization in the early modern era as the dismantling of an old urban structure and its replacement by a new one. An important feature of this process was that the constituent cities of these two structures remained the same. As a consequence, the histories of individual cities during these three centuries are largely concerned with their search for a place in a new urban environment. The transition involved many hazards and often resulted in failure. This danger was great precisely because the new urban structure was not primarily an administrative hierarchy or a central market system (although elements of both were, of necessity, present), but was shaped by the needs of a commercializing economy and came to be dominated by competitive mercantile centres.

In this light the conflicting claims of the advocates of the capitalist medieval city, the modern industrial city and the parasitic city of early modern times seem misdirected. The medieval city may have had many virtues, but the autarchic urban structure of the middle ages could not serve as the urban framework of a commercial and industrial society. The industrial city of the factory age was undoubtedly a novel and powerful organism, but it inserted itself into an existing urban system which it modified but did not transform.[1] In the intervening period many cities displayed parasitic characteristics (in the sense of living from tax revenues and land rents) or signs of decay (in the loss of industrial employment), but in this same period the whole – the system of cities – was becoming something different from the sum of its parts.

If the way cities functioned in the early modern period differed from earlier and later epochs, then the concept of urbanization appropriate to the period must also be distinctive. Following Lampard, I proposed that urbanization be decomposed into three elements – demographic, structural and behavioural – and that these could vary in their specific character and relative importance over time. What, then, were the features that distinguished early modern urbanization?

Demographic urbanization, at first glance, hardly existed, since the conventional measure, percentage of population resident in cities, crept upwards at a snail's pace. But the cities of this era exhibited internal demographic characteristics that caused them to exert, via migration, an often profound but highly variable impact on the rest of society. In the nineteenth century the demographic constraints that imparted a unique importance to rural–urban migration were lifted, permitting a new pattern of urban growth driven by natural increase. In this sense, the early modern era displayed a specific form of demographic urbanization.

Structural urbanization refers to the organizational innovations that increase the range of urban activities and increase the need for co-ordination and communications. It is here that the cities of Europe changed the most – a change reflected less in the size of the urban population than in the redistribution of population among cities of a developing urban hierarchy. The development of nation states, the control of colonial empires, the integration of regional marketing networks, and the co-ordination of a dispersed system of industrial production, all affected the nature of inter-urban links, and, hence, of the system of cities.

In the early modern era behavioural urbanization, the diffusion of an urban 'way of life' throughout society, was subject to severe limitations. The very largest cities surely affected the sociological character of extended areas,[2] but at the same time in smaller places one must still speak of the strong rural influences on town life. Behavioural urbanization remained highly uneven in its incidence. This of course stands in sharp contrast to the twentieth century, where in the advanced societies one can argue that urbanization has become essentially behavioural urbanization.

The primary achievement of an urbanization that was predominantly structural with an historically specific demographic element was the creation, by the early eighteenth century at the latest, of Europe's modern urban hierarchy. Contrary to the assertions of the 'modern-city versus traditional-city' school (which focuses its attention over much on the urban share of the total population), the modern urban system was an achievement of the 'pre-modern' era.

European urbanization has a longer past than is often thought, but that past was far from a linear progression. The historical process of urban hierarchy-formation can be summarized conveniently by dividing it into three distinctive phases. Such a periodization of early modern European urbanization, a sketch of which is presented in figure 11.1, requires some oversimplification and the suppression of regional variation, but standing opposite this 'cost' is the 'benefit' of a clear exposition of the principal elements of the urban achievement.

The long sixteenth century, 1500–1600/50

In the extended period of European demographic and economic recovery and expansion that stretched from the late fifteenth into the early seventeenth century, the stock of cities with which medieval civilization had endowed Europe was not significantly enlarged, but the growth of urban population was quite broadly distributed among cities of all types, sizes and locations.

CONCLUSIONS

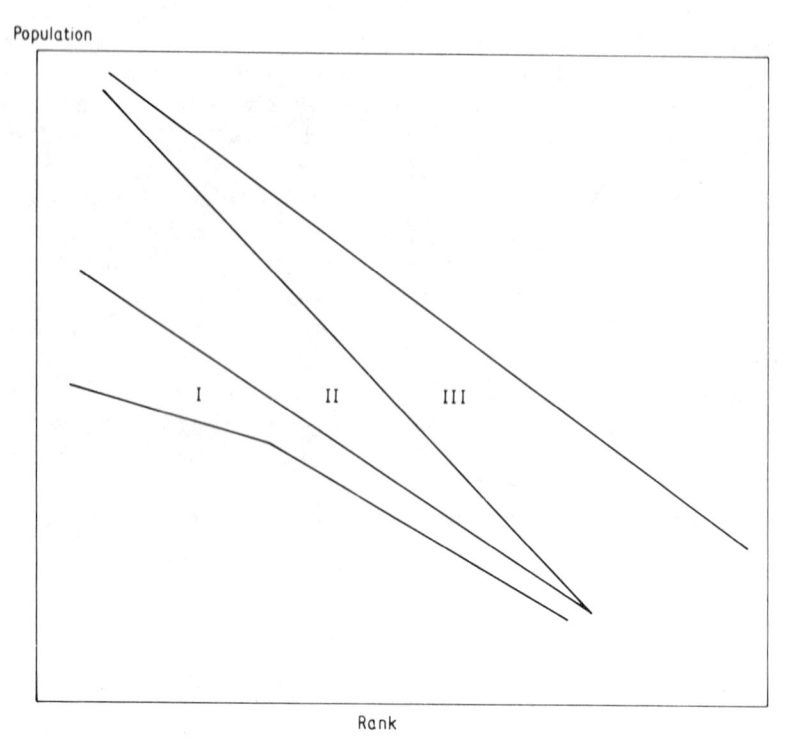

Figure 11.1 Three phases of early modern urbanization

Superimposed on this general urban growth was the work of state-building, most notably in England, France and Spain, that had the effect of undermining the independence and autonomy of many cities and subordinating their economic interests to those of the Renaissance monarchies. This, plus the impact of the Reformation on cathedral towns in newly Protestant lands and the impact of reduced demand for manufactured products brought on by rising agricultural prices, had the cumulative effect of undermining the viability of many cities at the same time that certain cities gained enormously in growth potential as the administrative centres of the new monarchies (Madrid, London, Paris and, in a sense, post-Trentine Rome) or as the economic handmaidens of imperial ambition (Genoa, Augsburg, Antwerp).

An old urban world was under attack, but the evidence for this in our data base is partly hidden by the overall economic and demographic vigour of the age. That economic vigour is associated with the connection with each other of Europe's trading areas and the growth in volume of interregional trade. This, together with the first steps towards the achievement of bureaucratic government, endowed the decentralized medieval urban structure still in evidence in 1500 with a novel element of hierarchy. But, since the growing cities were well distributed about Europe, this hierarchy was polycentric; no fewer than four important concentrations of cities vied for leadership in 1600.

The age of the rural proletariat, 1600/50–1750

No single date can be assigned to divide the first from the second period, for the shift is associated with the slowing or reversal of sixteenth-century population growth. This occurred earlier in the Mediterranean area (about 1600) than in central Europe (Thirty Years' War); central Europe in turn was hit before the north and west, where population growth was slowed but on the whole not reversed in the second half of the seventeenth century. From these varied dates until approximately the mid-eighteenth century urban growth was influenced by a unique combination of forces whose net effect was to bring about a sharper differentiation among the component parts of Europe's urban world.

This second period is shaped by the cessation of both the rapid growth of total population and of the expansion of the non-European areas of trade and colonization that had been so important in the preceding period. In this new environment, with seemingly fewer impulses stimulating urban growth, a series of organizational innovations affected state and society to the benefit of a highly selective group of cities, permitting them to assume new functions in the urban system. At the same time a larger group were being undermined sufficiently that they declined in relative standing and, often, in absolute population.

The selectivity of the urban growth process in this period assumed several forms. In the first place, urban growth was highly concentrated in large cities and cities that grew rapidly to become large. Two types of activity fuelled this growth: government and overseas trade. In absolutist and constitutional states alike, in big states and small, administration, the military and the legal apparatus provided for a major expansion of employment. The growing ports were, with only a few exceptions, engaged in the Atlantic trades. Among the exceptions were the Mediterranean ports that grew as outposts of north-west European merchant interests at the expense of 'indigenous' ports.

These activities had stimulated urban growth before, of course, and would be important in later eras as well. But in the seventeenth century they stood out because of the weakness of other growth impulses. A large portion of the 600 or so remaining cities with at least 5000 inhabitants, not to mention the thousands of smaller cities, stagnated or declined. There was a net de-urbanization of cities under 40,000 population, another way in which period II is unique in the three centuries under analysis here. The great bulk of inland trading centres, seats of ecclesiastical administration, and, particularly, industrial towns, suffered at least relative loss of standing between the early seventeenth and the mid-eighteenth centuries. The spread through the countryside of the putting-out system, or protoindustrialization, speeded the abandonment of cities as locations for many of the most labour-absorbing industries, while at the same time low agricultural prices, by lowering rental incomes, reduced upper-class demand for many of the services provided by regional towns. Compensating for this in some areas were the commercial opportunities arising through the growth of the markets in the exploding metropolises. Thus, while most small cities did not grow, their internal character changed.

The net effect of this pattern of urban growth and decay was to increase sharply the slope of Europe's rank-size distribution. This rigorous process of hierarchy-formation was most intense in northern Europe, for the urban growth impulses in the era of the rural proletariat were selective in a second respect: geographically. In the Mediterranean lands the urban growth of the sixteenth century, which caused the relative size of the urban population to be significantly higher than in the north, could not be sustained. In the hostile economic environment of the seventeenth century the blows struck suddenly and with great severity, and they were compounded by political setbacks to the region's dominant power, the Spanish Habsburgs. In a single fifty-year period the relative position of Mediterranean cities in general, and the leadership of the largest of them in particular, was swept away. The European urban system not only became more hierarchic, it also became unicentric.

The new urbanization, 1750–1800/50

Beginning around the mid-eighteenth century the basic factors underlying European urban growth and the nature of the urban hierarchy changed fundamentally. Rapid population growth, technical innovation, and changed relative prices that brought a new prosperity to the agricultural sector all combined to reverse a centuries-long process of urban population concentration in the largest cities. This 'new urbanization' (which becomes fully apparent in the Mediterranean area only after 1800) had the effect of shifting the rank-size distribution sharply to the right, but the shift was much more forceful in the lower tail of the distribution than in the highest ranks. Because total population rose rapidly, most cities grew substantially; but the net urbanization of the period 1750–1800 was, in fact, not unusually large and was disproportionately the result of the growth of smaller cities and the addition of new cities to the system.

The reduction of large-city growth to approximate proportionality with

CONCLUSIONS

total population growth for the first time in at least 250 years is not easily explained, since until now few historians have been aware of this check to large-city growth. It stems in part from the fact that the objective of state centralization had in large part been achieved in most states by 1750. In addition, the stimuli to urban growth provided by foreign and, particularly, inter-continental trade after 1750 may have been less potent than is asserted by the conventional wisdom, which has it that early industrialization moved forward on the strong back of colonial trade. It is not impossible that historians have exaggerated the importance of long-distance trade in this period.

The 'new urbanization' was an urban growth from below. Consequently, our task is to identify the new forces nurturing the 'grass roots' of Europe's urban system. An obvious factor was simply the rate of overall population growth. To the extent that the demographic variables acting upon the rate of natural increase did so in settlements of all sizes, many small cities were bound to find themselves in higher categories. But there were two basic additional factors at work that acted to expand the base of the urban system.

As is well known, the early stages of the Industrial Revolution tended to be played out in relatively small cities and in rural locations. Both institutional and technological factors encouraged this. As a consequence, many small cities with resource-based industries such as metallurgy grew as a consequence of technological innovation, and many rural places that had grown thick with people as protoindustrial textile production spread in the preceding era broke through to become industrial cities as technological change encouraged factory organization. This is the primary cause of the first concentrated wave of new city formation since the thirteenth century.

The Industrial Revolution of the eighteenth century was primarily a British phenomenon, and while British cities grew more vigorously than those elsewhere, the rise of small cities was by no means confined to that island. The rapid growth of small cities on the continent is often observed to begin somewhat later than in Britain; in the Mediterranean region it is in fact most pronounced in the period 1800–50, but the surprising universality of small-city growth indicates the need for another growth stimulus than the factory system alone. It can be found in the increase in agricultural incomes and the expansion of farm production. Regional marketing and administrative centres expanded their employment bases as the volume of marketed farm output grew, and the retailing and services sectors grew with the increase in landlords' rental incomes.

In the second half of the eighteenth century all these forces combined added some 200 cities to the size category of 5000–9900 inhabitants and over 100 cities to the 10,000–19,000 category, and the process of urban growth from below continued into the nineteenth century.

CONCLUSIONS

Ever since Adna Weber's pioneer analysis of urbanization, published in 1899, the proposition that modern urbanization is characterized by population concentration in large cities has seemed securely established.[3] Thus R. J. Johnson writes, in his recent interpretation of long-term urban growth, 'The factory system's impact [on the central place settlement pattern] was to accentuate the size and economic importance of the larger centres', and 'in effect, the gaps between different levels of the urban hierarchy opened up, with the large places benefiting disproportionately from the various growth impulses'.[4]

From the materials presented in this volume it now appears that the industrial age was inaugurated by an interval in which urban growth assumed a form that was the opposite of these conventional assumptions. Europe received, for the first time since the middle ages, a sizeable infusion of new cities. In fact, a truly iconoclastic interpreter of the data presented in this volume might argue that the post-1820/50 process of urban concentration in large cities has only restored the hierarchical characteristics imparted during the creation of Europe's modern urban system in the seventeenth century.

WHAT SORT OF URBAN SYSTEM DID EUROPE GET?

Figure 4.7, which brings together the available information on Europe's total and urban populations from the early fourteenth century to the present day, conveys a visual image of early modern urbanization as something intermediary or preparatory. It seems to stand between the small, stable but unintegrated urban world of the middle ages and the dynamic, ubiquitous urbanization of European society of the past 150 years. In this intermediate period, one might argue, cities grew substantially, but without dissolving the rural world in which they functioned; in addition, the cities fashioned loosely integrated networks, but without achieving the ideal integration of an efficient urban system. Both of these statements speaking to the character of Europe's urban system are misleading.

There is no need here to review in detail the characteristics of city growth uncovered in this study. It was found that this growth was, depending on the measure used, at once spectacular and lacklustre. Surely the most important discovery was that urban growth was highly selective of cities, and that the basis of selection changed – once around 1600, again in the mid-eighteenth century, and again a century later. No 'law of proportionate effect' governed the growth of Europe's cities in this period.

The second statement is more difficult to evaluate because 'integration' and 'efficiency' are terms that have unavoidable subjective elements. I have argued here that the cities of Europe came to form a single, albeit loosely coupled urban system, a system with sufficient integrity that the behaviour of national and regional subsystems cannot be well understood in isolation. In doing so I have had to consider the claims of others that the pre-modern urban systems were 'immature' or otherwise inadequate to achieve an efficient circulation of resources.

A problem with the assertion that Europe's cities formed an urban system is that the possibilities for comparative analysis are very limited. In comparing national subsystems, one can argue, for example, that the French cities formed a more coherent system than the Spanish, or one can compare the relative virtues of Neapolitan, English and Danish primacy. With the urban system of Europe as a whole I have based most claims on the evidence of its own historical development.

That historical development can be compared to the expectations of rank-size distribution theories, but in doing so I came to the conclusions that these theories had little merit. For example, the ideal of the rank-size rule could teach that the European urban system in the eighteenth century was still insufficiently integrated, or was in fact a conflation of several independent systems. But it cannot offer guidance in the exploration of the second possibility (see p. 92), and in the case of the first it stands powerless before the historical fact that the European urban system, and most national subsystems as well, never have and do not today conform to the rank-size rule. The slopes of these rank-size distributions are mostly substantially below -1, and have hovered in a rather narrow range since the mid-seventeenth century.

Another possibility is to compare the pre-industrial urban system of Europe with its contemporaries in other areas of the world. This is not the impractical suggestion it appears to be, for scholarly interest in pre-modern urbanization has been focused primarily on non-European societies. Of particular importance among recent studies are G. William Skinner's *The City in Late Imperial China* (1977) and two books by Gilbert Rozman, *Urban Networks in Ch'ing China and Tokugawa Japan* (1973) and *Urban Networks in Russia 1750–1800 and Premodern Periodization* (1976).

How can these urban systems be compared? Rozman, whose views about the stages of urban development have already been discussed (pp. 9–10), proposes that the relative efficiency of urban hierarchies be evaluated by comparing the number of central places per capita. The larger the average size of cities – the fewer the number of cities per capita – the more efficient is the system. Rozman defends his measure by arguing that 'ratios of the number of central places in adjoining levels [he groups cities into seven levels, based on size and function] measure the efficiency of moving goods up the urban hierarchy of settlements'.[5] This efficiency he supposes will differ according to the extent of administrative and commercial centralization. Although Rozman makes no use of rank-size distribution, his categorization of cities by 'level' can be translated into rank-size distribution without doing

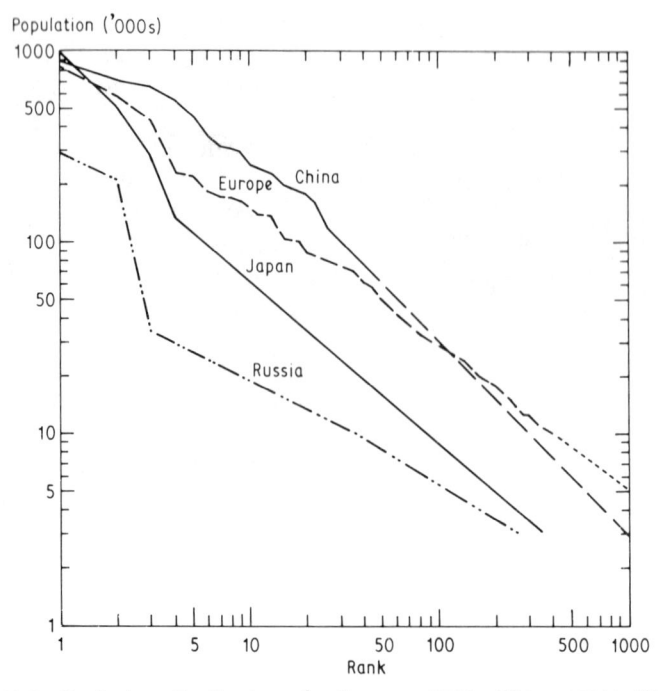

Figure 11.2 Rank-size distributions for Europe, 1800; China, 1843 (Skinner); Russia, *c.* 1800 (Rozman); and Japan, *c.* 1800 (Rozman)

too great violence to his concepts. When this is done, as in figure 11.2, one can readily see that efficiency in his terms is associated with a steeply sloped distribution. Of the three urban networks that he compares, Japan, Russia and China, the first is the most efficient network and 'the least efficient network for moving resources from the lowest to the highest level existed in China'.[6] He holds this view in part because of China's very large number of standard market towns, the smallest and most basic type of urban settlement.

Now, when the European distribution for 1800 is set beside the others, as in figure 11.2, we are led to the inescapable conclusion that it was the least efficient of them all. The number of very large cities (of at least 100,000 inhabitants) was much smaller than in China, while the number of very small ones (under 10,000) was much larger. It appears that the aggregate urban population of Europe and China did not differ enormously, but that the different distribution of that population among cities by size or level signified a fundamentally different design. In Rozman's parlance, Europe needed many more cities to 'move resources from the lowest to the highest level'.

CONCLUSIONS

Japan, by way of contrast, supported a complement of very large cities not much inferior to Europe with only a fraction of the intermediate cities and market towns found in Europe.

This surprising result is specious. The European urban system was not less 'efficient' for the simple reason that its purpose was not simply to 'move resources from the lowest to the highest level'. Rozman's concepts are based on the administrative needs of a well-ordered unitary state in which cities stand in a well-defined position of subordination or domination *vis-à-vis* one another. In Europe administrative centralization proved to be an important stimulus to urban growth, but of course Europe always remained, in contrast to the three societies examined by Rozman, a designation for a collection of states which themselves varied enormously in size and degree of internal centralization.

To speak of *an* urban system in such a collection of polities, as I feel justified in doing by the seventeenth century, implies that the basis of integration was other than political and administrative. It was an economic integration that bound the constituent elements of the urban systems together, one based on competitive relations among trading centres and, often, between regional centres and their hinterlands. The urban functions of controlling production and providing for the circulation of goods and services were not carried out *primarily* to fulfil the needs of a command structure 'at the top'. An urban hierarchy based on economic integration is, I suspect, unique to Europe and it calls for concepts that differ from those put forward by Rozman.

Europe's urban hierarchy cannot be labelled 'inefficient', but it certainly differed from the others displayed in figure 11.2. The very shallow slope at the top of the Chinese urban hierarchy reminds one of Europe in 1500 (although the scale is vastly different), and Skinner in fact argues that 'the cities of China [in 1843] did not form a single integrated urban system. . . . A unified urban system on such a scale was most likely simply infeasible in an agrarian society prior to the extension of mechanized transport'.[7] European integration occurred not so much through vertical links between cities of different levels in an administrative or marketing hierarchy as via horizontal links – competitive relationships – among functionally differentiated cities of several sorts. Such a unified system was feasible before the railway age wherever water-borne navigation could reach.

The shallow slope of the European rank-size distribution caused Europe, with a settled land area no larger than China, to be supplied with many more small cities. Rather than a sign of inefficiency, as Rozman has it, I regard this as a reflection of the higher level of local market organization and commercialization attained by Europe. A second even more striking indicator of the same difference is that the European rural population that supported an

CONCLUSIONS

urban structure of many more towns and nearly the same total urban population was in 1800 only one-third the size of the Chinese rural population.[8]

WHAT SORT OF URBAN SYSTEM WILL EUROPE GET?

Just as liberal clergymen are conditioned to abstain from making moral judgements, so are historians conditioned to refrain from calling attention to the contemporary implications of their work. Both have learned to do the forbidden through insinuation. I propose to conclude this book by breaking with tradition to discuss (openly) the present-day implications of the very long-term pattern of urban change uncovered in this study.

The three periods of early modern urbanization discussed above are part of a millennium-long history of European urbanization. It begins with the great age of medieval expansion which revived moribund ancient urban nodes and planted new cities by the hundreds. By the thirteenth century the creative, expansionary forces of the age had endowed most of Europe with a stock of urban settlements that was to serve as a framework for many centuries of urban growth. In the fourteenth and fifteenth centuries neither the number nor the size of cities experienced dramatic change, but, as we have seen, this was far from true in the 250 years after 1500. Then a process of rigorously selective city growth fashioned an urban system out of the medieval urban inheritance.

The century after 1750 stands out as a second period of 'city creation', a period in which urbanization takes the form of changing the functional character of hitherto non-urban or quasi-urban places. With an enlarged stock of cities, the process of consolidation, concentration and hierarchy-formation got under way again in the century after 1850. Figure 11.3 is a sketch of the family of rank-size distributions that outline this summary of a thousand years of urban change.

Viewed in this rather abstract way, urbanization assumes two distinct modes. In one, the city-creation mode, new forms of urban life penetrate society. Behind this process stand the requirements of technical and organizational innovations. One might associate this with 'unbalanced' economic growth, disrupting existing relationships through the rapid expansion of selected sectors of the economy.

In the second, the urban-concentration mode, the power and influence of the city confront society. This is made possible by innovations that cheapen the concentration of functions and make possible the consolidation of control of large-scale, widely spread activities. This might be associated with a 'balanced' growth path, bringing advances over a broad range of economic sectors.[9]

CONCLUSIONS

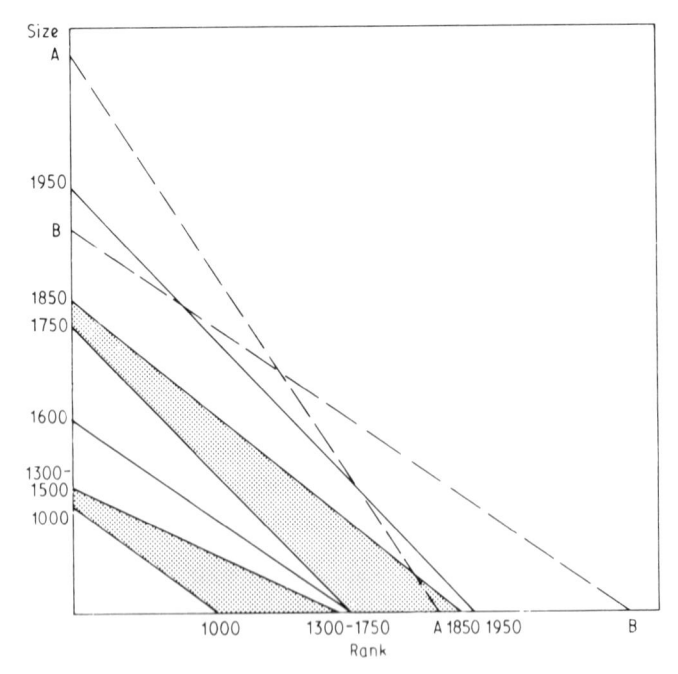

Figure 11.3 Two modes of European urbanization, 1000–the future

In the concentration mode urban growth is fed primarily by migration, people move to the cities; in the city-creation mode, transfers to the urban category play a significant role: urbanism is diffused to the country.

This is an interesting historical context in which to place contemporary utterances about 'the future of the city' Will the concentration mode of modern urbanization continue? Will it soon be superseded by a new city-creation mode? Indeed, has the concentration mode already ended, yielding to a future form of urban life we cannot yet wholly discern?

The belief that the future will bring ever larger agglomerations of human souls is probably still dominant. Since 1961, when Jean Gottman coined the term 'megalopolis' to refer to the chain of cities from Boston to Washington, the discovery of the embryos of the gargantuan megalopoli of the future has become a favourite activity of city and regional planners.[10] Not content with a London region embracing south-east England, or a Randstad Holland covering much of the Netherlands, planners now prefer to increase the scale of their urban units to 'Megalopolis England', stretching from Blackpool to Brighton, and the 'Northwest European Megalopolis', comprehending the Randstad Holland, the Rhine–Ruhr urban zones of Germany and other German metropolitan areas stretching up the Rhine and beyond to Ulm.[11]

CONCLUSIONS

The works of Peter Hall, C. A. Doxiadis and other prominent planners assume the irresistibility of, or urge upon us the desirability of, the formation of a small number of colossal urban zones.[12]

An alternative to this vision of the future city is not yet well articulated. It often seems to be assumed that the alternative to megalopolis is a bucolic, non-urban form of settlement. Such thinking is based on the expectation that technology will achieve 'frictionless space', while a continued rise in the demand for services rather than goods will further loosen the locational constraints imposed on economic activity. Since ever more people are becoming free to choose residential locations for personal pleasure rather than economic necessity, it is argued, we can expect 'a wholesale dissipation of existing urban clusters by the end of the century'.[13] This vision seems to imply the abandonment of cities rather than a new form of urban system.[14] Yet when this future is described as an 'urban civilization without cities' it is hard to suppress the thought that the visionaries are either talking nonsense or simply do not recognize the city's new form.

This latter possibility requires some thought. I noted earlier that a definition of the city is not a pressing matter when the stock of cities is constant, but it is critical to one's perceptions of the trend and timing of urbanization when the stock is being augmented. This phenomenon of city-creation fascinated Pirenne, who wrote provocatively about the origins of the medieval city of the west; it frightened the observers and disgusted the later interpreters of the industrial city, who spoke derisively of 'Coketowns'.[15] This study suggests that if future urbanization should take the form of city-creation rather than urban concentration it will not be for the first time, nor will it necessarily imply the wholesale abandonment of historic urban forms. The modern urban system has shown its capacity to adjust to major changes in the mode of urbanization without being utterly transfigured in the process.

In terms of figure 11.3, the future form of urbanization might be represented by either A (urban concentration) or B (city-creation). Both differ from earlier phases of urbanization in that an expansion in one direction – to either larger cities or more urban locations – will require outmigration from the other. In a very nearly fully urbanized society that is unavoidable. In this specific sense city-creation would occur in a unique environment that challenges the interpreter and the policy-maker to adapt the concept of the city to a new reality.

I have no wish to speculate about whether A or B will better represent the future course of urbanization, but if the city-creation mode should become dominant it would be foolish to interpret this as a 'ruralization', or as a symptom of post-industrial decay. Just as in the past it could be linked to a profound process of renewal.

APPENDICES

Appendix 1

THE DATA BASE

ALL CITIES WITH AT LEAST 10,000 INHABITANTS
DURING THE PERIOD 1500–1800

POPULATIONS ROUNDED TO THE NEAREST THOUSAND

Cities are listed alphabetically by territory. The complete name of the cities and, where necessary, the English names are listed in appendix 2. The cities are listed there in the same order as here and can easily be located with use of the identifying number. The territory code, listed after the city name, is as follows:

Code	Territory	Code	Territory
1	Scandinavia	9	Switzerland
2	England and Wales	10	Northern Italy
3	Scotland	11	Central Italy
4	Ireland	12	Southern Italy
5	The Netherlands	13	Spain
6	Belgium	14	Portugal
7	Germany	15	Austria and Czechoslovakia
8	France	16	Poland

The population columns make use of the following code:
   0   = populations below 10,000
   1–9 = populations below 10,000 presented for information only
   UNK = population unknown.
See the next section for further information.

APPENDIX 1

		Code	1500	1550	1600	1650	1700	1750	1800
1	BERGEN	1	0	0	0	UNK	UNK	14	17
2	COPENHAGEN	1	UNK	UNK	UNK	23	70	93	101
3	GÖTEBORG	1	0	0	0	4	6	8	13
4	KARLSKRONA	1	0	0	0	0	0	5	10
5	OSLO	1	0	0	0	0	0	7	12
6	STOCKHOLM	1	0	0	UNK	40	45	60	75
7	BATH	2	0	0	0	1	3	9	32
8	BIRMINGHAM	2	0	1	2	4	7	24	69
9	BLACKBURN	2	0	0	0	0	0	4	12
10	BOLTON	2	0	0	0	0	0	4	13
11	BRISTOL	2	10	10	11	20	25	45	64
12	CAMBRIDGE	2	0	0	0	9	9	6	10
13	CARLISLE	2	0	0	0	0	4	4	10
14	CHATHAM	2	0	0	1	0	5	5	11
15	CHESTER	2	0	0	0	8	10	13	15
16	COLCHESTER	2	5	0	0	10	10	9	12
17	COVENTRY	2	7	7	7	7	7	12	16
18	DERBY	2	0	0	0	0	0	6	11
19	EXETER	2	10	8	10	10	14	16	17
20	GREENWICH	2	0	0	0	0	0	UNK	14
21	HUDDERSFIELD	2	0	0	0	0	0	0	11
22	HULL	2	0	0	0	0	6	6	28
23	IPSWICH	2	0	0	0	UNK	8	12	11
24	KING'S LYNN	2	5	0	0	5	5	9	10
25	LEEDS	2	0	0	0	5	6	16	53
26	LEICESTER	2	4	3	5	5	6	8	17
27	LIVERPOOL	2	0	0	0	0	6	22	78
28	LONDON	2	40	80	200	400	575	675	865
29	MANCHESTER	2	0	0	0	5	9	18	70
30	NEWCASTLE	2	10	10	10	13	14	29	28
31	NORWICH	2	10	12	12	20	29	36	37
32	NOTTINGHAM	2	0	3	5	6	7	12	29
33	OLDHAM	2	0	0	0	0	0	0	12
34	OXFORD	2	5	0	0	9	8	8	12
35	PLYMOUTH	2	2	4	7	7	9	15	43
36	PORTSMOUTH	2	0	0	0	4	5	10	32
37	PRESTON	2	0	0	0	0	0	6	12
38	READING	2	0	0	0	0	0	7	10
39	SALFORD	2	0	0	0	0	0	0	14
40	SHEFFIELD	2	0	0	2	0	10	12	46
41	SHREWSBURY	2	5	0	0	0	10	13	15
42	STOCKPORT	2	0	0	0	0	0	3	15
43	SUNDERLAND	2	0	0	0	0	5	10	24
44	WARRINGTON	2	0	0	0	0	0	4	11

THE DATA BASE

		Code	1500	1550	1600	1650	1700	1750	1800
45	WENLOCK	2	0	0	0	0	0	UNK	15
46	WIGAN	2	0	0	0	0	0	4	11
47	WOLVERHAMPTON	2	0	2	0	4	0	7	13
48	WORCESTER	2	0	3	6	8	9	10	11
49	YARMOUTH	2	5	0	0	10	10	10	15
50	YORK	2	8	8	12	12	11	11	16
51	ABERDEEN	3	0	0	7	0	6	16	27
52	DUNDEE	3	0	0	7	UNK	UNK	12	26
53	EDINBURGH	3	UNK	UNK	30	35	40	57	82
54	GLASGOW	3	0	0	2	UNK	13	24	77
55	GREENOCK	3	0	0	0	0	0	4	17
56	INVERNESS	3	0	0	0	0	0	10	15
57	PAISLEY	3	0	0	0	0	0	7	17
58	PERTH	3	0	0	5	0	0	9	15
59	BELFAST	4	0	0	0	0	2	9	24
60	CORK	4	0	0	2	2	25	58	75
61	DUBLIN	4	0	5	5	17	60	90	168
62	GALWAY	4	0	0	4	0	5	0	12
63	KILKENNY	4	0	0	0	0	7	0	16
64	LIMERICK	4	0	0	3	0	11	UNK	39
65	NEWRY	4	0	0	0	0	0	0	15
66	WATERFORD	4	0	0	2	0	5	UNK	20
67	ALKMAAR	5	5	8	11	15	12	8	8
68	AMSTERDAM	5	14	30	65	175	200	210	217
69	ARNHEM	5	6	6	7	7	6	6	10
70	DELFT	5	14	14	20	24	18	15	17
71	DORDRECHT	5	11	11	15	20	22	16	18
72	ENKHUIZEN	5	4	8	17	22	14	7	7
73	GOUDA	5	11	11	13	15	15	15	12
74	GRONINGEN	5	14	19	19	20	20	21	24
75	HAARLEM	5	14	14	30	38	33	27	21
76	DEN HAAG	5	7	6	10	18	33	38	38
77	'S HERTOGENBOSCH	5	16	23	18	15	13	14	13
78	HOORN	5	6	8	12	16	13	10	10
79	LEEUWARDEN	5	4	7	11	15	15	14	16
80	LEIDEN	5	14	12	25	67	55	38	31
81	MAASTRICHT	5	10	10	12	18	26	18	18
82	MIDDELBURG	5	0	7	20	30	25	24	20
83	NIJMEGEN	5	12	12	12	11	11	11	13
84	ROTTERDAM	5	5	7	13	30	48	44	57
85	UTRECHT	5	20	25	25	30	30	25	32
86	ZAANDAM	5	7	10	16	24	26	28	25
87	ZWOLLE	5	0	0	0	0	10	12	12
88	AALST	6	0	7	7	7	8	8	11

APPENDIX 1

		Code	1500	1550	1600	1650	1700	1750	1800
89	ANTWERPEN	6	40	90	47	70	70	46	60
90	BRUGGE	6	30	35	27	34	38	28	32
91	BRUSSELS	6	35	40	50	69	80	60	74
92	DUNKERQUE	6	0	0	UNK	UNK	11	15	21
93	GENT	6	40	50	31	46	51	40	51
94	IEPER	6	10	10	UNK	13	11	11	12
95	KORTRIJK	6	5	0	0	UNK	UNK	12	14
96	LEUVEN	6	17	15	9	13	14	15	21
97	LIÈGE	6	20	UNK	UNK	35	45	57	55
98	LIER	6	0	0	0	0	5	6	11
99	LILLE	6	25	28	33	40	55	63	59
100	LOKEREN	6	0	0	0	0	0	0	11
101	MECHELEN	6	25	25	11	20	22	18	20
102	MONS	6	15	15	UNK	13	14	17	18
103	NAMUR	6	0	0	UNK	11	UNK	UNK	16
104	OOSTENDE	6	0	0	0	0	0	0	11
105	SINT NIKLAAS	6	0	0	2	4	6	8	11
106	TOURNAI	6	25	25	20	20	29	21	23
107	VALENCIENNES	6	UNK	15	15	18	19	16	17
108	AACHEN	7	15	UNK	UNK	12	15	UNK	24
109	ALTONA	7	0	0	2	3	12	15	23
110	ANSBACH	7	0	0	0	0	4	6	12
111	AUGSBURG	7	20	45	48	21	21	UNK	28
112	BAMBERG	7	0	10	12	7	10	12	17
113	BARMEN	7	0	0	0	2	2	4	13
114	BAUTZEN	7	0	5	0	0	0	8	11
115	BERLIN	7	12	UNK	25	12	55	90	150
116	BONN	7	0	0	0	0	0	0	11
117	BRANDENBURG	7	0	0	0	0	0	0	12
118	BRAUNSCHWEIG	7	18	16	16	16	UNK	21	27
119	BREMEN	7	18	UNK	UNK	UNK	27	28	36
120	BRESLAU (WROCLAW)	7	25	35	30	UNK	UNK	55	54
121	CHEMNITZ (K-MARX-ST)	7	0	4	5	0	4	11	11
122	DANZIG (GDANSK)	7	20	26	50	70	50	46	40
123	DRESDEN	7	5	8	12	15	40	52	55
124	DÜSSELDORF	7	2	0	0	5	5	UNK	20
125	ELBERFELD	7	0	0	0	2	3	0	10
126	ELBING (ELBLAG)	7	10	15	15	10	16	16	17
127	EMDEN	7	0	UNK	UNK	14	10	8	12
128	ERFURT	7	15	18	19	15	17	17	17
129	FLENSBURG	7	0	0	0	0	0	UNK	13
130	FRANKFURT A M	7	12	12	18	17	28	32	35
131	FRANKFURT A O	7	11	11	13	2	9	9	12
132	FREIBURG	7	5	0	10	6	0	0	9

THE DATA BASE

		Code	1500	1550	1600	1650	1700	1750	1800
133	FÜRTH	7	0	0	0	0	5	0	12
134	GOTHA	7	0	0	0	0	0	UNK	11
135	HALBERSTADT	7	0	0	0	0	0	UNK	12
136	HALLE	7	UNK	UNK	UNK	UNK	UNK	UNK	19
137	HAMBURG	7	14	29	40	75	70	75	100
138	HANAU	7	0	0	0	0	0	11	12
139	HANNOVER	7	0	6	7	9	11	17	17
140	HEIDELBERG	7	0	0	0	4	0	10	9
141	HILDESHEIM	7	11	0	0	0	0	0	12
142	KASSEL	7	0	0	6	0	10	19	18
143	KÖLN	7	30	35	40	45	42	43	42
144	KÖNIGSBERG	7	8	14	UNK	UNK	35	60	59
145	LEIPZIG	7	10	10	14	11	20	35	32
146	LÜBECK	7	24	25	23	31	UNK	UNK	23
147	LÜNEBURG	7	0	0	0	0	0	0	10
148	MAGDEBURG	7	18	40	40	5	10	18	37
149	MAINZ	7	6	UNK	20	10	20	24	22
150	MANNHEIM	7	0	0	0	1	13	20	22
151	MÜNCHEN	7	13	16	20	10	21	32	34
152	MÜNSTER	7	0	0	11	0	7	9	14
153	NÜRNBERG	7	36	40	40	25	40	30	27
154	POTSDAM	7	0	0	0	0	2	15	27
155	QUEDLINBURG	7	0	0	0	0	0	0	11
156	REGENSBURG	7	UNK	UNK	UNK	UNK	UNK	UNK	23
157	ROSTOCK	7	0	0	0	0	0	0	14
158	SOEST	7	12	15	10	5	5	5	5
159	STETTIN (SZCZECIN)	7	9	13	12	6	6	12	23
160	STRALSUND	7	0	0	0	0	0	UNK	11
161	STUTTGART	7	0	10	9	5	13	17	20
162	ULM	7	17	19	21	14	UNK	15	13
163	WÜRZBURG	7	10	9	10	11	14	15	16
164	ABBEVILLE	8	UNK	UNK	UNK	UNK	15	15	18
165	AGEN	8	0	0	UNK	UNK	10	10	10
166	AIX EN PROVENCE	8	UNK	UNK	UNK	UNK	28	25	19
167	ALBI	8	0	0	0	UNK	10	8	10
168	ALENÇON	8	UNK	UNK	UNK	UNK	12	12	13
169	AMIENS	8	UNK	UNK	UNK	27	30	33	36
170	ANGERS	8	UNK	UNK	25	32	27	23	25
171	ANGOULEME	8	0	0	0	0	0	0	14
172	ARLES	8	UNK	11	15	25	20	23	20
173	ARRAS	8	11	UNK	UNK	UNK	15	17	19
174	AUXERRE	8	0	0	0	0	0	0	12
175	AVIGNON	8	UNK	UNK	UNK	UNK	23	22	21
176	BAYEUX	8	0	0	6	8	7	8	10

273

APPENDIX 1

		Code	1500	1550	1600	1650	1700	1750	1800
177	BAYONNE	8	0	0	0	0	0	0	12
178	BEAUVAIS	8	UNK	UNK	UNK	UNK	12	12	13
179	BESANÇON	8	8	10	11	13	17	21	24
180	BEZIERS	8	UNK	UNK	UNK	UNK	12	13	14
181	BLOIS	8	UNK	UNK	UNK	UNK	11	11	11
182	BORDEAUX	8	20	20	40	40	50	67	88
183	BOULOGNE	8	2	0	0	0	0	UNK	12
184	BOURGES	8	UNK	0	UNK	UNK	15	25	18
185	BREST	8	0	0	0	0	7	20	22
186	CAEN	8	UNK	UNK	UNK	UNK	27	35	34
187	CAHORS	8	0	0	0	0	0	0	10
188	CAMBRAI	8	UNK	UNK	12	12	12	12	14
189	CARCASSONNE	8	0	0	UNK	UNK	11	12	14
190	CASTRES	8	0	0	0	0	9	9	13
191	CHALONS-SUR-MARNE	8	UNK	UNK	UNK	UNK	11	15	11
192	CHALONS-SUR-SAONE	8	0	0	0	0	0	0	11
193	CHARTRES	8	0	0	UNK	UNK	12	10	12
194	CHERBOURG	8	0	0	0	0	4	5	14
195	CLERMONT-FERRAND	8	0	0	0	UNK	12	24	30
196	COLMAR	8	5	0	0	8	7	0	13
197	DIEPPE	8	0	0	UNK	UNK	15	18	17
198	DIJON	8	13	UNK	UNK	20	22	22	22
199	DOUAI	8	UNK	UNK	UNK	UNK	13	21	18
200	FALAISE	8	0	0	0	0	9	0	10
201	GRENOBLE	8	0	UNK	UNK	UNK	20	24	23
202	LA ROCHELLE	8	UNK	UNK	23	17	14	16	18
203	LAVAL	8	UNK	UNK	UNK	UNK	10	10	12
204	LE HAVRE	8	0	0	0	0	9	14	19
205	LE MANS	8	UNK	UNK	UNK	UNK	17	16	18
206	LE PUY	8	0	0	0	UNK	10	10	12
207	LIMOGES	8	UNK	UNK	UNK	UNK	12	18	16
208	LISIEUX	8	0	0	0	0	0	0	11
209	LORIENT	8	0	0	0	0	0	0	15
210	LYON	8	50	70	40	75	97	114	100
211	MACON	8	0	0	0	0	0	0	10
212	MARSEILLE	8	UNK	30	40	66	75	68	78
213	METZ	8	15	UNK	19	15	22	29	39
214	MONTAUBAN	8	UNK	UNK	UNK	UNK	18	16	19
215	MONTPELLIER	8	6	UNK	UNK	UNK	25	35	31
216	MOULINS	8	0	UNK	UNK	UNK	11	11	13
217	NANCY	8	0	4	8	5	15	22	29
218	NANTES	8	14	19	25	40	42	57	74
219	NEVERS	8	0	0	0	0	0	0	11
220	NÎMES	8	0	UNK	10	15	19	30	40

THE DATA BASE

		Code	1500	1550	1600	1650	1700	1750	1800
221	NIORT	8	0	0	0	0	0	0	14
222	ORLEANS	8	UNK	UNK	UNK	UNK	30	37	43
223	PARIS	8	100	130	220	430	510	576	581
224	PERPIGNAN	8	0	0	0	0	0	0	13
225	POITIERS	8	UNK	UNK	UNK	UNK	18	18	20
226	REIMS	8	UNK	UNK	UNK	UNK	25	30	31
227	RENNES	8	12	UNK	22	UNK	30	30	28
228	RIOM	8	0	0	0	0	0	0	13
229	ROCHEFORT	8	0	0	0	0	10	0	15
230	ROUEN	8	40	65	60	82	64	67	81
231	SAINT-ETIENNE	8	0	0	0	0	0	UNK	18
232	SAINT-MALO	8	4	0	10	15	25	15	17
233	SAINT-OMER	8	11	0	0	UNK	15	UNK	20
234	SAINT-QUENTIN	8	0	0	0	0	0	0	10
235	STRASBOURG	8	20	24	28	23	30	40	48
236	TOULON	8	0	0	10	20	25	26	32
237	TOULOUSE	8	35	40	UNK	42	38	45	45
238	TOURS	8	UNK	UNK	UNK	UNK	30	22	23
239	TROYES	8	UNK	UNK	UNK	UNK	21	18	21
240	VERSAILLES	8	0	0	0	5	25	30	27
241	VIENNE	8	0	0	0	0	7	0	10
242	BASEL	9	9	9	10	10	11	14	16
243	BERN	9	3	5	0	0	0	11	11
244	GENÈVE	9	10	12	15	12	17	23	26
245	ZÜRICH	9	5	5	7	8	11	12	10
246	ALESSANDRIA	10	0	8	14	0	0	12	19
247	ASTI	10	0	8	10	UNK	10	13	11
248	BERGAMO	10	UNK	18	23	UNK	25	29	24
249	BRESCIA	10	49	41	42	25	35	29	28
250	CHIOGGIA	10	0	0	9	0	UNK	19	19
251	COMO	10	10	10	12	9	UNK	14	14
252	CREMA	10	UNK	11	14	7	0	9	9
253	CREMONA	10	40	34	37	15	22	24	25
254	CUNEO	10	0	6	11	UNK	UNK	13	18
255	FOSSANO	10	0	9	10	UNK	UNK	12	14
256	GENOA	10	60	65	71	90	80	87	91
257	LODI	10	0	9	14	UNK	UNK	14	16
258	MANTUA	10	28	38	31	14	21	24	26
259	MILANO	10	100	69	120	100	124	124	135
260	MODENA	10	18	16	21	15	19	18	22
261	MONDOVI	10	0	0	11	0	0	7	18
262	MONZA	10	UNK	UNK	12	UNK	UNK	UNK	12
263	NICE	10	UNK	UNK	16	UNK	15	16	13
264	NOVARA	10	0	7	0	0	0	9	12

APPENDIX 1

		Code	1500	1550	1600	1650	1700	1750	1800
265	PADOVA	10	27	32	36	25	30	31	32
266	PARMA	10	19	25	33	19	35	35	34
267	PAVIA	10	16	13	18	19	20	24	24
268	PIACENZA	10	UNK	27	33	17	UNK	31	28
269	REGGIO	10	UNK	13	11	10	15	16	18
270	SAVIGLIANO	10	0	0	10	UNK	UNK	11	13
271	TREVISO	10	UNK	12	14	9	UNK	10	11
272	TRIESTE	10	UNK	UNK	UNK	UNK	UNK	UNK	24
273	TORINO	10	0	14	24	37	42	57	82
274	UDINE	10	UNK	15	14	UNK	UNK	14	16
275	VENEZIA	10	100	158	139	120	138	149	138
276	VERCELLI	10	0	9	10	0	0	8	13
277	VERONA	10	38	52	49	30	41	43	41
278	VICENZA	10	UNK	21	37	25	26	28	29
279	VIGEVANO	10	0	7	8	0	0	9	12
280	ANCONA	11	0	0	0	10	9	10	15
281	BOLOGNA	11	55	62	63	59	63	69	71
282	FERRARA	11	UNK	42	33	25	27	30	30
283	FIRENZE	11	70	60	70	70	72	74	81
284	LIVORNO	11	0	0	4	12	16	32	53
285	LUCCA	11	UNK	24	24	25	23	21	17
286	PERUGIA	11	13	20	20	16	16	14	15
287	PISA	11	UNK	10	15	13	13	14	15
288	ROMA	11	55	45	105	124	138	156	163
289	SIENA	11	15	10	19	19	19	15	16
290	VITERBO	11	12	UNK	UNK	11	12	13	13
291	ACIREALE	12	0	0	14	9	12	13	15
292	ALTAMURA	12	0	0	UNK	0	UNK	UNK	18
293	BARI	12	8	8	15	15	13	18	18
294	CAGLIARI	12	0	0	0	12	17	19	18
295	CALTAGIRONE	12	0	10	13	11	12	17	20
296	CALTANISSETA	12	0	7	10	10	15	15	16
297	CASTELVETRANO	12	0	7	13	15	12	8	15
298	CASTROGIOVANNI	12	UNK	15	14	11	9	10	11
299	CATANIA	12	14	22	28	11	16	26	45
300	FOGGIA	12	0	0	0	0	UNK	UNK	13
301	GIRGENTI	12	UNK	13	10	9	11	18	18
302	LECCE	12	15	26	32	16	UNK	UNK	20
303	MARSALA	12	0	0	9	11	14	15	21
304	MASCALI	12	0	0	0	0	0	11	14
305	MAZZARINO	12	0	0	0	0	8	11	11
306	MESSINA	12	25	UNK	50	50	40	37	44
307	MODICA/POZZALLO	12	UNK	15	18	16	19	20	20
308	MONOPOLI	12	UNK	UNK	UNK	UNK	UNK	UNK	17

THE DATA BASE

		Code	1500	1550	1600	1650	1700	1750	1800
309	NAPOLI	12	150	212	281	176	216	305	427
310	NICOSIA	12	UNK	17	21	12	12	12	12
311	NOTO	12	0	0	8	10	7	11	11
312	PALERMO	12	55	70	105	129	100	118	139
313	PIAZZA (ENNA)	12	UNK	12	20	14	9	12	12
314	RAGUSA	12	0	0	9	9	9	12	17
315	REGGIO DI CALABRIA	12	UNK	UNK	UNK	UNK	UNK	UNK	UNK
316	SASSARI	12	13	UNK	14	UNK	14	15	17
317	SIRACUSA	12	UNK	12	12	14	17	18	16
318	TARANTO	12	12	21	17	UNK	UNK	UNK	17
319	TERMINI	12	UNK	UNK	10	9	7	10	14
320	TRAPANI	12	UNK	16	17	19	17	17	25
321	ALCALA LA REAL	13	UNK	UNK	10	UNK	UNK	UNK	12
322	ALCAZAR DE SAN JUAN	13	UNK	20	10	UNK	UNK	UNK	10
323	ALICANTE	13	0	0	11	11	0	0	13
324	ANDUJAR	13	UNK	UNK	12	UNK	UNK	UNK	10
325	ANTEQUERA	13	UNK	10	16	19	UNK	UNK	15
326	ARACENA	13	UNK	6	10	7	0	UNK	10
327	AVILA	13	UNK	16	14	6	5	0	0
328	BADAJOZ	13	UNK	UNK	11	UNK	UNK	UNK	10
329	BAEZA	13	UNK	18	21	12	7	UNK	10
330	BARCELONA	13	29	35	43	44	43	50	115
331	BILBAO	13	0	0	0	0	6	7	11
332	BURGOS	13	0	22	13	3	9	0	9
333	CADIZ	13	2	0	5	7	23	60	70
334	CARTAGENA	13	4	0	8	UNK	12	UNK	33
335	CORDOBA	13	27	33	45	32	28	UNK	40
336	CUENCA	13	UNK	14	25	0	0	0	0
337	ECIJA	13	UNK	17	22	20	10	UNK	28
338	GRANADA	13	70	UNK	69	UNK	UNK	UNK	55
339	JAEN	13	UNK	22	22	18	20	22	28
340	JEREZ DA LA FRONTERA	13	UNK	18	27	17	13	UNK	35
341	LUCENA	13	UNK	UNK	18	UNK	UNK	UNK	18
342	MADRID	13	0	30	49	130	110	109	167
343	MALAGA	13	UNK	13	13	UNK	30	32	36
344	MEDINA DEL CAMPO	13	UNK	16	14	3	5	0	0
345	MEDINA DE RIO SECO	13	UNK	11	10	6	7	0	0
346	MORON DE LA FRONTERA	13	UNK	UNK	8	0	0	0	11
347	MURCIA	13	10	13	17	20	25	32	40
348	OCAÑA	13	UNK	UNK	13	UNK	0	0	0
349	ORIHUELA	13	0	UNK	10	UNK	UNK	UNK	19
350	OSUNA	13	UNK	UNK	10	UNK	UNK	UNK	14
351	PALENCIA	13	UNK	8	12	4	4	0	10
352	PALMA	13	UNK	UNK	23	UNK	UNK	UNK	29

APPENDIX 1

		Code	1500	1550	1600	1650	1700	1750	1800
353	RONDA	13	UNK	8	8	UNK	UNK	UNK	15
354	SALAMANCA	13	UNK	20	25	15	12	UNK	9
355	SANTIAGO	13	4	1	1	10	UNK	UNK	25
356	SEGOVIA	13	UNK	22	28	16	8	0	0
357	SEVILLA	13	25	65	90	60	96	66	96
358	TOLEDO	13	UNK	30	50	20	20	UNK	25
359	UBEDA	13	UNK	13	19	12	10	UNK	14
360	UTRERA	13	0	UNK	11	11	8	UNK	0
361	VALENCIA	13	40	37	65	52	50	UNK	80
362	VALLADOLID	13	UNK	45	40	15	18	19	21
363	ZARAGOZA	13	UNK	18	25	30	30	UNK	40
364	COIMBRA	14	0	0	UNK	15	UNK	12	15
365	ELVAS	14	UNK	UNK	UNK	17	UNK	UNK	UNK
366	EVORA	14	UNK	UNK	UNK	17	UNK	15	UNK
367	LISBOA	14	30	98	100	130	165	148	180
368	PORTO	14	UNK	13	15	20	25	21	30
369	BRNO (BRÜNN)	15	0	0	0	9	UNK	15	23
370	GRAZ	15	5	0	8	UNK	UNK	20	31
371	INNSBRUCK	15	4	5	5	6	7	8	10
372	KLAGENFURT	15	0	0	4	0	0	7	10
373	LINZ	15	0	0	3	0	0	10	17
374	PRAHA	15	UNK	UNK	UNK	UNK	39	59	77
375	SALZBURG	15	UNK	UNK	10	10	13	15	11
376	WIEN	15	20	UNK	50	60	114	175	231
377	KRAKOW	16	0	0	0	0	UNK	UNK	24
378	POZNAN	16	0	0	0	0	0	0	16
379	WARSZAWA	16	0	10	15	20	15	23	63

CITIES IDENTIFIED BY SIZE CATEGORY

The following size categories are used throughout this study:

Code	Lower and upper limits
0	Under 10,000 (only those cities that at some point reach the 10,000 inhabitant level)
I	10,000 – 19,900
II	20,000 – 39,900
III	40,000 – 79,900
IV	80,000 – 159,900
V	160,000 – 319,900
VI	320,000 and over

THE DATA BASE

		Code	1500	1550	1600	1650	1700	1750	1800
1	BERGEN	1	0	0	0	0	0	1	1
2	COPENHAGEN	1	1	1	1	2	3	4	4
3	GÖTEBORG	1	0	0	0	0	0	0	1
4	KARLSKRONA	1	0	0	0	0	0	0	1
5	OSLO	1	0	0	0	0	0	0	1
6	STOCKHOLM	1	0	0	1	3	3	3	3
7	BATH	2	0	0	0	0	0	0	2
8	BIRMINGHAM	2	0	0	0	0	0	2	3
9	BLACKBURN	2	0	0	0	0	0	0	1
10	BOLTON	2	0	0	0	0	0	0	1
11	BRISTOL	2	1	1	1	2	2	3	3
12	CAMBRIDGE	2	0	0	0	0	0	0	1
13	CARLISLE	2	0	0	0	0	0	0	1
14	CHATHAM	2	0	0	0	0	0	0	1
15	CHESTER	2	0	0	0	0	1	1	1
16	COLCHESTER	2	0	0	0	1	1	0	1
17	COVENTRY	2	0	0	0	0	0	1	1
18	DERBY	2	0	0	0	0	0	0	1
19	EXETER	2	1	0	1	1	1	1	1
20	GREENWICH	2	0	0	0	0	0	0	1
21	HUDDERSFIELD	2	0	0	0	0	0	0	1
22	HULL	2	0	0	0	0	0	0	2
23	IPSWICH	2	0	0	0	0	0	1	1
24	KING'S LYNN	2	0	0	0	0	0	0	1
25	LEEDS	2	0	0	0	0	0	1	3
26	LEICESTER	2	0	0	0	0	0	0	1
27	LIVERPOOL	2	0	0	0	0	0	2	3
28	LONDON	2	3	4	5	6	6	6	6
29	MANCHESTER	2	0	0	0	0	0	1	3
30	NEWCASTLE	2	1	1	1	1	1	2	2
31	NORWICH	2	1	1	1	2	2	2	2
32	NOTTINGHAM	2	0	0	0	0	0	1	2
33	OLDHAM	2	0	0	0	0	0	0	1
34	OXFORD	2	0	0	0	0	0	0	1
35	PLYMOUTH	2	0	0	0	0	0	1	3
36	PORTSMOUTH	2	0	0	0	0	0	1	2
37	PRESTON	2	0	0	0	0	0	0	1
38	READING	2	0	0	0	0	0	0	1
39	SALFORD	2	0	0	0	0	0	0	1
40	SHEFFIELD	2	0	0	0	0	1	1	3
41	SHREWSBURY	2	0	0	0	0	1	1	1
42	STOCKPORT	2	0	0	0	0	0	0	1
43	SUNDERLAND	2	0	0	0	0	0	1	2
44	WARRINGTON	2	0	0	0	0	0	0	1

APPENDIX 1

		Code	1500	1550	1600	1650	1700	1750	1800
45	WENLOCK	2	0	0	0	0	0	0	1
46	WIGAN	2	0	0	0	0	0	0	1
47	WOLVERHAMPTON	2	0	0	0	0	0	0	1
48	WORCESTER	2	0	0	0	0	0	1	1
49	YARMOUTH	2	0	0	0	1	1	1	1
50	YORK	2	0	0	1	1	1	1	1
51	ABERDEEN	3	0	0	0	0	0	1	2
52	DUNDEE	3	0	0	0	0	0	1	2
53	EDINBURGH	3	1	1	2	2	3	3	4
54	GLASGOW	3	0	0	0	0	1	2	3
55	GREENOCK	3	0	0	0	0	0	0	1
56	INVERNESS	3	0	0	0	0	0	1	1
57	PAISLEY	3	0	0	0	0	0	0	1
58	PERTH	3	0	0	0	0	0	0	1
59	BELFAST	4	0	0	0	0	0	0	2
60	CORK	4	0	0	0	0	2	3	3
61	DUBLIN	4	0	0	0	1	3	4	5
62	GALWAY	4	0	0	0	0	0	0	1
63	KILKENNY	4	0	0	0	0	0	0	1
64	LIMERICK	4	0	0	0	0	1	1	2
65	NEWRY	4	0	0	0	0	0	0	1
66	WATERFORD	4	0	0	0	0	0	0	2
67	ALKMAAR	5	0	0	1	1	1	0	0
68	AMSTERDAM	5	1	2	3	5	5	5	5
69	ARNHEM	5	0	0	0	0	0	0	1
70	DELFT	5	1	1	2	2	1	1	1
71	DORDRECHT	5	1	1	1	2	2	1	1
72	ENKHUIZEN	5	0	0	1	2	1	0	0
73	GOUDA	5	1	1	1	1	1	1	1
74	GRONINGEN	5	1	1	1	2	2	2	2
75	HAARLEM	5	1	1	2	2	2	2	2
76	DEN HAAG	5	0	0	1	1	2	2	2
77	'S HERTOGENBOSCH	5	1	2	1	1	1	1	1
78	HOORN	5	0	0	1	1	1	1	1
79	LEEUWARDEN	5	0	0	1	1	1	1	1
80	LEIDEN	5	1	1	2	3	3	2	2
81	MAASTRICHT	5	1	1	1	1	2	1	1
82	MIDDELBURG	5	0	0	2	2	2	2	2
83	NIJMEGEN	5	1	1	1	1	1	1	1
84	ROTTERDAM	5	0	0	1	2	3	3	3
85	UTRECHT	5	2	2	2	2	2	2	2
86	ZAANDAM	5	0	1	1	2	2	2	2
87	ZWOLLE	5	0	0	0	0	1	1	1
88	AALST	6	0	0	0	0	0	0	1

THE DATA BASE

		Code	1500	1550	1600	1650	1700	1750	1800
89	ANTWERPEN	6	3	4	3	3	3	3	3
90	BRUGGE	6	2	2	2	2	2	2	2
91	BRUSSELS	6	2	3	3	3	4	3	3
92	DUNKERQUE	6	0	0	1	1	1	1	2
93	GENT	6	3	3	2	3	3	3	3
94	IEPER	6	1	1	1	1	1	1	1
95	KORTRIJK	6	0	0	0	0	1	1	1
96	LEUVEN	6	1	1	0	1	1	1	2
97	LIÈGE	6	2	2	2	2	3	3	3
98	LIER	6	0	0	0	0	0	0	1
99	LILLE	6	2	2	2	3	3	3	3
100	LOKEREN	6	0	0	0	0	0	0	1
101	MECHELEN	6	2	2	1	2	2	1	2
102	MONS	6	1	1	1	1	1	1	1
103	NAMUR	6	0	0	0	1	1	1	1
104	OOSTENDE	6	0	0	0	0	0	0	1
105	SINT NIKLAAS	6	0	0	0	0	0	0	1
106	TOURNAI	6	2	2	2	2	2	2	2
107	VALENCIENNES	6	1	1	1	1	1	1	1
108	AACHEN	7	1	1	1	1	1	1	2
109	ALTONA	7	0	0	0	0	1	1	2
110	ANSBACH	7	0	0	0	0	0	0	1
111	AUGSBURG	7	2	3	3	2	2	2	2
112	BAMBERG	7	0	1	1	0	1	1	1
113	BARMEN	7	0	0	0	0	0	0	1
114	BAUTZEN	7	0	0	0	0	0	0	1
115	BERLIN	7	1	1	2	1	3	4	4
116	BONN	7	0	0	0	0	0	0	1
117	BRANDENBURG	7	0	0	0	0	0	0	1
118	BRAUNSCHWEIG	7	1	1	1	1	1	2	2
119	BREMEN	7	1	1	2	2	2	2	2
120	BRESLAU (WROCLAW)	7	2	2	2	2	2	3	3
121	CHEMNITZ (K-MARX-ST)	7	0	0	0	0	0	1	1
122	DANZIG (GDANSK)	7	2	2	3	3	3	3	3
123	DRESDEN	7	0	0	1	1	3	3	3
124	DÜSSELDORF	7	0	0	0	0	0	1	2
125	ELBERFELD	7	0	0	0	0	0	0	1
126	ELBING (ELBLAG)	7	1	1	1	1	1	1	1
127	EMDEN	7	0	1	1	1	1	0	1
128	ERFURT	7	1	1	1	1	1	1	1
129	FLENSBURG	7	0	0	0	0	0	0	1
130	FRANKFURT A M	7	1	1	1	1	2	2	2
131	FRANKFURT A O	7	1	1	1	0	0	0	1
132	FREIBURG	7	0	0	1	0	0	0	0

APPENDIX 1

		Code	1500	1550	1600	1650	1700	1750	1800
133	FÜRTH	7	0	0	0	0	0	0	1
134	GOTHA	7	0	0	0	0	0	0	1
135	HALBERSTADT	7	0	0	0	0	0	0	1
136	HALLE	7	0	0	0	0	0	0	1
137	HAMBURG	7	1	2	3	3	3	3	4
138	HANAU	7	0	0	0	0	0	1	1
139	HANNOVER	7	0	0	0	0	1	1	1
140	HEIDELBERG	7	0	0	0	0	0	1	0
141	HILDESHEIM	7	1	0	0	0	0	0	1
142	KASSEL	7	0	0	0	0	1	1	1
143	KÖLN	7	2	2	3	3	3	3	3
144	KÖNIGSBERG	7	0	1	2	2	2	3	3
145	LEIPZIG	7	1	1	1	1	2	2	2
146	LÜBECK	7	2	2	2	2	2	2	2
147	LÜNEBURG	7	0	0	0	0	0	0	1
148	MAGDEBURG	7	1	3	3	0	1	1	2
149	MAINZ	7	0	1	2	1	2	2	2
150	MANNHEIM	7	0	0	0	0	1	2	2
151	MÜNCHEN	7	1	1	2	1	2	2	2
152	MÜNSTER	7	0	0	1	0	0	0	1
153	NÜRNBERG	7	2	3	3	2	3	2	2
154	POTSDAM	7	0	0	0	0	0	1	2
155	QUEDLINBURG	7	0	0	0	0	0	0	1
156	REGENSBURG	7	1	1	1	1	1	1	2
157	ROSTOCK	7	0	0	0	0	0	0	1
158	SOEST	7	1	1	1	0	0	0	0
159	STETTIN (SZCZECIN)	7	0	1	1	0	0	1	2
160	STRALSUND	7	0	0	0	0	0	0	1
161	STUTTGART	7	0	1	0	0	1	1	2
162	ULM	7	1	1	2	1	1	1	1
163	WÜRZBURG	7	1	0	1	1	1	1	1
164	ABBEVILLE	8	0	0	1	1	1	1	1
165	AGEN	8	0	0	0	0	1	1	1
166	AIX EN PROVENCE	8	1	2	2	2	2	2	1
167	ALBI	8	0	0	0	1	1	0	1
168	ALENÇON	8	0	0	1	1	1	1	1
169	AMIENS	8	2	2	2	2	2	2	2
170	ANGERS	8	2	2	2	2	2	2	2
171	ANGOULEME	8	0	0	0	0	0	0	1
172	ARLES	8	1	1	1	2	2	2	2
173	ARRAS	8	1	1	1	1	1	1	1
174	AUXERRE	8	0	0	0	0	0	0	1
175	AVIGNON	8	2	2	2	2	2	2	2
176	BAYEUX	8	0	0	0	0	0	0	1

THE DATA BASE

		Code	1500	1550	1600	1650	1700	1750	1800
177	BAYONNE	8	0	0	0	0	0	0	1
178	BEAUVAIS	8	1	1	1	1	1	1	1
179	BESANÇON	8	0	1	1	1	1	2	2
180	BEZIERS	8	1	1	1	1	1	1	1
181	BLOIS	8	1	1	1	1	1	1	1
182	BORDEAUX	8	2	2	3	3	3	3	4
183	BOULOGNE	8	0	0	0	0	0	0	1
184	BOURGES	8	0	0	1	1	1	2	1
185	BREST	8	0	0	0	0	0	2	2
186	CAEN	8	2	2	2	2	2	2	2
187	CAHORS	8	0	0	0	0	0	0	1
188	CAMBRAI	8	1	1	1	1	1	1	1
189	CARCASSONNE	8	0	0	0	0	1	1	1
190	CASTRES	8	0	0	0	0	0	0	1
191	CHALONS-SUR-MARNE	8	0	0	0	0	1	1	1
192	CHALONS-SUR-SAONE	8	0	0	0	0	0	0	1
193	CHARTRES	8	0	0	1	1	1	1	1
194	CHERBOURG	8	0	0	0	0	0	0	1
195	CLERMONT-FERRAND	8	0	0	0	0	1	2	2
196	COLMAR	8	0	0	0	0	0	0	1
197	DIEPPE	8	0	0	1	1	1	1	1
198	DIJON	8	1	1	2	2	2	2	2
199	DOUAI	8	1	1	1	1	1	2	1
200	FALAISE	8	0	0	0	0	0	0	1
201	GRENOBLE	8	0	1	1	1	2	2	2
202	LA ROCHELLE	8	1	1	2	1	1	1	1
203	LAVAL	8	0	0	0	0	1	1	1
204	LE HAVRE	8	0	0	0	0	0	1	1
205	LE MANS	8	0	0	1	1	1	1	1
206	LE PUY	8	0	0	0	0	1	1	1
207	LIMOGES	8	1	1	1	1	1	1	1
208	LISIEUX	8	0	0	0	0	0	0	1
209	LORIENT	8	0	0	0	0	0	0	1
210	LYON	8	3	3	3	3	4	4	4
211	MACON	8	0	0	0	0	0	0	1
212	MARSEILLE	8	2	2	3	3	3	3	3
213	METZ	8	1	1	1	1	2	2	2
214	MONTAUBAN	8	1	1	1	1	1	1	1
215	MONTPELLIER	8	0	1	2	2	2	2	2
216	MOULINS	8	0	0	0	0	1	1	1
217	NANCY	8	0	0	0	0	1	2	2
218	NANTES	8	1	1	2	3	3	3	3
219	NEVERS	8	0	0	0	0	0	0	1
220	NÎMES	8	0	0	1	1	1	2	3

APPENDIX 1

		Code	1500	1550	1600	1650	1700	1750	1800
221	NIORT	8	0	0	0	0	0	0	1
222	ORLEANS	8	2	2	2	2	2	2	3
223	PARIS	8	4	4	5	6	6	6	6
224	PERPIGNAN	8	0	0	0	0	0	0	1
225	POITIERS	8	1	1	1	1	1	1	2
226	REIMS	8	1	1	2	2	2	2	2
227	RENNES	8	1	1	2	2	2	2	2
228	RIOM	8	0	0	0	0	0	0	1
229	ROCHEFORT	8	0	0	0	0	1	0	1
230	ROUEN	8	3	3	3	4	3	3	4
231	SAINT-ETIENNE	8	0	0	0	0	0	0	1
232	SAINT-MALO	8	0	0	1	1	2	1	1
233	SAINT-OMER	8	1	0	0	0	1	1	2
234	SAINT-QUENTIN	8	0	0	0	0	0	0	1
235	STRASBOURG	8	2	2	2	2	2	3	3
236	TOULON	8	0	0	1	2	2	2	2
237	TOULOUSE	8	2	3	3	3	2	3	3
238	TOURS	8	1	1	2	2	2	2	2
239	TROYES	8	1	1	1	1	2	1	2
240	VERSAILLES	8	0	0	0	0	2	2	2
241	VIENNE	8	0	0	0	0	0	0	1
242	BASEL	9	0	0	1	1	1	1	1
243	BERN	9	0	0	0	0	0	1	1
244	GENÈVE	9	1	1	1	1	1	2	2
245	ZÜRICH	9	0	0	0	0	1	1	1
246	ALESSANDRIA	10	0	0	1	0	0	1	1
247	ASTI	10	0	0	1	0	1	1	1
248	BERGAMO	10	1	1	2	1	2	2	2
249	BRESCIA	10	3	3	3	2	2	2	2
250	CHIOGGIA	10	0	0	0	0	1	1	1
251	COMO	10	1	1	1	0	1	1	1
252	CREMA	10	1	1	1	0	0	0	0
253	CREMONA	10	3	2	2	1	2	2	2
254	CUNEO	10	0	0	1	0	0	1	1
255	FOSSANO	10	0	0	1	0	0	1	1
256	GENOA	10	3	3	3	4	4	4	4
257	LODI	10	0	0	1	1	1	1	1
258	MANTUA	10	2	2	2	1	2	2	2
259	MILANO	10	4	3	4	4	4	4	4
260	MODENA	10	1	1	2	1	1	1	2
261	MONDOVI	10	0	0	1	0	0	0	1
262	MONZA	10	1	1	1	0	0	1	1
263	NICE	10	1	1	1	1	1	1	1
264	NOVARA	10	0	0	0	0	0	0	1

THE DATA BASE

		Code	1500	1550	1600	1650	1700	1750	1800
265	PADOVA	10	2	2	2	2	2	2	2
266	PARMA	10	1	2	2	1	2	2	2
267	PAVIA	10	1	1	1	1	2	2	2
268	PIACENZA	10	2	2	2	1	2	2	2
269	REGGIO	10	1	1	1	1	1	1	1
270	SAVIGLIANO	10	0	0	1	0	0	1	1
271	TREVISO	10	1	1	1	0	0	1	1
272	TRIESTE	10	0	0	0	0	0	1	2
273	TORINO	10	0	1	2	2	3	3	4
274	UDINE	10	1	1	1	1	1	1	1
275	VENEZIA	10	4	4	4	4	4	4	4
276	VERCELLI	10	0	0	1	0	0	0	1
277	VERONA	10	2	3	3	2	3	3	3
278	VICENZA	10	1	2	2	2	2	2	2
279	VIGEVANO	10	0	0	0	0	0	0	1
280	ANCONA	11	0	0	0	1	0	1	1
281	BOLOGNA	11	3	3	3	3	3	3	3
282	FERRARA	11	2	3	2	2	2	2	2
283	FIRENZE	11	3	3	3	3	3	3	4
284	LIVORNO	11	0	0	0	1	1	2	3
285	LUCCA	11	2	2	2	2	2	2	1
286	PERUGIA	11	1	2	2	1	1	1	1
287	PISA	11	1	1	1	1	1	1	1
288	ROMA	11	3	3	4	4	4	4	5
289	SIENA	11	1	1	1	1	1	1	1
290	VITERBO	11	1	1	1	1	1	1	1
291	ACIREALE	12	0	0	1	0	1	1	1
292	ALTAMURA	12	0	0	0	0	0	0	1
293	BARI	12	0	0	1	1	1	1	1
294	CAGLIA	12	0	0	0	1	1	1	1
295	CALTAGIRONE	12	0	1	1	1	1	1	2
296	CALTANISSETA	12	0	0	1	1	1	1	1
297	CASTELVETRANO	12	0	0	1	1	1	0	1
298	CASTROGIOVANNI	12	1	1	1	1	0	1	1
299	CATANIA	12	1	2	2	1	1	2	3
300	FOGGIA	12	0	0	0	0	0	0	1
301	GIRGENTI	12	1	1	1	0	1	1	1
302	LECCE	12	1	2	2	1	1	1	2
303	MARSALA	12	0	0	0	1	1	1	2
304	MASCALI	12	0	0	0	0	0	1	1
305	MAZZARINO	12	0	0	0	0	0	1	1
306	MESSINA	12	2	2	3	3	3	2	3
307	MODICA/POZZALLO	12	1	1	1	1	1	2	2
308	MONOPOLI	12	0	0	0	0	0	0	1

APPENDIX 1

		Code	1500	1550	1600	1650	1700	1750	1800
309	NAPOLI	12	4	5	5	5	5	5	6
310	NICOSIA	12	1	1	2	1	1	1	1
311	NOTO	12	0	0	0	1	0	1	1
312	PALERMO	12	3	3	4	4	4	4	4
313	PIAZZA (ENNA)	12	1	1	2	1	0	1	1
314	RAGUSA	12	0	0	0	0	0	1	1
315	REGGIO DI CALABRIA	12	0	0	0	0	0	0	1
316	SASSARI	12	1	1	1	1	1	1	1
317	SIRACUSA	12	1	1	1	1	1	1	1
318	TARANTO	12	1	2	1	1	1	1	1
319	TERMINI	12	0	0	1	0	0	1	1
320	TRAPANI	12	1	1	1	1	1	1	2
321	ALCALA LA REAL	13	0	0	1	0	0	0	1
322	ALCAZAR DE SAN JUAN	13	1	2	1	0	0	0	1
323	ALICANTE	13	0	0	1	1	0	0	1
324	ANDUJAR	13	0	0	1	0	0	0	1
325	ANTEQUERA	13	0	1	1	1	1	1	1
326	ARACENA	13	0	0	1	0	0	0	1
327	AVILA	13	0	1	1	0	0	0	0
328	BADAJOZ	13	0	0	1	0	0	0	1
329	BAEZA	13	1	1	2	1	0	1	1
330	BARCELONA	13	2	2	3	3	3	3	4
331	BILBAO	13	0	0	0	0	0	0	1
332	BURGOS	13	0	2	1	0	0	0	0
333	CADIZ	13	0	0	0	0	2	3	3
334	CARTAGENA	13	0	0	0	0	1	2	2
335	CORDOBA	13	2	2	3	2	2	2	3
336	CUENCA	13	0	1	2	0	0	0	0
337	ECIJA	13	1	1	2	2	1	1	2
338	GRANADA	13	3	3	3	3	3	3	3
339	JAEN	13	1	2	2	1	2	2	2
340	JEREZ DA LA FRONTERA	13	1	1	2	1	1	2	2
341	LUCENA	13	1	1	1	1	1	1	1
342	MADRID	13	0	2	3	4	4	4	5
343	MALAGA	13	0	1	1	1	2	2	2
344	MEDINA DEL CAMPO	13	1	1	1	0	0	0	0
345	MEDINA DE RIO SECO	13	1	1	1	0	0	0	0
346	MORON DE LA FRONTERA	13	0	0	0	0	0	0	1
347	MURCIA	13	1	1	1	2	2	2	3
348	OCAÑA	13	0	0	1	0	0	0	0
349	ORIHUELA	13	0	0	1	0	0	1	1
350	OSUNA	13	0	0	1	0	0	0	1
351	PALENCIA	13	0	0	1	0	0	0	1
352	PALMA	13	1	1	2	2	2	2	2

THE DATA BASE

		Code	1500	1550	1600	1650	1700	1750	1800
353	RONDA	13	0	0	0	0	0	0	1
354	SALAMANCA	13	1	2	2	1	1	1	0
355	SANTIAGO	13	0	0	0	1	1	1	2
356	SEGOVIA	13	1	2	2	1	0	0	0
357	SEVILLA	13	2	3	4	3	4	3	4
358	TOLEDO	13	2	2	3	2	2	2	2
359	UBEDA	13	0	1	1	1	1	1	1
360	UTRERA	13	0	0	1	1	0	0	0
361	VALENCIA	13	3	2	3	3	3	3	4
362	VALLADOLID	13	2	3	3	1	1	1	2
363	ZARAGOZA	13	1	1	2	2	2	2	3
364	COIMBRA	14	0	0	1	1	1	1	1
365	ELVAS	14	0	1	1	1	1	1	1
366	EVORA	14	0	1	1	1	1	1	1
367	LISBOA	14	2	4	4	4	5	4	5
368	PORTO	14	0	1	1	2	2	2	2
369	BRNO (BRÜNN)	15	0	0	0	0	1	1	2
370	GRAZ	15	0	0	0	0	0	2	2
371	INNSBRUCK	15	0	0	0	0	0	0	1
372	KLAGENFURT	15	0	0	0	0	0	0	1
373	LINZ	15	0	0	0	0	0	1	1
374	PRAHA	15	2	2	2	2	2	3	3
375	SALZBURG	15	1	1	1	1	1	1	1
376	WIEN	15	2	2	3	3	4	5	5
377	KRAKOW	16	0	0	0	0	0	1	2
378	POZNAN	16	0	0	0	0	0	0	1
379	WARSZAWA	16	0	1	1	2	1	2	3

Appendix 2
SOURCES

The number and name of each city is presented in the same order as in appendix 1. The sources are listed per year. The notation 1500–1650, for example, indicates that the following source provided information for all dates between 1500 and 1650. The sources are presented in abbreviated form (author, year of publication and page). The full reference can be found in the bibliography.

SCANDINAVIA

1. BERGEN   *1750*: Humlum (1942); *1800*: Drake (1969a), 9.
2. COPENHAGEN   *1650*: Lassen (1965), 1–30; *1700*: Olson and Askgaard (1964–5), 436–47; Jeannin (1969), 95; *1750*: Lassen (1966), 134–57; Thestrup (1971), 132; *1800*: Degn (1977), 11.
3. GÖTEBORG   *1650*: Heckscher (1963), 111, 144–5; *1750*: Heckscher, 144–5; Ericsson (1977), 121; *1800*: idem.
4. KARLSKRONA   *1750*: Ericsson (1977), 121; *1800*: idem.
5. OSLO   *1750*: Humlum (1942); *1800*: Drake (1969a), 9.
6. STOCKHOLM   *1600*: Lager (1962), 145; *1650*: Heckscher (1949), II, 1; *1700*: idem.; Imhof (1975), 161–97; *1750–1800*: *Statistisk årsbok för Stockholms Stad 1964–5* (1965), 6.

ENGLAND AND WALES

7. BATH   *1650*: Chalkin (1974), 24; *1700*: Clark and Slack (1976), 33; Neale (1974), 253; *1750*: Law (1972), 25; Neale, 254; *1800*: Census of 1801.
8. BIRMINGHAM   *1550*: Court (1938), 43; *1600*: Court, 44; *1700*: Chalkin (1974), 22; Clark and Slack (1976), 38; *1750*: Law (1972), 26; Chalkin, 338; *1800*: Census of 1801; Chalkin, 338.
9. BLACKBURN   *1750*: Law (1972), 24; *1800*: Census of 1801.
10. BOLTON   *1750*: Law (1972), 24; *1800*: Census of 1801; Chalkin (1974), 35.

SOURCES

11 BRISTOL *1500*: Clark and Slack (1976), 46; Phythian-Adams (1979), 12; *1600*: McGrath (1955), ix; *1650*: Patten (1978), 114; Corfield (1976), 239–41; *1700*: Chalkin (1974), 15; Deane (1961), 359; *1750*: Law (1972), 23; *1800*: Census of 1801 (including Barton Regis Hundred).

12 CAMBRIDGE *1650*: Chalkin (1974), 18; *1700*: Clark and Slack (1976), map 2; Chalkin, 18; *1750*: Law (1972), 22; *1800*: Census of 1801 (including university population).

13 CARLISLE *1700*: Appleby (1978), 28; *1750*: Law (1972), 23; *1800*: Census of 1801; Krause (1969), 124; Chalkin (1974), 317.

14 CHATHAM *1600*: Clark and Slack (1976), 37; *1700*: Chalkin (1974), 23; Corfield (1976), 223; *1800*: Census of 1801.

15 CHESTER *1650*: Chalkin (1974), 18; *1700*: Chalkin, 18; *1750*: Law (1972), 23; *1800*: Census of 1801.

16 COLCHESTER *1500*: Clark and Slack (1976), map 1; Phythian-Adams (1979), 12; *1600*: Patten (1978), 115; *1650*: Doolittle (1975), 333–41; Chalkin (1974), 14; *1700*: Clark and Slack (1976), map 2; *1750*: Law (1972), 23; *1800*: Census of 1801.

17 COVENTRY *1500*: Harris (1907–13), 674; Phythian-Adams (1979), 12; *1600*: Patten (1978), 115; *1650*: Corfield (1976), 238; *1700*: Chalkin (1974), 4; Corfield, 223; *1750*: Chalkin, 20; Law (1969), 90–3; *1800*: Census of 1801.

18 DERBY *1750*: Law (1972), 23; *1800*: Census of 1801.

19 EXETER *1500*: Clark and Slack (1976), map 1; *1550*: Pickard (1947), 14–15; *1600*: Stephens (1958), 50; *1650*: Hoskins (1935), 114; *1700*: Harte (1938–9), 213; Hoskins (1938–9), 246–7; *1750*: Law (1972), 23; *1800*: Census of 1801 (city and county); Hoskins, 114; Chalkin (1974), 339.

20 GREENWICH *1800*: Census of 1801.

21 HUDDERSFIELD *1800*: Census of 1801.

22 HULL, KINGSTON-UPON- *1650*: Corfield (1976), 239, 241; *1700*: Chalkin (1974), 13; Victoria County History, Yorkshire, East Riding, 157–8; *1750*: Law (1972), 26; *1800*: Census of 1801; Jackson (1972), 2.

23 IPSWICH *1600*: Patten (1978), 115; *1700*: Corfield (1976), 223; Chalkin (1974), 10; *1750*: Law (1972), 25; *1800*: Census of 1801.

24 KING'S LYNN *1500*: Clark and Slack (1976), map 1; *1600*: Patten (1978), 115; *1650*: Chalkin (1974), 13; *1700*: Corfield (1976), 223; *1750*: Law (1972), 25; *1800*: Census of 1801.

25 LEEDS *1650*: Beresford (1974), 282; Rimmer (1967), 118; *1700*: Chalkin (1974), 21; *1750*: Law (1972), 22–6; *1800*: Census of 1801 (Town plus Liberty).

26 LEICESTER *1500*: Dury (1963), 247; *1550*: Dury, 247; *1650*: Chalkin (1974), 21; Dury, 247; *1700*: Simmons (1974), 98; Dury, 247; *1750*: Law (1972), 24; *1800*: Census of 1801; Simmons, 140.

27 LIVERPOOL *1700*: Wheeler (1836), 41; Chalkin (1974), 13; *1750*: Vigier (1970), 77; Law (1972), 24; *1800*: Census of 1801.

28 LONDON Thirsk (1967), 514; *1550*: Finlay (1981), 155–7; Wrigley (1967), 44; *1600–50*: Wrigley, 44; *1700*: Wrigley, 44; Corfield (1972), 8; *1750*: Wrigley, 44; Corfield, 8; Law (1972), 24; *1800*: Census of 1801. Figures cited for the

APPENDIX 2

population of London varying according to the boundaries assigned to the metropolis: 865,000 is published in the special recapitulation for London in the 1801 census.

29 MANCHESTER *1650*: Chalkin (1974), 22; *1700*: Clark and Slack (1976), 44; Vigier (1970), 95, 101; *1750*: Law (1972), 24; Vigier, 95; *1800*: Census of 1801; Vigier, 101. Other higher figures cited for Manchester are the result of including neighbouring Salford in the total. In this study Salford is listed separately.

30 NEWCASTLE-UPON-TYNE *1500*: Clark and Slack (1976), 46; *1550*: Howell (1967), 2; *1650*: Chalkin (1974), 14; Welford (1911), 55–6; *1700*: Chalkin, 14; *1750*: Law (1972), 14; *1800*: Census of 1801.

31 NORWICH *1500*: Clark and Slack (1976), 46; Patten (1978), 251; *1600*: Corfield (1972), 263–5; Patten, 251; *1650*: Corfield, 263–5; *1700*: Corfield, 263–5; *1750*: Patten, 251; Law (1972), 25; *1800*: Census of 1801; Patten, 251.

32 NOTTINGHAM *1550*: Dury (1963), 247; Gray (1953), 29; *1650*: Dury, 247; *1700*: Dury, 247; Chambers (1960), 334–53; *1750*: Law (1972), 24; *1800*: Census of 1801; Chambers, 334–53; Gray, 48.

33 OLDHAM *1750*: Law (1972), 24; *1800*: Census of 1801.

34 OXFORD *1500*: Clark and Slack (1976), map 1; *1550*: Hammer (1976), 196; *1650*: Chalkin (1974), 11; *1700*: Clark and Slack, map 2; Chalkin, 10; *1750*: Law (1972), 25; *1800*: Census of 1801.

35 PLYMOUTH *1550*: Clarkson (1971), 47; *1600*: Patten (1978), 115; *1700*: Corfield (1976), 223; *1750*: Law (1972), 23 (Plymouth and Devonport); *1800*: Census of 1801 (includes suburbs).

36 PORTSMOUTH *1650*: Chalkin (1974), 24; *1700*: Clark and Slack (1976), map 2; *1750*: Law (1972), 24 (includes Portsea); *1800*: Census of 1801 (includes Portsea).

37 PRESTON *1750*: Law (1972), 24; *1800*: Census of 1801.

38 READING *1750*: Law (1972), 22; *1800*: Census of 1801.

39 SALFORD *1750*: Vigier (1970), 95, 101; *1800*: Census of 1801; Vigier, 101.

40 SHEFFIELD *1700*: Chalkin (1974), 23; Law (1972), 26; Hoskins (1935), 17; *1800*: Census of 1801 (includes suburbs).

41 SHREWSBURY *1500*: Clark and Slack (1976), map 1; *1700*: Clark and Slack, map 2; Chalkin (1974), 10; *1750*: Chalkin, 34; *1800*: Census of 1801.

42 STOCKPORT *1750*: Law (1972), 22; *1800*: Census of 1801.

43 SUNDERLAND *1700*: Clark and Slack (1976), map 2; *1750*: Law (1972), 23; *1800*: Census of 1801; Chalkin (1974), 339.

44 WARRINGTON *1750*: Law (1972), 24; *1800*: Census of 1801.

45 WENLOCK *1800*: Census of 1801.

46 WIGAN *1750*: Law (1972), 24; *1800*: Census of 1801.

47 WOLVERHAMPTON *1550*: Palliser (1974), 55; *1650*: Palliser, 72; *1750*: Law (1972), 25; *1800*: Census of 1801.

48 WORCESTER *1550 – 1650*: Dyer (1973), 26; *1700*: Corfield (1976), 223; *1750*: Law (1972), 26; *1800*: Census of 1801; Chalkin (1974), 34.

49 YARMOUTH, GREAT *1500*: Clark and Slack (1976), map 1; Patten (1978), 251; *1600–50*: Patten, 251; *1700*: Corfield (1976), 223; *1750*: Law (1972), 25;

SOURCES

Patten, 251; *1800*: Census of 1801; Patten, 251.
50 YORK *1500*: Corfield (1976), 222; *1550*: Palliser (1974), 17–33; *1600*: Palliser (1972), 87; *1700*: Chalkin (1974), 18; Corfield, 223; *1750*: Law (1972), 26; *1800*: Census of 1801.

SCOTLAND

51 ABERDEEN *1550*: Lythe (1960), 117; *1750*: Kyd (1952), 1–81; *1800*: Census of 1801; Kyd, 1–81.
52 DUNDEE *1600*: Lythe (1960), 117; *1750*: Kyd (1952), 1–81; *1800*: Census of 1801; Kyd, 1–81.
53 EDINBURGH *1600*: Lythe (1960), 117; *1650*: Keir (1966), 98; *1700*: Keir, 98; *1750*: Kyd (1952), 1–81; Keir, 98; *1800*: Census of 1801.
54 GLASGOW *1600*: Lythe (1960), 117; *1700*: Cleland (1828), 2–3; Devine (1983), 98; *1750*: Cleland, 2–3; MacDonald (1937), 50; *1800*: Census of 1801; Kyd (1952), 1–81.
55 GREENOCK *1750*: Kyd (1952), 1–81; *1800*: Census of 1801; Hamilton (1963), 29.
56 INVERNESS *1750*: Kyd (1952), 1–81; *1800*: Census of 1801.
57 PAISLEY *1750*: Kyd (1952), 1–81; Hamilton (1963), 28; *1800*: Census of 1801.
58 PERTH *1600*: Lythe (1960), 117; *1750*: Kyd (1952), 1–8; *1800*: Census of 1801.

IRELAND

59 BELFAST *1700*: Butlin (1977), 97; *1800*: Cullen (1976b), 122; Vaughan and Fitzpatrick (1978), 28–41.
60 CORK *1600*: Cullen (1976b), 390; *1650*: O'Sullivan (1937), 85; *1700*: Butlin (1977), 102; *1750*: O'Sullivan, 85; *1800*: Cullen (1976a), 85; Vaughan and Fitzpatrick (1978), 28–41.
61 DUBLIN *1600*: Cullen (1976b), 390; *1650*: Simms (1964–5), 212; *1700*: Ogg (1957), 11; Cullen (1976a), 85; *1800*: Weber (1899), 66; Cullen (1976a), 121; Vaughan and Fitzpatrick (1978), 28–41.
62 GALWAY *1600*: Cullen (1976b), 390; *1700*: Butlin (1977), 93, 102; *1800*: Weber (1899), 66.
63 KILKENNY *1700*: Butlin (1977), 102; *1800*: Weber (1899), 66; Vaughan and Fitzpatrick (1978), 28–41.
64 LIMERICK *1600*: Cullen (1976b), 390; *1700*: Butlin (1977), 102; *1800*: Weber (1899), 66; Vaughan and Fitzpatrick (1978), 28–41.
65 NEWRY *1800*: Weber (1899), 66; Vaughan and Fitzpatrick (1978), 28–41.
66 WATERFORD *1600*: Cullen (1976b), 390; *1700*: Butlin (1977), 93, 102; *1800*: Freeman (1969), 120; Weber (1899), 66; Vaughan and Fitzpatrick (1978), 28–41.

THE NETHERLANDS

67 ALKMAAR *1500–50*: van der Woude (1972), III, 618–23; *1650*: van

APPENDIX 2

der Woude, I, 172-4; *1700*: estimate based on van der Woude, I, 172-9, and 'Familiegeld' tax of 1715; *1750*: van der Woude, I, 179; *1800*: Volks-telling van 1795.

68 AMSTERDAM   *1500*: van der Woude (1972), I, 187; de Vries (1974), 90; *1550-1600*: Schraa (1954), 29; *1650*: estimate based on Hart (1976), 118-20, 136-7; *1700*: de Vries (1981), 249; *1750*: van der Woude (1980), 138-9; *1800*: Volks-telling van 1795.

69 ARNHEM   *1500*: Roessingh (1964), 79-150; *1650*: idem.; *1750*: idem.; *1800*: Volks-telling van 1795.

70 DELFT   *1500*: Fruin (1866); *1550-1750*: Wijsenbeek-Olthuis (1983), 57-9; *1600*: van Dillen (1940), 167-89; *1650*: Rogier (1960), 193; *1700*: de Vries (1981), 249; *1750*: idem.; *1800*: Volks-telling van 1795.

71 DORDRECHT   *1500*: van der Woude (1972), I, 187; *1550*: de Vries (1974), 90; *1600*: van Dillen (1940), 167-89; *1650-1750*: de Vries (1981), 249; *1800*: Volks-telling van 1795.

72 ENKHUIZEN   *1500*: Fruin (1866); *1600*: van Dillen (1940), 167-89; *1650-1750*: estimate based on van der Woude (1972), I, 107-14; *1800*: Volks-telling van 1795.

73 GOUDA   *1500*: Fruin (1866); *1600*: van Dillen (1940), 167-89; *1650*: Kramer (n.d.); de Vries (1981), 249; *1700-50*: de Vries, 249; *1800*: Volks-telling van 1795.

74 GRONINGEN   *1550*: Keuning (1974), 38; *1600*: Matthey (1975), 251; *1750*: Tegenwoordige Staat der Vereenigde Nederlanden (1793), 10; *1800*: Volks-telling van 1795.

75 HAARLEM   *1500*: Fruin (1866); *1550*: de Vries (1974), 90; *1600*: van Dillen (1940), 167-89; *1650*: de Vries (1981), 249; *1700-50*: van der Woude (1972), I, 189; *1800*: Volks-telling van 1795.

76 DEN HAAG (THE HAGUE)   *1500*: Fruin (1866); *1600*: van Dillen (1940), 167-89; *1700*: Bureau voor statistiek en voorlichting der gemeente 's-Gravenhage (1948), 129-31; *1750*: de Vries (1981), 249; *1800*: Volks-telling van 1795.

77 'S HERTOGENBOSCH (BOIS-LE-DUC)   *1500*: van Houtte (1977), 136; *1550*: van der Woude (1980), 136; *1650*: van Houtte, 136; *1700*: van Xanten and van der Woude (1965), 3-91; *1750*: van Houtte, 240; *1800*: Volks-telling van 1795.

78 HOORN   *1500*: Fruin (1866); *1600*: van Dillen (1940), 167-89; *1700-50*: van der Woude (1972), I, 107-14; *1800*: Volks-telling van 1795.

79 LEEUWARDEN   *1500-1750*: Faber (1972), II, 405; *1800*: Volks-telling van 1795.

80 LEIDEN   *1500*: van der Woude (1972), I, 187; *1550*: Posthumus (1939), III, 1124-44; *1600*: van Dillen (1940), 167-89; Daelemans (1975), 137-215; *1650-1750*: Posthumus, III, 1197-1200; Noordam (1978), 105-7; *1800*: Volks-telling van 1795.

81 MAASTRICHT   *1500*: Kemp (1962), 341; *1600*: Kemp, 349; *1650*: Philips (1975), 1-48; *1700-50*: Kemp, 349; *1800*: Volks-telling van 1795.

82 MIDDELBURG   *1500-1750*: Fokker (1878), 81-100; *1800*: Volks-telling van 1795.

83 NIJMEGEN   *1500*: Gorissen (1956), 7; *1550*: Offermans (1972), 58-9; *1600-1750*: Nusteling, 41; *1800*: Volks-telling van 1795.

SOURCES

84 ROTTERDAM   *1500*: van der Woude (1972), I, 187; *1550*: estimate based on Ravesteijn (1933), 173; *1600*: van Dillen (1940), 167-89; *1650-1750*: van der Woude and Mentink (1965), 39; *1800*: Volks-telling van 1795.
85 UTRECHT   *1500*: estimate based on Berents (1972), 78-92; *1550*: Ramaer (1921), 37-8; *1650*: de Vries (1974), 97; *1750*: van der Woude (1980), 138; de Vries, 97; *1800*: Volks-telling van 1795.
86 ZAANDAM   Figures refer to the adjacent municipalities of Oostzanen, Westzanen, Krommenie, Jisp and Wormer; *1500-1750*: van der Woude (1972), I, 185; de Vries (1974), 90; *1800*: idem.; Volks-telling van 1795.
87 ZWOLLE   *1650-1750*: Slicher van Bath (1957), 61-8; *1800*: Volks-telling van 1795.

BELGIUM

88 AALST   *1550*: de Brouwer (1968), 111; *1650-1750*: idem.; *1800*: idem.; Franke (1922), 112.
89 ANTWERPEN   *1500*: Cuvelier (1912), 462-3; van Houtte (1962), 50-69; *1550*: Scholliers (1962), V, 610-17; *1600*: idem.; Klep (1981), 346-9; *1650*: Scholliers, V, 610-17; *1700*: Coseman (1939), 37; *1750*: Verbeemen (1957), 28; Klep, 349; *1800*: Klep, 402-3.
90 BRUGGE   *1500*: estimate suggested by evidence in de Smet (1933); *1600-1750*: Wyffels (1958), 1243-74; *1800*: idem.; Franke (1922), 112.
91 BRUSSELS (BRUSSEL, BRUXELLES)   *1500*: Henne and Wauters (1968), III, 22; Laurent (1963), 225-6; *1550*: Henne and Wauters, I, 363; van Houtte (1957), 130; *1650*: Charlier (1969), *passim*; *1700*: Cosemans (1939), 35-6; *1750*: Verbeemen (1962b), 205; *1800*: Cosemans (1966).
92 DUNKERQUE   *1700-50*: Mols (1954-6), II, 514; *1800*: Mols (1959), 491-511.
93 GENT   *1550*: Mols (1954-6), II, 522; *1600*: van Werveke (1940); *1650-1800*: idem.; Verbeemen (1956), 1051.
94 IEPER   *1500*: Demey (1950), 1031-48; Pirenne (1903), 1-32; *1700*: Demey, 1031-48; *1800*: Hélin (1963), 240-52.
95 KORTRIJK   *1500*: Pirenne (1903), 1-32; *1800*: Franke (1922), 112.
96 LEUVEN   *1500*: Cuvelier (1912-13), I, 432-3; *1600*: Cuvelier (1908), 347; *1650*: Verbeemen (1956), 1032; *1700*: Cosemans (1939), 35; Verbeemen (1954), 91; *1750*: van Houtte (1964), 159; Cosemans, 213-14.
97 LIÈGE   *1500*: Hélin (1963), 240-52; *1650*: Lejeune (1967), 27; *1750-1800*: Hélin, 240-52.
98 LIER   *1600*: Klep (1981), 351-2; *1700-50*: Cosemans (1939), 35; *1800*: Klep, 416-17.
99 LILLE   *1500-50*: Du Plessis (1977), 216; *1700-1800*: Deyon (1971), 495-508.
100 LOKEREN   *1800*: Franke (1922), 112.
101 MECHELEN   *1500-50*: Klep (1981), 349-50; *1600*: van Houtte (1977), 145; *1650-1750*: Verbeemen (1956), 1051; Klep, 351; *1800*: Klep, 400.
102 MONS   *1500*: Hélin (1963), 240-52; *1650*: idem.; *1700*: Hasquin (1975), 366; *1750*: van Houtte (1964), 159; *1800*: Hélin, 240-52.

APPENDIX 2

103 NAMUR *1650*: Hasquin (1975), 366; *1800*: Franke (1922), 112.
104 OOSTENDE *1800*: Franke (1922), 112.
105 SINT NIKLAAS *1600–50*: van Werveke (1940), 297; *1700*: van Houtte (1977), 240; *1750*: van Werveke, 297; *1800*: van Houtte, 240.
106 TOURNAI *1500–1650*: Wymans (1961), 111–34; *1700*: Hasquin (1975), 366; *1750*: Hélin (1963), 240–52; *1800*: Franke (1922), 112.
107 VALENCIENNES *1550*: Arnould (1951), 305; *1700*: Hélin (1963), 240–52; Robillard de Bearepaire (1872); *1750–1800*: Mols (1953), 201–20.

GERMANY

108 AACHEN *1500*: Keyser (1956), III.3, 32; *1650–1750*: Banck (1895), 224; *1800*: Franke (1922), 113.
109 ALTONA *1600–1750*: Lehe *et al.* (1967), 295; *1800*: Erichsen (1956), 99; Franke (1922), 114.
110 ANSBACH *1600–1750*: Bahl (1974), 173, 213; *1750*: Keyser (1971), V.1, 48; *1800*: Franke (1922), 112.
111 AUGSBURG *1500*: Zorn and Hellenbrand (1969), 73; *1550*: Zorn (n.d.), 183; *1600*: Zorn, 206; *1650*: Zorn, 218; *1700–50*: Schreiber (1939–40), 9–177; *1800*: Zorn and Hellenbrand (1969), 73.
112 BAMBERG *1550–1750*: Keyser (1971), V.1, 100–1; *1800*: Franke (1922), 114.
113 BARMEN *1650*: Köllmann (1960), 9; *1700–1800*: idem., and Köllmann (1974), 187.
114 BAUTZEN *1550*: Blaschke (1967), 138–41; *1750*: idem.; *1800*: Franke (1922), 113.
115 BERLIN *1500*: Keyser (1941), 376–7; *1600*: Dorwart (1971), 77–8; *1650*: Landry (1945), 111–12; *1700*: Dorwart, 232; *1750*: Dorwart, 235; Kisskalt (1921), 438–511; *1800*: Mols (1954–6), II, 512.
116 BONN *1650–1800*: Vogler (1983), 399; Ennen (1962), II, 300.
117 BRANDENBURG *1800*: Franke (1922), 113.
118 BRAUNSCHWEIG *1500*: Reincke (1951), 6; *1550*: Saalfeld (1960), 7; *1650*: idem.; *1750*: Buchholz (1966), 57; *1800*: Saalfeld, 7; Franke (1922), 114.
119 BREMEN *1500*: Reincke (1951), 6; *1700*: Reineke (1928); *1750–1800*: Schaeffer (1957), 35.
120 BRESLAU (WROCLAW) *1500*: Długoborski, Gierowski and Maleczyński (1958), 196, 206; *1550–1600*: Schmoller (1922), 95; Süssmilch (1775), I, 32–40; *1750*: Długoborski, Gierowski and Maleczyński, 738; *1800*: Franke (1922), 112.
121 CHEMNITZ (KARL-MARX-STADT) *1550*: Blaschke (1967), 138–41; *1600*: Schmoller (1922), 92; *1700*: idem.; *1750*: Blaschke, 138–41; *1800*: Franke (1922), 113.
122 DANZIG (GDANSK) *1500*: François (1978), 588; *1550–1600*: Mols (1954–6), I, 326; *1650*: Mols, II, 511; *1700*: idem.; *1750*: Mols, I, 180; *1800*: Mols, II, 512; Franke (1922), 114.
123 DRESDEN *1500*: Schmoller (1922), 92; *1550*: Blaschke (1967), 138–41; *1650*: estimated from *Philosophical Transactions of the Royal Society* (1723),

SOURCES

454-69; *1700*: Keyser (1941), 50; *1750*: Blaschke, 138-41; *1800*: Franke (1922), 113.
124 DÜSSELDORF *1500*: Weidenhaupt (1968), 33; *1650-1750*: Weidenhaupt, 60; *1800*: Weidenhaupt, 96.
125 ELBERFELD *1650-1800*: Köllmann (1960), 9.
126 ELBING (ELBLAG) *1500*: Carstenn (1937), 286; Olinski and Walden (1931), 81; *1550*: Carstenn, 286; *1650-1750*: Olinski and Walden, 81; *1800*: Franke (1922), 112.
127 EMDEN *1500-1650*: Keyser (1952), III.1, 123-4; *1650*: Franz (1961), 8; *1750*: Arends (1818-20), I, 6; *1800*: Aden (1964), 196.
128 ERFURT *1500*: Mols (1954-6), II, 509-11; *1550-1650*: Schrader (1921), 89; *1700-1750*: Schmoller (1922), 288; *1800*: Franke (1922), 114.
129 FLENSBURG *1800*: Erichsen (1956), 99; Franke (1922), 114.
130 FRANKFURT AM MAIN *1500*: Bücher (1886); *1550-1800*: Mauersberg (1960), 48-55.
131 FRANKFURT AM ODER *1500*: Reincke (1951), 6; *1600-50*: Schmoller (1922), 245; *1700-50*: Schmoller, 278; *1800*: Franke (1922), 112.
132 FREIBURG *1500*: Keyser (1959), IV.2, 224; *1600*: Schmoller (1922), 87; *1800*: idem.
133 FÜRTH *1600*: Keyser (1971), V.1, 208; *1700*: idem.; *1800*: idem.; Franke (1922), 113.
134 GOTHA *1800*: Franke (1922), 114.
135 HALBERSTADT *1800*: Franke (1922), 112.
136 HALLE *1800*: Schmoller (1922), 94; Franke (1922), 112.
137 HAMBURG *1500-1800*: Mauersberg (1960), 30-48.
138 HANAU *1750-1800*: Keyser (1957), IV.1, 219.
139 HANNOVER *1550-1800*: Mauersberg (1960), 54-64.
140 HEIDELBERG *1600*: Herrman (1974), 299; *1650*: Vogler (1983), 402; *1750*: Schremmer (1970), 172; *1800*: Franke (1922), 113.
141 HILDESHEIM Franke (1922), 114.
142 KASSEL *1650*: Lasch (1969); *1700-1800*: Keyser (1957), IV.1, 277; *1800*: Franke (1922), 114.
143 KÖLN (COLOGNE) *1500*: Reincke (1951), 6; *1550*: estimated from data in Kellenbenz and van Eyll (1975), I, 327; *1600*: estimated from Banck (1895), 331; *1700-1800*: Kellenbenz and van Eyll, II, 23.
144 KÖNIGSBERG (KALININGRAD) *1500-50*: Mols (1954-6), I, 320; *1700*: Keyser (1941), 375; Gause (1965-8), II, 293; *1750*: Keyser, 375; *1800*: Mols, II, 292; Franke (1922), 112.
145 LEIPZIG *1500*: Keyser (1941), 122; *1550*: Blaschke (1967), 138-41; *1600*: Schmoller (1922), 93; *1650-1700*: Keyser (1941), II, 123; *1750*: Blaschke, 138-41; *1800*: Franke (1922), 113.
146 LÜBECK *1500*: Arnim (1957), 25; *1600*: idem.; *1650*: Franz (1961), 7-8; *1800*: Franke (1922), 113.
147 LÜNEBURG *1800*: Franke (1922), 114.
148 MAGDEBURG *1500*: Reincke (1951), 6; *1550*: Schmoller (1922), 94; *1650-1750*: idem.; *1800*: Franke (1922), 112.

APPENDIX 2

149 MAINZ *1500*: Hegel (1882), 188; *1600–50*: Vogler (1983), 395; *1750–1800*: Dreyfus (1968), 248.
150 MANNHEIM *1600–1800*: Keyser (1959), IV.2, 113; Vogler (1983), 402; *1700*: Kruedener (1968), 291–347; *1750*: Herrman (1974), 300; *1800*: Franke (1922), 113.
151 MÜNCHEN (MUNICH) *1500–1800*: Mauersberg (1960), 64–72; *1800*: Schremmer (1970), 210.
152 MÜNSTER *1600*: Keyser (1954), III.2, 254; *1700–50*: idem.; *1800*: Keyser, III.2, 256; Franke (1922), 114.
153 NÜRNBERG *1500*: Hofmann (1975), 91–101; *1600*: Hofmann, 96–8; Schultheisz (1966), 63; *1650*: Hofmann, 96–8; *1700*: Müller (1967), 12; *1800*: Hofmann, 96–8.
154 POTSDAM *1700–50*: Schmoller (1922), 277; *1800*: Franke (1922), 112.
155 QUEDLINBURG *1800*: Franke (1922), 113.
156 REGENSBURG *1500*: Keyser (1974), V.2, 578–9; *1800*: Franke (1922), 113; Hable (1970).
157 ROSTOCK *1800*: Franke (1922), 114.
158 SOEST *1500*: Reincke (1951), 6; *1550*: Schmoller (1922), 78; *1650*: idem.; *1750*: Schmoller, 78, 278; *1800*: Franke (1922), 113.
159 STETTIN (SZCZECIN) *1500–1600*: Friederichs and Niessen (1931), 18; *1700–1800*: Schmoller (1922), 94; *1800*: Franke (1922), 112.
160 STRALSUND *1800*: Franke (1922), 114.
161 STUTTGART *1550*: Weber (1936); Abel (1978), 98; *1600*: Herrman (1974), 273–300; *1650–1750*: Keyser (1962), IV.2, 152, 226; *1800*: Franke (1922), 114.
162 ULM *1500–1800*: Keyser (1962), IV.2, 264; *1800*: Franke (1922), 113.
163 WÜRZBURG *1500–1750*: Seberich (1960), 49–68; *1800*: Franke (1922), 114.

FRANCE

164 ABBEVILLE *1700*: Mols (1954–6), II, 516; *1750*: Dupâquier (1979a), 195; *1800*: Le Mée (1971).
165 AGEN *1700*: Mols (1954–6), II, 516; *1800*: Le Mée (1971).
166 AIX EN PROVENCE *1700*: Carriere (1973), 251; Biraben (1968), 541; *1750*: Baehrel (1961), 234–6; *1800*: Le Mée (1971).
167 ALBI *1700–1800*: Frêche (1968), 404.
168 ALENÇON *1700*: Dupâquier (1979a), appendix; *1750*: Dupâquier, 195; *1800*: Le Mée (1971).
169 AMIENS *1650–1700*: Deyon (1967), 7; *1750*: Mols (1954–6), II, 514; *1800*: Le Mée (1971).
170 ANGERS *1600–1700*: Lebrun (1971); *1750*: Mols (1954–6), II, 514; *1800*: Le Mée (1971).
171 ANGOULEME *1800*: Le Mée (1971).
172 ARLES *1550–1700*: Baehrel (1961), 234–6; *1700*: Biraben (1968), 512; *1750*: Baehrel, 234–6; *1800*: Le Mée (1971).

SOURCES

173 ARRAS *1500*: Bocquet (1969), 179–81; *1700–50*: Mols (1954–6), II, 516; *1800*: Le Mée (1971).
174 AUXERRE *1800*: Le Mée (1971).
175 AVIGNON *1700*: Biraben (1968), 542; *1800*: Le Mée (1971).
176 BAYEUX *1600–1750*: El Kordi (1970), 152–5; *1800*: Le Mée (1971).
177 BAYONNE *1800*: Le Mée (1971).
178 BEAUVAIS *1700*: Mols (1954–6), II, 516; Dupâquier (1979a), 195; *1750*: Goubert (1960), 254; *1800*: Le Mée (1971).
179 BESANÇON *1500*: Fohlen (1964–5), I, 567; *1550–1600*: Fohlen, I, 568; *1650–1700*: Fohlen, II, 85; *1750*: estimated from data in Fohlen, II, 85–6, 156, 300; Mols (1954–6), II, 514–16; *1800*: Le Mée (1971).
180 BEZIERS *1700*: Mols (1954–6), II, 516; *1800*: Le Mée (1971).
181 BLOIS *1700*: Dupâquier (1979a), appendix, 324; *1750*: Dupâquier, 195; *1800*: Le Mée (1971).
182 BORDEAUX *1500*: Braudel and Labrousse (1977), I, 397; *1650*: Boutruche (1966), IV, 522; *1700–50*: Pousson (1968), V, 327; *1800*: Le Mée (1971).
183 BOULOGNE *1500*: Bocquet (1969), 179–81; *1750*: Bougard and Reinhard (1964), 21, 31; *1800*: Le Mée (1971).
184 BOURGES *1550*: Dupâquier (1979a), appendix; *1700*: Mols (1954–6), II, 515–16; Dupâquier, 195; *1750*: Mols (1954–6), II, 516; *1800*: Le Mée (1971).
185 BREST *1700*: Konvitz (1978), 136; Croix (1981), I, 142; *1750*: Mols (1954–6), II, 516; *1800*: Le Mée (1971).
186 CAEN *1700*: Perrot (1975), I, 148; *1750*: Perrot, I, 152; *1800*: Le Mée (1971).
187 CAHORS *1800*: Le Mée (1971).
188 CAMBRAI *1700*: Mols (1954–6), II, 516; *1750*: Bougard (1973), 79; *1800*: Le Mée (1971).
189 CARCASSONNE *1700*: Frêche (1968), 415; *1800*: Le Mée (1971).
190 CASTRES *1700–1750*: Frêche (1968), 418; *1800*: Le Mée (1971).
191 CHALONS-SUR-MARNE *1700*: Mols (1954–6), II, 516; Dupâquier (1979a), appendix; *1750*: Dupâquier, 195; *1800*: Le Mée (1971).
192 CHALONS-SUR-SAONE *1800*: Le Mée (1971).
193 CHARTRES *1700*: Mols (1954–6), II, 516; Dupâquier (1979a), 195; *1800*: Le Mée (1971).
194 CHERBOURG *1700–50*: Lefebvre (1965); *1800*: Le Mée (1971).
195 CLERMONT-FERRAND *1700–50*: Mols (1954–6), II, 516; *1800*: Le Mée (1971).
196 COLMAR *1500*: Waldner (1931), 734; *1650*: estimated from data in Fleurent (1922), annex; *1700*: Strohl (1950), 281; *1800*: Waldner, 734; Le Mée (1971).
197 DIEPPE *1700*: Mols (1954–6), II, 516; *1750*: Robillard de Bearepaire (1872); *1800*: Le Mée (1971).
198 DIJON *1500*: Bouchard (1953), 30–65; *1650*: Roupnel (1922), 118; *1700–50*: Bouchard, 30–65; *1800*: Le Mée (1971).
199 DOUAI *1700–50*: Lefebvre (1972), 399–409; *1800*: Le Mée (1971).
200 FALAISE *1700*: Dupâquier (1979a), 195; *1800*: Le Mée (1971).
201 GRENOBLE *1500*: Chartier and Neveux (1981), 23–50; Le Roy Ladurie and Quilliet (1981), 297; *1700*: Esmonin (1924), 177–202; Mols (1954–6), II, 516; *1750*: Mols, II, 516; *1800*: Le Mée (1971).

APPENDIX 2

202 LA ROCHELLE *1600–50*: Peronas (1961), 1131–40; *1700*: Mols (1954–6), II, 516; *1800*: Le Mée (1971).
203 LAVAL *1700*: Mols (1954–6), II, 516; *1800*: Le Mée (1971).
204 LE HAVRE *1700–50*: Dardel (1963), 313–14; Robillard de Bearepaire (1872); *1800*: Le Mée (1971).
205 LE MANS *1700*: Mols (1954–6), II, 516; Dupâquier (1979a), 195; *1750*: Mols, II, 515; *1800*: Le Mée (1971).
206 LE PUY *1700*: Mols (1954–6), II, 516; *1800*: Le Mée (1971).
207 LIMOGES *1700*: Mols (1954–6), II, 516; *1750*: Mols, II, 515; *1800*: Le Mée (1971).
208 LISIEUX *1700*: Dupâquier (1979a), 195; Zens and Delange (1974), 12–20; *1800*: Le Mée (1971).
209 LORIENT *1700*: Konvitz (1978), 138–9; *1800*: Le Mée (1971).
210 LYON *1500–50*: Braudel and Labrousse (1977), I, 397; *1650*: Garden (1970), 31; *1700–50*: Garden, 34; *1800*: Le Mée (1971).
211 MACON *1700*: Mols (1954–6), II, 516; *1800*: Le Mée (1971).
212 MARSEILLE *1550–1600*: Braudel and Labrousse (1977), I, 397; *1600*: Collier and Billioud (1951), III, 551; *1650*: Mols (1954–6), II, 36; Baehrel (1961), 234–6; *1700*: Carriere (1973), 198; *1750*: Carriere, 206; *1800*: Le Mée (1971).
213 METZ *1500*: Rigault (1951), 308; *1600–1750*: idem.; *1800*: Le Mée (1971).
214 MONTAUBAN *1700*: Mols (1954–6), II, 516; *1800*: Le Mée (1971).
215 MONTPELLIER *1500*: Russell (1962), 349–52; *1700*: Le Roy Ladurie and Quilliet (1981), 297; Mols (1954–6), II, 516; *1750*: Mols, II, 514; *1800*: Le Mée (1971).
216 MOULINS *1700–50*: Mols (1954–6), II, 515–16; *1800*: Le Mée (1971).
217 NANCY *1550–1700*: Carbourdin (1977) *passim*; *1600*: Herrman (1974), 299; *1700*: Pfister (1902–9), II, 166, III, 129; *1750*: Le Roy Ladurie and Quilliet (1981), 297; *1800*: idem.; Le Mée (1971).
218 NANTES *1500*: Croix (1974), 209; *1600–50*: Croix (1981), I, 135–7; *1700*: Croix (1974), 210; Martin (1928), 8; *1750*: Mols (1954–6), II, 514; *1800*: Le Mée (1971).
219 NEVERS *1800*: Le Mée (1971).
220 NÎMES *1600*: Kollmann (1956), III, 20; *1600–1800*: Teisseyre-Sallmann (1980), 967. *1800*: Le Mée (1971).
221 NIORT *1800*: Le Mée (1971).
222 ORLEANS *1700*: Dupâquier (1979a), 195; *1750*: Mols (1954–6), II, 514; *1800*: Le Mée (1971).
223 PARIS *1500*: Mols (1954–6), II, 47; *1550*: Russell (1958), 47; *1600*: Landry (1945), 106; *1650*: Meuvret (1956), 69–103; *1700*: Hélin (1963), 238–42; Dupâquier (1979a), 195; *1750*: Hélin, 238–42; *1800*: Armengaud, Reinhard and Dupâquier (1968), 244; Le Mée (1971).
224 PERPIGNAN *1800*: Le Mée (1971).
225 POITIERS *1700*: Mols (1954–6), II, 516; *1800*: Le Mée (1971).
226 REIMS *1500*: category assignment based on data in Desportes (1966), 463–509; *1700*: Mols (1954–6), II, 516; Dupâquier (1979a), appendix, 254; *1750*: Dupâquier, 195; *1800*: Le Mée (1971).
227 RENNES *1500*: Braudel and Labrousse (1977), I, 397; *1600*: idem.; *1700*: Le Roy

SOURCES

Ladurie and Quilliet (1981), 297; *1800*: Le Mée (1971).
228 RIOM   *1800*: Le Mée (1971).
229 ROCHEFORT   *1650–1750*: Konvitz (1978), 137–8; *1800*: Le Mée (1971).
230 ROUEN   *1500*: Cipolla (1976), 282; Mols (1974), 42; *1550–1750*: Bardet (1983), II, 34 (these new estimates, shown in appendices 1 and 3, introduce small changes which appeared too late to be incorporated in the body of the text); *1800*: Le Mée (1971).
231 SAINT-ETIENNE   *1800*: Le Mée (1971).
232 SAINT-MALO (including Saint-Servan)   *1500*: Chartier and Neveux (1981), 23–50; *1600–1750*: Croix (1981), I, 135–7; *1800*: Le Mée (1971).
233 SAINT-OMER   *1500*: Bocquet (1969), 179–81; *1550*: Brulez (1952), 224–5; *1700*: Mols (1954–6), II, 516; *1750*: category assignment based on Bougard and Reinhard (1964), 21, 31; *1800*: Le Mée (1971).
234 SAINT-QUENTIN   *1700*: Dupâquier (1979a), 195; *1800*: Le Mée (1971).
235 STRASBOURG (STRASSBURG)   *1500*: Ehebergs (1883), 297–314; *1550*: Hermann (1819), II, 87–108; Kintz (1975), 1053; *1600*: Cipolla (1975), 282; *1650*: Hermann, II, 87–108; *1700*: Lemoigne (1965), 13–44; *1750*: idem.; Dreyer-Roos (1969), 108; *1800*: Le Mée (1971).
236 TOULON   *1600–50*: Baehrel (1961), 234–6; *1700–50*: idem.; Biraben (1968), 541; *1800*: Le Mée (1971).
237 TOULOUSE   *1500*: Cipolla (1975), 282; *1550*: Braudel and Labrousse (1977), I, 397; *1650*: Wolff (1954), 253; *1700*: Coppolani (1963), 99–102; *1800*: Le Mée (1971).
238 TOURS   *1700*: Mols (1954–6), II, 516; Dupâquier (1979a), appendix, 672 (but this is contradicted on 195); *1750*: Mols, II, 514; *1800*: Le Mée (1971).
239 TROYES   *1700*: estimate based on baptism counts, 1701–20; *1750*: Dupâquier (1979a), 195; *1800*: Le Mée (1971).
240 VERSAILLES   *1650*: Lepetit (1977), 54; *1700*: idem.; Dupâquier (1979a), 195; *1750*: Lepetit (1978), 605, 611; *1800*: Le Mée (1971).
241 VIENNE   *1700*: Le Roy Ladurie and Quilliet (1981), 297; *1800*: Le Mée (1971).

SWITZERLAND

242 BASEL   *1500–1800*: Mauersberg (1960), 22–30.
243 BERN   *1500–1800*: Bickel (1947), 62.
244 GENÈVE   *1500*: Bickel (1947), 62; *1550*: Monter (1979), 402–3; *1600*: Piuz (1973), 460; *1600–1700*: Perrenoud (1979), I, 30; *1700*: Piuz, 460; Bickel, 62; *1750–1800*: Perrenoud, I, 9.
245 ZÜRICH   *1500–1600*: Bickel (1947), 62; *1650*: Schnyder (1925); *1700–1800*: Bickel, 62.

ITALY

246 ALESSANDRIA   *1550–1800*: Beloch (1937–61), III, 249.
247 ASTI   *1550–1600*: Beloch (1937–61), III, 279; *1700*: Cipolla (1975), 281; *1750–1800*: Beloch, III, 279.

APPENDIX 2

248 BERGAMO   *1550*: Beloch (1937–61), III, 145; Beltrami (1954), 69–70; *1600*: Beloch, III, 145; *1700*: Cipolla (1975), 281; *1750–1800*: Beloch, III, 145.
249 BRESCIA   *1500*: Beloch (1937–61), III, 357; *1550*: Beltrami (1954), 69–70; Beloch, III, 357; *1600–1800*: Beloch, III, 127, 359, 361.
250 CHIOGGIA   *1600–1800*: Beloch (1937–61), III, 24.
251 COMO   *1500*: Cipolla (1975), 281; *1550–1600*: Beloch (1937–61), III, 249; *1650*: Sella (1979), 52; *1750–1800*: Beloch, III, 249.
252 CREMA   *1550*: Beltrami (1954), 69–70; *1600–1800*: Beloch (1937–61), III, 159.
253 CREMONA   *1500–50*: Beloch (1937–61), III, 357; *1600–50*: Sella (1979), 52; Beloch, III, 203; *1700–1800*: Beloch, III, 205, 249.
254 CUNEO   *1550–1800*: Beloch (1937–61), III, 279.
255 FOSSANO   *1550–1800*: Beloch (1937–61), III, 279.
256 GENOA   *1500*: Beloch (1937–61), III, 357; *1550–1750*: estimated from data in Felloni (1977), 9; *1800*: Beloch, III, 360.
257 LODI   *1550–1800*: Beloch (1937–61), III, 249.
258 MANTUA   *1500–1800*: Beloch (1937–61), II, 290, 300; III, 357, 359, 361.
259 MILANO (MILAN)   *1500–50*: Beloch (1937–61), III, 357; *1600*: Sella (1979), 3; *1650–1800*: Beloch, III, 359–60.
260 MODENA   *1500*: Cipolla (1975), 281; *1550–1800*: Beloch (1937–61), II, 267.
261 MONDOVI   *1600–1800*: Beloch (1937–61), III, 279.
262 MONZA   *1600–1800*: Beloch (1937–61), III, 249.
263 NICE (NIZZA)   *1600–1750*: Beloch (1937–61), III, 279; *1800*: Le Mée (1971).
264 NOVARA   *1550–1800*: Beloch (1937–61), III, 249.
265 PADOVA (PADUA)   *1500*: Beloch (1937–61), III, 357; *1550*: Beltrami (1954), 69–70; *1600–1800*: Beloch, III, 357, 359, 361.
266 PARMA   *1500–1800*: Beloch (1937–61), II, 240, 243.
267 PAVIA   *1500*: Beloch (1937–61), III, 358; *1550*: Zanetti (1963), 46; *1600*: Beloch, III, 358; *1650*: Aleati (1957); Felloni (1960), 774–8; *1700*: Cipolla (1975), 281; *1750–1800*: Beloch, III, 361.
268 PIACENZA   *1550–1800*: Beloch (1937–61), II, 252.
269 REGGIO   *1550–1800*: Beloch (1937–61), II, 270–1.
270 SAVIGLIANO   *1600–1800*: Beloch (1937–61), III, 279.
271 TREVISO   *1550*: Beltrami (1954), 69–70; Beloch (1937–61), III, 52; *1600–1800*: Beloch, III, 52.
272 TRIESTE   *1800*: Franke (1922), 112.
273 TORINO (TURIN)   *1500*: Cipolla (1975), 282; *1550–1650*: Beloch (1937–61), III, 358–9; *1700*: Ghisleni and Maffioli (1971), 27; *1750–1800*: Beloch, III, 361.
274 UDINE   *1550–1800*: Beloch (1937–61), III, 49–50.
275 VENEZIA (VENICE)   *1500*: Beloch (1937–61), III, 357; *1550*: Beltrami (1954), 59; *1600–50*: Beloch, III, 359; Rapp (1976), 32–42; *1700*: Beltrami, 59; *1750–1800*: Beloch, III, 360.
276 VERCELLI   *1550–1800*: Beloch (1937–61), III, 279.
277 VERONA   *1500*: Beloch (1937–61), III, 357; *1550*: Beltrami (1954), 69–70; *1600–1800*: Beloch, III, 357, 359, 361.

SOURCES

278 VICENZA   *1550*: Beltrami (1954), 69–70; *1600–1800*: Beloch (1937–61), III, 357, 359, 361.
279 VIGEVANO   *1550–1800*: Beloch (1937–61), III, 249.

CENTRAL ITALY

280 ANCONA   *1650–1800*: Beloch (1937–61), II, 77.
281 BOLOGNA   *1500*: Beloch (1937–61), II, 98; *1550–1750*: Bellettini (1961), 88–96; Beloch, III, 359; *1800*: Beloch, III, 360.
282 FERRARA   *1550–1800*: Beloch (1937–61), II, 108–12; III, 357, 359–61.
283 FIRENZE (FLORENCE)   *1500–1650*: Beloch (1937–61), III, 357, 359; *1700*: Felloni (1977), 6, 9; *1750–1800*: Beloch, II, 147.
284 LIVORNO (LEGHORN)   *1600–1800*: Beloch (1937–61), II, 178; III, 361.
285 LUCCA   *1550–1800*: Beloch (1937–61), II, 166, 228, 358.
286 PERUGIA   *1500–1800*: Beloch (1937–61), II, 74; III, 358, 360.
287 PISA   *1550*: Herlihy (1958); Beloch (1937–61), II, 162; *1600–1800*: Beloch, II, 162.
288 ROMA (ROME)   *1500–1800*: Beloch (1937–61), II, 21; III, 357, 361.
289 SIENA   *1500–1800*: Beloch (1937–61), II, 156–7; III, 358, 360.
290 VITERBO   *1500–1800*: Beloch (1937–61), II, 57.

SOUTHERN ITALY

291 ACIREALE   *1600–1800*: Beloch (1937–61), I, 160–2.
292 ALTAMURA   *1550–1800*: Beloch (1937–61), I, 256–7.
293 BARI   *1550–1750*: Beloch (1937–61), I, 256; *1600*: Petraccone (1971), 68–86; *1800*: Beloch, I, 257.
294 CAGLIARI   *1650*: Felloni (1977), 5; *1700–50*: Beloch (1937–61), I, 17, 22; *1800*: Felloni, 7.
295 CALTAGIRONE   *1550–1800*: Beloch (1937–61), I, 161–2.
296 CALTANISSETA   *1550–1800*: Beloch (1937–61), I, 160–1.
297 CASTELVETRANO   *1550–1800*: Beloch (1937–61), I, 160–1.
298 CASTROGIOVANNI   *1550–1800*: Beloch (1937–61), I, 161–2.
299 CATANIA   *1500–1800*: Beloch (1937–61), I, 145, 162.
300 FOGGIA   *1600–1800*: Beloch (1937–61), I, 259.
301 GIRGENTI   *1550–1800*: Beloch (1937–61), I, 110, 115, 159.
302 LECCE   *1550–1800*: Beloch (1937–61), I, 258; III, 357, 359.
303 MARSALA   *1600–1800*: Beloch (1937–61), I, 161.
304 MASCALI   *1600–1800*: Beloch (1937–61), I, 162.
305 MAZZARINO   *1600–1800*: Beloch (1937–61), I, 162.
306 MESSINA   *1500*: Beloch (1937–61), III, 357; *1550*: Felloni (1977), 5; *1600–1800*: Beloch, I, 140; III, 357.
307 MODICA/POZZALLO   *1550–1800*: Beloch (1937–61), I, 161–2.
308 MONOPOLI   *1650–1800*: Beloch (1937–61), I, 256, 272.
309 NAPOLI (NAPLES)   *1500*: Pardi (1924), 66; *1550*: Beloch (1937–61), III, 357;

APPENDIX 2

1600: Coniglio (1955), 23-4; *1650*: De Seta (1973); Beloch, III, 359; *1700*: Petraccone (1974), 31, 149; *1750-1800*: Beloch, III, 359-60.
310 NICOSIA   *1550-1800*: Beloch (1937-61), I, 162; III, 358.
311 NOTO   *1600-1800*: Beloch (1937-61), I, 161-2.
312 PALERMO   *1500-1800*: Beloch (1937-61), III, 357, 359, 360.
313 PIAZZA (ENNA)   *1550-1800*: Beloch (1937-61), I, 162.
314 RAGUSA   *1600-1800*: Beloch (1937-61), I, 162.
315 REGGIO DI CALABRIA   *1550-1800*: Felloni (1977), 5-7.
316 SASSARI   *1700-1800*: Beloch (1937-61), I, 17, 21.
317 SIRACUSA   *1550-1800*: Beloch (1937-61), I, 161.
318 TARANTO   *1500-1600, 1800*: Beloch (1937-61), III, 258.
319 TERMINI   *1600-1800*: Beloch (1937-61), I, 161.
320 TRAPANI   *1550-1800*: Beloch (1937-61), I, 160-1.

SPAIN

321 ALCALA LA REAL   *1600*: Gonzalez (1829); *1800*: Miñano (1826), 87.
322 ALCAZAR DE SAN JUAN   *1550*: Vicens Vives (1969), 485; *1600*: idem.; Gonzalez (1829); *1750*: Artola (1971), 85; *1800*: Larruga y Boneta (1797).
323 ALICANTE   *1550-1650*: Dominguez Ortiz (1963), I, 153, *1800*: Nadal (1966), 107-8; Ringrose (1969), 65-122.
324 ANDUJAR   *1600*: Gonzalez (1829); *1800*: Miñano (1826), 204.
325 ANTEQUERA   *1550-1650*: Vincent (1977), 480-1; Gonzalez (1829); *1800*: Nadal (1966), 107-8.
326 ARACENA   *1550-1700*: Vincent (1977), 480-1; Gonzalez (1829); *1800*: Larruga y Boneta (1797).
327 AVILA   *1550-1700*: Bennassar (1967), 96, Vincent (1977), 480-1; Kamen (1971), 21; *1800*: Miñano (1826).
328 BADAJOZ   *1600*: Gonzalez (1829); *1750*: Artola (1971), 100; *1800*: Miñano (1826).
329 BAEZA   *1550-1700*: Vincent (1977), 480-1; *1800*: Miñano (1826), 358.
330 BARCELONA   *1500-1750*: Biraben (1975), I, 201, 203; *1800*: Ringrose (1970), 6; Landry (1945), 105.
331 BILBAO   *1700-1800*: Manleon (1961), 60, 79.
332 BURGOS   *1550-1700*: Vincent (1977), 480-1; Bennassar (1967), 96; Vicens Vives (1969), 485; *1800*: Ringrose (1970), 6.
333 CADIZ   *1500-1700*: Everaert (1973), 19-21; *1750*: Estrada (1748), II, 24; *1800*: Ringrose (1970), 6; Vicens Vives (1969), 485.
334 CARTAGENA   *1500-1600*: Gonzalez (1829); *1700*: Dominguez Ortiz (1963), I, 148; *1800*: Nadal (1966), 107-8.
335 CORDOBA   *1500-1600*: Fortea Pérez (1981); *1650-1700*: Vincent (1977), 480-1; *1800*: Nadal (1966), 107-8.
336 CUENCA   *1550*: Vincent (1977), 480-1; *1600*: Kamen (1980), 154; *1650-1700*: Vincent, 480-1; *1750*: Ringrose (1973), 74; *1800*: Miñano (1826), III, 249.
337 ECIJA   *1550*: Vincent (1977), 480-1; *1600-50*: Kamen (1980), 154; *1700*:

SOURCES

Vincent, 480-1; *1800*: revision of Nadal (1966), 107-8, in light of Junta central Estado (1857).

338 GRANADA *1500-1600*: estimates based on Vincent (1977), 480-1; Clark (1976), 74; *1700-50*: assignment of category based on Ringrose (1973), 72-3; *1800*: Nadal (1966), 107-8.

339 JAEN *1550-1650*: Vincent (1977), 480-1; *1700-50*: Dominguez Ortiz (1963), I, 147; *1800*: Miñano (1826), V, 85.

340 JEREZ DE LA FRONTERA *1550-1700*: Vincent (1977), 480-1; *1800*: Nadal (1966), 107-8.

341 LUCENA *1600*: Gonzalez (1829); *1800*: Miñano (1826), V, 269.

342 MADRID *1550-1800*: Ringrose (1983), appendix A, 28.

343 MALAGA *1550-1600*: Vincent (1977), 480-1; *1700*: Kamen (1980), 154; *1750*: Vicens Vives (1969), 485; *1800*: Nadal (1966), 107-8; Ringrose (1970), 6.

344 MEDINA DEL CAMPO *1550*: Bennassar (1967), 96; *1600-1700*: Vincent (1977), 480-1; *1800*: Miñano (1826), II, 384.

345 MEDINA DE RIO SECO *1550*: Vicens Vives (1969), 485; *1600-1700*: Vincent (1977), 480-1; Kamen (1971), 74.

346 MORON DE LA FRONTERA *1600*: Gonzalez (1829); *1800*: Nadal (1966), 107-8.

347 MURCIA *1550-1700*: Vincent (1977), 480-1; *1800*: Ringrose (1970), 6.

348 OCAÑA *1600*: Gonzalez (1829); *1750*: Artola (1971), 85; *1800*: Miñano (1826), VI, 281.

349 ORIHUELA *1500*: Vincent (1977), 480-1; *1600*: Gonzalez (1829); *1800*: Miñano (1826), VI, 344.

350 OSUNA *1600*: Gonzalez (1829); *1800*: Miñano (1826), VI, 365.

351 PALENCIA *1550*: Bennassar (1967), 96; *1600*: Gonzalez (1829); *1750*: category assignment based on Ringrose (1973), 72-3; *1800*: Miñano (1826), VI, 406.

352 PALMA *1600*: Dominguez Ortiz (1963), I, 156; *1800*: Minano (1826), VI, 409.

353 RONDA *1550-1600*: Vincent (1977), 480-1; *1800*: Minano (1826), VII, 361.

354 SALAMANCA *1550-1700*: Vincent (1977), 480-1; Bennassar (1967), 96; Vicens Vives (1969), 485; *1800*: Miñano (1826), VII, 402.

355 SANTIAGO DE COMPOSTELA *1500-1650*: Ruiz Almansa (1948), 243; *1800*: Miñano (1826), VIII, 131.

356 SEGOVIA *1550-1700*: Vincent (1977), 480-1; Bennassar (1967), 96; Vicens Vives (1969), 485; *1800*: Miñano (1826), VIII, 188.

357 SEVILLA (SEVILLE) *1500*: Batista I. Roca (1971), I, 318; *1550*: Pike (1972), 11; *1600*: Godinho (1969), 318; Gonzalez (1829); *1650*: Kamen (1971), 21; *1700-1750*: Godinho, 355; *1800*: Ringrose (1970), 6; Iglesias (1968).

358 TOLEDO *1550-1650*: Mauro and Parker (1977), 38; *1700*: Vincent (1977), 480-1; *1800*: Ringrose (1970), 6; Ringrose (1973), 765.

359 UBEDA *1550-1700*: Vincent (1977), 480-1; *1800*: Miñano (1826), IX, 102.

360 UTRERA *1550-1700*: Vincent (1977), 480-1; *1800*: Miñano (1826), IX, 134.

361 VALENCIA *1500*: Vincent (1977), 480-1; *1550*: Mauro and Parker (1977), 39; *1600*: Kamen (1980), 154; *1650*: Mauro and Parker, 39; *1700*: Kamen (1980), 51; *1800*: Ringrose (1970), 6.

362 VALLADOLID *1550-1700*: Bennassar (1967), 96; *1800*: Ringrose (1970), 6.

APPENDIX 2

363 ZARAGOZA *1550*: Dominguez Ortiz (1963), I, 155; *1600–1700*: Kamen (1980), 154; *1800*: Ringrose (1970), 6.

PORTUGAL

364 COIMBRA *1500–50*: Da Silva (1969), 268; *1650*: Godinho (1969), V, 384; *1750*: Godinho (1970), VI, 527; *1800*: based on Weber (1899), 120.
365 ELVAS *1500–50*: assignments based on Saunders (1982), 57; *1650*: Godinho (1969), V, 384; *1800*: category assignment based on Weber (1899), 120.
366 EVORA *1500–50*: assignments based on Saunders (1982), 57; *1650*: Godinho (1969), V, 384; *1750*: Godinho, VI, 527; *1800*: category assignment based on Weber (1899), 120.
367 LISBOA (LISBON) *1500*: Clark (1976), 14; *1550*: Saunders (1982), 95; *1600*: Armengaud *et al.* (1968), 117; *1650*: estimate based on Godinho (1969), V, 384; *1700–50*: Godinho (1970), VI, 542; *1800*: Mols (1954–6), II, 519.
368 PORTO *1550*: Saunders (1982), 95; *1600–50*: Godinho (1969), V, 384; *1700–50*: Godinho (1970), VI, 527; *1800*: Mols (1954–6), II, 519.

AUSTRIA-CZECHOSLOVAKIA

369 BRNO (BRÜNN) *1650*: Chandler (1974), 153; *1750*: idem.; *1800*: Franke (1922), 112.
370 GRAZ *1600–1750*: Klein (1973), 106; *1800*: Franke (1922), 112.
371 INNSBRUCK *1500–1800*: Mathis (1977), 20; *1800*: Franke (1922), 112.
372 KLAGENFURT *1600–1750*: Klein (1973), 106; *1800*: Franke (1922), 112.
373 LINZ *1600–1750*: Klein (1973), 106; *1750*: category assignment based on Franke (1922), 112; *1800*: idem.
374 PRAHA (PRAGUE) *1700*: Karnikova (1965), 59; *1750*: Peller (1920), 232–5; Bonnoure and Dupâquier (1966), 408–9; *1800*: idem.; Franke (1922), 112.
375 SALZBURG *1600–1700*: Mathis (1977), 175–7; *1750*: Klein (1973), 106; *1800*: Franke (1922), 114.
376 WIEN (VIENNA) *1500*: Cipolla (1975), 281; *1600*: Klein (1973), 106; *1650–1700*: Klein (1973), 90; *1650*: Keyser (1941), 375; *1700–50*: Weiss (1882–3), II, 95, 227; *1750*: Klein (1973), 106; *1800*: Franke (1922), 112.

POLAND

377 KRAKOW *1800*: Dabrowski (1957), 399.
378 POZNAN (POSEN) *1800*: Franke (1922), 114; Eisenbach and Grochulska (1965), 121.
379 WARSZAWA (WARSAW) *1550–1800*: Eisenbach and Grochulska (1965). 116–17.

Appendix 3
DISTRIBUTION OF CITIES BY SIZE CATEGORY, AGGREGATE URBAN POPULATION AND TRANSITION MATRICES, BY TERRITORY

For the identification of the size category codes, see appendix I.

APPENDIX 3
COUNTRY CODE 1   SCANDINAVIA

1550

	0	1	2	3	4	5	6	T
1500 0	5	0	0	0	0	0	0	5
1	0	1	0	0	0	0	0	1
2	0	0	0	0	0	0	0	0
3	0	0	0	0	0	0	0	0
4	0	0	0	0	0	0	0	0
5	0	0	0	0	0	0	0	0
6	0	0	0	0	0	0	0	0
T	5	1	0	0	0	0	0	6

1700

	0	1	2	3	4	5	6	T
1650 0	4	0	0	0	0	0	0	4
1	0	0	0	0	0	0	0	0
2	0	0	0	1	0	0	0	1
3	0	0	0	1	0	0	0	1
4	0	0	0	0	0	0	0	0
5	0	0	0	0	0	0	0	0
6	0	0	0	0	0	0	0	0
T	4	0	0	2	0	0	0	6

1600

	0	1	2	3	4	5	6	T
1550 0	4	1	0	0	0	0	0	5
1	0	1	0	0	0	0	0	1
2	0	0	0	0	0	0	0	0
3	0	0	0	0	0	0	0	0
4	0	0	0	0	0	0	0	0
5	0	0	0	0	0	0	0	0
6	0	0	0	0	0	0	0	0
T	4	2	0	0	0	0	0	6

1750

	0	1	2	3	4	5	6	T
1700 0	3	1	0	0	0	0	0	4
1	0	0	0	0	0	0	0	0
2	0	0	0	0	0	0	0	0
3	0	0	0	1	1	0	0	2
4	0	0	0	0	0	0	0	0
5	0	0	0	0	0	0	0	0
6	0	0	0	0	0	0	0	0
T	3	1	0	1	1	0	0	6

1650

	0	1	2	3	4	5	6	T
1600 0	4	0	0	0	0	0	0	4
1	0	0	1	1	0	0	0	2
2	0	0	0	0	0	0	0	0
3	0	0	0	0	0	0	0	0
4	0	0	0	0	0	0	0	0
5	0	0	0	0	0	0	0	0
6	0	0	0	0	0	0	0	0
T	4	0	1	1	0	0	0	6

1800

	0	1	2	3	4	5	6	T
1750 0	0	3	0	0	0	0	0	3
1	0	1	0	0	0	0	0	1
2	0	0	0	0	0	0	0	0
3	0	0	0	1	0	0	0	1
4	0	0	0	0	1	0	0	1
5	0	0	0	0	0	0	0	0
6	0	0	0	0	0	0	0	0
T	0	4	0	1	1	0	0	6

DISTRIBUTION OF CITIES BY TERRITORY

	Number of cities by size category						
	1500	1550	1600	1650	1700	1750	1800
1	1	1	2	0	0	1	4
2	0	0	0	1	0	0	0
3	0	0	0	1	2	1	1
4	0	0	0	0	0	1	1
5	0	0	0	0	0	0	0
6	0	0	0	0	0	0	0
Total	1	1	2	2	2	3	6
0	5	5	4	4	4	3	0

	Total urban population ('000s)						
	1500	1550	1600	1650	1700	1750	1800
1	13	13	26	0	0	14	52
2	0	0	0	23	0	0	0
3	0	0	0	40	115	60	75
4	0	0	0	0	0	93	101
5	0	0	0	0	0	0	0
6	0	0	0	0	0	0	0
Total	13	13	26	63	115	167	228

APPENDIX 3

COUNTRY CODE 2   ENGLAND AND WALES

1550

	0	1	2	3	4	5	6	T
0	39	0	0	0	0	0	0	39
1	1	3	0	0	0	0	0	4
2	0	0	0	0	0	0	0	0
3	0	0	0	0	1	0	0	1
4	0	0	0	0	0	0	0	0
5	0	0	0	0	0	0	0	0
6	0	0	0	0	0	0	0	0
T	40	3	0	0	1	0	0	44

(rows indexed by 1500)

1700

	0	1	2	3	4	5	6	T
0	33	3	0	0	0	0	0	36
1	0	5	0	0	0	0	0	5
2	0	0	2	0	0	0	0	2
3	0	0	0	0	0	0	0	0
4	0	0	0	0	0	0	0	0
5	0	0	0	0	0	0	0	0
6	0	0	0	0	0	0	1	1
T	33	8	2	0	0	0	1	44

(rows indexed by 1650)

1600

	0	1	2	3	4	5	6	T
0	38	2	0	0	0	0	0	40
1	0	3	0	0	0	0	0	3
2	0	0	0	0	0	0	0	0
3	0	0	0	0	0	0	0	0
4	0	0	0	0	0	1	0	1
5	0	0	0	0	0	0	0	0
6	0	0	0	0	0	0	0	0
T	38	5	0	0	0	1	0	44

(rows indexed by 1550)

1750

	0	1	2	3	4	5	6	T
0	22	9	2	0	0	0	0	33
1	1	6	1	0	0	0	0	8
2	0	0	1	1	0	0	0	2
3	0	0	0	0	0	0	0	0
4	0	0	0	0	0	0	0	0
5	0	0	0	0	0	0	0	0
6	0	0	0	0	0	0	1	1
T	23	15	4	1	0	0	1	44

(rows indexed by 1700)

1650

	0	1	2	3	4	5	6	T
0	36	2	0	0	0	0	0	38
1	0	3	2	0	0	0	0	5
2	0	0	0	0	0	0	0	0
3	0	0	0	0	0	0	0	0
4	0	0	0	0	0	0	0	0
5	0	0	0	0	0	1	0	1
6	0	0	0	0	0	0	0	0
T	36	5	2	0	0	0	1	44

(rows indexed by 1600)

1800

	0	1	2	3	4	5	6	T
0	0	21	2	0	0	0	0	23
1	0	8	3	4	0	0	0	15
2	0	0	2	2	0	0	0	4
3	0	0	0	1	0	0	0	1
4	0	0	0	0	0	0	0	0
5	0	0	0	0	0	0	0	0
6	0	0	0	0	0	0	1	1
T	0	29	7	7	0	0	1	44

(rows indexed by 1750)

DISTRIBUTION OF CITIES BY TERRITORY

	Number of cities by size category						
	1500	1550	1600	1650	1700	1750	1800
1	4	3	5	5	8	15	29
2	0	0	0	2	2	4	7
3	1	0	0	0	0	1	7
4	0	1	0	0	0	0	0
5	0	0	1	0	0	0	0
6	0	0	0	1	1	1	1
Total	5	4	6	8	11	21	44
0	39	40	38	36	33	23	0

	Total urban population ('000s)						
	1500	1550	1600	1650	1700	1750	1800
1	40	32	55	55	89	190	372
2	0	0	0	40	54	111	210
3	40	0	0	0	0	45	423
4	0	80	0	0	0	0	0
5	0	0	200	0	0	0	0
6	0	0	0	400	575	675	865
Total	80	112	255	495	718	1021	1870

APPENDIX 3

COUNTRY CODE 3   SCOTLAND

1550

1500 \	0	1	2	3	4	5	6	T
0	7	0	0	0	0	0	0	7
1	0	1	0	0	0	0	0	1
2	0	0	0	0	0	0	0	0
3	0	0	0	0	0	0	0	0
4	0	0	0	0	0	0	0	0
5	0	0	0	0	0	0	0	0
6	0	0	0	0	0	0	0	0
T	7	1	0	0	0	0	0	8

1700

1650 \	0	1	2	3	4	5	6	T
0	6	1	0	0	0	0	0	7
1	0	0	0	0	0	0	0	0
2	0	0	0	1	0	0	0	1
3	0	0	0	0	0	0	0	0
4	0	0	0	0	0	0	0	0
5	0	0	0	0	0	0	0	0
6	0	0	0	0	0	0	0	0
T	6	1	0	1	0	0	0	8

1600

1550 \	0	1	2	3	4	5	6	T
0	7	0	0	0	0	0	0	7
1	0	0	1	0	0	0	0	1
2	0	0	0	0	0	0	0	0
3	0	0	0	0	0	0	0	0
4	0	0	0	0	0	0	0	0
5	0	0	0	0	0	0	0	0
6	0	0	0	0	0	0	0	0
T	7	0	1	0	0	0	0	8

1750

1700 \	0	1	2	3	4	5	6	T
0	3	3	0	0	0	0	0	6
1	0	0	1	0	0	0	0	1
2	0	0	0	0	0	0	0	0
3	0	0	0	1	0	0	0	1
4	0	0	0	0	0	0	0	0
5	0	0	0	0	0	0	0	0
6	0	0	0	0	0	0	0	0
T	3	3	1	1	0	0	0	8

1650

1600 \	0	1	2	3	4	5	6	T
0	7	0	0	0	0	0	0	7
1	0	0	0	0	0	0	0	0
2	0	0	1	0	0	0	0	1
3	0	0	0	0	0	0	0	0
4	0	0	0	0	0	0	0	0
5	0	0	0	0	0	0	0	0
6	0	0	0	0	0	0	0	0
T	7	0	1	0	0	0	0	8

1800

1750 \	0	1	2	3	4	5	6	T
0	0	3	0	0	0	0	0	3
1	0	1	2	0	0	0	0	3
2	0	0	0	1	0	0	0	1
3	0	0	0	0	1	0	0	1
4	0	0	0	0	0	0	0	0
5	0	0	0	0	0	0	0	0
6	0	0	0	0	0	0	0	0
T	0	4	2	1	1	0	0	8

DISTRIBUTION OF CITIES BY TERRITORY

Number of cities by size category

	1500	1550	1600	1650	1700	1750	1800
1	1	1	0	0	1	3	4
2	0	0	1	1	0	1	2
3	0	0	0	0	1	1	1
4	0	0	0	0	0	0	1
5	0	0	0	0	0	0	0
6	0	0	0	0	0	0	0
Total	1	1	1	1	2	5	8
0	7	7	7	7	6	3	0

Total urban population ('000s)

	1500	1550	1600	1650	1700	1750	1800
1	13	13	0	0	13	38	64
2	0	0	30	35	0	24	53
3	0	0	0	0	40	57	77
4	0	0	0	0	0	0	82
5	0	0	0	0	0	0	0
6	0	0	0	0	0	0	0
Total	13	13	30	35	53	119	276

APPENDIX 3

COUNTRY CODE 4   IRELAND

1550

	0	1	2	3	4	5	6	T
0	8	0	0	0	0	0	0	8
1	0	0	0	0	0	0	0	0
2	0	0	0	0	0	0	0	0
3	0	0	0	0	0	0	0	0
4	0	0	0	0	0	0	0	0
5	0	0	0	0	0	0	0	0
6	0	0	0	0	0	0	0	0
T	8	0	0	0	0	0	0	8

(rows indexed by 1500)

1700

	0	1	2	3	4	5	6	T
0	5	1	1	0	0	0	0	7
1	0	0	0	1	0	0	0	1
2	0	0	0	0	0	0	0	0
3	0	0	0	0	0	0	0	0
4	0	0	0	0	0	0	0	0
5	0	0	0	0	0	0	0	0
6	0	0	0	0	0	0	0	0
T	5	1	1	1	0	0	0	8

(rows indexed by 1650)

1600

	0	1	2	3	4	5	6	T
0	8	0	0	0	0	0	0	8
1	0	0	0	0	0	0	0	0
2	0	0	0	0	0	0	0	0
3	0	0	0	0	0	0	0	0
4	0	0	0	0	0	0	0	0
5	0	0	0	0	0	0	0	0
6	0	0	0	0	0	0	0	0
T	8	0	0	0	0	0	0	8

(rows indexed by 1550)

1750

	0	1	2	3	4	5	6	T
0	5	0	0	0	0	0	0	5
1	0	1	0	0	0	0	0	1
2	0	0	0	1	0	0	0	1
3	0	0	0	0	1	0	0	1
4	0	0	0	0	0	0	0	0
5	0	0	0	0	0	0	0	0
6	0	0	0	0	0	0	0	0
T	5	1	0	1	1	0	0	8

(rows indexed by 1700)

1650

	0	1	2	3	4	5	6	T
0	7	1	0	0	0	0	0	8
1	0	0	0	0	0	0	0	0
2	0	0	0	0	0	0	0	0
3	0	0	0	0	0	0	0	0
4	0	0	0	0	0	0	0	0
5	0	0	0	0	0	0	0	0
6	0	0	0	0	0	0	0	0
T	7	1	0	0	0	0	0	8

(rows indexed by 1600)

1800

	0	1	2	3	4	5	6	T
0	0	3	2	0	0	0	0	5
1	0	0	1	0	0	0	0	1
2	0	0	0	0	0	0	0	0
3	0	0	0	1	0	0	0	1
4	0	0	0	0	0	1	0	1
5	0	0	0	0	0	0	0	0
6	0	0	0	0	0	0	0	0
T	0	3	3	1	0	1	0	8

(rows indexed by 1750)

DISTRIBUTION OF CITIES BY TERRITORY

Number of cities by size category

	1500	1550	1600	1650	1700	1750	1800
1	0	0	0	1	1	1	3
2	0	0	0	0	1	0	3
3	0	0	0	0	1	1	1
4	0	0	0	0	0	1	0
5	0	0	0	0	0	0	1
6	0	0	0	0	0	0	0
Total	0	0	0	1	3	3	8
0	8	8	8	7	5	5	0

Total urban population ('000s)

	1500	1550	1600	1650	1700	1750	1800
1	0	0	0	17	11	13	43
2	0	0	0	0	25	0	83
3	0	0	0	0	60	58	75
4	0	0	0	0	0	90	0
5	0	0	0	0	0	0	168
6	0	0	0	0	0	0	0
Total	0	0	0	17	96	161	369

APPENDIX 3

COUNTRY CODE 5   THE NETHERLANDS

1550

	0	1	2	3	4	5	6	T
0	9	1	0	0	0	0	0	10
1	0	8	2	0	0	0	0	10
2	0	0	1	0	0	0	0	1
3	0	0	0	0	0	0	0	0
4	0	0	0	0	0	0	0	0
5	0	0	0	0	0	0	0	0
6	0	0	0	0	0	0	0	0
T	9	9	3	0	0	0	0	21

(rows indexed by 1500)

1700

	0	1	2	3	4	5	6	T
0	1	1	0	0	0	0	0	2
1	0	6	2	0	0	0	0	8
2	0	2	6	1	0	0	0	9
3	0	0	0	1	0	0	0	1
4	0	0	0	0	0	0	0	0
5	0	0	0	0	0	1	0	1
6	0	0	0	0	0	0	0	0
T	1	9	8	2	0	1	0	21

(rows indexed by 1650)

1600

	0	1	2	3	4	5	6	T
0	2	6	1	0	0	0	0	9
1	0	6	3	0	0	0	0	9
2	0	1	1	1	0	0	0	3
3	0	0	0	0	0	0	0	0
4	0	0	0	0	0	0	0	0
5	0	0	0	0	0	0	0	0
6	0	0	0	0	0	0	0	0
T	2	13	5	1	0	0	0	21

(rows indexed by 1550)

1750

	0	1	2	3	4	5	6	T
0	1	0	0	0	0	0	0	1
1	2	7	0	0	0	0	0	9
2	0	2	6	0	0	0	0	8
3	0	0	1	1	0	0	0	2
4	0	0	0	0	0	0	0	0
5	0	0	0	0	0	1	0	1
6	0	0	0	0	0	0	0	0
T	3	9	7	1	0	1	0	21

(rows indexed by 1700)

1650

	0	1	2	3	4	5	6	T
0	2	0	0	0	0	0	0	2
1	0	8	5	0	0	0	0	13
2	0	0	4	1	0	0	0	5
3	0	0	0	0	0	1	0	1
4	0	0	0	0	0	0	0	0
5	0	0	0	0	0	0	0	0
6	0	0	0	0	0	0	0	0
T	2	8	9	1	0	1	0	21

(rows indexed by 1600)

1800

	0	1	2	3	4	5	6	T
0	2	1	0	0	0	0	0	3
1	0	9	0	0	0	0	0	9
2	0	0	7	0	0	0	0	7
3	0	0	0	1	0	0	0	1
4	0	0	0	0	0	0	0	0
5	0	0	0	0	0	1	0	1
6	0	0	0	0	0	0	0	0
T	2	10	7	1	0	1	0	21

(rows indexed by 1750)

DISTRIBUTION OF CITIES BY TERRITORY

Number of cities by size category

	1500	1550	1600	1650	1700	1750	1800
1	10	9	13	8	9	9	10
2	1	3	5	9	8	7	7
3	0	0	1	1	2	1	1
4	0	0	0	0	0	0	0
5	0	0	0	1	1	1	1
6	0	0	0	0	0	0	0
Total	11	12	19	19	20	18	19
0	10	9	2	2	1	3	2

Total urban population ('000s)

	1500	1550	1600	1650	1700	1750	1800
1	130	113	179	123	121	125	139
2	20	78	120	238	215	201	191
3	0	0	65	67	103	44	57
4	0	0	0	0	0	0	0
5	0	0	0	175	200	210	217
6	0	0	0	0	0	0	0
Total	150	191	364	603	639	580	604

APPENDIX 3

COUNTRY CODE 6 BELGIUM

1500 → 1550

	0	1	2	3	4	5	6	T
0	8	0	0	0	0	0	0	8
1	0	4	0	0	0	0	0	4
2	0	0	5	1	0	0	0	6
3	0	0	0	1	1	0	0	2
4	0	0	0	0	0	0	0	0
5	0	0	0	0	0	0	0	0
6	0	0	0	0	0	0	0	0
T	8	4	5	2	1	0	0	20

1650 → 1700

	0	1	2	3	4	5	6	T
0	5	1	0	0	0	0	0	6
1	0	6	0	0	0	0	0	6
2	0	0	3	1	0	0	0	4
3	0	0	0	3	1	0	0	4
4	0	0	0	0	0	0	0	0
5	0	0	0	0	0	0	0	0
6	0	0	0	0	0	0	0	0
T	5	7	3	4	1	0	0	20

1550 → 1600

	0	1	2	3	4	5	6	T
0	7	1	0	0	0	0	0	8
1	1	3	0	0	0	0	0	4
2	0	1	4	0	0	0	0	5
3	0	0	1	1	0	0	0	2
4	0	0	0	1	0	0	0	1
5	0	0	0	0	0	0	0	0
6	0	0	0	0	0	0	0	0
T	8	5	5	2	0	0	0	20

1700 → 1750

	0	1	2	3	4	5	6	T
0	5	0	0	0	0	0	0	5
1	0	7	0	0	0	0	0	7
2	0	1	2	0	0	0	0	3
3	0	0	0	4	0	0	0	4
4	0	0	0	1	0	0	0	1
5	0	0	0	0	0	0	0	0
6	0	0	0	0	0	0	0	0
T	5	8	2	5	0	0	0	20

1600 → 1650

	0	1	2	3	4	5	6	T
0	6	2	0	0	0	0	0	8
1	0	4	1	0	0	0	0	5
2	0	0	3	2	0	0	0	5
3	0	0	0	2	0	0	0	2
4	0	0	0	0	0	0	0	0
5	0	0	0	0	0	0	0	0
6	0	0	0	0	0	0	0	0
T	6	6	4	4	0	0	0	20

1750 → 1800

	0	1	2	3	4	5	6	T
0	0	5	0	0	0	0	0	5
1	0	5	3	0	0	0	0	8
2	0	0	2	0	0	0	0	2
3	0	0	0	5	0	0	0	5
4	0	0	0	0	0	0	0	0
5	0	0	0	0	0	0	0	0
6	0	0	0	0	0	0	0	0
T	0	10	5	5	0	0	0	20

DISTRIBUTION OF CITIES BY TERRITORY

Number of cities by size category

	1500	1550	1600	1650	1700	1750	1800
1	4	4	5	6	7	8	10
2	6	5	5	4	3	2	5
3	2	2	2	4	4	5	5
4	0	1	0	0	1	0	0
5	0	0	0	0	0	0	0
6	0	0	0	0	0	0	0
Total	12	12	12	14	15	15	20
0	8	8	8	6	5	5	0

Total urban population ('000s)

	1500	1550	1600	1650	1700	1750	1800
1	55	55	66	81	96	117	132
2	160	140	138	109	89	49	117
3	80	90	97	225	221	266	299
4	0	90	0	0	80	0	0
5	0	0	0	0	0	0	0
6	0	0	0	0	0	0	0
Total	295	375	301	415	486	432	548

APPENDIX 3

COUNTRY CODE 7 GERMANY

1550

1500 →

	0	1	2	3	4	5	6	T
0	27	6	0	0	0	0	0	33
1	2	13	1	1	0	0	0	17
2	0	0	4	2	0	0	0	6
3	0	0	0	0	0	0	0	0
4	0	0	0	0	0	0	0	0
5	0	0	0	0	0	0	0	0
6	0	0	0	0	0	0	0	0
T	29	19	5	3	0	0	0	56

1700

1650 →

	0	1	2	3	4	5	6	T
0	26	7	0	0	0	0	0	33
1	0	8	4	2	0	0	0	14
2	0	0	5	1	0	0	0	6
3	0	0	0	3	0	0	0	3
4	0	0	0	0	0	0	0	0
5	0	0	0	0	0	0	0	0
6	0	0	0	0	0	0	0	0
T	26	15	9	6	0	0	0	56

1600

1550 →

	0	1	2	3	4	5	6	T
0	25	4	0	0	0	0	0	29
1	1	12	6	0	0	0	0	19
2	0	0	2	3	0	0	0	5
3	0	0	0	3	0	0	0	3
4	0	0	0	0	0	0	0	0
5	0	0	0	0	0	0	0	0
6	0	0	0	0	0	0	0	0
T	26	16	8	6	0	0	0	56

1750

1700 →

	0	1	2	3	4	5	6	T
0	20	6	0	0	0	0	0	26
1	1	12	2	0	0	0	0	15
2	0	0	7	2	0	0	0	9
3	0	0	1	4	1	0	0	6
4	0	0	0	0	0	0	0	0
5	0	0	0	0	0	0	0	0
6	0	0	0	0	0	0	0	0
T	21	18	10	6	1	0	0	56

1650

1600 →

	0	1	2	3	4	5	6	T
0	26	0	0	0	0	0	0	26
1	6	10	0	0	0	0	0	16
2	0	4	4	0	0	0	0	8
3	1	0	2	3	0	0	0	6
4	0	0	0	0	0	0	0	0
5	0	0	0	0	0	0	0	0
6	0	0	0	0	0	0	0	0
T	33	14	6	3	0	0	0	56

1800

1750 →

	0	1	2	3	4	5	6	T
0	2	19	0	0	0	0	0	21
1	1	9	8	0	0	0	0	18
2	0	0	10	0	0	0	0	10
3	0	0	0	5	1	0	0	6
4	0	0	0	0	1	0	0	1
5	0	0	0	0	0	0	0	0
6	0	0	0	0	0	0	0	0
T	3	28	18	5	2	0	0	56

DISTRIBUTION OF CITIES BY TERRITORY

	Number of cities by size category						
	1500	1550	1600	1650	1700	1750	1800
1	17	19	16	14	15	18	28
2	6	5	8	6	9	10	18
3	0	3	6	3	6	6	5
4	0	0	0	0	0	1	2
5	0	0	0	0	0	0	0
6	0	0	0	0	0	0	0
Total	23	27	30	23	30	35	53
0	33	29	26	33	26	21	3

	Total urban population ('000s)						
	1500	1550	1600	1650	1700	1750	1800
1	230	259	211	181	191	260	370
2	155	150	193	157	226	276	483
3	0	125	258	190	297	331	250
4	0	0	0	0	0	90	250
5	0	0	0	0	0	0	0
6	0	0	0	0	0	0	0
Total	385	534	662	528	714	956	1353

APPENDIX 3

COUNTRY CODE 8 FRANCE

1550

	0	1	2	3	4	5	6	T
0	43	3	0	0	0	0	0	46
1	1	18	1	0	0	0	0	20
2	0	0	8	1	0	0	0	9
3	0	0	0	2	0	0	0	2
4	0	0	0	0	1	0	0	1
5	0	0	0	0	0	0	0	0
6	0	0	0	0	0	0	0	0
T	44	21	9	3	1	0	0	78

(1500)

1700

	0	1	2	3	4	5	6	T
0	23	10	1	0	0	0	0	34
1	0	19	4	0	0	0	0	23
2	0	0	14	0	0	0	0	14
3	0	0	1	3	1	0	0	5
4	0	0	0	1	0	0	0	1
5	0	0	0	0	0	0	0	0
6	0	0	0	0	0	0	1	1
T	23	29	20	4	1	0	1	78

(1650)

1600

	0	1	2	3	4	5	6	T
0	35	9	0	0	0	0	0	44
1	0	14	7	0	0	0	0	21
2	0	0	7	2	0	0	0	9
3	0	0	0	3	0	0	0	3
4	0	0	0	0	0	1	0	1
5	0	0	0	0	0	0	0	0
6	0	0	0	0	0	0	0	0
T	35	23	14	5	0	1	0	78

(1550)

1750

	0	1	2	3	4	5	6	T
0	21	1	1	0	0	0	0	23
1	2	21	6	0	0	0	0	29
2	0	2	16	2	0	0	0	20
3	0	0	0	4	0	0	0	4
4	0	0	0	0	1	0	0	1
5	0	0	0	0	0	0	0	0
6	0	0	0	0	0	0	1	1
T	23	24	23	6	1	0	1	78

(1700)

1650

	0	1	2	3	4	5	6	T
0	34	1	0	0	0	0	0	35
1	0	21	2	0	0	0	0	23
2	0	1	12	1	0	0	0	14
3	0	0	0	4	1	0	0	5
4	0	0	0	0	0	0	0	0
5	0	0	0	0	0	0	1	1
6	0	0	0	0	0	0	0	0
T	34	23	14	5	1	0	1	78

(1600)

1800

	0	1	2	3	4	5	6	T
0	0	23	0	0	0	0	0	23
1	0	21	3	0	0	0	0	24
2	0	3	18	2	0	0	0	23
3	0	0	0	4	2	0	0	6
4	0	0	0	0	1	0	0	1
5	0	0	0	0	0	0	0	0
6	0	0	0	0	0	0	1	1
T	0	47	21	6	3	0	1	78

(1750)

DISTRIBUTION OF CITIES BY TERRITORY

	Number of cities by size category						
	1500	*1550*	*1600*	*1650*	*1700*	*1750*	*1800*
1	20	21	23	23	29	24	47
2	9	9	14	14	20	23	21
3	2	3	5	5	4	6	6
4	1	1	0	1	1	1	3
5	0	0	1	0	0	0	0
6	0	0	0	1	1	1	1
Total	32	34	43	44	55	55	78
0	46	44	35	34	23	23	0

	Total urban population ('000s)						
	1500	*1550*	*1600*	*1650*	*1700*	*1750*	*1800*
1	262	279	299	313	384	332	646
2	236	235	364	362	523	609	558
3	90	175	220	263	231	341	328
4	100	130	0	82	97	114	269
5	0	0	220	0	0	0	0
6	0	0	0	430	510	576	581
Total	688	819	1104	1450	1745	1972	2382

N.B. See appendix 2, no. 230, Rouen, for clarification of small discrepancies between the data presented here and in the body of the text.

APPENDIX 3

COUNTRY CODE 9   SWITZERLAND

1550

1500 \	0	1	2	3	4	5	6	T
0	3	0	0	0	0	0	0	3
1	0	1	0	0	0	0	0	1
2	0	0	0	0	0	0	0	0
3	0	0	0	0	0	0	0	0
4	0	0	0	0	0	0	0	0
5	0	0	0	0	0	0	0	0
6	0	0	0	0	0	0	0	0
T	3	1	0	0	0	0	0	4

1700

1650 \	0	1	2	3	4	5	6	T
0	1	1	0	0	0	0	0	2
1	0	2	0	0	0	0	0	2
2	0	0	0	0	0	0	0	0
3	0	0	0	0	0	0	0	0
4	0	0	0	0	0	0	0	0
5	0	0	0	0	0	0	0	0
6	0	0	0	0	0	0	0	0
T	1	3	0	0	0	0	0	4

1600

1550 \	0	1	2	3	4	5	6	T
0	2	1	0	0	0	0	0	3
1	0	1	0	0	0	0	0	1
2	0	0	0	0	0	0	0	0
3	0	0	0	0	0	0	0	0
4	0	0	0	0	0	0	0	0
5	0	0	0	0	0	0	0	0
6	0	0	0	0	0	0	0	0
T	2	2	0	0	0	0	0	4

1750

1700 \	0	1	2	3	4	5	6	T
0	0	1	0	0	0	0	0	1
1	0	2	1	0	0	0	0	3
2	0	0	0	0	0	0	0	0
3	0	0	0	0	0	0	0	0
4	0	0	0	0	0	0	0	0
5	0	0	0	0	0	0	0	0
6	0	0	0	0	0	0	0	0
T	0	3	1	0	0	0	0	4

1650

1600 \	0	1	2	3	4	5	6	T
0	2	0	0	0	0	0	0	2
1	0	2	0	0	0	0	0	2
2	0	0	0	0	0	0	0	0
3	0	0	0	0	0	0	0	0
4	0	0	0	0	0	0	0	0
5	0	0	0	0	0	0	0	0
6	0	0	0	0	0	0	0	0
T	2	2	0	0	0	0	0	4

1800

1750 \	0	1	2	3	4	5	6	T
0	0	0	0	0	0	0	0	0
1	0	3	0	0	0	0	0	3
2	0	0	1	0	0	0	0	1
3	0	0	0	0	0	0	0	0
4	0	0	0	0	0	0	0	0
5	0	0	0	0	0	0	0	0
6	0	0	0	0	0	0	0	0
T	0	3	1	0	0	0	0	4

DISTRIBUTION OF CITIES BY TERRITORY

Number of cities by size category

	1500	1550	1600	1650	1700	1750	1800
1	1	1	2	2	3	3	3
2	0	0	0	0	0	1	1
3	0	0	0	0	0	0	0
4	0	0	0	0	0	0	0
5	0	0	0	0	0	0	0
6	0	0	0	0	0	0	0
Total	1	1	2	2	3	4	4
0	3	3	2	2	1	0	0

Total urban population ('000s)

	1500	1550	1600	1650	1700	1750	1800
1	10	12	25	22	39	37	37
2	0	0	0	0	0	23	26
3	0	0	0	0	0	0	0
4	0	0	0	0	0	0	0
5	0	0	0	0	0	0	0
6	0	0	0	0	0	0	0
Total	10	12	25	22	39	60	63

APPENDIX 3

COUNTRY CODE 10   NORTHERN ITALY

1500

1500\\1500	0	1	2	3	4	5	6	T
0	12	1	0	0	0	0	0	13
1	0	10	2	0	0	0	0	12
2	0	0	3	1	0	0	0	4
3	0	0	1	2	0	0	0	3
4	0	0	0	1	1	0	0	2
5	0	0	0	0	0	0	0	0
6	0	0	0	0	0	0	0	0
T	12	11	6	4	1	0	0	34

1700

1650\\1700	0	1	2	3	4	5	6	T
0	12	3	0	0	0	0	0	15
1	0	5	6	0	0	0	0	11
2	0	0	3	2	0	0	0	5
3	0	0	0	0	0	0	0	0
4	0	0	0	0	3	0	0	3
5	0	0	0	0	0	0	0	0
6	0	0	0	0	0	0	0	0
T	12	8	9	2	3	0	0	34

1600

1550\\1600	0	1	2	3	4	5	6	T
0	4	8	0	0	0	0	0	12
1	0	8	3	0	0	0	0	11
2	0	0	6	0	0	0	0	6
3	0	0	0	3	1	0	0	4
4	0	0	0	0	1	0	0	1
5	0	0	0	0	0	0	0	0
6	0	0	0	0	0	0	0	0
T	4	16	9	3	2	0	0	34

1750

1700\\1750	0	1	2	3	4	5	6	T
0	5	7	0	0	0	0	0	12
1	0	8	0	0	0	0	0	8
2	0	0	9	0	0	0	0	9
3	0	0	0	2	0	0	0	2
4	0	0	0	0	3	0	0	3
5	0	0	0	0	0	0	0	0
6	0	0	0	0	0	0	0	0
T	5	15	9	2	3	0	0	34

1650

1600\\1650	0	1	2	3	4	5	6	T
0	4	0	0	0	0	0	0	4
1	11	5	0	0	0	0	0	16
2	0	6	3	0	0	0	0	9
3	0	0	2	0	1	0	0	3
4	0	0	0	0	2	0	0	2
5	0	0	0	0	0	0	0	0
6	0	0	0	0	0	0	0	0
T	15	11	5	0	3	0	0	34

1800

1750\\1800	0	1	2	3	4	5	6	T
0	1	4	0	0	0	0	0	5
1	0	13	2	0	0	0	0	15
2	0	0	9	0	0	0	0	9
3	0	0	0	1	1	0	0	2
4	0	0	0	0	3	0	0	3
5	0	0	0	0	0	0	0	0
6	0	0	0	0	0	0	0	0
T	1	17	11	1	4	0	0	34

DISTRIBUTION OF CITIES BY TERRITORY

Number of cities by size category

	1500	1550	1600	1650	1700	1750	1800
1	12	11	16	11	8	15	17
2	4	6	9	5	9	9	11
3	3	4	3	0	2	2	1
4	2	1	2	3	3	3	4
5	0	0	0	0	0	0	0
6	0	0	0	0	0	0	0
Total	21	22	30	19	22	29	33
0	13	12	4	15	12	5	1

Total urban population ('000s)

	1500	1550	1600	1650	1700	1750	1800
1	169	149	201	162	112	209	249
2	120	177	275	142	241	255	296
3	149	227	162	0	83	100	41
4	200	158	259	310	342	360	446
5	0	0	0	0	0	0	0
6	0	0	0	0	0	0	0
Total	638	711	897	614	778	924	1032

APPENDIX 3

COUNTRY CODE 11   CENTRAL ITALY

1550

1500 \	0	1	2	3	4	5	6	T
0	2	0	0	0	0	0	0	2
1	0	3	1	0	0	0	0	4
2	0	0	1	1	0	0	0	2
3	0	0	0	3	0	0	0	3
4	0	0	0	0	0	0	0	0
5	0	0	0	0	0	0	0	0
6	0	0	0	0	0	0	0	0
T	2	3	2	4	0	0	0	11

1700

1650 \	0	1	2	3	4	5	6	T
0	0	0	0	0	0	0	0	0
1	1	5	0	0	0	0	0	6
2	0	0	2	0	0	0	0	2
3	0	0	0	2	0	0	0	2
4	0	0	0	0	1	0	0	1
5	0	0	0	0	0	0	0	0
6	0	0	0	0	0	0	0	0
T	1	5	2	2	1	0	0	11

1600

1550 \	0	1	2	3	4	5	6	T
0	2	0	0	0	0	0	0	2
1	0	3	0	0	0	0	0	3
2	0	0	2	0	0	0	0	2
3	0	0	1	2	1	0	0	4
4	0	0	0	0	0	0	0	0
5	0	0	0	0	0	0	0	0
6	0	0	0	0	0	0	0	0
T	2	3	3	2	1	0	0	11

1750

1700 \	0	1	2	3	4	5	6	T
0	0	1	0	0	0	0	0	1
1	0	4	1	0	0	0	0	5
2	0	0	2	0	0	0	0	2
3	0	0	0	2	0	0	0	2
4	0	0	0	0	1	0	0	1
5	0	0	0	0	0	0	0	0
6	0	0	0	0	0	0	0	0
T	0	5	3	2	1	0	0	11

1650

1600 \	0	1	2	3	4	5	6	T
0	0	2	0	0	0	0	0	2
1	0	3	0	0	0	0	0	3
2	0	1	2	0	0	0	0	3
3	0	0	0	2	0	0	0	2
4	0	0	0	0	1	0	0	1
5	0	0	0	0	0	0	0	0
6	0	0	0	0	0	0	0	0
T	0	6	2	2	1	0	0	11

1800

1750 \	0	1	2	3	4	5	6	T
0	0	0	0	0	0	0	0	0
1	0	5	0	0	0	0	0	5
2	0	1	1	1	0	0	0	3
3	0	0	0	1	1	0	0	2
4	0	0	0	0	0	1	0	1
5	0	0	0	0	0	0	0	0
6	0	0	0	0	0	0	0	0
T	0	6	1	2	1	1	0	11

DISTRIBUTION OF CITIES BY TERRITORY

	Number of cities by size category						
	1500	1550	1600	1650	1700	1750	1800
1	4	3	3	6	5	5	6
2	2	2	3	2	2	3	1
3	3	4	2	2	2	2	2
4	0	0	1	1	1	1	1
5	0	0	0	0	0	0	1
6	0	0	0	0	0	0	0
Total	9	9	9	11	10	11	11
0	2	2	2	0	1	0	0

	Total urban population ('000s)						
	1500	1550	1600	1650	1700	1750	1800
1	53	33	47	81	76	66	91
2	54	44	77	50	50	83	30
3	180	209	133	129	135	143	124
4	0	0	105	124	138	156	81
5	0	0	0	0	0	0	163
6	0	0	0	0	0	0	0
Total	287	286	362	384	399	448	449

APPENDIX 3

COUNTRY CODE 12 SOUTHERN ITALY

1550

	0	1	2	3	4	5	6	T
0	15	1	0	0	0	0	0	16
1	0	8	3	0	0	0	0	11
2	0	0	1	0	0	0	0	1
3	0	0	0	1	0	0	0	1
4	0	0	0	0	0	1	0	1
5	0	0	0	0	0	0	0	0
6	0	0	0	0	0	0	0	0
T	15	9	4	1	0	1	0	30

(rows labelled 1500)

1700

	0	1	2	3	4	5	6	T
0	8	2	0	0	0	0	0	10
1	3	14	0	0	0	0	0	17
2	0	0	0	0	0	0	0	0
3	0	0	0	1	0	0	0	1
4	0	0	0	0	1	0	0	1
5	0	0	0	0	0	1	0	1
6	0	0	0	0	0	0	0	0
T	11	16	0	1	1	1	0	30

(rows labelled 1650)

1600

	0	1	2	3	4	5	6	T
0	10	5	0	0	0	0	0	15
1	0	7	2	0	0	0	0	9
2	0	1	2	1	0	0	0	4
3	0	0	0	0	1	0	0	1
4	0	0	0	0	0	0	0	0
5	0	0	0	0	0	1	0	1
6	0	0	0	0	0	0	0	0
T	10	13	4	1	1	1	0	30

(rows labelled 1550)

1750

	0	1	2	3	4	5	6	T
0	4	7	0	0	0	0	0	11
1	1	13	2	0	0	0	0	16
2	0	0	0	0	0	0	0	0
3	0	0	1	0	0	0	0	1
4	0	0	0	0	1	0	0	1
5	0	0	0	0	0	1	0	1
6	0	0	0	0	0	0	0	0
T	5	20	3	0	1	1	0	30

(rows labelled 1700)

1650

	0	1	2	3	4	5	6	T
0	7	3	0	0	0	0	0	10
1	3	10	0	0	0	0	0	13
2	0	4	0	0	0	0	0	4
3	0	0	0	1	0	0	0	1
4	0	0	0	0	1	0	0	1
5	0	0	0	0	0	1	0	1
6	0	0	0	0	0	0	0	0
T	10	17	0	1	1	1	0	30

(rows labelled 1600)

1800

	0	1	2	3	4	5	6	T
0	0	5	0	0	0	0	0	5
1	0	16	4	0	0	0	0	20
2	0	0	1	2	0	0	0	3
3	0	0	0	0	0	0	0	0
4	0	0	0	0	1	0	0	1
5	0	0	0	0	0	1	1	1
6	0	0	0	0	0	0	0	0
T	0	21	5	2	1	0	1	30

(rows labelled 1750)

DISTRIBUTION OF CITIES BY TERRITORY

Number of cities by size category

	1500	1550	1600	1650	1700	1750	1800
1	11	9	13	17	16	20	21
2	1	4	4	0	0	3	5
3	1	1	1	1	1	0	2
4	1	0	1	1	1	1	1
5	0	1	1	1	1	1	0
6	0	0	0	0	0	0	1
Total	14	15	20	20	19	25	30
0	16	15	10	10	11	5	0

Total urban population ('000s)

	1500	1550	1600	1650	1700	1750	1800
1	147	123	177	224	228	281	313
2	25	96	101	0	0	83	106
3	55	70	50	50	40	0	89
4	150	0	105	129	100	118	139
5	0	212	281	176	216	305	0
6	0	0	0	0	0	0	427
Total	377	501	714	579	584	787	1074

APPENDIX 3

COUNTRY CODE 13 SPAIN

1550

	0	1	2	3	4	5	6	T
0	16	5	2	0	0	0	0	23
1	0	9	4	0	0	0	0	13
2	0	0	3	2	0	0	0	5
3	0	0	1	1	0	0	0	2
4	0	0	0	0	0	0	0	0
5	0	0	0	0	0	0	0	0
6	0	0	0	0	0	0	0	0
T	16	14	10	3	0	0	0	43

(rows labeled 1500)

1700

	0	1	2	3	4	5	6	T
0	17	1	1	0	0	0	0	19
1	4	7	2	0	0	0	0	13
2	0	1	5	0	0	0	0	6
3	0	0	0	3	1	0	0	4
4	0	0	0	0	1	0	0	1
5	0	0	0	0	0	0	0	0
6	0	0	0	0	0	0	0	0
T	21	9	8	3	2	0	0	43

(rows labeled 1650)

1600

	0	1	2	3	4	5	6	T
0	6	10	0	0	0	0	0	16
1	0	8	6	0	0	0	0	14
2	0	2	3	5	0	0	0	10
3	0	0	0	2	1	0	0	3
4	0	0	0	0	0	0	0	0
5	0	0	0	0	0	0	0	0
6	0	0	0	0	0	0	0	0
T	6	20	9	7	1	0	0	43

(rows labeled 1550)

1750

	0	1	2	3	4	5	6	T
0	19	2	0	0	0	0	0	21
1	0	7	2	0	0	0	0	9
2	0	0	7	1	0	0	0	8
3	0	0	0	3	0	0	0	3
4	0	0	0	1	1	0	0	2
5	0	0	0	0	0	0	0	0
6	0	0	0	0	0	0	0	0
T	19	9	9	5	1	0	0	43

(rows labeled 1700)

1650

	0	1	2	3	4	5	6	T
0	5	1	0	0	0	0	0	6
1	13	6	1	0	0	0	0	20
2	1	5	3	0	0	0	0	9
3	0	1	2	3	1	0	0	7
4	0	0	0	1	0	0	0	1
5	0	0	0	0	0	0	0	0
6	0	0	0	0	0	0	0	0
T	19	13	6	4	1	0	0	43

(rows labeled 1600)

1800

	0	1	2	3	4	5	6	T
0	8	11	0	0	0	0	0	19
1	1	5	3	0	0	0	0	9
2	0	0	6	3	0	0	0	9
3	0	0	0	2	3	0	0	5
4	0	0	0	0	0	1	0	1
5	0	0	0	0	0	0	0	0
6	0	0	0	0	0	0	0	0
T	9	16	9	5	3	1	0	43

(rows labeled 1750)

DISTRIBUTION OF CITIES BY TERRITORY

Number of cities by size category

	1500	1550	1600	1650	1700	1750	1800
1	13	14	20	13	9	9	16
2	5	10	9	6	8	9	9
3	2	3	7	4	3	5	5
4	0	0	1	1	2	1	3
5	0	0	0	0	0	0	1
6	0	0	0	0	0	0	0
Total	20	27	37	24	22	24	34
0	23	16	6	19	21	19	9

Total urban population ('000s)

	1500	1550	1600	1650	1700	1750	1800
1	169	204	254	183	115	125	202
2	134	271	218	149	203	247	260
3	110	165	361	211	150	286	245
4	0	0	90	130	206	109	291
5	0	0	0	0	0	0	167
6	0	0	0	0	0	0	0
Total	414	639	923	672	673	767	1165

APPENDIX 3

COUNTRY CODE 14 PORTUGAL

1550

	0	1	2	3	4	5	6	T
0	1	3	0	0	0	0	0	4
1	0	0	0	0	0	0	0	0
2	0	0	0	0	1	0	0	1
3	0	0	0	0	0	0	0	0
4	0	0	0	0	0	0	0	0
5	0	0	0	0	0	0	0	0
6	0	0	0	0	0	0	0	0
T	1	3	0	0	1	0	0	5

(rows labeled 1500)

1700

	0	1	2	3	4	5	6	T
0	0	0	0	0	0	0	0	0
1	0	3	0	0	0	0	0	3
2	0	0	1	0	0	0	0	1
3	0	0	0	0	0	0	0	0
4	0	0	0	0	0	1	0	1
5	0	0	0	0	0	0	0	0
6	0	0	0	0	0	0	0	0
T	0	3	1	0	0	1	0	5

(rows labeled 1650)

1600

	0	1	2	3	4	5	6	T
0	0	1	0	0	0	0	0	1
1	0	3	0	0	0	0	0	3
2	0	0	0	0	0	0	0	0
3	0	0	0	0	0	0	0	0
4	0	0	0	0	1	0	0	1
5	0	0	0	0	0	0	0	0
6	0	0	0	0	0	0	0	0
T	0	4	0	0	1	0	0	5

(rows labeled 1550)

1750

	0	1	2	3	4	5	6	T
0	0	0	0	0	0	0	0	0
1	0	3	0	0	0	0	0	3
2	0	0	1	0	0	0	0	1
3	0	0	0	0	0	0	0	0
4	0	0	0	0	0	0	0	0
5	0	0	0	0	1	0	0	1
6	0	0	0	0	0	0	0	0
T	0	3	1	0	1	0	0	5

(rows labeled 1700)

1650

	0	1	2	3	4	5	6	T
0	0	0	0	0	0	0	0	0
1	0	3	1	0	0	0	0	4
2	0	0	0	0	0	0	0	0
3	0	0	0	0	0	0	0	0
4	0	0	0	0	1	0	0	1
5	0	0	0	0	0	0	0	0
6	0	0	0	0	0	0	0	0
T	0	3	1	0	1	0	0	5

(rows labeled 1600)

1800

	0	1	2	3	4	5	6	T
0	0	0	0	0	0	0	0	0
1	0	3	0	0	0	0	0	3
2	0	0	1	0	0	0	0	1
3	0	0	0	0	0	0	0	0
4	0	0	0	0	0	1	0	1
5	0	0	0	0	0	0	0	0
6	0	0	0	0	0	0	0	0
T	0	3	1	0	0	1	0	5

(rows labeled 1750)

DISTRIBUTION OF CITIES BY TERRITORY

	Number of cities by size category							
	1500	1550	1600	1650	1700	1750	1800
1	0	3	4	3	3	3	3
2	1	0	0	1	1	1	1
3	0	0	0	0	0	0	0
4	0	1	1	1	0	1	0
5	0	0	0	0	1	0	1
6	0	0	0	0	0	0	0
Total	1	4	5	5	5	5	5
0	4	1	0	0	0	0	0

	Total urban population ('000s)							
	1500	1550	1600	1650	1700	1750	1800
1	0	40	55	49	40	40	42
2	30	0	0	20	25	21	30
3	0	0	0	0	0	0	0
4	0	98	100	130	0	148	0
5	0	0	0	0	165	0	180
6	0	0	0	0	0	0	0
Total	30	138	155	199	230	209	252

APPENDIX 3

COUNTRY CODE 15   AUSTRIA – CZECHOSLOVAKIA

1550

	0	1	2	3	4	5	6	T
0	5	0	0	0	0	0	0	5
1	0	1	0	0	0	0	0	1
2	0	0	2	0	0	0	0	2
3	0	0	0	0	0	0	0	0
4	0	0	0	0	0	0	0	0
5	0	0	0	0	0	0	0	0
6	0	0	0	0	0	0	0	0
T	5	1	2	0	0	0	0	8

(rows indexed by 1500)

1700

	0	1	2	3	4	5	6	T
0	4	1	0	0	0	0	0	5
1	0	1	0	0	0	0	0	1
2	0	0	1	0	0	0	0	1
3	0	0	0	0	1	0	0	1
4	0	0	0	0	0	0	0	0
5	0	0	0	0	0	0	0	0
6	0	0	0	0	0	0	0	0
T	4	2	1	0	1	0	0	8

(rows indexed by 1650)

1600

	0	1	2	3	4	5	6	T
0	5	0	0	0	0	0	0	5
1	0	1	0	0	0	0	0	1
2	0	0	1	1	0	0	0	2
3	0	0	0	0	0	0	0	0
4	0	0	0	0	0	0	0	0
5	0	0	0	0	0	0	0	0
6	0	0	0	0	0	0	0	0
T	5	1	1	1	0	0	0	8

(rows indexed by 1550)

1750

	0	1	2	3	4	5	6	T
0	2	1	1	0	0	0	0	4
1	0	2	0	0	0	0	0	2
2	0	0	0	1	0	0	0	1
3	0	0	0	0	0	0	0	0
4	0	0	0	0	0	1	0	1
5	0	0	0	0	0	0	0	0
6	0	0	0	0	0	0	0	0
T	2	3	1	1	0	1	0	8

(rows indexed by 1700)

1650

	0	1	2	3	4	5	6	T
0	5	0	0	0	0	0	0	5
1	0	1	0	0	0	0	0	1
2	0	0	1	0	0	0	0	1
3	0	0	0	1	0	0	0	1
4	0	0	0	0	0	0	0	0
5	0	0	0	0	0	0	0	0
6	0	0	0	0	0	0	0	0
T	5	1	1	1	0	0	0	8

(rows indexed by 1600)

1800

	0	1	2	3	4	5	6	T
0	0	2	0	0	0	0	0	2
1	0	2	1	0	0	0	0	3
2	0	0	1	0	0	0	0	1
3	0	0	0	1	0	0	0	1
4	0	0	0	0	0	0	0	0
5	0	0	0	0	0	1	0	1
6	0	0	0	0	0	0	0	0
T	0	4	2	1	0	1	0	8

(rows indexed by 1750)

DISTRIBUTION OF CITIES BY TERRITORY

	Number of cities by size category						
	1500	*1550*	*1600*	*1650*	*1700*	*1750*	*1800*
1	1	1	1	1	2	3	4
2	2	2	1	1	1	1	2
3	0	0	1	1	0	1	1
4	0	0	0	0	1	0	0
5	0	0	0	0	0	1	1
6	0	0	0	0	0	0	0
Total	3	3	3	3	4	6	8
0	5	5	5	5	4	2	0

	Total urban population ('000s)						
	1500	*1550*	*1600*	*1650*	*1700*	*1750*	*1800*
1	13	13	13	13	27	40	48
2	47	54	27	27	39	20	54
3	0	0	50	60	0	59	77
4	0	0	0	0	114	0	0
5	0	0	0	0	0	175	231
6	0	0	0	0	0	0	0
Total	60	67	90	100	180	294	410

APPENDIX 3

COUNTRY CODE 16   POLAND

1550

	0	1	2	3	4	5	6	T
0	2	1	0	0	0	0	0	3
1	0	0	0	0	0	0	0	0
2	0	0	0	0	0	0	0	0
3	0	0	0	0	0	0	0	0
4	0	0	0	0	0	0	0	0
5	0	0	0	0	0	0	0	0
6	0	0	0	0	0	0	0	0
T	2	1	0	0	0	0	0	3

(rows indexed 1500)

1700

	0	1	2	3	4	5	6	T
0	2	0	0	0	0	0	0	2
1	0	0	0	0	0	0	0	0
2	0	1	0	0	0	0	0	1
3	0	0	0	0	0	0	0	0
4	0	0	0	0	0	0	0	0
5	0	0	0	0	0	0	0	0
6	0	0	0	0	0	0	0	0
T	2	1	0	0	0	0	0	3

(rows indexed 1650)

1600

	0	1	2	3	4	5	6	T
0	2	0	0	0	0	0	0	2
1	0	1	0	0	0	0	0	1
2	0	0	0	0	0	0	0	0
3	0	0	0	0	0	0	0	0
4	0	0	0	0	0	0	0	0
5	0	0	0	0	0	0	0	0
6	0	0	0	0	0	0	0	0
T	2	1	0	0	0	0	0	3

(rows indexed 1550)

1750

	0	1	2	3	4	5	6	T
0	1	1	0	0	0	0	0	2
1	0	0	1	0	0	0	0	1
2	0	0	0	0	0	0	0	0
3	0	0	0	0	0	0	0	0
4	0	0	0	0	0	0	0	0
5	0	0	0	0	0	0	0	0
6	0	0	0	0	0	0	0	0
T	1	1	1	0	0	0	0	3

(rows indexed 1700)

1650

	0	1	2	3	4	5	6	T
0	2	0	0	0	0	0	0	2
1	0	0	1	0	0	0	0	1
2	0	0	0	0	0	0	0	0
3	0	0	0	0	0	0	0	0
4	0	0	0	0	0	0	0	0
5	0	0	0	0	0	0	0	0
6	0	0	0	0	0	0	0	0
T	2	0	1	0	0	0	0	3

(rows indexed 1600)

1800

	0	1	2	3	4	5	6	T
0	0	1	0	0	0	0	0	1
1	0	0	1	0	0	0	0	1
2	0	0	0	1	0	0	0	1
3	0	0	0	0	0	0	0	0
4	0	0	0	0	0	0	0	0
5	0	0	0	0	0	0	0	0
6	0	0	0	0	0	0	0	0
T	0	1	1	1	0	0	0	3

(rows indexed 1750)

DISTRIBUTION OF CITIES BY TERRITORY

Number of cities by size category

	1500	1550	1600	1650	1700	1750	1800
1	0	1	1	0	1	1	1
2	0	0	0	1	0	1	1
3	0	0	0	0	0	0	1
4	0	0	0	0	0	0	0
5	0	0	0	0	0	0	0
6	0	0	0	0	0	0	0
Total	0	1	1	1	1	2	3
0	3	2	2	2	2	1	0

Total urban population ('000s)

	1500	1550	1600	1650	1700	1750	1800
1	0	10	15	0	15	13	16
2	0	0	0	20	0	23	24
3	0	0	0	0	0	0	63
4	0	0	0	0	0	0	0
5	0	0	0	0	0	0	0
6	0	0	0	0	0	0	0
Total	0	10	15	20	15	36	103

Appendix 4
URBAN POPULATION OF EASTERN-MOST EUROPE c. 1800

The map opposite identifies the territory that was excluded from systematic consideration in this study. At the end of the eighteenth century it was ruled by the Ottoman empire and by the Hungarian half of the Austro-Hungarian empire. From the point of view of urban settlement the region is bounded on the west by the line Königsberg–Vienna–Trieste and on the east by the western-most cities of the Russian empire (as defined by Rozman): Riga–Minsk–Kiev–Black Sea (at latter-day Odessa).

The cities that are likely to have stood at or above the 10,000 inhabitant level in 1800 are listed below:

Hungarian empire		Ottoman empire	
Lvov (Lemburg)	39,000	Belgrade	17,000 (1854)
Przemyśl	?	Bucharest	42,000 (incl. rural pop.)
Budapest	54,000	Sofia	30,000 (1850)
Bratislava (Pressburg)	21,000	Philippopolis	40,000 (1850)
Debrecen	29,000	Sarajevo	?
Szeged	c. 20,000	Athens	31,000 (1853)
Subotica (Szobadka)	28,000	Salonica	60,000–70,000
Kecskemet	c. 20,000	Patras	16,000 (1853)
Hodmezövăsárhely	c. 20,000	Sérrai	20,000

Sources Philippe Wolff (ed.), *Guide international d'histoire urbaine*, vol. 1: *Europe* (Paris, 1977), 229, 252; Adna F. Weber, *The Growth of Cities in the Nineteenth Century: a Study in Statistics* (New York, 1899), 101, 120–2; Nikolaï Todorov, *La ville Balkanique aux XVe–XIXe siècles. Developpement sòcio-économique et démographique* (Sofia, 1972), *passim*.

For the period before 1800 the following can be said:
Greece   Around 1500 three cities may have exceeded the 10,000 level: Adrianople, Salonica and Athens. Six cities in Macedonia, three in central Greece and two on the Peloponnese are said to have contained between 1500 and 5000 inhabitants (Wolff *Guide international*, 229).

URBAN POPULATION OF EASTERN-MOST EUROPE c. 1800

Balkans In the second half of the sixteenth century the entire Balkan region possessed eight cities with over 1600 households (perhaps equivalent to 8000–10,000 inhabitants) and thirty-six cities of all sizes (Todorov, idem., 45). Elsewhere (in his 'Quelques aspects de la ville Balkanique aux XV^c et XVI^c siècles', in *La ville Balkanique sous les Ottomans (XV–XIXe siècles)* (London, 1977), 213), he lists the following cities as having at least 10,000 inhabitants in the mid-sixteenth century: Sarajevo, Nokopol and Skopje (each 10,000–15,000), Athens, Adrianople and Salonica (each 20,000–30,000) and Constantinople, with in excess of 100,000 inhabitants.

Around 1800 the Balkans plus Greece numbered seven or eight cities of 10,000 or

APPENDIX 4

more inhabitants, with an aggregate population of perhaps 100,000. The total population of the region is thought to have approached 5 million. (Constantinople and present-day European Turkey are excluded from these estimates.) The population resident in these cities did not far exceed 2 per cent of the total.

Hungary (the 'Greater Hungary' of the Austro-Hungarian empire) numbered 9.9 million inhabitants in 1800. Besides the cities listed above, there were other municipalities whose populations exceeded 10,000. One source (Weber *Growth of Cities*, 101) maintains there were thirty in all, with an aggregate population of 528,000, or 5.3 per cent of the total population. Apparently, the figures for many of these cities include the inhabitants of large rural districts (Jozsef Kovocsics, 'Situation démographique de la Hongrie à la fin du XVIIIe siècle', *Annales de démographie historique* (1965), 83–102). In view of the fact that the nine cities listed above together numbered some 220,000 inhabitants, the population of all cities of 10,000 or more could plausibly have reached 400,000, or 4 per cent of the total population.

For the entire territory, one can reckon on about twenty-five cities with about 500,000 inhabitants in a total population of 15 million. The overall urban percentage was thus about 3.3. per cent.

NOTES AND REFERENCES

CHAPTER 1   THE PROBLEM OF THE CITY IN EARLY
           MODERN EUROPE

1 H. J. Dyos, 'Agenda for urban historians', in H. J. Dyos (ed.), *The Study of Urban History* (London, 1968), 7.
2 Among the many studies are: Henri Pirenne, *Medieval Cities, their Origins, and the Revival of Trade* (Princeton, NJ, 1925); his collected works on this subject in Henri Pirenne, *Les Villes et les institutions urbaines*, 2 vols (Brussels, 1939); Max Weber, *Economy and Society* (New York, 1968).
3 Henri Pirenne, *Economic and Social History of Medieval Europe* (London, 1936), 239.
4 M. M. Postan, *The Medieval Economy and Society* (Berkeley and Los Angeles, Calif., 1975, 2nd edn), 212.
5 Fernand Braudel, *Capitalism and Material Life, 1400–1800* (New York, 1973), 396, 400.
6 For 'contemporary' views on the new industrial city see, among others, Robert Vaughn, *The Age of Great Cities* (London, 1843); P. Geddes, *Cities in Evolution* (London, 1915) and Ferdinand Tönnies, *Gemeinschaft und Gessellschaft* (trans. as *Community and Association*, London, 1955). For modern reviews of the discussion see Asa Briggs, 'The human aggregate', in H. J. Dyos and Michael Wolff (eds), *The Victorian City: Images and Realities*, vol. I (London, 1973), 83–104; Jürgen Reulecke (ed.), *Die deutsche Stadt im Industriezeitalter* (Wüppertal, 1978).
7 Leo Jakobson, 'Introduction', in Leo Jakobson and Ved Prakash (eds), *Urbanization and National Development*, vol. I (Beverley Hills, Calif., 1971), 15. Similar views can be found in: H. Carter, *The Study of Urban Geography* (London, 1976) and Peter N. Stearns, *European Society in Upheaval: Social History since 1750* (New York, 1975).
8 David Clark, *Urban Geography* (London, 1982), 48.
9 Not essentially different from this schema is the periodization and terminology

proposed by the urban historian Eric Lampard. He writes of a *primordial urbanization* ('the first achievement of incipient urban organization') and *definitive urbanization* ('the culmination of primordial tendencies . . . the organization and appropriation of an agricultural surplus'). Definitive urbanization Lampard divides into two subcategories: classic urbanization and industrial urbanization. In the former 'various constraints and circumstances combine to moderate the growth of population and cities, as it were, through "systemic" or built-in social checks and balances. In the latter, these constraints and conditions are relaxed through the final achievement of technological and organizational capacities for unprecedented population concentration.' Through his arrangement of categories, Lampard emphasized the early development of cities in settled agricultural societies over the lifting of the constraints to urban growth through industrial technology. Still, in view of the enormous length of these periods, it is hard to see how there is any practical difference between Lampard's categories and those of Sjoberg as presented by Clark. For Lampard's periodization see: Eric E. Lampard, 'Historical aspects of urbanization', in Philip M. Hauser and L. F. Schnore (eds), *The Study of Urbanization* (New York, 1965), 519-54.
10 Fernand Braudel, *The Mediterranean and the Mediterranean World in the Age of Philip II*, vol. I (New York, 1972), 326, 327.
11 ibid., p. 345.
12 Braudel, *Capitalism and Material Life*, 440.
13 John Merrington, 'Town and country in the transition to capitalism', *New Left Review* 93(1975), 71-92; reprinted in R. Hilton *et al.*, *The Transition from Feudalism to Capitalism* (London, 1978), 170-95.
14 ibid., 82-3.
15 ibid., 89.
16 ibid., 88.
17 The 'protoindustrialization' literature is cited in chapter 10, notes 40 and 43; see also Charles Tilly's argument in 'Flows of capital and forms of industry in Europe, 1500-1900', *Theory and Society* 12(1983), 123-42.
18 Philip Abrams, 'Towns and economic growth: some theories and problems', in Philip Abrams and E. A. Wrigley (eds), *Towns and Society: Essays in Economic History and Historical Sociology* (Cambridge, 1978), 24.
19 Gilbert Rozman, *Urban Networks in Ch'ing China and Tokugawa Japan* (Princeton, NJ, 1973); *Urban Networks in Russia, 1750-1800, and Premodern Periodization* (Princeton, NJ, 1976); 'Urban networks and historical stages', *Journal of Interdisciplinary History* 9(1978), 65-91; G. William Skinner, 'Regional urbanization in nineteenth century China', and 'Cities and the hierarchy of local systems', in G. William Skinner (ed.), *The City in Late Imperial China* (Stanford, Calif., 1977); Allan Pred, *Urban Growth and the Circulation of Information: the United States System of Cities, 1790-1840* (Cambridge, Mass., 1973); *Urban Growth and City-Systems in the United States, 1840-1860* (Cambridge, Mass., 1980); Brian T. Robson, *Urban Growth: an Approach* (London, 1973).
20 For a summary of the stages see Rozman, 'Urban networks and historical stages'.

21 Skinner, 'Regional urbanization', 211.
22 Abrams, 'Towns and economic growth', 31.
23 This insight is hardly new (it can be found in Lampard's articles repeatedly) but it is rarely acted upon. In this regard it is instructive to compare the subdisciplines of urban and agrarian history. The latter has the potential to be a chaos of particularism. After all, every field has its history. But, in fact, agrarian history is equipped with models and 'middle-level' generalizations – many of them developed internally by such historians as W. Abel, B. H. Slicher van Bath and E. Le Roy Ladurie, others borrowed from economics and demography – that have proved serviceable in integrating the details into comprehensive patterns. Consequently, one can distinguish the local fate of peasants or landowners from the functions of agricultural production and the transformations in regional specialization. Agrarian history is something other than local history. In urban history this sort of distinction is not easy to make since the middle-level generalizations are not yet up to the task.
24 Hope Eldridge Tisdale, 'The process of urbanization', *Social Forces* 10(1942), 311–16; reprinted in J. J. Spengler and O. D. Duncan (eds), *Demographic Analysis* (Glencoe, Ill., 1956), 338–43.
25 Among the many efforts to define the city, see Clark, *Urban Geography*, 17–37.
26 Philip M. Hauser, 'Urbanization: an overview', in Hauser and Schnore (eds), *The Study of Urbanization*, 7.
27 The behavioural aspects of urbanism are emphasized by the 'Chicago ecologists', notably L. Wirth, 'Urbanism as a way of life', *American Journal of Sociology* 44(1938), 1–24. Such behaviour as Wirth regarded to flow from life in an urban location is now often seen as disassociated from one's immediate environment. Thus 'There are some people who are in the city but are not of it (the urban villagers), whereas others are of the city but are not in it', R. E. Pahl (ed.), *Readings in Urban Sociology* (Oxford, 1968), 273.
28 John Patten, *English Towns, 1500–1700* (Folkestone, 1978), 17.
29 An essentially similar argument is presented in P. Kooij, 'Urbanization. What's in a name?', in H. Schmal (ed.), *Patterns of European Urbanisation since 1500* (London, 1981), 31–59.
30 That which follows is based on the definition offered in Charles Tilly, *The Vendée* (Cambridge, Mass., 1964), 16–20.
31 Jakobson, 'Introduction', 15.

CHAPTER 2   ASSEMBLING THE DATA BASE

1 The literature on this subject is now vast. For methodology see Louis Henry, *Manuel de démographie historique* (Paris, 1967); for a survey of family reconstitution research see Michael Flinn, *The European Demographic System, 1500–1820* (London, 1981); for inverse projection see E. A. Wrigley and R. S. Schofield, *The Population History of England, 1541–1871: a Reconstruction* (London, 1981).

NOTES TO PAGES 18-29

2 Roger Mols, *Introduction à la démographie historique des villes d'Europe du 14ᵉ au 18ᵉ siècle*, 3 vols (Leuven, 1954-6).
3 Tertius Chandler and Gerald Fox, *Three Thousand Years of Urban Growth* (New York, 1974).
4 Paul Bairoch, *Tailles des villes, conditions de vie et développement économique* (Paris, 1977). The data presented there have now been partially revised: see chapter 4, note 13.
5 Karl Julius Beloch, *Bevölkerungsgeschichte Italiens*, 3 vols (Berlin, 1937-61).
6 Paul M. M. Klep, *Bevolking en arbeid in transformatie* (Nijmegen, 1981); Karlheinz Blaschke, *Bevölkerungsgeschichte von Sachsen bis zur industriellen Revolution* (Weimar, 1967).
7 The inspiration for this part of the book is the pioneer study of urbanization *after* 1800 by Adna F. Weber, *The Growth of Cities in the Nineteenth Century: a Study in Statistics* (New York, 1899; republished, Ithaca, NY, 1963).
8 A defence for this distinction might be found in Rozman's treatment of Russian ubanization as an autonomous phenomenon and in Wallerstein's justifications for the boundaries of his 'European World Economy': Gilbert Rozman, *Urban Networks in Russia, 1750-1800, and Premodern Periodization* (Princeton, NJ, 1976); Immanuel Wallerstein, *The Modern World-System: Capitalist Agriculture and the Origins of the European World-Economy in the Sixteenth Century* (New York, 1973).
9 For a discussion of urban populations beyond the eastern borders used in this study, see appendix 4.
10 The boundaries that are used here for 'Poland' are roughly those of the Napoleonic 'Grand Duchy of Warsaw'. It covered an area of some 155,000 km² (compared to the 718,000 km² of Poland before the first partition of 1772).
11 United Nations, *Demographic Yearbook 1977* (New York, 1977), 182-6; cited in David Clark, *Urban Geography* (London, 1982), 26-8.
12 Eric E. Lampard, 'Urbanization and social change', in Oscar Handlin and John Burchard (eds), *The Historian and the City* (Cambridge, Mass., 1963).
13 Eric E. Lampard and Leo F. Schnore, 'Urbanization problems', in *Research Needs for Development Assistance Programs* (Washington, DC, 1961), 12.

CHAPTER 3   THE CONTOURS OF EUROPEAN URBANIZATION I

1 The Romans occupied territories beyond the Rhine-Danube line, notably Britain. But I have excluded these territories from 'Roman Europe' on the grounds of the strength and persistence of Roman urban traditions.
2 Fernand Braudel, *The Mediterranean and the Mediterranean World in the Age of Philip II*, vol. I (New York, 1972), 328-34; Henry Kamen, *Spain in the Later Seventeenth Century, 1665-1700* (London, 1980), 39-45; Günther Franz, *Der Dreissigjährige Krieg und das deutsche Volk* (Stuttgart, 1961, second edn);

Aksel Lassen, 'The population of Denmark in 1660', *Scandinavian Economic History Review* 13(1965), 1–30; Irena Gieysztorowa, 'Research into the demographic history of Poland: a provisional summing-up', *Acta Poloniae Historica* 18(1968), 5–17.
3 F. L. Ganshof, *Etudes sur le développement des villes entre Loire et Rhin au Moyen Age* (Paris, 1943); C. Haase, *Die Entstehung der westfälischen Städte* (Münster, 1960); H. A. Miskimin, *The Economy of Early Renaissance Europe, 1300–1460* (Cambridge, 1975, second edn), 75–7; M. Beresford, *New Towns of the Middle Ages* (London, 1967).
4 Henri Pirenne, *Medieval Cities, their Origins and the Revival of Trade* (Princeton, NJ, 1925), 53.
5 ibid.
6 Léopold Genicot, 'Les grandes villes de l'Occident en 1300', in *Économies et sociétiés au moyen age* (Paris, 1973), 199–219.
7 Josiah Cox Russell, *Medieval Regions and their Cities* (Bloomington, Ind., 1972).
8 Among the numerous publications, see: Adna F. Weber, *The Growth of Cities in the Nineteenth Century: a Study in Statistics* (New York, 1899; reprinted, Ithaca, NY, 1963); Peter Hall, *The World Cities* (London, 1977, second edn); Kingsley Davis, *World Urbanization 1950–1970*, 2 vols (Berkeley, Calif., 1969, 1972).
9 Peter Hall and Dennis Hay, *Growth Centres in the European Urban System* (Berkeley and Los Angeles, Calif., 1980), 85–8.
10 Whenever a fixed threshold level is used for an extended period of time, as I do in this study, the risk is run that the character of the settlements that are eligible for inclusion gradually changes. From 1500 to 1750 the slow overall pace of population growth makes it unlikely that this problem could be severe, but thereafter, and particularly in the nineteenth century, it cannot be ignored. I discuss this problem in chapter 7 (pp. 144–6). There is no simple or obvious solution to this problem. The specification of moving thresholds as developed in John R. Borchert, 'American metropolitan evolution', *Geographical Review* 57 (1967), 301–32, appears to me to be wholly arbitrary.

CHAPTER 4   THE CONTOURS OF EUROPEAN
URBANIZATION II

1 For an elementary presentation of the concept of the rank-size distribution see Peter Haggett, Andrew D. Cliff and Allan Frey, *Locational Models* (London, 1977), 110–26.
2 G. K. Zipf, *Human Behavior and the Principle of Least Effort* (New York, 1949), 364–76; and discussion in chapter 6.
3 That is, our interest in the rank-size distribution is not the usual one of assessing the position of the largest cities (primacy); our present concern is at 'the other end' of the distribution, specifically, to estimate the number of smaller cities, below the 10,000 population threshold.

4 In the regression equations, the slope (*b*) has the following values:

Year	Northern Europe	Mediterranean Europe	Europe
1500	−0.5391	−0.7505	−0.6305
1550	−0.6193	−0.8308	−0.7140
1600	−0.6216	−0.8508	−0.7246
1650	−0.7074	−0.8072	−0.7473
1700	−0.7699	−0.8392	−0.7976
1750	−0.7729	−0.8344	−0.7906
1800	−0.7498	−0.8467	−0.7822

5 Zipf, *Human Behavior*, 423; Brian J. L. Berry, 'City size and economic development: conceptual synthesis and policy problems, with special reference to south and southeast Asia', in Leo Jakobson and Ved Prakash (eds), *Urbanization and National Development*, vol. 1 (Beverly Hills, Calif., 1971), 119.

6 John Patten, *English Towns, 1500–1700* (Folkestone, 1978).

7 Karlheinz Blaschke, *Bevölkerungsgeschichte von Sachsen bis zur industriellen Revolution* (Weimar, 1967).

8 Aksel Lassen, 'The population of Denmark in 1660', *Scandinavian Economic History Review* 13(1965), 1–30; Aksel Lassen, 'The population of Denmark, 1660–1960', *Scandinavian Economic History Review* 14(1966), 134–57; Ole Degn, 'De nylagte byer og byudvikling en Danmark 1600–1800', in Grethe Authén Blom (ed.), *Urbaniseringsprosessen i Norden*, vol. 2 (Oslo, 1977).

9 A. M. van der Woude, 'Demografische ontwikkeling van de noordelijke Nederlanden 1500–1800', in *Algemene geschiedenis der Nederlanden*, vol. V (Haarlem, 1980), 137–9; Jan de Vries, *The Dutch Rural Economy in the Golden Age* (New Haven, Conn., 1974), 89–91; Jan de Vries, *Barges and Capitalism* (Utrecht, 1981), 248–50.

10 Peter Clark and Paul Slack, *English Towns in Transition 1500–1700* (Oxford, 1976), map 2; Patten, *English Towns*, 115; P. J. Corfield, 'Urban development in England and Wales in the sixteenth and seventeenth centuries', in D. C. Coleman and A. H. John (eds), *Trade, Government and Economy in Pre-Industrial England* (London, 1976), 223, 238–41; P. J. Corfield, *The Impact of English Towns, 1700–1800*, (Oxford, 1982), 8; C. M. Law, 'Some notes on the urban population of England and Wales in the eighteenth century', *The Local Historian* 10(1972), 13–26; Brian T. Robson, *Urban Growth: an Approach* (London, 1973), 53.

11 As cited in Clark and Slack, *English Towns in Transition*, 7–8. See also Peter Clark, 'Introduction', in Peter Clark (ed.), *English Country Towns, 1500–1800* (New York, 1981), 11–14.

12 Blom, *Urbaniseringsprosessen*, vol. 2, *passim*.

13 The evolution of the size and number of smaller cities that I have gone to some lengths to uncover is often ignored by investigators of urbanization, or is assumed by them to follow some predetermined path. It is, of course, convenient to suppose that the pattern observed for a small number of large cities also holds for the myriad smaller places. For example, Kingsley Davis observes that two indices of urbanization are commonly used: the percentage of popu-

NOTE TO PAGE 71

lation in places over 100,000 and the percentage in all places classified as urban in official statistics. He then goes on to claim that 'In practice the two indexes are highly correlated; therefore either one can be used as an index of urbanization' (Kingsley Davis, 'The urbanization of the human population', *Scientific American* 213(1965), 45.

In modern society Davis's claim is correct for the obvious reason that cities of over 100,000 account for the great bulk of urban population whatever the official definition. In the period being studied here such an assumption would be fatal to any effort to estimate the size of urban populations.

Paul Bairoch has recently published estimates of European urban population for the period 1500–1800. They differ substantially from mine, and one important reason for the difference resides in his method of estimating the population of small cities (cities of 5000–20,000 inhabitants). In 'Population urbaine et taille des villes en Europe de 1600 à 1970', *Revue d'histoire économique et sociale* 54(1976), 304–35, and his *Taille des villes, conditions de vie et développement économique* (Paris, 1977), he provides aggregative estimates of the number of cities of at least 20,000 inhabitants and of the total population of such cities. He then seeks to estimate the population of smaller cities. He writes in a methodological appendix (p. 326 of 'Population urbaine'): 'Le seul problème (mais très important) consistait en la détermination du rapport entre la population de villes de 5.000 à 20.000 habitants et celle des villes de 20.000 à 50.000. Nous avons décidé d'appliquer le *ratio* (légèrement modifié en hausse) qui découlait des données pour l'Europe de 1800.'

Bairoch's estimates of Europe's urban population, based on the application of a more-or-less fixed ratio, are vastly larger than mine. His method implies that the percentage of total urban population in cities of under 20,000 inhabitants, instead of falling from 64 to 40 per cent between 1500 and 1700 as I estimate, remains just over 50 per cent throughout the period.

Since publishing these figures Bairoch has set out to revise his tables, reducing substantially his estimates of the size of the urban population between 1500 and 1700 even while increasing his estimates of the number of cities with at least 20,000 inhabitants. The revisions imply a major change in his estimation of the population in the smaller cities; the new tables were kindly supplied to me by him, with permission to quote them, in advance of their publication in his forthcoming 'Les villes et le développement économique dans l'histoire: de l'origine du phenomene urbain aux villes du Tiers-Monde'. In the comparisons below, the 1976–7 publication is identified as 'Bairoch old', while the revisions are labelled 'Bairoch new'. The reader can observe here that Bairoch assumes cities of over 20,000 to have been much more numerous in earlier centuries than I have found. Moreover, his assumptions about small cities underestimate their importance in the sixteenth and seventeenth centuries. Ironically, the urban percentages that he presents are very close to mine. The reason for this is that his estimates of Europe's *total* population (in his case, all of Europe excluding Russia) are enormously in excess of those that I have been able to justify. The final similarity of our estimates is, thus, the consequence of a compounding of differences.

NOTES TO PAGES 71-3

	Total population in cities of 5000 and over ('000s)			
	1500	1600	1700	1800
Bairoch old	8,500	11,500	14,300	22,000
Bairoch new	7,040	9,920	12,130	—
De Vries	5,922	8,434	9,716	15,917

	Number of cities of 20,000 and over			
	1500	1600	1700	1800
Bairoch old	89	109	126	194
Bairoch new	93	112	128	—
De Vries	55	95	107	158

	Urban percentage of total population (in cities of 5000 and over)			
	1500	1600	1700	1800
Bairoch old	10.0	11.5	13.0	14.4
Bairoch new	9.4	10.4	11.9	—
De Vries	9.7	10.8	11.9	13.0

14 Eric E. Lampard, 'Historical contours of contemporary urban society: a comparative view', *Journal of Contemporary History* 4(1969), 3.

15 The statement that the world's urban population (in cities of over 5000 inhabitants) in 1800 totalled 27.2 million is a good example of a baseless number that gains authority through careless repetition. In 1954 and 1955 the demographer Kingsley Davis published accounts of world urbanization that included a table with the percentage of the world's population living in cities of 100,000 or more, and 20,000 and more. He also stated, in passing, that there were fewer than 900 cities of 5000 or more in the world in 1800 (Kingsley Davis, 'The origins and growth of urbanization in the world', *American Journal of Sociology* 60(1955), 433–4). The basis for these statements was described as 'statistical work . . . done as part of a continuing program of comparative urban research' (p. 433).

Philip Hauser drew the apparent implication of this information in his *Urbanization in Asia and the Far East* (UNESCO, 1957), 55–60. If all cities of 20,000 and over comprised 2.4 per cent of the world population, and if there were fewer than 900 cities of 5000 and over, the percentage in cities of 5000 and over could not be far from 3 per cent. A world population of 906 million in 1800 implies an urban population of 27.2 million.

Eric Lampard presented this conclusion in a table ('Historical aspects of urbanization' in Philip M. Hauser and Leo F. Schnore (eds), *The Study of Urbanization* (New York, 1965), 524). He cited Kingsley Davis and Hilda Hertz Golden *as cited by* P. M. Hauser. Hauser, in his introduction to the same volume, presented the same data (p. 7), citing Davis's *American Journal of Sociology* article.

Since then these 'back of the envelope' calculations have continued to circulate, although their provenance has been forgotten. We can find them repeated as facts not requiring substantiation in Gino Germani, *Modernization, Urbanization and the Urban Crisis* (Boston, 1973), 9; Jacques Lendert, 'The factors of urban population growth: net in-migration versus natural growth', *International Regional Science Review* 7(1982), 99; Andrei Rogers and Jeffrey G. Williamson, 'Migration, urbanization, and third world development: an overview', *Economic Development and Cultural Change* 30(1982), 463; and even in a Russian contribution to a Polish journal: Venyamin M. Gokhman, Grigorio M. Lappo, Issak M. Maergoiz and Yakov G. Mashbits, 'Characteristics of world urbanization and its features in individual countries', *Geographia Polonica* 37 (1977), 7-18.

Nor have the originators of these calculations turned their backs on them. Eric Lampard repeats them in his 'The nature of urbanization', in Derek Fraser and Anthony Sutcliffe (eds), *The Pursuit of Urban History* (London, 1983), 13; Hilda Hertz Golden puts forward a slight revision (the result of multiplying the sacred 3 per cent times a larger estimate of the world population) in her *Urbanization and Cities* (Lexington, Mass., 1981), 145.

Estimates of world urbanization before the twentieth century are bound to be speculative. But enough is known to show that the 'academic folk tradition' described above is very far from the mark. This study has demonstrated that Europe alone possessed more cities of at least 5000 in 1800 than Davis thought existed in the entire world. The following table summarizes recent scholarship on this issue, and shows that the world's 1200-odd cities of at least 10,000 inhabitants contained over 45 million people, while cities of at least 5000 certainly contained well over 60 million: more than double the 'traditional' estimate and, indeed, nearly equal to the urban population that Davis-Hauser-Lampard-*et al.* cite for 1850.

Region	10,000 and over Total population	Number	Aggregate urban population	Approximate percentage urban	Smaller cities Number	Aggregate urban population	Size category
1 China	400-330	310	12.0-10.0	3	1100	8.5	3000-10,000
2 Japan	32	83	3.8	12	250	1.3	3000-10,000
3 Russia	28	35	0.94	3	275	1.9	3000-10,000
4 Europe	123	363	12.2	10	545	3.7	5000-10,000
5 Europe-eastern	15	25	0.5	3			
6 Middle East	16	25	1.9	12			
7 India	200	c. 320	12.0	6			
8 Rest of eastern hemisphere	120	?	2.0	1.5			
9 North America	6	6	0.25	3			
10 South America	12	28	0.86	7			
11 Central America-Caribbean	7	?	0.25	3.5			
World	960-890	1195+	46.7-44.7	5			

1 *China* Gilbert Rozman, *Urban Networks in Russia 1750-1800, and Premodern Periodization* (Princeton, NJ, 1976), 242-4. The estimates are for the early nineteenth century, and are based on his *Urban Networks in Ch'ing China and Tokugawa Japan* (Princeton, NJ, 1973). G. William Skinner, in *The City in Late Imperial China* (Stanford, Calif.,

1977), 226, presents the following figures for 1893: a total population of 394 million (in China except Manchuria and Taiwan), with 877 cities of at least 4000 inhabitants, and an aggregate urban population of 20.8 million inhabitants. If Skinner's figures and Rozman's estimates are both accurate, the necessary conclusion is that neither the urban nor the total populations changed very much during the nineteenth century.

Other estimates place China's population around 1800 in the 320–40 million range: see Michael Cartier, 'La croissance démographique Chinoise du XVIII^c siècle et l'enregistrement des Pao-Chia', *Annales de démographie historique* (1979), 9–28; Louis Deriguy, *La China et l'Occident. Le commerce a Canton au XVIII siècle*, vol. II (Paris, 1964), 477–82. If the rate of urbanization were still 3 per cent, the urban population would be in the vicinity of 10 million.

2 *Japan* Rozman, idem.
3 *Russia* Rozman, idem. The figures are for Russia in 1782. At the time the Russian population was growing rapidly, so that by 1811 Rozman reckons there were 42 million inhabitants (50 per cent more than in 1782) and an urban population that was also 50 per cent greater than in 1782.
4 *Europe* This study, chapters 3 and 4. Note that Europe, too, was experiencing rapid growth at this time. The figures for 1780 or 1820 would be significantly different.
5 *Europe–eastern* Appendix 4.
6 *Middle East* Charles Issawi, 'Economic change and urbanization in the Middle east', in Ira M. Lapidus (ed.), *Middle Eastern Cities* (Berkeley and Los Angles, Calif., 1969), 101–4. The area covered in Issawi's survey embraces Egypt, Syria, Iraq and Turkey. See also Charles Issawi, *An Economic History of the Middle East and North Africa* (London, 1982), 100–1. There he appears to believe that in the areas stretching from Morocco to Iran, with some 30 million inhabitants in 1800, in excess of 3 million people lived in an unspecified number of cities of at least 10,000 inhabitants; 1 million of these lived in just seven large cities.
7 *India* Little is known about the population, let alone the urban population of the Indian subcontinent (modern India, Pakistan and Bangladesh), before the British-held census of 1881. Then over 6 per cent of the population of over 280 million inhabitants lived in 634 cities of at least 10,000 inhabitants. The most recent consideration of India's population before that date reckons that the population in 1800 stood at about 200 million (much higher than earlier guesses) and that the subcontinent had experienced de-urbanization in the course of the nineteenth century. The implication is that the urban population was relatively larger in 1800 than it is observed to have been at the end of the century (Irfan Habib, 'Population', in Tapan Raychaudhuri and Irfan Habib (eds), *Cambridge Economic History of India*, vol. I (Cambridge 1982), 163–71). The entry in the table makes the conservative assumption that the urban percentage in 1800 was no higher than in 1881. The number of cities is set at half the number at the end of the century. See also Kingsley Davis, *The Population of India and Pakistan* (Princeton, NJ, 1951).
8 *Rest of eastern hemisphere* In the absence of knowledge, I have adopted the minimal assumption of 1 per cent urbanization in Black Africa and south-east Asia. For North Africa and Iran I assume, following Issawi (see entry 6), an urban population of 1 million out of a total population of approximately 15–20 million.
9 *North America* The estimates refer to the United States and British North America. The indigenous populations beyond the eastern seaboard are not taken into account. For the United States see Allen Pred, *Urban Growth and the Circulation of Information: the United States System of Cities, 1790–1840* (Cambridge, Mass., 1973).
10 *South America* Richard M. Morse, 'Trends and patterns of Latin American urbanization, 1750–1920', *Comparative Studies in Society and History* 16(1974), 416–47. Morse's survey includes Argentina, Chile, Brazil, Peru, Columbia, Venezuela and Mexico. The remaining countries of Latin America plus the Caribbean islands are listed in entry 11.
11 *Rest of Latin America* see entry 10. In addition, see the collection of evidence presented in Woodrow Borah, 'Latin American cities in the eighteenth century: a sketch', in Woodrow Borah *et al.* (eds), *Urbanization in the Americas: The Background in Comparative Perspective* (Ottawa, 1980). Borah sets the total population of the New World south of the

NOTES TO PAGES 73-85

Rio Grande in 1800 at 20-22 million, and lists 29 cities of 10,000 or over with a total urban population of 933,000. His survey does not include the Caribbean except for Cuba.

CHAPTER 5   CITIES, SYSTEMS AND REGIONS

1 The literature on this concept is vast. See Brian J. L. Berry, 'Cities as systems within systems of cities', *Papers and Proceedings of the Regional Science Association* 13(1964), 147-63; Brian T. Robson, *Urban Growth: an Approach* (London, 1973), 16-41; Peter Hall and Dennis Hay, *Growth Centres in the European Urban System* (Berkeley and Los Angeles, Calif., 1980), 5-10; Allan Pred, *City-systems in Advanced Economies: Past Growth, Present Processes and Future Development Options* (New York, 1977); and the anthology of L. S. Bourne and J. W. Simmons (eds), *Systems of Cities: Readings on Structure, Growth, and Policy* (New York, 1978).
2 Allan Pred, *Urban Growth and City-systems in the United States, 1840-1860* (Cambridge, Mass., 1980), 2.
3 The above follows the discussion in Robson, *Urban Growth*, 16.
4 L. S. Bourne, *Urban Systems; Strategies for Regulation* (Oxford, 1975), 16.
5 Pred, *Urban Growth*, 2.
6 For an emphasis on national systems, see G. K. Zipf, *National Unity and Disunity* (Bloomington, Ind., 1941); and *Human Behavior and the Principle of Least Effort* (Cambridge, Mass., 1949), 417-44. For the relationship of systems to subsystems, see Chauncey Harris, *Cities in the Soviet Union* (Chicago, Ill., 1970), and G. William Skinner, 'Regional urbanization in nineteenth-century China', in G. William Skinner (ed.), *The City in Late Imperial China* (Stanford, Calif., 1977), 211-49. For daily commutation zones, see Brian J. L. Berry, *Growth Centers in the American Urban System*, 2 vols (Cambridge, Mass., 1973); Hall and Hay, *Growth Centres*, 1-26.
7 This is a central element in the 'world-economy' concept: see Immanuel Wallerstein, *The Modern World-System: Capitalist Agriculture and the Origins of the European World Economy in the Sixteenth Century* (New York, 1973), 301-4.
8 The importance of this aspect of the urban system is emphasized by Zipf, *Human Behavior*, in his explanation for London's large size (pp. 436-40), and more generally by R. J. Johnston, *City and Society: An Outline for Urban Geography* (London, 1980), 70-6.

CHAPTER 6   THE DEVELOPMENT OF AN URBAN HIERARCHY

1 A comprehensive and illuminating overview of the literature concerning theories of the distribution of city sizes is provided in Harry W. Richardson, 'Theory of the distribution of city sizes: review and prospects', *Regional Studies* 7(1973), 239-51. For a more elementary presentation consult Brian J. L. Berry and Frank E. Horton, *Geographic Perspectives on Urban Systems* (Englewood Cliffs, NJ, 1970), chapter 3.

2 While Zipf did much to popularize and apply this concept, he was not its discoverer. This honour probably goes to F. Auerbach, 'Das Gesetz der Bevölkerungskonzentration', *Petermann's Geographische Mitteilungen* 59(1913), 74–6. It was developed further in the work of A. J. Lotka, see particularly 'The law of urban concentration', *Science* 94(1941), 164.
3 G. K. Zipf, *Human Behavior and the Principle of Least Effort* (New York, 1949), 423.
4 Richardson, 'Review and prospects', 244.
5 Brian J. L. Berry, 'City size distribution and economic development', *Economic Development and Cultural Change* 9(1961), 587.
6 Two influential works advancing this position are H. Simon, 'On a class of skew distribution functions', *Biometrika* 42(1955), 425–40; B. Ward, 'City structure and interdependence', *Papers and Proceedings of the Regional Association* 22(1969), 207–21.
7 Berry, 'City size distributions'; Salah El Shakhs, 'Development, primacy and systems of cities', *Journal of Developing Areas* 7(1972), 11–36.
8 Berry and Horton, op. cit., 73–4.
9 Among many examples, see the historical application of this belief in Charles Tilly, *The Vendée* (Cambridge, Mass., 1964), 23–5.
10 Alejandro Portes. 'The economy and ecology of urban poverty', in A. Portes and J. Walton (eds), *Urban Latin America* (Austin, Tex., 1976); John Walton, 'Structures of power in Latin American cities', ibid.
11 E. A. J. Johnson, *The Organization of Space in Developing Countries* (Cambridge, Mass., 1970).
12 See, for example, Brian J. L. Berry, 'City size and economic development: conceptual synthesis and policy problems, with special reference to south and southeast Asia', in Leo Jakobson and Ved Prakash (eds), *Urbanization and National Development*, vol. I (Beverly Hills, Calif., 1971), 123, 132–4; J. R. Lasuen, A. Lorca and J. Oria, 'City-size distribution and economic growth', *Ekistics* 24(1967), 221–6.
13 El Shakhs, 'Development, primacy, and systems of cities'; P. J. M. Nes, *Stedenverdeling, nationale ontwikkeling en afhankelijkheid: een komparatief kwantatief benadering* (Leiden, 1976), pt II; Colin Clark, *Population Growth and Land Use* (New York, 1967), 321–7.
14 Carol A. Smith, 'Theories and measures of urban primacy: a critique', in Michael Timberlake (ed.), *Urbanization in the World Economy* (New York, forthcoming); Carol A. Smith, 'Modern and premodern urban primacy', *Comparative Urban Research* 11(1982), 79–96.
15 Smith, 'Modern and premodern urban primacy', 80.
16 Norton Ginsburg (ed.), *Atlas of Economic Development* (Chicago, Ill., 1961), 36.
17 J. Q. Stewart, 'The size and spacing of cities', *Geographical Review* 48(1958), 222–45; K. E. Rosing, 'A rejection of the Zipf model (rank-size rule) in relation to city size', *Professional Geographer* 18(1966), 75–82; Gregory A. Johnson, 'Rank-size convexity and system integration: a view from archeology', *Economic Geography* 56(1980), 234–47.
18 Brian T. Robson, *Urban Growth: An Approach* (London, 1973), 25.

19 Smith, 'Theories and measures of urban primacy', 7, note 11.
20 ibid., 16.
21 Robson, *Urban Growth*, 36–7.
22 For an account of how the depression affecting arable farming could redound to the benefit of the towns, see H. A. Miskimin, *The Economy of Early Renaissance Europe, 1300–1460* (Cambridge, 1975, second edn), 73–115.
23 Adna F. Weber, *The Growth of Cities in the Nineteenth Century: a Study in Statistics* (New York, 1899), 446.
24 Berry, 'City size and economic development', 144.
25 The data presented in figure 6.11 refer to all of Europe. The phenomenon of small-city growth was actually most pronounced in northern Europe in the period 1750–1800, and in Mediterranean Europe in the period 1800–50.
26 See David Ringrose, *Transportation and Economic Stagnation in Spain, 1750–1850* (Durham, 1970), and 'The impact of a new capital city: Madrid, Toledo, and New Castile, 1560–1660', *Journal of Economic History* 33(1973), 761–91.
27 The classic account is Fernand Braudel, *The Mediterranean and the Mediterranean World in the Age of Philip II*, 2 vols (New York, 1972).
28 See R. J. Johnston, *City and Society: an Outline for Urban Geography* (London, 1980), 66–74; P. J. M. Nes, 'Imperialism, city-size distribution and migration', *Sociologica Neerlandica* 10(1974), 219–32.
29 This position is advanced by Peter Hall in his much-consulted *The World Cities* (London, 1977, second edn), 118–49. He writes of the Rhine–Ruhr agglomeration as 'the greatest concentration of people on the European continent, including the U.S.S.R.' (p. 118). It numbers over 10 million inhabitants, but no single city of the region is truly large (Cologne has 848,000). Rather, the population is distributed among 22 cities of over 100,000 and many smaller municipalities.
30 Zipf, *Human Behavior*, 427–8.

CHAPTER 7 STABILITY AND DISCONTINUITY IN
EUROPEAN URBAN GROWTH

1 'The First Book, Entitled Clio', *The History of Herodotus*, trans. George Hawlinson (New York, 1882), vol. I, 121–2.
2 John Patten, *English Towns, 1500–1700* (Folkestone, 1978), 16.
3 Fernand Braudel, *Afterthoughts on Capitalism and Material Civilization* (Baltimore, Md, 1977), 85–6.
4 Allan Pred, *Urban Growth and City-systems in the United States, 1840–1860* (Cambridge, Mass., 1980), 2–3.
5 Arguably, a third city that does not now function as a capital should be included: Versailles.
6 The overall growth-rate of the 154 cities with at least 10,000 inhabitants in 1500 is distinctly lower than is that of the 216 'new' cities. But it must be borne in mind that these 216 are the rapid growers of a much larger set of cities. As a 'selected' group of rapid growers, their development cannot be directly compared to that of the overall category of larger cities.

NOTES TO PAGES 146-63

7 The size categories have been so arranged that the 'equivalent' categories for 1979 are five times the population of the 1800 categories.
8 The number of cities of 50,000-100,000 inhabitants is an estimate based on the number of such cities in those countries where one can be confident that the administrative boundaries do not drastically bias the count.
9 The disruptive effect of Madrid's rapid growth is described in David Ringrose, 'The impact of a new capital city: Madrid, Toledo, and New Castile, 1560-1660', *Journal of Economic History* 33(1973), 761-91. The position of Amsterdam as the dominant city of the northern Netherlands is unclear in 1500, is apparent only in retrospect by the 1560s, and was generally acknowledged by its competitors only in the 1590s.

CHAPTER 8   THE SPATIAL PATTERN OF EUROPEAN URBANIZATION

1 E. E. Arriaga, 'A new approach to the measurement of urbanization', *Economic Development and Cultural Change* 18(1969/70), 206-18.
2 Paul M. M. Klep, *Bevolking en arbeid in transformatie* (Nijmegen, 1981), 84-6.
3 For an elementary exposition of the concept, see Ronald Abler, John S. Adams and Peter Gould, *Spatial Organization* (Englewood Cliffs, NJ, 1971), 216-21.
4 I have adjusted two elements of the potential equation, a city's own potential (d_{ii}), and the effective effort required to communicate between any two cities (d_{ij}). The effect of the first adjustment is found at the centres of highest potential. If a large city's own potential were allowed to weigh very heavily, its total potential would be vastly greater than all other cities. The effect of the second adjustment is found at the margins – the precise shape of the isolines. A potential surface in which no account is taken of transport and communications costs would not differ from those presented here in the general location of zones of high and low potential. It would differ in the precise contours of the boundaries between such zones. Thus, my adjustments cause the isolines to include certain coastal cities in zones of higher potential, and certain inland towns in zones of lower potential than would be the case in the absence of adjustments. They do not relocate the centres of high potential, nor do they greatly affect the potential value of the high-potential centres.
5 Braudel, *Afterthoughts on Capitalism and Material Civilization* (Baltimore, Md, 1977), 85-6.
6 For data on Russian urbanization in the eighteenth century, see Gilbert Rozman, *Urban Networks in Russia, 1750-1800, and Premodern Periodization* (Princeton, NJ, 1976). See also appendix 4 for a review of data on urban populations east of the boundary used in this study.
7 In 1500 and 1600 about 45 per cent of all cities scored a potential value in excess of 50 per cent of the highest value. In 1750 about 60 per cent of all cities scored in excess of 30 per cent of the highest potential value.

CHAPTER 9 DEMOGRAPHY OF THE EARLY MODERN CITY

1 Alfred Perrenoud, *La population de Genève du seizième au début du dix-neuvième siècle. Etude démographique*, vol. I (Geneva, 1979), 411. For references to the concept of family reconstitutions see chapter 2, note 1.
2 See the classic work of Louis Henry, *Anciennes familles Genevoises: Etude démographique, 16e au 20e siècle* (Paris, 1956).
3 Roger Finlay, *Population and Metropolis: the Demography of London 1580–1650* (Cambridge, 1981), 12–13.
4 A. M. van der Woude and G. J. Mentink, *De demografische ontwikkeling te Rotterdam en Cool in de XVII en XVIII eeuw* (Rotterdam, 1965); a French summary is available in 'La population de Rotterdam au XVIIe et au XVIIIe siècle', *Population* 21(1966), 1165–90.
5 Alain Croix, *Nantes et le Pays Nantais au XVIe siècle. Etude démographique.* (Paris, 1974); Pierre Deyon, *Amiens, capitale provinciale. Etude sur la Société urbaine au 17e Siècle* (Paris, 1967); Maurice Garden, *Lyon et les Lyonnais au XVIIIe siècle* (Paris, 1970).
6 J. D. Chambers, 'Population changes in Nottingham', in L. S. Pressnell (ed.), *Studies in the Industrial Revolution, Presented to T. S. Ashton* (London, 1960); Herms Bahl, *Ansbach, Strukturanalyse einer Residenz vom Ende des Dreissigjährighen Krieges bis zur Mitte des 18. Jahrhunderts* (Ansbach, 1974), 213.
7 Ronald D. Lee, 'Estimating series of vital rates and age structure from baptisms and burials: a new technique, with applications to pre-industrial England', *Population Studies* 28(1974), 495–512; E. A. Wrigley and R. S. Schofield, *The Population History of England, 1541–1871: a Reconstruction* (London, 1981).
8 Wrigley and Schofield, op. cit., 733–5. Besides the vital events, one needs to know the ages at which migrants enter the city. They applied the migration age schedule for all Swedish towns in 1890.
9 Roger Mols, *Introduction à la démographie historique des villes d'Europe du 14e au 18e siècle*, 3 vols (Leuven, 1954–6).
10 ibid., vol. II, 183–99; Reinholt August Dorwart, *The Prussian Welfare State before 1740* (Cambridge, Mass., 1971); Mols, *Introduction*, vol. II, 198; A. Eisenbach and B. Grochulska, 'Population en Pologne (fin XVIIIe début XIXe siècle)', *Annales de démographie historique* (1965), 116–17; Fernand Braudel, *Capitalism and Material Life, 1400–1800* (New York, 1973), 422.
11 Karl Julius Beloch, *Bevölkerungsgeschichte Italiens*, vol. II (Berlin, 1937–61), 21.
12 For India, see Kingsley Davis, *The Population of India and Pakistan* (Princeton, NJ, 1951); for China, see G. William Skinner, 'Introduction: urban social structure in Ch'ing China', in *The City in Late Imperial China* (Stanford, Calif., 1977), 503–35.
13 Mols, *Introduction*, vol. III, 224–32.
14 John Graunt, *Natural and Political Observations and Conclusions made upon the Bills of Mortality* (London, 1662), reprinted in Peter Laslett (ed.), *The Earliest Classics: John Graunt and Gregory King* (Farnborough, 1973), 90.
15 Johann Peter Süssmilch, *Die Göttliche Ordnung in den Veränderungen des menschlichen Geschlechtes*, 3 vols, (Berlin, 1775, fourth edn).

16 ibid., vol. I, 75.
17 William Farr, *Vital Statistics* (London, 1885). Farr calculated mortality to vary with the twelfth root of the density of population (pp. 173–6).
18 Kingsley Davis, 'Cities and mortality', International Population and Urban Research, Institute of International Studies, University of California at Berkeley, reprint no. 433 (1973), 259–60. Davis holds that the inability of urban populations to reproduce themselves was not confined to the pre-nineteenth-century city. Using data from Stockholm he sought to show that this characteristic persisted into the twentieth century. In this he follows such observers as E. Levasseur, *La population Française* (Paris, 1889–92), vol. II, 386, and R. Boeckh, *Statistisch Jahrbuch Berlin* 19(1892), 94–5.
19 E. A. Wrigley, 'A simple model of London's importance in changing English society and economy', *Past and Present* 37(1967), 44–70.
20 Jan de Vries, *The Dutch Rural Economy in the Golden Age, 1500–1700* (New Haven, Conn., 1974), 115–17. Another exercise of this sort was made for France in Maurice Garden, 'La démographie des villes françaises du XVIIIe siècle: quelques approches', *Démographie urbaine XVe–XXe siècle*, Centre d'histoire économique et sociale de la région lyonnaise, no. 8 (Lyons, 1977), 43–85.
21 For efforts to tell a coherent story on the basis of the family reconstitution results, see Daniel Scott Smith, 'A homeostatic demographic regime: patterns in European family reconstitution studies', in Ronald D. Lee (ed.), *Population Patterns in the Past* (New York, 1977), 19–51; Michael Flinn, *The European Demographic System, 1500–1820* (London, 1981).
22 Allan Sharlin, 'Natural decrease in early modern cities: a reconsideration', *Past and Present* 79(1978), 127.
23 ibid. Sharlin's insight is foreshadowed in Adna F. Weber's discussion of urban demography in *The Growth of Cities in the Nineteenth Century: a Study in Statistics* (New York, 1899), 235.
24 ibid., 130.
25 A. M. van der Woude, 'Demografische ontwikkeling van de noordelijke Nederlanden 1500–1800', in *Algemene geschiedenis der Nederlanden*, vol. V (Haarlem, 1980), 143; see also his 'Population developments in the northern Netherlands (1500–1800) and the validity of the "urban graveyard" effect', *Annales de démographie historique* (1982), 55–75. An example of the viewpoint van der Woude is attacking is the following quotation from J. D. Chambers, *Population, Economy and Society in Pre-industrial England* (London, 1972), 103: 'The towns had been proverbial graveyards of successive generations of migrants . . . but . . . from about 1750 this trend was checked and before the end of the century was put into reverse. The urban population, *for the first time in its history*, was on the point of recruiting itself by a normal annual increment from its own natural increase' (my italics).
26 Van der Woude, 'Noordelijke Nederlanden', 143.
27 On the concept of 'secular trend' see Fernand Braudel and Frank Spooner, 'Prices in Europe from 1450–1750', in *Cambridge Economic History of Europe*, vol. IV (Cambridge, 1967), 379–486; B. H. Slicher van Bath, *Agrarian History*

of *Western Europe, 1500–1850* (London, 1963), pt III; E. Le Roy Ladurie and J. Goy, *Tithe and Agrarian History from the Fourteenth to the Nineteenth Century* (Cambridge and Paris, 1982); A. M. van der Woude, 'De "Nieuwe Geschiedenis" in een nieuwe gedaante', *Algemene geschiedenis der Nederlanden*, vol. V (Haarlem, 1980), 9–35.

28 Van der Woude, 'Noordelijke Nederlanden', 143.
29 David Ringrose, 'In migration, estroduras demograficas y tendencias economicas en Madrid a comiencos de la epocha moderna', *Moneda y crédito* 138(1976), 9–55; and his *Madrid and the Spanish Economy, 1560–1850* (Berkeley and Los Angeles, Calif., 1983), chapter 3.
30 Finlay, op. cit., 83–110; Alfred Perrenoud, 'L'inégalité sociale devant la mort à Genève au XVII^c siècle', *Population* 30(1975), numéro spécial, 221–43; Alfred Perrenoud, 'Croissance ou déclin? Les mécanismes du non-renouvellement des populations urbaines', *Histoire économie et société* 4(1982) 581–601.
31 For example, the demographic history of the Jews deserves special attention in view of the foregoing discussion.
32 Sharlin, op. cit., 137–8.
33 Ringrose, *Madrid and the Spanish Economy*, chapter 3.
34 Pierre Deyon 'Les sociétés urbaines', in Pierre Leon (ed.), *Histoire économique et sociale du monde*, vol. 2: *Les hésitations de la croissance, 1580–1730* (Paris, 1978), 302; E. Le Roy Ladurie and B. Quilliet, 'Baroque et lumières', in Georges Duby (ed.), *Histoire de la France urbaine*, vol. 3: *La Ville classique* (Paris, 1981), 301; Simon Hart, 'Geschrift en getal. Onderzoek naar samenstelling van de bevolking van Amsterdam in de 17e en 18e eeuw op grond van gegevens over migratie, huwelijk beroep en alfabetisme', in Simon Hart, *Geschrift en getal* (Dordrecht, 1976), 115–81.
35 Herman A. Diederiks, *Een stad in verval. Amsterdam omstreeks 1800* (Amsterdam, 1982), 75–85.
36 The words 'looking for' are not entirely correct. Since we can only observe persons seeking spouses who actually get them, nothing can be said about the characteristics of persons seeking spouses who never actually find them.
37 The causes of this relative shortage of young adult males can be sought in two areas. First, infant mortality among boys generally exceeds that among girls. Diederiks shows that this common pattern also obtained in Amsterdam around 1800 (pp. 35–6). The second and more important factor was migration. Many more young men than young women left the city. For a more detailed discussion of this phenomenon see pp. 210–12.
38 Diederiks, op. cit., 92.
39 ibid. Not only did migrants to the city marry later than native-born brides and grooms, but the more distant the birthplace of the migrant, the later the marriage age. This is indicated in a sample of marriages analysed by Diederiks for the years 1801 and 1806 (p. 97); Hart, op. cit., 205.
40 One is tempted to assume that migrants from afar arrive at their ultimate destination later than those migrating from nearby. This seems implicit in Ravenstein's 'second law of migration', that migration proceeds step-by-step (see D. B. Grigg, 'E. G. Ravenstein and the "laws of migration"', *Journal of*

Historical Geography 3(1977), 41–54). If this is true, then migrants from a distant place may be expected to have spent time in one or more smaller places before pushing on to a metropolis such as Amsterdam. One can then hypothesize that of a cohort born in a village, those who stay put will marry relatively young, those who find satisfactory opportunities in a nearby town will marry, on average, slightly later, and those who push on to more distant places take longer to 'settle down' and marry at more advanced ages.

41 Of all German men who married for the first time in Amsterdam in 1801 and 1806, fully 35 per cent were over 34 years of age. Among the Amsterdam-born only 6 per cent exceeded that age. Among women, 23 per cent of German-born were over 34 years of age while only 3 per cent of the Amsterdam-born were. A similar pattern of later marriage is evident when brides and grooms are categorized by church affiliation rather than birthplace. The Lutherans, including large numbers of German migrants, married later than the other denominations. Diederiks, op. cit., 93, 97.

42 Clear expositions of the effect of changes in the age at first marriage on total fertility can be found in Goren Ohlin, 'The positive and the preventative check', unpublished PhD dissertation, Harvard University (1955); E. A. Wrigley, *Population and History* (New York, 1969), 18–22. It is generally agreed that this variable was the single most important cause of change in the birth-rate in pre-industrial societies.

43 Bureau van statistiek der gemeente Amsterdam, *Statistiek der bevolking in Amsterdam tot 1921* (Amsterdam, 1923), 136, 179.

44 Diederiks, op. cit., 19, 60.

45 These statements are based on the following attempt to construct a life table for the late-eighteenth-century Amsterdam population. It makes the critical, and dangerous, assumption that the average pattern of births and deaths by age observed in the period 1777–97 can be taken to represent the annual flow of such events. The population of the city did not exhibit any long-term trend of growth or decline in this period, but there were fluctuations around the stable average number of annual births, deaths and marriages. The baptism and burial data were gathered in the *Nieuwe Nederlandsche Jaarboeken*, 1778–98; they are also represented in C. J. Nieuwenhuys, *Prove eener geneeskundige plaatsbeschrijving der Stad Amsterdam*, 3 vols (Amsterdam, 1820). The Jewish population of Amsterdam in the late eighteenth century was approximately 10 per cent of the total. Thus a Christian population of 198,600 plus 19,000 Jews would yield 217,000 inhabitants, which is the number arrived at by the 1795 census. This exercise implies that the average crude birth-rate stood at 32.3 per 1000, and the crude death-rate at 39.5 per 1000.

Note that the age-specific death-rates calculated for Amsterdam are very high for infants and children, exceeding even the third English life table level 4. From age 10 the pattern of deaths in Amsterdam conforms nicely to level 4, with its life expectancy at birth of 26 years. From age 55 the mortality suffered by Amsterdammers appears to become less severe. By age 70 it conforms best to the life table 10, with a life expectancy at birth of 40 years. It is possible, of course, that this pattern reflects an under-reporting of births and a tendency for older people to leave the city. The possible errors in this exercise are many. But it is interesting to observe that from ages 10 to 54, the simple net migration assumption (that net migration equalled the death surplus and was distributed over the age categories as shown in the table) yields a consistent, plausible pattern of age-specific deaths.

Age	Survivors at age	Average annual mortality	Assumed net immigration**	Age-specific death-rate 1000q_x	Wrigley–Schofield adaptation of third English life table			
					Level 3 $e_o 23.5$	Level 4 $e_o 26.0$	Level 6 $e_o 30.9$	Level 10 $e_o 40.7$
0	6437.0*	1879.5		292.0	279.2	255.8		
1	4557.5	1306.8		268.8	265.7	241.8		
5	3250.7	2299.0		91.4	91.9	83.7		
10	2951.4	146.7		49.7	49.3	45.0		
15	2804.7	146.8	732	52.3	58.3	53.5		
20	3389.9	236.7	366	69.8	77.6	71.4		
25	3519.2	236.7	366	67.3		79.3		
30	3648.5	304.5		83.5		87.7		
35	3344.0	304.6		91.2		97.8		
40	3039.4	348.1		114.5		109.0		
45	2691.3	348.1		129.3		124.5		
50	2343.2	343.5		146.6		146.7	126.5	
55	1999.7	343.5		171.8		191.0	164.9	
60	1656.2	366.7		221.4		256.4	223.4	
65	1289.5	366.7		284.4		353.4	310.7	
70	922.8	305.6		331.1			439.6	350.7
75	617.3	305.6		496.7			582.5	480.9
80	311.7	175.0		561.0				618.9
85	136.7	95.2		696.4				769.8
90	41.5	30.0		722.9				878.8
95	11.5	9.5		826.1				
100	2.0	2.0		1000.0				
105	0							

Implied population and age structure of Amsterdam: 1777–97 (Christian population only)

Age	Population	Percentage
0–19	64,100	31.0
20–59	113,713	57.3
60–over	20,805	10.5
Total	198,618	99.8

* Average annual baptisms.
** Difference between total baptisms and burials.

46 Perrenoud, 'Croissance ou déclin?' 581–601.
47 The data are drawn from Hart, op. cit., 136–43.

48 Van der Woude, 'Noordelijke Nederlanden', 149.
49 Nathan Keyfitz and Dimiter Philipov, 'Migration and natural increase in the growth of Cities', *Geographical Analysis* 13(1981), 288–9.
50 ibid., 288.
51 ibid.

CHAPTER 10 MIGRATION AND URBAN GROWTH

1 E. A. Wrigley and R. S. Schofield, *The Population History of England 1541–1871: a Reconstruction* (London, 1981), 268–9, 421–30.
2 ibid., 438–50. It must be emphasized that the demographic response to economic signals was not immediate. Wrigley and Schofield typically found the response delayed by many decades, provoking them to label the process of adjustment 'dilatory homeostasis'.
3 Allan Sharlin, 'Natural decrease in early modern cities: a reconsideration', *Past and Present* 79(1978), 126, note 2.
4 Bertrand Renaud, *National Urbanization Policy in Developing Countries* (New York and Oxford, 1981), 16–17.
5 This is the assumption underlying the analysis of urban growth found in Allan Pred, *Urban Growth and City-systems in the United States, 1840–1860* (Cambridge, Mass., 1980), 33–6.
6 John Patten, *English Towns, 1500–1700* (Folkestone, 1978), 127.
7 E. A. Wrigley, 'A simple model of London's importance in changing English society and economy', *Past and Present* 37(1967), 46–7.
8 Jan de Vries, *The Dutch Rural Economy in the Golden Age, 1500–1700* (New Haven, Conn., 1974), 116.
9 D. B. Grigg, 'E. G. Ravenstein and the "laws of migration"', *Journal of Historical Geography* 3(1977), 47.
10 Court records, in which witnesses are asked to state their past places of residence, are a good source for this sort of information. See Peter Clark, 'The migration in Kentish towns, 1580–1640', in Peter Clark and Paul Slack (eds), *Crisis and Order in English Towns, 1500–1700* (London, 1972), 117–63.
11 Throughout this exercise I use a straight-line method to estimate populations midway between two dates, or to estimate averages over fifty-year periods. Although this is a crude method, the data and the assumptions being made are such that more refined techniques would produce only a specious accuracy.
12 Jean-Claude Perrot, *Genèse d'une ville moderne. Caen au XVIIIe siècle*, vol. II (Paris, 1975), 160–5.
13 Henry Kamen, *Spain in the Later Seventeenth Century, 1665–1700* (London, 1980), 39.
14 J. R. Bruijn, F. S. Gaastra, I. Schöffer and E. S. van Eyck van Helsinga (eds), *Dutch–Asiatic shipping in the Seventeenth and Eighteenth Centuries*, vol. II: *Outward-bound Voyages from the Netherlands to Asia and the Cape (1595–1974)*; vol. III: *Homeward-bound Voyages from Asia and the Cape to the Netherlands (1597–1795)*, Rijksgeschiedkundige publicatieën, grote serie, nos 166 and 167 (The Hague, 1979); J. R. Bruijn, 'De personeelsbehoefte van de

VOC overzee en aan boord, bezien in Aziatisch en Nederlands perspectief', *Bijdragen en mededelingen betreffende de geschiedenis der Nederlanden* 91(1976), 218–48.
15 J. R. Bruijn and J. Lucassen, *Op de schepen der Oost-Indische Compagnie* (Groningen, 1980), 14. By their estimate, the VOC employed 11,000 sailors plus another 15,000 soldiers in 1725. At the same time 38,500 men functioned as sailors in the merchant marine, ocean fisheries and navy.
16 In a sample of 48,064 sailors who signed up with the VOC from 1637 to 1791, it was found that 60.2 per cent came from the Dutch Republic. Of those Dutch sailors, 88 per cent came from the maritime provinces. The vast majority of these in turn came from the cities; see the data presented in table 10.4. In the case of sailors in the Dutch navy, it is known that 85 per cent of the Dutch sailors came from the maritime provinces and 68 per cent from the cities. Bruijn and Lucassen, op. cit., 19, 139.
17 A. M. van der Woude, 'Demografische ontwikkeling van de noordelijke Nederlanden 1500–1800', in *Algemene geschiedenis der Nederlanden*, vol. V (Haarlem, 1980), 155.
18 For baptisms, Bureau van statistiek der gemeente Amsterdam, *Statistiek der bevolking in Amsterdam tot 1921* (Amsterdam, 1923), 136; for marriages, Simon Hart, 'Geschrift en getal. Onderzoek naar samenstelling van de bevolking van Amsterdam in de 17e en 18e eeuw op grond van gegevens over migratie, huwelijk beroep en alfabetisme', in Simon Hart, *Geschrift en getal* (Dordrecht, 1976), 136.
19 For a calculation of infant mortality see chapter 9, note 45. See also Herman A. Diederiks, *Een stad in verval. Amsterdam omstreeks 1800* (Amsterdam, 1982), 29–34.
20 As a general phenomenon see Wrigley and Schofield, op. cit., 225; H. S. Shryock and J. S. Siegel, *The Methods and Materials of Demography* (London, 1976), 228–9; for Amsterdam, see Diederiks, op. cit., 35–6.
21 Hart, op. cit., 136–43.
22 Wrigley and Schofield, op. cit., table 7.11.
23 See Michael Flinn, *The European Demographic System, 1500–1820* (London, 1981), 65–75, for an introduction to recent findings.
24 For glimpses of usually temporary war-induced migration see Myron Gutmann, *War and Rural Life in the Early Modern Low Countries* (Princeton, NJ, 1980), particularly 133–50.
25 This is the burden of the work of Peter Laslett, *The World We Have Lost* (London, 1965). See also the papers in Peter Laslett and Richard Wall (eds), *Household and Family in Past Times* (London, 1972).
26 John Wareing, 'Migration to London and transatlantic emigration of indentured servants, 1683–1775', *Journal of Historical Geography* 7(1981), 356–78. For the importance of short-distance migration see the survey in Grigg, op. cit., 44–7; for a detailed study of this phenomenon, see David W. Sabean, 'Household formation and geographical mobility: a family register study for a Württemberg village, 1760–1900', *Annales de démographie historique* (1970), 275–94.

27 Hart, op. cit., 170.
28 C. A. Davids, 'Migratie te Leiden in de achttiende eeuw: een onderzoek op grond van de acten van cautie', in H. A. Diederiks *et al.*, *Een stad in achteruitgang* (Leiden, 1978), 173-4; Herms Bahl, *Ansbach, Strukturanalyse einer Residenz vom Ende des Dreissigjährigen Krieges bis zur Mitte des 18. Jahrhunderts; Verfassung, Verwaltung, Bevölkerung und Wirtschaft* (Ansbach, 1974), 187.
29 Karl Marx, *Capital*, vol. I (Moscow, 1961), chapter 28, 734; see also chapter 30, 748-9; J. D. Chambers, 'Enclosure and labour supply in the Industrial Revolution', *Economic History Review* 5(1952-3), 319-43.
30 See B. H. Slicher van Bath, *Agrarian History of Western Europe, 1500-1850* (London, 1963), 340-56; Karlheinz Blaschke, *Bevölkerungsgeschichte von Sachsen bis zur industriellen Revolution* (Weimar, 1967), 190-1; E. L. Jones, 'The agricultural origins of industry', *Past and Present* 40(1968), 58-71; Joan Thirsk, 'Industries in the countryside', in F. J. Fisher (ed.), *Essays in the Economic and Social History of Tudor and Stuart England* (London, 1961), 70-88. For a general discussion of this issue, see Jan de Vries, 'Poverty and capitalism; review essay', *Theory and Society* 12(1983), 245-55.
31 Among the many works on the subject of migration see William McNeill (ed.), *Human Migration: Patterns, Implications, Policies* (Bloomington, Ind., 1978); F. Wilcox (ed.), *International Migration*, 2 vols (New York, 1931); *Annales de démographie historique* (1970), special number on migration; Paul White and Robert Woods (eds), *The Geographical Impact of Migration* (London, 1980); Peter A. Morrison (ed.), *Population Movements: Their Forms and Functions in Urbanization and Development* (Liège, 1980).
32 Nathan Keyfitz and Dimiter Philipov, 'Migration and natural increase in the growth of cities', *Geographical Analysis* 13(1981), 294.
33 E. J. T Collins, 'Labour supply and demand in European agriculture, 1800-1880', in E. L. Jones and S. J. Woolf (eds), *Agrarian Change and Economic Development* (London, 1969), 61-94.
34 Franklin Mendels, 'Social mobility and phases of industrialization', *Journal of Interdisciplinary History* 7(1976), 198.
35 Roger Finlay, *Population and Metropolis* (Cambridge, 1981), 156.
36 Brian Pullan, 'Wage-earners and the Venetian economy, 1550-1630', *Economic History Review* 16(1964), 407-26.
37 Richard T. Rapp, *Industry and Economic Decline in Seventeenth Century Venice* (Cambridge, Mass., 1976), 22.
38 Patten, *English Towns*, 132.
39 Pred, *Urban Growth*, 31.
40 For an introduction to this literature see Franklin Mendels, 'Proto-industrialization: the first phase of the industrialization process; *Journal of Economic History* 32(1972), 241-61; Peter Kriedte, Hans Medick and Jürgen Schlumbohm, *Industrialization before Industrialization: Rural Industry in the Genesis of Capitalism* (Cambridge and Paris, 1981); Pierre Deyon and Franklin Mendels (eds), 'La proto-industrialisation. Théorie et réalité', *Revue du Nord* 63(1981), special issue. To avoid confusion over nomenclature it will be of help to note here that my use of 'protoindustry' corresponds to rural industrial production

for non-local markets. It is a component part of a larger process of economic reorganization, 'protoindustrialization', that also involves commercial agriculture and urban marketing functions. I follow Mendels in using 'protoindustrialization' to refer to such a regional structure, and not simply to the spread of cottage industry.

41 See for instance Herbert Kish, 'The growth deterrents of a medieval heritage; the Aachen area woollen trades before 1790', *Journal of Economic History* 24(1964), 513–37; E. C. G. Brünner, *De ordre op de buitennering van 1531* (Amsterdam, 1921).

42 Rural industry existed much earlier, of course. The English textile industry exploited rural locations on a substantial scale in the Middle Ages. But the phenomenon becomes widespread and assumes a quantitatively important position in the course of the sixteenth and seventeenth centuries.

43 See Mendels, 'Proto-industrialization'; Rudolf Braun, *Industrialisierung und Volksleben* (Zurich, 1960); David Levine, *Family Formation in an Age of Nascent Capitalism* (New York, 1977).

44 J. Täck, *Hollandsgänger in Hannover und Oldenburg. Ein Beitrag zur Geschichte der Arbeiter-Wanderung* (Leipzig, 1902).

45 But even here we must be careful not to exaggerate the downward plunge involved in the switch from marginal farmer to cottage weaver with garden plot. The separation from the means of production involved in this change may well have been compensated for by an increased, and no less secure, income. For a clarifying discussion, see Paul M. M. Klep, *Bevolking en arbeid in transformatie* (Nijmegen, 1981), 310–11.

46 Keyfitz and Philipov, 'Migration and natural increase', 294.

47 Andrei Rogers, 'Migration patterns and population redistribution', *Regional Science and Urban Economics* 9(1979), 302.

48 Wilbur Zelinsky, 'The hypothesis of the mobility transition', *Geographical Review* 61(1971), 222.

49 The point at which natural increase becomes more important than migration as a source of population growth has been called a cross-over point. The more rapid the rate of growth, the sooner such a point is reached. Of course, if the rate of natural increase is negative, no cross-over point is ever reached. On this subject see Nathan Keyfitz, 'Do cities grow by natural increase or by migration?', *Geographical Analysis* 12(1980), 143–56.

50 Charles Tilly, 'Demographic origins of the European proletariat', Center for Research on Social Organization working paper no. 207, University of Michigan (1979); the argument is summarized in Charles Tilly, *As Sociology Meets History* (New York, 1981), 191–210. David Levine, 'The English proletariat makes itself', unpublished paper presented to the Conference on British Demographic History, Asilomar, Calif. (March 1982).

51 Notable among the few exceptions are Richard Goldthwaite, *The Building of Renaissance Florence* (Baltimore, Md, 1981); C. W. Chalkin, *The Provincial Towns of Georgian England: a Study of the Building Process, 1740–1820* (London, 1974).

52 W. Arthur Lewis, *Growth and Fluctuations, 1870–1913* (London, 1978), 145–9.

53 It must be emphasized that these rates are not based on the *total* population, but on the *urban* population. Thus, in the first half of the seventeenth century the urban population grew by 0.6 per cent per annum. This should not be confused with the rate of urbanization.
54 See Charles Tilly, 'Food supply and public order in modern Europe', in Charles Tilly (ed.), *The Formation of National States in Western Europe* (Princeton, NJ, 1975), 380–455.
55 See Jan de Vries, *The Economy of Europe in an Age of Crisis, 1600–1750* (Cambridge, 1976), chapter V, 146–75.
56 ibid., 34–6.
57 B. H. Slicher van Bath, 'The yields of different crops (mainly cereals) in relation to the seed, *ca.* 810–1820', *Acta historiae neerlandica* 2(1967), 26–106.
58 This argument is most forcefully presented in Michel Morineau, 'Y a-t-il eu une révolution agricole en France du 18ᵉ siècle?', *Revue historique* 486(1968), 299–326. For a summary of findings, see E. Le Roy Ladurie and J. Goy, *Tithe and Agrarian History from the Fourteenth to the Nineteenth Century* (Cambridge and Paris, 1982), pt II.
59 Le Roy Ladurie and Goy, op. cit., 133–5.
60 J. Topolski and A. Wyczanski, 'Les fluctuations de la production agricole en Pologne aux XVIᵉ–XVIIᵉ siècles', *Actes du colloque préparatoire* (Paris, forthcoming), cited in ibid., 93–4.
61 See N. F. R. Crafts, 'English economic growth in the eighteenth century: a re-examination of Deane and Cole's estimates', *Economic History Review* 29(1976), 226–35.
62 See the contributions of M. Aymard and J. Revel, among others, in *Actes du colloque préparatoire*, and of course Fernand Braudel, *The Mediterranean and the Mediterranean World in the Age of Philip II* (New York, 1972).
63 Thomas C. Smith, 'Pre-modern economic growth: Japan and the west', *Past and Present* 60(1973), 130.
64 ibid., 149.
65 ibid., 147.
66 Fernand Braudel, *Capitalism and Material Life, 1400–1800* (New York, 1973), 440.
67 See, for example, the classic of economic development theory, John C. Fei and Gustav Ranis, *Development of the Labor Surplus Economy* (Homewood, Ill., 1964).
68 Bert F. Hoselitz, 'The role of cities in the economic growth of underdeveloped countries', *Journal of Political Economy* 61(1953), 197.
69 J. G. Williamson and J. A. Swanson, 'The growth of cities in the American Northeast, 1820–1870', *Explorations in Entrepreneurial History* 4(1966), 44–67; J. G. Williamson, 'Antebellum urbanization in the American Northeast', *Journal of Economic History* 25(1965), 592–608.
70 A more extended discussion of this issue is presented in E. A. Wrigley, 'Parasite or stimulus: the town in a pre-industrial economy', in Philip Abrams and E. A. Wrigley (eds), *Towns and Society: Essays in Economic History and Historical Sociology* (Cambridge, 1978), 295–309.

NOTES TO PAGES 247–66

71 See David Clark, *Urban Geography* (London, 1982), 40–5.
72 Wrigley, 'Parasite or stimulus', 296–9.
73 David Ringrose, *Madrid and the Spanish Economy, 1560–1850* (Berkeley and Los Angeles, Calif., 1983).
74 F. J. Fisher, 'London as an engine of economic growth', in J. S. Bromley and E. H. Kossman (eds), *Britain and the Netherlands*, vol. IV (The Hague, 1971), 3–16; E. A. Wrigley, 'Simple model'.

CHAPTER 11 CONCLUSIONS

1 For an argument consistent with this viewpoint, see R. J. Johnston, *City and Society: an Outline for Urban Geography* (London, 1980), 98.
2 I argue this case in Jan de Vries, *The Economy of Europe in an Age of Crisis, 1600–1750* (Cambridge, 1976), chapter V.
3 Charles Tilly, *The Vendée* (Cambridge, Mass., 1964), 22–3; Adna F. Weber, *The Growth of Cities in the Nineteenth Century: a Study in Statistics* (New York, 1899), 155–229.
4 Johnston, op. cit., 98, 106.
5 Gilbert Rozman, *Urban Networks in Russia, 1750–1800, and Premodern Periodization* (Princeton, NJ, 1976), 283.
6 ibid., 250.
7 G. William Skinner, 'Regional urbanization in nineteenth century China', in G. William Skinner (ed.), *The City in Late Imperial China* (Stanford, Calif., 1977), 249.
8 Recent estimates of the population of China *c.* 1800 range between 350 and 400 million. See Michel Cartier, 'La croissance démographique Chinoise du XVIIIe siècle et l'enregistrement des Pao-Chia', *Annales de démographie historique* (1979), 9–28, whose estimate for 1818 is 375 million.
9 On the concept of 'balanced' and 'unbalanced' growth see Alfred O. Hirschman, *The Strategy of Economic Development* (New Haven Conn., 1958).
10 Jean Gottmann, *Megalopolis: the Urbanized Northeastern Seaboard of the United States* (New York, 1961).
11 These and other potential megalopoli are discussed in Peter Hall *et al.*, *The Containment of Urban England* (London and Beverley Hills, Calif., 1973), vol. I, 49–58.
12 Peter Hall, *The World Cities*:

> We have seen that in the century and a half since the industrial revolution, almost without exception all these metropolitan centres have shown continuous population growth, both absolutely and in relation to the countries of which they form a part. We have found this to be true in countries large and small, densely and sparsely populated, capitalist and communist; countries dedicated to laissez-faire, and countries wedded to the idea that planning may control growth.
>
> In the first edition (London, 1966) Hall hinted that we should expect this trend to persist into the future. In the second edition (London 1977) he adds: 'In

almost every respect, by the mid-1970s the world of the urban planner seemed quite different, even opposite, from that of the mid-1960s' (pp. 240, 252). C. A. Doxiadis argued that twelve great concentrations of urban population will characterize the United States by the year 2060. The futurologists Herman Kahn and A. J. Weiner in *The Year 2000* (New York, 1967) foresaw a United States with three gargantuan megalopoli (Boston–Washington, Chicago–Pittsburgh, and San Francisco–San Diego) which together would contain over half the United States population.

13 David Clark, *Urban Geography* (London, 1982), 69. This is the view of Brian J. L. Berry, expressed in *The Human Consequences of Urbanisation* (New York, 1973).

14 Thus Berry now writes of 'counterurbanization', for which he supplies a definition that is the mirror image of Tisdale's classic definition of urbanization: 'Counterurbanization is a process of population deconcentration; it implies a movement from a state of more concentration to a state of less concentration' (Brian J. L. Berry, 'The counterurbanization process: urban America since 1970', in Brian J. L. Berry (ed.), *Urbanization and Counterurbanization* (Beverley Hills, Calif., 1976), 17).

15 Lewis Mumford, *The City in History, its Origins, its Transformations, and its Prospects* (New York, 1961); E. P. Thompson, *The Making of the English Working Class* (London, 1963), 352–6.

BIBLIOGRAPHY

The bibliography consists of three parts. The first section lists all secondary works cited in appendix 2 and elsewhere as sources for the population estimates of cities and territories. The second section lists the censuses, census-like materials and major compendia that are cited as sources. The third section lists works that bear on the analysis. However, relevant works already listed in the first section are not listed again in the third.

Where more than one entry is listed for a single author, they are presented in *chronological* order.

SOURCES FOR POPULATION ESTIMATES

Abel, Wilhelm, *Agrarkrisen und Agrarkonjunktur* (Hamburg and Berlin, 1978, third edn); published in English as *Agricultural Fluctuations in Europe* (London, 1980).
Aden, Otto, *Entwicklung und Wechsellagen ausgewählter Gewerbe in Ostfriesland von der mitte des 18. bis zum ausgang des 19. Jahrhunderts* (Aurich, 1964).
Aleati, G., *La popolazione di Pavia durante il dominio spagnolo* (Milan, 1957).
Appleby, Andrew B., *Famine in Tudor and Stuart England* (Stanford, Calif., 1978).
Arends, F., *Ostfriesland und Jever in geographischer, statistischer und besonders landwirtschiftlicher Hinsicht*, 3 vols (Emden, 1818–20).
Armengaud, Andre, Reinhard, Marcel and Dupâquier, Jacques, *Histoire générale de la population mondiale* (Paris, 1968).
Armin, Volkmar von, *Krisen und Konjunkturen der Landwirtschaft in Schleswig-Holstein vom 16. bis zum 18. Jahrhundert* (Neumünster, 1957).
Arnould, Maurice, 'Les dènombrements de foyers en Hainaut, XIVe–XVI[e]siècle', *Bulletin de statistique* 37(1951).
Artola, Miguel, *La Espana del Antigua Regimen*, vol. VI: *Castilla La Nueva y Extremadura* (Salamanca, 1971).
Aubin, H. and Zorn, Wolfgang, *Handbuch der deutschen Wirtschafts- und Sozialgeschichte*, vol. I (Stuttgart, 1971).

BIBLIOGRAPHY

Baehrel, René, *La Basse-Provence rurale, fin XVIe siècle – 1789: une croissance, essai d'économie historique statistique*, 2 vols (Paris, 1961).

Bahl, Herms, *Ansbach, Strukturanalyse einer Residenz vom Ende des Dreissigjährigen Krieges bis zur Mitte des 18. Jahrhunderts; Verfassung, Verwaltung, Bevölkerung und Wirtschaft* (Ansbach, 1974).

Banck, R., 'Die Bevölkerung der Stadt Köln in der 2. Hälfte des 16. Jahrhundert', *Beiträge zur Geschichte Kölns und der Rheinlande zur 80. Geburstag G. v. Merissens* (Cologne, 1895).

Bardet, Jean-Pierre, *Rouen aux XVIIe et XVIIIe siècles. Les mutations d'un espace social*, 2 vols (Paris, 1983).

Batista I Roca, J. M., 'The Hispanic kingdoms and the Catholic kings', in *New Cambridge Modern History*, vol. I: *The Renaissance 1493–1520* (Cambridge, 1971), 316–42.

Bellettini, Athos, *La popolazione di Bologna dal secolo XV all unificazione italiana* (Bologna, 1961).

Beltrami, Daniele, *Storia della popolazione di Venezia dalla fine del secolo XVI alla caduta della Repubblica* (Padua, 1954).

Bennassar, Bartolomé, *Valladolid au siècle d'or. Une ville de Castille et sa campagne au XVIe siècle* (Paris, 1967).

Berents, D. A., 'Gegoeide burgerij in Utrecht in de 15e eeuw', *Jaarboek oud Utrecht* (1972), 78–92.

Beresford, Maurice, 'The making of a townscape: Richard Paley in the east end of Leeds, 1771–1803', in C. W. Chalkin and M. A. Havinden (eds), *Rural Change and Urban Growth, 1500–1800* (London, 1974).

Bickel, Wilhelm, *Bevölkerungsgeschichte und Bevölkerungspolitik des Schweiz, seit dem Ausgang des Mittelalters* (Zurich, 1947).

Biraben, Jean-Noël, 'La population de Reims et de son arrondissement et la vérification statistique, des recensements numériques ancients', *Population* 16(1961), 722–30.

——, 'Certain demographic characteristics of the plague epidemic in France, 1720–22', *Daedalus* 97(1968), 536–45.

——, *Les Hommes et la peste en France et dans les pays européens et méditerranéens*, 2 vols (Paris, 1975).

Blaschke, Karlheinz, *Bevölkerungsgeschichte von Sachsen bis zur industriellen Revolution* (Weimar, 1967).

Blockmans, W. P., Pieters, G., Prevenier, W. and van Schaïk, R. W. M., 'Tussen crisis en welvaart: sociale veranderingen 1300–1500', *Algemene geschiedenis der Nederlanden*, vol. 4 (Haarlem, 1980), 42–86.

Blom, Grethe Authén (ed.), *Urbaniseringsprosessen i Norden*, 3 vols (Oslo, 1977).

Bocquet, André, *Recherches sur la population rurale de l'Artois et du Boulonnais pendant la période bourguignonne, 1384–1477* (Arras, 1969).

Bonnoure, P. and Dupâquier, J., 'Anciennes statistiques Tchèques', *Annales de démographie historique* (1966), 401–10.

Borah, Woodrow et al. (eds), *Urbanization in the Americas: The Background in Comparative Perspective* (Ottawa, 1980).

Bouchard, G., 'Dijon au XVIIIe siècle. Les dénombrements d'habitants', *Annales de*

368

BIBLIOGRAPHY

Bourgogne 25(1953), 30-65.

Bougard, Pierre, 'Denombrement de la population du Cambresis', in Société de démographie historique, *Sur la population Française au XVIIIe et au XIXe siècles. Hommage à Marcel Reinhard* (Paris, 1973), 71-89.

—— and Reinhard, Marcel, *Les Sources de l'histoire démographique du département du Pas de Calais (1789-1815)* (Paris, 1964).

Boutruche, Robert (ed.), *Bordeaux de 1453 à 1715*, vol. 4 of Charles Higonnet (ed.), *Histoire de Bordeaux* (Bordeaux, 1966).

Braudel, Fernand and Labrousse, Ernest (eds), *Histoire économique et sociale de la France*, tome 1, vol. 1 (Paris, 1977).

Brouwer, J. de, *Demografische evolutie van het Land van Aalst, 1570-1800*, Pro civitate, historische uitgaven, vol. 18 (Brussels, 1968).

Brulez, Wilfried, 'Les difficultes financières de la ville de St-Omer dans la troisième quart du XVIe siècle', *Revue du Nord* 34(1952), 219-25.

Bücher, Karl, *Die Bevölkerung von Frankfurt am Main im XIV. und XV. Jahrhundert* (Tübingen, 1886).

Buchholz, Ernest, *Ländliche Bevölkerung an der Schwelle des Industriezeitalters. Der Raum Braunschweig als Beispiel* (Stuttgart, 1966).

Bureau van statistiek der gemeente Amsterdam, *Statistiek der bevolking in Amsterdam tot 1921* (Amsterdam, 1923).

Bureau voor statistiek en voorlichting der gemeente 's-Gravenhage, *Zeven eeuwen 's-Gravenhage* (The Hague, 1948).

Butlin, R. A., *The Development of the Irish Town* (London, 1977).

Carbourdin, G., *Terre et hommes de Lorraine, 1550-1635*, Annales de l'Est, memoire 55 (Nancy, 1977).

Carriere, Charles, *Negociants Marseillais au XVIIIe siècle* (Marseilles, 1973).

Carstenn, Edward, *Geschichte der Hansestadt Elbing* (Elbing, 1937).

Cartier, Michel, 'La croissance démographique Chinoise du XVIIIe siècle et l'enregistrement des Pao-Chia', *Annales de démographie historique* (1979), 9-28.

Chalkin, C. W., *The Provincial Towns of Georgian England: a Study of the Building Process, 1740-1820* (London, 1974).

—— and Havinden, M. A. (eds), *Rural Change and Urban Growth 1500-1800: Essays in English Regional History in Honour of W. G. Hoskins* (London, 1974).

Chambers, J. D., 'Population changes in Nottingham', in L. S. Pressnell (ed.), *Studies in the Industrial Revolution, Presented to T. S. Ashton* (London, 1960).

Chandler, Tertius and Fox, Gerald, *Three Thousand Years of Urban Growth* (New York, 1974).

Charlier, J., *La peste à Bruxelles de 1667 à 1669 et ses conséquences démographiques*, Pro civitate, historische reeks, vol. 20 (Brussels, 1969).

Chartier, R. and Neveux, H., 'L'armature urbaine', in Georges Duby (ed.), *Histoire de la France urbaine, tome 3, La ville classique* (Paris, 1981).

Cipolla, Carlo, *Before the Industrial Revolution: European Society and Economy, 1000-1700* (New York, 1976).

Clark, Peter, 'The migration in Kentish towns, 1580-1640', in Peter Clark and Paul Slack (eds), *Crisis and Order in English Towns, 1500-1700* (London, 1972), pp. 117-63.

—— (ed.), *The Early Modern Town: a Reader* (New York, 1976).
—— and Slack, Paul (eds), *Crisis and Order in English Towns 1500–1700* (London, 1972).
——, *English Towns in Transition 1500–1700* (Oxford, 1976).
Clarkson, L. A., *The Pre-Industrial Economy in England, 1500–1750* (London, 1971).
Cleland, James, *Statistical and Population Tables Relative to the City of Glasgow* (Glasgow, 1828).
Collier, R. and J. Billioud, '1480 à 1599', in Gaston Rambert (ed.), *Histoire du commerce de Marseille*, vol. 3 (Marseilles, 1951).
Coniglio, Guiseppe, *Ill viceregno di Napoli nel secolo XVII* (Rome, 1955).
Connell, K. H., *The Population of Ireland, 1750–1845* (Oxford, 1950).
Coppolani, Jean, *Toulouse au XXe siècle* (Toulouse, 1963).
Corfield, P. J., 'A provincial capital in the late seventeenth century: the case of Norwich', in Peter Clark and Paul Slack (eds), *Crisis and Order in English Towns 1500–1700* (London, 1972).
——, 'Urban development in England and Wales in the sixteenth and seventeenth centuries', in D. C. Coleman and A. H. John (eds), *Trade, Government and Economy in Pre-Industrial England* (London, 1976), 214–47.
——, *The Impact of English Towns, 1700–1800* (Oxford, 1982).
Cosemans, A., *De bevolking van Brabant in de XVIIde en XVIIIde eeuw* (Brussels, 1939).
——, *Bijdrage tot de demografische en sociale geschiedenis van de stad Brussel, 1796–1846*, Pro civitate, historische uitgaven, vol. 12 (Brussels, 1966).
Court, W. H. B., *Rise of the Midland Industries, 1600–1838* (London, 1938).
Croix, Alain, *Nantes et le Pays Nantais au XVIe siècle. Etude démographique* (Paris, 1974).
——, *La Bretagne aux 16e et 17e siècles; la vie – la morte – la foi*, 2 vols (Paris, 1981).
Cullen, L. M., 'Population trends in seventeenth-century Ireland', *Economic and Social Review* 6(1975), 149–65.
——, *An Economic History of Ireland since 1660* (London, 1976a).
——, 'Economic trends 1660–91', in T. W. Moody et al., *A New History of Ireland*, vol. III (Oxford, 1976b), 387–407.
Cuvelier, J., 'La population de Louvain au XVIIe siècle', *Annales de la société royale d'archeologie de Bruxelles* 22(1908), 337–76.
—— (ed.), *Les dénombrements de foyers en Brabant (XIVe–XVIe siècle)*, 2 vols (Brussels, 1912–13).
Dabrowski, J. (ed.), *Kraków. Studia nad rozwojem miasta* (Krakow, 1957).
Daelemans, F., 'Leiden 1581. Een socio-demografisch onderzoek', *A.A.G. Bijdragen* 19(1975), 137–215.
Dardel, P., *Navires et marchandises dans les ports de Rouen et Le Havre au XVIIIe siècle* (Paris, 1963).
Da Silva, José-Gentil, 'Au Portugal: structure démographique et développement économique', *Studi in onore di Amintore Fanfani*, vol. II (Milan, 1962), 490–510.
——, 'L'autoconsommation au Portugal (XIVe–XXe siècles)', *Annales E.S.C.* 24(1969), 250–88.

BIBLIOGRAPHY

Degn, Ole, 'De nylagte byer og byudviklingen Danmark 1600–1800', in Grethe Authén Blom (ed.), *Urbaniseringsprosessen i Norden*, vol. 2 (Oslo, 1977).

Demey, J., 'Bevolking en weefgetouwen in Ieper van de XIIIe tot de XVIIe eeuw', *Belgisch tijdschrift voor philologie en geschiedenis* 28(1950), 1031–48.

De Seta, Cesare, *Storia della citta di Napoli dalle origini al Settocento* (Bari, 1973).

Desportes, P., 'La population de Reims au XVe siècle d'après un dénombrement du 1422', *Le moyen-age* 3–4(1966), 463–509.

Devine, T. M., 'The merchant class of the larger Scottish towns in the seventeenth and early eighteenth centuries', in George Gordon and Brian Dicks (eds), *Scottish Urban History* (Aberdeen, 1983), 92–111.

Deyon, Pierre, *Amiens, capitale provinciale. Etude sur la société urbaine au 17e siècle* (Paris, 1967).

——, 'De dénombrements et structure urbaines', *Revue du Nord* 210(1971), 495–508.

Dillen, J. G. van, 'Summiere staat van de in 1622 in de provincie Holland gehouden volkstelling', *Economisch-historisch jaarboek* 21(1940), 167–89.

Długoborski, W., Gierowski, Jozef and Maleczyński, Karol, *Dzieje Wrocławia do roku 1807* (Warsaw, 1958).

Dominguez Ortiz, Antonio, *La sociedad española en el siglo XVII*, 3 vols (Madrid, 1963).

Doolittle, I. G., 'The effects of the plague on a provincial town in the sixteenth and seventeenth centuries', *Medical History* 19(1975), 333–41.

Dorwart, Reinholt August, *The Prussian Welfare State before 1740* (Cambridge, Mass., 1971).

Drake, Michael, *Population and Society in Norway, 1735–1865* (Cambridge, 1969a).

—— (ed.), *Population in Industrialization* (London, 1969b).

Dresden, 'The Bills of Mortality for the Town of Dresden for a whole Century, viz. from the Year 1617 to 1717, containing the Numbers of Marriages, Births, Burials, and Communicants', *Philosophical Transactions of the Royal Society* 32(1723), 454–69.

Dreyer-Roos, Suzanne, *La population Strasbourgeoise sous l'ancien régime* (Strasburg, 1969).

Dreyfus, François G., 'Prix et population à Trèves et à Mayence au XVIIIe siècle', *Revue d'histoire économique et sociale* 34(1968), 241–61.

Dupâquier, Jacques, *La Population rurale du bassin parisien à l'époque de Louis XIV* (Paris, 1979a).

——, *La Population française aux XVIIe et XVIIIe siècles* (Paris, 1979b).

Dupeux, Georges, 'La croissance urbaine en France au XIXe siècle', *Revue d'histoire économique et sociale* 52(1974), 173–89.

——, 'Maps of the cities of France, 1809–12', *Urbanism Past and Present* 3(1977–8), 5–8.

Du Plessis, Robert, 'Charité municipale et authorité publique au XVIème siècle: l'example de Lille', *Revue du Nord* 59(1977), 193–219.

Dury, George H., *The East Midlands and the Peak* (London, 1963).

Dyer, A. D., *The City of Worcester in the Sixteenth Century* (Leicester, 1973).

Dyrvik, Stale, 'Historical demography in Norway 1660–1801: a short survey', *Scandinavian Economic History Review* 20(1972), 27–44.

Ehebergs, K. Th., 'Strassburgs Bevölkerungszahl seit dem Ende des 15. Jahrhunderts bus zur Gogenwart', *Jahrbücher für national Okonomie und Statistik* 41(1883), 297–314; 42(1884), 413–30.

Eisenbach, A. and Grochulska, B., 'Population en Pologne (fin XVIII^c début XIX^c siècle)', *Annales de démographie historique* (1965), 105–25.

El Kordi, Mohamed, *Bayeux aux XVIIe et XVIIIe siècles* (Paris, 1970).

Ennen, E., *Geschichte der Stadt Bonn*, 2 vols (Bonn, 1962).

Erichsen, Ernest, 'Das Bettel- und Armenwesen in Schleswig-Holstein während der ersten Hälfte des 19. Jahrhunderts', *Zeitschrift der Gesellschaft für Schleswig-Holsteinische Geschichte* 80(1956), 93–148.

Ericsson, Brigitta, 'De anlagda städerna i Sverige (*ca.* 1580–1800)', in Grethe Authén Blom (ed.), *Urbaniseringsprosessen i Norden*, vol. 2 (Oslo, 1977).

Esmonin, Edmond, 'La revision des feux au Dauphiné en 1697–1706', *Annales de l'Université de Grenoble* 1(1924), 177–202.

Everaert, John, *De internationale en koloniale handel der Vlaamse firma's te Cádiz 1670–1700* (Bruges, 1973).

Faber, J. A., *Drie eeuwen Friesland*, 2 vols (Wageningen, 1972).

—— et al., 'Population changes and economic development in the northern Netherlands: a historical survey', *A.A.G. Bijdragen* 12(1965), 47–110.

Felloni, Giuseppe, 'Une monographie d'historie démographique: Pavia aux XVI^c et XVII^c siècle', *Annales E.S.C.* 15(1960), 774–8.

——, 'Italy', in Charles Wilson and Geoffrey Parker (eds), *An Introduction to the Sources of European Economic History 1500–1800* (Ithaca, NY, 1977).

Finlay, Roger, *Population and Metropolis. The Demography of London 1580–1650* (Cambridge, 1981).

Fleurent, Henri, *Essai sur la démographie et l'epidemologie de la ville de Colmar* (Colmar, 1922).

Fohlen, Claude et al., *Histoire de Besançon* (Paris, 1964–5).

Fokker, G. A., 'Iets over de bevolking van Middelburg vóór 1795', *Archief Zeeuwsch genootschap* 3 (second series) (1878), 81–100.

Fortea Pérez, José Ignacio, *Córdoba en el siglo XVI: las bases demográficas y económicas de una expansión urbana* (Córdoba, 1981).

François, E., 'Des républiques merchants aux capitales politiques: la hiérarchie urbaine du Saint-Empire', *Revue d'histoire moderne et contemporaine* 25(1978), 587–603.

Franz, Günther, *Der Dreissigjährige Krieg und das deutsche Volk* (Stuttgart, 1961, second edn).

Frêche, G., 'Dénombrements de feux et d'habitants de 2,973 communes de la région Toulousaine', *Annales de démographie historique* (1968), 389–421.

Freeman, T. W., *Pre-Famine Ireland* (London, 1969).

Friederichs, H. and Niessen, P., 'Die Bevölkerung stettins bis zu Ende der herzoglichen Zeit', *Monatsblätter der Gesellschaft für pommerische Geschichte und Altertumskunde* 45 (1931), 18–26.

Fruin, R. J. (ed.), *Informacie up den staet Faculteyt ende Gelegentheyt van de Steden*

ende Dorpen van Hollant ende Vrieslant . . . (1514) (Leiden, 1866).
Garden, Maurice, *Lyon et les Lyonnais au XVIIIe siècle* (Paris, 1970).
Gause, Fritz, *Die Geschichte der Stadt Königsberg*, 2 vols (Cologne–Graz, 1965–8).
Genicot, Léopold, 'Les grandes villes d'Occident en 1300', in *Economies et sociétés au moyen age. Mélanges offerts à Edouard Perroy* (Paris, 1973), 199–219.
Ghisleni, Pier Luigi and Maffioli, Maisa, *Il Verde nelle citta di Torino* (Turin, 1971).
Gieysztorowa, Irena, 'Research into the demographic history of Poland: a provisional summing-up', *Acts Poloniae Historica* 18(1968), 5–17.
Gille, H., 'The demographic history of the northern European countries in the eighteenth century', *Population Studies* 3(1949–50), 3–65.
Godinho, V. M., 'Portugal and her empire', *Cambridge Modern History of Europe*, vol. 5: *The Ascendancy of France 1648–88* (Cambridge, 1969), 384–97.
——, 'Portugal and her empire, 1680–1720', *Cambridge Modern History of Europe*, vol. 6: *The Rise of Great Britain and Russia 1688–1725* (Cambridge, 1970), 509–40.
Gorissen, F., *Stede-atlas van Nijmegen* (Arnhem, 1956).
Goubert, Pierre, *Beauvais et le Beauvaises de 1600 à 1730*, 2 vols (Paris, 1960).
Gray, Duncan, *Nottingham; Settlement to City* (Nottingham, 1953).
Hable, Guido, *Geschichte Regensburgs; eine Ubersicht nach Sachgebieten* (Regensburg, 1970).
Hamilton, Henry, *An Economic History of Scotland in the Eighteenth Century* (Oxford, 1963).
Hammer, C. I., 'The mobility of skilled labour in late medieval England: some Oxford evidence', *Vierteljahrschrift für Sozial- und Wirtschaftsgeschichte* 63(1976), 194–210.
Harris, M. D., *Coventry Leet Book*, vol. III (Oxford, 1913).
Hart, Simon, *Geschrift en getal*, Hollandse studiën 9 (Dordrecht, 1976).
Harte, W. J., 'Some data for assessing the population of Exeter at the end of the seventeenth century', *Devon and Cornwall Notes and Queries* 20(1938–9), 210–14.
Hasquin, Hervè (ed.), *La Wallonie, le pays et les hommes*, vol. I (Brussels, 1975).
Heckscher, Eli, *Sveriges ekonomiska historia fran Gustav Vasa*, 2 vols (Stockholm, 1935–49).
——, *An Economic History of Sweden* (Cambridge, Mass., 1963).
Hegel, C., 'Die Einwohnerzahl und der Gewerbestand in 15. Jahrhundert', *Chroniker der deutschen Städte* 18(1882).
Heidemann, H., *Bevölkerungszahl und berufliche Gliederung Münster in Westfalen am ende des 17. Jahrhunderts* (Münster, 1917).
Hélin, Etienne, *La Démographie de Liège aux XVIIe et XVIIIe siècles* (Brussels, 1963).
——, 'Size of households before the industrial revolution: the case of Liège in 1801', in Peter Laslett (ed.), *Household and Family in Past Time* (Cambridge, 1972), 319–34.
Henne, Alexandre and Wauters, Alphonse, *Histoire de la ville de Bruxelles*, 4 vols (Brussels, 1845; republished, 1968–9).
Henning, F.-W., *Das vorindustrielle Deutschland, 800 bis 1800. Wirtschafts-und Sozialgeschichte*, vol. 1 (Paderborn, 1977).
Herlihy, David, *Pisa in the Early Renaissance: a Study of Urban Growth* (New Haven, Conn., 1958).

Hermann, J. F., *Notices historique statistiques et littéraires sur la ville de Strasbourg*, 2 vols (Strasburg, 1819).

Herrman, Hans-Walter, 'Residenzstädte zwischen Oberrhein und Mosel', *Rheinische Vierteljahrsblätter* 38(1974), 273–300.

Hofmann, Hanns Hubert, 'Nürnbergs Raumfunction in der Geschichte', in *Stadt-land-beziehungen* (1975), 91–101.

Horska, Paula, 'L'état actuel des recherches sur l'évolution de la population dans les pays Tchèques aux XVIIIe et XIXe siècles', *Annales de démographie historique* (1967), 173–95.

Hoskins, W. G., *Industry, Trade, and People in Exeter, 1688–1800* (Manchester, 1935).

———, 'The population of Exeter', *Devon and Cornwall Notes and Queries* 20(1938–9), 242–5.

Houtte, Gisèle van, *Leuven in 1740, een krisisjaar. Economische, sociale en demografische aspekten*, Pro civitate, verzameling geschiedenis, no. 3 (Brussels, 1964).

Houtte, J. A. van, 'Die Städte der Niederlande im Übergang vom Mittelalter zur Neuzeit', *Rheinische Vierteljahrsblätter* 27(1962), 50–69.

———, *Economische en sociale geschiedenis van de Lage Landen* (Zeist, 1964).

———, *An Economic History of the Low Countries, 800–1800* (London, 1977).

Howell, Roger, jr, *Newcastle-upon-Tyne and the Puritan Revolution* (Oxford, 1967).

Humlum, J., *Befolkningstilvaeksten i den 10 Største Danske provinsbyer det Danske marked*, 3 vols (Copenhagen, 1942).

Imhof, Arthur, 'Der agrare Charakter der schwedischen und finnischen Städte im 18. Jahrhundert im vergleich zu Mittel- und Westeuropa', in *Stadt-land-beziehungen* (1975), 161–97.

Issawi, Charles, 'Economic change and urbanization in the Middle East', in Ira M. Lapidus (ed.), *Middle Eastern Cities* (Berkeley and Los Angeles, Calif., 1969).

———, *An Economic History of the Middle East and North Africa* (London, 1982).

Jackson, Gordon, *Hull in the Eighteenth Century* (London, 1972).

Jeannin, Pierre, *L'Europe du nord-ouest et du nord aux XVIIe et XVIIIe siècles* (Paris, 1969).

Kahk, J. et al., 'Sur l'histoire démographique de l'Estonie', *Annales de démographie historique* (1972), 425–46.

Kamen, Henry, *The Iron Century: Social Change in Europe, 1550–1660* (London, 1971).

———, *Spain in the Later Seventeenth Century, 1665–1700* (London, 1980).

Kaplow, Jeffrey (ed.), *New Perspectives on the French Revolution* (New York, 1965).

Kárniková, Ludmila, *Vývoj obyvatelstua v českých zemich 1754–1914* (Prague, 1965).

Keir, David (ed.), *Third Statistical Account of Scotland; the City of Edinburgh* (Glasgow, 1966).

Kellenbenz, Hermann and Eyll, Klara van (eds), *Zweijahrtausende Kölner Wirtschaft*, 2 vols (Cologne, 1975).

Kemp, A. G. H., 'Het verloop van de bevolkingscurve van Maastricht tot 1830', *Miscellanea Trajectensia Bijdragen tot de geschiedenis van Maastricht* (Maastricht, 1962).

Keuning, H. J., *De regio Groningen* (Groningen, 1974).

BIBLIOGRAPHY

Keyser, Erich, *Bevölkerungsgeschichte Deutschlands* (Leipzig, 1941).

—— (ed.), *Deutsches Städtebuch. Handbuch Städtischer Geschichte:* II, *Sächsisches Städtebuch* (Stuttgart, 1941); III.1, *Niedersächsisches Städtebuch* (Stuttgart, 1952); III.2, *Westfälisches Städtebuch* (Stuttgart, 1954); III.3, *Rheinisches Städtebuch* (Stuttgart, 1956); IV.1, *Hessisches Städtebuch* (Stuttgart, 1957); IV.2a, *Badisches Städtebuch* (Stuttgart, 1959); IV.2b, *Württembergisches Städtebuch* (Stuttgart, 1962); IV.3, *Städtebuch Rheinland Pfalz und Saarland* (Stuttgart, 1964); V.1–2, *Bayerisches Städtebuch* (Stuttgart, 1971–4).

Kintz, Jean-Pierre, 'Aspekte eines städtetypischen demographischen Verhaltnis im 17. und 18. Jahrhundert. Strassburg als Beispiel', in Arthur E. Imhof (ed.), *Historische Demographie als Sozialgeschichte* (Darmstadt and Marburg, 1975), 1049–57.

Kisskalt, K., 'Die Sterblichkeit im 18. Jahrhundert', *Zeitschrift für Hygiene* 93(1921), 438–511.

Klein, Kurt, 'Die Bevölkerung Österreichs von Beginn des 16 bis zur Mitte des 18 Jahrhunderts', in Helmond Helczmanovszki (ed.), *Beiträge sur Bevölkerungs- und Sozialgeschichte Österreichs* (Munich, 1973).

Klep, Paul M. M., *Bevolking en arbeid in transformatie. Een onderzoek in Brabant, 1700–1900* (Nijmegen, 1981).

Köllmann, W., *Raum und Bevölkerung in der Weltgeschichte* (Würzburg, 1956).

——, *Sozialgeschichte der Stadt Barmen* (Tübingen, 1960).

Konvitz, Josef W., *Cities and the Sea: Port City Planning in Early Modern Europe* (Baltimore, Md, 1978).

Kovocsics, Jozsef, 'Situation démographique de la Hongrie à la fin du XVIIIe siècle', *Annales de démographie historique* (1965), 83–102.

Kramer, J. M., 'De bevolkingsterkte van Gouda tussen 1550 en 1650', unpublished manuscript deposited in municipal archives of Gouda.

Krause, J. T., 'English population movements between 1700 and 1850', in M. Drake (ed.), *Population in Industrialization* (London, 1969).

Kruedener, J. Frh. von, 'Die Bevölkerung Mannheims im Jahre 1719', *Zeitschrift für Geschichte des Oberrheins* (1968), 291–347.

Lager, B., *Stockholms befolkning pa Johan IIIs tid* (Stockholm, 1962).

Landry, Adolphe, *Traité de démographie* (Paris, 1945).

Lasch, Manfred, *Unteruchungen über Wirtschaft und Bevölkerung der Landgrafschaft Hessen-Kassel und der Stadt Kassel vom Dreissigjährigen Krieg bis zum Tode Landgraf Karls 1730* (Kassel, 1969).

Lassen, Aksel, 'The population of Denmark in 1660', *Scandinavian Economic History Review* 13(1965), 1–30.

——, 'The population of Denmark, 1660–1960', *Scandinavian Economic History Review* 14(1966), 134–67.

Laurent, René, 'Les limites des paroisses a Bruxelles au XIV et XV siècle', *Cahiers Bruxellois* 8(1963), 161–234.

Law, C. M., 'Local censuses in the eighteenth century', *Population Studies* 23(1969), 87–100.

——, 'Some notes on the urban population of England and Wales in the eighteenth century', *The Local Historian* 10(1972), 13–26.

BIBLIOGRAPHY

Lebrun, F., *Les hommes et la mort en Anjou aux 17ᵉ et 18ᵉ siècles* (Paris, 1971).
Lefebvre, B., 'Les dénombrements douaniers de la révolution', *Revue du Nord* 54(1972), 399–409.
Lefebvre, Georges, 'Cherbourg à la fin de l'ancien règime et au début de la révolution', *Annales de Normandie* 4(1965), 1–296.
Leguay, J.-P., *Les villes bretonnes à la fin du moyen age (1364–v. 1514–1515)* (Bordeaux, 1978).
Lehe, Erich von et al., *Heimats chronik der Freien und Hansestadt Hamburg* (Cologne, 1967).
Lejeune, J., *Liège, de la principauté à la métropole* (Antwerp, 1967).
Lemoigne, Yves, 'Population and provisions in Strasbourg in the eighteenth century', in Jeffrey Kaplow (ed.), *New Perspectives on the French Revolution* (New York, 1965).
Lepetit, Bernard, 'Demographie d'une ville en gestation: Versailles sous Louis XIV', *Annales de démographie historique* (1977), 49–83.
——, 'Une création urbaine: Versailles de 1661 à 1722', *Revue d'histoire moderne et contemporaine* 25(1978), 604–18.
Le Roy Ladurie, E., 'De la crise ultimate à la vraie croissance, 1660–1789', in E. Le Roy Ladurie and M. Morineau (eds), *Historie de la France rurale*, vol. 2 (Paris, 1975).
—— and Quilliet, B., 'Baroque et lumières', in Georges Duby (ed.), *Histoire de la France urbaine*, vol. 3: *La Ville classique* (Paris, 1981).
Lythe, S. G. E., *The Economy of Scotland in its European Setting, 1550–1625* (Edinburgh, 1960).
MacDonald, D. F., *Scotland's Shifting Population, 1770–1850* (Glasgow, 1937).
McGrath, P., 'Merchants and merchandise in seventeenth century Bristol', *Bristol Record Society* 19(1955).
Manleon Isla, Mercedes, *La población de Bilbao en el siglo XVIII (Valladolid, 1961)*.
Martin, Gaston, *Nantes au XVIIIᵉ siècle* (Toulouse, 1928).
Mathis, Franz, *Zur Bevölkerungsstruktur österreichischer städte im 17 Jahrhundert* (Munich and Vienna, 1977).
Matthey, I. B. M., 'Op fiscaal kompas', in I. B. M. Matthey (ed.), *Westeremden. Het verleden van een Gronings terpdorp* (Groningen, 1975), 199–360.
Mauersberg, Hans, *Wirtschafts- und Sozialgeschichte zentraleuropäischer Städte im neuerer Zeit. Dargestellt an den Beispielen von Basel, Frankfurt a.M., Hamburg, Hannover und München* (Göttingen, 1960).
Mauro, Frédéric and Parker, Geoffrey, 'Spain', in Charles Wilson and Geoffrey Parker (eds), *An Introduction to the Sources of European Economic History* (Ithaca, NY, 1977).
Meuvret, J., 'Le commerce des grains et des farines à Paris et les marchands parisiens à l'époque de Louis XIV', *Revue d'historie moderne et contemporaine* 3(1956), 69–103.
Mika, Alois, 'On the economic status of Czech towns in the period of late feudalism', *Hospodářské Dějiny* 2(1978), 225–57.
Mols, Roger, 'Beschouwingen over de bevolkingsgeschiedenis in de Nederlanden', *Tijdschrift voor geschiedenis* 66(1953), 201–20.

BIBLIOGRAPHY

——, *Introduction à la démographie historique des villes d'Europe du 14ᵉ au 18ᵉ siècle*, 3 vols (Leuven, 1954–6).
——, 'Die Bevölkerungsgeschichte Belgiens im lichte der heutigen forschung', *Vierteljahrschrift für Sozial- und Wirtschaftsgeschichte* 46(1959), 491–511.
Monter, William, 'Demography and religious history in sixteenth-century Geneva', *Journal of Interdisciplinary History* 9(1979), 399–427.
Morqado, Nuno Alves, 'Portugal', in W. E. Lee (ed.), *European Demography and Economic Growth* (New York, 1979).
Morse, Richard M., 'Trends and patterns of Latin American urbanization, 1750–1920', *Comparative Studies in Society and History* 16(1974), 416–47.
Müller, A., 'Geschichte der Juden in Nürnberg, 1146–1945', *Beitrage zur Geschichte Nürnbergs* 12(1967).
Nadal, Jorge, *La población espanola (siglos XVI.à XX)* (Barcelona, 1966; fourth edn 1976).
Neale, Ron, 'Society, belief and the building of Bath, 1700–1793', in C. W. Chalkin and M. A. Havinden (eds), *Rural Change and Urban Growth, 1500–1800* (London, 1974).
Noordam, D. J., 'Bevolking, huishouden en gezin in Leiden in 1749', in H. A. Diederiks *et al.*, *Een stad in achteruitgang* (Leiden, 1978), 105–45.
Nusteling, Hubert P. H., *Binnen de vesting Nijmegen* (Zutphen, 1979).
Offermans, P. H. M. G., *Arbeid en levensstandaard in Nijmegen (1550–1600)* (Zutphen, 1972).
Ogg, David, *England in the Reigns of James II and William III* (Oxford, 1957).
O'Grada, Cormac, 'The population of Ireland, 1700–1900: a survey', *Annales de démographie historique* (1979), 281–99.
Olinski, H. and Walden, H., 'Beiträge zur elbinger Bevölkerungsstatistik der letzen drei Jahrhunderte', *Elbinger Jahrbuch* 9(1931).
Olsen, G. and Askgaard, F., *Danmarks historie, 1660–1721* (Copenhagen, 1964–5).
O'Sullivan, William, *The Economic History of Cork City from the Earliest Times to the Act of Union* (Dublin and Cork, 1937).
Palliser, David M., 'The trade guilds of Tudor York', in Peter Clark and Paul Slack (eds), *Crisis and Order in English Towns, 1500–1700* (London, 1972).
——, 'Dearth and disease in Staffordshire, 1540–1670', in C. W. Chalkin and M. A. Havinden (eds), *Rural Change and Urban Growth, 1500–1800* (London, 1974).
Pardi, Giuseppe, *Napoli attraverso i secoli disegno di storia economica e demografica* (Naples, 1924).
Patten, John, *English Towns, 1500–1700. Studies in Historical Geography* (Folkestone, 1978).
Peller, Sigismund, 'Zur Kenntnis der städtischen Mortalität im 18. Jahrhundert mit besonderer Berücksichtigung der Säuglings- und Tuberkulosesterblichkeit', *Zeitschrift für Hygiene und Infectionskrankheiten* 90(1920), 232–5.
Penner, T., 'Bevölkerungsgeschichtliche Probleme der Land-Stadt-Wanderung untersucht an der ländlichen Abwanderung in die Stadt Bruinschweig und Wolfenbuttel um die mitte des 18. Jahrhunderts', *Braunschweigisches Jahrbuch* 37(1965), 59–124.
Péronas, Louis, 'Sur la démographie rochelaise', *Annales E.S.C.* 16(1961), 1131–40.

Perrenoud, Alfred, *La Population de Genève du seizième au début du dix-neuvième siècle. Etude démographique*, 2 vols (Geneva, 1979).
Perrot, Jean-Claude, *Genèse d'une ville moderne. Caen au XVIIIe siècle*, 2 vols (Paris, 1975).
Petraccone, C., 'Le nascite a Bari dal pinizio del XVI secolo all'unificazione del regno d'Italia', *Studi di demografia* 8(1971), 68–86.
——, *Napoli dal '500 all' '800* (Naples, 1974).
Peyer, H. C., 'Die Wirtschaftliche Bedeutung der Fremden Dienste für die Schweiz', in J. Schneider (ed.), *Wirtschaftskräfte und Wirtschaftswege*, vol. II: *Wirtschaftskräfte in der europäischen Expansion* (Cologne, 1978).
Pfister, Christian, *Histoire de Nancy*, 3 vols (Nancy, 1902–9).
——, 'Nancy au début de règne de Charles IV (1624–1633). La siège de la ville par Louis XIII', *Annales de l'Est* (1907), 24–83.
Philips, J. F. R., 'Enige aanduidingen omtrent de bevolkingsontwikkeling van de 17e tet het einde van de 18e eeuw, in het gebied van de huidige provincie Nederlands Limburg', *Studies over de sociaal-economische geschiedenis van Limburg* (1975), 1–48.
Phythian-Adams, C., *Desolation of a City; Coventry and the Urban Crisis of the Late Middle Ages* (Cambridge, 1979).
Pickard, R., *The Population and Epidemics of Exeter in Pre-Census Times* (Exeter, 1947).
Pike, R., *Aristocrats and Traders. Sevillian Society in the Sixteenth Century* (Ithaca, NY, 1972).
Pirenne, Henri, 'Les dénombrements de la population à Ypres au XIVe siècle', *Vierteljahrschrift für Sozial- und Wirtschaftsgeschichte* 1(1903), 1–32.
Piuz, Anne-Marie, 'Marchands Genevois du monde méditerranéen (vers 1600–30)', in R. Aron *et al.* (eds), *Mélanges en l'honneur de Fernand Braudel* (Toulouse, 1973).
Posthumus, N. W., *De geschiedenis van de Leidsche lakenindustrie*, 3 vols (The Hague, 1939).
Pousson, Jean-Pierre, 'Les structures démographiques et sociales', in C. Higounet (ed.), *Histoire de Bordeaux*, vol. V: *Bordeaux au 18e siècle* (Bordeaux, 1968), 325–69.
Ramaer, J. C., 'Middelpunten van bewoning in Nederland voorheen en thans', *Tijdschrift van het koninklijk Nederlands aardrijkskundig genootschap*, second series, 38(1921), 1–38.
Rambert, Gaston (ed.), *Histoire du commerce de Marseille*, 6 vols (Marseilles, 1949–59): vol. III, Raymond Collier and Joseph Billioud (eds), *De 1480 à 1599* (1951); vol. IV, Louis Bergasse (ed.), *De 1599 à 1660* (1954); vol. V, Gaston Rambert (ed.), *De 1660 à 1789* (1954).
Rapp, Richard T., *Industry and Economic Decline in Seventeenth Century Venice* (Cambridge, Mass., 1976).
Ravesteijn, L. J. C. J. van, *Rotterdam tot het einde van de achttiende eeuw* (Rotterdam, 1933).
Reincke, Heinrich, 'Bevölkerungsprobleme der Hansestädte', *Hansische Geschichtsblätter* 70(1951), 1–35.

BIBLIOGRAPHY

Reineke, R., 'Geburten und Sterbefälle in der Stadt Bremen, 1700-1825', *Mitteilungen des statistischen Landesamtes Bremen* 2(1928).
Rigault, Jean, 'La population de Metz au XVII^c siècle. Quelques problemes de démographie', *Annales de l'Est* 2(1951), 307-15.
Rimmer, W. G., 'The evolution of Leeds to 1700', *Publications of the Thoresby Society*, no. 113, 50(1967), 91-129.
Ringrose, David, 'Madrid y Castilla, 1560-1850: una capital nacional en una economiá regional', *Moneda y crédito* 111(1969), 65-122.
——, *Transportation and Economic Stagnation in Spain, 1750-1850* (Durham, NC, 1970).
——, 'The impact of a new capital city: Madrid, Toledo, and New Castile, 1560-1660', *Journal of Economic History* 33(1973), 761-91.
——, *Madrid and the Spanish Economy, 1560-1850* (Berkeley and Los Angeles, Calif., 1983).
Robillard de Bearepaire, Charles de, *Recherches sur la population de la Généralité et du Diocèse de Rouen avant 1789* (Évreau, 1872).
Roessingh, H. K., 'Het Veluwse inwonertal, 1526-1947', *A.A.G. Bijdragen* 11(1964), 79-150.
Rogier, J., 'De betekenis van de terugkeer can de minderbroeders te Delft in 1709', *Archief voor de geschiedenis van de Katholieke Kerk in Nederland* 2(1960), 169-204.
Roupnel, Gaston, *La ville et la campagne au XVIIe siècle. Etude sur les populations du pays dijonnais* (Paris, 1922).
Ruiz Almansa, Javier, *La población de Galicia (1500-1945)*, vol. I: *Itinerario y cosmografia de Espana (1517-23)* (Madrid, 1948).
Russell, Josiah Cox, *Late, Ancient, and Medieval Population*, Transactions of the American Philosophical Society, vol. 43, no. 3 (Philadelphia, 1958).
——, 'L'évolution démographique de Montpellier au moyen age', *Annales du Midi* 74(1962), 345-60.
——, *Medieval Regions and their Cities* (Bloomington, Ind., 1972).
Saalfeld, Diedrich, *Bauernwirtschaft und Gutsbetrieb in der vorindustriellen Zeit* (Stuttgart, 1960).
Saunders, A. C. de C. M., *Social History of Black Slaves and Freedmen in Portugal, 1441-1555* (Cambridge, 1982).
Schaefer, Hans-Ludwig, *Bremens Bevölkerung in der ersten Hälfte des neunzehnten Jahrhunderts*, Veröffentlichungen aus dem Staatsarchiv der freien Hansestadt Bremen (Bremen, 1957).
Schmoller, Gustav, *Deutschen Städtewesen in älterer Zeit* (Bonn, 1922).
Schnyder, W., *Die Bevölkerung der Stadt und Landschaft Zürich vom 14.bis 17. Jahrnundert* (Zurich, 1925).
Scholliers, E., 'Un indice du loyer: les loyers anversois de 1500 à 1873', in *Studi in onore di Amintore Fanfani*, vol. 5 (Milan, 1962).
Schraa, P., 'Onderzoekingen naar de bevolkingsomvagn van Amsterdam tussen 1550 en 1650', *Jaarboek Amstelodamum* 46(1954), 1-33.
Schrader, F., 'Die Stadt Erfurt nach ihren wirtschaftslichen und sozialen Verhältnissen nach beendegung des Dreissigjährigen Krieges', *Mittelungen des Vereiens für Geschichte und Altertumskunde Erfurt* (1921).

BIBLIOGRAPHY

Schreiber, A., 'Die Entwicklung der augsburger Bevölkerung von Ende des 14. Jahrhunderts bis zum Beginn des 19. Jahrhunderts', *Archiv für Hygiene* 123(1939–40), 139–46.
Schremmer, Eckart, *Die Wirtschaft Bayerns* (Munich, 1970).
Schultheisz, W., *Kleine Geschichte Nürnbergs* (Nuremberg, 1966).
Schwippe, H. J., 'Zum Prozess der socialräumlichen Innerstädtischen Differenzierung im Industrialisierungsprozess des 19. Jahrhunderts', in H. I. Teuteberg (ed.), *Urbanisierung im 19. und 20. Jahrhunderts* (Cologne-Vienna, 1983).
Seberich, Franz, 'Die Einwohnerzahl Würzburgs in alter und neuer Zeit', *Mainfrank Jahrbuch* 12(1960), 49–68.
Sella, Domenico, *Crisis and Continuity* (Cambridge, Mass., 1979).
Simmons, Jack, *Leicester, Past and Present*, vol. 1: *Ancient Borough to 1860* (London, 1974).
Simms, J. G., 'Dublin in 1685', *Irish Historical Studies* 14(1964–5), 212–26.
Slicher van Bath, B. H., *Een samenleving onder spanning. Geschiedenis van het platteland van Overijssel* (Assen, 1957).
Smet, J. de, 'L'effectif des milices brugeoises et la population de la ville en 1340', *Revue Belge de philologie et d'histoire* 12(1933).
Société de démographie historique, *Sur la population francaise au XVIIIe et au XIXe siècles. Hommage à Marcel Reinhard* (Paris, 1973).
Stephens, W. B., *Seventeenth-century Exeter: a Study of Industrial and Commercial Development, 1625–1688* (Exeter, 1958).
Strohl, Henri, *Le Protestantisme en Alsace* (Strasburg, 1950).
Tegenwoordige staat der Vereenigde Nederlanden, 23 vols (Amsterdam, 1739–1803).
Teisseyre-Sallmann, L., 'Urbanisme et société: l'example de Nîmes aux XVIIe et XVIIIe siècles', *Annales E.S.C.* 35 (1980), 965–86.
Thestrup, Paul, *The Standard of Living in Copenhagen, 1730–1800* (Copenhagen, 1971).
Thirsk, Joan (ed.), *Agrarian History of England and Wales*, vol. 4: *1500–1640* (Cambridge, 1967).
Todorov, Nikolaï, *Studia Balcanica*, vol. 3: *La ville Balkanique XVe–XIXe siècles* (Sofia, 1970).
——, *La ville Balkanique aux XVe–XIXe siècles. Developpement sòcio-économique et démographique* (Sofia, 1972) [in Bulgarian].
——, *La ville Balkanique sous les Ottomans (XV–XIXe siècles)* (London, 1977).
Topolski, J. and Wyczanski, A., 'Les fluctuations de la production agricole en Pologne aux XVIe–XVIIe siècles', *Actes du colloque préparatoire*, 1977 conference in preparation for the seventh International Economic History Congress (Paris, forthcoming).
Toutain, J. C., *La Population de la France de 1700 à 1959* (Paris, 1963).
Verbeemen, J., 'De demografische evolutie van Leuven in de XVIIe en XVIIIe eeuw', *De schakel* 9(1954), 89–93.
——, 'De werking van economische factoren op de stedelijke demografie der XVIIe en XVIIIe eeuwen', *Revue Belge de philologie et d'histoire* 34(1956), 680–700, 1021–55.

——, 'Antwerpen in 1755. Een demografische en sociaal.economische studie', *Bijdragen tot de geschiedenis* 40(1957), 27 – 63.
——, 'Bruxelles en 1755. Sa situation démographique, sociale et économique', *Bijdragen tot de geschiedenis* 45(1962), 203 – 34; 46(1963), 65 – 134.
Vicens Vives, Jaime, *An Economic History of Spain* (Princeton, NJ, 1969).
Vigier, François, *Change and Apathy: Liverpool and Manchester during the Industrial Revolution* (Cambridge, Mass., 1970).
Vincent, B., 'Recents travaux de démographie historique en Espagne (XVIe – XVIIIe siècles)', *Annales de démographie historique* (1977), 463 – 91.
Vogler, Bernard, 'La Rhénanie', in J.-P. Poussou *et al.*, *Études sur les villes en Europe Occidentale*, vol. 2 (Paris, 1983), 389 – 469.
Vovelle, Michel, 'Formes de dependance d'un milieu urbain. Chartres à l'égard du monde rural', *83e Congrès soc. savantes Aix-Marseille* (1958), 483 – 512.
Vries, Jan de, *The Dutch Rural Economy in the Golden Age, 1500 – 1700* (New Haven, Conn., 1974).
——, *Barges and Capitalism* (Utrecht, 1981); originally published in *A.A.G. Bijdragen* 21(1978), 33 – 398.
Waldner, Euène, 'Aperçu de l'histoire de la ville de Colmar', *Revue d'Alsace* 78(1931), 416 – 31, 603 – 20, 718 – 37.
Weber, Adna F., *The Growth of Cities in the Nineteenth Century: a Study in Statistics* (New York, 1899; reprinted, Ithaca, NY, 1963).
Weber, S., *Stadt und Amt Stuttgart zur Zeit des Dreissigjährigen Krieges* (Tübingen, 1936).
Weidenhaupt, Hugo, *Kleine Geschichte der Stadt Düsseldorf* (Düsseldorf, 1968).
Weiss, Karl, *Geschichte der Stadt Wien*, 2 vols (Vienna, 1882 – 3).
Welford, R., 'Newcastle householders in 1665', *Arch. Aeliana* 7(1911), 55 – 6.
Werveke, H. van, 'Sint Niklaas', in R. van Roosbroeck (ed.), *Geschiedenis van Vlaanderen*, vol. V (Amsterdam, 1940).
Wheeler, J., *Manchester: its Political, Social, and Commercial History, Ancient and Modern* (London, 1836).
Wiaarda, D., *Die geschichtliche Entwicklung der landwirtschaftlichen Verhältnisse Ostfriesland* (Emden, 1880).
Wijsenbeek Olthuis, Thera, 'Delft in de 18^e eeuw, een stad in verval', in Stedelijk Museum het Prinsenhof, *De Stad Delft. Cultuur en maatschippij van 1667 tot 1813* (Delft, 1983).
Wilson, Charles and Parker, Geoffrey (eds), *An Introduction to the Sources of European Economic History, 1500 – 1800* (Ithaca, NY, and London, 1977).
Wolff, Philippe, *Commerce et marchands de Toulouse* (Paris, 1954).
Woude, A. M. van der, *Het Noorderkwartier. Een regionaal historisch onderzoek in de demografische en economische geschiedenis van westelijk Nederland van de late Middeleeuwen tot het begin van de 19e eeuw*, 3 vols (Wageningen, 1972; republished Utrecht, 1983).
——, 'Demografische ontwikkeling van de noordelijke Nederlanden 1500 – 1800', in *Algemene geschiedenis der Nederlanden*, vol. V (Haarlem, 1980), 102 – 68.
—— and Mentink, G. J., *De demografische ontwikkeling te Rotterdam en Cool in de XVII en XVIII eeuw* (Rotterdam, 1965).

BIBLIOGRAPHY

——, 'La population de Rotterdam au XVIIe et au XVIIIe siècle', *Population* 21(1966), 1165–90.
Wrigley, E. A., 'A simple model of London's importance in changing English society and economy', *Past and Present* 37(1967), 44–70.
—— and Schofield, R. S., *The Population History of England, 1541–1871: a Reconstruction* (London, 1981).
Wyffels, A., 'De omvang en de evolutie van het Brugse bevolkingscijfer in de 17e en de 18e eeuw', *Belgisch tijdschrift voor filologie en geschiedenis* 36(1958), 1243–74.
Wymans, G., 'Le déclin de Tournai au XVe siècle', *Standen en landen* 22(1961), 111–34.
Xanten, H. J. and Woude, A. M. van der, 'Het hoofdgeld en de bevolking van de Meijerij van 's-Hertogenbosch omstreeks 1700', *A.A.G. Bijdragen* 13(1965), 3–96.
Zanetti, Dante, 'L'approvisionnement de Pavie au XVIe siècle', *Annales E.S.C.* 18(1963), 44–62.
Zens, N. and Delange, J.-Y., 'Une reconstitution urbaine par sondage, Lisieux aux XVIIe et XVIIIe siècle. Resumé d'un mémoire de maitrise', *D.H. Bulletin d'information* 12(1974), 12–20.
Zorn, Wolfgang, *Augsburg, Geschichte einer deutschen Stadt* (Augsburg, n.d.).
—— and Hillenbrand, Leonhard, *Sechsjahrhunderte schwäbische Wirtschaft* (Augsburg, 1969).

CENSUS-LIKE SOURCES AND MAJOR COMPENDIA, LISTED BY COUNTRY

SWEDEN *Bidrag till Sveriges officiele statistik. Befolknings – statistik, Nyfolgd* I: 1805 population;
Statistik årsbok för Stockholms Stad, 1964–5 (Stockholm, 1965).
Statistisk årsbok, 1979. Sverges officielle statistik (Stockholm, 1979).
NORWAY *Folke- og Boligtelling 1970* (Oslo, 1974).
FINLAND *Suomen 1981 Tilastollinen Vuosikirja* (Helsinki, 1982).
ENGLAND AND WALES *British Parliamentary Papers. Session of 1801–2*, vol. VII: Census of 1801.
SCOTLAND Kyd, J. G., *Scottish Population Statistics*, Scottish Historical Society, third series, vol. XLIV (1952), 1–81.
Also, see England and Wales.
IRELAND Vaughan, W. E. and A. J. Fitzpatrick, *Irish Historical Statistics. Population, 1821–1971* (Dublin, 1978).
Statistical Abstract of Ireland, 1970–71 (Dublin, 1974).
THE NETHERLANDS *Volks-telling in de Nederlandsche Republiek*, compiled by order of the Commissie tot het ontwerpen van een plan van constitutie voor het volk van Nederland (The Hague, 1796).
Statistisch zakboek 1980 (The Hague, 1981).
GERMANY Franke, Wilhelm, 'Die Volkszahl deutschen Städte, ende des 18. und anfang des 19. Jahrhunderts', *Zeitschrift des preussischen statistischen Landesamts* 62(1922), 102–21.

BIBLIOGRAPHY

Oberman, K., 'Quelques donnés statistiques sur les états de la Confédération Germanique dans la première moitié du XIX siècle', *Annales de démographie historique* (1966), 79–95.
Reekers, Stephanie, *Westfalens Bevölkerung, 1818–1955* (Münster, 1956).
Uelschen, Gustav, *Die Bevölkerung in Niedersachsen, 1821–1961* (Hannover, 1966).
Statistisches Jahrbuch 1979 für die Bundesrepublik Deutschland (Stuttgart and Mainz, 1979).
Statistisches Jahrbuch 1980 der Deutschen Demokratischen Republik (Berlin, 1980).
FRANCE   Lee Mée, René, 'Population agglomérée et population éparse au début du XIX siècle', *Annales de démographie historique* (1971), 455–510.
Recensement général de la population de la France (Paris, 1975).
SWITZERLAND   *Eidgenössesches Volkszahlung, 1900* (Berne, 1904).
Statistisches Jahrbuch des Schweiz, 1979 (Basle, 1979).
ITALY   Beloch, Karl Julius, *Bevölkerungsgeschichte Italiens*, 3 vols (Berlin, 1937–61).
SPAIN   Gonzales, Tomás, *Censo de población de la provincias y partidos de la Corona de Castilla en el siglo XVI* (Madrid, 1829).
Estrada, J. A. de, *Población general de Espana*, 3 vols (Madrid, 1747).
Iglesias, Josep. (ed.), *El censo de comte de floridablanca*, Censo espanol executado de ordan del Rey communicada par el excelentisimo conde de Floridabalanca . . . 1787 (Barcelona, 1968).
Larruga y Boneta, Eugenio, *Utilizados en el Censo de Frutos y manufacturas* (Madrid, 1797).
Minaño, Sebastián de, *Diccionario Geográfico-Estadistico de Espana y Portugal*, Municipios de España (Madrid, 1826).
Junta central Estado, *Censo de población* (1897).
PORTUGAL   *Anuario Estatistico*, vol. I (Lisbon, 1973).
AUSTRIA   *Mittheilingen aus dem Gebiele des Statistik* (Vienna, 1852).
Statistisches Handbuch für der Republik Österreich, vol. 39 (Vienna, 1978).
CZECHOSLOVAKIA   *Statistická rocenka. Ceskoslovenské socialistické republiky, 1979* (Prague, 1979).
POLAND   *Annuaire statistique de la Republique Polonaise, 1923* (Warsaw, 1924).
GENERAL   *Geographical digest* (1981).
United Nations, *Demographic Yearbook* (1977–80).
Mitchell, B. R., *European Historical Statistics, 1750–1970* (London, 1975).

OTHER SOURCES

Abrams, Philip, 'Towns and economic growth: some theories and problems', in Philip Abrams and E. A. Wrigley (eds), *Towns in Societies: Essays in Economic History and Historical Sociology* (Cambridge, 1978), 9–33.
Arriaga, E. E., 'A new approach to the measurement of urbanization', *Economic Development and Cultural Change* 18(1969–70), 206–18.

BIBLIOGRAPHY

Auerbach, F., 'Das Gesetz der Bevölkerungskonzentration', *Petermann's Geographische Mitteilungen* 59(1913), 74–6.

Bairoch, Paul, 'Population urbaine et taille des villes en Europe de 1600 à 1970', *Revue d'histoire économique et sociale* 54(1976), 304–35.

——, *Taille des villes, conditions de vie et développement économique* (Paris, 1977).

Bardet, Jean-Pierre, 'La démographie des villes de la modernité (XVI^c–XVIII^c siècles): mythes et réalités', *Annales de démographie historique* (1974), 101–26.

Beresford, M., *New Towns of the Middle Ages* (London, 1967).

Berkner, Lutz and Mendels, Franklin F., 'Inheritance systems, family structure, and demographic patterns in western Europe, 1700–1900', in Charles Tilly (ed.), *Historical Studies of Changing Fertility* (Princeton, NJ, 1978).

Berry, Brian J. L., 'City size distribution and economic development', *Economic Development and Cultural Change* 9(1961), 571–87.

——, 'Cities as systems within systems of cities', *Papers and Proceedings of the Regional Science Association* 13(1964), 147–63.

——, 'City size and economic development: conceptual synthesis and policy problems, with special reference to south and southeast Asia', in Leo Jakobson and Ved Prakash (eds), *Urbanization and National Development*, vol. I (Beverly Hills, Calif., 1971).

——, 'Latent structure of the American urban systems', in B. J. L. Berry (ed.), *City Classification Handbook* (New York, 1972).

——, *The Human Consequences of Urbanisation: Divergent Paths in the Urban Experience of the Twentieth Century* (London, 1973).

——, *Growth Centers in the American Urban System*, 2 vols (Cambridge, Mass., 1973).

——, *Urbanization and Counterurbanization* (Beverly Hills, Calif., 1976).

—— and Horton, Frank E., *Geographic Perspectives on Urban Systems* (Englewood Cliffs, NJ, 1970).

Besch, Werner *et al.* (eds), *Die Stadt in der europaischer Geschichte: Festschrift Edith Ennen* (Bonn, 1972).

Borchert, John R., 'American metropolitan evolution', *Geographical Review* 57(1967), 301–32.

Borsay, Peter, 'The English urban renaissance: the development of provincial urban culture *c.* 1680–*c.* 1760', *Social History* 5(1977), 581–603.

Bourne, L. S., *Urban Systems; Strategies for Regulation* (Oxford, 1975).

Bourne, L. S. and J. W. Simmons (eds), *Systems of Cities: Readings on Structure, Growth, and Policy* (New York, 1978).

Braudel, Fernand, *The Mediterranean and the Mediterranean World in the Age of Philip II*, 2 vols, translation by Sian Reynolds of second edn (New York, 1972).

——, *Afterthoughts on Capitalism and Material Civilization*, translated by Patricia Ranum (Baltimore, Md, 1977).

—— *Capitalism and Material Life, 1400–1800*, translated by Miriam Kochan, New York, 1973; since published in revised edn as *Civilisation matérielle économique et capitalisme, XV–XVIII siècle*, vol. 1 (Paris, 1979).

—— and Spooner, Frank, 'Prices in Europe from 1450 to 1750', in *Cambridge Economic History of Europe*, vol. IV (Cambridge, 1967), 379–486.

BIBLIOGRAPHY

Braun, Rudolf, *Industrialisierung und Volksleben* (Zurich, 1960).
——, 'Early industrialization and demographic change in the Canton of Zürich', in Charles Tilly (ed.), *Historical Studies of Changing Fertility* (Princeton, NJ, 1978).
Briggs, Asa, *Victorian Cities* (London, 1963).
——, 'The human aggregate', in H. J. Dyos and Michael Wolff (eds), *The Victorian City: Images and Reality*, vol. I (London, 1973), 83–104.
Bruijn, J. R., 'De personeelsbehoefte van de VOC overzee en aan boord, bezien in Aziatisch en Nederlands perspectief', *Bijdragen en mededelingen betreffende de geschiedenis der Nederlanden* 91(1976), 218–48.
——, Gaastra, F. S., Schöffer, I. and van Eyck van Helsinga, E. S. (eds), *Dutch-Asiatic shipping in the Seventeenth and Eighteenth Centuries*, Rijksgeschiedkundige publicatieën, grote serie, nos 166 and 167 (The Hague, 1979).
—— and Lucassen, J., *Op de schepen der Oost-Indische Compagnie* (Groningen, 1980).
Brünner, E. C. G., *De ordre op de buitennering van 1531* (Amsterdam, 1921).
Burchharddt, Albrecht, *Demographie und Epidemiologie der Stadt Basel während der Letzten drei Jahrhunderten, 1601–1900* (Basle, 1908).
Carter, H., *The Study of Urban Geography* (London, 1976).
Chambers, J. D., 'Enclosure and labour supply in the industrial revolution', *Economic History Review* 5(1952–3), 319–43.
——, 'The Vale of Trent, 1670–1800, a regional study of economic change', *Economic History Review*, supplement 3 (Cambridge, 1957).
——, *Population, Economy and Society in Pre-industrial England* (London, 1972).
Clark, Colin, *Population Growth and Land Use* (New York, 1967).
Clark, David, *Urban Geography* (London, 1982).
Clark, Peter, 'Introduction', in Peter Clark (ed.), *English Country Towns, 1500–1800* (New York, 1981), 2–43.
Clarkson, L. A., *Death, Disease, and Famine in Preindustrial England* (Dublin, 1975).
Collins, E. J. T., 'Labour supply and demand in European agriculture, 1800–1880', in E. L. Jones and S. J. Woolf (eds), *Agrarian Change and Economic Development* (London, 1969), 61–94.
Crafts, N. F. R., 'English economic growth in the eighteenth century: a re-examination of Deane and Cole's estimates', *Economic History Review* 29(1976), 226–35.
Dainville, F. de, 'Grandeur et population des villes au XVIIIe siècle', *Population* 13(1958), 459–80.
Davids, C. A., 'Migratie te Leiden in de achttiende eeuw: een onderzoek op grond van de acten van cautie', in H. A. Diederiks *et al.*, *Een stad in achteruitgang* (Leiden, 1978), 146–92.
Davis, Kingsley, 'The origins and growth of urbanization in the world', *American Journal of Sociology* 60(1955), 429–37.
——, 'The urbanization of the human population', *Scientific American* 213(1965), 40–53.
——, *The Population of India and Pakistan* (New York, 1968; first published Princeton, NJ, 1951).

BIBLIOGRAPHY

——, *World Urbanization 1950–1970*, 2 vols (Berkeley, Calif., 1969, 1972).

——, 'Cities and mortality', International Population and Urban Research, Institute of International Studies, University of California at Berkeley, reprint no. 433 (1973).

Deurloo, M. C. *et al.*, *Zicht op de Nederlandse stad* (Bussum, 1981).

Deyon, Pierre, 'Les sociétés urbaines', in Pierre Leon (ed.), *Histoire économique et sociale du monde*, vol. 2: *Les Hésitations de la croissance, 1580–1730* (Paris, 1978).

—— and Mendels, Franklin (eds), 'La proto-industrialisation. Théorie et réalité', *Revue du Nord* 63(1981), special issue.

Diederiks, Herman A., *Een stad in verval. Amsterdam omstreeks 1800* (Amsterdam, 1982).

Dollinger, Phillipe and Wolff, Philippe, *Bibliographie des villes de France* (Paris, 1967).

Doxiadis, C. A., *Urban Renewal and the Future of the American City* (Chicago, Ill., 1966).

Du Bois-Melly, Charles, 'Les caractères originaux de l'histoire démographique francaise au XVIIIe siècle', *Revue d'histoire moderne et contemporaine* 23(1976), 182–202.

Dyos, H. J., 'Agenda for urban historians', in H. J. Dyos (ed.), *The Study of Urban History* (London, 1968).

—— and Wolff, M. (eds), *The Victorian City: Images and Realities*, 2 vols (London, 1973).

East, W. Gordon, *An Historical Geography of Europe* (London, 1950, fourth edn).

El Shakhs, Salah, 'Development, primacy and systems of cities', *Journal of Developing Areas* 7(1972), 11–36.

Everitt, A., 'The marketing of agricultural produce', in Joan Thirsk (ed.), *The Agrarian History of England and Wales*, vol. IV: *1500–1640* (Cambridge, 1967).

——, The food market of the English town, 1660–1760', *Third International Economic History Conference, Munich 1965* (Paris, 1968).

Farr, William, *Vital Statistics* (London, 1885).

Fei, John C. and Ranis, Gustav, *Development of the Labor Surplus Economy* (Homewood, Ill., 1964).

Finlay, Roger and Sharlin, Allan, 'Debate: natural decrease in early modern cities', *Past and Present* 92(1981), 169–80.

Fisher, F. J., 'London as an engine of economic growth', in J. S. Bromley and E. H. Kossmann (eds), *Britain and the Netherlands*, vol. IV (The Hague, 1971), 3–16.

Flinn, Michael, *The European Demographic System, 1500–1820* (London, 1981).

François, Etienne, 'La population de Coblence au XVIIIe siècle, deficit démographique et immigration dans une ville de résidence', *Annales de démographie historique* (1975), 291–341.

——, 'Coblence au XVIIIe siècle: une "ville de résidence" entre la tradition et les lumières', *Francia (Forschungen zur westeuropäischen Geschichte)* 4(1976), 391–407.

——, *Koblenz im 18. Jahrhundert* (Göttingen, 1982).

Ganshof, F. L., *Etudes sur le développement des villes entre Loire et Rhin au Moyen Age* (Paris, 1943).

Garden, Maurice, 'La démographie des villes francaises du XVIIIe siècle: quelques approches', *Démographie urbaine XVe – XXe siècle*, Centre d'histoire économique et sociale de la région lyonnaise, no. 8 (Lyons, 1977), 43 – 85.

Geddes, P., *Cities in Evolution* (London, 1915).

Germani, Gino (ed.), *Modernization, Urbanization and the Urban Crisis* (Boston, 1973).

Ginsberg, Norton, *Atlas of Economic Development* (Chicago, Ill., 1961).

Gokhman, Vanyamin M. *et al.*, 'Characteristics of world urbanization and its features in individual countries', *Geographia Polonica* 37(1977), 7 – 18.

Golden, Hilda Hertz, *Urbanization and Cities* (Lexington, Mass., 1981).

Goldstein, Sidney and Sly, David F. (eds), *Patterns of Urbanization: Comparative Country Studies*, 2 vols (Dolhain, Belgium, 1970).

Goldthwaite, Richard, *The Building of Renaissance Florence* (Baltimore, Md, 1981).

Gottmann, Jean, *Megalopolis: the Urbanized Northeastern Seaboard of the United States* (New York, 1961).

Graunt, John, *Natural and Political Observations and Conclusions made upon the Bills of Mortality* (London, 1662), reprinted in Peter Laslett (ed.), *The Earliest Classics: John Graunt and Gregory King* (Farnborough, 1973).

Grigg, D. B., 'E. G. Ravenstein and the "laws of migration"', *Journal of Historical Geography* 3(1977), 41 – 54.

Gschwind, Franz, *Bevölkerungsentwicklung und Wirtschaftsstruktur der Landschaft Basel im 18. Jahrhundert* (Liestal, 1977).

Guillaume, Pierre, *La Population de Bordeaux au XIXe siècle. Essai d'histoire sociale* (Paris, 1972).

Gutmann, Myron, *War and Rural Life in the Early Modern Low Countries* (Princeton, NJ, 1980).

Haase, C., *Die Entstehung der westfälischen Städte* (Münster, 1960).

Haggett, Peter, *Locational Models* (New York, 1977).

Hall, Peter, *The World Cities* (London, 1977, second edn).

——, Gracey, Harry, Drewett, Roy and Thomas, Ray, *The Containment of Urban England*, 2 vols (London and Beverly Hills, Calif., 1973).

—— and Hay, Dennis, *Growth Centers in the European Urban System* (Berkeley and Los Angeles, Calif., 1980).

Harris, Chauncey, *Cities in the Soviet Union* (Chicago, Ill., 1970).

Hasquin, Hervé, *Une Mutation. Le 'Pays de Charleroi' aux XVIIe et XVIIIe siècles* (Brussels, 1971).

Hauser, Philip M., 'Urbanization: an overview', in Philip M. Hauser and Leo F. Schnore (eds), *The Study of Urbanization* (New York, 1965).

Henry, Louis, *Anciennes familles Genevoises: Etude démographique, 16e au 20e siècle* (Paris, 1956).

——, *Manuel de démographie historique* (Paris, 1967).

Hirschman, Alfred O., *The Strategy of Economic Development* (New Haven, Conn., 1958).

Hoch, Irving, 'City size effects, trends, and policies', *Science* 193(1976), 856 – 63.

Hoselitz, Bert F., 'Generative and parasitic cities', *Economic Development and Cultural Change* 3(1954), 278 – 94.

——, 'The role of cities in the economic growth of underdeveloped countries', *Journal*

of Political Economy 61(1953), 195-209.
Hudson, J. C., 'Some observations on migration theory for an urban system', in L. A. Kosinski and R. M. Prothero (eds), *People on the Move: Studies on Internal Migration* (London, 1975), 67-74.
Imhof, Arthur E. (ed.), *Historiche Demographie als Sozialgeschichte. Giessen und Umgebung vom 17. zum 19. Jahrhundert*, Quellen und Forschung zur hessischen Geschichte, no. 31, 2 vols (Darmstadt and Marburg, 1975).
——, *Aspekte der Bevolkerungentwicklung in den nordischen Ländern, 1720-1750* (Berne, 1976).
Jakobson, Leo and Prakash, Ved (eds), *Urbanization and National Development*, 2 vols (Beverly Hills, Calif., 1971).
Jasper, Karlbernhard, 'Der urbanisierungsprozess dargestellt am Beispiel der Stadt Köln', *Rheinisch-Westfälischen Wirtschaftsarchiv zu Köln* 30(1977).
Johnson, E. A. J., *The Organization of Space in Developing Countries* (Cambridge, Mass., 1970).
Johnson, Gregory A., 'Rank-size convexity and system integration: a view from archeology', *Economic Geography* 56(1980), 234-47.
Johnston, R. J., *City and Society: an Outline for Urban Geography* (London, 1980).
Jones, E. L., 'The agricultural origins of industry', *Past and Present* 40(1968), 58-71.
Kahn, Herman and Weiner, A. J., *The Year 2000* (New York, 1967).
Kelly, Allen C. and Williamson, Jeffrey G., *Modelling Urbanization and Economic Growth* (Laxenburg, 1980).
Keyfitz, Nathan, 'Do cities grow by natural increase or by migration?', *Geographical Analysis* 12(1980), 143-56.
—— and Philipov, Dimiter, 'Migration and natural increase in the growth of cities', *Geographical Analysis* 13(1981), 288-99.
Kish, Herbert, 'The growth deterrents of a medieval heritage; the Aachen area woollen trades before 1790', *Journal of Economic History* 24(1964), 513-37.
Knaap, G. A. van der, *A Spatial Analysis of the Evolution of an Urban System: the Case of the Netherlands* (Utrecht, 1978).
Köllmann, Wolfgang, *Bevölkerung in der industriellen Revolution* (Göttingen, 1974).
Kooij, P., 'Urbanization. What's in a name?', in H. Schmal (ed.), *Patterns of European Urbanisation since 1500* (London, 1981), 31-59.
Kriedte, Peter, Medick, Hans and Schlumbohm, Jürgen, *Industrialisierung vor der Industrialisierung. Gewerbliche Warenproduktion auf dem Land in der Formationsperiode des Kapitalismus* (Göttingen, 1977); translated as *Industrialization before Industrialization: Rural Industry in the Genesis of Capitalism* (Cambridge and Paris, 1982).
Krug, Léopold, *Abriss der neuesten Statistik des preussischen Staats* (Halle, 1804).
Lampard, Eric E., 'The history of cities in the economically advanced areas', *Economic Development and Cultural Change* 3(1954), 81-136.
——, 'Ubanization and social change', in Oscar Handlin and John Burchard (eds), *The Historian and the City* (Cambridge, Mass., 1963).
——, 'Historical aspects of urbanization', in Philip M. Hauser and L. F. Schnore (eds), *The Study of Urbanization* (New York, 1965), 519-54.

BIBLIOGRAPHY

——, 'Historical contours of contemporary urban society: a comparative view', *Journal of Contemporary History* 4(1969), 3-25.

——, 'The nature of urbanization', in Derek Fraser and Anthony Sutcliffe (eds), *The Pursuit of Urban History* (London, 1983), 3-53.

—— and Schnore, Leo F., 'Urbanization problems', in *Research Needs for Development Assistance Programs* (Washington, DC, 1961).

Laslett, Peter, *The World We Have Lost* (London, 1965).

—— and Wall Richard (eds), *Household and Family in Past Times* (London, 1972).

Lasuen, J. R., Lorca, A. and Oria, J., 'City-size distribution and economic growth', *Ekistics* 24(1967), 221-6.

Lee, Ronald D., 'Estimating series of vital rates and age structure from baptisms and burials: a new technique, with applications to pre-industrial England', *Population Studies* 28(1974), 495-512.

Lendert, Jacques, 'The factor of urban population growth: net immigration versus natural increase', *International Regional Science Review* 7(1982), 99-125. Reprinted in Andrei Rogers (ed.), *Urbanization and Development: Selected Essays* (IIASA, Laxenburg, Austria, 1982).

Le Roy Ladurie, E. and Goy, J., *Tithe and Agrarian History from the Fourteenth to the Nineteenth Century* (Cambridge and Paris, 1982).

Levine, David, *Family Formation in an Age of Nascent Capitalism* (New York, 1977).

——, 'The English proletariat makes itself', unpublished paper presented to the Conference on British Demographic History, Asilomar, Calif. (March 1982).

Lewis, W. Arthur, *Growth and Fluctuations, 1870-1913* (London, 1978).

Lis, Catherine and Soly, Hugo, *Poverty and Capitalism in Pre-Industrial Europe* (Atlantic Highlands, NJ, 1979).

London, Bruce, 'Internal colonialism in Thailand: primate city parasitism reconsidered', *Urban Affairs Quarterly* 14(1979), 485-513.

McNeill, William H. (ed.), *Human Migration: Patterns, Implications, Policies* (Bloomington, Ind., 1978).

Mehta, Surinder, 'Some demographic and economic correlates of primate cities: a case for revaluation', *Demography* 1(1964), 136-47.

Mendels, Franklin, 'Proto-industrialization: the first phase of the industrialization process', *Journal of Economic History* 32(1972), 241-61.

——, 'Social mobility and phases of industrialization', *Journal of Interdisciplinary History* 7(1976), 193-216.

Merrington, John, 'Town and country in the transition to capitalism', *New Left Review* 93(1975), 71-92. Also in R. Hilton *et al.*, *The Transition from Feudalism to Capitalism* (London, 1978), 170-95.

Miskimin, H. A., *The Economy of Early Renaissance Europe, 1300-1460* (Cambridge, 1975, second edn).

Mokyr, Joel, *Industrialization in the Low Countries, 1795-1850* (New Haven, Conn., 1976).

Mumford, Lewis, *The City in History, its Origins, its Transformations, and its Prospects* (New York, 1961).

Nes, P. J. M., 'Imperialism, city-size distribution and migration', *Sociologica Neerlandica* 10(1974), 219-32.

——, *Stedenverdeling, nationale ontwikkeling en afhankelijkheid: een komparatief kwantatief benadering* (Leiden, 1976).

Okabe, Atsuyuki, 'An expected rank-size rule; a theoretical relationship between the rank-size rule and city-size distributions', *Regional Science and Urban Economics* 9(1979), 21–40.

Pahl, R. E. (ed.), *Readings in Urban Sociology* (Oxford, 1968).

Patten, John, 'Patterns of migration and movement of labour to three pre-industrial East Anglian towns', *Journal of Historical Geography* 2(1976), 111–29.

Perrenoud, Alfred, 'L'inégalité sociale devant la mort à Genève au XVIIe siècle', *Population* 30(1975), numéro spécial, 221–43.

——, 'La mortalité à Genève de 1625 à 1825', *Annales de démographie historique* (1978), 209–33.

——, 'Croissance ou déclin? Les mecanismes du non-renouvellement des populations urbaines', *Histoire économie et société* 4(1982), 581–601.

Perrot, Jean-Claude, 'Recherches sur l'analyse de l'économie urbaine au XVIIIe siècle', *Revue d'histoire économique et sociale* 52(1974), 350–83.

Pirenne, Henri, *Medieval Cities, their Origins and the Revival of Trade* (Princeton, NJ, 1925).

——, *Economic and Social History of Medieval Europe* (London, 1936).

——, *Les Villes et les institutions urbaines*, 2 vols (Brussels, 1939).

Pollard, Sidney (ed.), *Region und Industrialisierung: Studien zur Rollen der Region in der Wirtschaftsgeschichte der letzten zwei Jahrhunderte* (Göttingen, 1980).

Portes, Alejandro, 'The economy and ecology of urban poverty', in A. Portes and J. Walton (eds), *Urban Latin America* (Austin, Tex., 1976).

Postmus, J., *Een onderscheid naar de omvang en aard van de bevolkingsconcentratie in Nederland* (Amsterdam, 1928).

Pred, Allan, *Urban Growth and the Circulation of Information: the United States System of Cities, 1790–1840* (Cambridge, Mass., 1973).

——, *City-systems in Advanced Economies: Past Growth, Present Processes and Future Development Options* (New York, 1977).

——, *Urban Growth and City-systems in the United States, 1840–1860* (Cambridge, Mass., 1980).

Pullan, Brian, 'Wage-earners and the Venetian economy, 1500–1630', *Economic History Review* 16(1964), 407–26.

Renaud, Bertrand, *National Urbanization Policy in Developing Countries* (New York and Oxford, 1981).

Reulecke, Jürgen, 'Population growth and urbanization in Germany in the nineteenth century', *Urbanism Past and Present* 2(1977), 21–30.

—— (ed.), *Die deutsche Stadt im Industriezeitalter* (Wüppertal, 1978).

Richardson, Harry W., 'Theory of the distribution of city sizes: review and prospects', *Regional studies* 7(1973), 239–51.

Ringrose, David, 'In migration, estroduras demograficas y tendencias economicas en Madrid a comiencos de la epocha moderna', *Moneda y crédito*, 138(1976).

Robson, Brian T., *Urban Growth: an Approach* (London, 1973).

Rogers, Andrei, 'Migration patterns and population redistribution', *Regional Science and Urban Economics* 9(1979), 275–310.

BIBLIOGRAPHY

—— and Williamson, Jeffrey G., 'Migration, urbanization, and the third world: an overview', *Economic Development and Cultural Change* 30(1982), 463–82. Reprinted in Andrei Rogers and Jeffrey G. Williamson (eds), *Urbanization and Development in the Third World* (IIASA, Laxenburg, Austria, 1982).

Rosing, K. E., 'A rejection of the Zipf model (rank-size rule) in relation to city size', *Professional Geographer* 18(1966), 75–82.

Rozman, Gilbert, *Urban Networks in Ch'ing China and Tokugawa Japan* (Princeton, NJ, 1973).

——, 'Edo's importance in the changing Tokugawa society', *Journal of Japanese Studies* 1(1974), 91–112.

——, *Urban Networks in Russia, 1750–1800, and Premodern Periodization* (Princeton, NJ, 1976).

——, 'Urban networks and historical stages', *Journal of Interdisciplinary History* 9(1978), 65–91.

Sabean, David W., 'Household formation and Geographical mobility: a family register study for a Württemberg village, 1760–1900', *Annales de démographie historique* (1970), 275–94.

Schmal, H. (ed.), *Patterns of European Urbanisation since 1500* (London, 1981).

Sharlin, Allan, 'Natural decrease in early modern cities: a reconsideration', *Past and Present* 79(1978), 126–38.

Shryock, H. S. and J. S. Siegel, *The Methods and Materials of Demography*, 2 vols (Washington, DC, and London, 1975).

Simon, H., 'On a class of skew distribution functions', *Biometrika* 42(1955), 425–40.

Skinner, G. William, 'Introduction: urban social structure in Ch'ing China', in G. William Skinner (ed.), *The City in Late Imperial China* (Stanford, Calif., 1977).

——, 'Regional urbanization in nineteenth century China', in G. William Skinner (ed.), *The City in Late Imperial China* (Stanford, Calif., 1977).

Slicher van Bath, B. H., *Agrarian History of Western Europe, 1500–1850* (London, 1963).

——, 'The yields of different crops (mainly cereals) in relation to the seed, ca. 810–1820', *Acta historiae neerlandica* 2(1967), 26–106.

Smith, C. T., *An Historical Geography of Western Europe before 1800* (London, 1967).

Smith, Carol A., *Regional Analysis*, 2 vols (New York, 1976).

——, 'Modern and premodern urban primacy', *Comparative Urban Research* 11(1982), 79–96.

——, 'Theories and measures of urban primacy: a critique', in Michael Timberlake (ed.), *Urbanization in the World Economy* (New York, forthcoming).

Smith, Daniel Scott, 'A homeostatic demographic regime: patterns in European family reconstitution studies', in Ronald D. Lee (ed.), *Population Patterns in the Past* (New York, 1977).

Smith, Thomas C., 'Pre-modern economic growth: Japan and the west', *Past and Present* 60(1973), 127–60.

Stearns, Peter N., *European Society in Upheaval: Social History since 1750* (New York, 1975).

Stewart, C. T., 'The size and spacing of cities', *Geographical Review* 48(1958), 222–45.
Süssmilch, Johann Peter, *Die Göttliche Ordnung in den Veränderungen des menschlichen Geschlechtes*, 3 vols (Berlin, 1775, fourth edn).
Thirsk, Joan, 'Industries in the countryside', in F. J. Fisher (ed.), *Essays in the Economic and Social History of Tudor and Stuart England* (London, 1961), 70–88.
Thompson, E. P., *The Making of the English Working Class* (London, 1963).
Tijn, T. van, *Twintig jaren Amsterdam* (Amsterdam, 1965).
Tilly, Charles, *The Vendée* (Cambridge, Mass., 1964).
——, 'Food supply and public order in modern Europe', in Charles Tilly (ed.), *The Formation of National States in Western Europe* (Princeton, NJ, 1975).
——, 'Demographic origins of the European proletariat', Center for Research on Social Organization working paper no. 207, University of Michigan (1979).
——, *As Sociology Meets History* (New York, 1981).
——, 'Flows of capital and forms of industry in Europe, 1500–1900', *Theory and Society* 12(1983), 123–42.
Tisdale, Hope Eldridge, 'The process of urbanization', *Social Forces* 10(1942), 311–16; reprinted in J. J. Spengler and O. D. Duncan (eds), *Demographic Analysis* (Glencoe, Ill., 1956), 338–43.
United Nations, *Demographic Yearbook, 1977* (New York, 1977).
Vance, J. W., *The Merchant's World: the Geography of Wholesaling* (Englewood Cliffs, NJ, 1970).
Vaughan, Robert, *The Age of Great Cities. Modern Society viewed in its relation to Intelligence, Morals, and Religion* (London, 1843).
Vries, Jan de, *The Economy of Europe in an Age of Crisis, 1600–1750* (Cambridge, 1976).
——, 'Poverty and capitalism; review essay', *Theory and Society* 12(1983), 245–55.
Wallerstein, Immanuel, *The Modern World-system: Capitalist Agriculture and the Origins of the European World Economy in the Sixteenth Century* (New York, 1973).
Walton, John, 'Structures of power in Latin American cities', in A. Portes and J. Walton (eds), *Urban Latin America* (Austin, Tex., 1976).
Ward, B., 'City structure and interdependence', *Papers and Proceedings of the Regional Science Association* 22(1969), 207–21.
Wareing, John, 'Migration to London and transatlantic emigration of indentured servants, 1683–1775', *Journal of Historical Geography* 7(1981), 356–78.
Weber, Max, *Economy and Society* (New York, 1968).
Wee, Herman van der, 'Reflections on the development of the urban economy in western Europe during the late middle ages and early modern times', *Urbanism Past and Present* 1(1975–6), 9–14.
White, Paul and Woods, Robert (eds), *The Geographical Impact of Migration* (London, 1980).
Wilcox, F. (ed.), *International Migration*, 2 vols (New York, 1931).
Williamson, J. G., 'Antebellum urbanization in the American Northeast', *Journal of Economic History* 25(1965), 592–608.
—— and Swanson, J. A., 'The growth of cities in the American Northeast,

1820–1870', *Explorations in Entrepreneurial History* 4(1966), 44–67.
Wirth, L., 'Urbanism as a way of life', *American Journal of Sociology* 44(1938), 1–24.
Wolff, Philippe (ed.), *Guide international d'histoire urbaine*, vol. 1: *Europe* (Paris, 1977).
Woude, A. M. van der, 'Population developments in the northern Netherlands (1500–1800) and the validity of the "urban graveyard" effect', *Annales de démographie historique* (1982), 55–75.
Wrigley, E. A., *Population and History* (New York, 1969).
——, 'Parasite or stimulus: the town in a pre-industrial economy', in E. A. Wrigley and Philip Abrams (eds), *Towns in Society* (Cambridge, 1978), 295–309.
Zelinsky, Wilbur, 'The hypothesis of the mobility transition', *Geographical Review* 61(1971), 219–49.
Zipf, G. K., *National Unity and Disunity* (Bloomington, Ind., 1941).
——, *Human Behavior and the Principle of Least Effort* (Cambridge, Mass., 1949).

INDEX

Abrams, Philip, 9, 10
aggregative back projection, 177
agricultural productivity, 242–3; role of cities in, 244; role of protoindustry in, 244
agriculture: labour-absorbing capacity of, 220; stimulus to urban growth, 259
agrocities, 54
Amsterdam, 96, 123, 144, 150; age at marriage in, 190; causes of growth of, 234; excess male mortality in, 211; foreign migration to, 213; marriage partners in, 185; mortality rate in, 193; natural increase in, 195; parish registers of, 192, 210
Ansbach, long-distance migration to, 213
Antwerp, 96, 123, 168; potential value of, 158
Arriaga, E. E., 153
assignment, of city-size categories, 25
Augsburg, 150
Austria, 40; small cities of, 58

Bairoch, Paul, 18
Barcelona, 24, 108
Barmen, marriage partners in, 185, 190
basic urbanization, definition of, 168
Beloch, Karl Julius, 18
Berlin, 116, 178; causes of growth of, 234
Berne, 141
Berry, Brian J. L., 88, 102
Biraben, J. N., 24
Birmingham, 144
Black Death, 42–3

Blaschke, Karlheinz, 18, 60
Brabant, 168; urbanization of, 153
Braudel, Fernand, 4, 122, 159–61, 246
Bremen, 150
Brescia, 150
Bristol, 150
British Isles, urbanization of, 40, 134, 167–8
Brussels, 141

Cadiz, 141, 149
Caen, 205–6; 'gross permanent', urban migration, 206
capital cities, rapid growth of, 141–2
capital investment, 242
capitalism: in cities, 7; organized by cities, 122; role of dominant cities in, 160
celibacy rate, in Geneva, 190
central Europe: boundaries of, 21; transition matrices of, 129–33
Chalkin, C. W., 62
China, 9, 262
cities: continuity of, 144; creation of new, 69; definition of, 21–2, 53, 82; lower size threshold of, 22, 49, 53–4, 55, 58, 87; newly created, 62
city-creation urbanization, 264
city-size: categories, 25, 32–3, 85, 123; threshold in nineteenth century, 44
Clark, David, 5
Colchester, plague in, 218
Cologne, 96
Constantinople, 161
Copenhagen, 62, 96

INDEX

Cork, 149
counter-urbanization, 266
Czechoslovakia, small cities of, 58

Davis, Kingsley, 179
demographic urbanization, 32, 35
Denmark, small cities of, 62
de-urbanization, 76, 257; as shown by potential surfaces, 166; effect of protoindustrialization, 239; in Japan, 245
development economics, 246
Diederiks, Herman, 186, 189, 190, 192
Dortmund, 149
Doxiadis, C. A., 266
Dresden, 60, 142
Dublin, 144
Duisburg, 149
Dutch East India Company, 209–10
Dutch Republic: effect of urban mortality on, 180; small cities in, 62
Dyos, H. J., 3

East Anglia, urbanization of, 59
Eastern Europe, boundaries of, 21
Ecija, 24
economic base theory, 248
enclosures, 213
England, 9; as urban core, 171; decline of rural population, 44; mortality at sea, 212; small cities in, 62; small cities of, 58; urbanization of, 154
England and Wales, rank-size distributions of, 118
entropy maximization, 88
errors: in assignments, 27; in estimates of small cities, 66; in identifying rapid growers, 139; in interpreting rank-size distributions, 93, 120; in sources, 22–3; in urbanization estimates, 38
Essen, 149
Europe: boundaries of, 19–21; internal divisions, 19–21, 84; unity of, 84
Everett, Allan, 62

family reconstitution, 17, 175; representativeness of, 192
Farr, William, 179
fertility, in cities, 192; variability, 182
Finland, creation of new cities in, 69
Finlay, Roger, 184

Fisher, F. J., 248
Flanders, 168
food supply, 242
France, 9, 40; rank-size distributions of, 112–14; small cities in, 58, 66; urban system of, 167
Frankfurt-on-Main, 182

general systems theory, 83
Geneva: age at marriage in, 192; demography of, 184; marriage partners in, 189; net reproduction rate in, 194
Genicot, Leopold, 42
Genoa, 110, 123
German migrants, 186
Germany, boundaries of, 20; rank-size distributions of, 115–16; small cities of, 58; urbanization of, 153
Ghent, 150
Gonzalez, Tomas, 24
Gottman, Jean, 265
Granada, 25
Graunt, John, 179
Grenoble, marriage partners in, 185

Hague, The, 21
Hall, Peter, 266
Hamburg, 115
Hanseatic cities, 96
Harris, C. H., 91
Hart, Simon, 189–90
Hauser, Philip, 11
Herodotus, 122
Heurlingen, 222
historical demography, 17
Hungary, 19

industrial cities, 7; concept of, 5; limited impact of, 150; vulnerability of, 142
Industrial Revolution, 5, 98, 101, 119, 122, 150, 172, 259
interpolation, of city population, 25
inverse projection, 17, 177
Italy: plagues in, 209; rank-size distributions of, 109–12; urban subsystems of, 112

Japan, 9
Johnson, R. J., 206

Kamen, Henry, 24

395

INDEX

Keyfitz, Nathan, 198, 215
King's Lynn, 60
King, Gregory, 179
Klep, Paul, 18, 153

La Rochelle, 149
Lampard, Eric, 22, 73, 254
large cities: role in urban growth of, 137; urban growth concentrated in, 104–5
law of proportionate effect, 88, 102, 121, 260
Le Roy Ladurie, E., 243
Lee, Ronald D., 177
Leeds, 133
Leiden, foreign migration to, 213
Leipzig, 60
Levine, David, 238
Lewis, W. Arthur, 241
life expectancy at birth, 184
Lisbon, 162
Livorno, 141, 149
Lodz, 149
lognormal distribution, 87
London, 35, 96, 123, 152, 177, 248; fertility and mortality rates in, 193; long-distance migration to, 213; natural decrease in, 179; net migration to, 201; plague in, 218; potential value of, 159
long sixteenth century, 28
Lyons, 113, 141; marriage partners in, 185

Madrid, 108, 144, 150, 183, 248
Magdeburg, 150
main European axis, 172
Malaga, 141, 150
Manchester, 133, 144
marriage: age at, 190; controls on, 183; in pre-industrial cities, 181
marriage market, in Amsterdam, 196
marriage partners, in cities, 185–9
Marx, Karl, 214
medieval cities, 3–5; foundation of, 69; origins of, 41
medieval urbanization, 41–3
Mediterranean Europe: boundaries of, 21; lost predominance of, 31, 108, 158, 166, 258; net urban migration to, 207, 209; push migration in, 215; role of new cities in, 134; seventeenth-century stagnation of, 40, 98; small cities in, 54; transition matrices of, 129–33
Megalopolis, 265
Mendels, Franklin, 220
Mentink, G. J., 176
Merrington, John, 7
Middelburg, 149
migrants, marriage age of, 190
migration: demographic impact of, 222; effect of protoindustrialization on, 232; growth, 219; impact on urban demography of, 196–8; mortality consequences of, 181; potential, 217; push-pull, 214; regulator of urban population, 199; replacement, 218–19; temporary, 222; to Amsterdam, 186; to cities, 90
Milan, 110; potential value of, 158
Mobility Revolution, 234
mobility, in pre-industrial society, 213
Mols, Roger, 18, 177, 180, 245
mortality: at sea, 210; in Amsterdam, 211
Munich, 149

Naples, 35, 96; Kingdom of, 110; potential value of, 158
nation state, as unit of analysis, 152
natural decrease in cities: advocates of, 179–80; critics of, 180–2
natural increase, in cities, 231, 234
net migration, formula for, 201
net reproduction rate, 184
Netherlands, The, 40; birth and death rates in, 193; rank-size distributions in, 54, 116–18; small cities of, 58; urbanization of, 153; as urban core, 169
New York, 123, 160
new cities, role in urban system: to 1800, 142; to 1979, 149
Nimes, 144
north and west Europe: boundaries of, 21; transition matrices of, 129–33
northern Europe: net urban migration in, 204; push migration in, 215; role of new cities in, 136
Norway, creation of new cities in, 69
Norwich, 59–60
nuptiality: in cities, 192; regulator of total population, 199
Nuremberg, 96

396

INDEX

old-age pensioners, 181
Oslo, 141, 149
Ottoman Empire, 19, 107

Palermo, 112
parasitic cities, 247–8
Pareto distribution, 85–6
Paris, 35, 96; potential value of, 159
parish registers, weaknesses in cities, 176
partner choice, in urban marriage markets, 189, 190, 192
Patten, John, 58–9, 122
Perrenoud, Alfred, 176, 184, 190, 194
Perrot, Jean-Claude, 205
Philipov, Dimiter, 215
Pirenne, Henri, 4, 41
plague, 206
Plymouth, 133
Poland, 243; boundaries of, 20–1
population decline, in seventeenth century, 29
population reconstruction, 176
population of territories, 35, 38
port cities: rapid growth of, 141; relative decline of, 149
Portugal, mortality at sea, 212
Postan, M. M., 4
potential: definition of, 155; historical patterns of, 158–67; shifts toward Atlantic Ocean, 167
potential isolines, 161
pre-modern primacy, 89, 90–1; weaknesses of, 90–1
Pred, Allan, 9, 82, 123, 219
primacy, 88–90; of Amsterdam, 118; of London, 101; of Naples, 110; of Paris, 113
proletariat: emergence of, 8; origins of, 237–8
protoindustrial demographic regime, 221
protoindustrialization, 8, 220, 238–40

Randstad Holland, 265; net migration to, 201
rank-size distributions, 258, 264; and small cities, 51; formula for, 87; lower limb of, 54, 87; meaning of, 102; medieval, 95; of Europe, 95–101; pitfalls of, 93; techniques of, 91; theories of, 88–96
rank-size rule, 52, 88, 91, 261; definition of, 87; in Great Britain, 119

Rapp, Richard, 218
Ravenstein, E. G., 201
Reformation, 256
regions: as context of economic development, 249; definitions of, 83; differential urban growth of, 150
Reims, 150
reproductive value, definition of, 197
Ringrose, David, 183, 248
Robson, Brian, 9
Rochefort, 149
Rogers, Andrei, 234
Roman urbanism, 41
Roman urbanization, 28
Rome, 178
Rotterdam, 176; potential value of, 158
Rouen, 113
Rozman, Gilbert, 9, 10, 261, 263
Ruhrgebiet, 116, 149, 172
Russell, Josiah Cox, 42, 95
Russia, 9, 19, 107, 178

Saxony, Electoral, 60
Scandinavia, 40; small cities of, 58
Schofield, Roger, 177, 193, 199, 212
seamen, age at marriage of, 190
Seville, 162
sex ratios: in Amsterdam, 186; urban, 178
Sharlin, Allan, 180–1, 182, 192, 198, 200
Sheffield, 133
Sjoberg, Gideon, 5
Skinner, G. William, 9, 10, 89–91, 261, 263
small cities: census evidence about, 55, 57, 58–9, 60, 62, 66; estimates of number of, 69; estimation procedures for, 51–2; importance of, 51, 69; rapid growth among, 139; rapid growth of, 259; urban growth concentrated in, 101, 104–5
Smith, Carol, 89–91, 95, 108, 112
Smith, Thomas C., 245
social mobility, 222
southern Netherlands, as urban core, 171
Spain, 40; mortality at sea, 212; plagues in, 209; rank-size distributions of, 108; urbanization of, 154
Stockholm, 177; causes of growth of, 234
Sussmilch, Johan Peter, 179
Sweden, creation of new cities in, 69

Thirty Year's War, 132

INDEX

three-sector pre-industrial migration model, 221–3
Tilly, Charles, 12, 238
Tisdale, Hope Eldridge, 10, 11, 32
tourist cities, 149
transition matrices: after 1800, 144–6; by fifty-year period, 124; explanation of, 124–9; for twentieth century, 144–9; in very long run, 142–4; per era, 133
transportation costs, effect on urban potential, 156
Turin, 112, 142, 144

United Nations, 21
United States, 219
urban civilization, definition of, 168
urban core, rise of, 167–8
urban demographic transition, 234
urban differentiation, 76
urban growth: by city function, 141–2; by rank, 106–7; concentration of, 141; factors affecting, 107; instability of, 121–2; regional selectivity of, 151
urban history, concept of, 3–6
urban migration, 218; as percentage of rural surplus, 206–7; context of, 213; measurement difficulties of, 200; net, estimates of, 202, 204; of sailors, 210; role in nineteenth century, 233–4
urban population, percentage of total, 38, 71
urban systems: as prerequisite to protoindustry, 240; character of, 260–1; Chinese and European compared, 263; consolidation of, 167; definition of, 82; differentiation in, 77; discontinuity in, 150; efficiency of, 261; emergence of, 96, 107; functions of, 10; importance of, 253; integrity of, 107, 117, 120; of United States, 102, 123; political unification's role in, 114; polynuclear, 167; role of, 9, 10; stability of, 122–3; stages of development of, 10
urban-concentration urbanization, 264–5
urbanization: agricultural limits to, 243; behavioural, 12, 254–5; capital investment in, 241–2; ceiling of, 230; ceiling to, 91, 118; definition of, 10–13; demographic, 11, 253–4; demographic cost of, 230; determinants of, 231, 253; measurement of, 152–3; of the world, 73; phases of, 255–60; seventeenth-century discontinuity, 31, 129, 134, 136, 172; simulated impact of migration on, 223, 231; structural, 12, 254–5
urbanization index, 153
Utrecht, 96, 117

Venice, 110, 123; plague in, 218; potential value of, 158
Vital Revolution, 234

Warsaw, 178
Weber, Adna F., 101, 260
Weber, Max, 4
Woude, A. M. van der, 176, 182, 195, 198, 200, 210
Wrigley, E. A., 177, 180, 193, 199, 201, 212, 248
Würzburg, marriage partners in, 190

Yarmouth, Great, 60
Yield ratio, 242–3

Zelinsky, Wilbur, 234
Zipf, G. K., 87, 116
Zurich, 149